Teaching English as a Second or Foreign Language

Marianne Celce-Murcia

Lois McIntosh

Department of English—ESL Section
University of California, Los Angeles

EDITORS

Newbury House Publishers, Inc.
Rowley, Massachusetts 01969

Library of Congress Cataloging in Publication Data
Main entry under title:

Teaching English as a second or foreign language.

    Includes bibliographical references.
    1. English language--Study and teaching--Foreign
students. I. Celce-Murcia, Marianne. II. McIntosh,
Lois, 1908-
PE1128.A2T44   420'.7   78-16917
ISBN 0-88377-125-X

NEWBURY HOUSE PUBLISHERS, INC.

 Language Science
Language Teaching
Language Learning

ROWLEY, MASSACHUSETTS 01969

First printing: May 1979
Printed in the U.S.A.   12 11 10 9 8 7

To our students

who convinced us that such a textbook was
necessary and who did much to help complete it.

ACKNOWLEDGMENTS

We would like to thank our current colleagues and our frequent summer session colleague Harold Madsen for their kind and necessary collaboration in the preparation of this text. Special thanks also go to several of our former colleagues: Brad Arthur, Andy Cohen, Abdel-Messih Daoud, Tom Gorman, Jim Heaton, Diane Larsen-Freeman, and Anne Newton. They made very special contributions to this volume. We would also like to thank many of our former and current graduate students for their contributions and their commitment in the preparation of this text: Kathi Bailey, Bruce Cronnell, Richard Epting, Bill Gaskill, Mike Gasser, Suzanne Herschenhorn, Dorothy Lewis, Sue Mockridge-Fong, Brina Peck, Fred Rosensweig, Laura Thompson, and Ellyn Waldman.

We are also very grateful to Ms. Jo Alexander of Newbury House for her helpful suggestions during the organization and preparation of the manuscript and for her meticulous reading of the final draft.

Finally, we express deep appreciation to our current graduate student, Ms. Michiko Shintani, whose dedicated typing and retyping over a three-year period have made the final manuscript and several trial pre-publication versions possible. Her loyalty to this project has earned her our deepest gratitude.

M. C.-M.
L. M.

October 1978

CONTENTS

Acknowledgments   v
Introduction   ix
Biographical Statements on the Contributors   xi

I.   **Teaching Methods**   1
    An Outline of Language Teaching Approaches   3
      Clifford H. Prator *with* Marianne Celce-Murcia
    The Cornerstones of Method   5
      Clifford H. Prator
    Current Trends in Language Teaching   17
      Anne C. Newton
    Innovative Methodologies Applicable to TESL   26
      Harold S. Madsen
    An Audiovisual Method for ESL   38
      James Heaton
    Using Songs and Games in the ESL Classroom   49
      Michael Gasser *and* Ellyn Waldman

II.   **Language Skills**
    A. Listening   63
    Teaching Listening Comprehension Using Live Language   65
      Suzanne Herschenhorn
    Resurrecting the Language Lab for Teaching
    Listening Comprehension and Related Skills   74
      Richard S. Epting *and* J. Donald Bowen
    B. Speaking   81
    Linguistic and Social Aspects of Communicative Competence   83
      Russell N. Campbell
    Teaching the Speaking Skill   90
      Susan Mockridge-Fong
    Contextualizing Pronunciation Practice in the ESOL Classroom   101
      J. Donald Bowen

C. **Reading** 111

Preliteracy Activities for Adolescents and Adults 113
    Dorothy Lewis

Reading a Second Language 129
    Evelyn Hatch

The Teaching of Intermediate Reading in the ESL Classroom 144
    William H. Gaskill

Teaching Reading at the Advanced Level 154
    Thomas P. Gorman

The Teaching of Literature in Advanced ESL Classes 162
    John Povey

D. **Writing** 187

The Teaching of Composition 189
    Thomas P. Gorman

Spelling English as a Second Language 202
    Bruce Cronnell

E. **Grammar and Vocabulary** 215

Issues in the Teaching of Grammar 217
    Diane Larsen-Freeman

A Grammar Sequence for Teaching ESL to Beginners 229
    Lois McIntosh

Teaching Vocabulary in the ESL Classroom 241
    Marianne Celce-Murcia *and* Fred Rosensweig

III. **Students** 259

Differing Needs of ESL Students 261
    Sabrina Peck

Teaching English to Minority Groups 270
    Bradford Arthur

The Adult ESL Classroom 276
    James Heaton

IV. **Teachers** 293

Preparing Lesson Plans 295
    Marianne Celce-Murcia *and* Thomas P. Gorman

Selecting and Evaluating a Textbook 302
    Abdel-Messih Daoud *and* Marianne Celce-Murcia

Language Teaching Aids 307
    Marianne Celce-Murcia

Classroom Skills for ESL teachers 315
    Kathleen M. Bailey *and* Marianne Celce-Murcia

Second Language Testing 331
    Andrew D. Cohen

Keeping Up to Date as an ESL Teacher 360
    Laura Thompson

References 366
Index 381

INTRODUCTION

This volume represents our attempt to put together a comprehensive introduction to the profession of teaching English as a second or foreign language. We set out with the goal of maintaining a balance between theory and practice—between providing needed background information and relevant research, on the one hand, and providing many practical classroom suggestions, on the other. We also wanted to cover all of the areas that we consider critical to successful language instruction: knowledge of teaching methods, background on and strategies for teaching the language skills, an understanding of student factors, and information helpful to a teacher's performance and growth. We have tried to produce an introduction to the field that would be of sufficient depth and breadth to be suitable for students with some previous teaching experience, yet elementary enough not to needlessly bewilder the novice. We are preparing a second complementary volume dealing with more theoretical topics such as language acquisition, language policy, contrastive analysis and error analysis, attitude and motivation, syllabus design, etc. These topics are also important if the teacher wants to have a complete and balanced background in ESL/EFL. However, these topics are of less immediate practical value than the ones we have included in this basic volume since they are concerned with research issues that have not yet yielded any clear-cut answers or solutions, but which promise to do so in the future.

Two factors motivated us to undertake this task. First of all, we feel that the lack of a fully satisfactory introductory text has made both the teaching and learning of basic ESL skills and concepts somewhat difficult. There is general consensus among teacher trainers that an appropriate text designed to fulfill the needs of a basic and comprehensive methods course would go a long way toward meeting the challenges and solving the problems involved. The need for a such a text was, therefore, our primary objective in preparing this collection.

A second motivating factor was the belief that no one person or two people could, on their own, hope to write an adequate introduction to ESL. The field has simply become too vast. What we did as editors was to prepare a reasonable outline for the text and a pedagogically-motivated format for the chapters. We then approached appropriate individuals for contributions. Fortunately for us, many colleagues—former and present—have assisted us by writing a chapter in one or more of their areas of expertise. A remarkable number of our present and former graduate students have also made important contributions. A total of twenty-seven people have contributed to this thirty-chapter textbook. The common thread running through the experience of all the contributors has been time spent either studying or teaching (or both) in the ESL Section at UCLA. We thought that the reader might like to know something about the background and experience of the contributors, so we have included a short biographical statement on each of the twenty-seven in the section following this introduction.

With the exception of two chapters (i.e., those by Bowen and Newton) none of the chapters in the present collection has previously been published. Twenty-eight chapters have been written specially for this textbook; the materials have been piloted, expanded, and revised several times during the past four years. Each chapter concludes with a set of discussion questions, a number of suggested related activities, and some suggestions for further reading directed toward anyone who really gets interested in a given chapter's content and wants to find out more about the topic. A unified bibliography of all the references cited comes at the end of the book.

Although designed primarily as a textbook for a serious ESL methods course, we feel that it could be very useful as a resource and guide to individuals who are teaching ESL without having had specific training and to practicing teachers who received their training some time ago.

BIOGRAPHICAL STATEMENTS ON THE CONTRIBUTORS

Bradford Arthur (Ph.D., University of California, Berkeley, 1967) is Assistant Professor of Linguistics at the University of Michigan in Ann Arbor and has been associated with the English Language Institute at that university since 1975. Professor Arthur has also taught English linguistics and ESL at UCLA and the American Language Institute (USC). He is the author of several articles related to theoretical and applied linguistics and a book, *Teaching English To Speakers of English* (Harcourt Brace Jovanovich, Inc., 1973).

Kathleen M. Bailey (M.A., University of California, Los Angeles, 1976) was the Coordinator of, and teacher supervisor for the ESL Service Courses at UCLA from 1976-1978. She had previously taught several of these service courses in 1975-76. Earlier she taught reading courses for St. Louis High School, Korea (1974-75) and supervised teachers there. She is working on her Ph.D. in Applied Linguistics and has published articles dealing with teacher training, ESL curricula, and attitudes relating to speech accents. Her interests include teacher training and evaluation, curriculum development, and research on classroom interaction.

J. Donald Bowen (Ph.D., University of New Mexico, 1952) is a Professor of English in the ESL Section at UCLA, where he has been working since 1958. He has had extended overseas assignments in the Philippines (1959-63), East Africa (1968-70), and Egypt (1974-77), with shorter terms in Spanish-speaking America, South and Southeast Asia, and Eastern Europe. He has served a three-year term on the TESOL Executive Committee, was

a member of the UCLA English Teaching Advisory Panel (1964-74), and has been a member of NACTEFL since 1972. His publications have been in the areas of English and Spanish phonology and structure, contrastive analysis, language pedagogy, and language testing.

Russell N. Campbell (Ph.D., University of Michigan, 1964) is a Professor in the ESL section of the English Department at UCLA, where he has served as a teacher of methods and applied linguistics since 1964. For almost three years he has been the Vice-Chairman of the English Department in charge of the ESL section. He has had four long-term professional assignments overseas including Egypt (1972-74), Thailand (1959-61), Argentina (1956-58), and Costa Rica (1954-56). His publications include co-authorship of three ESL books and several articles. Professor Campbell has served on the Executive Committee of TESOL as Second Vice-President, First Vice-President, and President (1971-72).

Marianne Celce-Murcia (Ph.D., University of California, Los Angeles, 1972) is an Associate Professor of English in the ESL Section at UCLA, where she has been teaching courses in methods and English grammar since 1972. She has also taught ESL for two years in Lagos, Nigeria, and from 1974 to 1976 she was in charge of the ESL service course program at UCLA. Areas in which Professor Celce-Murcia has published articles include English grammar, language testing, teaching composition, contrastive analysis and error analysis, and language acquisition. She was presented the UCLA Distinguished Teaching Award in 1976, appointed to the Danforth Associate Program for 1977-1983, and served as Associate Chair for the 1978 TESOL Convention in Mexico City.

Andrew D. Cohen (Ph.D., Stanford, 1972) is Senior Lecturer in Applied Linguistics at the Hebrew University, Jerusalem, Israel, and is Director of the Centre for Applied Linguistics at the University. He has also taught in the ESL Section at UCLA (1972-75). Professor Cohen has published articles in the fields of language testing, error analysis, sociolinguistics, language education, and evaluational research in bilingual education. His publications include the book, *A Sociolinguistic Approach to Bilingual Education* (Newbury House, 1975).

Bruce Cronnell (Ph.D., University of California, Los Angeles, 1973) is a Senior Member of the Professional Staff at the Southwest Regional Laboratory, Educational Research and Development Division, Los Alamitos, California. Since 1968 his work at SWRL has involved research into vocabulary and spelling-sound relations; in addition, he has developed spelling materials for use in elementary school. He has also taught ESL in Nigeria and in various universities in the United States. Dr. Cronnell has published articles and monographs on reading, spelling, Black English, and vocabulary.

Abdel-Messih Daoud (Ph.D., Ain Shams University, Egypt, 1970) is Professor of Teaching English as a Foreign Language in the Faculty of Education at Ain Shams University in Cairo, where he has taught courses in English teaching methodology since 1955. He has co-authored eleven English language textbooks prescribed by the Egyptian Ministry of Education for students in secondary schools and teacher training institutes. Professor Daoud recently co-authored two teacher's manuals for the use of teachers of English in Egyptian preparatory and secondary schools. He studied in England for two years, and spent seven months as a Fulbright Visiting Scholar at UCLA in 1977.

Richard S. Epting (M.A., University of California, Los Angeles, 1974) is currently a teacher of English in the English Language Division at Robert College in Istanbul, Turkey, where he has been teaching since 1974. Mr. Epting had an earlier experience as an ESL teacher in Turkey when he was there as a Peace Corps Volunteer from 1966 to 1968. While carrying out his M.A. studies at UCLA, he served as the ESL Section's Language Laboratory Assistant.

William Gaskill (M.A., University of California, Los Angeles, 1977) is currently working toward a Ph.D. in applied linguistics at UCLA and is employed by the American Language Center, UCLA Extension, as a curriculum specialist. Mr. Gaskill spent two and a half years in Tehran, Iran, where he was first an instructor and a teacher supervisor at the Iran America Society and where he subsequently taught ESL at Damavand College and with RCA Globcom. In addition to teaching reading to ESL students, Mr. Gaskill's interests include ESL curriculum development, teacher training, classroom interaction and conversational analysis. He has made oral presentations at national conferences dealing with his research in the latter two areas.

Michael Gasser (M.A., University of California, Los Angeles, 1979) is currently an ESL instructor in the American Language Center, UCLA Extension Division. While in the Peace Corps he taught ESL from 1970 to 1972 in Ethiopia, where he also acted as a supervisor of ESL instruction for the Ministry of Education from 1972 to 1973.

Tom Gorman (Ph.D., University of East Africa, University College, Nairobi, 1971) is a Principal Research Officer at the National Foundation for Educational Research, the United Kingdom. He is currently director of the research team that has been set up by the Department of Education and Science to monitor student performance in language in the schools of England and Wales. Before joining the Foundation he taught in the Department of Language and Linguistics at the University of Essex. From 1972 to 1975 he was a Visiting Professor in the ESL Section at UCLA. Dr. Gorman has published books and articles on topics relating to the teaching of reading and writing, literacy, language planning, and the lexicography of East African languages.

Evelyn Hatch (Ph.D., University of California, Los Angeles, 1969) is an Associate Professor of English in the ESL Section at UCLA. She has taught English as a foreign language in Egypt (1964-66) and was again in Egypt during the 1977-78 academic year on a State Department Project at Ain Shams University in Cairo. She has taught classes in methodology, linguistics, psycholinguistics, language acquisition, and reading at UCLA. Her major area of research is second language acquisition, both developmental bilingualism and the acquisition of a second language by adults. A second interest is the teaching of reading in a second language. Her publications include *Second Language Acquisition* (Newbury House, 1978), a book of readings of which she was the editor.

James Heaton (M.A., University of California, Los Angeles, 1967) is a lecturer in ESL at Woodbury College in Los Angeles. Previous to that he had been a lecturer in the ESL Section at UCLA where he had taught and worked on various materials development projects from 1973 to 1978. Before that, Mr. Heaton worked on a curriculum development project for the Ford Foundation in Uganda and then taught ESL for adults at a community junior college in California. He is currently developing several video ESL courses.

Suzanne Herschenhorn (M.A., University of California, Los Angeles, 1974) is the Curriculum Coordinator for the Indochinese Education and Employment Project, a federally funded program under the direction of the Career and Continuing Education Division of the Los Angeles Unified School District. Ms. Herschenhorn has been with LAUSD for three years. She began as an ESL instructor with the Evans Community Adult School, where she implemented a new language laboratory program. Her ESL teaching experience also includes two years at El Camino Junior College and two years at the American Language Institute at the University of Southern California, where she both taught and helped develop materials for the spoken English courses. Her overseas experience consists of working 18 months for the American University Alumni Association, a binational school in Bangkok, and the Royal Thai Navy.

Diane Larsen-Freeman (Ph.D., University of Michigan, 1975) teaches at the Experiment in International Living's School for International Training in Brattleboro, Vermont. From 1975 to 1978 she was an Assistant Professor of English in the ESL Section at UCLA. Prior to teaching at UCLA, Dr. Larsen-Freeman taught ESL for two years in Malaysia as a Peace Corps Volunteer and then for two years at the University of Michigan's English Language Institute. Her major area of research is second language acquisition. She has published in the *TESOL Quarterly, Language Learning,* and the *Modern Language Journal,* and currently is editor of the Research Notes section of the *TESOL Quarterly.* She is also a member of the TOEFL Research Committee of the Educational Testing Service, Princeton, New Jersey.

Dorothy Lewis (M.A., California State University, Long Beach, 1973) is an ESL Consultant and an ESL/Bilingual Specialist for the elementary and adult levels in the Long Beach Unified School District. She served as a reading specialist for the District from 1969-73. Mrs. Lewis has been an active member of CATESOL (the California Affiliate of TESOL) and has served both as presenter and as chairperson at state and local conferences. She is co-author of *Learning Center Activities for Beginning ESL Language and Reading Development* and *Learning Center Activities for Beginning SSL Language and Reading Development* (SSL = Spanish as a Second Language), both published by Harris Press, Long Beach.

Harold S. Madsen (Ph.D., University of Colorado, 1965) is Professor of TESL in the Linguistics Department at Brigham Young University, where he has taught intermittently since 1956. From 1966 to 1970 he taught university ESL classes in Ethiopia and served as Assistant Dean, as well as USAID Contract Chief of Party and Advisor on TEFL at the Ministry of Education. During 1976-77, he was a visiting TEFL Professor in Egypt and advisor on TEFL testing at the Ministry of Education. He was a visiting professor in the UCLA summer programs for Soviet teachers of English from 1973 to 1975. Former President of the Intermountain TESOL Affiliate from 1973 to 1975, Dr. Madsen has published articles on testing and methodology in the *TESOL Quarterly*, the *English Language Teaching Journal*, and other publications.

Lois McIntosh (Ph.D., University of Michigan, 1953) retired with the title of Professor of English in 1975 from UCLA, where she had been teaching in the ESL Section since 1960. Before coming to UCLA, Professor McIntosh had also taught ESL at the University of Michigan's English Language Institute and at the American Language Institute at Columbia University. She was a visiting professor of English in the Philippines from 1958 to 1959. She later went abroad again to Japan as a Fulbright Exchange Teacher in 1967-68. Until 1974, she was responsible for the ESL Service Course Program at UCLA. Her specialty is the teaching of grammar. She is a co-author of *English as a Second Language with Special Applications to Hungarians* (Rinehart and Co., 1957) and *Advancing in English* (American Book Co., 1970). She also worked with William Slager on revising Books One and Two of the *English for Today* series, Second Edition (McGraw-Hill, 1972 and 1973 respectively).

Susan Mockridge-Fong (M.A., University of Wisconsin, 1969) is an M.A. candidate in the ESL Section at UCLA, where she was a teaching assistant from 1972 to 1974. Since 1975, she has served as an Evaluator for the Seattle Public Schools, charged with evaluating the District's *Lau Compliance Plan* for students from non-English language backgrounds. She has taught ESL at Shoreline Community College (Seattle) and at the University of Wisconsin, Madison, and has led workshops in composition for ESL students at conferences of the Washington Association for teachers of English as a Second or Other Language (WAESOL).

Anne C. Newton (M.A., University of California, Los Angeles, 1962) is editor of the *English Teaching Forum*, a publication of the U.S. Information Agency. She was an NDEA Fellow in Near Eastern languages, 1960-61, at UCLA, where she subsequently taught ESL for several years. In 1962-63 she served as Fulbright lecturer in linguistics and TESL at the Philippine Normal College in Manila, and the following year as a staff member of the Philippine Center for Language Study. In 1966 she became an English teaching consultant for the U.S. Information Agency and, for several years prior to undertaking her present assignment in 1975, wrote English teaching materials and conducted videotaped interviews on teaching and testing techniques in EFL.

Sabrina Peck (M.A., University of California, Los Angeles, 1977) is a doctoral candidate in Applied Linguistics at UCLA. She taught ESL and first grade in a bilingual school (Spanish-English) in Boston from 1972 to 1975. For two summers she worked as an ESL teacher trainer in Arequipa, Peru, where she also taught ESL to high school students. She has published articles on child-child discourse and on the role of play in child second language acquisition. In 1977 she was chairperson of the Los Angeles Second Language Research Forum.

John Povey (Ph.D., Michigan State University, 1964) is a Professor of English in the ESL Section at UCLA, where he has been teaching since 1964. Prior to his doctoral studies he had taught English in many areas of Africa. His research interests focus particularly on advanced language usage—the secondary skills of reading and writing and the role of literature in language learning. He has conducted projects and workshops in ESL creative writing both in Africa and on American Indian Reservations and has also been involved in assistance programs and faculty training in Francophone Africa. His most substantial publication is *African Literature in English* (State University of New York Press, 1975).

Clifford H. Prator (Ph.D., University of Michigan, 1939) is a Professor of English at UCLA, where for almost thirty years he was responsible for the direction of all ESL work. He has also been instrumental in the development of the Philippine Center for Language Study in Manila, the Instituto Colombo-Americano in Bogotá, and the Center for Developing English

Language Teaching at Ain Shams University in Cairo, Egypt. In 1967-68 he was Field Director of the survey of Language Use and Language Teaching in Eastern Africa, sponsored by the Ford Foundation. His major interests at present are the training of teacher-specialists in ESL and questions of language policy. His *Manual of American English Pronunciation* (Holt, Rinehart, and Winston, 1958) and the *English-Language Policy Survey of Jordan,* of which he was a co-author (Center for Applied Linguistics, 1975) are perhaps his best known publications. He has been awarded the Philippine Legion of Honor for his services to Philippine education.

Fred Rosensweig (M.A., University of California, Los Angeles, 1974) is presently Associate Director of Education for the U.S. Peace Corps in Tunisia. Previous Peace Corps experience includes teaching EFL in Senegal and Cameroun from 1969 to 1972. Mr. Rosensweig has also trained two groups of Peace Corps EFL teachers in Cameroun. In the U.S. he has taught ESL while serving as an instructor at the American Language Institute at USC from 1975 to 1977, and as a teaching assistant at UCLA

from 1972 to 1974. He gave presentations at the 1976 TESOL and NAFSA Conventions on improving the speaking ability of intermediate and advanced ESL students, one of his major research interests.

Laura Thompson (Certificate in TESL, UCLA, 1976) has taught intensive ESL classes at the University of California, Davis, and also served as a teaching assistant at UCLA for two years from 1975 to 1977. Her area of specialization is the teaching of composition, and techniques for improving the essay writing skills of students—both native and non-native speakers of English.

Ellyn Waldman (M.A., University of California, Los Angeles, 1975) is working toward a doctorate in the UCLA School of Education. She is teaching in the Intensive ESL Program in the American Language Center, UCLA Extension Division. Ms. Waldman is an accomplished folk guitarist and has used music and songs as teaching aids for many years now in her ESL classes. In Fall 1978 she opened up her own ESL school in Los Angeles.

Teaching English as a Second or Foreign Language

PART I
TEACHING METHODS

In this section of the textbook Prator and Celce-Murcia provide, first of all, an outline of the five major language teaching approaches that have been used in the United States during this century. Then, in the next chapter, Prator identifies and discusses the three foundations of ESL methodology: the nature of the language, the nature of the learner, and the aims of instruction. He also gives background on the growth and consolidation of the TESL profession in the United States. In the following chapter, Newton provides us with perspectives on the way that pressures develop—social and theoretical—that in turn cause teaching methods to come and go. In the fourth chapter Madsen reviews many unique current methodologies that the ESL teacher should be familiar with. The last two chapters involve fairly specific methodological suggestions: Heaton proposes that an audiovisual method be used in teaching ESL, and Gasser and Waldman show us how songs and games can be used to teach ESL and to have fun, too.

Taken collectively, we hope that these six chapters give the reader a good idea of where TESL has been, where it is, and where it may be headed.

NOTE: *All notes appear at ends of chapters in this book.*

AN OUTLINE OF LANGUAGE TEACHING APPROACHES

Clifford H. Prator *with*
Marianne Celce-Murcia

The following is a brief outline of the various language teaching approaches that have been used in the United States during the 20th century. It is hoped that by stating the defining features of each, comparison and contrast with other approaches (and with methods based on them) will be facilitated.

GRAMMAR-TRANSLATION APPROACH

Typically used in teaching Greek and Latin, and generalized to modern languages.

1. Classes are taught in the mother tongue, with little active use of the target language.
2. Much vocabulary is taught in the form of lists of isolated words.
3. Long elaborate explanations of the intricacies of grammar are given.
4. Grammar provides the rules for putting words together, and instruction often focuses on the form and inflection of words.
5. Reading of difficult classical texts is begun early.
6. Little attention is paid to the content of texts, which are treated as exercises in grammatical analysis.
7. Often the only drills are exercises in translating disconnected sentences from the target language into the mother tongue.
8. Little or no attention is given to pronunciation.

DIRECT METHOD (actually an APPROACH)

A reaction to the extension of the above approach to the teaching of modern languages.

1. Lessons begin with a brief anecdote or dialogue in the target language, and in modern conversational style.
2. This material is first presented orally with actions or pictures.
3. The mother tongue is never, never used (i.e., there is no translation).
4. The preferred type of exercise is a series of questions in the target language based on the anecdote or dialogue, and answered in the target language.
5. Grammar is taught inductively; rule generalization comes only after experience.
6. Verbs are used first, and systematically conjugated much later.
7. Advanced students read literature for comprehension and pleasure; literary texts are not analyzed grammatically.
8. The culture associated with the target language is also taught inductively.

READING APPROACH

This approach is selected for practical reasons; for people who do not travel abroad, reading is the one usable skill.

1. The objectives in priority order are (a) reading ability, (b) current and historical knowledge of the country where the target language is spoken.
2. Only the grammar necessary for reading is taught.
3. Minimal attention is paid to pronunciation.
4. From the beginning, a great amount of reading is done, both in and out of class.
5. The vocabulary of the early readings is strictly controlled.
6. Vocabulary is expanded as fast as possible, since the acquisition of vocabulary is considered more important than grammatical skills.
7. Translation reappears as a respectable classroom procedure.

AUDIOLINGUAL APPROACH

A reaction to the Reading Approach; much is taken from the Direct Method, the rest from behaviorism.

1. New material is presented in dialogue form.
2. There is dependence on mimicry, memorization of set phrases, and overlearning (i.e., it is believed that language learning is habit formation).
3. Structures are sequenced, and taught one at a time.
4. Structural patterns are taught using repetitive drills.
5. There is little or no grammatical explanation: grammar is taught by inductive analogy rather than deductive explanation.
6. Skills are sequenced—listen, speak, read, write.
7. Vocabulary is strictly limited and learned in context.
8. Teaching points are determined by contrastive analysis.
9. There is much use of tapes, language labs, and visual aids.
10. There is an extended pre-reading period at the beginning of the course.
11. Great importance is attached to pronunciation, with special attention being paid to intonation.
12. The cultural background of the target language is stressed.
13. Some use of the mother tongue by teachers is permitted.
14. Successful responses are immediately reinforced.
15. There is a great effort to prevent student errors.
16. There is a tendency to manipulate language and disregard content.

COGNITIVE APPROACH

A reaction to the behaviorist features of the Audiolingual Approach.

1. There is emphasis on communication, or communicative competence (i.e., being able to use the language).
2. Language acquisition is seen as rule (not habit) formation; deductive explanation of grammar is preferred.
3. Pronunciation is de-emphasized, since it is considered futile for most students to try to sound like native speakers.
4. Group work and individualized instruction are encouraged.
5. There is a renewed interest in vocabulary, especially the expansion of passive vocabulary for reading purposes.
6. The teacher is viewed as a facilitator rather than a figure of absolute authority.
7. The importance of comprehension—especially listening comprehension—is emphasized.
8. Errors are seen as an inevitable by-product of language learning; systematic study, interpretation, and—where possible—remediation are of concern.
9. The written language skills (reading and writing) and the spoken language skills (listening and speaking) are viewed as being of equal importance, rather than the former secondary and the latter primary.
10. Repetition in and of itself is discouraged; silence is recognized as useful and often necessary.
11. There is contextualization of all teaching points through the use of audiovisual aids, stories, or other appropriate means.
12. The use of the mother tongue and translation are permitted.
13. There is increased interest in the affective domain: the attitude of the teacher and student are seen as important, human sensitivity crucial, and the quality of interaction a significant variable.
14. Bilingual-bicultural proficiency is seen as an ideal goal.

DISCUSSION QUESTIONS

1. What has been the attitude toward the teaching of (a) pronunciation, (b) grammar, (c) vocabulary in the five approaches discussed in this chapter? Has there been a swinging of the pendulum? Why or why not?

2. What changes have occurred regarding the position of speech and writing in the various approaches?

SUGGESTED ACTIVITIES

1. Select an integrated skills ESL/EFL text that you have used or expect to use. Examine its contents to determine which approach it seems to follow most closely. Support your decision with examples. Discuss any mixing of approaches that you observe.

2. Examine any English language proficiency test—standardized or otherwise. See if you can detect a methodological bias in the test. Support your conclusion(s) with examples.

SUGGESTIONS FOR FURTHER READING

Louis G. Kelly (1969)
Twenty-five Centuries of Language Teaching. Rowley, Mass.: Newbury House.
Provides excellent historical perspective on the language teaching methodologies that have been employed from the time of the Greeks to the present.

William Mackey (1965)
Language Teaching Analysis (Chapter 5). Bloomington, Indiana: Indiana University Press.
This is a clear and concise overview of the interplay of language analysis and method, of the development of language teaching; it also describes 15 types of methods and reflects on what methods are made of.

Edward M. Anthony (1963)
"Approach, Method, and Technique," *ELT*, Jan., 1963, 63-67. Reprinted in Allen and Campbell (1972). A good, concise discussion of the difference in meaning of the three terms given in the title.

THE CORNERSTONES OF METHOD *

Clifford H. Prator

THE SEARCH FOR A METHODOLOGY

A first dip into the literature on methods of teaching foreign languages is likely to be a puzzling, even a disheartening, experience. Conscientious teachers-to-be would presumably hope to find there a coherent system of ideas, built up in an orderly fashion by the contributions of successive generations of authorities who made every effort to base their recommendations on experimental evidence and scientific fact. What they actually discover, if they sample the works on the subject written over the last fifty years, is something quite different.

In fact, the most striking feature of the history of language instruction, especially in the United States, appears to be the great diversity of the methodologies that have been propounded. At relatively brief intervals one highly touted "method" or "approach" has succeeded another in the favor of educators, and the proponents of each have tended to deny the validity of all that preceded. The use of the mother tongue in the foreign language classroom has been successively emphasized, banned, required, and barely tolerated. The ability to speak the foreign tongue was once regarded as irrelevant. Then came the Direct Method, which made speaking its primary aim. But this was followed by the Reading Approach, whose proponents believed that the only language skill which could really be taught within the available time was reading. And later the triumphant Aural-Oral or Audiolingual Approach once again insisted on the primacy of speech. There have been similarly violent swings of the pendulum with regard to many other elements of language teaching: the role of rules, the use of phonetic symbols, vocabulary control, and the like.

The new teacher will probably also be struck by the highly individualistic tone of much methodological literature. S/he will note that great prophets have arisen—Gouin, De Sauzé, Berlitz, West, Kaulfers, Ogden, Fries— who have built up large and often blindly enthusiastic groups of followers and who have been able to impose their somewhat closed systems of thought on a generation or more of disciples by their personal prestige and authority. Unlike the prophets of the Bible, however, these prophets of the language teaching profession have developed no coherent body of doctrine; indeed their dominant ideas are to a considerable extent mutually exclusive.

As these facts become clear to the student, s/he is left with a series of deeply disturbing questions. Why does the pendulum swing so widely and rapidly from one extreme to another? Why have language teachers been able to achieve so little balance and continuity in their work? Is progress possible if it is continually necessary to begin over again? What reason is there to believe that the currently approved methodology will last any longer than have its predecessors? In short, in what is one to have faith, and why?

LANGUAGE TEACHING, AN ART OR A SCIENCE?

To judge by its pattern of development, language instruction has up to the present been rather more of an art than a science. That is to say, it has been largely intuitive, dependent on the personal skill and convictions of the teacher, and hence particularly subject to fads and abrupt about-faces. It has hardly been possible to see in it the characteristics of a systematically arranged body of knowledge developed through the use of time-tested and generally accepted methods.

Perhaps this is to some extent inevitable; the element of human nature and behavior, precisely the element that is most difficult to treat with scientific rigor, is so prominent in

language teaching that it can probably never be made entirely explicable in scientific terms. The new teacher would do well, as a matter of principle, to distrust any methodologist who claims that enough is now known about the process of learning a language to permit the teaching of it in an absolutely scientific way.

Yet few thoughtful teachers would be willing to take the opposite position, that their profession is purely an art, basically unanalyzable and unteachable, to be improved only through the exercise of greater personal gifts of insight and imagination. In today's world, any educators worthy of the name are deeply uncomfortable if they cannot believe that their work bears some demonstrable relationship to established scientific fact. They cannot be happy in a situation where they can justify their actions only by their confidence in their own abilities, or by an appeal to the prestige of authority. They need a more durable and confidence-inspiring basis on which to build their work than the pronouncements of a single prophet.

The answer to the question that stands at the beginning of this section seems, then, to be that language teaching must be both an art *and* a science. To the extent that it remains an art, it permits the individual teacher to exercise such personal gifts as s/he may be endowed with. To the extent that it can be related to a science or sciences and thus itself become an applied science, it can be developed in a coherent way, be given continuity, and be taught.

The most successful teacher will always be something of an artist. But the art will be enhanced rather than destroyed if it is exercised within a framework of scientifically established guidelines. Therein lies the possiblity of faith.

THE CORNERSTONES OF METHOD

The belief that it is necessary to relate language teaching to an established scientific discipline is certainly not new. Indeed, it has been an important feature of several of the later methods and approaches mentioned above. Until recently, however, there has been little agreement as to *which* discipline or disciplines are the essential ones. West, and particularly the Americans associated with him in developing the Reading Approach, looked almost exclusively to the psychologists for guidance. Kaulfers tried to bring something of the aims and subject matter of the social sciences into language instruction. Ogden and Richards found the ideas which led to their Basic English in semantics and logic. Fries based his concept of English teaching on structural linguistics. Since these leaders of the profession were looking in different directions for their inspiration, it is hardly surprising that their common interest in a scientific approach failed to result in compatible methods.

It is only during the last few years that the realization has begun to emerge that past methodologies, in general, have been too narrowly based, that more than one cornerstone is necessary for the development of a type of teaching which will be both flexible enough to meet the manifold language needs of modern society and sufficiently scientific to avoid the abrupt about-faces that have characterized previous language instruction. It is an encouraging fact that this realization has not been the work of any one individual but appears to have forced itself almost simultaneously upon a large number of the leaders of the profession on both sides of the Atlantic. The fact is encouraging because it seems to hold out the promise of a methodology that will not harden into a closed system but will remain open to new ideas arising from the advances made in several related scientific disciplines.

The emerging consensus among methodologists arises from a set of relationships so fundamental and self-evident that they may be regarded as axiomatic. The basic elements in any teaching situation are the teacher, the subject matter, the learner, and the aims of instruction. These elements are related to one another in a way very similar to the terms of an equation. As in any equation, the value of the first term—in this case the behavior of the teacher—should vary as different values are assigned to the other terms.

This is, of course, another way of stating that *methods of language teaching should be based on at least three cornerstones:*

a. *What is known about the nature of the language.*
b. *What is known about the nature of the learner.*
c. *The aims of instruction.*

The science which analyzes the nature of language in general as well as that of particular languages is linguistics. The science that has studied the processes of human learning deeply is psychology. The aims of instruction are not scientifically determined but depend on the needs felt by the society and the individual at a given moment; a number of scientific and humanistic disciplines can, however, throw some light on these needs.

LANGUAGE TEACHING AND LINGUISTICS

Though there are still some skeptics, most creative methodologists now agree, then, that one of the cornerstones on which language instruction must be built—perhaps the most useful one—is the science that deals with the nature of language itself: linguistics. Of the various branches of linguistics, that which treats most directly the kind of problems which teachers must concern themselves with, at least in the elementary stages of instruction, is *synchronic* or *descriptive* linguistics. *Diachronic* or *historical* linguistics deals with the development of languages, chiefly written languages, over long periods of time and with the discovery of the genetic relationships among them. Descriptive linguistics, on the other hand, was developed in order to provide a rigorous method for analyzing living languages as they are used today. Since little has been written in the majority of such tongues, the descriptivists have learned to work with them directly in their spoken form.

Though descriptive linguistics is now known and cultivated in many parts of the world, it has had its stronghold in the United States, and Americans like to credit Bloomfield with having brought it to the dignity of a science by the publication of *Language* in 1933. The first large-scale attempt to apply linguistics to the teaching of English to speakers of other languages was made at the University of Michigan accompanying and following the appearance of Fries' *Teaching and Learning English as a Foreign Language* in 1945.

In spite of the irrefutable logic of establishing a close relationship between methods of teaching language on the one hand, and the best established body of facts available about language on the other, the battle to convince teachers of the necessity for such an orientation has been long and arduous and has as yet been only partially won.

Much of the resistance has been due, without doubt, to the very dogmatism and excessiveness of the claims that some linguists, mostly young disciples of the masters, have felt confident enough to make. The less cautious among them have allowed to be seen their belief that linguistics can supply all the needed answers and that language instruction can be regarded as a mere appendage of descriptive linguistics. Not content with their basic role as analysts of language, and with having teachers look to their science as a source of ideas, some of which might be applicable to instructional purposes, they have sometimes urged that their techniques should be taken into the classroom practically unchanged. There have been those who argued that a Ph.D. in linguistics was a perfectly adequate—indeed the only adequate—preparation for a specialist in language instruction, even if the degree work was organized without reference to teaching. There has even been a tendency to substitute the phrase "applied linguistics" for "language teaching" as the name of the profession.[1]

As any people who have spent many years of their lives training and supervising teachers know, however, the best linguists are not necessarily the best language teachers. Quite the reverse may often be true. Some of the teachers of English to speakers of other languages who have been most undeniably successful know, regrettably, little or nothing about linguistic science. And some of the most brilliant graduate students of linguistics seem hopelessly inept as apprentice teachers. What can be safely asserted is no more than that the teacher who has the firmest grasp of the fundamentals of linguistics, all other things being equal, will probably be the most effective in his or her work.

That it should appear desirable to make such statements in an article on methodology reflects, of course, a conviction that the effort to wed language teaching and linguistics has been, in some respects, entirely too successful. This has been particularly true in the case of American teachers of English to speakers of other languages, perhaps because they have appeared only recently as a professional group. They have had no large body of methodological literature of their own, have not always realized the fundamental identity of their work with that of teachers of other languages, and have been largely unaware of the long history of foreign language instruction.

The chief disadvantage of an exclusive relationship with linguistics is that the latter, by definition, casts very little light on the human element in the language teaching equation, the nature of the learner. That element is, however, much too important to be slighted. Perhaps the best way to convince oneself of the truth of this statement is to attempt to use in a classroom situation certain of the materials that have been developed directly by narrowly-oriented linguists who lacked classroom experience. Such materials—with their pages of drill on meaningless sounds, their excessive reliance on unfamiliar terminology and symbolism, their disconnected sentences unrelated to reality, their indifference to true communication—may be very sound indeed linguistically, but they are certainly no models of teachability.

Nevertheless, it would not be fair to lay at the door of the linguists all the blame for the many troubles that have attended their *affaire de coeur* with the language teachers. The teachers themselves, in large numbers, have been perfectly willing to forget what their experience has taught them and to adopt uncritically everything the linguists had to offer, without testing, without looking elsewhere for additional guidance. In other words, they seem to have given up any idea they may once have had of standing on their own feet as creative scholars with a basically independent profession of their own to develop.[2]

This is almost certainly the reason for the long inability of teachers of English to speakers of other languages, especially in the United

States, to cope with the problems of advanced instruction. They have been relatively successful in classes for beginners, and the list of elementary textbooks they have written is very long. But until recent years there have been practically no good materials available for teaching advanced students of English. The descriptive linguists, as has been pointed out, are primarily concerned with the spoken language; they have as yet had little to offer that could be applied to the teaching of composition and the advanced skills of reading. And where the linguists could not lead, the English teachers were apparently unwilling to go alone or in other company.

In the current state of affairs, then, the relationship between linguistics and language teaching is confused and even somewhat paradoxical. On the one hand, the many teachers in the United States who reject linguistics as mechanical and unnecessary, as well as many abroad who hardly know of its existence, need to be convinced that the tie is essential. On the other hand, there is the necessity to caution teachers against the dangers of a relationship that can be too dependent and too exclusive. In doing both things, the methodologist must try to make the difference between a theoretical science and an applied art-science, between unquestioning adoption and judicious application, crystal clear.

LANGUAGE TEACHING AND PSYCHOLOGY

No such ambivalence is involved in the relations between language teachers and psychologists. These were, by and large, relatively slight during the two decades between 1940 and 1960, roughly the period of greatest linguistic hegemony. During the fifteen years preceding 1940, however, they had been close and beneficial. Perhaps because of the very wide range of problems with which psychologists are concerned, the latter seem never to have developed the feeling of possessiveness about language instruction that has been shown at times by linguists.

1925-40 were the years of the Reading Approach. The methodologists responsible for its popularity—West and his followers in the British Commonwealth, and the American and Canadian Committees on Modern Languages in North America—were determined to reduce the role of guesswork in language teaching. They hoped, as we still hope today, to be able to replace guesswork by experimental evidence. They therefore invited as many psychologists as they could interest to participate with them in their work.

The result was an explosive increase in the amount of evaluative experimentation dealing with the teaching of languages. In fact, a large proportion of the total literature on such experiments dates from this period, much of it still quite pertinent.[3] But with the advent of linguistically oriented language teaching, this literature came to be neglected. It was the product of a group that had approved of the reading aim and hence was suspect to the champions of the Aural-Oral Approach.

Thus, with the repudiation of the reading aim came an unfortunate tendency to minimize the potential relevance of psychology to language instruction. Actually, there was little if any demonstrable connection between the work of the psychologists who collaborated with the American and Canadian Committees on Modern Languages and the fact that the Committees concluded that an ability to read was the only foreign language skill likely to be achieved under the conditions then prevailing in American schools. Critics of the Reading Approach have pointed out more than once that the evidence gathered clearly did not support the recommendations made in the name of the Committees.[4] The role of the psychologists in the matter was essentially neutral.

There were more substantial reasons, however, for doubting that psychology had a great deal of help to offer foreign language teachers, reasons arising from the state of the science in general and from its methods of developing learning theory in particular. For one thing, psychologists were divided in rapidly changing schools, each of which disputed the validity of their rivals' analysis of mental and behavioral processes. The behaviorists were attempting to discredit the introspective method; the gestalt group approved of introspection but were unwilling to accept Thorndike's connectionism.[5] Confusing differences in terminology made it very difficult for an outsider to decide whether or not the plethora of investigation had indeed established a modicum of fact.

For reasons obvious to the psychologists, experiments dealing with learning theory were carried out mostly with animals; to apply the results to human learning it would have been necessary to extrapolate. When the experimental subjects were human, they were set to performing tasks which bore no resemblance a language teacher could see to the kinds of activities central to studying a foreign tongue: tasks such as learning to associate pairs of nonsense words or to distinguish between sounds of varying intensity and pitch. Joint attempts by teachers and psychologists to measure the effectiveness of one method of language teaching against another in an actual classroom situation over an extended period of time proved inconclusive because of lack of clarity in the definition of methods, inability to control variables, and insufficient rigor of design.[6]

But these objections have become less valid in recent years. The area of agreement among psychologists regarding the nature of learning seems to have grown progressively larger as new theorists have deliberately attempted to work out a synthesis of the controversial points and thus act as a bridge between schools of thought. "While it remains true that research findings will be somewhat differently expressed and explained within different theoretical frameworks, the findings themselves are fairly solid," says a Columbia professor who set himself the job of explaining "what psychology we can trust." He was able to prepare a list of fifty propositions about children and learning with which he thought few knowledgeable psychologists of any school of thought would disagree (Watson, 1961, p. 1).

It is also encouraging that more and more psychologists are becoming specifically interested in language learning and even in foreign language learning. One major cause of this is certainly the fact that there has been a perceptible shift of the center of gravity of linguistics itself toward psychology. The generative-transformational approach to the analysis of language, which has become dominant since the appearance of Chomsky's *Syntactic Structures* in 1957, is very much concerned with the possibility that there may be a direct connection between grammatical rules and a human being's competence to produce speech. Analysis of this kind has given psychologists for the first time a linguistic model whose validity can perhaps be tested experimentally. A new term, "psycholinguistics" (apparently dating from about 1950), has come into wide use to describe the work of those whose investigations are carried out in the border area between psychology and linguistics. Methodologists and language teachers generally have been impressed by the value and relevance of these investigations and are showing unmistakable signs of renewed confidence in the helpfulness of psychologists.

The trend toward a rapprochement may have begun in 1955, when Carroll demonstrated that a leading educational psychologist can also be an excellent linguist by publishing his survey of linguistics and related disciplines. It was greatly strengthened by the passage of the National Defense Education Act (NDEA), which made available funds both for linguistic analysis and for psychological experimentation. In 1959 under NDEA auspices, a Conference on Psychological Experiments Related to Second-Language Learning was held at the University of California, Los Angeles. The research designed or suggested there was later carried out by investigators all over the country.[7] Especially favorable attention has been attracted by Berko's work (1958) on the child's learning of English morphology, which was widely popularized in a series of films on language teaching, and by Lambert's investigation (1961) at McGill of the roles of attitudes and motivation in foreign language learning. By 1961 enough material on psycholinguistics had accumulated to make possible the publication of a sizable anthology under that title by Saporta (1961).

The great interest in programmed learning gave impetus toward a reestablishment of the former close working relationship between language teachers and psychologists. Much of the development of programmed materials for language instruction—see Lane (1964)—has been based on the theoretical foundation supplied by Skinner (1957), leader of the strict behaviorists.

One of the foremost benefits that should accrue from such a close working relationship is a reawakening of the scientific spirit among language teachers. To be sure, the latter have tried hard at the urging of the linguists to be more scientific in their analysis of language itself, but this has been accompanied by an unmistakable tendency to accept on faith the linguists' dictums regarding methodology. There is an obvious need for more experimental testing of such tenets as "never are the students assigned a lesson in advance for silent study before coming to class," and "reading in the foreign language . . . is deliberately postponed until the structure of the new language is firmly grasped, and it may never become an important part of the study" (Fries, 1945, p. 7).

Though much past experimentation has been inconclusive, we seem at least to have learned *why* this has been the case. It should be possible through joint effort to devise experiments which would involve the acquisition of skills or the answering of questions that any teacher would regard as directly pertinent to foreign language instruction. And there appears to be no reason why these could not be carried out with sufficient rigor to satisfy the most exacting psychologist. Carroll believes that a particularly helpful type of experimentation that is now entirely feasible would be one designed not merely to differentiate two methods of instruction in terms of their overall results, but also to reveal *the conditions under which each method succeeds best* (1955, pp. 178-9, 187-9).

Even in its present state of development, learning theory is a valuable counterpoise to linguistic theory. In a study that should be widely read, *The Psychologist and the Foreign-Language Teacher*, Rivers (1964) shows how each major assumption of the Audiolingual Approach can be checked and often rendered more accurate and sophisticated by a confrontation with appropriate psychological literature.

But the greatest benefit to be hoped for is undoubtedly a better understanding of and a stronger emphasis on the human element in the language-teaching equation. Language learners are, in the main, rational human beings. They seem to be proud of their ability to analyze data and make generalizations. They do not normally enjoy speaking unless they understand what they are saying, but they do get great satisfaction from communicating their thoughts through speech. They like their sentences to come out in logical sequence, and hope that they bear some relationship to the real world around them. They are easily baffled by new names for old things or abstract representations of the concrete. They are deeply averse to the performance of tasks that seem meaningless to them. They dislike endless mechanical repetitions. They come in many different shapes and sizes, and appear to learn things in various ways. No matter what they are forced to do, they do not learn at all unless they want to do so. Language teachers have been in grave danger of losing sight of some of these apparent truths. Only the psychologists could perhaps tell us whether they are really facts, or merely beliefs held to be self-evident.

One must add that, if the necessary humanization is to be effected, it will probably not be through the influence of the Skinnerian behaviorists, with their view that a person is the mere site of verbal behavior rather than one of its causes. Contacts with this group may be of value in other ways, but their view of language and people does not seem to lead in the direction of greater feeling for the learner as an element of language teaching.[8] Fortunately, there are many other behaviorists who believe—along with other psychologists such as the gestalt group and even some of Pavlov's countrymen[9]—that the speaker does play a significant role in the generation of human speech.

THE AIMS OF LANGUAGE INSTRUCTION

Of the three cornerstones of method—whether it be in the teaching of English to speakers of other languages or in any other type of foreign language teaching—the aims of instruction are in one sense the most important. That is to say, in the teaching situation it is the methods used, more than any other factor, that determine the results achieved. And if results do not coincide with objectives, the teaching is at least partially unsuccessful. In any given classroom the teacher should have as clear an idea as possible of what s/he wants to accomplish and should choose his or her techniques and materials accordingly.

The aims of instruction are thus an overriding consideration. If they conflict with methodological conclusions drawn from another source, then these latter must be disregarded to the extent that they cannot be reconciled with the aims set up. A class made up of students who need, above all else, to learn to pronounce English well so as to become radio announcers can serve as an example. Because of the very definite nature of these students' needs, objectives can be precisely formulated in terms of a scientific skill. How shall the class spend its time? The teacher may have learned in a phonetics course that the ability to pronounce English depends primarily on being able to recognize one English sound as different from another. S/he may therefore be tempted to conclude that all classes in oral English, including this one, should be devoted to hearing and discrimination drills. But his or her objectives point in another direction, toward having the class spend its time in actually pronouncing English of the sort used by radio announcers. In this case, a reconciliation is certainly possible, since there is clear justification for both types of activity: both can be included in the class hour, but most time should be given to the type which most resembles the terminal behavior prescribed by the objectives.

Should any serious consideration of methods not begin, then, with the drawing up of a generally acceptable statement of objectives from which the most promising teaching techniques could be deduced in a step-by-step analysis? This is indeed the way the planning for any particular class or any single meeting of a class should begin. It would not be a very useful procedure for a textbook on methods of teaching English, however.

The difficulty lies in drawing up a statement that will win general acceptance. Language teachers have argued endlessly about objectives. Shall we aim at a speaking knowledge, a reading knowledge, or both? Shall we work toward a native-like perfection in pronunciation or content ourselves with reasonable intelligibility? Is it enough to develop practical language skills, or must we also impart an understanding of how language works? Should literature be taught for appreciation alone or for the insights it can give into a new culture? The list of questions could be prolonged almost indefinitely.

To gain even a moderate degree of acceptance, a statement of objectives would have to be so general, so vague, so devoid of any indication of priorities, as to be practically worthless as a basis for methodological decisions. Total agreement could probably be achieved on nothing more definite than that all those enrolled in English classes should learn English.

This is another way of saying that *instructional aims are useful as an indication of method only to the extent that they are specific.* Many general methodological principles can be deduced from the nature of language and some from what we know about the nature of the learner but none from the aims of instruction *en masse.* Objectives can play their dominant role only under circumstances which permit their being clearly defined; they should insure the modification of general methods in specific situations.

There is no intention here to suggest that, in refusing to agree on aims, language teachers are simply being perverse or stubborn. The chief reason they cannot agree is that languages must be taught for a great variety of purposes and there is never enough class time to achieve all the ends that would be desirable. The needs for English felt around the world today, and hence the reasons for teaching it, are particularly diverse and pressing. In the United States it is taught to give children a mastery sufficient to enable them to obtain a complete education in American schools, to make it possible for adult immigrants to function effectively in a new society, to put foreign students in a position to cope with university lectures and examinations, to familiarize pilots with a few spoken expressions so they can land a plane safely, etc. Overseas still other aims are pursued, equally valid and sometimes prescribed by law.

The clearest conclusion to be drawn from a study of the aims of teaching English to speakers of other languages is *the necessity for variety and flexibility of methods*.

There is much evidence that English teachers have tended to forget or ignore the overriding importance of specific objectives. Methods calculated to achieve one objective have been used in an attempt to achieve some other avowed or implicit objective that was quite different. Most new foreign students in American universities badly need help in learning to read rapidly and to express their thoughts in writing. Yet the only English courses provided for them in many institutions offer a diet made up almost exclusively of oral pattern practice and pronunciation drills. The justification given for this anomaly would presumably be that a mastery of the spoken language is an essential prerequisite to learning to read and write it. However sound such a principle may be in the abstract, when applied to this concrete case to the exclusion of all other considerations it leaves the teacher in the absurd position of never knowing whether or not s/he is making progress toward his or her reading-and-writing objectives. S/he hopes so, but mere hope is not sufficient. If a course aims to improve mastery of all the different language skills, it should include some practice in all of them.

Similar anomalies arise when textbooks developed to achieve a specific set of objectives are taken over and used with students whose needs are altogether different. At the English Language Institute of the University of Michigan, a series of texts was produced to meet the highly specialized needs of a group of adult Latin Americans living on campus and studying the language full-time so as to be able to enroll in an American university.[10] Because of their success in their original setting and their prestige, these texts were widely adopted, often without modification, for use in many parts of the world at various levels of instruction by students with very disparate needs. The expla-

nation usually given was that they were the best books available. In each such situation, a clear formulation of immediate and ultimate objectives would have enabled the teacher to see the extent and nature of the risk s/he was running and to plan the modifications necessary to make his or her work fully productive.

Teachers must often be reminded that aims, and hence methods, do and must vary. There is no one method, immutable, universal, eternal.

TESL, TEFL, AND TESOL

One of the clearest and most significant examples of the necessity for such modification stems from the differences between the objectives of teaching English as a second language and teaching it as a foreign language. In conclusion, then, it seems useful to try to clear up certain difficulties of terminology.

Those who teach English to students who speak some other language as their mother tongue have never found it easy to label their own profession. If they simply call themselves "teachers of English," they run the risk of having people think their work is no different from that of any other teacher of English in American or British schools, a very common and harmful confusion. But the attempt to find a more meaningful descriptive phrase always seems to produce terms that are either too long for current use (like that which stands at the beginning of this paragraph) or are awkward, ambiguous, or fraught with undesirable connotations.

The first phrase to gain currency in this country was "teachers of English as a *foreign* language," often abbreviated to TEFL. It was soon realized, however, that people like the Filipinos or the Nigerians, who receive most of their education through the medium of English and use it extensively in their everyday life even though it is not their mother tongue, do not like to think of the language as something foreign or alien to their culture.

To meet this objection, "teachers of English as a *second* language" (TESL) was proposed and became quite popular. "Second" was intended to mean simply that English was not the first language the students learned in point of time. It was thought that no word could be freer of emotional overtones than a colorless numerical term. Unfortunately, "second" turned out to have connotations of unimportance, especially when people began making the easy mistake of saying "secondary" instead of "second." Furthermore, it was objected that English might actually be the third or fourth language of students in a so-called second language situation; therefore, what was really needed was a phrase meaning any language other than the first.

In recent years still other terms have been suggested such as "teachers of English to speakers of other languages" (TESOL) and "teachers of English to non-English speakers" (TENES).[11] So far, no one appears to have discovered undesirable connotations in the first of these, but its meaning is certainly not completely clear: "speakers of other languages" seems to include any Americans who have learned to speak a foreign language in addition to English. The second, "teachers of English to non-English speakers," is awkward and one cannot be sure whether the reference is to speakers who are not English or to those who do not speak it. And how long do "non-English speakers" remain such? Are they still to be referred to in the same way in intermediate and advanced classes?

Obviously, no generally understood terminology has yet emerged. American members of the profession tend to use the various expressions interchangeably or according to personal preference.

It seems quite possible that the best solution of the problem may lie, not in attempting to win acceptance for one of the possible alternative terms as a general label and rejecting the others, but in assigning specific and much-needed meanings to those that are already best established. Undesirable connotations may disappear if the several different denotations can be made sufficiently clear.

There is already considerable precedent, especially in the United Kingdom, for assigning such a specialized meaning to "teachers of English as a *second* language." They are those who teach it in systems *where English is the partial or universal medium of instruction for other subjects in the curriculum.* On the other hand, "teachers of English as a *foreign* language" are those who work in systems *where instruction in other subjects is not normally given in English.* In this sense English is typically taught as a second language to Africans in Kenya or to Spanish-speaking children in the American Southwest, and as a foreign language in France. The distinction is thus based on the uses to which the language is to be put, on ultimate objectives. As was pointed out at the beginning of this section, this is a useful and important distinction. It also seems to be a reasonably clear one.

If specific meanings are assigned to "teachers of English as a second language" and "teachers of English as a foreign language," then there is still need for a term which can be applied to both groups jointly but which will distinguish them from those who teach English to children for whom it is the mother tongue. Such a term is useful, for example, in the name of a national association which embraces both former groups. Faced with this problem, those who organized such an association decided to use "teachers of English to speakers of other languages" (TESOL) as a name which would include all teachers who teach English to students who speak another language as their mother tongue.

Anyone who has read through this article will understand, without further explanation, the need for using an abbreviated form of these three expressions: TESL, TEFL, and TESOL. Each of the three abbreviations will stand for the type of work done ("the teach*ing* of . . .") as well as for those who do the work ("teach*ers* of . . .").

SUMMARY AND CONCLUSION

As this chapter indicates, there exist controversies in our profession ranging from the search for a reasonable language teaching methodology to the search for an appropriate professional name. Three "cornerstones" that are parts of the foundation in the development of any acceptable methodology have been proposed, with the third viewed as somehow being more basic than the other two:

a. Linguistics: the nature of language in general, and also the English language and the language(s) of the learner in particular.

b. Psychology: the nature of the learner, the nature of the teaching/learning process.

c. The aims of instruction: i.e., what things must the learner be able to do in or with English?

Current intellectual trends, which encourage the development of syllabi based on needs, and which encourage interdisciplinary research as well as healthy skepticism with respect to doctrinaire proposals, suggest that our profession is coming of age and will perhaps make better progress in the near future than it has in the past.

Various names (and acronyms) that have been suggested as professional labels have been listed and discussed; of these, the following appear to have gained relatively permanent acceptance:

TEFL (Teaching/Teachers of English as a foreign language): used in educational situations where instruction in other subjects is not normally given in English.

TESL (Teaching/Teachers of English as a second language): used in educational situations where English is the partial or universal medium of instruction for other subjects.

TESOL (Teaching/Teachers of English to speakers of other languages): a cover-term for teachers working in either of the above situations.

This relative consensus in terminology is also a healthy development.

NOTES

*This article, which has not been published previously, was first written in 1964-65 when the author was on sabbatical leave. Since an extensive up-dating was not a possible undertaking, the author at first did not want the article to appear as a chapter in this volume. However, the editors feel that the article is timeless in nature and contains much valuable information not found elsewhere in the literature. In addition, the information needed to update the article is contained in the two following chapters by Newton and Madsen.

Thus the author has agreed to permit the publication of the article in this volume with the qualification that it is—with only a few minor changes—the 1964-65 version.

1. There is a clear need for the term "applied linguistics" when it is properly used. Each year new possibilities of applying linguistics are being discovered in a large number of fields: machine translation, information retrieval, the analysis of literature, literacy campaigns, the treatment of aphasia, etc. But to equate "applied linguistics" with "language teaching" is a gross misuse of the term. Linguistics may be applied for many purposes and certainly much more is involved in language teaching than the application of linguistics.

2. The attempt to sort out the respective roles of linguists and language teachers has given rise to much impassioned writing on both sides. For an example of excessive linguistic claims see Cornelius (1953). A typical protest from an indignant teacher is that of Heise (1961).

3. This material was analyzed in some detail by Coleman and Fife (1933-49).

4. The Committees' formal report was made by Coleman (1929). The lack of correlation between recommendations and data was pointed out by Mercier (1930), Carroll (1955, p. 172) and others.

5. A concise survey of the various schools of psychology at mid-century was made by Woodworth (1948) and an analysis of the different approaches to learning theory by Hilgard (1956).

6. The most extensive such attempt was the Investigation of the Teaching of a Second Language reported by Agard and Dunkel (1948), and briefly assessed by Carroll (1955, pp. 177-9). A characteristic linguist's reaction to psychological experimentation dealing with language learning is that of Lado (1964b, pp. 35-45).

7. The conference report was prepared by Pimsleur (1959). Research completed by the end of 1964 is listed by the National Defense Language Development Program, U.S. Office of Education (1964).

8. See Chomsky's review (1959) of Skinner's *Verbal Behavior*.

9. See Chapters I and II of Belyayev (1964).

10. English Language Institute (1943).

11. Ohannessian (1965) suggests that the original appearance of the first of these expressions was in her *Interim Bibliography on the Teaching of English to Speakers of Other Languages* (1960) and that the second originated with Harold B. Allen's 1966 *Survey of the Teaching of English to Non-English Speakers.*

DISCUSSION QUESTIONS

1. When certain of the profession are referred to in Sections 1 and 2 of this article as "prophets," what meaning is attached to this term? Do you think the use of this word is justifiable?

2. Is it desirable that language instruction should become entirely explicable in scientific terms?

3. Do you agree that "the aims of instruction are not scientifically determined but depend on the needs felt by the society and the individual at a given moment"?

4. Why does the Skinnerian psychologists' view that people are the site of verbal behavior rather than one of its causes make it unlikely that they will contribute to the humanization of language teaching?

5. Can you explain the decision to consider the three cornerstones of method in the particular order followed in this section?

6. Do you think it is ever true that the best way to learn a given skill is to practice a different but related skill?

SUGGESTED ACTIVITIES

1. Ask several TESOL or other language teachers about specific ways in which a knowledge of linguistics or psychology has been helpful in their work, and try to find out their judgment as to the relative value to them of the two sciences. Report your findings to the class.

2. Conduct a poll among your fellow students in order to determine (a) the expression they prefer as a general label for all those that teach English to students who speak another language as their mother tongue and (b) the chief reason for their preference.

SUGGESTIONS FOR FURTHER READING

Belyayev, B. V. (1964)
The Psychology of Teaching Foreign Languages (translated from the Russian). New York: Macmillan.
Summarizes many interesting Soviet experiments that have pedagogical relevance to the teaching of foreign languages.

Fries, Charles C. (1945)
Teaching and Learning English as a Foreign Language. Ann Arbor: University of Michigan Press.
The earliest American exposition of language teaching methodology that follows the principles of structural linguistics. It was a classic (a "Bible" of sorts) up until the early 1960s.

Rivers, Wilga (1964)
The Psychologist and the Foreign-Language Teacher. Chicago: University of Chicago Press.
Focuses on the influence that various schools of psychology have had on language teaching methodology.

CURRENT TRENDS IN LANGUAGE TEACHING*

Anne C. Newton

INTRODUCTION

A few years ago language teaching methodology seemed monolithic. There were, to be sure, a few dissenting voices. But, on the whole, methodologists solidly favored the Audiolingual Approach.

Then came a voice "crying in the wilderness" of linguistic theory: Chomsky with his transformational-generative grammar, which challenged the very foundations that supported the entrenched methodology. At first this linguistic challenge seemed not to affect language teaching methodology itself: the controversies it engendered remained on the plane of rarified theoretical discussion. Chomsky himself pointedly denied the claim that his grammatical theory included or specifically implied a language teaching methodology.

Today, however, the confrontation between Chomskyan and structural linguistics causes us to ask—and try to answer—such questions as these: What impact, if any, have Chomsky's theories of linguistics and language acquisition had on language teaching methodology? What other influences are currently affecting the methodology? What has been the effect of these trends on the use of the Audiolingual Method? In what direction is language teaching headed?

The history of language teaching suggests two sources that, flowing together, produce the currents of methodological thought. One source is the changing concept of the nature of mind, which determines not only learning theory but also the form and direction of theory in the social sciencies—including psychology and linguistics. The other source consists, quite simply, of the practical concerns of language teaching, which vary according to the changing

needs of the language learner. These practical concerns may exist wholly apart from theoretical considerations. They reflect the changing social, political, economic, and other conditions that determine the motives and purposes for language study at any given time.

In order to understand the changing currents of thought in language teaching methodology, we need to recognize the effect of both influences, the theoretical and the practical. And the teacher who would choose his course wisely through the ebb and flow of the various tides of methodological thought must have a perspective based on some knowledge of the source and direction of these diverse currents. In order to acquire such perspective, let us look back for a moment to see where the audiolingual method came from.

THE AUDIOLINGUAL METHOD

We can trace the Audiolingual Method directly to the "scientific" linguistics of Bloomfield and his followers in the 1920s and 1930s and to the assumptions of behavioristic psychology, which had at that time come into vogue. Both behavioristic psychology and structural linguistics constituted a reaction against the theories that preceded them—against a vague and unscientific approach to the questions of human behavior, including the acquisition of knowledge. In the behaviorist-structuralist view nothing was truly scientific except empirical knowledge—whatever could be physically observed and measured. The "mentalism" of the past was to be rigorously avoided. Twaddell (1935), an enthusiastic exponent of the new approach, expressed this demand succinctly: "The scientific method is quite simply the convention that mind does not exist."

Theoretical factors

As applied to linguistics the "scientific method" meant that language was to be described only as *form*; any description in terms of meaning was prohibited. (That this ideal was ever fully achieved is questionable, and many linguists have asserted that language cannot be described wholly apart from meaning, since meaning—and its relation to mind—is inherent in the very nature of language.) This dictum of formalism led to such usages as numbered classifications for word categories in place of the traditional designations *noun, verb, adjective*, etc. By this means the linguist (and teacher) could avoid, it was thought, all reference to meaning or meaning-related definitions. Such purity of adherence to the empirical, or structural, method seems to have been early abandoned. But language continued to be viewed as a collection of discrete items to be put together like building blocks. This putting together was not a creative process: it was a matter of classifying and arranging.

Behaviorist psychology described all learning (including language acquisition) as a matter of conditioning—as the formation of habits through responses to outside stimuli. Thus one learned a language through *mimicry and memorization* ("mim-mem") and through *analogy*. It follows that the two basic techniques of audiolingual methodology are: (i) various kinds of mimicry and memorization, and (ii) pattern drills based on analogies. Clearly, such methodology is in accord with both structural linguistics and behaviorist psychology.

Practical factors

To gain a proper perspective on the Audiolingual Method, however, we need to appreciate the practical as well as the theoretical climate within which it developed. We may begin by listing the five slogans by which Moulton (1961) summed up the basic principles of the Audiolingual Method:

a. Language is speech, not writing.
b. A language is a set of habits.
c. Teach the language, not facts about the language.

d. A language is what native speakers say, not what someone thinks they ought to say.
e. Languages are different.

We have already considered how the second point ("a language is a set of habits") relates to the theoretical bases of structural linguistics and behaviorist psychology. The other slogans are also compatible with those theoretical foundations, though less obviously derived from them. Perhaps more importantly, however, they are clearly understandable in terms of our second "stream of influence"—the practical factors outside of linguistic or psychological theory. As Moulton points out, the origin of these principles lies mainly in three facts:

a. The linguists whose work underlies the development of this methodology were, by and large, anthropologists who had come into intimate contact with *nonwritten* American Indian languages (as opposed to the several European languages commonly taught in American schools).

b. This methodology was developed at a time when the United States was beginning to emerge from linguistic isolationism into an awareness of the desirability of learning to speak other languages.

c. This methodology was given initial impetus during World War II in a language teaching program that had the specific purpose of equipping the learners with a practical speaking knowledge of a number of "exotic" languages as quickly as possible, with virtually no relation to literature or the written language.

The relationship of the above three facts to the five slogans of the Audiolingual Method is apparent. The change in purpose and motivation for language learning—from a scholarly pursuit to a practical means of oral communication—was a decisive factor in the change to a new methodology.

Perhaps another factor was the expansion of "universal" education—the increased number of secondary school students with less scholarly interests and abilities. The curriculum in American schools underwent a marked change in the 1940s: from the traditional college-oriented classical education to the inclusion of courses concerned with the problems of "everyday life." A de-emphasis of literary matters of the traditional sort, and of rhetoric and formal composition, also characterized that period. We must recognize the importance of such non-theoretical considerations in seeking the "reasons" for adopting a methodology. Such recognition will provide a perspective that can help us guard against an unquestioning acceptance of any methodological dogma on the basis of theoretical arguments alone.

THE CHALLENGE

When Chomsky first published his theory of transformational generative grammar in 1957, it caused a stir in linguistic circles. Far from being just another theoretical aside, his work challenged the very foundations of structural grammars. Chomsky's linguistic theory had little impact on language teaching, however, for its methodological implications were not immediately apparent. His earliest writings on the subject dealt almost entirely with the forms of grammars rather than with the question of language acquisition.

However, in the introductory chapter of Chomsky (1965), he made it clear that he was challenging behavioristic theories of language acquisition as well as phrase-structure grammars. Language learning is not a matter of habit and conditioning, he asserted, but a creative process—a rationalistic, cognitive activity rather than a response to outside stimuli. Once again, the combined forces of a new linguistic theory and a new psychological theory were challenging existing methodology. But this time it was the linguistic and psychological theories underlying the Audiolingual Method that were under attack.

Practical considerations

Again, however, we cannot fully understand methodological change on the basis of theory alone; we must also consider the practical needs and reactions of language teachers and students. Simultaneous with, or even long before, their acquaintance with new theoretical influences,

many teachers using the Audiolingual Method had wished for some improvement or modification of the accepted methodology. Although they found the memorization and pattern-practice exercises useful for the early stages, they felt a need to build a bridge from those highly structured activities to the freer, more creative use of language at the intermediate and advanced levels. The Audiolingual Method and its proponents did not provide a satisfactory solution to this important problem.

Creative teachers, who early saw that a potential drawback of the Audiolingual Method was its tendency to be dull and uninspiring (for both student and teacher), tried to make the drills more interesting by varying their form, by providing a meaningful context, and by using visual aids. Resourceful teachers often succeeded admirably by such means. But there was a limit to what they could accomplish without making use of more "cognitive" activities.

Other sources of disillusionment with the audiolingual approach were its emphasis on speech (and consequent deemphasis of reading and writing), and the rigid order it prescribed for teaching the skills: listening, speaking, reading, and writing. Viewing it in historical perspective, we may see this rigid ordering as a reaction (perhaps overreaction) against the traditional Grammar-Translation Approach that had preceded it, which was almost wholly devoted to reading and writing (that is, translating) and learning rules of grammar.

Among other prescriptions of the Audiolingual Method that have been challenged on both theoretical and practical grounds are these: (a) that the student's native language should never be used in the classroom,[1] and (b) that classroom activities should be structured in such a way as to preclude the possibility for a student to make a mistake.

CURRENT TRENDS

The practical teacher may well ask: But what are the effects of this theoretical challenge and the expressed desire for something better? What is the current methodology? Do we have to abandon all we have learned of the Audiolingual Method and start anew? Are we to go back to the old Grammar-Translation Method? Or worse: Are we left without any guidance at all, to flounder among the currents of varying methodologies?

It is a hopeful sign—perhaps an indication of methodological maturity—that the reaction to one dogmatic approach has not resulted in another method equally arbitrary and inflexible. Thus far, the suggestions for change have been gentle, and we have not been left with a vacuum to be filled. Judging from techniques and trends of the past few years, we can see that current thinking in methodology seems to be in the direction of: (a) relaxation of some of the more extreme restrictions of the Audiolingual Method, and (b) development of techniques requiring a more active use of the students' mental powers.

Let us examine these two trends in some detail.

Relaxation of restrictions

Teachers have found that a close adherence to the listening-speaking-reading-writing order has not always brought the desired results—nor has a lack of such adherence necessarily proved harmful. They have also called into question the theory that speech is primary, and that reading and writing are secondary manifestations. Such theoretical and experimental rethinking has resulted in the current trend toward teaching and testing the various language skills in a more integrated way. We find a renewed interest, for example, in tests of the dictation and cloze types.[2] And teachers no longer feel the need to defer or widely separate reading and writing lessons from listening and speaking activities.

Similarly, the prohibition against using the student's native language has been considerably relaxed. It is just more efficient to give explanations and instructions in the native language—and this affords more time for really meaningful practice in English.

Notable among current trends is a more practical recognition of the varying needs of students. If, for instance, a student needs a reading knowledge of English above all else, then reading must have first priority, and the student must learn that skill through specific guided practice in reading.

More closely related to theoretical considerations is the question of whether the teacher must structure the student's participation so rigidly that s/he has almost no chance of making a mistake. That "prohibition" of errors was due largely to the fear that the slightest mistake uttered by the student would contribute to the creation of a bad habit. Now that the "habit theory" of language acquisition has been so strongly challenged and the creative aspects of language learning emphasized, the teacher is largely freed from that fear. The current thinking considers the student's creative involvement more important to the learning process than the mere avoiding of errors. (This does not mean, of course, that the teacher should abandon the standard of correctness or should fail to correct the student and provide necessary drill when appropriate.)

Moving toward communication

As mentioned above, teachers have for some time felt a need to move from the rigidly structured practice prescribed by the early proponents of the Audiolingual Method to a less controlled situation in which the student can communicate his or her own ideas. Prator (1965) described this problem and suggested a practical solution to it in an article entitled "Development of a Manipulation-Communication Scale." In this article Prator points out that all language learning activities can be classified as either purely manipulative, purely communicative, or some combination of the two. He suggests that it may be helpful to think of classroom activities as falling into at least four major categories: (a) those that are *completely manipulative*, (b) those that are *predominantly manipulative* (this kind of exercise would have a little communicative value), (c) those that are *predominantly communicative*, and (d) activities that are *completely communicative*.

Examples of completely manipulative activity would be: (a) a drill in which the students merely repeat sentences after the teacher, (b) a simple substitution drill. The latter exercise could be made into a predominantly manipulative drill if the teacher indicated the word to be substituted by showing a picture that suggests the word rather than actually saying the word, or by having the students supply the word from their own knowledge or experience. For example, instead of doing a routine substitution drill in which the student substitutes in the sentence a cue word given by the teacher (*My father is an engineer, a doctor, a merchant, a teacher*), the student may respond with the name of his or her father's real profession.

In a more advanced class, an element of communication might be brought in by having the students retell, after a lapse of time, a story the teacher has given them. Various kinds of question-and-answer exercises, paraphrases of dialogues, and other oral and written activities can become *predominantly communicative* as they move away from simple repetition or memorization toward a freer expression of the student's own knowledge and ideas. Finally, an example of pure communication would be a free conversation among the members of the class.[3]

The trend toward cognitive activity

The trend toward a more active use of the student's mental powers probably represents the most important effect of the cognitive theory of language acquisition. This *mental activity* goes well beyond the more passive "activity" that the Audiolingual Method called for. Advocates of the Audiolingual Method often advised the teacher to keep students "active"—since, they said, when a student is active s/he is learning. They advised the teacher to have all the students saying things aloud in English during as much of the class period as possible. This was the chief reason for doing so much choral work. In this way the greatest number of students could be actively participating—"using the language," as it was called.

But the utility of such "active" use of language has been challenged by proponents of cognitive-code learning. They point out that the mere mechanical repetition of language forms is in reality *passive* rather than *active* learning, for it is primarily—sometimes almost entirely—a physical, mechanical sort of activity. It does not begin to engage the student's full mental powers.

Viewing language learning as a natural creative process rather than as habit formation suggests that the teacher should provide guided practice in thinking in the language rather than mere repetitive drill. Such mental involvement tends to make language learning more enjoyable for the student, which must itself be a positive factor contributing to improved attitudes and better results.

We should note, too, that this kind of mental activity is quite different from memorizing grammar rules, as in the old Grammar-Translation Method. Nor is it simply the manipulation of examples of grammar rules—an activity that was largely discredited by the early proponents of the Audiolingual Method.

An illustration of mental involvement

At the 1973 convention of the TESOL organization, Rutherford presented a modest illustration of how the teacher can use the student's natural curiosity and mental energies. While his exercises are basically similar to those in many textbooks, they contain an element of interest not usually found in such exercises. Here are some of Rutherford's examples (slightly modified) for practicing sentences linked by *and so*, *and neither*, and *but*:

Teacher: *I'm thinking of taking a trip, but I don't want to go to Europe this time. I think I'll go to Spain and Portugal instead.*
Student: *Spain is in Europe, and so is Portugal.*
Teacher: *What countries border on Spain besides Germany and Belgium?*
Student: *Germany doesn't border on Spain, and neither does Belgium.*
Teacher: *My first stop is Madrid, but I haven't decided whether to go there by boat or by plane.*
Student: *The plane goes to Madrid, but the boat doesn't.*
Teacher: *I'm studying French and Italian so I'll be able to communicate a little when I get to Spain.*
Student: *French isn't the language of Spain, and neither is Italian.*
Teacher: *At first I thought I'd be back by the 31st of August, but the trip has been delayed. So I'll return on the 31st of September.*
Student: *August has 31 days, but September doesn't.*

In doing these exercises the student has to listen carefully for the meaning and then decide what is wrong with the statement, or with some part of it. Even the students who don't have an opportunity to give their answers aloud must be mentally involved all along the way. They have received guided practice in thinking in English.

Gattegno's "Silent Way"

A method of language teaching that seems to reflect the influence of the cognitive-code theory of learning is the system developed by Gattegno (1972) called the "Silent Way." The name is somewhat misleading, because the students do make oral statements and responses in the language they are learning. But the teacher, especially, speaks much less than in the average Audiolingual classroom, and the students do not mimic and repeat aloud so frequently. Rather, they are motivated to "think and say" the appropriate sentence(s) to accompany actions performed under the guidance of the teacher.

Ideally, the "silent spaces" between utterances are filled with the student's activity of thinking in the language s/he is learning, as s/he mentally repeats and recalls words and phrases and puts them together to form appropriate new sentences. Perhaps the most remarkable characteristic of Gattegno's method is the keen attention with which the student watches the actions and listens to the utterances of the teacher and his or her fellow students, as s/he strives to grasp the meaning as well as the form of those utterances.

The advantage of the "Silent Way" is that it combines a high degree of mental involvement and interest with actual use of the language. This combination of close interest and intensive listening with actual practice in producing the language would seem to include almost all the elements required for efficient language learning. It has not yet been demonstrated, however, how such a method would work in the average classroom situation, or how successfully it might be used at more advanced stages.

The "lecturette" technique

In the 1972 *UCLA Workpapers in TESL* Bowen describes a technique that embodies several ideas of current interest in language teaching: integration of skills, carefully planned listening exercises, attention to meaning, and active participation on the part of the student. This technique is based on short presentations prepared for student listening, called "lecturettes." It is designed to provide practice in several language skills: listening and reading comprehension, copying and taking dictation, and writing and spelling.

The lecturettes are written in two forms, *full* and *simplified*. *Full* means normal English prose of a certain difficulty. *Simplified* means a paraphrase written in somewhat easier form and with a limited vocabulary. Each of these versions is recorded on tape in two forms: *regular* and *deliberate*. *Regular* is the normal speed of delivery for a public lecture. *Deliberate* is a somewhat slower delivery. This makes four variations altogether:

a. simplified deliberate,
b. simplified regular,
c. full deliberate,
d. full regular.

The idea is to take the student through these four versions in graded sequence, from simple deliberate to the full form at normal speed. The teacher provides for the student's active participation by giving him or her a modified dictation task, as follows: The text of the lecturette is prepared with every tenth word deleted (the cloze technique). The students then listen to the tape with their mind as well as their ears, and write in each blank space the word they hear that belongs in that space. For each of the four variations, different words are deleted from the written text.

The above procedure constitutes a kind of comprehension/dictation technique that integrates the language skills. This reflects a current trend toward teaching the four skills together rather than one after another.

Selective listening

In line with the emphasis on a fuller use of the student's perceptive and cognitive faculties is a new interest in *meaningful listening*. This interest is reflected in the recent reprinting of an article by Nida (1952-53) entitled "Selective Listening" in a 1972 anthology prepared by Allen and Campbell.[4] In this article Nida emphasizes the usefulness of carefully planned listening, in which the learner concentrates in a systematic way on certain features at a time.

Nida lists five general principles of selective listening, as follows:

a. Selective listening should begin from the very moment that one first hears a language.
b. One should listen for only one feature (or one set of features) at a time.
c. One should listen successively to all the features of a language.
d. The order of listening to different features should be systematic.
e. One should concentrate particularly on those features that cause the learner difficulty in understanding and speaking.

Nida further suggests that the order of features to be listened for should usually be as follows: first, phonetic features (that is, sounds); then vocabulary; then grammar (elements of morphology and syntax). More specifically, Nida suggests that the learner should begin by listening at length for the principal intonational characteristics: the typical rise and fall of the voice, the staccato effect of syllable sequence, types of pauses, rhythms of long and short vowels, and types of emphatic forms—not necessarily to know the meaning of these distinctions, but just to discover the patterns.

Next, the student should listen for particularly striking or "strange" consonants—that is, consonants that are not present in his or her native language. After that, s/he should tackle the vowels, first listening to the extremes (like /iy/ and /uw/), then the lower and more central vowels.

In listening for vocabulary, the student can listen for words and phrases that s/he has already learned. S/he can also discover expressions that s/he has not learned but which recur in the text.

Nida points out that as the student listens for grammatical elements s/he can begin to predict certain forms or words that will follow from the occurrence of certain other forms. This kind of predicting is, of course, what the native speaker does constantly when listening to the language.

As a supplementary activity to selective listening, Nida suggests *selective reading*—that is, concentrating on certain features as one reads, and building up an awareness of them.

Individualized instruction

We have heard much in recent years about "individualized instruction." However, individualized instruction is not a technique, or set of techniques, that one can readily describe. It is, rather, the recognition that students have different needs and different abilities, that they learn at different rates of speed, and that a single method or technique is not equally successful or appropriate for all learners.

For example, various studies reported in Chastain (1970) have indicated that the Audio-lingual Approach is more successful with students of low verbal ability, while the Cognitive Approach is more successful with students of high verbal ability. At this date, most activities described under the general heading of "individualized teaching" are still in the experimental stages. They consist primarily of dividing classes into various groups and providing activities for interaction of the students within each group.

Most experiments in "individualized instruction" that have been reported have been developed to meet the unique needs of a particular group of students.[5] Such experiments do more to indicate current trends in thought than to provide a generalizable solution to specific problems. While some techniques that have proved successful for one group of students might also be useful for another group, the principal message of these experiments would seem to be "Adapt, don't adopt"—which might serve as a general slogan for today's trends in language teaching.[6]

A recent experiment

Many experiments in so-called "individualized instruction" reflect a current interest in two pedagogical ideas: the idea of group interaction, and the idea that the individual learner should be allowed to progress at his or her own pace and in his or her own way. An experiment at the University of Michigan that seems to combine these two ideas was described by LaForge (1971).[7] The participants in this series of experiments were groups of five graduate and undergraduate students and professional people.

These learners, who were native speakers of English, sat in a circle, with a microphone in the center of the room. Also present was a native speaker of the language the group was studying (say, French). When one of the participants wished to say something, he said it in English and the French speaker said it in French for him. In this way a free conversation developed, with the speakers' utterances translated into the target language. The conversation, which was limited to fifteen minutes, was recorded on tape and played back to the group, which then analyzed it.

The participants noted that the periods of silence that occurred from time to time were in fact moments of intense mental activity as they reflected on what they had said. During most of these silent periods, each one was verbalizing to him- or herself the sentences s/he had heard another person say. The tape recording revealed that the participants often drilled themselves intensively on the utterances produced by the native-speaker assistant. In reflecting on the experience, members of the group felt that the entire procedure had provided them with a double experience in the learning process—a direct and a reflex experience.

As LaForge readily admits, this experiment raises many questions of both a theoretical and a practical nature and presents difficulties that would seem to preclude its duplication in a normal classroom situation. Nevertheless, it provides a useful example of the recent inclination to think of language learning in terms of group interaction in an informal situation rather than in terms of an individual experience within a highly structured group context.

Perhaps one of the significant results of this experiment is the realization (characteristic of a number of recent experiments) that this kind of procedure works better for some kinds of learners than for others. Responding least favorably to the Michigan experiment were linguistically sophisticated participants and those who found the informality unacceptable.

LOOKING AHEAD

Current thinking in language teaching methodology seems to show a trend toward eclecticism—that is, toward "choosing what appears to be the best from diverse sources, systems, or styles." This trend is in many ways the direct opposite of the monolithic approach mentioned at the beginning of this article.

Eclecticism is sometimes misunderstood to mean that all approaches are equally valid, and that therefore it is not important to know about various methods or ideas or new experiments or trends. This would seem to suggest that the training and continuing education of teachers might not be necessary. But in fact the opposite is true.

An approach that is truly eclectic makes the greatest demands on teachers. It requires them to know enough about the various sources, systems, and styles of teaching to choose wisely between what is good for their particular purposes and what is not useful. It requires of them both an intelligent skepticism and a ready enthusiasm; a willingness to reject both old and new techniques that seem unsuitable and an eagerness to refresh their teaching with useful adaptations of techniques both new and old. To do this intelligently, they must be well informed about the methods and techniques that are available to them. Then they can wisely "adapt, not adopt."[8]

As a concluding note, it seems appropriate to remind ourselves that teaching involves much more than a knowledge of methods. However well versed a teacher may be in psychological and linguistic theories, in techniques and methodologies, this knowledge alone will not assure success. An even more basic ingredient of all good teaching is the teacher's attitude toward his or her students and work.

In his article "English through Drama," Via (1972) stated this fact in the simplest terms: "You must love your students. Or you must love the subject you are teaching. It's best if you can love them both." More than ever, we must recognize the teacher's compassionate, intelligent, individual approach to his or her work as the essential factor in successful language teaching.

NOTES

*This article was originally published in the *English Teaching Forum*, 12:1, Jan-March, 1974. It is reprinted in this volume with the journal's permission.

The Discussion Questions, Suggested Activities, and Suggestions for Further Reading are original.

1. Although the origin of this prohibition is traceable to the Direct Method rather than to the Audiolingual Approach, it became closely identified with the latter and was recommended and practiced in varying degrees by many proponents of Audiolingualism.

2. A cloze test is one in which words are omitted from a text at regular intervals (every 5th, or 7th, or 10th word, for example). The student must supply the missing words according to his understanding of the text and his knowledge of English structure and vocabulary. In this connection see Bowen (1972).

3. Two other useful discussions about introducing elements of communication into pattern drill are Palmer (1971) and Cosgrave (1971).

4. This anthology contains a number of interesting articles about current thought in language-teaching methodology.

5. An example is Sprenger (1973).

6. This slogan is by no means a new one. Prator, of the University of California, Los Angeles, used it frequently in his classes in the late 1950s.

7. I am indebted to my colleague Julia Dobson for references on this and other recent innovations, as well as for her comments on the article as a whole.

8. See, for example, Paulston (1974), which combines a discussion of twelve important books on language teaching methodology based on the author's personal experience in using the books in teacher-training courses with a listing of ten other books in specialized fields, such as testing and language laboratories.

5. Why do you think the reaction to the Audiolingual Approach has not resulted in a similarly dogmatic approach as its successor?

6. (a) Permitting students to use languages creatively, on the one hand, and (b) preventing students from practicing errors, on the other hand, seem to be conflicting goals. How does current thinking regard this seeming dilemma? What is your view?

7. What is meant by "active" participation in the language classroom (a) in the Audiolingual sense? (b) in the Cognitive sense? Do you think the distinction is real and/or useful?

8. How does the "mental involvement" called for by the Cognitive Approach differ from the "mental involvement" of the Grammar-Translation Method?

9. Do you think that using an eclectic approach makes greater or fewer demands on the teacher than following a single method? Why or why not?

10. What two major considerations combine to produce the methodology at a particular time and place? How, in particular, did this produce the Audiolingual Approach?; the reaction to the Audiolingual Approach?

11. What are the two basic techniques of the Audiolingual Approach, and how do they reflect the influence of behaviorist psychology and structural linguistics?

DISCUSSION QUESTIONS

1. In what ways were Bloomfield's "scientific" linguistics and behavioristic psychology a reaction against the theories that preceded them?

2. How did the "scientific method" affect the description of languages?

3. In what ways did practical factors produce a climate of acceptance for the Audiolingual Approach?

4. In what ways did the Audiolingual Approach fail to meet the expectations of teachers who used it?

SUGGESTED ACTIVITIES

1. Explore and describe in detail the background and practical implications of one of the following trends: (a) the movement toward cognitive activity/mental involvement; (b) the movement toward improving listening comprehension; (c) the movement toward communication; (d) the movement toward individualized instruction.

2. Read Paulston's "A Biased Bibliography" (1974). Select one of the twelve language teaching methodology texts she reviews. Read the text yourself carefully, and then write your own review stating whether or not you agree with Paulston and why.

3. Write an essay outlining some of the important questions that must be answered if a new, improved and unified language methodology is to be achieved in the future. Make your priorities obvious.

4. Read Gattegno's *Silent Way* and Stevick's review of it in *TESOL*, Vol. 8, No. 3, Sept. 1974, pp. 305-14. Write an essay giving your own reaction to this approach as well as showing how the "Silent Way" reflects trends toward cognitive involvement on the part of the student.

SUGGESTIONS FOR FURTHER READING

Diller, Karl Conrad (1978)
The Language Teaching Controversy. Rowley, Mass.: Newbury House.
A survey of the recent history of language teaching focusing on currently controversial issues.

Kelly, L. G. (1969)
25 Centuries of Language Teaching 500 BC-1969. Rowley, Mass.: Newbury House.
Provides excellent historical perspective on the language teaching methodologies that have been employed from the time of the Greeks to the present.

Moulton, William G. (1961)
"Linguistics and Language Teaching in the United States," in Mohrmann, Sommerfelt, and Whatmough (eds.). *Trends in European and American Linguistics 1930-1960.* Utrecht: Spectrum Publ.
An overview of structural linguistics and audiolingual method that dominated European and American language teaching during this period.

Paulston, Christina Bratt (1974)
"A Biased Bibliography," *Language Learning*, 23 (June, 1973), pp. 129-43.
A useful and subjective evaluation of twelve texts concerned with language teaching methodology that can be used as references or in teacher-training courses.

INNOVATIVE METHODOLOGIES APPLICABLE TO TESL

Harold S. Madsen

INTRODUCTION

With the decline of that blissful Ptolemaic era during the 1950s and 1960s when Audiolingualism was the center of our methodological universe, language teachers—particularly in this country—began to give thought to new methodology. But there was no heir apparent in either the ranks of transformational-grammar or of cognitive psychology. During the transition period of the late '60s and early '70s, psychologist Carroll made a significant plea for moderation and reconciliation.[1] He pointed out practical values in both the behavioristic and cognitive schools, suggesting that a synthesis of methodologies was possible. Some agreed that synthesis was both possible and desirable (cf.

Ney, 1973). Marckwardt also supported the idea that the time was ripe for "a prudent eclecticism."[2] But Diller (1975) held that eclecticism was untenable and unable "to endure for long." His rather optimistic view was that "responsible teachers" could fashion their own method consistent with the present understanding of what language is and how it is learned.

Some independent methodologies were fashioned, as they had been during the Audiolingual era, but most tended to be in-house efforts in government, business, and higher education. Specialized approaches emerged in Work Incentive programs as they had in the Foreign Service Institute; distinctive methodological approaches were devised in corporations ranging from Mobil Oil in Japan to IBM

France, as well as in language training schools such as Berlitz and English Language Services. Some universities also formulated their own system, one of the most innovative being the PLATO computerized TESL program at the University of Illinois, a self-instruction program capable of transmission to terminals in other institutions.

Most teachers, on the other hand, have tried either to remodel their old approach somewhat, or to select a text with a more contemporary orientation. Their British counterparts, who have been in the second language business for so many decades, have long used a pragmatic-intuitive approach to methodology, drawing on linguistic science when it seemed appropriate. American language teachers seem at last to be achieving a similar independence—perhaps the "methodological maturity" spoken of by Newton: one dogmatic monolithic approach has not been abandoned in favor of "another method equally arbitrary and inflexible."[3]

Methodological alternatives have been suggested in areas such as individualized instruction.[4] And another broad area of great interest with immediate implications for methodology is the whole concern with communicative competence.[5] Moreover, much has been written on limited areas ranging from vocabulary acquisition to testing.

But despite this volume of literature, not to mention the writings of transformational grammarians and psycho- and sociolinguists, there seemed to be something of a vacuum in methodology during the early post-Audiolingual period. It was natural that innovations should appear. As they emerged, some teachers embraced them with an almost religious fanaticism, while the majority scrutinized them with cautious interest to find what insights or techniques might be gleaned from them. Our objective in this chapter will be to survey the approach used in some of the most significant innovations, and to look at their rationale and limitations.

We will consider "innovations" that have been around for a decade or more—though with little public exposure—as well as some which have been only recently conceived. In the former category are methodologies such as St.

Cloud and microwave; in the latter are Harrison's Structured Tutoring and the Winitz-Reeds approach. Following a brief overview of seven innovations, we will examine three in more depth.

THE ST. CLOUD METHOD

The St. Cloud method is far less familiar to TESL teachers than to teachers of foreign languages. Its inception was in 1951 at a teacher training college in St. Cloud, France.[6] It is a carefully structured course in which students are immersed in multi-media language presentations. Since oral communication in particular depends on more than mere linguistic skill, it was felt that cultural, non-verbal, situational ingredients should permeate the presentation. Film strips are the dominant medium, though films are used for passive review. The Direct Method is employed; initially students watch a picture sequence, then repeat the material chorally. Students do not see the written language until after sixty hours of instruction. St. Cloud appears to be most successful during the earlier stages and most appreciated by non-native teachers who are not completely secure in the language they are teaching. It produces better phonological than communicative competence; and it has proven more satisfactory with younger students than with those of college age.[7]

THE MICROWAVE DEVICE

The microwave or Cummings device was conceived of in 1964 by Stevick when he was developing teaching materials for exotic languages at the Foreign Service Institute and in the Peace Corps. In the writings of Cummings (e.g., Cummings, 1916), he recognized the power of a small corpus of questions and answers in generating new vocabulary and bona fide communication. He found "true, important, and ... autobiographical" material to be most effective. The microwave format consisted of an utterance (generally a question and four to eight replies); the cycle of instruction included an M-phase (mimicry, manipulation, mechanics) and a C-phase (communication, conversation and continuity). His format was employed in a wide variety of teaching materials and utilized in practical overseas situations where U.S. personnel had to communicate in a cluster of foreign language situations within a very short period of time. Though produced commercially as a "method" by his imitators, according to Stevick, it is too limited for such a wide application. He feels it should play "a supporting role, or at most a co-starring role" in language materials" (Stevick, 1971, pp. 310-64; see also Schumann, 1972).

HALL'S SITUATIONAL REINFORCEMENT

At the close of the last decade, Hall assailed the Audiolingual Approach; its dialogues, he said, failed to approximate actual language. He charged that "almost no language learning takes place in the average language classroom." First in Saudi Arabia and later in Washington, D.C. he developed strategies and materials to remedy this situation. First, he prepared lessons that would involve the students in "authentic communication" (as Stevick had done). Second, he built in cognitive choices in order to avoid mere mechanical repetition; and finally, he incorporated analogy. A principal aim was to have students involved in doing what they were talking about. Hall discarded the sequenced grammar approach; the only sequencing is a gradual one from situations that are related exclusively to concrete objects to those involving more abstract ideas. The minimal grammar instruction grows entirely out of the situation. His widely used S-R *Orientation in American English* series, written with Costinett, is easily used by teachers with minimal training in TESL; students enjoy the realistic situations which lend themselves easily to field trips and use of relevant realia. Personal experience has shown that in addition to excessive repetition in the lesson format, the unstructured-unsequenced material can give students the feeling that they are not making any real progresss. In actual fact, however, students learn to communicate quite soon with these materials (see also Hall, 1978).

WINITZ-REEDS' AURAL DISCRIMINATION METHOD

In 1973, Winitz and Reeds introduced a visually-cued listening approach to language instruc-

tion. In their material for learning German Winitz and Reeds introduce vocabulary at least four or five times as fast as is possible in regular classes, and they teach inflectional mastery, phonology, and syntax as well. The strategy consists of having the students listen to an utterance and then from a group of four pictures select the one which best represents what they have heard. Students do not begin to speak until they have mastered the basic structure and vocabulary of the language. While interest is apparently high, this Aural-Discrimination Approach lacks the variety of some methods and the relevance inherent in Stevick and Hall. Because of its similarity to Total Physical Response, to be discussed later, one might well anticipate some of the temporary pronunciation difficulties that TPR experienced when speech was introduced. The main question is whether there is adequate variety to sustain this as a total method. For more discussion of this method see Winitz and Reeds (1975) and Ney (1976), a review of the 1975 monograph.

LIPSON'S STYLIZED MNEMONICS

Lipson's Stylized Mnemonics, unlike the previous methods discussed, utilizes translation at the outset of instruction (Lipson, 1971). A corpus of sentences is learned through choral repetition and translation. But drawings replace translation almost immediately. Interesting, culturally relevant vocabulary is combined in exotic situations. Following are typical symbolic representations used by Lipson:

Some grammatical explanations are presented, but from the outset the emphasis is on communication. The situations become more and more involved; novel combinations of language are constantly generated. The approach is cognitive, culturally oriented, systematic, and interesting. The limitations in Lipson include the bizarre situations which can create an amused detachment on the part of the learner; the need at least initially of a linguistically homogeneous group; and the requirement of a bilingual teacher (although native informants could be used).

HARRISON'S STRUCTURED TUTORING

Several years ago instructional psychologist Harrison developed a highly successful method to teach disadvantaged children how to read. It involved volunteer tutors—adult or peer. Literate, native speakers were accepted for the assignment, provided they were warm and supportive of the person being tutored. Carefully prepared instructions guided every move of the volunteer teacher. In recent years, Harrison has extended his tutorial approach to include English, Spanish, and French (with German and Japanese in the formative stages) (Harrison, 1976 and 1977). The students, who must be literate in their native tongue, receive four one-hour tutorial visits a week and work four to six hours on their own. Designed for adults and youths on the secondary level, the materials can be covered in one and a half to two months, with reading and writing introduced even to beginners during the second week of instruction. Tutors spend 80 percent of their time on grammar during seven out of the eight units. The balance of the time is divided among activities ranging from the eliciting of novel utterances to careful mastery checks of language achievement. Pilot programs in Latin America and the United States are reporting dramatic language acquisition with only a few weeks of instruction. Other advantages include the negligible costs involved (simply administrative and materials charges) and the good will that is generated. Limitations include (according to one administrator) the lack of continuity when volunteers outside the school are used and some drop out because of lack of time; the

difficulty in finding volunteer native-speaking tutors overseas; and occasional chafing by experienced teachers under the tightly controlled tutorial materials.

ASHER'S TOTAL PHYSICAL RESPONSE

Widely cited in journals on foreign language instruction, Asher's Total Physical Response methodology (see Asher, 1977) reportedly provides rapid, permanent instruction through the use of commands accompanied by a physical response. TPR (as the method is called) is still in the development stage, although four major controlled experiments have been conducted in TPR during the past dozen years. Languages taught include Japanese, Russian, German, and Spanish. Within thirty minutes school children and adults were able to carry out commands ranging from single-word imperatives to those of this complexity: *Isu kara tatte, kokuban no anata no namae o kese.* These volunteer subjects demonstrated virtually perfect retention after two weeks had elapsed and again after a period of a year. Moreover, they outstripped the performance of high school and college students, who had received three to four times as many hours of instruction as TPR students (Asher, 1964, 1965, 1972; Asher et al., 1974). While demonstrating impressive results, the Total Physical Response approach is still in the process of development. Asher recognizes that he now needs to develop advanced-level techniques, "fine tuning," as he calls it. He feels that the Winitz-Reeds approach discussed earlier might well contribute the refinement needed in TPR. Some concerns of interested observers include the following: Thus far, TPR has been an experimental model with volunteer students; does it have the characteristics needed to meet the learning needs of less well-motivated students? Initial TPR experiments were measured in minutes rather than hours; the latter extended instruction to 32 and then to 90 hours. Is TPR viable as a teaching methodology through the advanced level? Stevick felt his microwave technique did not offer sufficient variety to constitute a thoroughgoing methodology. Are TPR commands in the same category? Regardless of the answers to these questions, TPR has demonstrated its effectiveness in providing rapid and rather permanent language gains on early levels; and a somewhat surprising transfer effect on reading and writing skills.

While widely different in approach, each of the seven methods discussed above departs in various ways from traditional instruction of the past two decades. In most of them, situation plays a highly significant role in relation to the linguistic matter presented. And in most, meaning and cognition are predominant; in several, students are required to use and respond to novel combinations of the language.

The three methodologies that we shall now look at in somewhat greater detail are significant because their rationale is compatible with our present understanding of language acquisition and because of their increasing influence on language teaching. At the same time they are new enough that many language teachers in the country have had little or no exposure to them. The three are Lozanov's Suggestology, Gattegno's Silent Way, and Curran's Counseling Learning. Each of these "innovative" methodologies has been around for over a decade; and interestingly, each of the three (like TPR) was developed by someone outside the language teaching discipline.

SUGGESTOLOGY

Suggestology (sometimes referred to as Suggestopedia) was developed in Eastern Europe by psychiatrist Lozanov of Sofia, Bulgaria. Like Gattegno, Lozanov indicates that his methodology transcends the language classroom and can be applied in other school subjects as well. He even notes applications that can be made in psychiatry, business, and medicine. As applied in the school, Lozanov's methodology is designed to counteract the many negative "suggestions" or fears which purportedly inhibit learning: feelings of incompetence, fear of making mistakes, apprehension of that which is novel or unfamiliar. One means is through the prestige of the method and the authority and reputation of the instructor. "Infantilization" is fostered, or, in other words, a child-like trust in the system. A second and related means is through student self-confidence stemming from increasing language facility as well as the "authority" and prestige of method and teach-

er. Learner confidence and inclination to communicate are provided both through relaxed but direct instruction, and through subtle covert communication, essentially non-verbal, suggesting that learning is progressing well, and that it is easy and pleasant. An interesting adjunct is the use of aesthetic principles, notably the arts. This key feature in Suggestology includes not only the use of music, which is so universally associated with the method, but also the sensitive presentation of the teacher and (as in Counseling Learning) a close interaction of class members and instructor. Breaking down the inhibiting fears of learners is said to result in "hypermnesia" or heightened memory as well as uninhibited communicative competence (see Racle, 1977).

In practice, how does this work? Suggestion begins with the selection of an appropriate setting. Since it is felt that classrooms call to mind the frustration, failure, and artificiality of many previous learning efforts, Suggestology classes are conducted in a living-room atmosphere with carpeted floors and easy chairs. Such a setting is designed to encourage informal contact and free, natural communication. The aesthetic element is integrated through judicious use of music or even elements of art, lecture, and theater. To suggest that the language to be learned is easy, scores of lines of dialogue are introduced every few days (introducing only a few lines at a time would supposedly concede that the language was so difficult it could be digested only a small bite at a time). Homework is minimal: simply a request to read over (but not memorize) the lines of the dialogue before retiring and upon arising in the morning. Finally, the orientation is on communication. Content and exchange of ideas precede the full mastery of form. Accurate pronunciation and grammar are to come in due course. Students are provided a new name and role on the first day of class. As the course proceeds, they live out a new identity rather than wrestle with a foreign language. As in Counseling Learning, student initiative is paramount; as in the Silent Way, correction is minimal (Madsen and Bushman, 1976).

Typically, six hours of class time are required to cover each lesson. The two-part division of the lesson includes the language presentation through dialogue and communication activities. The dialogue for a lesson is a surprising ten to fourteen pages long; although students have no text, they do receive a copy of the dialogue. These somewhat rambling conversations based on common themes serve as resource material for language assimilation through listening, for grammatical explanations in a simple-to-complex scheme, and for communication activities. There is considerable built-in redundancy.

The dialogues are presented to the students in three phases: explicative reading, intonational reading, and concert. In the *explicative* reading, the teacher moves through the entire dialogue, commenting on the meaning of words, on pronunciation, grammar, or whatever s/he anticipates may cause the student difficulty. Explanations are simple, avoiding technical language. Students follow along on their handouts without repeating, though they are free to ask questions if they choose. In the *intonational* reading, the teacher again reads the whole new dialogue aloud, but this time without comment. The reading begins and ends with mood music. Three special intonations alternate throughout the selection: normal, hushed, and strong. After reading a line or phrase with one intonation, and then giving the native language translation in a low, neutral voice, the teacher proceeds to the following line, using the text intonation of the cycle, and so forth. Pauses and variations in rhythm heighten the contrasts of the lines. Students follow along on their handouts, but there is no interaction·with the teacher. The third phase of dialogue presentation is the *concert.* After a short break, the students are invited to put away their dialogues, sit back, and enjoy the concert of music that is played. They may close their eyes, but are not to sleep; they need *not* pay attention to the reading of the dialogue that will be presented along with the music. After a few minutes of musical introduction, the entire dialogue is read through in expressive form, without translation, but to the accompaniment of beautiful classical music. During subsequent periods, students engage in interaction activities incorporating lexical and thematic material recalled from the dialogue, but involving novel utterances as much as possible.

Despite promising results, several limitations have been identified: for one thing, Suggestology has been developed for classes in which all students share a common native language. Teachers must be proficient not only in the target language but also in the students' native language. There are indications that the system may not work as well with some types of students as with others; and it most certainly requires teachers with the right temperament and philosophical persuasions. A common cricitism of Suggestopedic students is that their speech is somewhat inaccurate grammatically and phonologically. But these criticisms must be weighed against the remarkable fluency and lack of inhibition observed in Suggestology students. Willing and able to communicate, they have been shown to acquire language proficiency far more rapidly and with greater positive affect than have students taught by traditional methods. These advantages alone recommend a careful look at this approach.

The final two methodologies—the Silent Way and Counseling Learning—are more than teaching "strategies"; they embody a new approach to education in general, a respect for the individual (the latter in particular), and an awareness of the individual's extraordinary cognitive powers.

GATTEGNO'S SILENT WAY

It was 1963 when Gattegno first published *Teaching Foreign Languages in Schools the Silent Way,* but it was more than a decade before a sizable minority of the nation's language teachers had even heard of the new methodology.[8] It is unique among methodologies. Not only is the teacher silent more than 90 percent of the time but there are frequent occasions when the students, too, are silent— not reading or daydreaming or watching a film—but concentrating intensely on some piece of language they have heard. The teacher uses no realia, simply a few wooden rods. S/he indulges in no praise; "It is unnecessary," says Gattegno. S/he makes no oral corrections. "Mistakes," he says, "are precious indicators of the discrepancy between what is and what should be."

A cardinal principle of the Silent Way is respect for the students' capacity to work out language problems and recall information on their own with no verbalization and minimal help from the teacher. Gattegno frequently urges "throwing the learner on himself." Charles Curran, to be discussed next, speaks of "learner space"—that space which the learner is "expanding into." While using different terminology, both Curran and Gattegno would agree that this must not be invaded. Moreover, the teacher is to answer no questions. Complementing the notion that students require minimal teacher assistance is the non-competitive atmosphere which stimulates students to help one another.

Related to this self-reliance principle is the decision (similar to Asher's and Lozanov's) to let students err. Only in this way, it is felt, can they develop criteria of correctness. Whatever the mind produces is psychologically correct, though perhaps out of tune socially at the outset. In time the mind will "transform the material until it becomes adequate." One of the great imperfections of most teaching, says Gattegno, is the compulsion to require perfection at once. But no true domination of a field is possible without exploring it, and this exploration can result in occasional errors.

According to Gattegno, both reflection and sleep are creative periods and should be utilized adequately. In this he reflects the thinking in Ghiselin's *The Creative Process,* in which noted scientists, mathematicians, artists, and writers analyze how the creative process works for them; the most prevalent explanation is that the subconscious generates solutions to problems which have initially been reflected on.

In 1976, Gattegno in New York and in Vancouver contrasted his "new" Silent Way with the "old" Silent Way. Formerly, he said, the principal question was, "How can I make people speak?" The new question, he said, is, "How can I make my students free?"—so that they will react to the new language as they do to the old one. Like Lozanov, he now seeks to rid instruction of the "foreign language syndrome." He devotes two to three hours to freeing the student so that language might "flow" naturally (see also Gattegno, 1976b).

Advocates of the Silent Way feel that more important than the techniques, and more important even than the language learning results, is the process, the change that occurs in individuals. This includes understanding and tolerance of one another—"acceptance of others as contributors to one's own life. . . ."

Turning to its specific methodology, we find that the first major phase of instruction introduces an absolute minimum of vocabulary. The focus is on the "melody" and structure of the language. The printed word comes very early. Essentially the only objects used in the lessons are a number of colored wooden rods of various lengths. These are used not simply to illustrate spatial relationships and related prepositions but virtually every aspect of language, ranging from comparisons to tense, the conditional, and the subjunctive. Phonic charts utilize standard spelling and identify identical sounds through color coding. Wall charts contain the words that have been introduced—initially a mere 28. By the time the focus shifts to vocabulary acquisition, students have acquired four hundred words.

As instruction begins, concentration is intense (and for that matter it is usually intense) since students realize that what is said will not be repeated. The teacher lifts one rod and says simply, *A rod*; s/he repeats this while lifting rods of other colors. Then s/he introduces a few colors. Next s/he motions for two students to come forward and says to one, *Take a (blue) rod*; when this is performed, s/he says, *Give it to (her)*. Cueing takes the form of mime, gesture and assistance from other students. Without verbal explanation, the teacher changes places with one of the students and the student begins making requests. (Note that at this point there seems to be a superficial similarity to TPR; in actual fact the two bear almost no resemblance.) The teacher gradually says less and less, the students more and more, but the linguistic situation is always under teacher direction. The native language of the students is always avoided. Very quickly students are responding to and using twelve to fifteen word sentences. The printed word is introduced through "visual dictation." With a pointer, the teacher indicates words that have already been used in sentences; new combinations can now be uttered as the teacher points out the word sequence s/he wants. Then the teacher produces an utterance him- or herself, and students point on the chart to the words s/he has said. An unusual way in which the rhythm of the language is worked on is through the use of taped passages from various languages; the students do not yet have the vocabulary to understand what is said, but they learn to identify the sounds of their new language when they hear it.

Finally the time comes for extensive vocabulary acquisition, in clusters of related words. Specially prepared drawings and pictures plus Silent Way worksheets are utilized. The latter contain miniature pictures that enable the student to label the words which he is interested in. Transparencies with corresponding worksheets are also employed. Other Silent Way materials used in teaching reading and advanced skills include controlled readers, anthologies which focus on contrasting styles of writing, and films. It should be pointed out that no text is used during the entire time spent on the basics of the language.

This approach, which is supposed to be flexible enough for seven year olds or adults is claimed to provide as much instruction in one year as students normally acquire in four or five. The Silent Way has been used in teaching Arabic, Portuguese, Cantonese and Mandarin Chinese, Danish, English as a second language, Farsi (i.e., Persian), French, German, Hebrew, Hindi, Hungarian, Italian, Japanese, Russian, Serbo-Croatian, Spanish, and Thai. The last half of Gattegno's text is devoted to testimonials and examples from a variety of language teachers who are now Gattegno devotees.

What are some of the limitations? First, Gattegno's book on the Silent Way is unsettling. Since the world's educators have been unable to come to grips with "what learning actually entails," Gattegno kindly explains the matter. While he's at it, he uses his experience with one child and shows how language is learned. Seemingly bent on ignoring contributions by researchers and experts in every field, he quietly turns his back on linguists as well, talking at length about the spirit of the language, the need to "surrender to its melody,"[9] and also to its breathing requirements. Moving uneasily through his slightly mystical and intuitive background material, one wonders if the following page will contain a black-strap molasses and yogurt remedy or foot massage treatment for sagging language learners. Then suddenly in chapter 3 we are back to the twentieth century and reality.

For some learners, one limitation is the approach to language basics which begins with seemingly irrelevant discussions about rods, and which involves silence and concentration and "games with the teacher" about meaning. An experienced and able inner-city teacher who had been introduced to Gattegno's and to Curran's methodologies indicated to me recently that neither method would work for his volunteer evening school students (the number per class ranged from 35 to 50 students). Their expectations and need for immediately relevant language learning forced him to abandon each approach in turn. For other teachers the rigidity of the system (no repetitions by the teacher, no answers by the teacher, the closed system indicating precisely which words will be introduced) seems stultifying.

But the results are notable, though they have not yet been verified in controlled experiments such as those reported by Asher. I have seen the method used effectively in a large-scale intensive foreign language program. Moreover, demonstrations of the method are impressive in illustrating how rapidly the language can be learned. Stevick (1974) reports seeing it used "brilliantly" in a class of one and a class of 70; he himself used it with Turkish instructors who had not received previous instruction in the Silent Way, and with them he taught a beginning class for 150 hours. Stevick comments on one of the several classes in the Silent Way he has observed during the past five years ("an actual Spanish class in its seventh hour of instruction"): "That session was one of the most impressive I had ever seen, not only for the amount of language that the students controlled, but also for the variety and intensity of the personal energies that were released." While not willing to concede that it is the "one methodological pearl of great price," he does regard it as "possibly the most under-valued pearl on the market today."

CURRAN'S COUNSELING-LEARNING METHOD

Of all the methodologists referred to so far, none is less concerned with technique and more concerned with human relationships than Curran, who introduced Counseling-Learning methodology in 1961. While his text on Counseling-Learning understandably focuses on the learner, Curran devotes a surprising amount of space to the needs of the teacher. In 1973 when I first presented a lecture-discussion on Counseling-Learning, a visiting scholar from England sought me out to discuss insights from this methodology. He was particularly interested in Curran's concern for the teacher. He mentioned in passing that his wife, a highly capable EFL teacher, was then undergoing one of her most difficult assignments—the teaching of some adults from the Middle East who were in a program that they found unsuitable. Without the positive reaction she normally experienced, his wife felt that her teaching was disintegrating. We discussed, then, Curran's position on this matter. From his counseling point of view, Curran describes the sense of belonging needed by both student and teacher. The latter, he says, "enters the learning situation faced with [an] unpredictable situation." The teacher should work to create an atmosphere in which his own anxieties can be allayed through mutual understanding and acceptance. He discusses as well the necessity for student initiative: "It is not only the teacher . . . who is responsible for understanding; the students also have a responsibility to recognize the state of threat and anxiety that they too can constitute for the knower" (Curran, 1972, p. 113). He demonstrates ways in which students themselves can shift to a "counseling" role; and he takes up repeatedly the supportive, empathic role that students can learn to play, not only for the teacher's personal benefit but also for the improved clarity and insight possible from the teacher's presentation.

In an exhaustive rationale for Counseling-Learning, Curran underscores the unique-ness of each individual. He feels that there has been an unnecessary dichotomy between counseling and teaching—the former being interested in the individual's achieving insights and self-awareness that can stimulate personal development, fulfillment and improved relations with others; the latter being too exclusively concerned with the intellectual learning process. In Counseling-Learning, he feels, the two are merged. In addition, learning is greatly stimulated through the development of self-worth and through a feeling of belonging and sharing with others.

The emphasis on shared task-oriented activity has led some, including Curran himself, to refer to the method as "community learning." For Curran, such activity is far more than a group process; it involves a deep commitment to others. Our problem, he feels, is an inclination to deal with problems rather than to relate to people.

Strategies for learning that he rejects include the "doubting, questioning" stance, excessive concern for labeling and diagnosing, and tendencies toward mere intellectualizing or mere universalizing.

Curran sees a cycle of development and learning somewhat as follows: The counselor-teacher recognizes each individual's need for personal fulfillment. Such fulfillment requires interaction with others which can result in mutual appreciation and understanding. One form of such interaction, especially in the language classroom, is communication resulting from joint learner efforts directed toward completing a task. Achievement of this requires the teacher to step down from his or her pedestal and for the student to step out of his or her protective shell of non-involvement. And the interest, trust, and openness implicit in this realignment of roles becomes easier as one's sense of personal worth and fulfillment increases.

The procedure followed in a Counseling-Learning language class is deceptively simple (see Curran, 1976). The students ("clients" in Curran's terminology) sit in a circle. The teacher or teachers ("knowers" or "counselor-experts" or "counselor-teachers") are outside the circle. There may be one knower for each client or one for every three, or just one knower for the entire group. With multiple knowers it is possible to include clients who do not even speak the same language. However, it is advantageous to have a group that can all communicate in the same language.

During the first stage, a tape recorder is normally used. However, the only voices taped are those of the student-clients when they are speaking in the target language. Curran feels this increases their new identity in the foreign language and helps sublimate the role of the counselor-expert.

Of the several methods discussed in the present chapter, this is the least structured (though the demands on the teacher are great). The students are simply told to communicate with one another on any subject and in any sequence they choose. They initiate the conversation in their native language, and the knower, outside the circle, translates it into the target language. They then say in the target language what they have heard the knower say. Since the knower is considered to be non-existent in the communicating circle of clients, naturally questions cannot be directed to him or her; if s/he is asked something, someone in the circle will attempt a reply. At this stage "overhear" is important. Even though a group of Spanish speakers, for example, is communicating in English from the outset, what they *overhear* between client and knower is very important. As in the Silent Way, there are periods of silence or reflection when each individual mulls over what s/he has heard (see LaForge, 1977). It is felt that there is little or no time in the regular classroom for this sort of thing. If a tape recording has been made, it is played back near the end of class. Clients can have the knower write these dialogues on the blackboard and clarify points of grammar. This is handled simply and briefly.

Though not directly relevant to this discussion, it should be pointed out that Curran has likewise developed a Counseling-Learning approach for lecture classes. He utilizes four rotating counselors from among the students. Throughout the lecture these persons paraphrase or summarize what has been said. If their perception is satisfactory, the teacher can proceed. Students report an intense involvement and teachers a freedom from the anxiety of wondering whether or not they have been understood.

The thing that surprises and usually delights the language learner is the discovery that s/he is completely in charge of his or her own learning. S/he can *use* the teacher when there is a need and "turn him or her off" when there isn't a need. As in the Silent Way, students assist each other. When they begin to acquire the target language, conversation can become animated—momentarily reverting to the native language for clarification and then back to the target language. The knower provides translation only when someone signals by raising his or her hand.

In the final stage, color coded signals are used. If red is flashed, an error has been made; if amber, there is a more suitable idiom or better way of phrasing the expression; if green, the utterance is acceptable. Blue indicates native expertise. Students have commented on the satisfaction they feel in speaking sentence after sentence with someone else in the circle while receiving "only the warm support of silence and an approving symbolization."

In a good knower-client relationship, there quickly develops a warm, sympathetic attitude of mutual trust and respect. The client emulates the language and person of the knower; the knower is fulfilled and enriched through the counseling-teaching experience. It has been demonstrated in actual Counseling-Learning situations that rapport and mutual understanding are essential in order for the knower to be utilized adequately (Stevick, 1973, pp. 259-71). Just as in a counseling situation, it is not unusual for the client (and sometimes even the knower) to express anger—for example, on occasions when the knower "butts in" when s/he is not needed. As indicated earlier, this "learner space" must not be encroached on. The learner uses it "until s/he reduces the knower to silence or 'nonexistence'."

Curran identifies five stages in the client's development. The first he calls the "Embryonic Stage," where there is almost total dependence on the teacher. Second is the "Self-Assertion Stage" (the mother feels "life" in the womb) as the student-client begins to show some independence and tries out the language. Next is the "Birth Stage," when the client speaks independently, though imperfectly. It is now that s/he is most likely to resent what s/he feels is unnecessary assistance from the knower. Fourth comes the "Reversal Stage" when s/he is secure enough to take correction; s/he is in a position to exchange roles periodically with the knower and as student-counselor extend warmth and understanding to his or her mentor. In the final or "Independent Stage," as we have indicated, interruptions are infrequent; they occur occasionally for correction but more often for enrichment and improvement of style.

What are some possible limitations in this approach? One is the training required for the ideal knower. While slightly exaggerated, this reaction is close to the mark:

He would have to have a perfect command of the foreign language if he were not a native speaker. Besides, he would have to be professionally competent in both psychology—for the interpersonal problems which could arise—and linguistics to deal with the phonological and grammatical problems of the foreign language in a scientific way. It was noted that a doctorate in both psychology and linguistics, plus a perfect command of one foreign language, could hardly be expected of many individuals. (LaForge, 1971)

We have already noted its limitations in a large-group situation with one teacher. In a demonstration I observed with adult learners, I recall a doubt expressed by one of the clients as he asked someone else in the circle, "Do you think we'll ever be able to learn Spanish this way?" Particularly at the beginning when clients have not yet learned to simplify their utterances, the sounds, syntax, and lexicon seem hopelessly confusing and difficult. Then, too, there is the need (though not a definite requirement) for clients who speak a common language. Finally, Curran's book, like Gattegno's, takes some adjusting to, though for different reasons. His penchant for theological terms and side trips into philosophy and philology make the journey rocky at times.

The method's strengths are both affective and cognitive. LaForge, who conducted demonstrations in Counseling-Learning at the University of Michigan during a six-month period, has reported on the high motivation of clients. He

corroborates the value of periods of silence for learning and understanding what has been said. Students could move at their own pace, he observed, yet those lagging were encouraged and aided by their peers. He was impressed with the initiative students assumed in this approach ("Students drilled themselves!" he noted with surprise). In addition they strived to identify culturally with the language being learned. And the sheer volume of language consumed was impressive. More important to many learners is the freedom and initiative they are permitted in the Counseling-Learning approach; it is a unique and fascinating learning experience. Stevick regards Curran's text as so important that he would "like to see it read and discussed by everyone who trains language teachers" (Stevick, 1973).

Concluding her article on "Current Trends in Language Teaching," in this volume, Newton observes that the teacher's attitude toward his or her students is an even more basic ingredient than his or her method. In Counseling-Learning the most basic ingredient *is* a mutual interest, respect and concern of teacher for student and student for teacher. Perhaps this is one reason for its success. It is certainly a characteristic that helps qualify the method, together with the others we have surveyed, as deserving of our attention. For these methodologies can provide valuable insights to the ESL teacher who is attempting to fashion a coherent cognitive methodology of his or her own.

NOTES

1. Carroll made his plea in a keynote address at the 1971 TESOL Convention in New Orleans.

2. Marckwardt made his suggestion at the 1973 NAFSA Convention in Detroit—advice that had been advanced for several years by this time.

3. Newton, "Current Trends in Language Teaching," in this anthology, p. 20.

4. Reference texts include Altman and Politzer (1971) and Gougher (1972); one of the several conferences is discussed in ERIC (ED 063 823); some of the many articles include Burns (1971), Disick (1973), Fisher (1973), Mills (ERIC), and Rosenthal (1973).

5. Numerous publications and papers in this area include a reference text by Savignon (1972) who did

her doctoral dissertation on the same subject, writings by Rivers (1972a and 1973), Schumann (1972), Wingfield (1972), and convention papers by Paulston and others.

6.   Cuyer (1972) published a review of St. Cloud in a British TESL journal; Schumann (1972) examined it in an American TESL journal, though Renard and Heinle (1969) wrote a book on it in the United States (but referred to it as "Voix et Images de France"). The Centre de Recherche et d'Etude pour la Diffusion du Français was installed in the Ecole Normale Supérieure de Saint-Cloud, France; development of the educational principles undergirding the method was by George Gougenheim, Paul Rivenc and Peter Guberina; an elementary French course was created—*Voix et Images de France*—in 1962; the Center for Curriculum Development in the United States set out to adapt these materials for use in America.

7.   "Description and Evaluation of the St. Cloud Method," a lecture-demonstration by Slade, February 5, 1975; see also Cuyer (1972).

8.   I am indebted to colleague Robert W. Blair (who had been informed by Stevick) for information about the Silent Way in 1973, and also to students such as Virginia Cresap and Tom Howard who urged him on me, particularly after attending bootleg "Silent Way" sessions at the 1974 TESOL Convention. It has been Stevick more than any other single person who has popularized Gattegno in TESL circles.

9.   Gattegno says: "It is of interest here to mention the relationship of our flesh to music being heard. The true listener yields to the complexes that we call music and is actually affected by it to the point where all parts of his body can indicate its presence. . . . Since babies learn to talk their mother tongue first by yielding to its 'music,' I think that we can trace the first elements of the spirit of a language to the unconscious surrender of our sensitivity to what is conveyed by the background of noise in each language. . . . Surrender to the melody of language, as to music, will bring to our unconscious all of the spirit of a language that has been stored in the melody. It cannot be reached otherwise." (Gattegno, 1972, p. 22).

DISCUSSION QUESTIONS

1.   (preparatory) What do you understand "method" to mean? How does it contrast with "technique," for example? For clarification see Anthony (1963).

2.   (preparatory) There are many applications of the Audiolingual Approach. Generally speaking, what kinds of classroom activities characterized this methodology? (For assistance see Newton, in this volume, and Allen-Campbell, Chastain, and Rivers under *Suggestions for Further Reading.*)

3.   Diller, among others, feels that several of the methodologists discussed in this chapter use one form or another of the Direct Method, which avoids the vernacular and close attention to grammar. Which methods that we have discussed here do you feel meet these specifications?

4.   From our discussion, why does it seem logical that Asher would consider the Winitz-Reeds approach as more complementary to his method than any of the others we have discussed?

5.   While different in application, the Silent Way and Counseling-Learning have a number of characteristics in common. What are they? Consider also ways in which these two differ.

6.   Which one of the six methodologies discussed at the beginning of the chapter shares the affective concern that Counseling-Learning has for the relationship between teacher and student?

7.   Discuss the several methodologies in relation to the teacher's role in carrying them out. Which seems to expect most (and which least) from the teacher? Which is most concerned about the teacher? Should "how the teacher feels" enter into a methodological discussion?

SUGGESTED ACTIVITIES

1.   Investigate in some detail one of the methods presented (preferably one of the six presented early in the chapter); if possible, interview a teacher who has used the method or seen it in operation (note, for example, that French teachers will generally be more familiar with St. Cloud than will other teachers). Assess its strengths and limitations, and whether or not it makes a definite break with the Audiolingual Approach.

2.   (optional) Investigate the University of Illinois PLATO computerized approach to TESL instruction. Has the "software" kept up

with the "hardware"? How is evaluation carried out? Does it provide "individual" or "individualized" instruction?

3.	Read either Curran or Gattegno (both texts are short). Then write a two-page critique of the book.

4.	Participate in a classroom demonstration of TPR, the Silent Way, or Counseling-Learning. (or) Prepare a seven-minute micro-teaching demonstration incorporating one of these three methodologies.

SUGGESTIONS FOR FURTHER READING

Allen, Harold B., and Russell N. Campbell (1972)
Teaching English as a Second Language. New York: McGraw-Hill (Second edition).
Note particularly Part One on Theories and Approaches.

Chastain, Kenneth (1971)
The Development of Modern Language Skills: Theory to Practice. Philadelphia: The Center for Curriculum Development.
See Chapter 2 for a discussion of the Audiolingual Method and assumptions underlying the Method.

Diller, Karl C. (1978)
The Language Teaching Controversy. Rowley, Mass.: Newbury House.
See his overview of language teaching methodology and assumptions underlying the same.

Postovsky, Valerian A. (1974)
"Effects of Delay in Oral Practice at the Beginning of Second Language Learning," *The Modern Language Journal,* 58:5-6, 229-39.

Rivers, Wilga M. (1964)
The Psychologist and the Foreign Language Teacher. Chicago: University of Chicago Press.
See this for the historical interest implicit in the presentation. A decade ago she carefully spelled out all of the psychological assumptions underlying the audiolingual approach.

AN AUDIOVISUAL METHOD FOR ESL

James Heaton

Media, by altering the environment, evoke in us unique ratios of sense perceptions. The extension of any one sense alters the way we think and act—the way we perceive the world.
— McLuhan, 1967

Since the great hurrahs of the language lab and its Skinnerian associate, programmed learning, a great deal of heat and thunder has been generated around the use of the new media in education. Some of these media, such as television, are not really new any more but seem to be enjoying a prolonged infancy. It is safe to say that nobody yet understands what electronics has to do with education. The projected media, on the other hand, have been around for more than a century but are still being adapted in various ways. With the exception of motion pictures, these also have not been significantly exploited in the classroom. But impressive changes are taking place on the surface. The bare-plastered classroom with rows of desks, hard chairs, and a picture of George Washington at the front, has in many instances been transformed into a comfortable and colorful multi-purpose room, with areas set aside for special subject materials, and with a variety of audio and visual materials available through which students can experience many modes of learning. Although audio cassettes, individual filmstrip viewers, language masters, film cassette projectors, and video apparatus are all commonly found these days—frequently in the same classroom—the areas of reading/writing and "language arts" seem to be the most dependent on the use of media.

It was said at one time that the old lock-step version of the language lab was the most appropriate medium for the language learning process, but it seems to be in this area that a multitude of media have recently blossomed. Public school students have available cassette machines to facilitate "read-along" materials, improved language masters for vocabulary and spelling, and student-operated filmstrip viewers and phonographs. These are used in addition to display media and the more accessible placement of conventional print media. *Variety* and *availability* seem to be the current watchwords of audiovisual utilization.

There is an important distinction between the use of audiovisual aids to facilitate the classroom teaching of substantive material such as literature, arithmetic, and science, and the integration of appropriate media into a program to help students acquire the communication skills involved in using a language. The need for audiovisual materials in the ESL classroom arises from the fact that language is ultimately inseparable from the real world—and there is precious little of the real world in a classroom. This problem has been with us ever since learning was abstracted out of the streets, shops, and courts into a special building called a school. It has been compounded, moreover, by the universal use of the print medium. School grammars, until this century, held the written form of the language as the primary model and mode of learning spoken language. The printed text remains unchallenged as the central focus for language learning even now, after the audiolingual revolution has come and gone.

On the other hand, the real world practically inundates us with media for potential language use. Everybody, including a foreign student, is constantly deluged with advertisements, T.V. broadcasts, newspapers, application forms, lectures, and film. Within education in general, there is even a technology which is exclusively concerned with *mediating* material; i.e., making learning experiences take place

through the exploitation of multiple sensory modes. However, the message of the language classroom is still mediated almost exclusively by the following:

a.   the teacher
b.   the students
c.   the blackboard
d.   the classroom
e.   the textbook

Usually a lesson is built around one or more of these "Basic Five," depending upon the preferences of the teacher. Other materials, such as tape-recorded drills, realia, flash cards and pictures, may (or may not) be used, but generally these latter account for a small portion of language teaching activity. Other media, such as overhead projection, though depended upon greatly in other areas of education, are often entirely absent from the ESL scene. The attitude persists among language teachers that audiovisual techniques are imprecise and difficult to execute and should not, therefore, be depended upon. Media other than the Basic Five are considered as peripheral to language learning as the term "audiovisual *aid*" would suggest.

Let's examine what the traditional or basic classroom media are meant to do. The teacher is a medium of sorts since s/he usually speaks a bona fide dialect of the target language and acts and relates to the students in a way which typifies the culture of the target language. The teacher is also able to reinforce the meaning of the language with a set of gestures typical of the culture. Such things as beckoning, kissing, hand-shaking, and head-shaking often vary in style and communicative content from one language and culture to another. Such types of actions and reactions are the things that students depend on the teacher to demonstrate; they cannot be derived from the print medium. Vocabulary such as the verbs *walk, open, close, write, point to, look at* and nouns for the parts of the body have typically required the teacher as the chief audiovisual aid in the classroom.

It may be obvious that the teacher would be unable to function as an educational medium without students. But especially in language teaching, the physical participation of the learners themselves is an essential adjunct to the teaching process. Participation is necessary not only in the traditional modes of class drill, dialogue, question-answer, and chain drill, but also in the more genuine language experiences of role playing, and self-evaluatory group work. Language originates with people, and the activities of the lesson must always reflect this.

The teacher's ubiquitous ally, the blackboard, is also an economical and durable audiovisual aid. Even the poorest primary schools in "underdeveloped" countries have them, though the blackboards may consist only of black paint over mud brick. And, if teachers are given any training at all, they will likely know how to make the best use of this written and pictorial medium.

The chief problem with blackboard illustration is the same as the problem with even the most well-illustrated textbook: lack of reality—or, more precisely, lack of the kind of psychological impact which, in a classroom, might pass for reality. This is especially true for children who have had little exposure to two-dimensional representations at all. To them, line drawings are abstract and often meaningless. The same effect exists even among adults. The strongest advantage of the blackboard is that it enables the temporary display of the written word. But in this age of psychedelic billboards and fluorescent cereal boxes, we need a stronger resource to teach something as contextually loaded as language.

To be sure, our present system of learning from abstracted experience depends on a kind of isolation from the experience itself. Thus, we attend classes instead of doing an apprenticeship for our "higher" education. Such isolation is doubtless appropriate for certain types of subjects such as mathematics or philosophy. But in learning language some means must be found to compensate for the spatial and psychological removal of the students from the real world. The classroom does furnish artifacts such as doors, windows, chairs, lights, and blackboards to aid the teaching process but when you have identified and talked about all these things, the students have all introduced themselves and greeted one another, and you have covered the first six pages of *Easy English* with blackboard footnotes—where does the pursuit of reality in the language classroom go from there? In most cases, the answer is "nowhere." Without an imaginative teacher, it stays right where it is, recycling through the Basic Five.

Even with the best of teachers working within limited media, the correct learning of abstract vocabulary items, such as *surprise, sadness,* and *thought* is miraculous. The problem is analogous to the way the chimpanzee Washoe, upon being taught the American Sign Language word for "baby" (in the presence of one), quickly applied the word to dolls, as a human might do. However, she also applied it to photographs and miniatures of all kinds. She had correctly assimilated the feature "miniaturization" for the word but, given a rather limited context for applying "baby," she began using it for many things which lack the flesh-and-blood features we generally add. Errors of overgeneralization are almost a certainty when teaching is done with minimal context, even if humans are considered more sophisticated than chimpanzees in organizing their semantic features.

Teaching greetings, identification of concrete nouns for available objects, and the correct use of numbers, time, days, and dates can probably be accomplished within the conventional media. Extension to more abstract language commonly relies on reading material— i.e., the textbook—as the artificial context. If this occurs at the university level, the result is a student trained in classroom-and-library survival who has great difficulty dealing with restaurants, movies, and landlords. A host of nagging problems including monolingually extending vocabulary and grammar so that one can function well in the community simply can't be dealt with without calling upon more realistic teaching media. In fact, it is extremely doubtful that any of the Basic Five—save the teacher and the students—is essential for teaching linguistic survival in a foreign country. For students who are well equipped with learning strategies, even the teacher might be dispensed with.

It may be, then, that we should turn to other media, when their particular expressive value warrants it. For example, language situations take on a new dimension when presented in a projected medium, and a great deal of information is presented very compactly. The purely verbal presentation of the sentence, "Ramon had a dead battery," may get the meaning across if the students are shown a picture of a battery and if they are used to some of the weird conventions of English. That is, the students will have to know that we sometimes substitute ourselves for cars (Ramon has . . . , I'm parked . . .), and that dead and die can by extension refer to certain inanimate objects (My car died, The phone is dead). But the additional dramatic redundancy of a lesson based on slide visuals of Ramon's dead battery, how he came to have it, and what he did about it, would ensure that passive understanding is achieved for the vocabulary coextensive with the situation. If the presentation includes dialogue practice (Ramon and his cousin Julio, who is a garage mechanic) and participatory role playing (What would you say to the garage mechanic if . . . ?), the students will have a good chance of actively associating the vocabulary/grammar with the situation just as a native speaker would do.

Only lessons which exploit a variety of media can approach the kind of information density that is required if the language is to be effectively contextualized within the allotted constraints of time and place. Locations, objects, labels, comparative sizes and capacities, facial expressions, and actions can be accurately captured and "described" by a photograph in a way which is impossible to do as efficiently in a conventional Basic Five-type classroom. An accompanying sound tape supplies an additional dimension of contrasting voice qualities, intonation, volume (signifying relative distance), and contextual sound effects. In addition to the sound material itself, a sound tape can carry synchronization signals to advance slides automatically in step with the sound, freeing the teacher to monitor or test the students' responses.

If media are properly exploited, the resulting form of the lesson will bear little resemblance to a traditional lesson with audio-visual aids. The language will stem more from situations, and, depending on the sequencing of the situations, some of the grammar may not be taught in the traditional order. For example, the present perfect and the possessive have are of such high frequency of occurrence that these will be presented earlier than they would be in a purely "structural" course. Moreover, vocabulary will be taught in "situational clusters" resulting in many words of frequent occurrence in typical conversations being taught before those of "classroom" significance. Bread, coffee, registration form, student union, bathroom, and checking account are much more important items to college-level foreign students than table, chair, desk, read, or sit—even at the beginning level. Similarly, vital situations will be allowed to dictate a considerable proportion of the vocabulary for adult learners attempting to cope with life in this country.

Following are (1) an example of a narrative lesson, focusing on comparison; (2) a dialogue lesson on infinitives; and (3) a "drill" lesson on mass/count nouns. All three use 35mm color slides, with taped or live voice sound.

1. Narrative (see Chart 1)

Intermediate level: The comparison is introduced and a few and a lot are reviewed.
Method: First the slides are presented at a moderate speed with taped or live voice sound. Then the slides are shown a second time with questions (What does Henry have to buy at the supermarket? What is expensive? etc.) to cue the students to reconstruct the narrative. Following this reconstruction stage, the lesson can be branched into contextual drill (with objects or a full-page newspaper advertisement), dialogue, or composition work, depending on the needs of the class. The homework assignment is, of course, to check out the newspaper for the prices of a list of items and to report on which items are more expensive than other items, and which supermarket of two or three is more expensive.

2. Dialogue (see Chart 2)

Advanced level: Pseudo-auxiliaries: want to /wɔnə/ or /wánə/; going to /gánə/; have to /hǽftə/; get to /gɛ́ttə/.
Method: The visuals and sound are presented several times, as in the previous example. The

Chart 1

Sound	Visual
1. Henry has to buy a lot of things at the supermarket,	1. Wide Angle Shot of Henry in a supermarket interior.
2. but everything is very expensive.	2. Medium Shot of Henry looking at vegetable prices.
3. Mushrooms are expensive	3. Close Up of mushroom display, including price prominent near the top.
4. and avocadoes are expensive.	4. Same with avocado display.
5. But apples are cheap.	5. Same with apple display.
6. Oranges are cheap,	6. Same with orange display.
7. but onions are cheaper than oranges.	7. Same with onion display.
8. Henry is getting a few oranges and a lot of onions.	8. Medium Shot of Henry lifting a large bag of onions into a shopping cart already containing a small bag of oranges.
9. Mushrooms are more expensive than avocadoes.	9. Medium Shot of Henry standing by the mushroom and avocado displays looking perplexed.
10. So Henry is getting a few mushrooms and a lot of avocadoes.	10. As in 8, substituting mushrooms and avocadoes.
11. This canteloupe is heavy,	11. Medium Shot of Henry lifting cantalope.
12. but this watermelon is heavier.	12. Medium Shot of Henry trying to lift an enormous watermelon.
13. These mushrooms are light,	13. Close Up of Henry's bag of mushrooms on the scale, which reads ¾ pound.
14. but these beansprouts are lighter.	14. Same with bag of beansprouts. Scale reads ½ pound.
15. These apples aren't ripe. They're green.	15. Medium Shot of Henry scowling at a green apple, with the display in the background.
16. These apples are ripe. They're riper than the others.	16. Medium Shot of Henry looking satisfied at a ripe red apple. Display in background.
17. Now Henry has a lot of groceries.	17. Medium Shot of Henry and his full shopping cart.
18. He has meat, milk, eggs, bread, fruit, and vegetables.	18. Close Up of shopping cart in which the new items are identifiable.
19. But Martha has more groceries. She has six children.	19. Medium Shot of Martha and cart, which is overflowing.
20. She has a lot more groceries than Henry.	20. Medium Close Up of cart only.
21. Henry is paying for his groceries. They cost a lot.	21. Medium Shot of Henry at check stand, showing $25 on cash register.
22. But Martha's cost more than Henry's!	22. Same of Martha, showing $40 on cash register.

Chart 2

Sound	Visual
1. (George): Do you want to go to the movies, Hilda?	1. Medium-Long Shot of George and Hilda standing on a sidewalk downtown.
2. (Hilda): I'd like to, but I'm broke. You'll have to pay for both of us.	2. Medium Shot of Hilda, face to camera.
3. (George): Well, I'm nearly broke, too. Maybe we could get something to eat anyway.	3. Reverse angle to George.
4. (Hilda): Oh, good! I never get to eat out!	4. Two Shot, Hilda facing camera, looking pleased.
5. (George): Where would you like to go?	5. Two Shot, reverse angle with George facing camera.
6. (Hilda): I'd like to eat at the Pizza Palace.	6. Medium-Long Shot of Hilda, pointing to Pizza Palace sign in background.
7. (George): The sign says it's closed. We'll have to go somewhere else.	7. Close Up of hand-lettered sign in window.
8. (Hilda): Do you want to get a hamburger at Woody's?	8. Medium Shot of Hilda and George, Hilda pointing out of picture in the direction of Woody's.
9. (George): Yeah, let's do that. Then we won't have to wait so long.	9. Two Shot, George facing camera.
10. (Hilda): And Woody's is cheap. We'll get to go to the movies, too!	10. Two Shot, reverse angle, Hilda looks joyful.

students take the roles in the second and third presentation by groups. This choral stage is followed by handing out a ditto of the dialogue, which the students practice in pairs. The teacher will check linguistic performance during this paired practice. When the students perform the dialogue before the class in pairs, they will be encouraged to use their own words and to improvise on the dialogue as if it were a role play. In this stage, the visuals will be superseded by the "real" improvised situation. The aim is for the students to be able to deal with the language in a related manner—not to simply "model" the language for the others. Whatever losses in accuracy may occur will be exchanged for confidence in communicative ability. At this stage of improvised dialogue, videotaping has been found to be an excellent means of providing the students with feedback on the quality of their performance.

3. Drill (see Chart 3)

Beginning level, review: Mass/count nouns; past tense

Method: This will be a situation where the language is typically, and naturally, limited to one structure: *Rafael drove his brother's car to the filling station yesterday.* How much *gasoline did he get?* How many *quarts of oil did he put in?* The presentation will be followed by question-answer and improvised dialogue. When Rafael gets home, his brother, Pablo, asks him all the *how much/how many* questions to make sure he didn't forget anything. After practicing the improvised dialogue, the class will do a written fill-in exercise of the cloze type with one possible dialogue (either on a prepared ditto, or from the blackboard). This lesson will follow a lesson on food nouns, and will precede work with nouns for building materials (wood, glass, glue, plaster, nails), clothes (cloth, soap,

Chart 3

Sound	Visual
1. This is the Pacific Avenue Filling Station.	1. Long Shot of filling station.
2. Fred and Bill work here, and they sell gasoline, oil, tires, and sparkplugs.	2. Medium Shot of Fred and Bill servicing a car.
3. Yesterday, Rafael drove his brother's car to the filling station.	3. Medium Shot of Rafael driving into the station.
4. First he got some gasoline.	4. Close Up of gas hose in filler.
5. How much gasoline did he get?	5. Black slide (no image).
6. He got 10 gallons.	6. Close Up of meter on gas pump showing ten gallons.
7. Then he got some oil.	7. Medium Shot of front of car, hood up, with Fred holding dip stick.
8. How much oil did he get?	8. Black slide.
9. He got two quarts.	9. Medium Shot of Fred carrying two cans toward the camera.
10. Oh, oh! He needed a tire.	10. Close Up of Rafael looking worriedly at a worn out tire.
11. How many tires did he get?	11. Black slide.
12. He got two tires.	12. Long Shot of Fred wheeling out tires.
13. He needed some spark plugs.	13. Close Up of Fred examining spark plugs.
14. How many spark plugs did he get?	14. Black slide.
15. He got six spark plugs.	15. Close Up of spark plugs on fender beside engine, waiting to be put in.
16. That will cost Rafael a lot of money.	16. Medium Shot of Rafael and Fred, the latter smiling, and Rafael looking doubtfully into wallet.
17. How much money did he pay?	17. Black slide.
18. He paid $53.	18. Close Up of money.

dye, thread) and abstract nouns (politics, dishonesty) around which more contexts will be built.

Though the examples have been based on the projected medium with 35mm slides and sound tape, there are many other possible media in which one can construct or adapt lesson materials. The slide medium was chosen for illustration because the amount of lesson equipment required is minimal, relative to the amount and kind of information this medium can communicate. Though the choice of materials and equipment and the production of photographic materials may require additional skill, the exploitation of existent media for the audiovisual lesson is limited in general only by the teacher's imagination. Newspapers and magazines are a rich source of pictorial, graphic, and print material for ESL application. Appropriate material can also be found in realia, such as application blanks, instruction sheets, maps, and brochures. Such material may be used in small groups in original form, or it can be duplicated on ditto masters, overhead transparencies, or slides for whole-class work. The advantages of such "found" media are obvious in forming an associative bridge between the classroom and the world.

Most schools have access to a variety of motion picture films. Few of these will be entirely suitable for any but advanced students. But within a properly planned lesson, including pointer questions given before the film presentation and well-prepared discussion afterwards, quite a lot of appreciation can be gained of complex film topics, even at intermediate English levels. However, the teacher has more adaptive control over filmstrip materials, whose visual and sound impact can be almost as good as that of films. Many commercial filmstrip kits are now available, dealing with current issues as well as survival matters. Since filmstrips can be run at a variable rate and the teacher can provide "live" commentary, the students have a much greater chance of understanding the experience. Some audiovisual kits include sound discs or cassettes which can be adapted to ESL by re-recording, editing and providing voice-over supplementation.

Other projected media make unique contributions to the types of lesson material that can be presented. The overhead projector has long been used especially in public schools for presenting print medium exercises, illustrations, and graphics. Since an overhead (O.H.) transparency can be manipulated while it is being projected, this medium lends itself naturally to composition work, test correction feedback, and certain types of "instant animation" for dialogue presentation. Line drawings and printed matter can be converted into transparencies by the thermofax process, or clear acetate can be drawn or written on with felt-tip pens to make multi-colored transparencies. The projection of O.H. transparencies can be further modified by overlays—additional transparencies which add complementary detail or color. Thus, the answers to a fill-in exercise can be instantly plugged in, or certain words in a composition can be highlighted with transparent color for vocabulary work or controlled rewriting. An opaque piece of cardboard can be used to mask part of the transparency prepared for reading exercises so that only one sentence or word is revealed at a time.

For non-verbal material, O.H. transparencies can be animated by using silhouette puppets against a fixed background. If the background is projected to a large size in a well-darkened room, live students could take the place of the puppets. Another way to produce animation is by using a polarizing wheel in front of the O.H. projector lens. When the transparency is made with layers of stressed acetate in the appropriate areas, color and motion effects are created. There are also conventional photographic techniques for producing color or monochromatic transparency copies.

Video, as a representative of the student's extracurricular media experience, has a psychological effect which is distinct from any of the projected media. The television image signifies immediacy and gives one the sense of being allowed to eavesdrop on a relatively unedited segment of experience. It suggests involvement in a way which is impossible with a delayed and finished film. This gives videotape the properties of a tool for unique kinds of communication, as well as expression. Perhaps the following list can give an idea of some of the *dimensions* of classroom video. It is by no means exhaustive.

1.   Prepared lesson presentations
     a. Studio recorded dialogue/drill.
     b. "Verité" material, real or simulated impromptu, with background noise, etc.
     c. Lectures: for comprehension/ composition/note-taking:
        i.   unedited,
        ii. edited,
        iii. edited with voice-over glosses.
     d. Non-recorded image magnification in class (as in opaque projection):
        i.   reading material,
        ii. pictures,
        iii. correction of tests and dictations.
     e. Broadcast material (taped from regular programming):
        i.   educational T.V.,
        ii. news/documentary,
        iii. cultural/drama,
        iv. any of the above with appropriate editing.

2. Feedback of students' performance (recorded in class)
   a. Role-playing for:
      i. fluency,
      ii. gestures,
      iii. appropriateness.
   b. Pronunciation by:
      i. reading/drill/dialogue,
      ii. role-playing.
3. Information
   a. "Cultural exchange" between classes in different locations. Material selected and taped by the students.
   b. Other documentary material done by students as in-class project.

Though video is considered an expensive Big Medium,[1] the technology is a good deal less complex, expensive, and fallible than the language lab. But, as with the language lab, a crucial problem with video will be materials—often referred to in the trade jargon as "software." There are many videotape machines withering away in school closets for lack of inspiration as to how to make use of them. Hopefully, imaginative teachers will be able to overcome this problem with good recorded materials, scripts, and ideas, and will not be reluctant to let the students participate in exploiting the medium themselves. (An experiment along these lines was described in Lopate (1973).) Unprepared though we may be, if present trends continue, the availability of video recording equipment will soon be as universal as that for sound.

We cannot as yet say that there is any one medium that is best for teaching a given language skill, but certainly each medium leaves its particular imprint on the learning that takes place. A lesson which uses a visual medium leaves a visual impression of the situation associated with the language. A lesson which is taught only through a sound medium omits this visual association. This would be an appropriate choice when dealing with a class for telephone operators or airline pilots, but it would not fit more typical language objectives. If even "abstract" media, such as print, are appropriate for "abstract" objectives, such as learning to read, a number of modes should be exploited for

getting the same material across. Even print is learned differently when projected, depicted on signs, derived from instructions, or advertisements, or shown on other realia. The teacher's task is to handle adeptly a variety of such possibilities. This may involve switching from realia to slides to role-playing to videotape during a one-hour period. One needn't overwhelm the class with media in order to provide some representation of language as it is normally encountered, but one should make use of the associative quality of each medium and choose it to conform to the students' needs. As in most types of learning, the experience is the message, and ESL is no exception.

NOTE

1. See Schramm (1973) for an important discussion on the relative effectiveness of using "big" versus "little" media in the classroom.

DISCUSSION QUESTIONS

1. What are the Basic Five classroom media discussed in this article? Do you agree with this list or not?

2. Why is it especially important to go beyond these Basic Five in teaching ESL?

3. What are some of the other useful audiovisual media the ESL teacher should be prepared to exploit?

4. Which of the audiovisual media elicited by question 3 are you sufficiently familiar with to use in the ESL classroom?

5. Is there a feasibility criterion involved in the use of audiovisual media? I.e., are certain teachers or teaching situations so limited that it would be better to use "little media" such as the blackboard, pictures from magazines, newspaper cartoons, etc., rather than the complicated machinery inherent in "big media" such as language labs, videotape, etc.?

6. What do you feel the relative effectiveness of using "big media" versus "little media" would be in the ESL classroom? (See Schramm (1973) on this question.)

7. Think of five more uses of video to add to the list given in the article.

8. What should the evaluation criteria for ESL use of films or other audiovisual material be? For instance, what would a film evaluation checklist look like?

SUGGESTED ACTIVITIES

1. Find a comic strip of four to six frames which would be useful for teaching oral or written composition. White out the words and look carefully for any ambiguities that might be evident to a foreign student "reading" the cartoon—or get an ESL student to identify problems for you. How might such ambiguities be made use of?

2. Assemble six photographic prints into a situation and write a short dialogue around the sequence. Use the present progressive tense or the past tense as exclusively as possible.

3. Sketch a composition lesson plan around 1. or 2. Include any of the following student activities: (a) preliminary oral composition; (b) writing alternate versions; (c) filling in a composition frame; (d) supplying the ending to a dictated narrative about the pictures; (e) changing a dialogue to an indirect-quoted narrative.

4. Record an actual unrehearsed conversation between you and a friend. Write a transcription of a representative portion. How could such verité material be used in the ESL classroom?

5. Similarly, how could a lesson be built around videotaped verité material—e.g., a conversation involving registration? What application would it have and at what level? How important would cultural content be in such material?

6. Look at three T.V. soap operas and determine whether these would have useful cultural or language content. How would you edit a videotape of such material?

7. From an audiovisual catalogue, find several films or filmstrips which would fit into a particular class. Preview them if possible. What language objectives might they fulfill? What non-language objectives? How would you sequence them?

8. Sketch a lesson in note-taking or comprehension for an advanced class using a film or filmstrip which you are familiar with. What composition topics might it lead to?

9. Find five current popular or folk songs which would fit within the language taught in a particular class. Check the lyrics used by the Beatles, Cat Stevens, Pete Seeger, early Joan Baez, or others in your record collection. You'll find quite a range of complexity, but most folk music tends to be at least linguistically easy—though a good many dialect variations may be illustrated.

10. Write a "survival English" dialogue dealing with one of the following. Keep the dialogue to within ten lines and use English appropriate to intermediate university ESL level.

    a. Buying a shirt, sweater, or pair of shoes.
    b. Calling up the local movie theater to ask what's playing.
    c. Asking for something at the supermarket.
    d. Buying books.
    e. Politely asking noisy neighbors to be quiet.
    f. Registration at the university.
    g. Calling up a utility company to report a broken appliance.
    h. Asking for directions to the Recreation Center from somewhere on campus.
    i. Asking a librarian how to find information about a topic.

11. Make one of the survival dialogues of 10 into a slide lesson. Refer to comic strips for ideas about types of shots. Keep pictures as simple as possible. About a dozen slides would be sufficient for a short presentation.

12. Make one of the following games or realia.

    a. A map of some part of your city.
    b. A job application blank for Mucky Supermarket, Inc.
    c. A housing contract or apartment lease (with appended comprehension questions).

d. A bingo game using names of common foods.

e. A crossword puzzle using vocabulary from current events or local place names.

f. A Monopoly type of game emphasizing vocabulary or tense practice.

SUGGESTIONS FOR FURTHER READING

Battung, Diane (1972)
A Pilot Study for the development of a learning resource center format. MA TESL, UCLA.
Carries the argument for media one step further, to individualized instruction.

Brown, James et al. (1973)
A-V Instructions: Technology, media, and methods, 4th edition. New York: McGraw-Hill.
Good source of ideas for video, graphic materials, and photography.

Purves, Alan C., ed. (1972)
How porcupines make love. Lexingon, Mass.: Xerox.
How media relate to the response-centered curriculum.

Kemp, Jerrold E. (1968)
Planning and producing audiovisual materials, 2d edition. Scranton, N.J.: Chandler.
Includes a brief summary of research and much data on photographic techniques, mounting visuals, design and printing.

Lopate, Philip (1973)
"How to use Videotapes when you don't know the first thing about it," *Teachers and Writers Collaborative Newsletter,* 4:4 (Spring), 81-104.

McLuhan, Marshall, and Quentin Fiore (1967)
The Medium is the Message. New York: Random House.

——— (1964)
Understanding media. New York: McGraw-Hill.
Both these volumes furnish appropriately formed insights into what makes media affect us—a necessary purgative for those of us who were brought up in traditional ways.

Postman, Neil, and Charles Weingartner (1969)
Teaching as a subversive activity. New York: Delacorte Press.
A fundamental textbook on survival.

Rivers, Wilga (1968)
Teaching Foreign Language Skills. Chicago: University of Chicago Press, pp. 174-83.
A discussion of the audiovisual approach to language teaching, pro and con.

Schramm, Wilbur (1973)
Big Media, Little Media, A Report to the Agency for International Development. Palo Alto: Stanford Univ. Press. Also available through ERIC. (ED 077-186)
Discusses research on evaluating educational media in developing countries, and the arguments for and against the application of complex technology.

Wittich, W.A., and Charles Schuller (1973)
Instructional technology: Its nature and use, 5th edition. New York: Harper & Row.
Probably the most up-to-date and comprehensive book on techniques and resources.

Other references:

Filmstrips and sound materials

Denoyer-Geppert Audio-Visuals
Chicago, 1972. Filmstrips and discs: *Power of my spirit—the American Indian* (includes Buffy Saint-Marie); *Women: the forgotten majority* (includes interview with Gloria Steinem); *Is democracy alive and well?*; *New York City: an environmental case study*; *Lifestyle 2000: what will we take to the future?*

Images of Man
Inglewood Cliffs, N.J.: Scholastic Magazines Inc., 1972. Cassettes, filmstrips, and pictures. On major changes in society from the viewpoints of selected photographers: *Toward the Margin of Life* (Cornell Capa); *Voyages of Self Discovery* (Bruce Davidson); *The Uncertain Day* (Don McCullin); *Between Birth and Death* (W. Eugene Smith).

Modern Consumer Education
New York: Grolier Educational Corp., 1974. Cassettes, filmstrips, wall charts, workbooks. "Interviews" with high-pressure salesmen and similar episodes. A bit overdone for the purpose of entertainment, but usable.

USING SONGS AND GAMES IN THE ESL CLASSROOM

Michael Gasser *and*
Ellyn Waldman

INTRODUCTION

Few instructors would question the value of using songs and games when teaching ESL to children. Many instructors, however, seem reluctant to employ songs or games when teaching adolescent or adult ESL students. Aside from the potential pedagogical value of songs or games, Richards points out that, "Pleasure for its own sake is an important part of language learning, a fact which is often overlooked by the teacher in his quest for teaching points, or by the course designer focussing on presentation or repetition" (Richards, 1969). In this chapter we present a rationale for including songs and games in the ESL curriculum and we suggest some presentation strategies. We will then offer some examples of songs and games which have been used successfully with ESL students at all levels of English proficiency.

SONGS

When to teach songs

Using songs in the ESL classroom can be both enjoyable and educational. As pure diversion, group singing provides a change of pace in the classroom. From a pedagogical standpoint, songs can be incorporated into the curriculum for a variety of reasons. Richards (1969) suggests that songs can be used, "as a useful aid in the learning of vocabulary, pronunciation, structures, and sentence patterns." Pomeroy (1974) suggests that songs can also be used to teach aspects of culture.

Songs can provide an excellent means for introducing or reviewing vocabulary, including idiomatic expressions. For example, the song *Colours* (words and music by Donovan; see p. 51) can be used at the beginning levels to review colors and at a more advanced level to introduce expressions such as *mellow* and *to be low.*

Another value of songs is in teaching pronunciation. The song can be an aid in teaching individual sounds or stress and rhythm patterns in words and sentences. At the beginning level, a simple song like *Everybody Loves Saturday Night* (traditional; see p. 51) can be used to reinforce the /l/ and /r/ sounds. At the advanced level, the /l/ sound can be reviewed in *The Old Lady Who Swallowed a Fly* (traditional; see p. 53). As far as stress and rhythm are concerned, the song *The Fox* (traditional; see p. 52) is an excellent tool to use for this purpose at an advanced level. If the student wants to fit the words into the melody line, s/he must use proper stress and rhythm.

In teaching structures and sentence patterns, songs provide a novel way of presenting or reviewing material. *Michael Row the Boat Ashore* (traditional; see p. 51) is a good song to use for the imperative. *Colours* can be used for the simple present tense, and *The Drunken Sailor* (traditional; see p. 52) can be used at the intermediate level for presenting or reinforcing the modal *shall.*

Finally, songs can be a way of introducing various aspects of American culture or of stimulating a conversation on cultural contrasts and similarities. For example, *Oh, Susanna* (words and music by Stephen Foster; see p. 51) can be used to introduce a discussion of the Gold Rush, of Stephen Foster and his era, or of American folk humor. On the other hand, with *Everybody Loves Saturday Night* students can be encouraged to translate the words into their own language and teach the verse in their language to the class. There can then be some discussion as to whether or not Saturday night is the night everybody loves in all countries (i.e., is it the night for going to parties, movies, dances, etc.?).

Aside from all these pedagogical benefits, however, there are affective bonuses unmatched by any other activity. Foreign students have told us that learning their first song in English was one of the most pleasurable and satisfying experiences they ever had in using the language. The combined sense of accomplishment and aesthetic enjoyment that these students reported should be utilized by more ESL teachers.

What criteria should be used in selecting songs?
The following are guidelines we have developed for choosing appropriate songs to teach:

1.   To ensure the pedagogical value of the song, the ESL teacher should be able to use it to teach points in at least one of the four previously mentioned categories (grammar, pronunciation, vocabulary, culture).

2.   The tune should be simple and easy to learn.

3.   It helps if the lyrics are repetitive. If they are not, it helps if the song has a chorus which is easy to learn. In this way even the slowest students can master at least part of the song relatively quickly.

4.   The lyrics should be as representative as possible of standard, spoken English. *Greensleeves* is a lovely melody but no one today would actually say, *Alas, my love, you do me wrong, to cast me off so discourteously.*

5.   It should not be necessary to change the lyrics to make them more standard or to enhance their pedagogical value.

Finally, it should be pointed out that adult students are often familiar with a number of American folk and popular songs. In selecting songs, while it is important to take the above guidelines into consideration, it is of equal importance to take the taste and wishes of the students into consideration. We have found that students tend to participate much more enthusiastically in group singing when they have played an active role in selecting the songs.

How should songs be presented?
It is usually a good idea to save singing for the end of the class period. In presenting a new song, we suggest the following steps:

1.   Introduce the song by telling a little about it: when it was written, who composed it, etc.

2.   Pass out copies of the lyrics to the students or write the lyrics on the board. One variation of this is to pass out sheets which have some words missing (i.e., the cloze technique). The students then have to listen to the song a few times and try to fill in the missing words.

3.   Sing or play the song all the way through.

4.   Read the lyrics out loud and ask the class questions about the storyline, the vocabulary, etc., to check for comprehension.

5.   Sing or play the song verse by verse. Let the class listen to each verse before attempting to sing it. If the song has a chorus, teach it first.

6.   Sing the whole song through a few times with the class.

Some songs to teach
The following are songs which we have used successfully with ESL students. The songs are presented alphabetically. We have indicated the level that each song is appropriate for (note: songs marked "beginning" or "intermediate" are also appropriate for more advanced levels) and the teaching points that should be stressed for each song. For some songs, recommendations or comments are included that are based on our experience in teaching the songs.

Beginning level
1. *Bingo*
(traditional camp song)
Teaching Points:
Vocabulary   Individual letter sounds
Pronunciation   Being able to sing all the

words in the first line in the time allotted by the phrase.

Miscellaneous:
This is an excellent first song to teach. It relaxes the students and is very easy to learn.

Lyrics:
Once a farmer had a dog and Bingo was his name
B-I-N-G-O, B-I-N-G-O, B-I-N-G-O
And Bingo was his name

2. *Colours*

Teaching Points:
Grammar   Non-count noun + *be*: contraction *that's*
Pronunciation   /l/ and /r/
Vocabulary   *rarely, low, mellow*
Miscellaneous:
Once the students learn this song, they sometimes enjoy making up new verses on their own.

Lyrics:
Yellow is the colour of my true love's hair
In the morning when we rise, in the morning when we rise
That's the time, that's the time, I love the best.
Blue is the colour of the sky-y-y
In the morning when we rise, in the morning when we rise
That's the time, that's the time, I love the best.
Green is the colour of the sparkling corn
In the morning when we rise, in the morning when we rise
That's the time, that's the time, I love the best.
Mellow is the feeling that I get
When I see her —mm-hm, when I see her -mm-hm
That's the time, that's the time, I love the best.
Freedom is a word I rarely use
Without thinking -mm-hm, without thinking -mm-hm
Of the time, of the time, when I been low.[1]

3. *Everybody Loves Saturday Night*

Teaching Points:
Grammar   *everybody* with singular verb
Pronunciation   /l/ and /r/
Culture   Does *everybody love Saturday night* in all cultures or is some other evening used for recreation and socialization elsewhere?

Lyrics:
Everybody loves Saturday night
Everybody loves Saturday night
Everybody, everybody, everybody, everybody
Everybody loves Saturday night.

4. *Michael Row the Boat Ashore*

Teaching Points:
Grammar   imperative
Pronunciation   /l/, /r/, /s/, and /h/
Vocabulary   *row, ashore, Hallelujah, lend a helping hand*
Miscellaneous:
Students can be encouraged to make up their own verses, using the imperative.

Lyrics:
Michael row the boat ashore, Hallelujah.
Michael row the boat ashore, Hallelujah.

Sister help to trim the sails, Hallelujah.
Sister help to trim the sails, Hallelujah.

Brother lend a helping hand, Hallelujah.
Brother lend a helping hand, Hallelujah.

Sinner row to save your soul, Hallelujah.
Sinner row to save your soul, Hallelujah.

5. *Oh Susanna*[2]

Teaching Points:
Grammar   simple past tense
Vocabulary   *banjo, buckwheat*
Culture   Discuss in terms of Stephen Foster (his place in American culture) and the fact that this was the "theme song" of the California Gold Rush (Boni, 1947).

Lyrics:
I come from Alabama, with my banjo on my knee,
I'm going to Louisiana, my Susanna for to see.
It rained all day the night I left, the weather was so dry,
The sun so hot, I froze myself, Susanna don't you cry.

Chorus:
Oh Susanna, Oh don't you cry for me,
For I come from Alabama, with my banjo on my knee.

I had a dream the other night, when everything was still,

I thought I saw Susanna, a-coming down the hill.
The buckwheat cake was in her mouth, the tear was in her eye;
Says I, "I'm coming from the South," Susanna don't you cry.

Chrous

Intermediate level
6. *I've Been Workin' on the Railroad* (Traditional)
Teaching Points:
Grammar   present perfect continuous tense; contraction *can't.* So common is this contraction and this form of question, that you may wish to use the question as the basis for a substitution drill, with the students either singing or speaking the new questions, or both (*Songs to Sing in Class,* 1966).
Lyrics:
I've been workin' on the railroad, all the livelong day,
I've been workin' on the railroad, just to pass the time away.
Can't you hear the whistle blowin', rise up so early in the morn?
Can't you hear the captain shouting, "Dinah blow your horn"?
Dinah, won't you blow, Dinah, won't you blow, Dinah, won't you blow your horn?
Dinah, won't you blow, Dinah, won't you blow, Dinah, won't you blow your horn?

7. *Red River Valley* (Traditional)
Teaching Points:
Grammar   simple present; future; and present perfect tenses; modals *may* and *would*
Pronunciation   /ð/, /l/, and /r/
Vocabulary   *brighten, pathway, hasten, bid me adieu, leave her behind, unprotected*
Culture   Many students are anxious to learn an authentic cowboy song and this is a perfect example of one.
Lyrics:
From this valley they say you are going,
We will miss your bright eyes and sweet smile,
For they say you are taking the sunshine
That has brightened our pathway awhile.

Chorus:
Come and sit by my side if you love me,
Do not hasten to bid me adieu,
But remember the Red River Valley
And the cowboy (cowgirl) who loves you so true.

From this valley they say you are going;
When you go, may your darling go too?
Would you leave him/her behind unprotected
When s/he loves no other but you?
I have promised you darling, that never
Will a word from my lips cause you pain,
And my heart it will be yours forever
If you only will love me again.

Chorus

8. *The Drunken Sailor*
Teaching Points:
Grammar   modal *shall* in question form
Pronunciation   /š/, /r/, and /l/
Vocabulary   *drunken, sober, long boat, plug*
Lyrics:
What shall we do with the drunken sailor?
What shall we do with the drinken sailor?
What shall we do with the drunken sailor, early in the morning?

Chorus:
Hooray and up she rises, hooray and up she rises,
Hooray and up she rises, early in the morning.

Put him in the long boat until he's sober,
Put him in the long boat until he's sober,
Put him in the long boat until he's sober, early in the morning.

Chorus

Pull out the plug and wet him all over,
Pull out the plug and wet him all over,
Pull out the plug and wet him all over, early in the morning.

Chorus

Advanced level
9. *The Fox*[3]
Teaching Points:
Pronunciation   The challenge for the advanced student in singing this song is to reduce sounds to make the word fit the melody line.

Ideally, the song should be sung very fast.

Vocabulary *bin, dangle, cocked her head, shrill, flee, cozy, den strife*

Lyrics:

The fox went out on a chilly night
He prayed for the moon to give him light
For he'd many a mile to go that night
Before he reached the town-o, town-o, town-o
For he'd many a mile to go that night
Before he reached the town-o.
He ran till he came to a great big bin
Where the ducks and geese were kept therein
"A couple of you will grease my chin
Before I leave this town-o, town-o, town-o
A couple of you will grease my chin
Before I leave this town-o."
He grabbed the grey goose by the neck
Throwed a duck across his back
He didn't mind their quack, quack, quack
And their legs all dangling down-o, down-o, down-o
He didn't mind their quack, quack, quack
And their legs all dangling down-o.
Then old mother Flipper-Flopper jumped out of bed
Out of the window she cocked her head
Crying, "John, John, the grey goose is gone
And the fox is on the town-o, town-o, town-o."
Crying, "John, John, the grey goose is gone
And the fox is on the town-o."
Then John, he went to the top of the hill
Blowed his horn both loud and shrill;
The fox he said, "I better flee with my kill
Or they'll soon be on my trail-o, trail-o, trail-o."
The fox he said, "I better flee with my kill
Or they'll soon be on my trail-o."
He ran till he came to his cozy den;
There were the little ones eight, nine, ten.
They said, "Daddy you better go back again,
'Cause it must be a mighty fine town-o, town-o, town-o,
Daddy you better go back again
'Cause it must be a mighty fine town-o."
Then the fox and his wife without any strife
Cut up the goose with a fork and knife;
They never had such a supper in their life
And the little ones chewed on the bones-o, bones-o, bones-o,
They never had such a supper in their life
And the little ones chewed on the bones-o.

10. *The Old Lady
Who Swallowed A Fly*

Teaching Points:

Grammar relative clauses; review of simple past tense

Pronunciation /l/, /j/, and vowels

Vocabulary *wriggle, jiggle, absurd, what a hog* Lyrics:

There was an old lady who swallowed a fly
I don't know why she swallowed a fly
Perhaps she'll die.

There was an old lady who swallowed a spider
That wriggled and wriggled and jiggled inside her
She swallowed the spider to catch the fly
I don't know why she swallowed a fly
Perhaps she'll die.

There was an old lady who swallowed a bird
Have you ever heard, she swallowed a bird! etc.

There was an old lady who swallowed a cat
Well, fancy that, she swallowed a cat!
She swallowed the cat to catch the bird, etc.

There was an old lady who swallowed a dog
What a hog, to swallow a dog!
She swallowed the dog to catch the cat, etc.

There was an old lady who swallowed a cow
I don't know how she swallowed a cow!
She swallowed the cow to catch the dog
She swallowed the dog to catch the cat
She swallowed the cat to catch the bird
She swallowed the bird to catch the spider
That wriggled and wriggled and jiggled inside her
She swallowed the spider to catch the fly
I don't know why she swallowed a fly
Perhaps she'll die.

There was an old lady who swallowed a horse
She's dead of course.

GAMES

Writers who discuss ESL games most often justify their use with reference to the motivation which they can provide students. Games are, by definition, fun, and nearly everyone would agree that if learning can be made enjoyable, then students will learn more. What is perhaps not always realized is that adolescents and adults enjoy games as much as children and, if the purpose of a game is explained to them, do not feel that it is childish or out of place to participate in a game in the language classroom.

There is, however, an even better reason for including games in a language class. As Johnson (1973) has stated, "the use of language in games is task-oriented . . . and has a purpose which is not, in the end, the correct or appropriate use of language itself." In games, language use takes precedence over language practice, and in this sense games help bring the classroom closer to the real world, no matter how contrived they may be.

This is not to say that language is not practiced in ESL games. On the contrary, each game, by its nature, will focus on one or more aspects of English; say, a grammar point, a vocabulary area, or a communication skill. Teachers may expect their students to be concerned not only with the object of the game but also with the correctness of their language, at least in those aspects which the game is intended to practice. In this way, a game can be the logical follow-up after students have been given explanation and drill on a particular point; the game is a good deal further toward communication on Prator's manipulation-communication scale (Prator, 1965) than most other language classroom activities.

Thus games should be more than something which teachers use to provide relief from the classroom routine, to get their students' attention, or to take up the extra minutes at the end of class. Games can teach, and there is no reason why they cannot be legitimately included as an integral part of a lesson.

A number of writers have discussed the value of games in second language learning, and there are at least two small books devoted entirely to the subject (Lee, 1968; Dorry, 1966). Current interest in this area is reflected in the appearance of packaged games designed specifically for ESL, such as *Jabberwocky*, developed by Longman.[4] Unfortunately, many of the games described in the literature seem to have been designed for the enjoyment factor alone, as they require little or no real language use on the part of the students. For example, it is difficult to see the point of a game in which

the object is to think of words beginning with various letters of the alphabet.

It is possible to devise games which practice any of the language skills. In the games described below, the emphasis is on grammar, listening comprehension, vocabulary, and communication skills (such as giving directions), because these are the areas where there seems to be the greatest need for activities which involve language use. Spelling games have been omitted; most teachers probably know at least one way to do this, and both Dorry and Lee have included a number of them in their collections. For pronunciation practice, it is not difficult to create games out of contextualized minimal pair work. And many of the games below, though not designed specifically for pronunciation, will help expose those phonological errors which hinder communication and, at the very least, make students aware of the importance of pronunciation.

For the most part, the procedure to be followed with a game depends on the teacher's purpose in using it, the level of the class and the nature of the game itself. Usually some practice with sentence patterns and vocabulary is advisable before a game begins. Explaining the rules of a game is not always easy; this can constitute a listening comprehension exercise in itself. It is, of course, up to the individual teacher whether s/he corrects students' language errors during a game. In any case, interruptions should be as infrequent as possible so as not to detract from the students' interest in the game. An alternative to immediate correction is to make note of errors and discuss them when the game is over. Games can also be recorded on tape and then played back for the class for discussion and correction.

The word *game* is used here in a fairly broad sense. All of the games described below meet the following criteria: they have a goal (the "task" Johnson (1973) refers to), they are governed by rules, and they are meant to be fun. Most of them also contain an element of competition. Teachers who would rather discourage competition among their students can alter most of the games so as to make them non-competitive. It is sometimes best to avoid having winners and losers when individual students, as opposed to teams, are playing, because the weaker students may tend to become discouraged by never winning. Whether or not competition works in a class probably depends more than anything else on the relationship that exists among the students. Four different groups of games are described and illustrated below to give the ESL teacher a good idea of the possibilities that games offer.

Games involving some listening comprehension
1. *Commands*
Level:

Any

Teaching Points:

Comprehension of imperatives, and a range of vocabulary depending on the commands used. In this simple game the teacher gives commands which the students must obey. There are basically two types of commands which can be used in this game, those which call for overt physical response (*Stand up. Put your right hand behind your back. Shake hands with your neighbor.*) and those which require the students to write or draw something (*Write a three-letter word beginning with the letter B. Draw a large circle with a small square in the middle.*). The physical response commands may include some which can be mimed. (*Pretend you're playing the guitar. Pretend you have a headache.*) This game is well suited to practice with prepositions (*Put your pencil in/on/beside/under your book. Draw a line next to/above/through/between the circles.*). For competition it is enough to see who is the first to obey a command. Students can also be given instructions for drawing the parts of a picture without knowing what it is they are drawing. In this case they can compete to see who can guess first what the picture is. With a young class, the game can be made more interesting by having the students obey only those commands which are preceded by *Simon says.*

2. *Traveler Puzzle*
Level:

Intermediate to advanced.

Teaching Points:

Listening comprehension and note-taking; vo-

cabulary related to traveling; task-oriented conversation among students.

In this game information is read to the students, who take notes and then solve a problem using the information. Maps of a fictitious country are distributed to the students. The maps show towns, roads, railroads, a river, and a lake. There is a scale of miles at the bottom. The teacher explains that a traveler begins at one particular town and must get to another as fast as possible. The students are told how much money the traveler has at the beginning of the trip. The teacher then gives the students information about routes and fares for all of the means of transportation in the country (buses, trains, planes and ships) while the students take notes. The problem can be made more complicated by including cars, bicycles and boats, which can be bought or rented for a specific fee and are available only in certain towns. In addition, bridges may be out or roads closed. After all the information has been given, the students work together in groups to come up with the fastest possible route for the traveler to take. This stage is perhaps even more valuable than the listening part, as the students must use a good deal of English to solve the problem together, though they will, of course, be tempted to resort to their first language if they are with others of the same language background. The language they use will be relatively unpredictable, but the students should have had prior practice in using both the simple present tense (*It takes one day to go from here to here.*) and simple conditionals (*If he takes the bus, he'll get there sooner.*). This game requires a good deal of preparation on the part of the teacher but is an interesting challenge to many students.

3. *Crossword Puzzles*
Level:

Any

Teaching Points:

Whatever vocabulary the teacher includes in the puzzle, definitions, relative clauses and noun clauses, spelling.

Students are given copies of the blank crossword puzzle. The definitions are then given to the class orally. These should be more colloquial than the average dictionary definitions, e.g., *What you do with soap* (a definition for *wash*). A puzzle becomes more personalized and more interesting if names of students or local places are included (*The student who gave a speech yesterday. The street this school is on.*). Practice with informal definitions like these is useful for second-language learners, because they sometimes find themselves in situations where they must define a word that they either haven't learned or can't remember (*You know, those little things that you put in your eyes instead of glasses.*). Note that definitions often include relative clauses or noun clauses. After some experience with crossword puzzles, relatively advanced students should be able to create their own puzzles. This can be done by individuals or groups of students.

Questioning games

4. Twenty Questions

Level:
Any
Teaching Points:
Questions (mainly *yes-no*), the tense depending on the topic chosen.
A slip of paper with a word on it is given to a student, or the student writes down his or her own word. The other students must then ask him or her questions in order to guess the word. There is a limit on the number of questions that can be asked (usually twenty) and students are restricted to *yes-no* questions. The game is repeated with other students' words. Various categories of words may be used, each practicing particular structures and vocabulary:

Object in the room—present tense of *be* (third person singular), prepositions, comparative (*Is it heavier than this book?*).

Any object—present tense of *be*, simple present tense (*Do you use it every day? Does it move?*), comparative.

Places—present tense of *be*, prepositions.

Occupations (the game is conducted as if these are the students' own jobs)—simple present tense, second person (*Do you work in an office?*); present tense of *be*, second person; vocabulary relating to jobs.

People (living)—same as for occupations.

People (dead)—simple past tense.

In one variation of the game from an article by Deyes (1973:161), occupations or names of people are printed on students' backs. The students circulate around the room, asking other students questions in order to guess who or what they are. There need be no limit on the number of questions asked; the winner is the student who first figures out his job or identity. This variation practices first person singular questions.

5. Charades

Level:
Any
Teaching Points:
Questions in present continuous and simple past, vocabulary (mainly verbs of action).
In the ESL version of this game, individual students mime actions while the rest of the class guesses what they are doing. The actions may be written on slips of paper for the students, or they may come up with their own ideas. Actions which are completed quickly practice past tense questions (*Did you fall off a horse? Did you wake up?*). More durative actions practice the present continuous tense (*Are you eating spaghetti? Are you repairing a watch?*).

6. Alibi
(from Lee, 1968:58-9)

Level:
Intermediate to advanced
Teaching Points:
Past tense questions, reported speech.
The teacher explains that a bank was robbed the day before at a particular time and that two of the students are under suspicion. The two suspects claim that they were together at that time and nowhere near the bank. They then leave the room to prepare their alibi. While they are outside, the other students and the teacher discuss what kinds of questions they will ask the suspects. (*Where did you meet each other yesterday? Where did you go then?*) After five minutes or so, one of the suspects is called in for questioning. If possible, each of the students should ask at least one question. When the class is satisfied that they have asked

enough questions, the first suspect is sent out and the other called in for interrogation. The idea is to try to expose inconsistencies in the alibi. Finally the first suspect is brought in again, and the class must explain whatever contradictions they discovered. (*Yoshiko said they had Coke in the restaurant, but Juan said they drank beer.*) The suspects may even try to account somehow for the inconsistencies.

Games in which students provide clues, information, or directions

In the following games some students give information while others listen and then make a guess or a decision or perform a task using the information. For more games of this type, see Heaton's chapter on *The Adult ESL Classroom* (in this volume).

7. *Definition Game*

Level:
Intermediate to advanced
Teaching Points:
Definitions, relative and noun clauses, listening, whatever vocabulary is used.
The class is divided into two or three teams. Each student is given a word on a slip of paper. Normally all of the words will belong to one class; say, adjectives, concrete nouns, or action verbs. The students are given a few minutes to think over how they will define their words. A timekeeper tells the first player when to begin, and s/he then gives a definition for his or her word. The other members of the team have to guess the word. The teacher records on the blackboard the length of time it took for them to guess the word. A student from the other team then defines his or her word for his or her team. After all of the students have had a turn, the times are added up and the team with the lowest total time wins.

Another variation of this game works best with more advanced students. Instead of one word, each student is given eight words, all belonging to a particular category; for example, "things having to do with movies," "words that begin with W," or "things that are red." Students may choose the category they want from a list on the blackboard. They may or

may not be given time to prepare their definitions, as the teacher wishes. Each student must get his or her team members to guess as many of the eight words as possible in two minutes. The score is the number of words guessed within the time limit. After all the students have had turns, the teams' scores are totaled. In this case, the highest score wins.

8. *Password*
(From the TV game of the same name)
Level:
Any
Teaching Points:
Vocabulary (depending on words used), pronunciation.
This game works best with a small class. The students are first divided into two teams. One student from each team is called outside, where the teacher tells them the "password." The students return to the room and flip a coin to decide who goes first. (The winner of the toss may choose to go first or second.) The first player gives his or her team a clue. A clue must consist of only one word and may not be related morphologically to (i.e., may not use the same word root(s) as) the password. The team members may consult with each other and must then make a guess within a certain time limit, say, 15 seconds. If the first team fails to guess the password, the player from the other team gives his or her team a clue. Note that the clues are audible to both teams, but only one may guess. The two students continue to alternate giving clues until one team guesses the password. The score depends on how many clues a team needed before it guessed the word. If a team guesses correctly after the first clue, it receives ten points, after the second clue, nine points, and so on. A maximum of ten clues may be given for each word. Two more players, one from each team, are told a new password, and they proceed in the same way, except that this time the student from the team which is behind in points has the choice of whether to go first or second. The game is over when all of the students have had a turn, and the teams' scores are totaled. Note that if players are allowed to say a clue only once, they will have to be very careful about their pronunciation.

9. *Picture Matching Game*

Level:
Elementary to intermediate
Teaching Points:
There is/are, present continuous, indefinite and definite articles.

Preparation for this game should include some examples of describing pictures. Normally the first sentence will contain *there is* or *there are*, and there will be at least one example of the present continuous tense (*In this picture there are two women and a man. The women are talking, and the man is reading a newspaper.*). Note that there is also plenty of opportunity to practice articles here.

Photographs or cartoons are handed out, a different one to each student. Students are told not to let others see their picture. They have five or ten minutes to prepare descriptions of their pictures. During this time the teacher helps individuals with vocabulary if necessary. One student then describes his or her picture while the others listen and take notes, including the student's name so as to remember later which picture s/he described. After all of the students have talked about their pictures, the teacher collects the pictures and mixes them up. S/he then shows them to the class one by one, giving each a number. The students must refer to their notes and match the number of each picture with the name of the student who described it. If the teacher wants to make the game more competitive, the students can be awarded one point for each picture correctly identified.

10. *Recipes*

Level:
Intermediate to advanced
Teaching Points:
Simple present, articles, giving directions, vocabulary (cooking terms, use of the verb *put*), pronunciation.

Preparation for this game should include a discussion of verbs used in recipes (*boil, fry, bake, mix, stir,* etc.) and perhaps also of patterns with the verb *put*, which gives many ESL students trouble and is useful in recipes.

The students should use the simple present tense with subject *you* in their recipes.

The class is divided into groups of about four students. Each group is given a list of ten ingredients. The lists may be the same or different. This game can involve pronunciation practice as well if the teacher chooses words containing troublesome sounds (e.g., for *l* and *r—flour, lard, milk, rice,* etc.). Each group creates a meal from its list of ingredients, adding others if desired. The meal may, of course, include a number of courses. It will take the students at least twenty minutes to put together their recipes. When they finish, each team gives its recipe orally to the others. The class can then vote on which meal would be the tastiest and which the least appetizing.

11. *Paper Hunt*

Level:
Any
Teaching Points:
Giving and following directions.
A slip of paper, and a piece of tape or a tack, are given to each student. The class is divided up into pairs of students. One student from each pair leaves the room and attaches the piece of paper somewhere with the tack or the tape. S/he then returns and gives his or her partner directions on how to find the piece of paper. The partner goes out to search for the paper. If s/he cannot locate it, s/he may return to the classroom for more or better directions. After s/he finds the paper, it is his or her turn to hide the slip of paper and then give directions on how to locate it. There are no winners or losers in this game.

12. *Map Game*

Level:
Any
Teaching Points:
Giving and following directions.
City maps are distributed to the students. The maps show streets, some of them with names, and a number of buildings. There are two versions of the map, one with half of the buildings identified and one with the other half identified. The names of the buildings which

are not identified on a map are listed at the bottom. Students with one version of the map are paired up with those with the other version. Each pair of students must sit back to back or have an upright divider between them so that they cannot see each other's map. A starting point is indicated in one corner of the map. Students must ask their partners for directions from that point to one of the buildings from the list at the bottom of their map. Their partners give them directions until they have located the building. The students in each pair take turns asking for and giving directions in this way until all of the buildings on both maps have been identified.

13. *Drawing Game*
Level:
Any
Teaching Points:
Vocabulary related to shape and orientation.
For this game students work in pairs. Each student is given five drawings of simple figures on small separate pieces of paper. The figures differ from those his or her partner has, and the students must not look at each other's figures. One student from each pair begins by telling his or her partner how to draw one of the figures. No gesturing is allowed. When they are finished, the drawing is compared with the original. The students take turns telling each other how to draw the figures. If competition is desired, the winning pair can be the one which comes closest to reproducing the original drawings in a specified span of time.

This game normally requires some preparation. A good deal of vocabulary is necessary to describe even the simplest figures. The teacher should also go over some examples with the class before distributing the figures.

Games involving less predictable language
In these games the students' language is less bound to particular structures and vocabulary than in those already described. Thus in a sense they are even less manipulative than the other games. The point here is simply to get the students to communicate in their second language, and these games give them something to communicate about.

14. *Debates*
Level:
High intermediate to advanced
The best debates are probably those that involve the whole class. Deyes (1973:161) describes one type in which all of the students participate. Each student chooses a person, living or dead, whom s/he considers to be very important. The teacher then explains that all of the people chosen by the class are passengers in a balloon which is falling so fast that all but one passenger must jump out in order for it to land safely. Each student has to argue for one minute why the person s/he has chosen should be the one to remain in the balloon. The class then votes on which passenger is to be saved, each student voting for someone other than the person s/he argued for.

15. *Interviews*
Level:
Intermediate to advanced
The class is divided into teams of three students. Within each team one student portrays a famous person, living or dead. The other two are to interview him or her. The teams have ten minutes or so to prepare and rehearse their interviews. After the students hear all of the interviews, they vote on which was the most interesting or humorous, each student voting for an interview in which s/he did not take part. Alternatively, one student from each team may be interviewed regarding an interesting experience of his or her own.

16. *Board Games*
Level:
Any
Most standard board games elicit lots of language from the players. Radice (1973) has considered in some detail the language that arises out of the game of Monopoly and how this game can be used in an ESL class. If teachers object to the values that this game might encourage in their students, a game called Anti-Monopoly is also available.

Reading and writing games
Games 1, 3, 10, and 11 above become reading and/or writing games if written, instead of

spoken, cues or information are used. In addition, many board games, including Monopoly, involve some reading. Here are a few other ideas.

17. *Treasure Hunt*

Level:
Elementary to intermediate
An object has been hidden somewhere on the campus. Sets of clues leading to the "treasure," one set for each team, have also been hidden in various places. The class is divided into several teams. Each team is given a slip of paper with the first clue in its set. Each clue leads the students to the next clue in the set and eventually to the treasure. Alternatively, one group of students may hide the treasure and write the clues for the rest of the class.

18. *Book Hunt*

Level:
Intermediate to advanced readers
Teaching Points:
Some reading, use of the card catalogue.
This game is played in the library. The class is divided into teams of two or three students each. Each team is given a topic, e.g., Russian cooking, the history of Chile, Korean grammar. The first team to return to the teacher with a book on the given topic is the winner.

19. *Information Hunt*

Level:
High intermediate to advanced
Teaching Points:
Reading for information, use of the library.
This game is also played in the library. Each student is given a slip of paper with an information question (*What's the main export of Paraguay? Where was Charles Darwin born? What's the main ingredient of toothpaste?*). If necessary, students may consult with a librarian in their search. The first student to answer his or her question correctly wins.

Some areas have certainly been neglected in this list of games. In particular, there is little that is applicable for young children in their first years of English. Teachers of such students are referred to the work of the Teaching English as a Second Language Materials Devel-

opment Center (Dykstra, 1967), which has devised a series of fifteen "communication activities." Similar to some of the games described above, these activities divide the class into groups of four, and place the students in situations where they must communicate with the others in their group, using basic patterns they have practiced, in order to accomplish certain tasks.

CONCLUSION

The songs and games described here and countless others, not mentioned, have a place in the ESL classroom which goes beyond their entertainment function. While this chapter has suggested some of the ways in which songs and games can be included in a lesson, other possibilities are numerous. There is plenty of room for the creativity of the individual teacher not only in devising new games and discovering songs which can help teach particular aspects of the language, but also in developing ways of presenting and using them. The dual potential that songs and games have—that they can be simultaneously instructive and enjoyable—should be exploited more by ESL teachers.

NOTES

1.   The teacher should point out this non-standard form to students: the standard form would be *when I have been low.*

2.   The teacher should point out the non-standard grammar and archaisms in this song, e.g., *for to see, a-coming.*

3.   There are three non-standard forms in this song, which you may want to point out to your students: *throwed* (line 14), *blowed* (line 26), and *I better flee* (line 27), which would probably be expressed in current colloquial English as *I had better get* (or *run*) *away.*

4.   See the advertisement in the *ELT*, 29:1, Oct. 1974, for details concerning this packaged card game designed for use in ESL classes.

DISCUSSION QUESTIONS

1.   In a class of adults, do you believe it is worth taking the time to explain to the students how songs or games can be a useful part of the language learning curriculum?

2. In every class there are a few students who are shy and reluctant to sing. What would be the best way to encourage these students to participate in the singing?

3. Using the birthday song as an example (*Happy birthday to you, happy birthday to you, happy birthday dear . . . , happy birthday to you*) discuss to what extent it fits the five criteria mentioned above for selecting songs to be used in the ESL classroom.

4. In an intensive English program, what would be the advantages and disadvantages of having a separate games class as opposed to including games as part of the other classes?

5. *Hangman* is a well-known game in which one student writes spaces on the blackboard in place of the letters of a word s/he has thought of, and the other students take turns guessing the letters in the word. They must guess the word before they have named six letters which are not in the word, or the student at the board wins. Discuss the potential usefulness of this game in a language classroom.

6. On the *College Bowl* television program, two teams of students were asked a variety of questions on academic subjects. A team received points when one of its members was able to answer a question before someone from the other team did. Discuss ways in which this game might be adapted for use in a language classroom and what teaching points it might be used to practice.

SUGGESTED ACTIVITIES

1. Students often like to learn popular songs as well as traditional folk songs. Choose one popular song and explain why it would or would not be a good song to use in the ESL classroom (refer to specific points of grammar, vocabulary, pronunciation, and culture that could be taught or reinforced using the song).

2. Think of an example of a grammar point that beginning, intermediate, or advanced students often have trouble with, and find a song which would illustrate this grammar point.

Explain how you would include the song in the grammar lesson.

3. Devise a game which practices a particular structure; e.g., present perfect, passive, or mass and count nouns.

4. Consider the suitability for the language classroom of a board game you are familiar with. What structures and vocabulary areas, if any, does the game focus on?

SUGGESTIONS FOR FURTHER READING

Boni, M. B. (ed.) (1947)
Fireside Book of Folk Songs. New York: Simon and Schuster, Inc.
Gives a short history for each folksong, which would be useful to the teacher in presenting the song to an ESL class. It also provides piano music and guitar chords.

Hill, L. A., and R. D. S. Fielden (1974)
English Language Teaching Games for Adult Students. Vol. 1: Elementary, Vol. 2: Advanced. London: Evans.
Each of the games practices a particular structure and there are suggestions for how to drill the structure before beginning the game.

Olsen, J. E. W-B. (1977)
Communication-starters and Other Activities for the ESL Classroom. San Francisco: Alemany Press.
This book contains a number of games of the type described in this chapter. Included is a useful index of the structures which the games and activities focus on.

Richards, J. (1969)
"Songs in language learning." *TESL Quarterly* 3:2.
A detailed rationale and methodology for using songs in the ESL classroom.

Recommended Song Books

Boni, M. B. (ed.) (1947)
Fireside Book of Songs. New York: Simon and Schuster, Inc.

The Burl Ives Song Book (1953)
New York: Baltimore Books.

Haufrecht, H. (ed.) (1960)
Folksing. New York: Berkeley Medallion Books.

Sing-a-long (1977)
Los Angeles: UCLA Extension, American Language Center. (Available on request. Write: Ellyn Waldman, Language Learning Center, 1377 Westwood Blvd., Los Angeles, CA 90024.)

There was an old lady who swallowed a fly (1973)
New York: Grosset and Dunlap.

PART II
LANGUAGE SKILLS
A. Listening

Until recently the skill of listening comprehension had been somewhat neglected since the teaching strategy of audiolingualism had been to make students *listen and repeat* rather than *listen and understand*. Listening comprehension is now felt to be a necessary preliminary to oral proficiency, and these two chapters—one by Herschenhorn, and one by Epting and Bowen—reflect this current concern. Both chapters stress the need to prepare students, from the start, to understand the speech of native speakers of English speaking at a normal rate, in a normal manner. Their methods differ somewhat, but they agree that prolonged exposure to the slow, overly precise speech sometimes characteristic of ESL "teacherese" will not prepare students to understand the natural spontaneous speech of native speakers, which, of course, is one of the major goals of ESL instruction. In both articles strategies for achieving this goal are described.

TEACHING LISTENING COMPREHENSION USING LIVE LANGUAGE

Suzanne Herschenhorn

Because a student can utter a lot of sentences in a foreign language is no guarantee that he will understand them in the mouth of a native speaker. There is a virtual chasm between the performance of native speakers engaged in a conversation and what a student expects a conversation to sound like.

—Belasco, 1967

LISTENING COMPREHENSION IN THE LITERATURE

Listening comprehension is one of the most important and fundamental of the four skills in language learning; yet, it is probably the least stressed skill in the language classroom. Reasons for this may lie in the lack of emphasis on teaching listening comprehension in language textbooks in general, as well as in the lack of available material specifically developed for and focused on the teaching of listening skills. In a brief overview of some early prominent works in language teaching, it can be noted that some mention is made of the importance of listening comprehension. Until recently, however, little is offered in terms of methodology or practical application for helping the ESL[1] student develop these important aural skills.

In *Teaching and Learning English as a Foreign Language* (1945), an influential methodology for decades, Fries attempts to develop materials based on scientific studies of the English language (p. vi). Fries holds that mastery of any language is on two levels: *"production* and *recognition"* (p. 8). He states that the two, production and recognition—and he puts them in that order—must be considered separately when it comes to teaching and learning a language in the initial stages. In almost the same breath, he says that "the two interact and

condition one another and in the actual practice of the language can hardly be separated." Consequently, Fries does not separate production from recognition, i.e., teaching the speaking skills from the listening skills, in his methodology and materials.

In learning a new language, Fries holds that the first problem to consider is "mastery of the sound system" (p. 3). He explains further that one must not only be able to hear "distinctive sound features" but also be able to "approximate their production." For example, Fries suggests that one of the best ways for a student to learn to *hear* differences in the English language is to be able to discriminate in the production of minimal pairs such as *leak, lick, lack, lake, lock, luck, look* (p. 8). The remainder of Fries' discussion on the topic of recognition is based on a description of the phonemes and allophones of the spoken language as well as on stress, intonation, rhythm, structural forms and arrangements within a limited range of vocabulary (pp. 8, 9, 10-26 ff.).

To familiarize students with the sounds or features of pause, stress, rhythm and intonation, Fries suggests oral reading to the class of fairly lively dialogues from literature. Such dialogues are to be read, almost acted out, in as natural a conversational manner as possible to make them "much more alive, interesting and meaningful to the listener" (p. 62).

Fries stresses the importance of basing one's studies on a descriptive analysis of real or natural language as is "used by native speakers in carrying on their affairs—the exact reproduction of all parts of whole utterances as they appear in the normal conversation of native speakers" (p. 3). Furthermore, he advocates the use of contractions and reduced forms since they are "more accurate in the speed of usual conversation." Fries reveals some vital information about natural or live language, but for the purpose of production not recognition. He never really distinguishes between the two in his methodology and materials (pp. 68-80). Rather, Fries implies that since the two, production and recognition, "are interdependent, recognition, i.e., the listening skills, will develop as a result of learning the speaking skills" (pp. 3, 8, 10-27). He never really deals directly with the important area of teaching listening comprehension.

In *Language Teaching, A Scientific Approach* (1964), Lado, in his opening remarks, firmly states that the goals of language learning "have broadened to include spoken communication with an understanding of native speakers on the widest range of human interests" (p. 3). However, nowhere in his text does he deal with the problem of understanding native speakers or in other words, the area of listening comprehension.

Lado sets forth "laws of learning," "hypothetical laws of learning," theories and techniques for language teaching and information on technological aids including the language lab (pp. 36ff., 49ff., 173ff.). But in none of his writings, not even in the section on theories and techniques for language teaching where he states "teach listening and speaking first, reading and writing next" does he deal directly with the area of teaching listening (p. 50).

Lado does stress teaching various aspects of pronunciation: phonemes, intonation, rhythm, consonants and vowels (pp. 70-89). One might infer then that Lado, like Fries, believes that imitation or good production will help develop the aural skills.

In his *Language and Language Learning* (1960), Brooks is one of the first to recognize and emphasize the importance of developing listening skills apart from oral skills. The skills must be ordered, he says, and "ear training must come first" (p. 107). Brooks suggests that 50% of class time at the first level of language learning should be devoted to listening. In the second and third levels, he recommends that 30% and 20% of class time respectively be spent on listening (pp. 122-9). Brooks discusses vital points for the student to be made aware of, such as contractions and omissions—aspects of sandhi-variation (changes which occur in natural speech as a result of environment, stress, intonation, rate of speed and so forth). Though Brooks does not specifically refer to the term "sandhi-variation," he does refer to the phenomenon of sandhi in his examples: *Jeet jet?* (*Did you eat yet?*) (p. 50). According to Brooks, native speakers in an informal situation "habitually reduce the clarity of speech signals to the minimum required for comprehension." Brooks believes that it is necessary to give consideration also to the interdependence of language and culture; for example, register, expletives, verbal taboos, culture-bound vocabulary. And he also mentions the need to clarify and point out the differences between written and spoken English—a point not stressed enough in most texts (pp. 87-90).

With regard to aiding the student to develop aural skills, Brooks suggests five-minute monologues, cultural "hors d'oeuvres" presented by the teacher (a native speaker) at the beginning of each class, on topics ranging from national and ethnic holidays to verbal taboos (pp. 86-92). He also recommends use of dialogues as well as reading from plays in class to provide students with varied, interesting, and useful models for listening (pp. 86, 127).

Brooks does not offer specifics or provide special procedures or graded exercises for teaching how to listen, though he does offer suggestions for aural presentations in class. One could infer, then, that Brooks assumes that by listening to the language in large doses, by sufficient exposure to readings and other oral presentations, listening skills will develop.

In a positive contribution to language learning, Belasco has written numerous articles on the importance of teaching listening comprehension with emphasis on the phonology, syntax, semantics, sandhi-variation and culture of a language. In a series of studies, Belasco discovered that even when a student had learned to speak or vocalize in a foreign language, s/he was not necessarily able to comprehend the spoken language in the mouth of a native speaker (1969, p. 194). Reasons for this, he holds, are: insufficient emphasis placed on listening comprehension; and reluctance of the teacher to expose him- or herself "to so-called 'details' characteristic of a sound pattern—sandhi-variation in the initial stages of language learning" (1969, p. 195; 1967, p. 88). Students are being taught "language" not "speech" (1969, p. 196). Belasco says that using solely contrived materials will not get the student to a level where he can understand natural language. Materials used in the classroom "must be supplemented with 'live' materials before the gap between *basic* foreign language performance and *real* foreign language performance can be bridged" (ibid., pp. 198-9).

Belasco stresses the importance in the initial stages of language learning of internalizing basic phonological, syntactic, and sandhi-variation patterns of the language (1965, p. 485). He emphasizes the need to use live language in helping the student to internalize these basic essentials (1972, p. 36). He stresses some of the basic differences between real language and contrived speech with an emphasis on sandhi-variation (1969, pp. 214-16; 223-4).

Further reasons for upholding the need to use live language in the classroom stem first of all from the fact that "the 'creative' aspect of language is its essential characteristic" (1965, p. 484). Since the student will be expected to create and recognize new sentences which can be "theoretically infinite in number," s/he needs to have internalized basic patterns to be enabled to do so (ibid., p. 484). S/he also needs to be prepared for a "state of expectancy" for hearing and comprehending live language as spoken by natives (1972, p. 16). Contrived language can never fully prepare the student to reach this level since it does not expose him or her to the real elements of live language, nor does it offer the infinite variety of combinations of live language. "Omission of redundant elements, retention of important elements, these are the characteristics of normal speech" (1965, p. 486). And these elements are precisely what the student needs to become accustomed to hearing, which can only be done through learning to listen to live language.

Belasco makes it clear that listening can and ought to be taught apart from speaking. He elucidates the necessity of using real or live language in teaching listening to help get the students to a level where they can understand and converse with native speakers (ibid., p. 485). Belasco recommends the use of "interviews, newscasts, speeches, popular songs, excerpts from original plays, etc., recorded live for developing listening skills" (1972, p. 19).

In her text, *Teaching Foreign-Language Skills* (1968), Rivers offers the most complete and clear-cut presentation to date on the theoretical and practical aspects of teaching listening comprehension. Listening comprehension has been neglected too long, says Rivers. Since oral communication involves listening and decoding as well as speaking, then it is necessary to be able to comprehend as well as speak (pp. 135-6).

In learning to listen, there are two basic levels to be considered, according to Rivers: (a) the level of recognition, and (b) the level of selection (pp. 142-3). When first confronted with a foreign language, the student hears only a barrage of meaningless noise. Gradually, after continued exposure to the language, s/he begins to recognize elements and patterns such as phonemes, intonation, words and phrases. When s/he is able to recognize the phonological, syntactic, and semantic codes of the language automatically, s/he has reached the first level, that of recognition (pp. 140-1). Before going on with Rivers' theory, it is useful to note the basic features a native speaker recognizes unconsciously in his or her language. These same features must be learned with conscious effort by the ESL student. They include:

a.   The phonological code:
  i.   phonemes,
  ii. rhythm,
  iii. stress,
  iv. intonation patterns and emotional overtones (e.g., anger),
  v.   sandhi-variation (including reflections of regional, social and dialectical variations).
b.   The syntactic code:
  i.   word classes (including affixes and exceptions),
  ii. word order (including stylistic variations),

iii. inter-relationship of words (including stylistic variations).
c. The semantic code:
    i. word meaning (including variations within the context),
    ii. connotation (culture-tied and often dependent upon region as well as individual speaker),
    iii. culture (national, regional, ethnic),
    iv. idioms, expletives, clichés, colloquialisms,
    v. false starts, pauses, fillers (redundancies).

(Rivers, 1968, p. 144; Belasco, 1965, p. 485; Brooks, 1960, pp. 85-6).

After looking over this list, an instructor can perhaps realize and appreciate the difficult tasks the student must perform in learning to listen and comprehend in another language. When the student is able to recognize these elements automatically, s/he should next be able to sift out the message-bearing units for retention and comprehension without conscious attention to individual components. This is the level of selection (Rivers, 1968, pp. 140-1). In conjunction with her levels of recognition and selection, Rivers points out Broadbent's theory of perception and retention.

According to Broadbent, the human organism can only absorb so much information at a time. Thus the relevant or important matter needs to be sifted out from the whole and sent to the short-term memory. In order for this information to be retained for decoding or comprehension, it must be recirculated "through the perceptual processes at regular intervals" (Rivers, 1968, p. 142; Broadbent, 1958, pp. 216-42). In this way, important information, or the message, can be gleaned from the incoming sounds, recirculated and passed on to the long-term memory allowing time for cognitive processing.

Rivers suggests four stages for teaching the listening skill in the elementary, intermediate, and advanced levels of language learning. They are: (a) identification; (b) identification and selection without retention; (c) identification and guided selection with short-term retention; and finally, (d) identification, selection,

and long-term retention (pp. 148-51). She also suggests a list of activities which could be used for teaching listening comprehension.

Rivers gives listening comprehension its rightful prominence and attention and she deals directly with teaching listening skills. She states that "listening comprehension has its peculiar problems which arise from the fleeting, immaterial nature of spoken utterances" (p. 136). And she even points out the significant differences between live and contrived language, such as variances in intonation, redundancy, in terms of morphological and syntactic elements, as well as pauses, fillers, and false starts (1966, pp. 196-7). But she does not stress the importance of using live language in the classroom to teach listening skills, as does Belasco.

In his book *The Development of Modern Language Skills* (1971), Chastain nicely summarizes some of the major premises of both Rivers' and Belasco's philosophies on listening comprehension. He also includes some points from Brooks and Fries. Chastain stresses that what is most important is for a student to be able to understand the language when spoken by a native, "at normal speed in unstructured situations" (p. 163).

According to Chastain, the three components which make up the levels or stages of developing listening skills are: (a) sound discrimination (e.g., recognizing minimal pairs, phonemes); (b) auditory memory, and (c) comprehension. Chastain recommends going from the simple to the complex in terms of difficulty factors and from short to long in terms of content for developing memory span. He tends to emphasize developing auditory memory. Though Chastain offers no specific directions as to the actual steps to follow in teaching listening comprehension, he does offer a list of activities which could be used to help to develop listening skills. These activities include minimal pair drills, games, impromptu conversations, dialogues prepared with classmates, oral reports, and so forth (pp. 169-73).

Finally, Chastain recommends that, since there is a dearth of good listening materials now, besides buying whatever materials may be available on the market, the teacher can and should begin to make and save tapes of visiting speakers, dramatizations, readings, descriptions of cultural topics, guessing games, anecdotes, radio and short-wave broadcasts, and so on, to use with his classes (p. 173). Thus he emphasizes the need for giving special attention to teaching listening comprehension in the classroom as well as the need for using live language to supplement materials.

AVAILABLE MATERIALS

To date, two of the best sets of materials on the market specifically prepared for teaching listening comprehension to ESL students are Morley's *Improving Aural Comprehension* (1972) and Finocchiaro and Lavenda's *Selections for Developing English Language Skills* (1966).

Morley's materials offer a step by step set of exercises to help students train their ear to listen for specific items, including stress and intonation, as well as to aid them in developing their memory span, since the exercises become longer and more complex. One of her exercises, for example, consists of dictating a series of sentences containing numerical information. E.g., *Our seats are in the 19th row. Bob bought four new ties.* After dictating these sentences, the instructor is then to ask related questions in a random order to see if the students heard the information correctly. E.g., *How many ties did Bob buy? Where are our seats?* The emphasis in this particular lesson is listening not only for specific information, but also for the cardinal and ordinal numbers which often present a problem for non-native speakers. The exercises progress in difficulty and length and include such items as mathematical figures, acronyms, times, dates, places, specific words, technical terminology, and so forth. There is a workbook to go with the text, and an additional attraction may be the fact that Morley's materials have been reproduced on tape.

Finocchiaro and Lavenda's *Selections for Developing English Language Skills* offers a series of short readings which gradually increase in length and difficulty. The readings are followed by an inference-type question based on the main idea, plus multiple-choice answers. For example,

A patient came to consult his doctor. He said, "Doctor, I'm very nervous. Every time I sing, tears come to my eyes. What can I do?"

The doctor replied, "Put cotton in your ears."

Q: What advice did the doctor give his patient?
1. Stop singing.
2. Don't be sad.
3. Don't listen to your own voice.
4. Clean your ears.

The instructor should read the question as a pre-question; then read the paragraph; repeat the question; and finally, read the multiple-choice answers. The student, therefore, must rely heavily on his memory and a certain amount of interpretive ability since the answers provided are not identical on a word for word basis to the answer found in the paragraph. This would be, perhaps, an exercise for intermediate or advanced ESL students who are learning to listen.

The problem remains, however, that though both texts mentioned above are good for dealing with certain aspects of developing aural skills, neither attempts to solve the problem of teaching students to comprehend live or natural language in the mouth of a native speaker of American English in an informal situation.

SOME PRACTICAL APPLICATIONS USING LIVE LANGUAGE

Nearly all of the exercises already mentioned can be helpful in teaching listening in the ESL classroom since the students need to learn to focus their attention during a listening exercise. In the following suggestions, however, the emphasis is on teaching listening comprehension using live or natural language mainly in an informal monologue or dialogue. Here the language is presented in full and is totally integrated with all its features of phonology, semantics, syntax, and, more particularly, sandhi-variation.

Exercise I: Relating anecdotes to your class about personal experiences, your family, friends, pets, funny incidents, or even details about current events or controversial issues, not only exposes the students to very natural language with its infinite variety of structures, new vocabulary, idiomatic expressions, collo- quialisms, sandhi-variation, and changes in regis- ter (as opposed to typical classroom register), but it also adds a lot in terms of meaningful cultural exchanges. As problems arise—for ex- ample, new vocabulary or a misunderstanding due to sandhi-variation—they can be explained on the spot. Such explanations may be better received or more clearly understood than if they had been offered in isolation, since they are based on problems arising from a contextu- alized monologue in progress or recently heard. When speaking to the class this informally, a great deal of eye contact is essential, not only to help hold your audience but also to check on whether the students are really listening hard. Afterwards, be sure to ask questions, particu- larly questions which might elicit references to similar experiences the students may themselves have had or at least experiences that they have heard or read about. Additional topics to relate might include "hot" issues (national, local or objective), cultural items such as holidays, family gatherings, weddings, births, deaths and even funerals. An example of the range of topics covered in some of my classes included the recent arrival of Vietnamese refugees to the United States and their dilemma, as well as an anecdote about a humorous experience I had as a child with my pet canary and my mother who is afraid of birds. (If you can serialize some childhood experiences, this can be very effec- tive and will probably be well received.) Whether it is the topic or the presentation, my experience has been that the attentiveness and involvement on the part of the students regard- less of new vocabulary items, rate of speech, sandhi-variation, and so forth, as well as their participation during and after the presentation with questions and discussion, and their relating of similar experiences, were extremely high. As to the best time to offer such an informal monologue, the beginning of class has worked well for me—a kind of cultural "hors d'oeuvre" à la Brooks.

Exercise II: A second technique or ap- proach which can be more controlled, at least

initially, is teaching students to listen by teaching them how to take or leave messages, make appointments and get information via the telephone. Depending on the level of the class, you may wish to prime the students with a basic dialogue such as the following.

Operator: Directory Assistance, for what city?
Caller: Los Angeles.
O: Yes?
C: Could I have the phone number for Ameri- can Airlines?
O: 274-6185.
C: 274. . . .
O: 6185.
C: 6185?
O: That's correct.
C: Thank you.
O: You're welcome.

Once the students feel confident with the basic structures, it should be made clear to them that whenever they are giving or receiving informa- tion via telephone, they ought to repeat it to be sure that they or the other party involved has heard the information correctly. If props are available (some telephone companies loan "tele- trainers" to educational institutions), use them. If walkie-talkies are available or students are able to rig up some other ingenious device, make use of those, too. Otherwise, have stu- dents sit back-to-back and "phone" each other. The exercises could include dialing Directory Assistance (information) for a phone number; an airline for a flight arrival or departure; an airline or trucking company for information about shipping animals or freight; a movie theater, museum, tour agency, train or bus line for time schedules; directions to a museum, restaurant, place of interest; a department store for a specific item; a doctor or dentist for an appointment; and whatever else you can think of that could be of practical value to your students. Have the students use pencil and paper to take down the information so that they can repeat the message accurately. While the students are practicing with each other, walk around monitoring their conversations. Also, talk to as many students on the "phone" as possible to give them practice with a native speaker. If other native speakers are available—friends, neighbors, aides—have them come to class for a brief period to give the students additional practice "on the phone." And if time and situation permit, assign individuals to make real phone calls to inquire about certain information (e.g., phone numbers, directions, schedules) for homework. (If you are teaching in a country where English is not used on the telephone, see if it is possible to make use of American or other English-speaking agencies or companies abroad without becoming bothersome, e.g., American Express, business companies, and so forth.)

Exercise III: Another exercise using live language to help students learn to listen involves interviews. (In a less advanced class, this assignment could be done in class with students grouped in pairs.) After priming students on a particular topic with a reading assignment, a class discussion, or a field trip, prepare questions—with suggestions from the students—designed to interview native speakers on that topic. The topic could range anywhere from eating habits (*How many meals a day do you usually eat? How about weekends? What do you usually eat for breakfast? What's brunch? Do you eat lunch out, at home, or do you "brown-bag" it?*), to recreation in spare time, holidays and vacations, celebrating holidays, and so on. For best results, particularly the first time and with less advanced students, keep the questions to the simple-information type, i.e., *who? what? where? when? how many?* Once your questionnaire is completed, be sure the students understand everything by going over each question for pronunciation, intonation and vocabulary. Also make it clear that the students are to interview native speakers (friends, neighbors, tourists, the man on the street, whoever is most readily available—even other teachers), and are not to just give them the questionnaire to fill out. Also, prepare students with an approach. For example: *Excuse me, please. I'm studying English and have an assignment to interview Americans. If you have a few minutes, could you answer some questions for me?* Explain to your students that some people may refuse for any number of reasons, and they, the students, should not be

offended. The students can interview native speakers at random, in school, on the street, in their neighborhood, at informal gatherings. If you are teaching overseas, the students can interview whoever is available—other teachers, tourists, employees of American Express. Have the students use their ingenuity to find a subject. You could also use personal resources to provide the students with a subject. Invite friends, co-workers, representatives from American businesses or organizations for coffee and an informal afternoon of conversation with your students. It should prove to be a mutually educational and rewarding, as well as a delightful experience.

Exercise IV: Another useful technique in teaching listening using live language is using short taped segments of radio or T.V. news and weather reports, talk shows, even cooking programs. Assignments can be prepared for in-class use with an instructor or in the language lab on an individual basis. For news and weather reports, prime students with pre-questions, information, questions such as *who? what? where? when?* For talk shows, the focus could be the main idea, examples given, and/or descriptions. The questions would depend on the content of that particular taping. For more advanced classes, the focus could be on structures, vocabulary, idiomatic expressions, even register. For a cooking program, have students take down steps and ingredients (you may need to go over measurements and vocabulary items in advance) for preparing a specific dish. You might try having students give recipes for simple favorite dishes to the class or to each other using the same technique for taking down steps and ingredients.

Exercise V: One final suggestion for teaching listening comprehension using live language would be to use short taped live conversations or dialogues between native speakers in unrehearsed, typical situations where natural language, with its pauses and fillers, false starts, idioms, natural intonation patterns with emotional overtones, sandhi-variations, and so forth, is reflected. You can tape yourself or others in various situations, e.g., ordering food in a restaurant, buying gas at a station, cashing a check in a bank, and so on. Again, use the technique of pre-questions, *who? what? where? when?* and *what's the main idea?* (If the class is advanced, the focus can be on structures, vocabulary, register, sandhi-variation. See Herschenhorn, 1975.)

CONCLUSION

Within the last few years, the ESL market has offered only a few materials specifically prepared to teach listening comprehension in ESL classes. These include the Morley and Finocchiaro-Lavenda texts discussed above. In addition, another approach to teaching listening comprehension—this one using the language laboratory—is discussed in the Epting and Bowen chapter in this volume. To date, however, I have seen nothing on the market in the United States specifically prepared to teach listening comprehension using live language. And this is precisely what is needed to bridge the gap between the language heard in ESL classrooms and the real language that is spoken by native speakers in informal situations. Until such materials are available, it will be up to the ESL teacher to help students make that transition.

The suggestions I have made are a few that might work for you and your students. The exercises or techniques can be used at most levels with some modifications or a little extra help on the part of the teacher. If students are real beginners, you may be able to use the phone, role-play, or interview. Don't discourage students by giving them an impossible task; on the other hand, if you never give them a challenge, neither you nor they will know how far they can stretch their minds or ears. Given that in many instances people have learned a second language merely by intensive exposure to that language as spoken by natives, it does not seem unrealistic to teach listening comprehension using live language at any level.

DISCUSSION QUESTIONS

1.   Explain why you agree or disagree with the statement "Listening comprehension is one of the least stressed skills in the language classroom." Give reasons to support your answer.

2.   Compare and contrast treatments of the area of listening comprehension by Fries, Rivers, and Belasco.

3.   Define "sandhi-variation." Give at least one original example.

4.   Be prepared to discuss some of the differences between contrived and live language.

5.   Realistically, how much emphasis could you or would you give to teaching listening comprehension in the classroom at beginning, intermediate, and advanced levels? Cite some ways you might teach listening at the various levels.

6.   Develop at least one original exercise or technique you might use to teach listening comprehension and present it to your methods class for discussion.

7.   What advantages or disadvantages can you see in using live language for teaching listening comprehension?

SUGGESTED ACTIVITIES

1.   With a little thought and one or two notes on an index card, if necessary, give an off-the-cuff anecdote regarding some aspect of American culture or your personal life, e.g., your family, friends, pets, an incident with your car, and so on. If you are able to present this in a classroom situation, answer questions from students as they arise and ask questions of them afterwards to stimulate student participation.

2.   Prepare a brief dialogue to prime students for a "real" telephone exercise as a follow-up.

3.   Look through Finocchiaro and Lavenda's *Selections for Developing English Language*

Skills and select about twenty-five of the readings most suited to your class. Choose two of approximately equal difficulty as pre- and post-tests. Try the exercises daily in class for a three-week period. Analyze the results of your pre- and post-tests and make a report on your findings.

4. Refer to Morley's *Improving Aural Comprehension.* Try a limited but broad selection of the exercises in the classroom and decide which would be best used at the elementary, intermediate and/or advanced levels.

5. Tape a radio or T.V. news or weather report, talk show, etc., for use in the classroom. Prepare a lesson with pre-questions of the information type, i.e., *who? what? where?*

6. Tape a short live dialogue spoken in a "survival" situation: in a restaurant, bank, etc. Prepare pre-questions, *who? what? where?* to be asked in class. Be ready to explain any difficulties which may arise due to the false starts, fillers (e.g., *you know, see what I mean*) and, more particularly, sandhi-variation used by the speakers.

SUGGESTIONS FOR FURTHER READING

Belasco, Simon (1967)
"The plateau: or the case for comprehension: the concept approach." *Modern Language Journal, 51,* pp. 82-86.

Belasco, Simon (1972)
"Language teaching—help or hindrance." *The Canadian Modern Language Journal Review, 28,* pp. 10-20. All five Belasco articles in the references would be helpful; however, these two strongly stress the need for development of aural skills using live language.

Bowen, J. Donald (1975)
Patterns of English Pronunciation. Rowley, Mass.: Newbury House.
A unique source of exercises on common assimilation and palatization rules that occur in American English.

Brooks, Nelson (1960)
Language and language learning: theory and practice. New York: Harcourt, Brace and Co.
Interesting because this is one of the first texts in which listening comprehension is given due notice. Some practical suggestions, too.

Chastain, Kenneth (1976)
Developing Second Language Skills: Theory to Practice (2d ed.). Chicago: Rand McNally.
A good summary of the position others have taken on listening comprehension with some added discussion.

Meyer, George A. (1965, reprinted 1968)
Speaking Fluent American English. Palo Alto: The National Press.
Observes some interesting facts about sandhi-variation in English not systematically treated elsewhere.

Rivers, Wilga (1968)
Teaching foreign-language skills. Chicago: Univ. of Chicago Press.
Gives listening comprehension proper emphasis and makes some useful suggestions.

RESURRECTING THE LANGUAGE LAB FOR TEACHING LISTENING COMPREHENSION AND RELATED SKILLS

Richard S. Epting *and*
J. Donald Bowen

THE DIMINISHING ROLE OF THE LANGUAGE LABORATORY

Recent developments in linguistics and psychology have greatly influenced foreign language teaching methodology. A brief look at the relevant bibliographic materials published in the last six years illustrates this point. Journal articles and monographs extolling the virtues of audiolingual theory, habit-formation, and rigid pattern drills have all but disappeared. Instead, foreign language educators and researchers are examining the merits of cognitive-code theory, contextualization and communicative exercises. This change has been genuinely applauded by English as a second language teachers and students alike, for any move toward openness, human interaction, and meaningful learning is a marked improvement over some of the restrictive and unimaginative pattern drills which permeated language teaching in the 1960s. Unfortunately, this philosophical change within ESL has resulted in numerous casualties, one of the most prominent being the language laboratory.

The language laboratory's diminishing role in the ESL curriculum is the result of many interrelated factors. The operation and maintenance of a laboratory are extremely expensive, and the time and effort involved in developing useful laboratory materials is difficult to justify, especially when many instructors believe their own classroom presentations are far more productive. Also, since the overwhelming majority of ESL students in the United States are taught by native English speakers, this eliminates one of the language laboratory's major advantages—that of providing a native model. Another factor to be considered is that commercially prepared tape recordings designed specifically for language learning are not plentiful, and those that exist are of such questionable quality that it is unlikely that they would meet the needs of most ESL students, particularly those attending American universities. These students have come to this country from diverse linguistic backgrounds, and although most exhibit a certain amount of proficiency in the English language, they do have weaknesses in various phonological, structural, and skill areas (Ross, 1967, p. 16). The commercial tapes that are available are generally planned for beginning instruction; however, it would seem that the most productive materials would be those developed after specific problems and weaknesses have been diagnosed by individual teachers. But since ESL instructors have generally assumed that the language laboratory reflects the theoretical orientation of audiolingual theory, a methodology which is to some degree incongruous with present classroom procedures, research into the development and preparation of laboratory materials exploiting current learning theories and communicative skills has been minimal.

It is no wonder then that many ESL educators have begun to question whether the language laboratory is making a valuable contribution to the teaching of English as a second language. If there is indeed a scarcity of high quality laboratory materials, there is no logical reason to use the language laboratory, or to subject students to inferior materials. And if there is any doubt as to the validity of the preceding statements, a brief examination of the relationship between language laboratory hardware (the equipment) and software (the tapes, scripts, etc.) should provide convincing evidence. Throughout the laboratory's rather haphazard development, this relationship has been dominated by laboratory machinery. One has only to examine a general bibliography on the language laboratory to understand this point. On the one hand, there are a large number of references dealing with the advantages and disadvantages of laboratory use, methods of laboratory study, and the capabilities of laboratory equipment; while on the other hand, there are only a few isolated sources which describe laboratory materials or the methods and guidelines for developing such materials. This overemphasis on language laboratory hardware and the relative neglect of laboratory materials may well be the main reasons the laboratory is presently in such an impoverished state (Smith, 1971, p. 21). In an attempt to rectify this serious imbalance, this article will concentrate on the development of laboratory materials and will provide some encouraging examples of language laboratory utilization in the field of English as a second language.

Before we begin to discuss language laboratory materials, it is important to note that from a pedagogical viewpoint language laboratory hardware does have some rather acute shortcomings. For even beyond the more obvious mechanical and technological problems, there are certain educational limitations which have tended to inhibit laboratory use and which must be recognized before any effective materials can be developed. First, the language laboratory with its elaborate system of booths and equipment isolates the students from the teacher, and thus it is extremely difficult for an instructor to accurately evaluate an individual student's performance or to diagnose his or her problems (Reed, 1970, pp. 25-8). Second, the laboratory's built-in mechanism for self-evaluation, the delayed comparison cycle, has proven to be fairly ineffective, and there is reason to believe that most students do not benefit from listening to their own responses (Allen, 1968, p. 59). Finally, the language laboratory is somewhat restrictive in relation to the types of

materials it can present. This is certainly true at advanced ESL levels, where teachers are no longer just concerned with the manipulation of grammatical structures, but are instead devising exercises which enable students to use English as a vehicle for communication. At this level, most teachers would agree that classroom presentations and exercises should be based upon the premise that students need an opportunity to respond to contextually meaningful utterances which require a natural speaker-hearer exchange. There is no question that the language laboratory is ill-suited for presentation of highly communicative exercises, since information flows only in one direction, from the sender (the console) to the receiver (the student). However, this is not to say that the language laboratory cannot be used to systematically develop those language skills which are essential for communication—that is to say, to some extent speaking; but, much more specifically, listening comprehension.

GUIDELINES FOR LABORATORY SOFTWARE

Once the language laboratory's limitations have been recognized, the next step is to formulate some basic guidelines for developing appropriate materials. Obviously, the most important issue is the nature of the drills and exercises that will be used. In the past, language laboratory materials have been severely criticized for being mechanical and repetitious. In most cases this criticism is justified, for writers of materials have generally over-emphasized the laboratory's mechanical attributes in the belief that all mechanical operations involved in language learning could be successfully relegated to the laboratory. We grant that at beginning levels of instruction many exercises must of necessity be largely manipulative. But language is much more than a mechanical skill, and since most foreign students who have come to the United States have progressed far beyond the manipulative state, any exercise that is overly mechanical will most likely be met with indifference. It is true that many of these students do have an inadequate control of the English language. But at the same time, we are addressing ourselves to the needs of a particular group of students whose academic and intellectual level demands materials that are of a more complex and stimulating nature than repetition drills and pattern practice (Evans, 1970, pp. 109-11). In the classroom, most teachers have been able to avoid this problem by devising or adapting challenging exercises which deal with specific problems. We argue that those procedures which have proved successful in the classroom can, with some modification, be similarly effective in the language laboratory.

A second guideline for preparing laboratory materials, one that takes into account many of the limitations of laboratory hardware, relates directly to the problem of evaluation. There is no question that the effectiveness of any language laboratory program depends to a large extent on the degree of participation of the students. By themselves, language laboratory materials do not necessarily motivate students to listen with a high degree of concentration, nor do they lend themselves to active student participation. Thus, the one way to make language laboratory materials more meaningful and induce active participation is to include written exercises at the end of each tape assignment. Whether it is in the form of a special assignment or short examination, this type of exercise will serve as a powerful stimulus, for if the students are aware that their work will be evaluated by their instructors, their attention span and participation level will almost certainly increase. More importantly, these written exercises will enable the instructor to better evaluate each student's performance while at the same time the students will be able to judge for themselves which areas need more attention. Campbell (1967) has examined this facet of laboratory learning and has made a realistic assessment:

For a number of students of modern languages, the long-range goal of eventually learning the language and the anticipated satisfaction of being able to communicate in it is sufficient motivation for their sustained interest and study. For a yet larger number, there is an apparent need for a more immediate objective if they are to apply their skills in the classroom or language laboratory. (p. 152)

A final consideration is that taped materials should possess a high technical quality, particularly in relation to sound reproduction, naturalness of voice, and pacing. This is an extremely critical point, for if the tapes are poorly constructed, with a high distortion level or inadequate pacing, their educational value will be limited. Certainly the time and effort involved in producing quality materials is considerable, but there seems to be no viable alternative. Fortunately, magnetic tapes are extremely flexible and easily edited; thus teachers can experiment with different modes of delivery, voices, and equipment. Also, there are some excellent bibliographic materials available which deal with the technical aspects of recording language laboratory exercises, and anyone interested in this subject would certainly benefit from the expertise that is offered. These articles include Holmes (1966), Stack (1971) Capretz (1971), and Green (1973). Of particular interest are the articles by Holmes and Green, which give a detailed account of many of the procedures involved in recording, such as microphone placement, voice alternation, and splicing. The purpose of presenting these guidelines has been to establish a general format for preparing laboratory materials, and although this list is rather brief, it does include some of the more basic aspects of materials development. Once these guidelines have been established, the next step is to examine some successful laboratory programs and hopefully from this examination gain some insights into what can be done with the ESL language laboratory.

EXAMPLES OF LABORATORY PROGRAMS

The first laboratory presentation model that we would like to discuss was used at UCLA during the Spring Quarter of 1974. Many of the instructors at UCLA were dissatisfied with their students' progress in the general area of listening comprehension, specifically listening to lectures and taking notes. To improve these important skills a series of classroom lectures with accompanying tapes was prepared. After each short "live" classroom lecture, each of which dealt with a specific comprehension problem (e.g., name the four communicable diseases mentioned in the lecture), the students were asked to listen to a taped lecture on topics ranging from the history of science to 19th century British literature. Each tape was followed by a series of comprehension questions in which the students were asked to identify the main idea and supportive evidence. Later, the students were divided into two general interest groups, one representing science majors and the other humanities and liberal arts. In this sense, the laboratory's dual channel capability, which provides two programs simultaneously, can play a useful role, for it allows the students to concentrate on their own specialized academic interests. After the students had completed the written exercises, they broke up into various groups and continued to discuss what they had heard. This type of laboratory program, which relies on a classroom lecture followed by taped exercises and discussion groups proved to be fairly effective mainly because the objective of this program was to improve two very important and relevant skills, listening comprehension and note-taking.

Another program which is rather ingenious is described by Swales (1968). While teaching in the Middle East, Swales found that many of the commercial tapes the students were using were inappropriate to both their academic needs and interests. Also, he noticed that although many of the students had an adequate background in English, very few had any training in the comprehension or production of scientific English, particularly in regard to scientific description or explanation. According to Swales, many of the students did not even know how to write up a simple scientific experiment—and since they were now taking science courses in English, this presented some major problems (p. 39). To combat this situation, Swales decided to produce his own specialized materials that would involve certain skills similar to those the students were using in their science classes.

One taped exercise that was particularly effective was a scientific explanation followed by a non-verbal response. The students were given a short lecture on a scientific subject such as the human heart or how to make a mosquito trap. Next, the students were required to make a drawing from the description that was given

on the tape. Finally, the students had to describe the function and operation of the item under discussion. Swales believes this type of exercise was extremely popular with his students because it not only established a link between their language and science courses, but also simulated many of the experiments that were conducted in their science classes. Swales' program illustrates that language laboratory materials, if they are carefully devised for specific purposes, can be very effective in helping students improve certain language and academic skills.

Because of the renewed interest in teaching listening comprehension, it is not surprising that many language laboratory materials are in some way related to this important skill. One scholar who is particularly concerned with using the language laboratory for teaching listening comprehension skills is Dickinson. In her article, "The Language Laboratory and Advanced Teaching" (1970), she describes a method for teaching listening comprehension which she believes motivates the students to listen with a high degree of concentration (pp. 39-40). To accomplish this she has divided listening comprehension into three distinct problem areas: phonological factors which consist of background noise and surface structure manifestations; syntactic factors such as complex or rambling sentences; and semantic and lexical features which include unfamiliar vocabulary items and idioms. The procedures that the students follow are very similar to the other models that have already been discussed. First, the students listen to a short ten-minute lecture in the language laboratory. Then, the same lecture is repeated, but this time a buzz appears at various intervals and the students stop their machines and refer to their worksheets. The multiple choice questions on the worksheets relate to those problem areas that have already been discussed. For example, the student might be asked, *In the last sentence, what does "left his mark" mean?* or *In the last sentence, did the speaker say, "It is interesting" or "It'd be interesting?"* At the end of the second tape, the answers are given to the students so they are able to evaluate their performance. Finally, the tape is played for a third time, and the students are asked general comprehension questions about the main idea of the passage or the speaker's purpose. There might be some question as to the advisability of having the students hear the same passage for three consecutive times. This format is fairly flexible, however, and modifications can easily be made. The essential point here is that by having a series of relevant tasks to perform the students are actively participating in the laboratory and should become more aware of their various comprehension problems.

Another interesting method for presenting listening comprehension materials can be found in Bowen (1972). At the American University in Cairo, it was noted that many of the management students, mid-career adults, complained about the quality of the English materials that were being used. These students were highly motivated and were critical of materials they felt were neither challenging nor relevant to their professional interests. In response to this criticism a materials workshop team devised six individualized teaching projects which are excellent examples of how the language laboratory can be effectively used for advanced learners.

The most interesting result of this project, the lecturette, was designed to give the students practice in listening and reading comprehension. These so-called lecturettes are brief comprehension exercises whose content was guided by student interests, in this case, topics dealing with management. Each lecturette was recorded in four modes. The rationale for this division was "to take the students through materials in contexts that are graded in terms of lexical/grammatical complexity and rate of delivery, from a form most easily interpreted to a form that represents the demands and challenges of normal English lecture style" (p. 4). Also, to ensure that the students were actively participating in these listening comprehension exercises, they were given a modified dictation exercise in the form of a cloze test in which every tenth word was deleted. After each taped dictation, the students were given a series of comprehension questions to determine if they had understood the meaning of the entire passage. As the students proceeded to the more

advanced levels, there were discussion questions, written summaries, and oral reports. Like Swales' work, Bowen's article illustrates how materials can be devised for a specific group of students, and also how the laboratory can be utilized in advanced learning:

Lecturettes offer the further promise of something to do in a laboratory setting that cannot be well controlled in a *viva voce* classroom situation. Hopefully, we will, through the experimental use of a variety of classroom laboratory activities, gradually develop useful insights into how students can more efficiently be given the skills of thought and expression in a second language. (p. 10)

(See also Newton's chapter in this volume, pp. 22 and 23.)

There are many different ways to present listening comprehension materials and possibly one of the most helpful for foreign students is to combine listening comprehension and note-taking skills. Since foreign students in the United States are using English as the medium of their university education, they must learn how to organize and evaluate the course material presented in their classes. Yorkey (1970a) gives a thorough description of how to teach foreign students to take rapid and accurate notes while listening to a college lecture. He emphasizes such essentials as basic outline form, using abbreviations, and recognizing delivery cues. To help the students develop their note-taking abilities, he has provided taped paragraphs in which the organization is prompted by grammatical and electrical sound cues. As the lectures begin, each organizational point is signaled by a different electrical sound. For example, a bell might signify a Roman numeral, or a buzz a capital letter. As the lecture continues, these electrical sounds are gradually deleted so that the student is relying solely on the delivery cues. It should be noted that this problem, like the others, could easily be adapted to a library laboratory, whereby individual students would be able to work on their own to improve either their note-taking or listening comprehension skills.

These articles illustrate the different types of activities that can be effectively presented in an ESL language laboratory. But certainly there are many other activities that can be equally effective and enriching. These would include dictations, plays, poems, songs, short stories and possibly even discussions on culture-related topics. Unlike traditional structural drills, these materials are readily available, and if need be, are also not difficult to produce. This paper has attempted to show that the language laboratory has a potential role and value in the ESL curriculum, but again, it must be emphasized that this role can only be viable if pedagogically sound materials and tapes are available. If ESL teachers and administrators are reluctant to either develop or purchase quality lab materials, the language laboratory will continue to be an expensive and ineffective teaching device.

DISCUSSION QUESTIONS

1. What has been the relationship between the language laboratory and audiolingual teaching? Has this relationship had a negative effect upon the laboratory's development?

2. What are some of the advantages that might be devised from using a language laboratory?

3. Can a student evaluate his or her own performance in a language laboratory? Can performance criteria be stated equally well for grammatical structure and for pronunciation? Elaborate.

4. Be prepared to discuss several effective student-involvement activities that you feel could be used to advantage with a language laboratory. What kind of "communication" is possible between a laboratory program and a student?

SUGGESTED ACTIVITIES

1. Arrange with the professor, technician, or graduate student in charge to learn how to run a language laboratory or to learn about the procedures involved in producing tapes. Write up a report on your experiences.

2. From the following list choose one area and explain how you would devise a tape lesson: (a) listening comprehension, (b) pronunciation, (c) dictation, (d) grammatical structure.

3. Describe in essay form how you would circumvent the problem of laboratory evaluation. What type of exercises would you include?

4. Prepare at least one tape covering a teaching point in a language area or skill area that interests you.

SUGGESTIONS FOR FURTHER READING

Cole, L. R. (1966)
"Advantages and Limitations of Language Laboratory Learning," *Journal of Applied Linguistics and Language Teaching Technology*, Vol. V, No. 2, pp. 59-74.
An excellent article on many of the advantages and limitations of language laboratory use.

Hayes, Charles (1973)
"The Language-Lab 'Love Story,'" *English Teaching Forum*, Vol. XI, No. 4, pp. 15-22.
Hayes offers a rather interesting and insightful analysis of the language laboratory's development.

Reed, J. (1970)
"Improving the Effectiveness of Language Laboratory work," *Journal of Applied Linguistics and Language Teaching Technology*, Vol. III, No. 1, pp. 25-37.
A discussion of some of the ways in which the laboratory can be more effectively utilized.

Ross, Janet (1967)
"The Language Laboratory in a Small TESOL Program," *TESOL*, Vol. 1, No. 1, pp. 15-24.
An analysis of the relationship between laboratory hardware and software with an emphasis on the latter.

Stack Edward (1971)
The Language Laboratory and Modern Language Teaching. New York: Oxford University Press.
The most comprehensive study on laboratory mechanics, type production and language laboratory study.

B. Speaking

This sub-section focuses on how the ESL teacher can facilitate the oral expression skills of his or her students. Campbell's chapter gives the reader a basic understanding of the linguistic and social aspects of communicative competence. More specifically, however, the teacher needs to know dozens of strategies and exercises to ensure that each student is getting enough relevant practice in speaking English to develop fluency and confidence. This is not easy, especially in large classes, but Mockridge-Fong addresses herself to such problems in her chapter and offers the ESL teacher a multitude of suggestions that have been successfully implemented by others. Fluency, however, is not the only objective of oral proficiency and Bowen's chapter, which outlines a contextualized approach to the teaching of pronunciation, shows the ESL teacher how reasonable accuracy of pronunciation can be achieved along with fluency.

LINGUISTIC AND SOCIAL ASPECTS
OF COMMUNICATIVE COMPETENCE

Russell N. Campbell

INTRODUCTION

The essence of language is human activity—activity on the part of one individual to make himself understood by another, and activity on the part of that other to understand what was on the mind of the first.

—Jespersen, 1924

Jespersen's characterization of language, written over a half century ago, is eloquent in its simplicity. It is a definition that emphasizes the role of language as a means by which human beings communicate with each other. While involved in this human activity, individuals inform each other of their desires, their plans, their ignorance of certain facts, their feelings about certain objects or events, their ambitions; in short, about what is on their minds.

We should note that implicit in Jespersen's definition is that the individuals involved in this activity must be speaking the same language; otherwise, the activity could not succeed in its objective—that is, to communicate what each individual has on his or her mind. Consider the following:

1. Mr. Smith: *Excuse me, sir.*
2. Sr. Garcia: *¿Cómo?*
3. Mr. Smith: *Can you tell me where the post office is?*
4. Sr. Garcia: *Ay de mí! Lo siento señor, no le entiendo. María! Ven aca!*
5. Maria: *¿Qué quieres, papá?*
6. Sr. Garcia: *Aquí hay un señor que quiere algo. Parece que no habla español.*[1]

It is obvious that Mr. Smith and Mr. Garcia will not succeed in communicating with each other although each was speaking what is clearly a language.

Jespersen's definition, again, speaks to the role of language. But what is language? Perhaps by examining the continuation of the above conversation we can begin to answer that question.

7. Maria: *What you want, meester?*
8. Mr. Smith: *I'm sorry to bother you, but can you tell me where the post office is?*
9. Maria: *Yes. One go dis estreet two handred yars, turn to the lefta. Is dere.*
10. Mr. Smith: *Thank you very much. I appreciate your help.*
11. Maria: *For nothing.*

The first thing that we might notice is that this exchange between Maria and Mr. Smith fits Jespersen's characterization of language. Two individuals have successfully let each other know what is on their respective minds. However, if Maria had said in the beginning, *Jess, guar jew wan?* it may well have been that Mr. Smith would not have known what was on her mind, and the attempt at communication would have ended in failure. In observing Maria's speech, speakers of English will have noted that even though the question *What you want?* communicates, it somehow violates what we know about English. That is, we know that speakers of English would typically have formed that question by asking *What do you want?* Even though Mr. Smith apparently understood what was on her mind, Maria's instructions, *One go dis estreet...,* is readily recognized as approximate but clearly non-English, or let us say, clearly ungrammatical English. English speakers would probably agree that the closest English equivalent to Maria's instructions would be either *You go up this street...,* or, less likely, *One goes up this street....*

It is apparent that speakers of English have little difficulty recognizing sentences or even parts of sentences, for example, *one go,* that are ungrammatical. This would suggest that speakers of English have some norm or standard of grammaticality against which they can compare utterances to determine whether or not the utterances are like those that a native speaker of English would produce. This capacity appears to be similar to that of someone who knows the rules of chess and can judge whether or not a particular move made by a player conforms to the rules of the game. A speaker of English knows that in some way Maria broke the rules of English question formation when she produced the question *What you want?* This does not mean that the native speaker of English could immediately inform Maria in what way the sentence was ungrammatical; that is, s/he might not be able to quote her a rule for question formation, but intuitively s/he would know that it was ungrammatical. It follows that this subconscious knowledge of the rules of English that permits the speaker of English to judge grammaticality is precisely the set of rules that s/he adheres to in producing English utterances. When Mr. Smith said, *I appreciate your help,* he followed rules of English that determined the order of the words, the pronunciation of those words and even the choice of the words. Since *your appreciate help I* or *help appreciate I your* or many other arrangements of those four words are non-English, we must assume that he followed a set of rules which determined that the order should be *I appreciate your help.* Rules such as those that determined the grammar (including the pronunciation) of that sentence must also be instrumental in all the English utterances that Mr. Smith has produced or will produce in the future.

To summarize these introductory remarks, we can easily agree with Jespersen that language is an activity that permits people to communicate with each other. Communication can be accomplished if the interlocutors share at least some of the same rules of a particular language. Exactly how much of a common language is required for communication is not known. We readily understand *What you want?*

but perhaps would not understand *Guar jew wan?* as equivalent to *What do you want?* Furthermore, even though we understand *What you want?* we know that it does not conform to the rules of English which require the addition of *do* to produce *What do you want?* If teachers of English to speakers of other languages are to help students acquire the ability to communicate successfully with people who speak English, then they must provide the opportunity for the students to acquire the rules of sentence production and sentence comprehension that native speakers of English possess. The closer the student comes to complete mastery of those rules, the greater becomes the chance that s/he can successfully enter into the communicative activity called language described by Jespersen.

The notion that language is rule-governed, as suggested by the preceding discussion, helps us to comprehend the remarkable ability which people have to produce the endless number of sentences required to deal with the endless number of situations in which they become involved during their lives. It also helps us understand how it is that we are capable of comprehending sentences that we have never heard before in our entire lives. It is almost a certainty that the sentence *Richard Nixon resigned from the office of the Presidency of the United States,* was never uttered by anyone before August 1, 1974. Yet anyone who shares the knowledge of the rules of English grammar understands immediately who did what. In the sections that follow we shall briefly examine various kinds of rules found in languages that begin to explain this remarkable capacity that humans have to produce and understand sentences thus making it possible for them to speak and to communicate what is on their minds.

RULES OF PRONUNCIATION

The human vocal apparatus—which includes the lungs, vocal cords, tongue, teeth, uvula, and the oral and nasal cavities—is physically capable of producing a huge variety of sounds. However, it is characteristic of that huge potential that only a small subset of sounds is systematically used in speaking any one language. Furthermore, the subset of all possible sounds used in one language will not coincide completely with the subset of sounds used in any other language. Even when certain sounds are used in two or more languages there may be differences in the possible distribution of those sounds in the two languages. A suggestion of this difference in distribution of sounds for Spanish as contrasted with English is found in Maria's pronunciation of *street* as *estreet*. In English there are hundreds of words that begin with the consonantal sequence *st-* as in *star, stone, steer,* and *stop*. This combination of sounds conforms to the pronunciation (phonological) rules of English. However, in Spanish the sequence *st* at the beginning of a syllable is "ungrammatical"; that is, it does not conform to the phonological rules of that language. According to the rules of Spanish there are no words that begin with this cluster. It is apparent that Maria is following Spanish phonological rules when she produces *estreet* for *street*; that is, she avoids a combination of sounds that would violate the rules of Spanish by separating the *s* and the *t*. She does this by adding a vowel to which the *s* can be attached in a separate syllable.

There is no question here of a Spanish speaker's physical ability to produce the cluster *st*; rather, what we have observed is one of the peculiarities of natural languages; namely, that there are rules in each language that restrict or govern the distribution of a limited number of sounds used in the pronunciation of the words, phrases, and sentences of that language. Exactly how or why the particular set of rules for each language evolved as it has can only be discussed from an historical point of view. There are no logical explanations why any sound or combination of sounds that are physiologically possible for any human to produce are employed in some languages but not others. The fact remains, however, that differences such as the one described above do exist.

There are many other examples of phonological constraints that are found in natural languages. For instance, Mr. Smith said to Maria, *I appreciate your help*. The word *help* contains the sequence *lp*. According to the rules of English phonology this is an acceptable cluster, but only if it occurs at the end of a

syllable. The same cluster at the beginning of a word would be rejected as non-English. The phonological rules of English simply do not permit words that begin with *lp-*. Those same consonants, however, in the order *pl* are not only possible, but are found in hundreds of words such as *please, play,* and *plan*.

Another example of difference in distribution of sounds in two languages can be seen when we consider the last sound in the English word *song* (spelled *ng*). According to the phonological rules of English this sound is not used at the beginning of words. In Thai, and many other languages of the world, the sound represented by *ng* can be produced at the end of words as in English, but also at the beginning of words, such as *ngu* (snake).

There are other interesting comparisons that can be made between Thai and English. For example, included in the subset of sounds used in English is the initial sound in the word *go*. This sound is not found in the Thai subset of sounds. On the other hand, there is a sound in Thai found in the word *cai* (heart) that is not found in English. Also, although English uses pitch on words or strings of words as in:

He's a doctor,

as contrasted with

He's a doctor?

pitch is not used on the same sequence of consonants and vowels to form separate words. In Thai the sequence *maa* with one pitch means *horse*, with another, *dog*, and with a third, *come*. Thus *mǎa maa* means *The dog is coming*, but *máa maa* means *The horse is coming*.

From the above examples we begin to gain some insight into the nature of phonological rules in natural languages. It must be emphasized that we have just barely scratched the surface. The phonological rules of any one language as well as those that might apply to all languages are many and they are complex. Part of the complexity lies in the fact that the pronunciation of particular words and phrases depends upon their grammatical function in different contexts. We will look at some of those contexts a little later. For now, we can conclude this brief discussion of phonological rules by restating these broad principles:

a.   All normal human beings are capable of producing a very large number of sounds with their vocal apparatus.

b.   The subset of all possible sounds and the distribution of the sounds in that subset used in the production of words, phrases, and sentences in any one language is relatively small.

c.   The phonological rules of natural languages are arbitrary in that there is no logical reason why certain sounds and their distribution are in evidence in one language but not another.

RULES OF WORD GRAMMAR

In the preceding section we freely used the term *word* when we talked about rules of pronunciation. It is doubtful that any reader took exception to this because it appears that speakers of all languages are capable of subdividing their language into linguistic units which they label with terms equivalent to *word*. In spite of this seemingly universal capability, it remains extremely difficult for linguists or grammarians or lexicographers to give a precise, succinct, scientific definition of *word* (cf. Falk, 1973, Chap. 3). Most speakers of English would agree most of the time if they were asked to specify the number of words in a given utterance. Thus, most would readily agree that the sentence, *John quickly picked six green apples*, contains six words. There might be less agreement on the number of words in *I'm sorry he's not here*. How are the contractions *I'm* and *he's* to be counted? And what about words like *nevertheless, matchbox, (match box? matchbox?), himself, strawberry, icecream?* There would surely be those who would want to count some of these examples as two words. In spite of possible disagreement on examples such as these, the concept of *word* is sufficiently clear that we can consider some aspects of the grammar of words without too much concern for a concrete definition of the term itself.

Consider again the sentence, *John quickly picked six green apples*. Probably no one would have considered *apples* in this sentence as two words, yet it obviously contains two bits of information: one is that segment that carries the meaning "a kind of fruit" and the other that means "more than one": thus, *apple + plural*. Similarly, *picked* would not be considered as two words even though it contains two concepts; one, the "act of collecting from plants" and the other "the act took place in the past": thus, *pick + past*. The word *quickly* in the same sentence is easily analyzed as containing the concepts "rapid" and "manner," or "way." From just these three English examples we can see that words often have an internal grammar. Rules of English demand that the two concepts found in *apples* occur in the order *noun + plural* rather than *plural + noun*. This is a general rule for English that applies to thousands of occurrences of countable *nouns plus plural*. However, even though many other languages of Western Europe have a similar rule, it is not universal by any means. For example, in Swahili for certain classes of nouns, number, both singular and plural, is signaled by a prefix; thus *u-bawa* (wing) and *m-bawa* (wings), which could be represented as *singular + noun* and *plural + noun*.

In a language of the Philippines, Ilocano, the plural marker is frequently a reduplication of part of the singular form; thus, *talon* (field) and *taltalon* (fields), *pingan* (dish) and *pingpingan* (dishes). If these Ilocano rules were applied to English, we would have *table* and *tatable*, or *basket* and *basbasket*.

In Thai there is no modification of nouns to signal number: *mǎa* would be translated into English as *dog* in *mii mǎa nỳng tua* (There is one dog) and as *dogs* in *mii mǎa sǒng tua* (There are two dogs). The notion of number, i.e., singular and plural, in Thai is communicated by number words such as *one, two, some, many, several*, etc., or not at all if that information is not important in a particular communicative act.

Referring back to Maria's speech once again (line 9), it is interesting to note the utterance, *One go. . . .* In English there is a general rule that verbs in the present tense that co-occur with a third person subject (e.g., *one, he, she, it, George, Mary*) are marked with the ending (suffix) -s or -es. Thus we find *I go* (without the suffix) but *one goes* or *he goes* with the suffix. In Spanish, typically, the co-occurrence of a verb in the present tense with a third person singular subject does not call for the ending -s or -es but the second person singular does; thus *tu vas* (you go) but *el va* (he goes). It is not surprising that Maria produces near-English utterances such as *one go.* We might expect her to also produce *he eat, she like,* etc. Such "ungrammatical" productions would further demonstrate the point being considered here; namely, any natural language can be characterized (described) as a set of rules. The rules, in this instance of word formation, for one language will not necessarily correspond to those of another. Maria's ungrammatical rendition of English calls our attention to a rule of English that has been violated (i.e., no third-person singular suffix) and suggests rules that might be characteristic of her native language.

In the preceding section we mentioned the possibility of different pronunciations of words in different contexts. Just one example from English will serve as example of this phenomenon. Compare the pronunciation of *sign* in the utterances *Sign this,* and *What does this signify?* Obviously, in the first occurrence the pronunciation of *sign* does not contain the sound we might represent as /g/ but the second occurrence of *sign,* with the suffix -*ify* does contain that sound. This one example suggests that we cannot consider the rules of pronunciation and the rules of word formation independently.

The pronunciation of words and parts of words in utterances can be characterized by generalizations or rules. Let's return just briefly to our discussion of *apples,* that is, *apple + plural.* "Plural" here, in the environment of the last sound of *apple,* is spelled *s,* but pronounced /z/, just as it is in *cars, boys, bugs,* and other environments. However, plural is pronounced /s/ in *cats, trips, tacks,* and elsewhere. A third pronunciation (/əz/) of plural is found in *peaches, bushes, kisses,* and elsewhere. We have identified three different pronunciations of plural. The distribution of these different pronunciations is not haphazard. Speakers of English adhere to rules of English in their employment of one or the other of these pronunciations of plural depending on the last sound of the noun to which it is suffixed. Similar rules govern the pronunciation of other affixes in English and similar rules are found in all languages. Again, pronunciation and word grammar are interdependent. It would be virtually impossible to say anything significant about one without considering the other. Teachers of English as a second language in their efforts to provide students with the ability to speak and communicate in English must consider how they can help those students acquire these inter-related rules.

RULES OF SENTENCE FORMATION

We have already briefly compared Maria's ungrammatical question *What you want?* with the English question, *What do you want?* We noted that she omitted the word *do* in her rendition. From our previous discussion of Maria's pronunciation and her use of the sequence *one go* we can almost predict that her "error" can be accounted for, in part, in terms of the differences that exist between the rules for question formation in Spanish and English. However, equally important, we can once again deduce that if we can recognize the ungrammaticality of *What you want?* there must be rules that would characterize the grammatical utterance *What do you want?*

A detailed study of English questions would explain the occurrence of *do* in *What do you want?, Which do you want?, Why do you smoke?,* etc. It would also explain why these *wh-* words (i.e., *what, which, who, why,* etc.) typically occur at the beginning of the question in English. Maria's question *What you want?* suggests that the rules of Spanish would not require the addition of a word like *do* (e.g., *¿Qué quiere usted?* (*What want you?*) *¿Dónde trabaja él?* (*Where work he?*)). And, if we were to study the rules of Thai, we would find that neither the insertion of a word comparable to *do* nor the location of the question word at the beginning of the question is required (e.g., *khun tôngkhan àraj?* (*You want what?*) *khun pay mŷaraj?* (*You go when?*)). Investigation of other types of sentences (statements, imperatives, negatives, passives, conjoined, etc.) in various languages would only reinforce our observations that the grammar of those sentences in each language can be specified by sets of rules to which speakers of those languages adhere.

We have reviewed here a small sample of the kinds of rules that can be used to characterize language. All speakers of a given language in some sense know the rules of their respective languages and it follows that they generally adhere to them in order to communicate with each other. It also follows that foreign language teachers have the responsibility to provide the student with the best possible conditions for the acquisition of such rules. This is not to imply that students must or should learn to state the rules that govern the sentences of the language they wish to learn any more than the typical native speaker of English could state the rules for the insertion of *do* in the formation of questions. However, as we have seen, the native speaker of English does "know" that *What want you?* is ungrammatical. It is this level of "knowing" that is the goal that modern language teachers have for their students. The degree to which rules of the foreign language are explicitly presented by the teacher to his or her students depends a great deal on the age, experience, and goals of the students. But explicit knowedge of the rules that characterize the language of the student and the language to be acquired—on the part of the teacher, the curriculum designer, and the textbook writer— can greatly facilitate the fulfillment of their goals. Fortunately, grammarians and linguists of the past and the present have provided us with a tremendous amount of information on specific languages and language in general that will help in the acquisition of that knowledge.

CONCLUSION

This paper has considered two notions about languages. One is that language is an activity that humans participate in when they wish to communicate with each other. The other is that a language can be characterized as a set of inter-related rules that govern the form and distribution of sounds, words, and phrases which make up the sentences of that language. We have pointed out that every normal native speaker of a given language knows—subconsciously—that set of rules for his or her language. This kind of knowledge has been called linguistic competence. If a student is to participate in the communicative act with speakers of another language, then s/he must acquire linguistic competence in that language. Our job as language teachers is, in part, to facilitate that acquisition.

Clearly linguistic competence is not all there is to successful communication. As we have seen, it is quite possible to produce a series of ungrammatical utterances that succeeds in letting someone else know what is on our minds. The opposite of this is also true. It is possible to produce perfectly grammatical sentences, yet fail to communicate. One possible explanation has to do with the manner in which we speak to different people. Speakers of all languages have available to them a variety of styles and registers in which they can communicate what is on their minds. Clearly the English that a father uses with his child will be different from that which he uses with his wife, and both will be different from the English he uses when he gives a formal speech to his professional associates. Part of language learning is the development of a knowledge of "how and when one speaks to whom about what." For further discussion of this see Joos (1962).

Language learning, then, includes both linguistic competence and this second kind of knowledge that concerns the appropriate choice of language for the many social situations in which people find themselves. Together these two kinds of knowledge can be termed *communicative competence* (Savignon, 1972). The most important task language teachers have is the presentation of instructional programs that will permit students to acquire a sense of linguistic and social appropriateness in the use of the language they are striving to learn.

NOTE

1.   English translation for what the Spanish speakers said.

2. Mr. Garcia: What?

4. Mr. Garcia: Good gosh. I'm sorry sir, I don't understand you. Mary. Come here.
5. Mary: What do you want, daddy?
6. Mr. Garcia: There's a man here who wants something. It seems he doesn't speak Spanish.

DISCUSSION QUESTIONS

1. How would you modify Jespersen's definition of language to make it include the minimal "linguistic" requirements for communication?

2. Explain the statement "... if we can recognize the ungrammaticality of *What you want?* there must be rules that would characterize the grammatical utterance *What do you want?*"

3. What does the term "rule-governed" mean? What evidence other than is found in this paper can you give that language is "rule-governed"?

4. If a Thai speaker says *sekin, kit* and *pan* for *skin, kiss* and *plan*, what assumptions could be made about the phonological system of Thai?

5. What is your estimate of how much of a second language one needs to know in order to communicate what is on his or her mind?

6. How do you think a student acquires the "rules" of a second language?

SUGGESTED ACTIVITIES

1. Listen to a non-native speaker of English and try to identify five phonological and five grammatical errors that you would consider violations of the rules of English. What should be done to correct them?

2. First write a short message (i.e., one paragraph) on any topic directed to a seven-year-old child. Then write a second paragraph with precisely the same message but directed to a university professor. Compare the style used in the two paragraphs. Is there a difference in the selection of vocabulary in the kinds of sentences you used? Would the paragraph written for the child be appropriate for the professor? Why or why not?

3. Cite your own example of a case where two individuals have failed to communicate in English despite the fact that there was no linguistic error committed. What was the cause of the breakdown in communication? Were the speakers native or non-native speakers of English? What implications are there for the language teacher?

SUGGESTIONS FOR FURTHER READING

Falk, Julia S. (1973)
Linguistics and Language: A Survey of Basic Concepts and Applications. Lexington, Mass.: Xerox.
Provides the linguistic background prerequisite to serious and effective language teaching.

Joos, Martin (1962)
The Five Clocks. IJAL Publ. No. 22, Vol. 28. Part 2, Research Center in Anthropology, Folklore, and Linguistics, Indiana University.
An extended discussion of the five registers used by speakers of English (i.e., frozen, formal, consultative, informal, and intimate).

Savignon, Sandra (1972)
Communicative Competence: An Experiment in Foreign Language Teaching. Philadelphia: The Center for Curriculum Development, Inc.
Reminds us of the many extra-linguistic factors of communication that the language teacher must keep in mind in order to be optimally effective.

TEACHING THE SPEAKING SKILL

Susan Mockridge-Fong

A review of recent literature which discusses the teaching of the speaking skill in ESL classes reveals a recurrent concern, which Rivers (1972a) has stated succinctly: "In almost a quarter of a century we still have not come to grips with our basic problem: 'How do we develop communicative ability in a foreign language?' " Stevick (1967b) blames this problem on the gap between our linguistic expertise and our teaching methodology:

Speaking, without communicating, is a tale told by an idiot. How often do we ask adults to play structural games with toy information? How often do our students ask us for meat and drink, and we give them a grammatical vitamin pill. We are becoming more and more sophisticated in isolating delicate points of grammar and preparing them for student use, but when we get them ready for shipment, why must we pack them in communicational styrofoam?

Many recent articles link increasing concern for communication to the need for greater emphasis on contextualization, early integration of receptive and productive skills, and student experimentation in language use. In addition, there are continuing reminders that (a) fluency in speaking is probably the most difficult of all second language skills to develop; (b) because speaking practice cross-cuts so many other classroom activities, it must begin at the earliest stages of instruction; and (c) activities requiring manipulation of syntactic patterns and vocabulary supplied by the teacher must be carefully distinguished from those which allow students to choose these items themselves to fulfill communicative needs which *they* have designated.

Studies in first and second language acquisition repeatedly note a considerable gap between the language learner's understanding and production, that is, between his skills in *decoding* and *encoding*. Jakobovits (1968) states that there is no adequate psychological theory to explain either phenomenon, yet we know that children learning their first language typically can understand many more vocabulary items and more complex grammatical structures than they can actually use in utterances of their own. This observation has led to the assumption that ESL students should have practice in listening to structures and vocabulary before they repeat items at the direction of the teacher and then produce them independently.

Neurologically, *decoding* seems to demand chopping up the stream of incoming sound into phonological, morphological and syntactic units, linking these to their corresponding semantic features, and following that with understanding of the relationships among the individual units. The number of steps required in *encoding* a message is even more formidable: Jakobovits explains the difference by noting that decoding is primarily an analytical process, whereas encoding requires synthesis. Although we can say little about the precise order of steps the producer of spoken language follows, at a minimum s/he must complete the following processes (Mackey, 1965): (a) select the raw content of his or her utterance; (b) choose the syntactic patterns; (c) plug in lexical items; (d) add inflectional forms; (e) compose the sequence of the utterance; (f) group the sounds; and (g) utter the sounds. The native speaker quickly learns to complete these steps in a split second; however, even his or her performance is oftentimes flawed by false starts, pauses, meaningless fillers, faulty choice of vocabulary, or "semi-grammatical" forms. The difficulty of becoming a fluent speaker is thus obviously compounded for the second language learner, who must cope not only with these performance factors, but also more seriously with limited grammatical competence, with cultural differences, and with the wide range of socio-linguistic features which determine the context for speaking.

The ESL teacher's growing concern over meaning and communication seems largely a reaction against the most extreme practices of the Audiolingual Method, which, although emphasizing oral skills, tended to dichotomize language structure and content. The behaviorist theory of learning on which this method was based stressed the development of automatic, conditioned responses to teacher-directed cues. Memorization of short dialogues and oral repetition of controlled structural drills became the activities through which students were to develop phonological and syntactic habits so automatic that eventually they would be free to concentrate on the meaning of their utterances. It was further assumed that students would be able to infer general rules and patterns in the foreign language from the model sentences drilled in class and thus extend their control by recognizing semantic and structural similarities which had never been explicitly presented to them. Instead, teachers found to their horror that there was precious little carry-over from drills to free conversation, and that students who could flawlessly repeat classroom dialogues were unable to speak in analogous contexts.

It was this separation of structure and meaning that Prator (1965) criticized fairly early:

In their effort to develop more rigorous methods of linguistic analysis, the Bloomfieldians have tended to downgrade the importance of meaning as an element of language. However healthy this de-emphasis of meaning may have been in analytical work, it should never have been extended to the practical activities of the language classroom. In following the linguists too trustingly on this point, we language teachers have often fallen into grievous error: extended drills on nonsense syllables, failure to make sure that our students understand the sentences they are so assiduously repeating, the use of language that bears no relationship to the realities of the situation, exercises made up of totally disconnected sentences.

Prator then suggests that classroom activities might be ranked along a continuum which runs from *manipulation* to *communication*: "Communicative activities are those that allow the student himself to find the words and

structures he uses. The other type of activity, in which he receives the words and structures from teacher, tape, or book, may be called—for want of a better word—a manipulative activity." His purpose is two-fold: (a) to remind teachers that even the most manipulative activities can and must incorporate useful, meaningful content, and (b) to suggest a balanced, cyclic approach to the development of speaking skills, in which *each* activity at each level of instruction fulfills the movement from manipulation to communication before another activity is begun.

Though dialogues sometimes fulfill the requirement of meaningful *content*, Prator cautions us that memorization can only be evaluated as highly mechanical language use:

The recitation of freshly memorized dialogue whether it be recited with full comprehension by both participants or not, whether it be in perfectly authentic conversational form or not, cannot be said to involve any considerable element of communication as that term is defined here. It is almost pure manipulation, since the opportunity for the speakers to supply all or part of the language is practically nil. On the other hand, if the teacher encourages students to paraphrase all or portions of a dialogue, then they can certainly move into the area of communication. One wonders why our textbooks so seldom contain versions of dialogues that leave blank some portions of sentences, to be filled in by student improvisation.

Prator (1967) later notes that because "manipulation has pejorative overtones and suggests something that one would like to avoid altogether," we might consider Stevick's phrase, "muscular habituation," as a more satisfactory description of what is accomplished when students memorize dialogues and make guided substitutions in specified structures. According to Stevick (1967a), "drills and exercises of a highly systematic repetitive kind" contribute primarily to the "development of *muscular habits* in sound production or in the use of grammatical patterns" (my emphasis). Because the student has chosen neither form nor content himself, Lee et al. (1970) states that "it can be reasoned that drill-stimulated oral performance is language behavior minus the semantic component, visual cues and speaker intent."

I doubt that any one of the experienced language teachers currently writing about the need to develop communicative ability was ever guilty of ignoring the importance of meaningful practice, any more than s/he relied entirely upon slot substitution drills. The problem is largely one for new and inexperienced teachers, suddenly faced with five or six classes a day, three preparations, and textbooks which explicitly delineate manipulative drills but then become wretchedly vague about communicative activities. Many student texts and methods handbooks for ESL teachers seem to stress what are supposedly the briefest instructional segments, leaving the heart of the lesson—extending students' ability to use the new forms actively in sentences of their own—largely to the ingenuity of the insecure teacher.

Almost all methodology handbooks include extensive descriptions of different types of oral drills, invariably arranged in an order which moves from "most" to "least" controlled. Almost all explicitly warn the teacher that slot substitution is not communication, and that the sequence of drills must gradually allow greater student choice among lexical and structural items. Most end with advice similar to that presented in Stockwell, Bowen and Martin (1965):

Sequencing of activities should include a consideration of semantic transition. Between drill sets—and more important—between sentences of a single set, sentences should be logically relatable to each other. This relation need not be strictly contextual, but it should at least suggest a common semantic component. Unmotivated and abrupt switches in the reference of drill sentences are distracting and unnecessary.

Unfortunately, a number of textbooks still in wide use patently ignore these suggestions. In addition, the substitution drill scheduled as a three-minute exercise in "muscular habituation" has a way of stretching itself out to ten minutes, in which case it is all too tempting to move on to the next activity, without taking time for student practice.

Despite our feeling that the transformational-generative theory of grammar has provided a far more accurate description of the syntax and to some extent of the semantics of English than structuralist grammar offered, we still face the same problems of contextualizing materials and providing meaningful practice that we had before. Since we now view language acquisition as a process in which the learner formulates and refines successive hypotheses about underlying rules and structures, we are very careful in teaching adults to include examples and explanations which might hasten the development of accurate hypotheses. However, we have perhaps erred in the opposite direction from the audiolingual proponents by now relying too heavily on extensive presentations of the rules, particularly in intermediate and advanced classes. Bolinger (1968) reminds us of the constant need for a balance:

Being given a rule is like being introduced to a stranger; we may be able to recognize him on later encounters, but cannot be said to know him. Teaching a rule involves not just the phase of grasping but the phase of familiarizing. To imagine that drills are to be displaced by rule-giving is to imagine that digestion can be displaced by swallowing. We have to return to the lowly origin of drills, which was in the humble setting of the classroom, before anybody thought of dressing them up in behaviorist philosophy. We have pragmatic reasons for retaining them, and retain them we should. This says nothing of the limitless need for improving them.

Probably the most profound changes which we need to make in teaching speaking or any other second language skill have little to do with the behaviorist versus the cognitive-code theories of language learning. A central issue in recent TESL articles seems to parallel a major topic in pedagogical literature in general: the problem of the teacher-centered classroom and the student passivity which this arrangement has engendered. Manifestos such as Silberman (1970) and Postman and Weingartner (1969) document in painful detail the battery of methods by which well-intentioned teachers reduce thinking students into passive mimics, afraid or incapable of stating their own opinions. This problem is crucial in ESL classrooms, in which teacher domination all too easily reaches new extremes. Rivers (1973) speaks of the schizophrenia which we unconsciously foster in student roles: though our ultimate objective is ostensibly that students be able to create novel utterances in communication with native speakers, much of our classwork is so tightly directed that they are negatively conditioned against free participation. She states that "our failure in the past has been in our satisfaction with students who perform well in pseudo-communication. . . . We may have encouraged some sketchy attempts at autonomous interaction, but always with the supporting hand: the instructor or the native speaker leading the group, drawing the student out, directing the interchange."

This problem is hardly confined to beginning levels, nor does it evolve only from reliance on manipulative drills. It seems obvious that as students' proficiency increases, the teacher should do far less of the talking, but I wonder if this is consistently true. So long as we view our own role as "imparter of information" or "initiator of all meaningful activities," the focus of attention remains on us. Furthermore, we have been well-schooled in the importance of preparing our lessons thoroughly and of keeping activities moving at a snappy pace. Too often, perhaps, we tend to dismiss students' questions and comments as irrelevant to the lesson and to cut them off in order to move on. A *few* questions probably are irrelevant; I would merely suggest that we think quite a bit longer before brushing aside what are at least genuine, student-initiated attempts to communicate.

In discussing changes needed in ESL teaching, Wardhaugh (1969) states that:

The emphasis . . . should be less on the teacher and the course or text and more on the student himself. We should attempt to stimulate him to use the language and encourage him to use the innate processes of language acquisition that he has. This means, of course, that in our methods it will be necessary to be eclectic rather than single-minded and monolithic. It means that we cannot rely on any single narrow pedagogical approach. It means too that we must respond to the different needs of students, the different learning patterns they exhibit, and the different inclinations and motives that they have in learning. Obviously, in such a setting the teacher's role is less one of providing something absolutely sure, certain and definite, for such certainty does not exist, and more one of trying to create an atmosphere in which the teacher's enthusiasm for learning, desire for his students' success and overall commitment to his task somehow rub off on his students. Consequently, I see a need for lots of examples, lots of variety, and lots of context-oriented work.

A number of recent articles outline specific methods by which we might develop lots of examples, lots of variety, and lots of context-oriented work in teaching students to communicate more effectively. The majority depend upon the obvious fact that in order to increase what West (1968) terms I.P.T.T., or "individual pupil talking time," the teacher must be vitally concerned, from the beginning, about developing student-to-student interaction. Efforts to increase I.P.T.T. might well begin with a careful analysis of just how much time the teacher talks, since all of us probably talk more than we think we do. Marks' (1972) modification of the Flanders system of Interaction Analysis for ESL classes provides one method of evaluating the amount and kind of teacher influence and student response generated within each class activity.

Of course, the teacher can begin to estimate I.P.T.T. simply by examining the types of activities planned for each class session. Consider for a moment a sixty-minute class hour and a class of thirty students. If the teacher plans only whole-group activities but somehow manages not to say a word him- or herself, s/he has allotted a maximum I.P.T.T. of two minutes. In reality, it is probably considerably less. If, on the other hand, s/he plans one twenty-minute activity to be completed in groups of five, s/he has already allotted four minutes per student, although s/he must still ensure equal participation. If a second twenty minutes is given over to working in pairs of roughly equal proficiency, another ten minutes per student has been allotted. This sounds very simple, but in practice it requires a commitment to planning activities—and a variety of them—just as thoroughly as we now plan content, and to specifying the kinds of speaking skills we intend to practice as precisely as we now state how many readings and compositions we will work into a course.

In determining content for speaking activities, Rivers (1972a) suggests that we provide practice in which students choose language to fulfill the following communicative purposes:

a. establishing and maintaining social relations,
b. seeking information,
c. giving information (about oneself or a well-known subject),
d. learning to do or make something,
e. expressing reactions: to a TV show or a movie, a slide presentation, an art exhibit, or a single picture,

f. hiding one's intentions from others,
g. talking one's way out of trouble,
h. problem-solving,
i. sharing leisure activities,
j. conversing on the telephone,
k. entertaining,
l. displaying one's achievements.

Development of this range of communicative skills obviously requires a cyclical approach to lesson planning; just as obviously, practice can be encouraged through a wide variety of activities, many of which incorporate practice in listening, reading, and writing as well as in speaking. Rivers stresses that to a greater extent than has been evident in the past, we must give students the choice of "their own way, place, time and company" to complete such assignments.

Increasing the opportunities for student-student interaction clearly require simultaneous concern for content and methods. Palmer (1970) suggests that teachers committed to providing practice in communication will look for texts which introduce all question patterns fairly early and which sequence grammar according to its "usefulness in establishing quick communication." Stevick (1967a) notes that "any content that is general enough to get into a published text is at least a little musty" and in a separate article (1972) offers detailed guidelines for evaluating and adapting classroom materials. His "socio-topical matrix" is one tool for systematically evaluating the content of texts and materials with respect to students' immediate communicative needs. Both Stevick (1967a) and Jakobovits (1970) suggest that further questions about course objectives are in order. In Jakobovits' view:

Some fundamental rethinking on the definition of goals of particular language courses needs to be effected. It may be that we should not be thinking about language skills per se (listening, reading, etc.) but rather about limited communicative skills. Thus we might develop courses designed to enable an individual "to converse with a native on travel or shopping" or "to understand foreign movies," or "to be able to read newspapers," or "to listen to radio broadcasts"—i.e., courses in "how to do something in a Foreign Language."

At the very least, the teacher will search for texts which represent the best possible combinations of a sequenced approach to syntax and a simultaneous emphasis on contextualization, so that, as far as possible, s/he can direct his or her own energies to providing a variety of activities which incorporate these materials by maximizing opportunities for student participation.

Specific techniques and aids through which the teacher can encourage student-student interaction begin with expansion of materials used in beginning level classes for dialogues and drills. Rivers (1972a) offers helpful distinctions between manipulative and communicative activities and suggests immediate emphasis on chain drills, student-led small groups, competitive team activities, games, and work in pairs as helpful in channeling the language of flow from student to student rather than from student to teacher. Finnochiaro (1964) provides detailed illustrations of question-answer drills and examples of visual aids which can be used to cue students' own comments on topics they choose themselves. When used in conjunction with what we now know about sequencing vocabulary and syntax, Hornby's (1950) situational lessons based on picture series offer one method of speeding the transition from drill to free response in beginning classes. McIntosh (1967) illustrates a number of concrete ways in which the teacher can encourage meaningful, contextualized practice in oral grammar lessons.

Charts, diagrams, symbols, and realia can all become powerful aids in diverting the focus of attention away from the teacher. The international symbols used for road signs and public notices can often be modified for classroom use. A simple diagonal slash or an X to signal "negative," for instance, has the dual advantage of eliminating the necessity for verbal cues from the teacher and of serving as one among several optional symbols offered to students as guides in beginning to formulate sentences of their own. Lipson (1971) advocates the use of symbolic drawings as a kind of "second voice" for the teacher and offers contextualized illustrations of their use. Although Schumann (1972) finds Lipson's hooligan stories "surrealistic," they do suggest ways in which humor and language play can be incorporated into communicative activities for adult learners.

A sequence of pictures or a chart signaling the main points in a narrative can often be used to complete the movement from manipulation to communication in oral grammar activities. For example, the teacher of a low intermediate ESL class at UCLA used a circular chart to introduce and drill prepositions of direction. The diagram told a story: Pedro walked *out of* the house, *across* the street, *over* the bridge, *to* the park, *down* the street, *to* and then *into* the store, etc. The students could visualize the spatial relationships signaled by each preposition as they practiced the patterns, first separately and then in contrast. Because the narrative had no explicit beginning or end, each segment made sense in itself. After a little choral repetition and individually cued response, students went to the front one by one and completed a segment designated by the teacher. Soon students chose the segments themselves and asked a classmate to relate the sequence as *they* checked his/her use of the forms. To prevent mere memorization of any part of the narrative, the teacher quickly randomized the selection of segments to be described orally. Finally, the students used the diagram as a guide in formulating sentences about their own daily routines which included the prepositions drilled. Similar pictures and diagrams can be used to introduce and contrast verb tense and aspect combinations, relative clauses, phrasal verbs and so on.[1]

The teacher of an advanced ESL section at UCLA used simple diagrams as an oral pre-writing activity: to provide student practice in stating analogies, he divided students into two teams, each consisting of several pairs of two. One person in each pair was given a simple drawing which s/he had to explain verbally to his or her partner, using phrases such as *it's like a . . .* or *it resembles a. . . .* His or her partner then had to draw a picture of the item. Individual pairs on the two teams were competing against each other, with the prize going to the pair whose combination of verbal cue and finished drawing most closely matched the original drawing.

Many recent articles discuss not only communication but the need to develop communicative competence, the term which Hymes (1962) popularized in distinguishing between raw knowledge of the syntactic and semantic rules of a language and the additional knowledge of social and psycholinguistic factors which govern their use in specific contexts. A number of writers suggest that we must prepare students for a variety of communicative settings and for the variations in intonation, pause fillers, facial expressions, and gestures which they will encounter in attempting to talk with native speakers. That elusive word "context" has received a great deal of attention in recent years, primarily in stylistic analyses. Enkvist (1969) offers the following as "a very tentative illustration . . . of lists of features in the contextual spectrum" (edited here to omit those features unique to writing):

a. linguistic frame:
   i. phonetic context (voice quality, speech rate, etc.)
   ii. phonemic context
   iii. morphemic context
   iv. syntactic context (including sentence length and complexity)
   v. lexical context
b. compositional frame:
   i. beginning, middle or end of utterance
c. extratextual context:
   i. type of speech
   ii. speaker
   iii. listener
   iv. relationship between speaker/listener in terms of sex, age, familiarity, education, social class and status, common stock of experience, etc.
   v. context of situation and environment
   vi. gesture, physical action
   vii. dialect and language.

The profusion of texts, courses, and sessions currently available in communication theory, sensitivity training, T-groups, effective listening, non-verbal communication, kinesics, and proxemics confirms that native speakers are becoming increasingly aware of "the sounds of silence" and of the need to distinguish between talking and communicating. It is rather ironic that at the same time that theoretical linguists have been emphasizing "novel utterances" and the need to account for our ability to produce and understand them, communications experts have disparaged the triteness and ineffectiveness of much ordinary conversation. As ESL teachers, we have to recognize this disparity, I think, avoiding the worst of our common clichés and jargon at the same time that we develop students' awareness of a variety of communicative contexts. Chiu (1972) provides a useful summary of recent work, done largely in England, concerning the sociolinguistic features of various communication settings and their relevance for advanced ESL classes.

Of the methods suggested for developing communicative competence, role-playing and verbal problem-solving are now most frequently mentioned. Dacanay (1963), Newmark (1966), and Rivers (1972b) were among the earlier proponents of role-playing. In Newmark's words, "by creating a dramatic situation in a classroom—in part simply by acting out dialogues, but also in part by relabeling objects and people in the room (supplemented by realia if desired) to prepare for imaginative role-playing—the teacher can expand the classroom indefinitely and provide imaginatively natural contexts for the language being used." He suggests that after students have acted out one role in a dialogue, the situation should be changed slightly (e.g., a shift in the time of action; a change from playing a satisfied customer to playing a disgruntled one) and then re-enacted.

Similarly, Ball (1968), based on earlier work reported in Ball (1966), has constructed several series of dialogues, each of which incorporates possible variations of statements, questions, commands, and explanations characteristic of two-way conversations in British English. Each series has a common topic but introduces variations in the speaker-listener relationship, which in turn offer possibilities for emphasizing changes in intonation, gestures, and facial expressions. In one series, the conversants discuss the fact that a road has been blocked due to a landslide, a topic which recognizes the opportunity for asking and answering *wh-* questions: *when? where? how? how long?* etc.

The interest in materials which synthesize useful vocabulary, realistic context, and the complex of social and psycholinguistic features which vary with context has led to the development of a number of exercises suitable for small group work or work in pairs. Rosensweig (1974) carefully outlines the procedures which a teacher might use in presenting role-playing exercises to intermediate and advanced ESL classes. In order that students may concentrate on communicative behavior as they act out their roles, he advocates that the situation and key vocabulary be presented to them in advance, with each small group charged with working out the role-play in its own way. He urges that the teacher become a skillful listener and observer, noting student errors in word choice, syntax, and intonation as they occur, but withholding correction of the majority of errors until role-playing has been completed. The situations which he has developed represent problems which high school and college ESL students in the United States are very likely to encounter, including meeting with an advisor, being stopped by a policeman, and going to a doctor's office for treatment.

The growing availability of video-tape equipment has added a new dimension to role-playing activities. Because the taped performance can be replayed as many times as the students and teacher desire, specific problems in grammar, vocabulary, intonation, and gestures can be analyzed and discussed separately. This allows graduated, cyclical attention to a number of inter-related features, at the same time that students have the distinct advantage of seeing themselves as they really are in contexts which require behavior which is different from that typical in the classroom.[2]

Materials which focus on problem-solving offer further opportunities for students to work in pairs or small groups to share information and opinions on topics which are meaningful to them. The primary objective in such activities may change significantly as students' oral proficiency develops: in beginning classes, the teacher may be trying to provide opportunities for sharing concrete facts and information; at the advanced level, s/he may be more concerned that students experience the difficulties of arriving at some consensus on a controversial topic. In beginning classes, students can be divided into pairs, each supplied with simplified maps illustrating a neighborhood or campus area in the vicinity of the classroom. Each pair of maps can be designed to present incomplete but complementary information, so that the two members of each pair must trade information about streets and buildings marked on their maps but not on their partner's in order to fill in the gaps on their own. They can be asked to drill each other on grammar or vocabulary, with dittos of the correct alternatives supplied by the teacher, or to work together to discuss and write grocery lists, or very simple narratives to describe picture series.

White (1971) suggests that more advanced students can be given problems which require going out into the community or on campus to interview people who can supply concrete information about the problem. Classroom activities include the preparation of informal "scripts" to be used as guides during the interviews. After the students have completed their research, they present their findings to the class by re-enacting the interview and then answering questions from the group in the guise of the persons whom they interviewed. Rosensweig (1974) presents five detailed exercises for small-group work in verbal problem-solving, in which students learn to defend their own opinions while working toward group consensus without resorting to simplistic solutions such as taking a majority vote. Lawrence (1972) offers a number of exercises which, like Rosensweig's, provide opportunities for discussion, debate, and finally for individual writing assignments. Connected activities such as these introduce the students to the problems of developing contexts and anticipating their audience's reactions—features critical in effective writing as well as in speaking.

More traditional oral activities also require careful attention to the possibilities they offer for student interaction. As experienced teachers know, "free" discussions are very likely to fail if the teacher hasn't planned them in advance (think of the problems that native speakers, even graduate students, evidence if they are suddenly asked to discuss a topic they supposedly know well). Valette (1973) designates specific discussion techniques for intermediate and advanced classes, emphasizing that, above all, the teacher must learn to become an effective listener and to avoid excessive contributions to discussion. She insists that students generate their own questions on a short reading or essay, rather than providing such questions him- or herself. "Discussion training" begins with two or three whole-group sessions, in which students sit in a circle and offer their questions one by one to the rest of the group. If a speaker gropes for a word or grammatical form, or if no one in the group can understand his or her question, s/he is responsible for paraphrasing and re-working his or her remarks until a fellow student follows him or her well enough to help out, i.e., the teacher will not supply the information. After these initial whole-group sessions, intended to familiarize students with a routine which emphasizes equal participation and lots of it, further sessions are conducted in small groups. The students can select their own leaders for discussion and meet together as a large group later in the period to summarize their conclusions.

It is perhaps in the teaching of writing that we most need to increase our emphasis on speaking activities. Too often, in more advanced classes, we tend merely to supply the general topic for assignments, leaving the student with total responsibility for generating the details and supporting material. The majority of topics need very thorough talking out in advance, whether they are based on general observation or on a common reading assignment. It is helpful to begin by asking students to observe a scene or to look at a picture very carefully and to jot down as many factual and descriptive phrases as they can think of. Several students can then write their lists on the board for group discussion of similarities, differences, and possible ways in which the details could be categorized in writing paragraphs. To further students' recognition of the importance of concrete details, the teacher can assign oral compositions to be worked out in small groups and then written on a ditto. Students thus gain the advantage of discussing alternative methods of organization and of drawing upon more than one source for details and examples. Before completed papers of any sort are submitted to the teacher, students can exchange papers in pairs or small groups to discuss the ways in which they have approached the assignment.

Hatch (1971) offers concrete suggestions and an excellent bibliography of sources for the teacher concerned about increasing student participation and communication in writing activities.

In addition to becoming a "collector of contexts"[3] and of methods which encourage student-student interaction, the teacher committed to improving speaking skills must become acutely conscious of his or her own question-asking techniques. Frequently, our introductory activities turn into needlessly difficult exercises in listening comprehension, simply because we haven't been able to phrase questions concretely. We shouldn't be surprised if students sit dumbly when they are presented with examples of passive and active sentence constructions and then asked, *Now, why have we done this?* (done *what? where? we* haven't done anything; could a native speaker answer this question?). Similarly, many reading discussions planned to generate enthusiastic student participation never get off the ground, because the teacher opens the questions with *Well, what did you think about this story/article?* Gurrey's (1955) carefully graded question sequences and Igarashi's (1971) modifications of them offer insights into the difficulty of responses required by a variety of question patterns.

Effective questioning plays an equally important part in oral activities used to introduce writing assignments. Materials developed at CITE (1974) offer some useful reminders of the ways in which we might state questions more precisely. CITE's "key question" technique provides a procedure for the oral analysis of paragraphs and essays, in which students are asked to formulate the question which the topic sentence answers and then, through successive questions, to paraphrase the details which support that generalization. This question-answer method is then applied to their own writing assignments: they first state a "key question" as precisely as possible, the answer serving as their topic sentence. They then ask themselves a series of questions in order to generate examples and details. In discussing types of topic sentences and key questions, the writers note that:

If the topic sentence offers an opinion, the key question elicits the reasons for holding that opinion.

For example: *Why do you say that? What are your reasons?* However, these may be too general to be useful, particularly for beginning students. These are better because they are more specific:

1. *What happens/happened/will happen that shows that . . . (opinion)?*
2. *What happened that made you think that . . . (opinion)?*

To elicit details which support the reader or writer's feelings about a person s/he is discussing, CITE suggests that the teacher ask students:

1. *What does X do that shows . . .* (fact or opinion)?
2. *What does X say that shows . . .* (fact or opinion)?

In both Gurrey and CITE's work, the suggestion is that although eventually students must be able to answer questions which demand personal opinions, we ought to be much more careful in leading up to these, grounding our discussions on detailed comments about objective facts and observations, and developing a very clear sense of the types of response which our questions will in fact elicit.

Two final points concerning the teaching of speaking skills need brief consideration: the extent to which we emphasize totally "correct" utterances and the methods by which we can evaluate what we have taught. Hypersensitivity to student errors is hopefully diminishing as we wean ourselves away from mechanical drills. As Jakobovits (1968) reminds us,

the fluent speech of most native speakers does not consist totally (or even in the majority of instances) of well-formed sentences. One would imagine that the imposition of a requirement to utter exclusively well-formed sentences would seriously hinder the fluency of most native speakers. The logical implication of this observation would be that no language teacher should ever force his pupils to use only well-formed sentences in practice conversation whether it be in the classroom, laboratory or outside.

Rivers (1972a) further notes that our emphasis on correctness has perhaps stifled the adventurous spirit in language use, when in fact students must be encouraged to experiment from the early stages of instruction if they are ever to face communicative situations outside the classroom with any degree of confidence.

In testing, too, the tendency has been to look for specific errors, rather than to evaluate total communicative proficiency. Perren (1967) describes the limitations of discrete items which test pronunciation and those which truly test oral skills. He suggests that all exercises be pretested with native speakers, in that we "must beware of requiring second-language users . . . to attain standards of so-called correctness not habitual to mother-tongue speakers." In recent years, a number of tests have been developed which require the examinee to relate a narrative in his or her own words and sentences about a picture series presented to him or her. Others require him or her to formulate responses in the context of an interview. Though the need for special equipment such as tape recorders and the difficulty of establishing objective criteria for evaluation continue to be major problems in testing oral proficiency, exercises are now being developed which afford a more comprehensive analysis of speaking ability than were available through discrete item tests (Upshur, 1971; Beardsmore and Renkin, 1971).

Although I have tried to offer some specific suggestions for teaching speaking skills, obviously none is a panacea. Recurrent emphasis in recent articles on contextualization and communicative competence suggest that we are now concerned with early synthesis of a number of discrete skills which were once taught fairly much in isolation supposedly to be combined at some later time for the purposes of real communication. Since that time never came, we are now attempting to simulate *total contexts* which require more immediate integration of basic skills. The extent to which we are successful may well depend upon our own ability to let go—to recognize that active practice requiring students to choose among lexical and syntactic options must supplant controlled drill and rule-giving as our primary classroom activities, and that we will probably control far less of what goes on in the classroom than we once did. Above all, we have to learn to keep quiet and let our students do the talking; though they need practice in listening to native speakers, our primary objective must be to encourage active *use* of the forms we teach.

NOTES

1. Lawrence (1972) provides several excellent examples of charts illustrating biological, economic, and historical processes which could be used to generate discussion and student-student questions in intermediate and advanced classes.

2. For teachers concerned about their own classroom role, video-taping becomes an additional tool for evaluating their effectiveness.

3. The tasks of collecting and creating contexts for language practice are discussed in Slager (1973).

DISCUSSION QUESTIONS

1. Teachers anxious to increase student participation in ESL classes frequently complain that their students' near reverence for authority and their fear of losing face add to the difficulties of establishing a warm, receptive classroom atmosphere. How would you attempt to handle such situations? Should the teacher attempt to modify students' sociocultural attitudes or accept them as they are?

2. What is your own reaction to Jakobovits' argument that language teachers should never force students to use *only* complete sentences either in class or in the language laboratory? Does such an argument suggest a disparity between the teaching of speaking and writing skills? To what extent should the teacher settle for some "minimum adequate" (West) comprehensibility in his or her students' oral work?

3. The article lists some of the advantages frequently stated to support the use of role-playing and verbal problem-solving exercises in the ESL classroom. From your own experience, what are some of the *dis*advantages and shortcomings of such activities?

4. Discuss the advantages and disadvantages of sequencing speaking activities through primary emphasis on (a) syntactic patterns or (b) students' immediate communicative needs. Is one emphasis more systematic than the other? Do the two goals necessarily conflict?

SUGGESTED ACTIVITIES

1. Following are the Situational Practice activities listed in the first lesson of a 1973 text for beginning ESL students. Students have learned three basic sentence patterns: (a) statements beginning with *This is a . . . That is a . . .*; (b) negative statements with *This/That + be*; (c) questions beginning with *be*: *Is this*

a . . . ?/Is that a . . . ? Nouns used in slot substitution drills are: *shirt, house, pen, dress, school, pencil, shoe, bank, school, house, town, family.* Situational Practice proceeds according to these instructions:

a. One student goes to the front of the room, picks up a picture card and asks a question with *this.* Other students answer the questions.

 Examples: Student A: *Is this a book?*
  Student B: *Yes, it is.*

  Student A: *Is this a pen?*
  Student B: *No, it isn't.*
   (continue)

b. Follow the directions for 1 above but use real objects in the room rather than pictures. If you have mastered the vocabulary for this lesson, your teacher may teach you the names of other things in the room and you can practice with new words.

c. Follow the directions for (a) and (b) above, but stand away from the picture or object, point to it with your finger, and ask questions with *that.*

Devise situations in which native speakers would actually use the questions students are asked to practice here. What could the teacher concerned with the immediate communicative value of sentence patterns and vocabulary do to modify these text exercises?

2. Write out the general differences in socio-topical matrices (Stevick) which you would anticipate for classes comprising the following kinds of ESL and EFL students: (a) adult immigrants in the United States; (b) university students in the United States; (c) high school students abroad (distinguish between those in second language and foreign language settings); and (d) technicians studying EFL abroad.

SUGGESTIONS FOR FURTHER READING

Theory and general studies

Carroll, J. (1966)
"The contributions of psychological theory and educational research to the teaching of foreign languages," in A. Valdman (ed.), *Trends in language teaching.* New York: McGraw-Hill, pp. 93-106.

Delineates the limitations of audiolingual teaching methods; suggests teaching procedures based on current learning theory.

Hymes, D. (1967)
"Models of the interaction of language and social setting," *Journal of Social Issues, 23,* 8-28.
Specific discussion of sociolinguistic features which vary with setting, some of which apply to the development of materials which emphasize communicative competence.

Jakobovits, L. (1970)
"Prolegomena to a theory of communicative competence," in R. Lugton (ed.), *English as a second language: current issues.* Philadelphia: Center for Curriculum Development, pp. 1-39.
A detailed discussion of attempts to date to combine generative semantics with work in syntax. Stresses general applications for the language classroom.

Methods and materials

Abbs, B., V. Cook, and M. Underwood (1970)
Realistic English. London: Oxford University Press.
Exercises in verbal problem-solving for ESL students. Procedures include researching problems, devising appropriate solutions, and presenting both the problem and solution through role-playing.

Allen, E., and R. Valette (1972)
"Speaking," in *Modern language classroom techniques: a handbook.* New York: Harcourt Brace, pp. 160-88.
Both this chapter and Chapter Two, "Preparing Supplementary Materials," contain very explicit descriptions of a wide range of classroom procedures.

Altschuler, T. (1970)
Choices. Englewood Cliffs, N.J.: Prentice-Hall.
Contains a number of activities designed for work in pairs or small groups which are adaptable for ESL classes.

Chastain, K. (1976)
"Speaking," in *Developing Second Language Skills: theory to practice.* 2d ed. Chicago: Rand McNally College Publishing.
A general overview of pedagogical considerations and methodology.

Rivers, W. (1968)
"The speaking skill: learning the fundamentals," and "The speaking skill: spontaneous expression," in *Teaching foreign-language skills.* Chicago: University of Chicago Press, pp. 158-212.

Testing

Beardsmore, H., and A. Renkin (1971)
"A test of spoken English," *IRAL, 9,* 1-11.
Stresses the need to eliminate discrete item tests of oral proficiency; discusses the shortcomings of tests

based on picture series and interview methods. Describes one method of testing which is based on a fictitious dialogue.

Perren, G. (1967)
"Testing ability in English as a second language: 3. Spoken language," *English Language Teaching, 22,* 22-9.
Outlines the problems of constructing adequate tests and lists the shortcomings of some traditional methods.

ods. Emphasizes need to distinguish among tests of aural comprehension, pronunciation, and oral production.

Upshur, J. (1971)
"Objective evaluation of oral proficiency in the ESOL classroom," *TESOL Quarterly, 5,* 47-59.
Illustrates techniques through which oral tests can be improved.

CONTEXTUALIZING PRONUNCIATION PRACTICE IN THE ESOL CLASSROOM*

J. Donald Bowen

The teaching of pronunciation in ESOL classes has not always been as successful as other aspects of English teaching, possibly because pronunciation has been considered a separate skill and has not been well integrated in language courses. If pronunciation can be presented in meaningful contrasts and in situations that are both relevant and interesting to the students—in other words, if instruction in pronunciation can be contextualized—perhaps achievement can be improved. Productive contextualization suggests: (a) pronunciation features and contrasts should carry meaning with minimum redundancy that will offer additional clues affecting interpretation; i.e., the student should have to rely on what s/he hears (and produces) rather than on an intelligent estimate of what the situation calls for; (b) situations should be meaningfully related to student interest and/or experience; (c) the repetition of specific drills and situations should be minimized; (d) the language and style of pronunciation exercise material should be convincingly natural and realistic; and (e) at least some exercises should be designed to give practice when the students' attention is on the content rather than the form of the message.

Some thirty years ago, foreign language classes in the United States were largely concerned with teaching students to read. Pronunciation was a low priority skill, usually presented by a quick run through the alphabet to illustrate the characteristic sound or sounds associated with each letter. It did not really matter if the sounds of the new language were not authentically produced, since any contact with the foreign culture would be almost exclusively through reading, using the familiar visual symbols of a Roman alphabet. In fact, pronunciation hints were not offered in terms of the new language sound system, but framed in terms of the native language in such instructions as: pronounced like the *i* in *machine*, or like the *g* in *get*.

Today the purposes of language teaching more often include face-to-face contact with live speakers. Indeed oral communication has come to be one of the central purposes of language study, and the philosophy on which classroom activities are based has correspondingly changed to reflect the present oral emphasis. The Audiolingual Method of foreign language teaching accords pronunciation a central role in pedagogy, and the mystery of an adequate command of the spoken language is a goal seriously taken.

With respect to linguistic theory, pronunciation enjoyed an estimate of maximum importance as the phonology component of language analysis of structural linguistics, which flourished in the 1940s and 1950s. Later, when transformational analysis caught the imagination of the theorists, phonology was relegated to a minor role. The linguistic primitives were syntactic or perhaps semantic units, which were interestingly and creatively controlled, manipulated, and combined to encode a message, after which a relatively uninteresting set of morphophonemic rules were applied to produce a sequence of spoken sounds. These rules are less interesting to the theoretical linguist because they are applied automatically and mechanically once the underlying syntactic elements are in place.

This new theoretical alignment has not so far had a significant effect on pedagogy. In the contemporary classroom, pronunciation has not experienced the same diminished interest as has phonology in linguistic theory. Pronunciation remains the entrée to the linguistic system of a new language, and a student cannot be said to have mastered a second language unless s/he has a command of its spoken symbols. The ideal is to be able to pronounce and speak with native-like competence, though in most classrooms and with most students this remains an ideal, a goal to shoot at, the approximation to which serves as a measure of student achievement. In actual practice the teaching of pronunciation has been a frustrating experience. Pre-puberty-aged students need only a model and an incentive to follow that model to acquire an authentic native-speaker pronunciation. A well-planned pronunciation component in the foreign language course is unnecessary. Post-puberty students are essentially unsuccessful when they attempt to speak like natives. A pronunciation component is usually quite unproductive of satisfactory results.

Most frustrating is the observation that when mature students try seriously to imitate a foreign pronunciation model, and when the expertise is available to offer technical assistance, they will demonstrate the physical capacity for a quite satisfactory production. But the minute the students' attention is diverted to the content of the message, the pronunciation control loosens, and native language influence reappears to produce a heavy speech accent. Adult learners seem to have their cultural identification firmly implanted, and their language follows this identification. Only rarely does one find an adult student of unusual language acquisition aptitude who is the exception to this rule.

What are the implications for language teachers in this observation of the difficulty of teaching native speaker proficiency in pronunciation? Should we abdicate formal responsibility, given the prediction that full success is highly unlikely? Or should we conclude that "man's reach must exceed his grasp," and use native speaker competence only as an ideal to guide students of limited aptitude toward whatever approximation to the model they are capable of achieving?

My own belief is a retreat to eclecticism, taking the best of each theoretical possibility in a compromise. For most adult students a reasonable goal is the ability to communicate orally with ease and efficiency, but without expecting to achieve a competence in pronunciation that would enable them to conceal their own different language background. At the same time it should be possible to achieve a consistent production of the basic contrasts of the sound system, to speak fluently and understandably in a form that requires minimum adjustment on the part of one's listeners. And of course students must be capable of understanding native pronunciation under normal circumstances of production, and not require of their interlocutors a special style. They should, for example, be capable of understanding two native speakers addressing each other in informal speech.

It is my opinion that improvements can be made in the teaching of the pronunciation component in a language course. It is my further opinion that one way to effect an improvement would be to find a means of better integrating pronunciation instruction with other elements of instruction.

In too many language classes the teaching of pronunciation is something that is done with an approach that identifies pronunciation as something to be taught separately. It is traditionally advised that the "pronunciation lesson," that segment of the full lesson to be devoted to pronunciation, should be limited to about five minutes, moving then to other aspects. But when attention is shifted, gains disappear.

It is true that there are different aspects to a language lesson, that a teacher must devote attention to grammatical forms, to the sequence of words, to the transformation of patterns, and to the meaning of related sentences used to transmit a message. But perhaps there is a way of incorporating some of these elements in a lesson segment designed to improve pronunciation. I suggest an effort to contextualize the pronunciation lesson. What I mean by this should become clear with the discussion and examples that follow.

Pronunciation instruction has been presented in various ways. First there is model and imitation. The teacher (or a recording playback device) sets a model which the student attempts to reproduce. If this were adequate, no problems would appear. But experience has shown that habits of one's first language will interfere in ways that can be explained by a knowledge of the specific differences in the pronunciation patterns of the first and second languages.

A second technique for teaching pronunciation is explanation. The teacher tries to guide the student by telling him or her how to produce troublesome sounds, how to manipulate his or her speech organs, or what characteristics the sounds should have when produced. This method may help some students, but many fail to respond, either because the explanations tend to be esoteric or because students have no effective experience in controlling speech production on the basis of instructions. Another possible limitation is that explanations usually involve labels, so that sounds can be referred to and discussed. Often these labels will be the names of letters used to represent the sounds. But since letter names may in fact repeat the minimal difference of the sounds in a pair of words, they can pose the same problem of identification. It is not very enlightening to differentiate the two words *base* and *vase* by saying that one begins with a *b* and the other with a *v*.

A third technique is practice. Applications are seen in example sentences that provide multiple opportunities to produce a sound, such as the famous *Erre con erre cigarro* example for the Spanish trilled *rr*. It has never been satisfactorily explained how a sound difficult to produce becomes any easier when it appears in multiple form. If one *rr* is a problem, surely the solution is not a series of twelve. In my opinion the tongue-twister approach to problem sounds is wholly without merit.

A fourth technique is comparison and contrast—an application to pedagogy that has been recognized as the analytical tool par excellence of phonological research. Two similar but significantly contrasting sounds are taught together, with an effort to highlight the feature that differentiates them. Thus *p* and *b* are contrasted by voicing (voiceless vs. voiced), *d* and *g* by point of articulation (alveolar vs. velar), and *sh* and *ch* by manner of articulation (fricative vs. affricate). This kind of comparison helps pinpoint the difference, but doesn't always guarantee efficient acquisition of the two contrasting sounds. If the contrast is a new aural experience, the fact of contrast will not necessarily become simple to interpret and produce. Let me illustrate by offering a contrast from Tagalog, the two words *bata* meaning *bathrobe* and *bata* meaning *child*. Most American speakers of English experience difficulty even hearing this distinction, let alone understanding, producing, and assimilating it. Yet for Tagalog speakers the distinction is every bit as clear as the one in the English pair *cart* and *card*.

The contrast can be made clear by a fifth technique, which I'll refer to as a combination (of modeling, explanation, comparison, mimicry, and practice). A model of *bata-bata* has been given. The explanation is that one ends in an aspirate, the other in a glottal closure (conveniently not shown in the spelling, but illustrable in a special transcription, as /bataʰ-bata?/. A comparison would perhaps involve the closest native language phenomenon, in this case English *uh huh* and *uh uh*, transcribable as /ʔəhə-ʔəʔə/, calling attention to the fact that the contrast occurs syllable initially in English but syllable finally in Tagalog; and this is precisely the reason why English speakers have perception difficulties: they have no experience with a meaningful contrast involving these sounds in final position. Finally, with this explanation as guidance, students would attempt to mimic and practice.

But this procedure (combining the techniques of modeling, explanation, contrast, comparison, mimicry and practice) more often than not fails to internalize the new habits to make them actually part of the students' new-language pronunciation. When they listen, they'll fail to distinguish (unless prompted by powerful contextual clues), and when they speak, they'll fail to consistently produce the contrast (unless close attention exaggerates the distinction). Why this difficulty internalizing a new contrast? I think it is to a significant extent because the presentation has been disembodied from a meaningful context.

Obviously there are problems of motivation involved. When communication is possible, why strive for perfection? Or as a Japanese student once confided to me: "I get along, with some difficulty to be sure, but why should I invest a tremendous effort in an attempt to sound like an American when I'm really Japanese?" Motivation can be materially heightened by increasing the chance of success.

We need reasonable and realistic goals, and these need to be tied to students' views of their own objectives. A Basque-speaking student from Spain working under my supervision once reported experiencing, while on a date, a headache that was so severe she went into a drugstore and asked the manager if he had any aspirin. He answered that he did, and asked how many she wanted, to which she answered two. The manager invited her and her boy friend to be seated. In two minutes he reappeared with two dishes of rice pudding. In reporting this event the next day, this young woman demonstrated a very strong motivation to improve her command of English pronunciation.

The young Basque woman was motivated by a context that demonstrated rather vividly that she could be misunderstood. How can we build a similar motivation into our classroom presentations? I believe that we should seek to introduce contextualization into pronunciation teaching and that it is quite possible to do so. The remainder of this paper is devoted to examples that will hopefully illustrate at least some of the ways this can be done, how drill activities can be devised that will reinforce the pronunciation aspects of what has been termed "communicative competence."

The minimal pair concept has been widely applied to teaching pronunciation contrasts that have been found empirically to cause trouble for students in specific first and second language situations. Typically a contrast is illustrated, such as *base-vase*, possibly explained, and then presented for identification by the students. Usually they are asked to do something overt to signal their reaction to the pair. Two words will be given, sometimes alike (*base-base*) and sometimes different (*base-vase*). Students will be asked to respond *same* or *different*. Or the words will be given one at a time, with instructions to raise the left arm if *base* is heard, the right arm if *vase*. Or the identification can be made by saying A or B, or one or two, or by raising one or two fingers, etc. Or three pronunciations can be given, with the students instructed to identify by number (one, two, or three) the word that is different from the other two. Later students practice the contrast by imitating the teacher: *base-vase* (*base-vase*), *bile-vile* (*bile-vile*), *ban-van*, (*ban-van*), *boat-vote* (*boat-vote*), etc.

There may be other activities used in a typical minimal pair drill, including production of the words in illustrative sentences, such as: *They are going to vote on the boat.* One might say this is a form of contextualization, but if so it is not a very powerful example, since there is no indication of who is going to vote, what the occasion of the vote is, why a boat should be voted on (or, since the sentence is grammatically ambiguous, why people should be on a boat when they vote), etc. In other words, this is meaningless context, and it will not serve to fix the contrast in the mind or habits of the student. Minimal-pair sentences are sometimes employed, such as *This is a base. This is a vase.* These may be a little better, especially if the concepts are picturable and appropriate pictures can be shown. Pictorial illustration can be difficult—which interpretation of *base* should be pictured, for example? Even when pictures are appropriate, the context is still minimal, and identification frames are not really very interesting. This pattern is typically used to teach vocabulary, not pronunciation. Of course there may be other frames than the identification *This is a . . .* , but rarely are effective ones employed in a classroom.

I suggest that the context for the minimal pair should be an entire situation, supported and reinforced by reasonable and credible visual images, and placed in a setting that can hope to provide a measure of intellectual stimulus and interest. The dull recitations that characterize most pronunciation lessons need to be markedly upgraded if there is to be any hope of solid improvement in classroom performance and any promise of carry-over in out-of-class competence.

The following sequence of activities describes a pronunciation lesson I have used several times as a demonstration. I begin by asking if anyone in the class is good at drawing. If no one responds immediately, I ask who is the best artist in the class, hoping somebody will volunteer, either him- or herself or another student. When an artist is finally identified, I invite him or her to the front of the class and whisper my first request in his or her ear—to draw a horse. Not letting the other students know what s/he is to draw usually builds a bit of interest, and I ask class members to tell me as soon as anyone can guess what the volunteer is drawing. Depending on the skill of the artist they may say *dog* or *cow* or something, but we finally arrive at *horse*. Then I whisper a second instruction: *fire*. We go through the same process, with guesses such as *grass, bush*, and eventually *fire*. I thank my collaborator and then I draw a *horse shoe*. (This is safely within my artistic competence; I might do all the drawing myself if I were more talented.) I ask if anyone can identify what I have drawn and then, if the class level permits, have a brief discussion of what a horse shoe is, why it is used, how it is affixed to the horse's hooves, etc. As this is given, or as I give it, I am drawing a picture of a *hammer*. Then I explain how the metal shoe can be heated to white hot on a forge and bent by pounding so it will fit the horse. Together we identify the profession of the person who does this job—the blacksmith.

This detail can be omitted, with a general reference *he* or *she* if the new vocabulary load seems to be getting too high. (We will refer to the blacksmith simply as *he* throughout this example.)

I show that the blacksmith first heats the shoe, then pounds it with a hammer to shape it. Then I ask the class to identify the means the blacksmith uses for each of two tasks:

He's heating the shoe.
   With a fire.

He's hitting the shoe.
   With a hammer.

I now have the statement and rejoinder to serve as model and response for a meaningful identification drill. I have purposely not put the contrasting sound pair in sentence-final position where they will get the extra emphasis of sentence stress, because I want the students to have practice with the minimum of differentiation that will be presented in a real-life use, where rarely will there be an overt, specific contrast (that is, with *both* of the contrasting sentences in the same conversation or situation). Note that both interpretations are reasonable in an overall context; one does not overshadow the other in probability of occurrence.

(This balance of probability is very important. Consider for a moment an example of minimal-pair sentences that lack balance. The sentence frame is *He came back from Paris on a . . .* with *ship-sheep* as candidates for the blank. In this example *ship* is infinitely more likely than *sheep*. In cases like this one, students and native speakers alike will correct *sheep* to *ship* in their own interpretation if the wrong stimulus is offered, since people expect language to make sense. Lack of balance is a common weakness of minimal-pair sentences used for pronunciation drills, and students usually pay scant attention to the crucial features if the probabilities make one interpretation silly. And if they are not listening, they do not learn.)

After I've produced the full sentence several times—*He's heating the shoe with a fire.*

He's hitting the shoe with a hammer—I then give just the first part of the sentence and ask the class to give the final phrase as a rejoinder. If, as often happens, there is a disagreement, I stop and ask for a show of hands: *How many say* fire? *How many say* hammer? Then I announce which one I said by indicating which response I expected. As confidence builds, I get a volunteer to come to the front of the room and work with me. I make my statement, and s/he offers his or her rejoinder. Then I ask how many in the class agree with him or her; then announce what my intention was.

Then I ask the class to produce the statement in chorus, following my cue as I point alternately to the pictures of the fire and the hammer. Often it is difficult to tell if the production is accurate, so I ask individuals to produce the appropriate rejoinder on cue. If there is any doubt in my mind as to the accuracy of the production, I ask the class if they agree. After a few experiences they are conditioned to consider my query as evidence that *I* do *not* agree, so I recapture initiative by questioning a production that is perfectly satisfactory. I find this introduction of the unexpected into a class routine an excellent way to keep interest and attention. Students soon come to know "that I can't be trusted" and they are encouraged to keep a more careful check, which is of course just what I want.

Finally I ask for another volunteer, who comes to the front of the room. I mark a figure 1 over the fire and a figure 2 over the hammer. Then I go to the back of the room where only the volunteer can face me. I insist that other students face front, away from me. Then with arms folded or extended I briefly signal an intention to the volunteer. If I flash one finger, s/he is to say *He's heating the shoe*; if two fingers, *He's hitting the shoe*. The class is to respond with the appropriate rejoinder. In this way I retain the initiative, I decide the intention. After the rejoinder of the class indicates their interpretation, I ask the volunteer if s/he agrees. I'm then in a very strong position to judge his or her performance. I know what s/he was instructed to say, and I can agree or disagree with the interpretation of the class. In case of a mismatch of statement and rejoinder,

if I agree with the volunteer (assuming s/he confirms my signaled intention), the mistake is one of aural interpretation (by the class). If I agree with the class, the mistake is one of production (by the volunteer).

This last step doesn't always go right, since it depends for success on a good performance by the volunteer. S/he is expected to take an abstract symbol (one or two, gathered from seeing one finger or two) and convert it into a performance based on an arbitrary association. S/he may get confused. If the student is apt, the procedure usually goes well. But note that this is the only point at which an arbitrary meaning association is introduced, and it comes *after* logical associations have been established: *heating* with *fire*, *hitting* with *hammer*. This is much less an artificial signal than the left hand/right hand or A/B so frequently used in minimal-pair identifications. And the use I propose is purposeful. Even this last bit of arbitrariness could be avoided if one prepared a couple of flash cards with a fire and a hammer to use in the back of the room, or these two items could quickly be drawn on the rear blackboard with signals given by pointing to one or the other.

One might observe that this technique gives production practice to only one student, and that in a large class there will not be time to repeat the sequence for each student. Even if several repetitions were feasible, there is some question about the advisability of repeating the same procedures; it is possible that the loss in motivation is greater than the gain from additional practice. But the problem remains of how to generalize effective practice. Production is an individual matter, and if meaningful guidance to students is to be offered, choral practice has serious limitations beyond a very general kind of tongue-loosening activity. Students must perform one at a time with the techniques discussed here, or with any others I am familiar with. Options are (a) to repeat the last phase of the exercise with different students, or (b) to follow the exercise as described with other activities that involve individual performance. As an example of the second alternative I suggest a short reading passage that embeds the pronunciation problem in various ways, preferably ways not fully expected. This makes it possible to maximize variety and to avoid excessive repetition of the elaborate procedure described earlier. As students read, individually and audibly, they can be recorded for subsequent review and analysis as a separate class activity. Rehearsing a sentence or phrase or word is helpful in case there is disagreement on just what pronunciation was used. Brief discussion following the recorded readings can answer queries on interpretations and possible misinterpretations.

A suggested selection which students can take turns reading into a recording microphone, a sentence or two at a time, is as follows:

If a blacksmith wants to shoe a horse, he must first heat the shoe over a hot fire. Then he will put it on an anvil and hit it with a large hammer. He must heat the shoe before he hits it so the metal will be soft enough to shape. If he hits it first, the cold shoe will not take a new shape, and after hitting it, there's no point in heating it. So after first heating the shoe he will beat it into the right shape, in case it's a little bit too big or too little. Then the shoe can be attached to the horse's hoof. The blacksmith does this by driving several long nails through the shoe into the hoof. He probably uses a smaller hammer to hit the nails than he did on the heated shoe. In any event, we'll easily see that it's a lot of work, and a blacksmith needs to be very strong to do his job.

The aim in preparing this reading is to produce something that is natural-sounding English prose, but that still incorporates the teaching points. It should also be reasonably interesting in content. It is quite likely that the class will notice that forms of *heat* and *hit* (five each) appear in the reading and that a special effort will be made to produce these forms correctly. These are distributed as follows:

If a blacksmith wants to shoe a horse, he must first *heat* the shoe over a hot fire. Then he will put it on an anvil and *hit* it with a large hammer. He must *heat* the shoe before he *hits* it so the metal will be soft enough to shape. If he *hits* it first, the cold shoe will not take a new shape, and after *hitting* it, there's no point in *heating* it. So after first *heating* the shoe, he will beat it into the right shape, in case it's a little bit too big or too little. Then the shoe can be attached to the horse's hoof. The blacksmith does this by driving several long nails through the shoe into the hoof. He probably uses a smaller hammer to *hit* the nails than he did on the *heated* shoe. In any event, we'll easily see that it's a lot of work, and a blacksmith needs to be very strong to do his job.

There is of course no objection to this attention to the forms of *heat* and *hit*. Not only is it desirable that they be learned and produced accurately, but they serve as a temporary screen to other, more important items in the reading, that test and practice the same contrast of /iy/ and /ɪ/ in other words. There are 53 of these, 21 for /iy/ and 32 for /ɪ/. There are two minimal pairs fully represented, *beat-bit* and *we'll-will*, and four minimal pairs partially represented, *eat-it, eats-it's, deed-did, he's-his*. The other examples of one or the other sounds occur in words that do not occur as minimal pairs. The relevant syllables are marked in the version of the reading that follows:

If a black**smith** wants to shoe a horse, **he** must first *heat* the shoe over a hot fire. Then **he will** put **it** on an an**vil** and *hit* **it with** a large hammer. **He** must *heat* the shoe before **he** *hits* **it** so the metal **will be** soft enough to shape. **If he** *hits* **it** first, the cold shoe **will** not take a new shape, and after *hitting* **it**, there's no point **in** *heating* **it**. So after first *heating* the shoe, **he will beat it into** the right shape, **in** case **it's** a **little bit** too **big** or too **little**. Then the shoe can **be** attached to the horse's hoof. The black**smith** does **this** by driving several long nails through the shoe **into** the hoof. **He** probably uses a smaller hammer to *hit* the nails than **he did** on the *heated* shoe. **In** any event, **we'll easily see** that **it's** a lot of work, and a black**smith needs** to **be** very strong to do **his** job.

In using a reading of this kind to check (and encourage) the contrast that is being taught, good use should be made of juxtapositions of two words with different members of the contrast. In the reading the following opportunities occur: *he will, will be, if he hits, in heating it, he will beat it, he did, in any, smith needs.* Also useful are sequences of several examples of the same sound, to check for consistency: *in case it's a little bit too big or too little, in any event we'll easily see.*

In spite of the relatively large number of examples of the sounds being drilled and learned (66 if everything is counted), it is important not to overload the reading question, or at least not to give the impression of overloading. When a contrast drill becomes too conspicuous it is felt to be ridiculous, and this damages the atmosphere for efficient learning. As an example of something that would be too overloaded to be used effectively, consider the following portion:

The blacksmith did the deed so that the horse shoes would fit the feet of the horse. He takes the shoe, first heats and then hits it. He usually has to beat it a bit. This is what he does to eat; it is his job.

This is too forced, and the contrasts are unnatural. The fact that the contrasts are conspicuous means that special attention may be given them, and the conditions of generalization are violated: that accuracy of pronunciation be extended to language use where the student's attention is on the message rather than the form. Even if the student could do the above segment satisfactorily, there is no assurance that a carryover would improve his or her general use of the language.

My experiences with the techniques described and illustrated above have been that they capture and hold class interest. I have no controlled, experimental evidence that they teach pronunciation, but at least that first giant step toward learning is taken: getting the ears and eyes of the students focused on a problem, since when there is no attention, there is no learning.

Many pronunciation problems can be handled by the techniques of contextualized pronunciation practice: all that is necessary is a bit of imagination and ingenuity to devise an appropriate situation, one that is (a) meaningful, (b) picturable, (c) balanced, and (d) if possible, relevant to the experience and/or interest of the students. I can suggest two or three possibilities. A pedagogue and a cook complain that:

This pen leaks.
    Then don't write with it.

This pan leaks.
    Then don't cook with it.

Pedagogues write and cooks cook, and neither likes a leaky utensil. The differentiaters *write* and *cook* are clearly distinct, and will serve to identify members of the pair *pen-pan*. All concepts are concrete and readily picturable. Both pens and pans fit the instrumental use after the preposition *with* and both have been known to leak. This contrast drills the vowel pair /ɛ-æ/, which causes difficulties for students of English as a second language with many language backgrounds.

Another contrast is:

What's this pool for?
    For swimming.

What's this spool for?
    For sewing.

This pair illustrates and drills two features: (a) a single vs. a double *s*, signaled by length, and (b) the presence and absence of aspiration with the voiceless stop consonant *p*. The feature of a lengthened consonant occurs only across word boundaries in English. The aspiration is present when the /p/ is initial in the word *pool*, but absent when /p/ follows /s/ in the word *spool*. This pair is perhaps a little weaker pedagogically, since while spools of thread are certainly associated with sewing, the sequence *spool—for sewing* is not quite as convincing as *pool—for swimming*. However, it's not a bad match, and the balance, picturability, and relevance are satisfactory.

A pair that illustrates a stress contrast is:

Where can I buy côld créam?
    At the dairy.
Where can I buy cóld crèam?
    At the drugstore.

In this pair a normal adjective-noun sequence is compared with a noun compound or construct. The minimal stress contrast influences the pitch pattern by placing the highest pitch on the syllable with the strongest stress: *cream* in the first sentence and *cold* in the second:

côld créam vs cóld crèam.

A possible difficulty with these two concepts is their picturability. *Cream* may come in a bottle or a paper carton, or perhaps in an aerosol can, and the student may not be personally familiar with the container. *Cold crèam* is a women's cosmetic product that might not be commonly known to men students. If this disadvantage of being unfamiliar is too great, there are many other pairs illustrating the same stress contrast that can be used:

What's a hêad dóctor?
  He's an administrator.
What's a héad dòctor?
  He's a psychiatrist.

or to produce a more easily handled rejoinder:

A hêad dóctor works
  at a desk.
A héad dòctor works
  at a couch.

If you disagree with the levity implicit in the use of an informal designation *head doctor* for a psychiatrist, pick another pair. There are plenty of them available.

This, then, is an example of contextualized pronunciation practice. Students work with familiar (or specifically learned but relevant and reasonable) concepts, which are associated with easily distinguished clues. The activities carry messages that are not arbitrary, and the sequence has been demonstrated to hold the interest of a wide variety of students. This, hopefully, is a step toward making all of our language teaching activities more meaningful and relevant to the lives, interests, and experience of our students.

Perhaps there are other ways of using meaning and meaningful communication to make teaching more effective; that is, perhaps there are other ways of contextualizing teaching materials. We know that schools do not provide the most productive language learning, that learning in an immersion situation, where a need for communication is strongly felt and sympathetic encouragement is offered, is much more efficient. In such an environment every utterance ever heard or used is meaningful and relevant to the situation it is used in. It is, to use the word I have chosen, contextualized.

I have indicated one way to contextualize a pronunciation presentation. Perhaps there are other, maybe better ways. Surely something must be done to win and hold the attention of students, to organize materials for learning in a way that is compatible with the development of skills needed for communication. Our record of success in the schools is not an enviable one. Perhaps we can do better.

Editor's note: Exercises for extending this contextualization technique to all aspects of teaching pronunciation are available in Bowen (1975).

NOTE

*This article has been reprinted from the *TESOL Quarterly*, Vol. 6, No. 1, pp. 83-94, 1972, by permission of the Executive Committee. The Discussion Questions, Suggested Activities, and Suggestions for Further Reading are original.

DISCUSSION QUESTIONS

1. Why should we be concerned with pronunciation, since it is so hard to teach? Why is pronunciation mastery developed under controlled circumstances likely to be lost in more general use of the language?

2. Will audiolingual (behaviorist) emphasis or transformational (cognitive) emphasis likely pay more attention to pronunciation? Why?

3. Do you agree that a student cannot be said to have mastered a language unless s/he controls its spoken form? Why?

4. Is generalization of a pronunciation contrast more likely to be accomplished by practice that directs the students' attention to form or to content?

5. Discuss various techniques of teaching pronunciation with the advantages and disadvantages of each.

6. Discuss the value of paraphrases and pictorial representation as opposed to such arbitrary designations as 1, 2 or (a), (b) for identifying members of a contrasting pair.

7. Comment on the importance of balanced probability of occurrence for two interpretations of a contrast.

SUGGESTED ACTIVITIES

1. Prepare a lesson (explanation, exercises, generalization, etc.) for a specific problem of

pronunciation in English involving stress contrasts, such as *The army was reformed/ reformed* (formed again/improved).

2.	Prepare a lesson to teach some specified common English consonant cluster, using a contrasting pair such as *He is supporting/ sporting a new wife* (assuming expenses of/ showing off).

3.	Define what you think is an important pronunciation problem in English for students of a particular background language and develop a lesson to adequately teach in context the sound or feature identified.

SUGGESTIONS FOR FURTHER READING

Bowen, J. Donald (1975)
Patterns of English Pronunciation. Rowley, Mass.: Newbury House.
Provides contextualized drills and exercises for a large number of pronunciation problems.

Campbell, R. N., and Judith Lindfors (1969)
Insights Into English Structures. Englewood Cliffs, N.J.: Prentice-Hall.
Part I (pp. 1-62) is a programmed introduction to the sound system of English—urgently needed by any prospective ESL teacher not already thoroughly familiar with the English sound system.

Nilsen, Don, and Alleen Pace Nilsen (1967)
Pronunciation Contexts in English. New York: Regents Publ. Co.
An excellent repository of minimal pair contrasts in English—useful to the ESL teacher, who can select from Nilsen the most readily contextualizable pairs for lesson development.

Prator, Clifford H. (1971)
"Phonetics vs. phonemics in the ESL Classroom: When *is* Allophonic Accuracy Important?" *TESOL*, Vol. 5, No. 1, pp. 61-72.
Establishes priorities for the teaching of English pronunciation and makes use of both the generative and the structural viewpoints.

C. Reading

Teaching the reading skill involves unique problems and challenges at all conceivable levels of instruction. ESL teachers working with illiterate adolescents and adults are often ill-prepared to teach language and literacy simultaneously. Lewis's chapter with all of its tried and tested activities will be helpful in such situations. For the ESL teacher who has never had a course in reading instruction, Hatch's chapter, with its description of all the initial reading instruction methods that have been used with children and adults, is indispensable. For the teacher dealing with those intermediate students who have mastered initial reading skills but still need supervision and guidance, Gaskill's chapter is very useful. Similarly, for teachers of those advanced ESL students who still need improved reading speed and better reading strategies, Gorman's chapter provides valuable suggestions. Finally, Povey's chapter deals with the teaching of literature to ESL students. He takes into account the linguistic and cultural barriers that the ESL teacher must deal with, in addition to the usual problems inherent in the teaching of literature. The procedures suggested by Povey are designed firstly to facilitate understanding and then aesthetic appreciation on the part of the students.

PRELITERACY ACTIVITIES FOR ADOLESCENTS AND ADULTS

Dorothy Lewis

INTRODUCTION

Literacy is one of the most important components that contribute to a person's sense of dignity and personal worth.

The non-English-speaking adolescent or adult who is illiterate in his or her first language has many obstacles to overcome. S/he probably had a wavering self-image in the country of his or her origin because s/he could neither read nor write. If s/he wants to succeed in his or her new English-speaking environment, s/he realizes that s/he must prepare him- or herself to communicate in a new language. Success in a language can mean many things—a job, easier adaptation to a new environment, friends to communicate with, etc.

This chapter deals with the adult or teenage ESL student who is in the very beginning stages of English language development. S/he also shares a common problem with many other immigrants in the United States. His or her previous education was minimal and s/he is either unable to read and write in his or her first language, or s/he is extremely limited in these skills.

There are many reading techniques with materials accompanying them which are used to teach initial reading in English. However, most of these techniques and materials were prepared for native-speaking children and do not apply to preliterate ESL adolescents and adults.

We know that adult students choose to attend ESL classes because they want to learn a new language. They arrive with high hopes and high motivation. This is probably true of most adolescent students also. It is true that some teenagers are in school only because they are required by law to be there. Regardless of the reason for attending the class each ESL student needs and wants to experience success. If s/he is in a multi-level class, s/he realizes that others know more than s/he does. Most of the other students are literate in their first language. A sensitive preliterate student is already a potential drop-out. The teacher's role is extremely important right from the beginning of the first class. A sensitive teacher is prepared to meet the needs of these special students.

A good language development program for all ESL students should include listening experiences; concept and vocabulary development; opportunities for the student to speak both with teacher direction and spontaneously; instruction in correct grammatical usage; and pronunciation drill.

The activities described in this chapter are a result of my own experience of working with preliterate adults and adolescents. These activities have worked well with students in this situation.

The following activities are intended to provide opportunities for the beginning student to successfully learn simple concepts such as numerals, colors, and common nouns. As s/he acquires a beginning vocabulary, s/he is ready to learn simple language patterns both orally and by reading the written forms. The tasks are learning center activities which can be done by one or more students at any given time. The tasks in each section are sequenced in order of difficulty. They move from the concrete to the abstract because this is how most learning takes place. They can be used as worksheets or mounted on tagboard for durability and used as manipulative lessons. For more effective learning, it is recommended that the students verbalize the task they have just completed. Pictures with stick-figure people are used throughout because students of all ages can relate to them without feeling intimidated. They are also easier for the unartistic teacher and student to draw.

LEVEL I ACTIVITIES:
NUMBER WORDS AND COLOR WORDS

Numbers

With these activities the students will learn to say, read, and write the numerals and corresponding words.

Task 1: Match the number word, the numeral, and the concept. The concept is represented by dots, which is particularly helpful if the students' native orthography differs from English. These puzzles serve as a self-directing aid until the students are able to recognize the words. Students can progress at their own pace in mastering the concept, the numeral, and finally the number word. Cut on the lines and instruct the students to reconstruct a portion or all of the page. The students are now ready for the next task where the aid (i.e., the puzzle element) has been removed.

Task 2: Match the number word and numeral without the aid of visual clues. This task will reinforce the students' ability to associate a numeral with its written symbol. The students can continue to use the aid of Task 1 if they wish. As in Task 1, cut on the lines and instruct the students to reconstruct a portion or all of the page.

Task 3: Match the numeral with the correct number word. Request the students to circle the correct word on the right that represents the numeral on the left. A master copy with the correct answers circled can be used as a self-check for the students.

Task 4: Crossword puzzle. This is a concluding number activity designed for more reinforcement and satisfaction. A master copy with completed answers can serve as a correction

Numbers—Task 1

Numbers—Task 2

1	five	four	(one)	eight
2	(two)	nine	six	five
3	seven	eight	ten	(three)
4	one	four	two	eight
5	five	two	nine	seven
6	ten	one	six	three
7	four	one	nine	seven
8	six	five	eight	two
9	three	nine	six	seven
10	ten	seven	four	nine

Numbers—Task 3

ⲡⲡⲡNUMBERالسⲡⲡⲡ

ACROSS
1. 6   6. 9
3. 2   7. 8
5. 5

DOWN
1. 7   4. 1
2. 10   5. 4
3. 3

Answer Bank

one   four   eight
two   five   nine
three   six   ten
         seven

Numbers—Task 4

key. An "answer bank" is included to aid the students with spelling, and to ensure success. It can be eliminated if the teacher feels the students can manage without it.

Numbers eleven through twenty follow the same format and tasks as numbers one through ten. For variation, colors can be introduced at this time, and when the color tasks have been completed, teach numbers eleven through twenty.

Colors

With these activity pages, the students will recognize ten colors and say, read, and write the color words.

Task 1: Match the color word with the correct color by use of an aid. This task is done in the same manner as the number puzzle with an aid. In this case, the aid is a small black notch which must match properly for the answer to be correct. It will be necessary for the teacher, aide, or student helper to color in the squares so they correspond with each color word.

COLORS

1.	red	
2.	blue	
3.	brown	
4.	orange	
5.	green	
6.	yellow	
7.	black	
8.	purple	
9.	white	
10.	pink	

Colors—Task 1

Task 2: Match the color word with the color without the aid of visual clues. This activity can be used to further reinforce the students' ability to associate a color with its written symbol. Color the squares to correspond with

COLORS

1.	red	□
2.	blue	□
3.	brown	□
4.	orange	□
5.	green	□
6.	yellow	□
7.	black	□
8.	purple	□
9.	white	□
10.	pink	□

Colors—Task 2

the color words. Cut them apart and instruct the students to match them correctly. The teacher can either correct the students' work or provide an answer key.

Task 3: Color by number. This is an enjoyable activity where the students color the picture with the color assigned to each numeral. If they do it correctly, they have indicated that they are able to read the color words. The students can check their work against a master copy provided by the teacher.

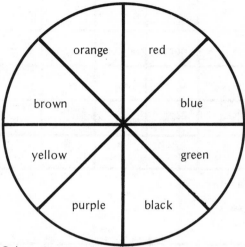

Colors—Task 4

Color by NUMBER

1. red	4. green	8. black
2. blue	5. orange	9. white
3. brown	6. yellow	10. pink
	7. purple	

Colors—Task 3

Task 4: Color the wheel. The color wheel can be utilized in a number of different ways to help students learn and reinforce their knowledge of color words. The students can begin by coloring in the appropriate colors on the wheel. The wheel can then be turned into a spinner type game as follows: (a) Cut an arrow-shaped strip from a piece of tagboard or a plastic milk carton. (b) Punch a hole in the center and affix the arrow to the center of the color wheel with a brass fastener. (c) The student spins the arrow and identifies the color to which the arrow points. (d) At a more advanced level, the game can be played without coloring the wheel (i.e., just with the names of the colors).

Task 5: Color the shape and write the color name. This activity allows the students to match colors and words independently. After they have colored in a square, they choose and write the corresponding color word. For self-checking the students can refer to a sheet or chart which shows matched colors and words.

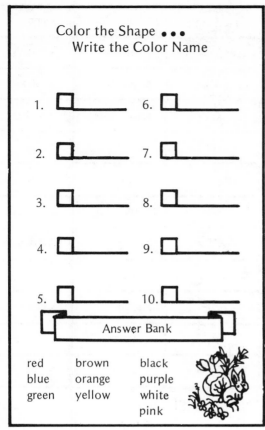

Color the Shape ... Write the Color Name

1. ☐ _____   6. ☐ _____

2. ☐ _____   7. ☐ _____

3. ☐ _____   8. ☐ _____

4. ☐ _____   9. ☐ _____

5. ☐ _____   10. ☐ _____

Answer Bank

red	brown	black
blue	orange	purple
green	yellow	white
		pink

Colors—Task 5

Task 6: Color puzzle. This is another reinforcement activity. The attached teacher key provides the necessary cues for coloring the ovals. Fold under or remove the key before presenting the puzzle to the students. This can serve as a self-checking device when the students have completed the puzzle. If desired, a master copy can be used for a correction key.

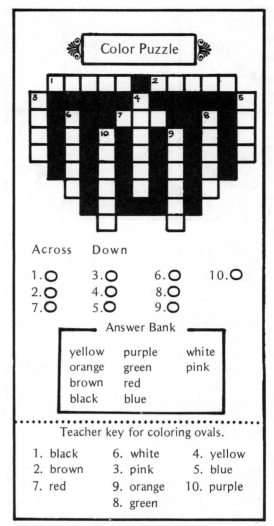

Color Puzzle

Across   Down

1. ○   3. ○   6. ○   10. ○
2. ○   4. ○   8. ○
7. ○   5. ○   9. ○

Answer Bank

yellow	purple	white
orange	green	pink
brown	red	
black	blue	

Teacher key for coloring ovals.

1. black   6. white   4. yellow
2. brown   3. pink   5. blue
7. red   9. orange   10. purple
            8. green

Colors—Task 6

LEVEL II ACTIVITIES: VOCABULARY 1 AND READING 1

Vocabulary 1

Because most ESL classes are held in typical classrooms, pictures of classroom objects are suggested for this activity. However, a teacher may choose to use any pictures or objects s/he desires. Staying within a specific classification, such as food and clothing, is recommended. Realia representing the pictures should be used as often as possible for concrete reinforcement. It is advisable to teach the articles while teaching the nouns. Although there are rules relating to articles, they would probably be too difficult to comprehend at this time. As the students advance in their knowledge of the language, begin to teach the rules.

Task 1: Classroom objects. In this task the students will learn to say the names of the objects with teacher direction. Ideally, each student should have his or her own set of pictures. To ensure that they are mastering the names correctly, the students should always practice with the supervision of a teacher, aide, or student tutor.

Vocabulary 1—Task 1

	(a book)	a pen
	an eraser	(a ruler)
	a pencil	a ruler
	some paste	a book
	a clock	a ruler
	a book	a ball
	a ruler	a book
	a pencil	some paper
	some scissors	a clock
	a ruler	a clock
	a clock	some chalk
	a ruler	a ball

Vocabulary 1—Task 2

Task 2: Match the picture with the correct word. This is done in the same manner as *Numbers,* Task 3. In this case the students match the classroom object with the correct word.

Task 3: Writing: Classroom objects. This activity provides the students with an opportunity to write the names of the classroom objects. Instruct the students to select the correct word from the answer bank and write it beneath the appropriate picture. If the teacher feels that the students can master the task without an aid, the answer bank can be eliminated.

Reading 1

These reading lessons are designed to offer beginning students early and instant success in reading English. Simple language patterns are used. Other approaches to the teaching of reading, such as phonics, can be introduced later. Lessons will cover the following:

A. Parts of speech:
   i. Nouns—singular and plural of nouns previously introduced.
   ii. Verbs—*want* and *have.*
   iii. Adjectives—numbers and colors.
   iv. Pronouns—*I, you* (singular), *he, she,* and *they.*
   v. Articles—*a, an,* and *some.*
B. Verb forms:
   i. The present tense of *want* and *have.*
   ii. The auxiliaries *do* and *does.*
   iii. Question formation—*wh*-questions beginning with *What.*

Task 1: The Dialogue. A specific language pattern is taught orally, utilizing vocabulary covered in *Vocabulary 1,* and augmented by the vocabulary used to teach the language pattern. Place the classroom object pictures face-up on a table. Teach the pattern as follows:

a crayon	some chalk
a ball	some paste
(a clock)	a book
a ruler	a pencil
some paper	a pencil
a pencil	an eraser
a clock	a crayon
a pen	a ruler
a ruler	a book
a pen	a pencil
a book	a ruler
a clock	an eraser

Vocabulary 1—Task 2 (continued)

1.____ 2.____ 3.____

4.____ 5.____ 6.____

7.____ 8.____ 9.____

10.____ 11.____ 12.____

Answer Bank

clock	book	chalk
pen	ball	paper
pencil	crayon	paste
ruler	eraser	scissors

Vocabulary 1—Task 3

Teacher: (picking up a picture card)
I want a/an/some . . .
What do you want?

Student: (picking up another picture card)
I want a/an/some . . .
What do you want?

This process is continued until all the cards have been picked. It should be pointed out that this seemingly simple task often takes the beginning student quite a while to master. This is true for most newly introduced dialogues. When the students have mastered the above pattern, expand the dialogue as follows:

Teacher	Student
What does he want?	*He wants. . . .*
What does she want?	*She wants. . . .*
What do they want?	*They want. . . .*

These patterns should be repeated by the teacher and student(s), as well as student and student(s), until the concept and vocabulary are clearly understood. Pay careful attention to correct and contextualized use of the pronouns and verb forms.

Note: In the beginning, it is advisable to work only with the above forms. The patterns *What do I want?*, *What do we want?*, and *What do you want?* (plural) are too difficult to comprehend at this early stage. They can be taught later.

Task 2: Picture cards with sentence patterns that have been learned orally. These can be used to further enhance the previously learned dialogues. They also serve as an introduction to reading sentences. The pictures are intended to provide contextual clues to the written sentences. The blank faces can be completed by the students, picturing themselves, to allow them to internalize the first person singular.

Reading 1—Task 2

Cut out the picture sentence cards and use them in the same manner as *Vocabulary 1*, Task 1. In this case, however, the students read the language patterns.

Task 3: Big Book. With this book the students will read orally the language patterns (with pictures) which they have just mastered. At this stage many of the students will not recognize the individual words but merely repeat the patterns they have memorized. The four pages of the book are numbered 1 to 4. After reproducing pages 1 and 4 on a ditto machine, reverse the copies and reproduce pages 2 and 3 on the other side. This makes it possible for the

Reading 1—Task 3 (Front)

Reading 1—Task 3 (Back)

book to be printed on one sheet of paper. Fold on the dotted line after reproducing.

Scrambled Sentences. These sentences can be used to ensure the recognition and correct positioning of the words used in the sentence patterns. This can be done in two ways—Task 4 and Task 5, which follow. After completing each of these tasks, the students should demonstrate mastery by reading each of their sentences correctly.

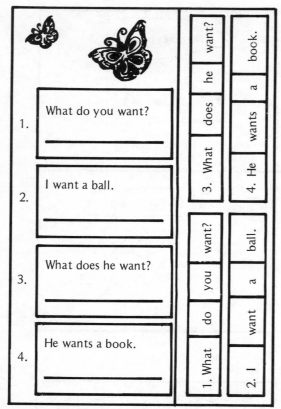

1. What do you want?

2. I want a ball.

3. What does he want?

4. He wants a book.

1. What	2. I
do	want
you	a
want?	ball.

3. What	4. He
does	wants
he	a
want?	book.

Reading 1—Task 4 (page 1)

5. What does she want?

6. She wants an eraser.

7. What do they want?

8. They want some paper.

5. What	6. She
does	wants
she	an
want?	eraser.

7. What	8. They
do	want
they	some
want?	paper.

Reading 1—Task 4 (page 2)

1. want you What do
_____ ?

2. a ball I want
_____ .

3. does want What he
_____ ?

4. He book a wants
_____ .

5. want she does What
_____ ?

6. pencil wants She a
_____ .

7. they do What want
_____ ?

8. paper some They want
_____ .

Reading 1—Task 5

Task 4: Match the sentence parts with the sentences. This is a tactile activity that allows the students to manipulate the words in the sentences they have been learning. This task consists of two sentence boards plus sentence strips. The boards are to be left intact, cutting only around the outer border. The sentence strips on the right should be cut apart and used as follows: (a) a matching activity with word-to-word correspondence, (b) a cut-and-paste activity. The students can then read their sentences to the teacher, aide, or tutor.

Task 5: Unscramble the sentences. This is a writing activity where the students rewrite the sentence correctly on the line beneath the scrambled sentence.

Task 6: Word list. This is a list of forty words covered in previous lessons. They can be read by the students or, ideally, made into flashcards. The students can also say each word in a sentence or form their own sentences with the word cards. Instead of using all of the words in

WORDS

what	some	eraser	brown
do	does	book	black
you	wants	chalk	white
want	pencil	ball	pink
I	ruler	paste	green
he	scissors	red	one
she	paper	blue	two
they	pen	yellow	three
a	crayon	orange	four
an	clock	purple	five

Reading 1—Task 6

—1—
What does he want?
He wants a ball.

What do you want?
I want a pencil.

LITTLE BOOK

By _____

—2—
What do they want?
They want a ruler.

What does she want?
She wants a book.

What does she want?
She wants a clock.

What does he want?
He wants some paper.
—3—

Reading 1 — Task 7

one lesson, the teacher may choose to group the words into categories—colors, classroom objects, numbers, and words from sentence patterns.

Task 7: Little book. Here we have the same language patterns as the big book, but without pictures (contextual clues). Fold each copy on the dotted lines after reproducing. The students do their own illustrating (with colors, if desired). If they have mastered the previous reading tasks, the students should have no problem comprehending the sentences in the little book. The illustrations will indicate the degree of comprehension.

LEVEL III ACTIVITIES: VOCABULARY 2 AND READING 2

At this time another series of vocabulary items may be taught. This can be done in the same manner as *Vocabulary 1,* Tasks 1, 2, and 3. As soon as the nouns are learned, a new dialogue should be introduced. Utilizing the new vocabu-lary and the classroom nouns, the following dialogue should be taught after each student is given a picture to hold.

Teacher	Student
What do you have?	*I have. . . .*
What does he have?	*He has. . . .*
What does she have?	*She has. . . .*
What do they have?	*They have. . . .*

These patterns should be repeated by the teacher and student(s) and student and student(s) until the dialogue is clearly understood. As in the dialogue in *Reading 1,* pay careful attention to the correct use of pronouns and verb forms. A series of tasks, similar to *Reading 1,* Tasks 2, 3, 4, 5, 6, and 7 can follow the mastery of the new dialogue.[1]

As the students progress, teach new dialogues and accompanying tasks. The patterns included could be questions with affirmative and negative answers using the present tense of *want* and *have.* Begin to add numbers and color words.

Teacher	Student
Do you have a pencil?	*Yes, I do.* or *No, I don't. I have a book.*
Does she want an eraser?	*Yes, she does.* or *No, she doesn't.*
	She wants some paper.
Do they have a clock?	*Yes, they do.* or
	No, they don't. They have a book.
Do you want two red pencils?	*Yes, I do.* or *No, I don't. I want a*
	brown pencil.
Does he have four purple pens?	*No, he doesn't. He has three blue books.*
I have two blue pens. Do you have a	*No, I don't. I have a black pen.*
blue pen?	
Do you want some white paper?	*Yes, I do*

These patterns can be followed through in the same manner as previously taught dialogues. Tasks and teacher-made books will continue to increase the students' reading power.

As the students succeed in reading these controlled vocabulary items and dialogues, the teacher can begin to introduce material from the class text. Through listening, repeating, and looking at the words, the students will discover that these symbols which represent words are not so difficult to tackle. Although they have a long way to go, these students are no longer illiterate.

ADDITIONAL ACTIVITIES FOR THE PRELITERATE ESL STUDENT

It is advisable to arrange for areas of diversity such as listening centers and writing centers. This is particularly necessary in a multi-level class. These centers offer a change of pace for the students and an opportunity for the teacher to work with smaller groups.

Listening and reading

Listening comprehension is, without a doubt, the most important skill in learning a new language. Understanding a language is a prerequisite to speaking, reading, and writing that language. Commercial or teacher-made tapes accompanied by written texts can provide preliterate students with opportunities to hear their new language and see the written words that they are hearing. We can't expect them to become readers from this experience, but these students need all of the opportunities we can offer them to come in contact with words. As they listen to a tape recorder and attempt to follow the spoken words in written form, the students may experience a sense of personal worth. They probably aren't reading, but they are working with a book and they appear to be reading. There are fringe benefits, too. Each time students participate in this exercise, they will add a few more words to their reading vocabulary.

Handwriting practice

Preliterate ESL students will need a great deal of practice in handwriting. Since most of the texts they will encounter are in printed form, they should probably begin their handwriting practice by learning to write both upper case and lower case printed letters. State adopted handwriting textbooks are among the best resources for the teaching of handwriting. Contact your State Superintendent of Education if you would like to have a list of adopted or approved texts. If students encounter extreme difficulty in writing, they should be encouraged to trace the letters. As they progress with their handwriting skills, they should begin to copy familiar words and sentences. These can be the vocabulary items and language patterns they have learned during their ESL lessons. Further handwriting practice can be provided by having students complete simple personal data forms and application blanks. As they become more competent, the students can begin to take dictation of familiar words and sentences given by the teacher.

Personal information

All students should become familiar with words commonly found on employment application forms and school registration forms. They will encounter many personal data forms as they venture into their new environment, and it will be necessary for them to be able to read and fill out these forms. The teacher should provide the

Sample Personal Data Form

Name: Mr.
Mrs. _____
Miss   (last)   (first)   (middle initial)
Ms.

Address: _____
            (number)   (street)   (apt. no.)

            _____
            (city)   (state)   (zip code)

Telephone: _____

Birthday: _____
           (month)   (day)   (year)

Age: _____

Social Security Number: _____

Sex: _____ Male

     _____ Female

Signature: _____

students with a great deal of practice in this area. Understanding what they are doing is of prime importance to the students.

Reading signs

It is important for everyone to recognize signs essential to daily living and to associate these signs with their meanings. State motor vehicle code books are an excellent source for street and highway signs. Some states publish these books in Spanish. Introduce no more than ten words (signs) during a lesson. Demonstrate the meanings with actions, pictures, chalkboard drawings, and signs around the room. An imaginative teacher can help the students derive meanings from these written symbols. Each student should be provided with his or her own list of these words. An excellent way to reinforce the recognition of these signs is to make or acquire a set of language-master cards with pictures and words of these important signs. The students can learn at their own pace as they read, listen to, and repeat the words. Following are some of the signs all ESL students should learn to read:

Danger	*Men (Gentlemen)*
Caution	*Ped Xing*
Watch Your Step	*No Ped Xing*
Stop	*Crosswalk*
Entrance	*In*
Exit	*Out*
Up	*Hospital*
Down	*Fire Escape*
Do Not Enter	*No Smoking*
Poison	*Pull*
Keep Out	*Push*
No Trespassing	*Stairway*
Information	*For Sale*
Wait	*For Rent*
Restrooms	
Ladies (Women)	

Language experience

A popular technique for the teaching of reading is referred to as the "language experience approach." The students dictate their sentences or story individually to the teacher, who writes the words on the chalkboard or on paper. The theory behind this approach is that the student can read what s/he can think and say. Each student's language (in this case—his or her new language) and experiences are unique to him or her. The students' command of the language is limited and this approach promises them that their early English reading experience will be based upon the language skills and experiences they possess at a given time. When they see their own words in written form they are able to read and understand what has been written. In the beginning, their dictation will probably be limited to what they have learned in simple dialogues. As their oral language expands, so will their dictated stories. After a student has dictated a story, allow him or her to read it and then copy it. Eventually the dictated stories of two or more students can be shared by a small group or the entire class.

Learning to read through music

Everyone likes to sing. Devote a portion of each ESL class to music, preferably the last ten or fifteen minutes. Give your students reproduced copies of folk songs, western ballads, and holiday songs. Adolescents especially enjoy the current popular songs. Songs with repetition like *Where Have All the Flowers Gone?* are especially good for beginners. Provide accompanying music with records or tapes or a guitarist, if one is available. In the beginning the students will probably memorize the lyrics. Eventually they will begin to associate the written words with the words they are singing. Sometimes students are reluctant to begin singing. Don't give up. As the melodies become more familiar and the words more comprehensible, the entire class will join in.

Reading games

Games can be used for fun and reinforcement. Both checkers and Bingo can be played in the ESL classroom to strengthen the student's word recognition skills.

Checkers—The teacher reproduces a checkerboard with black and white squares. Any words the teacher chooses can be written in the white squares. These should be words that have been previously introduced to the students. Two

WORD CHECKERS

identical words are written in each white square with one word facing each player. Before a player can move a checker to a white square, s/he must read the word in that square. S/he can also be requested to use the word in a sentence. The teacher can adapt the rules of checkers to suit his or her needs.

Bingo—The teacher reproduces a blank bingo board and writes a word in each square. These should be words that have been taught in earlier lessons. By rearranging the words, the teacher can provide bingo boards for several players. The caller can be a more advanced student who draws each word from a box. The winning student must read the words s/he has covered.

For some more suggestions regarding the use of songs and games in the ESL classrooms, see the chapter by Gasser and Waldman beginning on page 49 of this volume.

High frequency word lists

There are several high frequency word lists which are used by reading teachers in various ways. The Kučera-Francis list (1967), Dolch (1941), and the Thorndike-Lorge list (1944) are examples of high frequency word lists. These lists can be valuable when teaching important "sight words," especially words which are commonly used in our language. However, these essential words are useful to beginning ESL students only if they understand their meanings and can use them in context. It is important to recognize high frequency words such as *the, of, and, to,* and *a,* but it is more important to know their meanings and how they fit into our language. The more advanced beginner and the intermediate student would probably benefit from exercises and lessons utilizing these high frequency words.

two	white	eight	blue	ten
green	black	yellow	red	three
nine	orange	◇	one	want
purple	four	brown	six	she
he	seven	they	five	I

NOTE

1. The aforementioned activities come from Eley and Lewis (1976).

DISCUSSION QUESTIONS

1. The preliterate student is one of our greatest drop-out potentials. Discuss.

2. Would it be a good idea to teach preliterate adolescents and adults to read in their native language first? Give reasons pro and con.

3. What are the advantages and disadvantages of multilevel ESL classes?

4. It was suggested in this chapter that newly introduced vocabulary items should be within specific classifications such as classroom objects, food and clothing. Which do you consider some of the most important classifications that beginning adolescent and adult ESL students should learn? Why?

5. Discuss the advantages and disadvantages of teaching printed writing or cursive writing.

6. If you were provided with an ESL classroom aide to help you with a multilevel adult class (consisting of some preliterate students) how would you utilize this person during class sessions?

SUGGESTED ACTIVITIES

1. Using your own format, design a series of tasks for the preliterate student.

2. Devise a lesson for teaching street and traffic signs for beginning ESL students.

3. Ask a preliterate ESL adolescent or adult to dictate a short story to you. What are your observations regarding his or her acquisition and use of the English language?

4. Share with your class some published materials that can be adapted to a listening-read-along lesson for the beginning student.

5. Prepare a detailed personal information form. Invite some beginning students to fill it out. After analyzing the forms, make a list of the items which indicate a lack of understanding by the student. Develop a lesson plan to teach these concepts.

6. Prepare a list of twelve vocabulary items which fall within a specific classification. Discuss why you chose these particular items and how you plan to present them.

SUGGESTIONS FOR FURTHER READING

Not much material which relates directly to the preliterate adolescent and adult has been published. The following references offer a variety of suggestions which may be helpful to the teacher of preliterate ESL students.

Allen, R. V., and C. Allen (1966)
An Introduction To A Language-Experience Program—Levels I and II. Chicago: Encyclopaedia Britannica Press.

——— (1967)
Language Experiences In Reading. Chicago: Encyclopaedia Britannica Press.
These are three sequential teacher resource books on the language-experience approach to reading, written for teachers of elementary age students. The foundation for a language-experience approach is the student's own oral-language background and personal experiences. Many sections of these guides can be adapted to the preliterate adolescent and adult student.

Carroll, J. B., P. Davies, and B. Richman (1972)
The American Heritage Word Frequency Book. New York: American Heritage Publishing Company, Inc.
A word-frequency study based upon textual samples from published materials to which English-speaking students are exposed in grades 3 through 9.

Goodman, Y. M., and K. S. Goodman (1971)
Linguistics, Psycholinguistics and the Teaching of Reading. Newark, Delaware: International Reading Association.
The selections referred to in this annotated bibliography include a full range of topics, points of view, and authors' special fields. Especially helpful to the ESL teacher are the suggested reading materials dealing with instruction and theory in reading, the relationship between oral and written language, and intonation as it relates to reading.

Horn, T. (ed.) (1970)
Reading for the Disadvantaged—Problems of Linguistically Different Learners. A project of the International Reading Association. New York: Harcourt, Brace, and World, Inc.
A group of reading specialists, linguists, sociologists, and psychologists contributed their views and expertise to this book. It was written for elementary

through high school students, but there are many instructional implications that also apply to non-English-speaking adults.

Paine, M. J. (1971)
"Drill Charts and Reading Cards," *English Language Teaching, Volume XXVI, 1,* 56-9.
Suggestions using stick-figure-people drawings for teaching speaking and reading simple language patterns.

Seward, B. H. (1972)
"Teaching Cursive Writing to EFL Students," *English Language Teaching, Volume XXVI, 2,* 169-78.
Step by step suggestions in teaching cursive handwriting. This approach can be used with any group of students but it was developed primarily for Arab learners.

Shaw, A. M. (1970)
"How to Make Songs for Language Drills," *English Language Teaching, Volume XXIV, 2,* 125-32.
This selection offers some interesting ways to teach language patterns through singing.

Steeves, R. W. (1969)
Handbook for Teachers of English as a Second Language. Americanization—Literacy. California State Department of Education, Sacramento.
This handbook was designed to give useful suggestions to teachers of ESL adults. Especially helpful is the section of "Selected References," pages 73-80. Most of these reference works deal with the beginning ESL adult.

Thonis, E. (1970)
Teaching Reading to Non-English Speakers. New York: Collier-Macmillan International.
This book is a comprehensive study of the teaching of initial reading to non-English-speaking children. Although it does not specifically apply to adults and adolescents, the book offers many sound psychological, linguistic, and practical suggestions that should be helpful to the teacher of the more mature preliterate ESL student.

Adult education curriculum guides dealing with ESL students have been published by many school districts throughout the United States. Some of them offer helpful suggestions for the beginning ESL adult. Following are three adult education ESL curriculum guides.

Scope and Sequence in the Teaching of English as a New Language to Adults—Beginning Level. Curriculum Bulletin 1967-1968, Series No. 22. Bureau of Curriculum Development, Board of Education of the City of New York.

English as a Second Language. Department of Adult Education. Board of Education, Newark, New Jersey, 1967.

Teaching English as a New Language. Adult Basic Education. Board of Education, City of Chicago, 1967.

READING A SECOND LANGUAGE

Evelyn Hatch

INTRODUCTION

ESL students are not just concerned with speaking; they want to be able to read and write English as well as speak it. Even in audiolingual programs which stress listening and speaking, the student needs to know how to read. In fact, in most programs it is assumed that the student can read. Obviously this is not

true in elementary school ESL classes. And ESL teachers working in community adult schools know that more and more of their students want to learn to read English though some of these students are illiterate in their first language. For many university foreign students reading skills are perhaps even more important for academic success than speaking ability. Reading is a skill that everyone needs whether s/he is a student in elementary, secondary, university, or adult school. Yet it is a skill that gets slighted in most ESL teacher-training programs.

Reading instruction means different things to different teachers. For learners it may also mean problems which are specifically their own. In a single adult class there may be students who need basic reading skills. They need to know how to read traffic signs, labels, grocery ads, classified ads, job applications, and bank loan applications. There may also be students in the same class who want help in speed-reading and comprehension skills suitable for reading American history books, biochemistry texts, or *War and Peace.*

How can the teacher be prepared to meet these very different needs? A first step is to understand the basic methods of reading instruction. This is important because the methods make assumptions about the reading process, assumptions that are not age specific. Even if you do not teach basic literacy, i.e., beginning reading, most remedial reading activities are also based on the four methods. Your choice for reviewing and consolidating beginning skills depends on what reading methods you (or the writer of your textbook) advocate.

INITIAL READING INSTRUCTION

Basic methods

(a) *Phonics.* The phonics method teaches the learner to "sound out" the squiggles on the page. The method is also called "teaching the alphabetic principle" or "teaching the phoneme-grapheme correspondences." The individual letter-sound, the phoneme, is the perceptual unit. Letter-sounds are blended to form words. Thus, the sound system is assumed to mediate between symbol and meaning. Emphasis is on this letter-to-sound correspondence rather than on meaning. This presupposes that one knows the sounds of the language to start with. For example, if the student hears no difference between /r/ and /l/—and many Japanese speakers don't—we can expect him or her to have difficulty in learning the correspondence of letters to sounds s/he cannot distinguish. If s/he hears no difference between /iy/ and /i/—and many Spanish speakers don't—it may be difficult to teach him or her the letter symbols for these sounds. And when the task is complicated by a variety of spelling patterns for these same sounds, the situation becomes exceedingly difficult for the student. The following example from Arthur (1973) should make this problem clear:

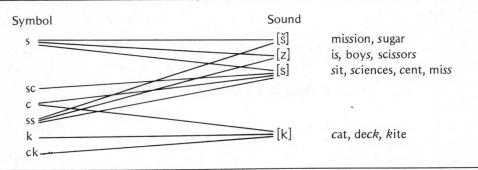

Symbol		Sound	
s		[š]	mission, *sugar*
		[z]	i*s*, boy*s*, sci*ss*ors
		[s]	*s*it, *s*ciences, *c*ent, mi*ss*
sc			
c			
ss			
k		[k]	*c*at, de*ck*, *k*ite
ck			

While ESL teachers know about pronunciation problems and have thought through the implications of splits, coalesced categories, and so on for pronunciation lessons, they have seldom been asked to apply such information to the teaching of reading. Perhaps because of our heavy emphasis on speaking skills, pronunciation problem areas are not considered as reading problem areas. Or perhaps we have not asked teachers to read the research that shows pronunciation problems do transfer to reading.

The research does show, in fact, that students misread and misinterpret words containing sounds which they cannot discriminate. That is, if they cannot hear the difference between /r/ and /l/, they may read *light* for *right*, *cloud* for *crowd*. Following a study by Serpell (1968), we tested Spanish-speaking children using the multiple-choice technique Serpell advocated. We wanted to know whether the Spanish child, on seeing the word *cat*, could interpret it as *cot*. Given *bit*, might s/he interpret it as *beet*? In the following examples, the item in italics is the test item:

Which of these are parts of your body?
hands   when   *fit*   eyes   shoes

Which of these are colors?
blue   *grin*   happy   yellow   red

As we expected, many of the students did misread *fit* as *feet* and *grin* as *green*. The test does contain a Type I research error. Students don't normally read passages set up to trap them like this. That is, it is not likely that in a passage about tuna boats, the student would misinterpret a sentence like *The ship docked at the harbor* as *The sheep docked at the harbor*. Just as in listening, the problem may cause a temporary slow-down in comprehension but it does not always mean that misunderstanding will take place.

Tests of ability to discriminate among similar sounds (Wepmann Auditory Discrimination Test) have been used to predict reading difficulty for Anglo children. And Clark and Richards (1966) have shown that economically disadvantaged children score far lower on such discrimination tests than the Anglo population. A quick check of the learner's ability to discriminate sounds should help the teacher know where to expect problems in using the phonics method. Plans to spend additional time on these particular sound-symbol correspondences seem mandatory.

Another criticism of the phonics method is that in teaching *b* and *t* we say *buh* and *tuh* as though we were accurately isolating a sound of English. To blend *puh-ah-tuh* to get *pot* is a formidable task for ESL (and any other) students. Most teachers give their top reading group the phonics approach because they are the only students who can do the activities. Some educators have suggested that if students can really do this, they probably already know how to read.

To overcome some of the problems of phonics, an initial teaching alphabet (ita) was devised. It works on the one sound-one symbol format (see illustration 1). Until recently it had not been used with ESL students. It is being used in a few California schools now; no reports are available on its effectiveness. Anglo children acquire reading skills very rapidly with ita. However, gains made wash out once the student is expected to transfer to regular orthography. That is, the transfer period is long enough to allow students instructed by other methods to catch up.

(b) *Syllabary*. On the basis of work in speech perception (Savin, 1972; Bever, 1970; Schankweiler and Liberman, 1972), the syllable has been chosen as the natural reading unit of this method. The syllable can be pronounced in isolation and it is easier to blend syllables than it is to blend phoneme-letter units (Gleitman and Rozin, 1973). That is, it is easier to arrive at *paper* by blending *pa-per* than it is by blending *puh-ah-puh-eh-er*, or even *puh-aper*. Languages which use syllabaries rather than alphabets are reportedly easier to read. Makita (1968), for example, has shown a very low rate of illiteracy in Japanese, which uses a combination logograph and syllabary system. In fact, many Japanese children have learned the syllables before beginning school. Unfortunately, English has a complex syllable structure with consonant clusters both in initial and final positions, so there would be thousands of separate syllables to learn plus spelling variations for many of them.

Nevertheless, syllable reading instruction has proven to be effective in helping non-readers from the inner-city to learn to read (Gleitman and Rozin, 1973). The method begins with a rebus (see Illustration 2) similar to that in the Peabody Rebus Reading Program (Woodcock, 1968). After about fifteen separate syllables have been taught, the learner reads and writes sentences by placing word cards in a row. With twenty-four syllables it is possible to write small books (but with small sense). The most productive syllables are introduced first. This results in a strong emphasis on morphology. In this sense, syllable reading programs would reinforce much of the grammar taught in most

a gaem ov baull

"cum on, paul.
hit the baull," sed ted.
"see if you can hit it.
see if you can hit the baull
with the bat."

Illustration 2

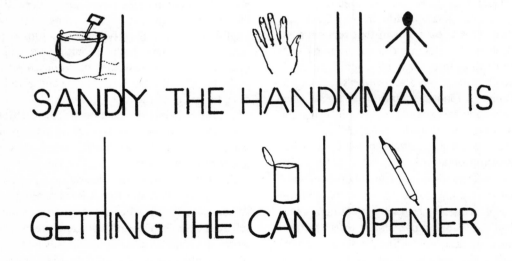

SANDY THE HANDYMAN IS
GETTING THE CAN OPENER

beginning ESL programs (plurals, tense, etc.). The method is used, though not exclusively, in reading materials for Adult Basic Education programs (cf. the Mott Series) and in remedial secondary materials.

(c) *Linguistic.* The linguistic method (named for its originator, Bloomfield, and for Charles Fries, who also worked on reading materials) teaches recognition of frequently-occurring patterns in words (see Illustration 3).

Illustration 3

The Cat on the Van

Dan is on the van.

Nat is on the van.

The pan is on the van.

The cat can bat the pan.

Dan can pat the cat.

The man ran the van.

Again, meaning is not the central focus; the patterns are. Very few visuals are included and guessing is not encouraged. A pattern such as *at* is learned and then initial consonants are blended onto it, producing *cat, bat, sat, rat, fat, hat.* The *it* pattern is taught and initial consonants are blended onto it, producing *bit, fit, sit, lit.* Final consonants are also blended onto patterns as in *ma, man, map, mat,* even though the phonological resemblance in many such patterns is lost.

The linguistic method is the most popular method for inner-city, ESL, and remedial programs. The Miami Linguistic Series, the first set written especially for ESL students, uses this method. In remedial programs one finds many exercises such as those mentioned above, nonsensical stories about *The man fans the van,* and the use of flip charts and pull charts (see Illustration 4).

To show how effective this method is, let's use a new alphabet. The sentence (borrowed from Virginia French Allen, 1975) is *Nan and Dan want a cat.*

C·C ·C□ □·C λ·C△ ·M·△

If I tell you that C = *n* (it's a nose), □ = *d* (it's a door), M = *c* (it's a crown), △ = *t* (it's

Illustration 4   Pull, Flip and Pocket Charts

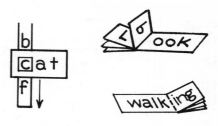

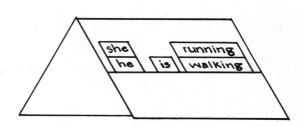

a tree trunk), and λ = *w* (it's a wave), you should be able to use the mnemonic connection between descriptor symbol and sound to reconstruct the sentence. But if I give you practice in *Nan, Dan, tan* several times with a flip chart and practice

·△, M·△, C·△,

you should be able to recognize these patterns very rapidly and, hopefully, be able to blend new combinations onto the learned patterns.

(d) *Whole word.* This method, also called "look-say" or basal reading, uses the word as the perceptual unit. The method is meaning-centered, that is, each word is taught with reference to its meaning in what is actually a memorization process. The new word is presented first on the board or on word cards. The word cards are used as labels for objects when possible. The word shape is pointed out and the student practices reading it and writing it. After the learner is familiar with the word on the

Illustration 5

word card, s/he goes to the text where the new word (or several new words) are repeated over and over in a short story. There are plentiful picture cues to help where memory fails and the reader is encouraged to guess what s/he has forgotten. Since this method circumvents direct sound-symbol correspondence, it is frequently used with second language learners who may have difficulty hearing differences between many English sounds.

Teachers who believe that learners should read only words which interest them also use the whole-word approach, giving learners a word card for each new word they want to be able to read. Students learn their stack of word cards and use them in combination to create their own reading stories. The whole word approach is used in many adult classes where language master cards are used at the reading station. The word is printed on the card and a picture is added whenever possible. The word is recorded on the tape below (see Illustration 5). The student accumulates his or her own sight-word card deck, and practices associating the sound of the word, by playing the tape, with the word printed on the card. To help retain more and more sight words, the words for such cards are usually chosen in sets of high association vocabulary (*dog, cat, mouse*) rather than for pattern similarity (*house, mouse, louse,* or *cat, mat, sat*) as in the linguistic method. (There is nothing to prevent using them for any method, but most students seem to prefer lexical sets rather than word patterns.)

Only so many words can be memorized easily; the memorization problem rapidly becomes intrusive unless the learner uses other strategies. Whole-word primers use words with very different word shapes like *Dick, Jane, Sally* and *oh, oh.* The shape of the word makes it easy to discriminate and memorize. But words like *pan, pen, pin* are so similar that they are difficult to remember unless some reference is made to vowel sounds. As differences in shape become smaller and smaller, it becomes very difficult to use shape alone for memorization. The student has no recourse but to refer to the sound equivalents, if not single letters, rather than the frequently-occurring patterns.

(f) *Other strategies.* There are a variety of other methods but they are actually variations on the four discussed above. The four methods make four different hypotheses as to what will best allow the learner to abstract meaning from the symbols on the page: (a) sound out each letter and blend the sounds of the letters to form words; (b) learn syllables and combine them to form words; (c) learn the most frequently-occurring patterns, and blend initial or final consonants onto the patterns to form words; or (d) memorize words by associating word shapes with meanings. A great deal of research (cf. Chall, 1967) has been done on the relative effectiveness of these methods. There is no clear cut evidence favoring one over all others. This could be due to the usual problems with classroom research or it may show that learners, in fact, read by strategies of their own creation rather than by what the teacher asks them to do. Different students use different strategies; certainly a combination of methods must be tried with students who have difficulty with reading tasks.

If the student is not literate in his or her first language, another possibility presents itself: why not teach him or her to read in his or her first language and hope for a strong transfer of skills to reading in English? A great deal of rhetoric has been directed toward this question but insufficient definitive research has been reported. It should be easier to learn to read in a language you know well than one you don't. To verify this, Modiano (1968) conducted an experiment with children from three Mexican Indian tribes. Children in the experimental group were taught reading in the vernacular. When they had mastered the primers, they entered first grade where all reading texts were in Spanish. The students were evaluated against control groups both on formal tests and informally by their teachers. Teachers felt the experimental group showed greater comprehension in reading the second language (Spanish) than students who had been taught reading from the beginning in Spanish. And the test data supported the teachers' judgments.

The Tarascan study (Barrera-Vasques, 1953) showed that children introduced to reading in their first language were better readers by the end of the second year than students who had all their instruction in Spanish, their second language. Osterberg (1961) found that children taught to read in their local dialect of Swedish first and then transferred to standard Swedish were able to read standard Swedish better than those who began reading in the standard dialect. Thonis (1970), discussing the Marysville project, claimed success for children taught to read in Spanish first and then transferred to reading English. She states that children, once they have learned what reading is all about, do not have to learn to read again in the second language; they only have to learn a new code.

These studies suggest that a wise policy would be to introduce reading in the child's first language or dialect and then transfer to the second language. The claim is that there is a strong transfer in skills; that reading a new code is not a difficult new task. That is, once having learned that the letter a stands for /a/ in Spanish, it will not be an insurmountable problem to learn that it can stand for /æ/ or /a/ or /ey/ or /e/ or /ə/ or /ɔ/ in English. While ESL teachers would consider such splits as extremely difficult in pronunciation, in vocabulary, and even in syntax, the issue is ignored when it comes to teaching reading. The transition, it is claimed, is not as traumatic as learning the correspondence first in English.

There are, of course, findings to support the other side as well. The St. Lambert Study (Lambert et al., 1970), the Toronto study (Barik and Swain, 1972), and the Culver City project (Cathcart, 1972; Cohen, 1973) seem to suggest that learning to read in a new language is not as difficult as we might imagine. After two years, both of the Canadian projects found that English-speaking children receiving all school instruction in French do as well as the control groups in reading readiness and reading achievement. They do report a lag in the first year of reading instruction. The Culver City project shows the same results for English-speaking children instructed in Spanish. Since the question is a political issue, emotional commitment to one side or the other is strong. As more and more bilingual programs are evaluated, we should have more definite answers.

Of course, it is not always possible to teach reading first in the native language. Second, many students do read well in their first language but not in the second. So, let us turn away from basic word-attack skills and look to the literature on reading for comprehension.

BEYOND BASIC READING

After initial word-attack skills have been acquired, how does one go from word naming to reading a psychology textbook? We seem to feel the process takes place automatically. Yet research shows that it does not. California reading test scores for schools with large second-language populations show that ESL students are not becoming proficient in reading. Macnamara and Kellaghan (1967) documented a similar situation when they showed that 12- and 13-year-old English-Irish bilinguals who had received most of their school instruction in Irish, their second language, read very little Irish. They found students read faster in their first language and that they were able to solve problems written in English more accurately than identical problems written in Irish, even though tests showed they understood the vocabulary and syntax of the Irish passages.

How can one learn to read rapidly and with comprehension in a second language? The usual first answer is practice and, in order to be sure the student does practice, strong motivational devices. A second answer is to work through a carefully sequenced set of reading materials which incorporate research findings on first and second language reading. We will discuss sequence first and then look at suggestions for motivating extensive reading practice.

Sequence

Once the learner has acquired some way of dealing with the relationship between print and sound, s/he must work out some way of processing what s/he sees on the page. That "some way" is probably similar to what Goodman (1970), Hochberg (1970) and others have called the "psycholinguistic guessing game." As we read, our eyes do not sweep in a steady movement across the print. Rather, we move our eyes in jumps called eye fixation movements. We scan a line, fixate at a point to permit eye focus. We pick up graphic cues and make a guess, a prediction about what appears on the printed page. While the guess is partly based on graphic cues, it is also subject to our knowledge about the language and on what we have read up to that point. If the guess makes semantic and syntactic sense, we continue to read. If it does not—especially if it doesn't make semantic sense—we recheck and make an amended guess. Neisser (1967) has even suggested that at each focus point, the reader must be able to recognize which features seen in peripheral vision are uninformative in order to move efficiently to the next fixation point. This guessing process model assumes the reader

can identify important words in reading, and can make semantic predictions about their relationship to one another. It assumes s/he has acquired enough language to predict syntactic relationships and that somehow these two systems (semantic and syntactic) allow him or her to hold passage content in memory for further guesses.

Tullius (1971) suggested that one reason ESL students take longer to read a passage is that they make more eye fixations per line and they frequently regress to check back on information when they do not understand what they read. To test this, he conducted an eye movement study with university-level ESL students. He found, to his surprise, that they did neither. Instead, the difference in their eye movements compared to that of monolingual students was in the duration of each fixation. The duration was almost three times that of monolingual students. If we believe in the Goodman model, we could say foreign students take much longer to arrive at a guess about passage content. ESL students are obviously unable to make such predictions rapidly.

In fact, the second language learner is not able to predict at all in the beginning stage of reading with much accuracy. As s/he becomes more proficient in word recognition, s/he seems to use semantic cues to make his or her guesses. S/he seems much more skilled at making guesses using the semantic system. For many students, the syntactic system seems to be "noise" that gets in their way. Schlesinger, in a series of impressive studies (1968), found this to be true even for native speakers of English. That is, in reading very complex syntactic structures we use a lexical strategy to understand what we read rather than a syntactic one. For example, in the following sentence from Schlesinger's work—*This is the hole that the rat, which our cat, that the dog bit, made, caught.*—most people, reading such a sentence, would claim something made a hole, and it was probably the rat. If they used syntactic processing, they would discover they were wrong. The conclusion is that we can, and do, read without attending to the syntax when syntax becomes extremely complex. (This accounts for the lack of difference found in experiment after experiment where syntactic complexity is varied in an attempt to show that syntactic complexity equals reading difficulty.) If we can identify content words and if we use our knowledge of the real world, we can make fairly successful guesses about what we read without always paying attention to syntax.

We know that ESL students do this, at least those students at beginning levels. They may recognize words in sentences and try to figure out some logical connection between them. The sentence structure is probably ignored in many instances. Once the subject discovers that the first noun is usually the subject, s/he can make fairly accurate (if slow) predictions about the rest of the content words and their relationships to one another.

Macnamara (1966) worked out an ingenious way to get at the effect of syntax (as word order probabilities) on reading speed. Using Miller and Selfridge's approximation to English procedure (1950), he constructed passages which closely approximated English syntax (e.g., *road in the country was insane especially in dreary rooms where they have some books to buy for studying . . .*) and passages where word order was random (e.g., *road house reins women bought scream especially much said cake love that to school a they in is . . .*). He also prepared passages for Irish, the second language, in the same two orders of approximation to Irish. He hypothesized that students would read the close approximation to English rapidly since the passages would be somewhat predictable, and they would read the random order slowly. Second, students reading the approximations to Irish would show no speed difference for the two versions. That is, the syntax of any approximation to Irish—whether close or random—would be Greek to them. His predictions held. Students were not able to use their knowledge of Irish syntax for prediction in the same way that they used their knowledge of their first language.

Despite this finding, Macnamara attributes much more importance to word recognition problems than to lack of syntactic processing. Using the information from several experiments, he estimated that his Ss took 3.9000 sec. per 20 words longer to read in their second language than in their first. Of this, he claimed 1.799 seconds was due to articulation, .785 was due to syntax, and the remaining 1.316 secs. he attributed to word recognition and other factors. However, we have found that university ESL students are very good at word recognition tasks such as the following from Harris (1966): *sing/sink sins sang sing sign; cheese/crease choose chess cheats cheese,* where the student matches the test word with the identical word in the list. They are also good at word-pair tasks such as *poor day poor pay* S D; *new chair new chair* S D, where they must check the *S* if the pair members are identical and the *D* if they are different. Visual perception is obviously not a problem. Yet they do not excel when asked to find a synonym: *shut/watch close sleep need; speak/point talk hope see.* Nor are they able to perform a same-different task for synonyms: *stop go* S D; *speak talk* S D, with any speed. While word recognition is important, we should not waste time on visual perception since this is a skill students already possess at this level. While exercises on word meanings are helpful, it is more important to recognize words in context than in isolation. We should relax our emphasis on recognition of small units at some point and concentrate on the larger process.

In addition to the Macnamara study mentioned above, there is other evidence that ESL students are more puzzled than helped by syntactic clues as to the relationship between content words in reading passages. Using the Corcoran procedure (1966), we (Hatch, Polin and Part, 1974) approached the effect of syntax somewhat differently. If you turned to the beginning of this paper and crossed out as quickly as possible every letter *e* on the first page, you would miss a large number of *e*'s if you were a native speaker of English. We found that ESL university students were highly successful at the task, much more so than native speakers of English. Once we started looking at where letters went unnoticed for the two groups, an interesting pattern appeared. First, Anglos marked letters when they appeared in content words but not in function words. The ESL students marked them everywhere; they paid as much attention to letters in words which show grammatical relationships (prepositions, articles, conjunctions, etc.) as they did to letters in content words. Second, native speakers crossed out letters which appeared in strongly stressed syllables. That is, asked to cross out the letter *a*, they marked the first *a* but not the second in *vocabulary*; they marked the second but not the first in *apparently*. ESL students showed no pattern as to stressed or unstressed syllables. Since ESL students marked letters in function words, we might suppose that they were paying attention to grammatical relationships expressed by them. This, once we looked at their answers on comprehension questions, did not seem to be the case. Their answers were based, for the most part, on semantically-based interpretations which did not always turn out to be correct.

Perhaps a clearer example occurs in a study reported by Johnston (1972). In the pilot study for her project, Johnston found that university ESL students did not attend to graphic cues which signal stress and intonation information. This allowed them to misread sentences in a variety of ways. For example, after reading a sentence from a passage on the San Diego Zoo about Monkey Mesa and the Great Ape Grotto, students ignored the capital letters on *Great Ape Grotto* and changed *grotto* from a noun to a verb; they thought the great ape was grottoing (even though *grotto* was mentioned earlier in the passage as the place where apes live). Having read about the Children's Zoo where one can pet friendly little deer, camels, and backyard animals, they responded that you could pet dear little camels. They ignored periods, thus assigning time clauses from one sentence to another. They misinterpreted pronoun reference, word group boundaries and misread clause groups.

From these two studies it is clear that these students were not able to create a grammatical structure out of the series of images their eye fixations gave them. Some people would call this a problem of not "reading by structure." Amble and Muehl (1959) found that extensive practice in reading short phrases was a very effective way to give Anglo fifth-grade children help in learning to "read by structure." Plaister (1968) suggested

Illustration 6

Until about
four hundred years ago
nothing like
a modern microscope
existed.
Then
spectacle makers
in Holland
noticed that
when certain lenses
are used in pairs
at the right distance
apart
they magnify things.
The first man
to make
a powerful microscope
was a Dutchman
named Leeuwenhoek,
who was born
in 1632.
His instruments
could magnify things
to three hundred times
their actual size.

we also give ESL students practice in reading by phrases. His system required rewriting passages so that each column is one phrase wide. This doesn't mean that students read a column per eye fixation; instead it gives students information of what words should be grouped together. In a sense, it teaches the syntax of the passage. (See Illustration 6.)

Johnston suggested a variety of ways to help students with phrase reading. Some of these are similar to Plaister's. She also experimented with marking phrase boundaries with slashes and parentheses, and by using darker type for word groups that go together. (See Illustration 7.) Perhaps the most effective method for less proficient readers is total input. In this method, short passages are marked for phrase boundaries in one of the above ways. The student takes the written passage to the

Illustration 7   Phrase Reading Example

High above the zoo canyons/ a new aerial tramway/ the Skyfari whisks you/ on an exciting 5-minute ride/ over the grottos and mesas/

(Lions roam freely) (on the other side) (of good-sized moats) (and) (exotic birds) (fly free) (in a tropical rain forest). (You may see) (a guinea fowl)

Joshua Tree National Monument   covers more than 850 square miles   and is located   east of Palm Springs   about an hour's drive from Los Angeles.

Notice that the underlined syllables in this reading passage are the syllables that would be stressed, or read more strongly, if you were reading it outloud.

Illustration 8   Cloze Passages

Easy:

    There was a small _____ in Northern California yesterday. _____ shook buildings and broke _____ from Santa Rosa to San Rafael, _____ there wasn't any serious _____. No one was killed, but _____ woman was hurt when _____ boxes fell on her. _____ earthquake was very short. _____ man who lives in _____ area said, "I was _____ in the store when _____ felt the earth move. _____ started to go to _____ safe place, but it _____ over before I got _____."

Difficult:

    Studies made by physicians on _____ brains of multilingual _____ have shown that some _____ of the brain near _____ center of speech are _____ developed, the proterior portions _____ the second and third _____ convolutions acting as a _____ for their large vocabulary. _____ there are no centers _____ separate languages, there _____ a center of multilingualism _____ acts as a "switchboard." _____ center is near _____ speech center, near the _____ limit of the _____ Silvus and the _____ part of the parietal _____; the latter findings have _____ confirmed several times by _____ of aphasia in _____ subjects. The psychological law _____ aphasia in such subjects _____ formulated first by _____ and is still considered _____.

language lab and listens to a recording of a native speaker reading the passage as s/he reads the passage silently to him- or herself.

According to our current model of reading behavior, good readers are able to predict what they will read on the basis of their knowledge of English syntax and semantics. The closest practice to this kind of prediction is the use of cloze passages. The cloze technique is very simple. A reading passage is selected and every fifth or sixth word is omitted to force the student to make a prediction about what might be seen in the blank (see Illustration 8). These exercises should be sequenced from short to long passages and from high frequency structures to low probability sentences. The vocabulary should range from high association sets in beginning passages to low association probabilities in more advanced materials. There is a great deal of research in first language reading to support this sequence (Morton, 1964; Tulving and Gold, 1963; Samuels, 1968). The cloze

Illustration 9

Sometimes I Talk With Myself

The first day of school we went together to a bookstore in Harvard Square. We bought some books, French books, on the first day. I think it was Monday. I got a ticket on my car.

I feel now that my English isn't very good, but I feel it's better. My tutor, she's a nice girl. She goes with me to the O.I.C. to find out about jobs. We also went to the aquarium.

I want to speak English all the time, but I don't speak it all the time. It's not good for me. I finish school right now and I will go to my sister's. We talk French or Creole, you know, and I go to work after that at night.

I don't have anyone to talk to. Sometimes my Supervisor goes to visit my job. Sometimes he talks to me, sometimes not. He just passes by and looks. Sometimes I talk with myself and I listen to the radio. It's not good for me. I don't speak.

Maybe if I changed shifts to work in the morning. It would be good for me because on the day shift there are many people working together and we could talk. It would be very good.

procedure (a) forces the reader to be active and constructive; (b) requires guesses based on both semantic and syntactic clues of the language; (c) requires retention of content in order for the reader to continue guessing. Bloomer (1962) reported that the cloze technique improved reading comprehension in remedial college classes. Best (1971) found it improved reading comprehension in young children. In neither study was reading speed increased.

Cloze materials are easy to make yourself; the difficult part is selecting an appropriate reading passage. It takes some practice before students are able to do them easily. Preparatory exercises in the use of the cloze are available (cf. the Special Skills Series). These exercises, appropriate for beginners, consist of very short and interesting paragraphs with blanks for some of the words. Possibilities for the blanks are listed either at the end of each paragraph reading or at the bottom of the page. After using these short simple preparatory exercises, paragraphs with cloze procedure can be introduced. Controls can gradually be relaxed and at advanced levels materials from the newspaper or short articles from magazines can be used.

High interest level should be as important a criterion for passage selection as language complexity.

Motivation

The need for motivating students to read has led to the LEA approach (Language Experience Approach). In this approach, students write their own reading materials. First devised in San Diego as a way of turning students on to reading, the idea has spread to almost every school in the country. Students tape record a story that they want to share with the class. The teacher (or aide) types them up (usually in primary type). The student may illustrate his or her story. The stories are bound and covered with contact paper and a library card check-out pocket is glued inside the cover. Then, with the author's permission, the story becomes part of the reading collection for the class. This method has been popular with all age groups. (See adult example, Illustration 9.) The students share their ideas with each other as a class; they want to know each other and they want to read what each person has decided to share.

The teacher and/or aide must decide whether to correct language "errors" when s/he types the story. The notion is that it will be easier to read what has been actually said and that if drastic changes are made it may no longer be easy to read. Rudell (1965), for example, found that it is easier to read a selection that reflects one's own natural speech than it is to read a passage that does not correspond to one's own language. (For an extension of this concept to the language of testing, see Kennedy, 1973.) The LEA approach has led many teachers to produce their own class dialect readers. Other teachers, believing that one should not allow learners to see "mistakes," carefully correct all "errors" before giving the materials to students to read. In some adult classes (Taylor, 1971) teachers use the students' readers as a base for comparing standard English to dialect or interlanguage forms in the stories.

Extrinsic motivational devices—M and M's, "good work" stickers, poker chips, blue chip stamps—have also been found effective in motivating students to practice their reading skills but a discussion of their use is beyond the scope of this paper.

Reading machines can also be considered motivation devices. Students frequently are willing to read on a machine (especially if it includes a timed pacer) because they believe in the power of machinery. Some reading materials include tapes, film strips, a reading text and a workbook in conjunction with special machine programs. Again, there are no materials specifically for ESL students but many learning centers have adult basic reading programs which can be used. Some California adult schools are also using computer-assisted reading programs such as the CED program. The fun of having a computer talk to you by name and tell you how many comprehension questions you got right is irresistible to most ESL students. There are beginning reading programs and advanced literature programs available at present.

For many students, no motivational devices are necessary beyond the student's own evaluation that s/he is improving. In adult classes using the station approach, it is often difficult to pry students who are learning to read for the first time away from the reading center. In university classes, students who keep track of their reading speed and comprehension scores are highly motivated to continue making progress that they themselves can see. Reading is important to most students; the motivation is there.

CONCLUSION

Students have wide-ranging needs in reading skills. One might divide these needs into four stages: word reading, phrase and sentence reading, paragraph reading, and advanced reading. At each level, the teacher must have materials which will help rather than harm the student.

(a) At the word level, the teacher should choose a combination of linguistic, whole word, syllable and phonics methods, probably in that order. S/he should be prepared for problems with the phonics method, and spend additional time on sound-symbol correspondences which are difficult for his or her particular students. S/he should have a wide variety of reading games available, since they are not age-specific and add variety to reading practice. The words read should be important to the student. Adult students may want to learn animal words. The Language Master should be used as much as possible with ESL students.

(b) At the phrase and sentence level, the teacher should give students massive practice in phrase reading. The students should practice reading simple high-frequency sentence structures and high word-association bond vocabulary. Word reading should continue as well and heavy work on reading vocabulary should be stressed. The students should be given preparation for cloze passage reading.

(c) At the paragraph level, the teacher should continue word recognition, phrase- and sentence-reading exercises, and begin massive practice with cloze passages. Materials should be of high interest and sequenced for difficulty. The students should make a speed reading chart as a self-check on progress. They should also have a chance to practice reading paragraphs marked for phrase boundaries in a variety of ways. They should have the chance to hear what they are reading on tapes in the language laboratory. Students should be encouraged to begin reading short stories available in the ESL program. Depending on the students' ages, these might be Reading Attainment or SRA (Science Research Associates) materials. Students should also begin to write and share using the LEA approach to produce their own reading materials.

(d) At the fourth level, students should continue activities from all the previous stages and, in addition, be taught how to skim articles for information. The SQ3R study technique, which helps students retain information in textbooks, should be taught using texts that the students are reading for their classes whenever possible. A summary of the method can be found in Yorkey (1970a, p. 130). Short stories should be an important part of the reading program as well.

This chapter has outlined some of the processes for teaching one of the most important, and most neglected, language skills. I do not mean the guidelines listed above to be anything other than guidelines. Students have very different needs in the field of reading; different students respond to different techniques. The important thing is to be flexible in your approach, to try everything at least once, and hope that your students will find at least some of your techniques helpful. Certainly, more attention needs to be paid to the teaching of reading in ESL classes. Special materials to bridge the gap from beginning to advanced reading need to be developed. Reading is an important part of second language learning. As Murielle Saville-Troike said in her "State of the Art" speech at a TESOL conference in the early 1970s, it is time to put the "R" back into TESOL.

DISCUSSION QUESTIONS

1. The teacher of an adult class has labeled everything in the classroom with word cards. Is this a reading activity or vocabulary reinforcement? Would it be better to write a sentence label instead? Why, or why not?

2. The class is on a beginning lesson teaching: *in* the morning, *in* the afternoon, *at* night, *at* 8:00, *on* Monday, etc. The reading lesson is the TV guide. What kind of lesson plan could the teacher create? Would pronunciation and spelling also be included in such a lesson? (Assume the students are all from one language background, maybe Spanish.)

3. Under what circumstances would you consider using the ita system in an ESL class?

4. One ESL adult program uses this sequence. What are its strong and weak points?

Step 1: Introduce new vocabulary, give translations where possible.

Step 2: Students listen; teacher reads short reading passage.

Step 3: Students read the passage which is presented in phrase-wide columns.

Step 4: Teacher checks comprehension by asking questions.

Step 5: Students read sentences from the passage and mark them true or false.

Step 6: Students circle answers on multiple-choice questions from the passage.

Step 7: Students match fragments of sentences to form complete sentences. They copy these to form the passage anew.

Step 8: A sentence completion exercise (written or oral) from the passage.

Step 9: Cloze passage version of the story. Students write in missing words.

Step 10: Students write sentences given word cues (including the new vocabulary) from the story.

5. What advantages and disadvantages are there in using older people (say 6th grade students from the same language background, or parents) to help teach reading to second and third grade ESL students?

6. A reading workbook has the following kinds of exercises:

We went to the library *before the meeting.*
   (Italicized phrase printed in red.)
   why   who   how   when

Do you know your bike has *two flat tires*?
   who   what   where   why

I liked your story *because it was exciting.*
   how   why   where   what

What are such exercises for? At what level would they be appropriate?

7. Some people read "Dear Abby" every day, and it has been used in adult schools. Do you think the vocabulary/sentence structure/content make it appropriate reading for an ESL class? If so, what kinds of activities could be invented around such a column? Could you do the same thing with articles from *Psychology Today*, the campus newspaper, etc.?

8. Foreign students frequently spend time reading material which may be included in a course syllabus as "suggested reading." In a first language situation they might quickly skim an article and say "I've read all that before." In the second language situation they spend hours poring over old material. Do you think a course including skimming techniques would be sufficient to overcome this habit or are there other factors involved?

9. Would you ever have a class do choral reading (oral reading)? What would be your objectives if the answer is yes?

10. Would you consider teaching illiterate ESL students to read in their native language even though your class was an English class?

SUGGESTED ACTIVITIES

1. Prepare a set of Language Master cards for an adult ESL class using either (a) high-frequency word-association vocabulary, or (b) linguistic-method pattern sets. Add visual reinforcement where possible.

2. Prepare a set of slides to teach reading of signs (e.g., traffic, warning labels, shop signs) or simple instructions (e.g., laundromat, post office directions) for an adult class which is illiterate in the first language.

3. Using available materials, make a collection of timed word recognition exercises. Sequence them for difficulty.

4. If you have access to a class, try the LEA approach. Type up and distribute reading materials to the class. How much editing did you do?

5. Examine a simplified short story. Compare it with the original. What has been lost and gained? Is the sentence structure really simple?

Try simplifying part of one of your favorite short stories. How did you judge sentence simplicity and vocabulary frequency?

6. Go to the Reading Lab and try out some of the reading machines. Would you advise acquiring such machines if you were in charge of an ESL language lab?

7. Prepare cloze passages for beginning, intermediate, or advanced students. How long should each be? Which kinds of sentences and vocabulary are appropriate to each level?

8. Time your reading speed in your first language. Try to find a comparable passage in your second language. How much difference in reading speed did you find? If reading tests are available in both languages, check your comprehension as well. How much difference is there between your scores on each language?

9. Practice writing phrase exercises, one for each of three levels. What phrase types did you select? Was it easy to mark all phrase boundaries for the advanced level?

10. Survey ESL elementary schools in your area. What materials are· used? What basic method is reflected in the materials? Or, watch either Electric Company or Sesame Street on television. Are the reading activities graded? Would any be appropriate for your students?

SUGGESTIONS FOR FURTHER READING

Andrews, A. (1970)
The characteristics of efficient reading and implications for remedial reading techniques with foreign students. Unpublished M.A. TESL thesis, UCLA.
This is an excellent survey of research on the reading process. It also contains some suggestions on how research findings might be used in an ESL class.

Arthur, B. (1973)
Teaching English to speakers of English. New York: Harcourt, Brace Jovanovich, Chapter 3, 29-54.
This gives the reader a good background in three areas: the reading process, the strategies children use in reading, and the methods teachers use. While it is not directed toward ESL specifically, almost everything in this book has direct application to the ESL classroom. Look at some of the other chapters as well.

Cruz, Victor (1974)
Using Television to Teach Reading Skills to University-level EFL Students. Unpublished M.A. TESL thesis, UCLA.
An evaluation of the use of media in teaching advanced student reading skills. Like many teachers overseas, Cruz is faced with the problem of finding ways to work with classes of over 100 students, usually from the fields of science and engineering. This project should give the reader an idea of possible solutions to teaching reading in such situations.

Fisher, J. (1972)
Materials for developing the reading skills of junior high ESL students. Unpublished M.A. TESL thesis, UCLA.
An example of LEA in the ESL classroom.

Hamel, P. J. (1974)
English of Science and Technology. Unpublished M.A. TESL thesis, UCLA.

This evaluation of materials is concerned with texts which concentrate heavily on reading skills. A good bibliography of science reading materials.

McKinley, C. A. (1974)
A study of ESL reading difficulties. Unpublished M.A. TESL thesis, UCLA.
The literature review for this thesis discusses a number of studies in reading and how they relate to reading in a second language. The study itself looks at the effect of reading proficiency on academic success.

Yorkey, R. C. (1970a)
Study skills for students of English as a second language. New York: McGraw-Hill.
The chapters on reading and study skills give examples of various kinds of exercises that help to improve reading skills at the college level.

THE TEACHING OF INTERMEDIATE READING IN THE ESL CLASSROOM

William H. Gaskill

INTRODUCTION

Although much has been written about reading in a first or second language, most writers conclude that we really know very little about the reading process and perhaps less about what should be done in first or second language study to facilitate it. The following paper is intended to assist the ESL instructor in developing and teaching an intermediate level reading course. The comments made here are intended primarily for the high school and adult age student.

The discussion is plagued from the onset by the ambiguities of the term *intermediate*. In narrowing the frame of reference, I appeal to the reader's intuition by suggesting some characteristics of the intermediate student discussed here. The intermediate student has completed at least one basic course similar in content to a college level, first-year foreign language course in that s/he has, at least, been exposed to most of the basic grammar. S/he has learned to read in the second language, but probably has read only very short, simplified or graded selections. Although the student makes many mistakes and has real difficulty in participating in native English conversation, s/he is able to make him- or herself understood in the classroom. S/he is generally unable to consistently produce a well-organized English paragraph.

The major proposal here is not a new one but rather a reiteration and synthesis of ideas proposed by writers dealing with reading in the ESL context such as Norris (1970) and Chastain (1976), and ESL textbook writers such as Yorkey (1970a) and Harris (1966). This paper is influenced additionally by the author's experience gained at Damavand College in Tehran, Iran. There students participated in four hours of instruction per day, five days a week. Each day they spent one hour in a "reading lab" using SRA materials (Yorkey, 1970a), and one hour reading "literary texts" drawn from a wide variety of materials and selections, few of which were specially adapted for ESL.

Essentially, the proposal outlined in this paper concerns designing the intermediate ESL reading program so that there are two distinct components: (a) *reading skills*, directed toward the development and improvement of skills which are thought to aid in the reading process; and (b) *reading comprehension*, directed toward exposing students to a wide variety of reading selections and reading experiences in such a way as to foster independence in dealing with reading in the second language. Ideally, separate but closely coordinated class periods for each of these components would be established. Gradually, as goals are realized and students become more independent, the nature of the components may change. However, throughout most of the intermediate level, the idea in one component is to talk to students about skills which need to be developed, and to practice them; while in the other component the goal is to provide reading activities which attempt to parallel those that the student will one day pursue on his or her own.

LITERATURE RELEVANT TO INTERMEDIATE READING IN ESL

Before further delineating the nature of the components mentioned above, it may be helpful to briefly mention some of the activities which are thought to assist students in developing and improving reading skills. A number of the activities mentioned below have been discussed in the context of advanced reading in ESL, but it is felt that they are also appropriate for, or can be adapted for, intermediate ESL students.

Several writers recommend that ESL instructors repeatedly discuss with their students what they should do to become efficient readers (e.g., Chastain, ibid.; Plaister, 1968). Such discussions ought to focus on reading

skills which the instructor feels are most important for his or her class. Regardless of whether the skill be related to identifying main ideas, determining meaning from the context, or improving reading speed, students should be regularly reminded of the importance of the activity and why it is being practiced. Essentially this process amounts to a conscious attempt to establish good reading habits.

There is wide agreement that ESL students need to increase their vocabularies and to develop strategies for coping with unfamiliar words. The value of studying word derivations, cognates, and word formation has long been cited, along with the need for regular practice in determining lexical meaning from the context (e.g., Norris, Yorkey, and Chastain). Chastain also recommends practice in the use of bilingual and monolingual dictionaries.

Been (1975) encourages students to guess the meaning of unfamiliar words and to use contextual redundancies in determining lexical meaning; she reminds the instructor that to accomplish these goals students must feel free to guess, and that wrong guesses, as well as right ones, should be positively reinforced. In the initial phases of reading instruction, Been suggests the use of specially prepared reading selections with cues in boldface type which are intended to point out lexical and/or structural redundancies. With these selections Been attempts to lead students away from a word-by-word decoding process. In addition to providing practice in using contextual clues, the specially printed passages are used for a variety of other purposes, including reading for specific information, for main ideas, and for skimming. An example, modeled after Been's material, is presented here:

Assumptions:
Key words are familiar.
Aims:
To discourage linear reading and to encourage searching for specific information (i.e., to train the learner to ignore anything which is not directly relevant to the question).
Question:
First reading   What kind of store is described in this passage?

The aisles are wide and the store is very large. Canned goods, bottled goods, dry goods, and many other things fill the shelves along each aisle. Meat, fish, and dairy products are in the rear. On the right there are fresh fruits and vegetables, and on the left you'll see an area with breads, cakes, pies, and cookies. Large signs indicate the location of all of these items.

Question:
Second reading   Is it easy to find something you want in this store?

The aisles are wide and the store is very large. Canned goods, bottled goods, dry goods, and many other things fill the shelves along each aisle. Meat, fish, and dairy products are in the rear. On the right there are fresh fruits and vegetables, and on the left you'll see an area with breads, cakes, pies, and cookies. Large signs indicate the location of all of these items.

Based on her research in tutoring ESL students in reading and in using Goodman and Burke's (1972) reading miscue inventory, Stafford (1976) found intermediate ESL students especially in need of strategies to deal with unfamiliar vocabulary, as well as needing practice in syntax, and in reading for different purposes. Stafford recommends the use of Been's exercises and points out the usefulness of regular practice with cloze passages as a means of determining the student's ability to anticipate vocabulary and to demonstrate knowledge of structural relationships.

A number of writers on advanced reading in ESL have expressed the belief that syntax has been neglected and should play a more important role in advanced reading programs. Many of the exercises recommended for advanced students can also be practiced with intermediate students. Wilson (1973) believes that ESL students rely too much on lexical meaning and that a better understanding of syntax will yield more clues to the meaning of individual vocabulary items. She urges that students be encouraged to acquire a better passive understanding of such patterns as *there* + *be* + complement, the passive and relative clauses. Berman's (1975) recommendations for advanced students can also be modified for use with intermediate students. Her exercises selec-

tively require students to reduce complex sentences to simpler component sentences, to trace antecedents where relative clauses occur, and to explain what various connectors and punctuation marks signal. Pierce (1973) recommends talking to students about what she calls the "embedding game," which authors play as they attempt to fit a number of ideas into one sentence. To further student understanding of the embedding process, she gives them a number of related short sentences to combine for themselves.

Also writing for the advanced ESL reading instructor, Norris (1970) takes a more global stance and details a wide variety of activities designed to improve student performance in the following areas: (a) reading speed, (b) vocabulary comprehension, (c) sentence structure and comprehension, (d) paragraph structure and comprehension, and (e) comprehension of the whole reading selection. Most of his techniques and examples lend themselves to adaptation with intermediate students. To improve reading speed, Norris suggests word recognition exercises and reading by structures. As mentioned above, his vocabulary exercises include practice with word formation, with word derivation, and with contextual clues. For complex sentences, Norris recommends comprehension exercises involving short answer responses and/or fill-ins. He strongly recommends practice in identifying types of paragraph organization, in locating main ideas, and in scanning for specific information. Norris describes various types of comprehension questions which can be used to follow up reading selections; these range from simple *yes/no* questions to questions oriented toward inference and evaluation.

A TWO-COMPONENT APPROACH TO THE ESL INTERMEDIATE READING PROGRAM

Having considered activities which can be incorporated into ESL reading instruction at the intermediate level, let us return to the idea of two separate but closely coordinated components in the intermediate ESL reading program, those of reading skills and reading comprehension. While there is much to be said for the importance of specific activities and of combinations of activities, nothing takes the place of actual reading and exposure to a variety of reading selections. On the subject of reading comprehension, Chastain (1976, p. 313) reminds the instructor, "The teacher cannot play an active role while the students are practicing reading comprehension. If she does, reading becomes some other related activity." Thus, the recommendation here is that the reading skills component should provide students with an opportunity to practice activities which are believed to aid in the reading process; the reading comprehension component should provide students with opportunities to read in class the way we want them to read on their own—silently, efficiently, and for overall comprehension.

The reading skills component

At first, considering the variety of skills which could be included, the task of preparing a reading skills course seems overwhelming. Regardless of the exact format, the activities should be integrated, contextualized, and frequently recycled. Initially, the intermediate reading skills component will usually have to be carefully structured with the instructor playing a major role in introducing activities, discussing them with students, and guiding them in exercises. It is more likely, especially at lower intermediate levels, that students will need a lot of guidance; conceivably, however, with time, the reading skills classroom could take on the form of a reading laboratory or resource center where students could proceed at their own pace in areas where they need practice.

Reading for the main idea: Since the goal of the reading program should be getting students to read independently, efficiently, and for overall comprehension, the first step and perhaps a central part of the intermediate program should be reading paragraphs for the main idea. Such practice might logically include a discussion of the ways in which paragraphs are organized and of the concept of a topic sentence. The instructor should have a large collection of paragraphs, including many which are short and relatively simple, for the beginning stages of the intermediate program. Students may be asked to choose the main idea in

a multiple choice format or to state the main idea on their own. For most students, selecting the main idea is a difficult task and this is all the more reason for making it a regular part of the reading skills component. Introductory lessons in selecting the main idea might involve getting the class to come to a decision as a group or, alternatively, carrying out this task in smaller groups. A general policy should be established that words or structures will be discussed only after students have attempted to identify the main idea.

Such paragraphs can be provided on multiple copies, shown on the overhead projector, or shown with slides as Stevenson (1973) has described. In the early stages, techniques which direct students' attention to one copy projected on a screen may give the instructor more control in presenting specific techniques as well as in assessing the progress of individual students who might otherwise have their heads buried in the text or handout.

While there are a number of texts which provide exercises in determining the main idea of paragraphs, it is doubtful that a single text could provide enough exercises of this type. Therefore, it becomes necessary to resort to a variety of sources. Once they have been located or collected, such paragraphs can also be used for other purposes such as identifying topic sentences, outlining, scanning, and determining meaning from the context.

Vocabulary: Once students have identified the main idea of a paragraph, it is then appropriate to consider specific problems which caused difficulty. Vocabulary items will most likely be the largest source of difficulty. Here it is important to encourage students to use what they already know about the passage to help determine the meaning of unknown words. Concurrent discussion and practice in determining the meaning of words and structures from the context will be vital in encouraging students to be more self-reliant. The following example which is modeled on many similar exercises in Yorkey (ibid.) is one type of exercise which might be used to familiarize students with what is meant by deriving meaning from the context:

This psychologist's approach to research is *eclectic*. He has familiarized himself with all the currently relevant theories, and he is trying to develop a new model of animal behavior that will integrate the best features of other narrower models representing only one school of thought.

   a.   He creates something totally new.
   b.   He follows a fixed point of view.
   c.   He selects from many available sources.
   d.   He criticizes all other theories.

In such exercises, students should be asked to explain how they arrived at the correct answer, thereby possibly clarifying the process for others. Again, such exercises are seldom found in sufficient number; thus, it is necessary for the instructor to collect or generate examples for practice exercises. Also, when students ask for definitions of words in context, the instructor should encourage students to try to answer the question themselves by returning to the context. The problem is often one of persuading students to be content with a general idea instead of insisting on a precise definition. Patience and persistence are required on the part of the instructor in fostering student acquisition of more independent vocabulary comprehension strategies.

In addition to context clues, there should be other systematic approaches to vocabulary instruction integrated with the reading skills component. Emphasis is placed on the word *systematic*; students should feel that they are being given a fair opportunity to learn new words according to a plan. One strategy might include learning several prefixes, stems, and suffixes each week along with practice in attempting to decide what a word means using some knowledge of etymology. Students should also be given contextualized practice with word forms; Hirasawa and Markstein (1974) provide numerous exercises of this type:

to discriminate, discriminating, discriminatory, discrimination

   a.   The speaker was accused by many listeners in the audience of having made unfounded and . . . . . . remarks.
   b.   Give two women $50.00 each to buy a dress, and one of them will come back with a much nicer dress than the other because of more . . . . . . taste.
   c.   Employers doing business with the U.S. government may not . . . . . . on the basis of race, religion, sex or age when hiring employees.
   d.   Despite recent progress in the U.S. in the area of civil rights, many Americans still feel that they are experiencing subtle forms of . . . .

It may also be valuable to pursue another organized approach to vocabulary based on one of a variety of programmed materials which are available in book or kit form. Some of these are reading kits or "laboratories" which offer vocabulary practice integrated into the reading program, and others which offer separate practice in vocabulary.

Many instructors ask their students to learn vocabulary items which are found in their reading selections. This can be helpful if the number of words is held to a reasonable ten to twenty words per selection and if the list of words is accompanied with contextualized examples and practice. Preparing lists of vocabulary items and contextualized practice requires additional preparation on the part of the instructor. In addition to the initial decision of which items to include, one must also decide whether to indicate the part of speech, other related word forms, synonyms, antonyms, information on register, not to mention other meanings the word may have. Discussion of and practice with such lists takes a lot of class time.

Another technique which is helpful in dealing with unfamiliar vocabulary in a reading selection is to categorize items according to whether they (a) should be learned and incorporated into the students' active vocabulary, (b) should be learned as passive vocabulary, or (c) should be ignored because they are too specialized, too rare, or too difficult to be worthy of consideration at the particular level in question. Naturally such categorization is highly arbitrary and very much dependent on the level; a word which would fall in category two at the intermediate level might easily be placed in category one at the advanced level. Furthermore, such a system still requires that words in category one and two be further discussed and that students have an opportunity to practice category one words in other contextualized exercises. This system is very helpful in illustrating that some words are more important than others and in gradually helping students to be discriminating, given their concern about unfamiliar vocabulary.

Our discussion of choosing vocabulary items from reading selections points up a way in which the reading skills component can be used to support work being done in the comprehension component. Rather than take valuable time from the reading comprehension component, vocabulary from reading selections can be discussed and practiced in the reading skills component. If this is done, I recommend that vocabulary be discussed once the selection has been started or when it is finished rather than before students begin to read. Previewing vocabulary from reading selections seems counter to the goal of fostering self-reliance in the student.

Syntax: The reading skills component can also be used to reinforce and discuss specific syntactic structures which have caused difficulty in the reading comprehension component. In addition to treating structures which have caused problems, regular reading skills practice might also be provided in such areas as the use of connectives, adverbials, and other syntactic structures. Practice of the type discussed above (e.g., Wilson, Berman, Pierce, and Norris) can also be incorporated. For example, questions can be posed to check understanding of various types of phrases and clauses and how they relate to their respective sentences. In choosing reading materials, it is worthwhile to look for texts which index syntactic structures occurring in individual selections and which also provide supplementary practice in those structures.

Other activities: Although activities in the reading skills component will mainly consist of reading for the main idea, developing vocabulary strategies, and working with syntax, other reading-related activities can be pursued. Intermediate students can be introduced to various types of written organization such as that found in textbooks. Practice can be provided in the use of the table of contents, the index, charts, graphs, and footnotes. Discussion and practice of reading strategies can also be included in the reading skills component. In his article on advanced reading in this volume, Gorman discusses scanning, reading for the main idea, and study reading—all of which can be discussed and practiced at the intermediate level, too.

Some writers recommend that instructors preface individual reading selections by discuss-ing the general idea of the selection in addition to vocabulary and structures. I feel that it is important to have some foreknowledge of the reading selection, but I have found it more satisfactory to have students themselves do as much of the preparatory work as possible. To do this in the reading skills component I show students how to use a modified SQ3R[1] approach to scan a reading selection in order to get a general idea of what the selection is about before beginning the actual reading. In this procedure students are first asked to look at the title of the selection to see what information it conveys. Sometimes the title provides little information, but often it is quite revealing. Next, students are asked to silently read the first paragraph as quickly as possible without stopping to ponder words or structures which they do not understand; the goal is to get the main idea. Upon completion of the first paragraph, students should write down the main idea in as few words as possible. When it appears that all have read the first paragraph and jotted down the main idea, the main idea is discussed in class and then written on the board in as brief a form as possible. Then students are instructed to quickly read the first sentence of the second paragraph and restate the main idea of the sentence. This information is also written on the board in telegraphic fashion. This procedure of reading the first sentence of each paragraph is repeated until the end of the selection or far enough into the selection until students begin to get an idea of what the selection is about. Making brief notes on the chalkboard helps to keep in clear view the information that has been established. The scanning procedure detailed here is at first a slow and cumbersome process. The first few times it is practiced, the instructor should take students through the process step by step, making sure that all are reading in the same place. Initially, for many students the activity seems strange and foolish. Remind them that this activity is not an end in itself nor a substitute for reading the selection; rather it is a means of establishing a frame of reference and of making it easier to begin reading the selection. As a foreign language student, I often found my best intentions about reading an assignment thwarted before the end of the first page, largely because I had no idea where the selection was headed, and I got bogged down in the details and the unfamiliar vocabulary. After some practice with this scanning process, students should be asked to scan a selection on their own and report their findings. It should be pointed out to students that there is no one particular method of scanning. The first sentence in a paragraph is not always the topic sentence, and it may reveal little about the content of the paragraph. In a number of instances it will still be appropriate for the instructor to make introductory comments about a selection, especially regarding cultural information which may be crucial to understanding. The idea is again to encourage students to be as independent as possible in their approach to reading.

Once a general frame of reference has been established, students should return to the beginning of the reading selection and read it paragraph by paragraph. However, this reading will generally take place in the reading comprehension component. At the beginning of a course, and especially at the beginning of each selection, it is generally wise to proceed slowly, making sure that students focus first on the main idea of each paragraph. Students should be reminded not to worry about specific lexical items or other questions until they have first attempted to identify the main idea.

The reading comprehension component
Reading comprehension, the other component of the reading program discussed here, should focus on as much exposure to reading materials as time and individual student ability allow. The reading comprehension component should build on and reinforce the skills being concurrently developed and improved in the reading skills component. Like the reading skills component, reading comprehension will probably require more teacher guidance and assistance in the early intermediate levels, but in the upper intermediate levels, and wherever possible, students should be encouraged to work independently.

Intensive and extensive reading: In the reading comprehension component it is mean-ingful to follow the example of Norris and others who make a distinction between intensive and extensive reading. For our purposes, intensive reading consists of short reading selections which can be read and discussed in one class period. These intensive selections should provide students with practice in improving skills being developed in the reading skills component. Intensive readings, although shorter, can be somewhat more difficult so as to enable the student to encounter and solve problems while the instructor is present. Extensive reading assignments should generally involve longer selections which are read outside of class. It may be advisable to delay extensive reading until one is sure that students are grasping and employing concepts being presented and reinforced in both components of the reading course. Extensive assignments should be easier than intensive assignments to enable students to concentrate on main ideas and to build self-confidence.

Reading materials: Even if there were a wide variety of really excellent reading materials, it is hard to imagine choosing any one text or set of materials which would be truly responsive to the heterogeneity of backgrounds, reading abilities, interests, and personal objectives found in most intermediate ESL reading classes. Selections should be chosen with regard for the interests of the individuals in the class. At the beginning of a course, the instructor should try to assess the students' interests as well as their objectives in terms of the kinds of reading they will need to do in the future. Although it is unlikely that all selections will be met with the same degree of enthusiasm by each student, the use of many short selections on a variety of topics should tend to reduce the chances of boredom. Throughout most of the intermediate level, particularly in the case of intensive reading, brevity should be a prime consideration. Often adult ESL students are unable to attend every class meeting and they should not be penalized or frustrated by reading selections which are drawn out over several class periods.

In the earliest stages of intermediate reading, selections that are one or two paragraphs long may be best suited to the students' abilities and to the time allotted. Such selections may be specially prepared for ESL students or they may be carefully chosen from other sources. The occasional use of carefully chosen selections from newspapers and magazines often increases interest and builds confidence. Extensive reading may vary in the early stages of intermediate reading from ESL textbook selections to graded readers and in later stages from carefully chosen short stories and articles to short novels. It is appropriate to add a word about flexibility. Inevitably, there are intermediate students whose abilities either exceed or fall behind those of the majority. The instructor should be prepared for such instances and provide alternative reading assignments rather than insisting that all students adhere to the same program.

The instructor's attitude is very important. All reading assignments should be presented positively and with enthusiasm. Students should feel that the instructor has selected readings with their interests and capabilities in mind as well as concern for their overall improvement. Integrating a variety of selections from different sources should further convince students that the instructor is making a special effort to make reading both interesting and enjoyable.

Procedures for intensive reading: As mentioned earlier, reading selections for either intensive or extensive reading can be previewed in the reading skills component. The following suggestions are offered to describe how intensive reading might be carried out in class. Students should be instructed to read a paragraph silently and as quickly as possible. The instructor should point out that it may be necessary to read a paragraph several times to get the main idea. There should be a general rule that lexical and syntactic difficulties will only be discussed after students have attempted to identify the main idea. Depending on the selection, after students have identified the main idea, it may be best to first ask some comprehension questions before turning to specific problems regarding vocabulary and structure. Having established the main idea and possibly other points of reference, students should be encouraged to exploit this informa-

tion in attempting to figure out the meaning of unfamiliar words. When the discussion turns to specific lexical problems, strategies fostering independence should be encouraged. Students should be discouraged from blurting out definitions of words which are unfamiliar to others. Contextual redundancies should always be examined first and students should be encouraged to guess. Again, Been's advice regarding classroom atmosphere is well taken: students must feel free to indicate what they do not understand, and they should feel that it is "safe" to make incorrect guesses.

As soon as questions have been answered, students should proceed to the next paragraph, read silently, select the main idea, and attempt to solve any problems they have on their own. The instructor is reminded that the reading comprehension component should focus on reading. If a particular passage or selection requires extensive discussion, it may be too difficult, and it should perhaps be presented and discussed again in the reading skills section.

It is recommended that once the instructor feels that the class is making progress with a given selection, students should be allowed to work independently or in groups. In groups, students can silently read either a paragraph at a time or a section including several paragraphs and then discuss the main ideas and any problems they encountered. On some occasions it may be advantageous to assign people to groups such that stronger students work with weaker students. When students work alone or in groups on the same selection, it is usually wise to reserve the last part of the class period to go over the main ideas and to resolve any problems which may have arisen. Comprehension questions can also be posed and again it is wise to follow the advice of Norris and Been in posing a variety of questions which not only ask for information but also encourage students to express their opinions of the selection.

Procedures for extensive reading: Once the instructor begins to feel certain that students have a grasp of reading for the main idea, of using context clues, and of developing a sense of confidence and self-reliance, it is time to make extensive or outside reading assignments. These selections should be previewed before students are sent out to complete an assignment, and students should feel convinced that they not only know something about the assignment but that they can complete it. Study questions can be provided initially to help focus attention on main ideas. As time goes on, students might be asked to list the main ideas themselves. Care should be taken in making the assignment long enough to discourage translating or looking up all the words in a dictionary but not so long as to seem impossible. Chastain (1976) emphasizes the importance of being consistent in follow-up activities. He suggests providing a time when students can ask precise questions citing exact page and line references. He believes that activities should be planned which require student preparation and that the instructor should not compromise these assignments by reading or discussing the assignment in class, thus enabling some students to get by without working. Chastain also reminds the instructor not to lose sight of the goal of reading for overall comprehension by asking questions which are too precise or which make students feel that they should have looked up more words in the dictionary.

Thus the reading comprehension component has the double goal of giving students as many opportunities to read as possible and of encouraging students to read as independently as they can. These goals are facilitated through the use of carefully chosen intensive and extensive reading assignments and by encouraging students to employ the skills they have been practicing in the reading skills component.

ADDITIONAL ASPECTS OF INTERMEDIATE READING

There are many aspects of intermediate reading which have not been discussed here. Among these are speed reading, cultural issues, and testing.

Speed reading: With regard to speed reading, I respect Norris who feels that emphasis should be placed on "efficient reading" rather than on speed reading. However, as Norris maintains, students should be encouraged to try to improve their reading rate. Timed reading exercises may be helpful in improving reading speed and efficiency. However, speed reading should not have high priority at the intermediate level.

Cultural issues: While it is generally impossible to find reading materials which are not in some way culture-bound, I believe there are enough skills and problems to be dealt with at the intermediate level that materials should be selected which require minimal cultural explanation. Working in Iran, Stevenson (1973) found that materials which are based on the student's own cultural experience or which are less culture-bound allow him or her greater flexibility in focusing on the development of reading skills.

Testing: Nothing has been said here about testing or evaluation in reading. First, I personally am reluctant to assign grades to such an important skill while it is in its developmental stages. I want to encourage the student and consciously refrain from any activity which might interfere with his or her progress. Second, due to the heterogeneous nature of most intermediate classes, I find traditional grades meaningless. Ideally, I favor the use of self-paced materials in both components of the reading program (see "Suggestions for Further Reading"). Such materials allow the student to chart his or her own performance in areas such as reading rate, reading level, comprehension, and vocabulary. If grades must be given, I would base them on performance in certain discrete skills such as learning vocabulary, finding the main idea, and general participation in the reading program. As suggested earlier, I favor viewing the reading program as a kind of workshop where students can pursue activities according to their needs. The practice activities they pursue should reflect the goals of the program.

CONCLUSION

The major implications here are perhaps addressed as much to the curriculum planner and materials writer as to the ESL instructor. But it often happens that the ESL instructor is engaged in all three activities. Our field is greatly in need of materials which are designed to teach and review reading skills and which at the same time provide a variety of short reading selections. The heterogeneous nature of our business, our students, and their needs makes the creation of such materials extremely difficult if they are to be used by a wide audience. The answer probably lies in programmed, self-paced materials which integrate and recycle reading skills and vocabulary, and which include a large variety of graded reading selections on a wide range of topics.

Those responsible for curriculum design in ESL programs at all levels of reading instruction should be sensitive to the needs of the student. An hour of reading instruction per class meeting day is not enough. The reading program should consist of a closely coordinated program of reading skills and of actual reading. It is ideal if the teacher of one component also teaches the other component, so that continuity is maintained and teacher expectancies are consistent with student preparation. If the two components cannot be taught by the same instructor, then either the two instructors need to coordinate their activities closely or a syllabus needs to be designed and followed which will ensure continuity in the reading program.

NOTE

1. Survey, Question, Read, Recite and Review: cf. Robinson (1946), as reviewed in Yorkey (1970a), p. 130.

DISCUSSION QUESTIONS

1. What do you believe to be the single most difficult aspect of teaching intermediate reading in ESL? Explain why and propose ways of handling the difficulty.

2. Based on the activities proposed under the reading skills component, can such topics as reading for the main idea, syntax, vocabulary, and study skills be ranked in terms of their importance? Give reasons for your opinion.

3. There are opinions about whether vocabulary items should be introduced before the reading selection or not. Explain and justify your opinion on this matter.

4. Briefly characterize what is meant by *intensive* and *extensive* reading. Are these distinctions meaningful? How do these terms relate to the reading skills and reading comprehension components?

5. Due to a variety of factors, many ESL programs do not offer the kind of reading curriculum the author recommends. Given the following weekly time constraints, how would you teach ESL reading at the intermediate level? (a) one hour a day; (b) one hour a day, three days a week; (c) one hundred-minute class period, two days a week.

SUGGESTED ACTIVITIES

1. Be on the alert for short, interesting, and well-written paragraphs. File them according to difficulty, and according to their best possible use in class, e.g., reading for the main idea, outlining, contextual clues, or as a supplement or complement to another reading selection. Encourage colleagues to do the same and make a practice of sharing materials which have proved effective for specific purposes.

2. Make a list of interesting and relatively easy reading selections which the average intermediate ESL student could read outside of class. Note whether the selection is related to other lessons and activities. Again, encourage colleagues to do the same and share your materials and your reactions to these materials.

3. Along with your colleagues, take a reading selection two or three pages in length and individually select twenty-five words which are likely to cause difficulty for a hypothetical intermediate ESL reading class. Categorize the items under the following headings: (a) should be learned and incorporated into the students' active vocabulary; (b) should be learned as passive vocabulary; (c) should be ignored because the item is too specialized, too rare, or too difficult to be worthy of discussion at this level. Then formulate an efficient teaching strategy for the words in category one which will take a minimum of class time. Compare and discuss your choices with your colleagues and react to one another's teaching strategies.

4. Outline your own approach to teaching intermediate reading in ESL and discuss your ideas with others who are interested. In addition to clarifying your philosophy on teaching reading, such an outline may help you in formulating your own lesson plans.

SUGGESTIONS FOR FURTHER READING

Binner, V. O. (1966)
American Folktales I: a structured reader. New York: Thomas Y. Crowell (see also *American Folktales II* and *International Folktales I* and *II*).

These ESL texts provide a wide variety of short reading selections, each focusing on specific grammatical structures and accompanied by grammar exercises. Sections on vocabulary and idioms are also included, but they are less well integrated and lack contextualization. These materials could be used in the reading comprehension component of an intermediate ESL reading class for either intensive or extensive reading.

Dimensions: countries and cultures
Chicago: Science Research Associates, 1970 (see also other SRA materials including *Multi-Read 2: a multi-level reading kit*).

Typical of many of the SRA materials, this is a self-paced programmed set of reading materials ranging from reading level 4.5 to 9.5. The selections range in length from 500 words at the lowest level to 1,250 at the highest. The kit is distinguished by the international flavor of the reading selections. The selections correspond to skill cards which are suitable for discussion and composition.

Reading attainment system (sets 1 and 2)
New York: Grolier Educational Corp., 1974 and 1970. These sets of self-paced, programmed reading materials consists of six levels each. They are intended for remedial use at the junior and senior high school and adult levels. The sets include reading selections with comprehension questions and corresponding skill cards which cover such areas as antonyms, synonyms, prefixes, suffixes, punctuation, and alphabetization.

The reading practice program: a self-paced program for reading skill improvement
New York: Center for Curriculum Design, Harcourt, Brace and Jovanovich, 1973.

This self-paced, programmed set of materials might be appropriate for some aspects of a reading skills program. It is designed to offer remedial practice in decoding, word study, and sentence patterns for upper elementary and junior high school students. Especially relevant are units 5-8 on vocabulary study and units 9-13 involving sentence patterns and comprehension. The materials are not contextualized.

Yorkey, R. C. (1970a)
Study skills for students of English as a second language. New York: Mc-Graw Hill.

This ESL text offers many valuable exercises which are suitable for the reading skills component of intermediate and advanced ESL reading programs. The chapters entitled "Vocabulary" and "Improving Your Reading" are especially valuable and many of the exercises can serve as models for follow-up exercises which the instructor may wish to develop.

TEACHING READING AT THE ADVANCED LEVEL

Thomas P. Gorman

PROBLEMS ENCOUNTERED BY THE ADVANCED READER

For many advanced students of English as a second or foreign language, reading English is both the primary means by which they become acquainted with the content of the subject area they are studying and the most important way in which they continue to develop their knowledge of the language itself. It will be apparent that the needs of students in Iran or Chile, for example, who may be required to read specialized literature of a technical nature in English, are very different from those of foreign students in the United States or the United Kingdom all of whose instruction is in English; but in their reading tasks they are likely to share a number of problems and, initially, there is some point in attempting to review what these might be.

Numerous commentators have attempted to delineate the problem areas in relation to the reading needs of university students. Many of them have drawn attention to problems that supposedly result from syntactic complexity encountered in writing (Eskey, 1971; Wilson, 1973; Pierce, 1973). Other scholars have discussed problems due to a lack of extensive vocabulary or a range of terminology specific to a specialized field of study; and there have been several attempts to detail syntactic and lexical features that are characteristic of registers associated with particular subject areas (Cowan, 1974). Increasingly, in the last decade, attention has been given to features of discourse structure and in particular to features of paragraph organization that might present students with problems of interpretation in particular content areas (Lackstrom et al., 1970). Problems of interference from a first language or dialect at a phonological, syntactic, and semantic level have frequently been referred to, but relatively little basic research has been focused on these matters in their relation to reading (see Hatch, 1975, with regard to the possible effects of phonological interference in the process of initial reading). Much has also been written about the difficulties that arise from the interpretation of content that is unfamiliar for cultural or other reasons, particularly with respect to works of a literary nature. Finally, many commentators have remarked on differences between native and non-native readers with regard to rates of reading and flexibility in adjusting rates to different purposes and materials (McKillop, 1966; Langmuir, 1967; Unoh, 1968; Macmillan, 1968; Gorman, 1968). The latter problems are generally considered ancillary to those mentioned earlier, as are "problems" supposedly related to subvocalization. Langmuir and others have also drawn attention to other "attendant problems of the reading handicap" consequent upon "the gap between student reading ability and the difficulty level of textbooks." These problems are said to include reduced learning due to anxiety and frustration, and the development of rote memory rather than the development of genuine understanding (Lee and Bowers, 1967).

A number of investigators have supported their observations regarding student reading difficulties in a second or foreign language with self reports from students relating to what they consider to be their major reading problems (Yorio, 1971). In 1974 questionnaires relating to these issues were administered to advanced ESL students at UCLA. They were asked to indicate what they considered to be their major reading problems in tasks relating to academic work. Sixty-eight percent attributed their major difficulty to what they considered to be deficiencies in vocabulary; nineteen percent to complexities of syntax; six percent to problems relating to pronunciation, and seven percent to problems related to rate of reading. In terms of "attendant" difficulties, sixty percent reported difficulty in completing parts of required textbooks, and forty percent reported difficulty in completing assigned reading (McKinley, 1974). A similar investigation was undertaken in the following year by a different researcher, and the general range of problems as interpreted by the students themselves was remarkably similar (Walsleben, 1975).[1]

Before taking up further discussion of the teaching of reading, I would like to comment briefly on the outline of reading problems itemized so far. Since many commentators have identified what might be termed syntactical complexity as a central area of difficulty it might be appropriate to focus initially on this issue. Most commentators who have discussed the question have, in practice, tended to ignore or underplay the difficulties involved in delineating the relations between the semantic and syntactic components of a grammar. The matter has generally been discussed in terms of a limited number of features of surface structure which are said to cause difficulties of interpretation.[2] However, there is some evidence to indicate that syntactic complexity at the level of surface structures is unlikely to be the primary cause of our students' difficulties. The work of Schlesinger (1958) provides one indication as to why this might be the case (cf. Hatch's discussion in this volume). McKinley (ibid.) found that syntactical complexity did not appear to be a significant variable in his study of variables adversely affecting his class of advanced ESL students on a standardized test of reading. There is then some preliminary evidence that, as students become more proficient in a second language, problems caused specifically by syntactical variation become less significant. However, exposure to exercises intended to increase students' familiarity with specific syntactic features that are recurrent in the prose they are likely to read may be helpful, particularly when a systematic attempt has been made to identify such recurrent features.

In view of the emphasis that students themselves tend to lay on problems that ensue from what they interpret as vocabulary deficiency, it might be argued that emphasis should be given in advanced programs to exercises that develop vocabulary; but again there are certain qualifications that need to be made in this connection. First, it is generally impossible to ensure that students have been presented in advance with lexical items they are likely to encounter in advanced texts (Twaddell, 1973). Moreover, any vocabulary extension program should not leave the student with the idea that it is essential for him or her to understand the meaning of every individual word in isolation before reading a text for meaning. Furthermore, as a general procedure new items should be presented in an appropriate context, so that in practice it is not usually feasible to isolate the learning of vocabulary from the comprehension of subject matter generally. It is the practice in many programs to provide students with information regarding such features as prefixes and derivation, or suffixes, or root words in languages such as Latin, in the hope that such procedures will facilitate the comprehension of words derived from these languages. There is, however, no conclusive evidence that a knowledge of such interesting etymological details will in itself aid the student in developing an extensive vocabulary in English, but such exercises may be useful, and it has been plausibly argued that they are of direct assistance to students in certain specialized areas such as medicine.

READING SPEED AND FLEXIBILITY

Reading speed, however determined, is generally regarded as a symptom rather than as a cause of other reading problems but the issue is more complex than this. To indicate why this is the case it will be necessary to refer briefly to some characteristics of the reading process as this is currently interpreted by a number of research workers.

Goodman (1967) has popularized the view of reading as a "psycholinguistic guessing game." While this designation is undoubtedly a misleading simplification,[3] it is evident, as Goodman argues, that fluent reading is dependent to a considerable degree on the reader's ability to exploit redundancies in the text to reduce uncertainty. By using his or her knowledge of the graphemic, morphophonemic, syntactic, and semantic rules, the reader samples the text and meaning and interprets it in the light of this contextual-pragmatic knowledge of the situation, the function of the text, and intentions of the writer (Goodman, ibid.). Because many readers of English as a foreign language lack the awareness of transitional probabilities possessed by native speakers, there is some evidence that they tend to concentrate attention on each word serially and, in a few cases, to consistently reinforce their impressions by sounding out words as they read.

Smith (1971) argues convincingly that any attempt to identify individual letters while reading for words, or to identify words when the aim is comprehension, must inevitably result in delay and disruption of both identification processes. Smith recognizes that there will be times when all readers find it necessary to focus on letters or individual words but maintains that the decoding a skilled reader performs does not consistently involve operations of this nature. He further suggests that it is necessary to distinguish between what he terms "immediate meaning identification," in which the reader moves from feature identification to comprehension of meaning, and "mediated meaning identification," which refers to a more laborious process where the reader moves from feature to letter to word identification and eventually to meaning. Finally, he suggests that fluent reading insofar as this involves immediate meaning identification cannot be done efficiently at less than 200 words a minute (and optimally at a rate of 500 words a minute, i.e., two word identifications in every fixation at a rate of four fixations a second).

It would, of course, be wrong to deduce from these observations that the fast reader is necessarily an efficient reader or the slow reader an inefficient one. Nevertheless there is independent evidence available that students who are obliged to read more slowly than they customarily do make significantly more errors in comprehension than if the rate is increased (Buswell, 1957). Macnamara's (undated) studies of English-speaking children reading in a second language (i.e., Irish) have also yielded information relevant to this particular issue. He found differences between reading in the native language and reading in the second language in the rate at which individual words were interpreted, and in the ability of the students to anticipate the sequence of words—the total effort of such differences being that the students read more slowly in Irish than English. Macnamara then went on to ask, "What does it matter if a man reads French a little more slowly than he reads English or whatever the pair of languages may be?" He answered the question by suggesting that there is an optimal rate at which any particular person can digest comfortably what s/he reads. He recognized that the rate would vary from person to person and according to the nature of the materials read and the constraints placed on the reader.[4] He surmised that if a reader reads too quickly s/he may miss some relevant points of information; if s/he reads too slowly and does not employ extra time for processing the information, some relevant points may slip his or her mind. Macnamara concludes that the slower rate in which a weaker language is read does not allow the reader the time required for thinking about what s/he has read as the extra time is fully employed on the task of decoding the language. Consequently some important points may be ignored and the reader may have added difficulty in determining what is important, since to do so presupposes some idea of the problem as a whole (cf. also Kellaghan and Macnamara, 1967).

The above comments could be interpreted to support the suggestion that reading improvement courses for non-native speakers of English might include a speed reading component, but it has frequently been argued that speed in reading should not be emphasized at all until basic comprehension skills have been adequately developed (Smith and Dechant, 1961; Harris, 1961). This cannot be taken as axiomatic. It seems to be apparent that students at all levels of attainment could be appropriately encouraged to read materials quickly in carrying out certain tasks such as finding the answer to a specific question of a factual nature contained in a newspaper or an article.

It has been also taken as axiomatic by many who teach speakers of English as a second language that it is necessary for students to obtain prior skills in oral expression and listening comprehension if reading is to be efficient, and it is widely accepted that initial reading activity should be postponed until the material to be read is orally controlled (Thonis, 1970). There are a number of reasons why such an approach is appropriate in circumstances in which students are learning to read initially in a second language. It cannot, however, be assumed that this approach would necessarily be applicable in situations in which the students were already literate in their first language; and it is possible to envisage circumstances in which, for example, university students were being taught to read specialized texts in science and technology, in which it would be inappropriate to require higher oral mastery of the material being read. The view that such mastery is essential in all circumstances tends to be supported by those who accept a model of the reading process that postulates that readers go from print to meaning, as it were, by way of speech; that is, that the seen word is converted to the heard word, or some representation of it, and the reading process is then carried on by whatever mechanisms are used to process speech.

I have already given some indications as to why I consider this interpretation of the reading process to be inadequate to account for some facets of fluent reading. Bower (1970) has suggested additional cogent reasons why such an interpretation of the reading process is generally unacceptable. Bever and Bower (1970) have argued that reading can and should be taught as a visual skill, so that readers are able to analyze written sentences without auditory mediation. They also argue that visual readers comprehend faster and better than non-visual readers, though experimental evidence to support this hypothesis is needed. There is, however, considerable empirical evidence that readers can learn to read a language efficiently which they do not articulate with any degree of proficiency; and this is to be expected as it is apparent that "encoding and decoding a language are not symmetrical operations" (Kolers, 1966). Conversely, there are large numbers of students who are good "decoders" in the sense that they pronounce written materials accurately, but who are inefficient readers in the sense that they do not comprehend what is read.

Finally, in discussing questions relating to rates of reading, it might be appropriate to refer to the numerous reading improvement projects that have involved the use of mechanical devices such as the tachistoscope to bring about changes in oculomotor skills, such as an alteration of apprehension span or duration of fixation.[5] Other instruments such as reading accelerators, shadowscopes, and pacers have been used to compel students to read faster. Reading films, such as those developed by Perry and Whitlock and their collaborators at Harvard, and Gorman were intended to be used for both purposes (Perry and Whitlock, 1957; Gorman, 1965). The value of such instruments, if any, is primarily motivational. They have a secondary value in that they serve to prevent habitual perceptual motor behavior which in some cases may be retarding the development of new reading habits. Such effects can, however, be obtained equally effectively through the use of timed reading passages (Tinker, 1965).

It is, of course, sensible to maintain a considerable degree of skepticism with regard to the claims made by those involved in reading improvement courses, particularly if there is an element of commercialism involved. Nevertheless there is abundant objective evidence that both with native speakers and speakers of English as a second or foreign language it is possible for a marked increase in reading rate to be achieved over a period of time and in certain tasks without a significant loss of comprehen-

sion. Numerous studies have also shown that while a decline in rate may be anticipated after such a course there is a degree of retention of gain in reading rate in the majority of cases (Ray, 1964; Wright, 1968; Cosper and Kephart, 1955; Dumler, 1958; Staton, 1950).

This lengthy commentary on issues related to rates of reading should not be interpreted as suggesting that rate of reading should be valued as an end in itself. The concern should be with rate of comprehension, i.e., the optimal rate at which students can fulfill the purposes for which they are reading a particular passage. What is to be aimed at is reading flexibility—a term that refers to "a characteristic possessed by the mature efficient reader which enables him to adjust or vary his rate of reading in order to deal effectively with different reading situations" (Braam, 1963). Flexibility should not, however, be regarded as a characteristic simply related to reading rate, as is generally the case (Laycock, 1958; Bowman, 1966). Efficient readers exhibit flexibility of attentional strategies in reading for different types of information, and these strategies can vary according to characteristics of the text (Rothkopf, 1972), the familiarity of content, their personal interests, and the instructions given them regarding the kind of information they should derive from the passage being read. Flexibility might appropriately be defined, therefore, as a characteristic that enables the reader to adjust his or her attentional strategies and rate of reading according to the materials being read and the purposes for which they are being read.

READING COMPREHENSION

Perhaps this issue can be best discussed initially in terms of a number of subskills that research has indicated may be considered independent components activated in the process of understanding a text. Spearritt (1972), for example, has suggested that such components include recalling word meanings, drawing inferences from the context, recognizing the writer's purpose, tone and mood, and following the structure of a passage—that is, recognizing salient features of paragraph organization. Davis

(1968) also reports evidence that such skills additionally include finding the answers to specific questions, selecting relevant information, and disregarding irrelevant data. On the basis of his own research, Thorndike (1971) informally summarized certain significant processes associated with comprehension and his comments are frequently cited: "Understanding a paragraph is like solving a problem in mathematics. It consists in selecting the right elements of the situation, putting them together in the right relations, and also with the right amount of weight or influence or force for each. The mind is assailed as it were, by every word in the paragraph. It must select, repress, soften, emphasize, correlate and organize, all under the influence of the right mental set of purpose or demand."

What we may infer from this is that purposeful reading entails the selection and interpretation of facts significant in terms of the reader's aims. For reasons hinted at in Macnamara's comments cited above, it seems likely that students reading in a language other than their first might experience a degree of difficulty in isolating such facts. There is, in fact, abundant evidence that university students reading a second language do encounter such difficulties. McKinley, for example, found that a considerable proportion of the students he studied had difficulty in identifying the central issue or theme of a passage presented in a standardized test and in distinguishing significant detail and irrelevant issues. He also found that, if students were asked to draw inferences from the information provided, they frequently found this difficult, whereas, if asked to locate specific items of information they tended to do this accurately but slowly. Such difficulties are not of course confined to non-native readers.

For students engaged in academic work there are also a considerable number of specialized reading skills that may have to be specifically practiced, e.g., locating information in source books; using dictionaries or encyclopedias; and interpreting charts, maps, and tables. For such students, a whole set of ancillary study skills may need to be developed with regard to the subject area studied with reading as a central component.

SOME PRACTICAL SUGGESTIONS

After this outline of some of the issues that need to be taken into account in a discussion of reading in a second language, it might be appropriate to outline some practical suggestions deriving from the writer's experience in developing reading courses of limited duration for university students in Africa and the United States. In each case the primary objective of the courses was that of providing an opportunity for advanced ESL students to develop for themselves learning strategies that would enable them to extract information from unsimplified texts in accordance with the purposes for which the text was being read.[6] The task of the instructor was conceived as being that of motivating the students to read, providing the opportunity and materials for them to do so, and providing appropriate feedback and encouragement.

The framework of the course developed consisted of ten sections each of which contained a number of reading passages relating to a single theme of contemporary interest. Each passage of expository prose was accompanied by a glossary of less common terms which students were advised to refer to, if they found it necessary, in extracting such information from the passage as they required. The sets of passages in each section comprised four relatively short passages that required what I termed "Directed Reading," in which the students were asked to find the answer to an explicit question given in advance. Two further passages in each section required "Exploratory Reading," where students were asked to identify the propositional core or main idea of the passage and to ignore secondary details; and, finally, each section concluded with a passage in which students were involved in what I term "Study Reading," on conclusion of which they were asked to make deductions from the information given and to relate information given in the passage to information given earlier in the section.[7] They were instructed to read the study passages carefully and asked to make inferences about the writer's intentions and attitudes and to detect bias and illogicality, to guess or project the meaning of individual words or phrases using the information available in the text, and to detect specific cases of ambiguity at sentence level and above.

Since at the University of California the reading course was one component in a more general course in English as a second language, the passages were followed by a series of supplemental sections involving (a) analysis and discussion of the text, which ultimately involved the requirement that students come to a conclusion about the truth or falsity of arguments advanced in passages discussed. Such discussion also had the aim of drawing students' attention to the logical and rhetorical structure of the passage as a whole; (b) listening comprehension exercises, including a passage of dictation related thematically to the rest of the section; (c) a series of written exercises that required students to paraphrase or summarize information provided in the text and to present in writing their own views on the topic under consideration; (d) supplementary exercises relating to study skills involving reading and writing. The reading component therefore provided the core element in a more general course for advanced ESL students.

A later version of the course incorporated a form of cloze exercise in each supplementary section. The general purpose of these exercises was to encourage students to recall omitted elements that contributed directly to textual "cohesion," in the sense that this term is used by Halliday (Halliday and Hasan, 1976).[8] To take account of individual interests and to provide additional practice in reading, such a course should be supplemented by thematically related materials that can be read by students outside class periods. If possible, such materials should be drawn from a wider range of genres than the course materials proper. Numerous commentators have suggested methods of organizing such extensive reading (e.g., Carroll, 1967), and the only suggestions I have to make in this connection are that the exercise should be voluntary; that students who read the supplementary materials should have the opportunity of discussing these individually or in groups; and that participants in the course should be invited to add to the collection of materials—and to propose for addition—passages or books that they have themselves found enlightening and entertaining.

NOTES

1. The following profile of a particular student might be taken in some respects as typical of this particular group. "Miss X is a First-Year Japanese student majoring in economics. She reads and speaks English 'very well.' She considers that she reads English better than she speaks it or writes it. She has considerable difficulty in completing assigned reading though she reads an average of 4½ hours a day, and she considers the reason for this difficulty to be 'because I don't have much vocabulary.' In one respect she differs from the majority of her colleagues. Since coming to the University she has read one book *not* associated with the subject area of her studies."

2. Such additional studies as I am aware of that have concerned themselves with difficulties of interpretation of native speakers in which the researchers have attempted to distinguish in a principled way between syntactic and semantic properties of sentences have tended to yield inconclusive results—which is to be expected in the present state of knowledge regarding lexical, syntactic and semantic processing (cf. for example, Forster and Olbrei, 1974).

3. I agree with Gough that "the good reader need not guess; the bad should not" (Gough, 1972).

4. The idea of an optimal rate comes from the fact that human nature places certain constraints on all human performances, among them the span of short-term memory. This span is not more than a few seconds and can embrace no more than about eight or nine separate units. Macnamara suggests that if a person is to function within these constraints and solve a particular problem s/he has to reduce the total information in the material read to manageable proportions and hold it in his or her short-term memory.

5. Problems involved in processing meaning are reflected to a degree in the students' eye movements. In scanning lines efficient readers tend to regress to the left approximately once every two lines; non-native readers tend to regress more frequently. In the scanning process native speakers tend to focus or fixate about six times in each line and each fixation lasts about 250 milliseconds. The duration of fixation of non-native speakers tends to be longer, possibly because they tend to require significantly more time than natives for the short term memory processing being enacted during a fixation (Andrews, 1970; Tullius, 1971). It has also been frequently maintained that the apprehension span (the amount seen at each individual fixation) of non-native speakers tends to be more restricted than that of fluent native speakers.

6.   It has been frequently suggested that simplified materials should be used in reading exercises provided for students at intermediate and advanced level (Eskey, 1973); and in the course prepared at the University of Nairobi passages were graded according to a number of criteria including the Farr-Jenkins-Patterson Adaptation of the Flesch reading ease formula. However, our research indicated that there was no significant correlation between the difficulty level of the passage, so measured, and students' scores on questions relating to the content of the passage. However, there was a significant correlation between these scores and the type of question asked, e.g., whether these were questions requiring students to draw inferences from what had been read or to locate special items of information, etc. (McKinley, 1974). In the revision of the course, attention was therefore focused on establishing and controlling question difficulty primarily through successive item analyses.

7.   The mean length of Directed Reading Passages was approximately 250 words; and that of Exploratory Reading and Study Reading passages 430 and 850 words respectively. The Study passages were untimed; students were asked to take note of the time taken to read the four Directed and two Exploratory Reading passages.

8.   Such elements include referents of anaphoric and cataphoric devices and other elements contributing to lexical cohesion and conjunction. The emphasis was laid on this last category and, in particular, on devices for expressing logical relations between sentences. In focusing on such features I was influenced by suggestions made by Freeman and McDonough (1975).

DISCUSSION QUESTIONS

1.   Discuss the validity of the writer's suggestion that syntactic complexity at the level of surface structure is unlikely to be the primary cause of students' difficulties of interpretation in most cases.

2.   In your own experience, what are the major cases of such difficulty?

3.   What is the nature of the distinction that Smith makes between immediate meaning identification and mediated meaning identification?

4.   The writer rejects an interpretation of the reading process that suggests that "the seen word is converted to the heard word, or some representation of it, and the reading process is then carried on by whatever mechanisms are used to process speech." What arguments can you suggest that would seem either to support or reject this interpretation?

5.   What do you understand by the term "reading flexibility"?

SUGGESTED ACTIVITIES

1.   Taking into account the comments of Davis (1968) and Spearritt (1972) regarding subskills related to reading comprehension, suggest additional types of exercises that might be devised to practice these.

2.   Invite a group of students to submit suggestions regarding reading materials that they think would be generally enjoyed by other students in the group. Attempt to establish whether the materials suggested have any common characteristics with regard to such factors as theme, length, or difficulty level. In the light of your discussion attempt a definition of the term "readability" with respect to these materials and to your students.

SUGGESTIONS FOR FURTHER READING

Gibson, E. G., and H. Levin (1975)
The Psychology of Reading, M.I.T. Press.
This book comprises a survey of research on reading and an interpretation of it from the point of view of two psychologists. It is an essential reference work.

Smith, F. (1971)
Understanding Reading, A Psycholinguistic Analysis of Reading and Learning to Read. Holt, Rinehart and Winston.
This is an original and very readable contribution to the theory of reading.

Gunderson, D. V. (1970)
Language and Reading, An Interdisciplinary Approach, Center for Applied Linguistics.
This is a useful anthology including important articles by Wiener and Cromer, Goodman, Carroll and others, together with useful practical papers by Shuy and Reed. (Note: Reed's discussion of the so-called "linguistic readers" betrays a somewhat odd interpretation of how reading courses might be organized "from the point of view of linguistics.")

Levin, H., and G. P. Williams (1970)
Basic Studies on Reading, Basic Books, Inc.
This is another excellent anthology with useful articles by Chomsky, Venezky, Bower, Bever, and Brown among others.

Kavanagh, G. F., and I. G. Mattingly (1972)
Language by Ear and Eye, M.I.T. Press.
Most of the contributions in this text are again by psychologists. The articles by Gough and Mattingly are of particular interest.

Melnik, A., and T. G. Merrit (1972)
Reading Today and Tomorrow. University of London Press Ltd., and Open University Press.
A useful and inexpensive anthology of twenty-two articles on the nature of reading and the teaching of reading.

THE TEACHING OF LITERATURE IN ADVANCED ESL CLASSES

John Povey

Editor's note: Before reading this chapter it would be helpful to familiarize yourself with Robert Frost's poem "Mending Wall" and Willa Cather's short story "The Sculptor's Funeral." Both selections are included in English For Today, *Vol. 6, New York: McGraw-Hill (several editions have appeared since 1964).*

INTRODUCTION

The desirability and need for literature in advanced ESL classes appears obvious. There is a significant distinction between the primary elements of language; listening and speaking, and the secondary skills; reading and writing. Most crucially, foreign students differ from native speaking children with whom they are often identified, because they have already accomplished the second stage in their own language. It seems safe enough to assert that English literature would make a valuable transitional material. Literature gives evidence of the widest variety of syntax, the richest variations of vocabulary discrimination. It provides examples of the language employed at its most effective, subtle, and suggestive. As literature sets out the potential of the English language it serves as encouragement, guide, target to the presently limited linguistic achievement of the foreign student.

Yet some theoretical and practical complications have developed when literature has been introduced into ESL and its basically utilitarian activities. This dilemma has made the arguments on both sides specious and contradictory, even when honestly and sincerely advanced. Does ESL provide the need for dividing language and literature—tool from target? Literature has traditionally been defended on firmer ground than its linguistic practicality. For those who want to acquire English for writing reports or attending business conferences, it is likely that literature will not be particularly useful. More accurately, for these limited purposes many other things will do as much with far fewer additional problems. Accept that fact and then the task can be defended on surer grounds as simply the teaching of literature—for its own qualities, with all the desirable corollaries of that decision.

The natural enough question has been "how to *use* literature in ESL classes?" This establishes that literature has regularly been considered a means and not an end. The difficulties deriving from this attitude are as much philosophical as methodological. Unfortunately, the sequence in the discussion has not always been maintained in that order. Frustrating arguments about methodology exasperate primarily because they are not associated with any defined intention that could establish the needs that the methodology should deliver. If we can confirm the aim of our introducing literature into our classes then the most effective approaches will become substantially evident. Technique cannot survive in the abstract. It is efficient only when it is applied to some certain target.

Teachers of literature, albeit and significantly teachers of literature to foreign students, share a single concern. The important distinction that the additional phrase supplies rests largely in the priorities rather than direction that it establishes. It does not mean that one ceases to be a teacher of language—in TESL that obligation is never terminated—but that one ceases setting literature primarily at the mercy of language teaching in a way that largely destroys the educational values of both. Seek a story through which to teach vocabulary, and one teaches a story with the students learning only vocabulary. When one reverses this sequence, the aim of the vocabulary exercises and explanations become the comprehension of the story. This is both the justification and the solution of the methodological problem. There is no artificial non-functional learning. Overall motives fall into the pattern of literature teaching in all its educational fulfillment. The story selected is then good not because it includes certain words which the teacher for some reason has deemed to be significant, but because it touches on questions of deep human concern, perhaps deriving specific response from being set deeply into the American social and cultural context. Its discussion requires individual self-examination and classroom interaction. Such things are highly dependent on vocabulary and are stimulating in the search for self-expression. Thus new vocabulary is initiated by the need to communicate the new discovery induced by the literature and is not merely memorized from the piece itself.

One teaches literature because one believes the activity valuable in itself, and any other advantage to be derived from that occupation is a by-product. One assumes that regardless of their linguistic capacity the students have the maturity and awareness to share the concerns of the author, subject to sensible selection of material. There will be limitations of both language and cultural knowledge but these can be substantially eliminated by sensible teaching methods.

THE COURSE

There can be little justification for presenting a foreign student with a historical overview of American or British literature: more particularly since our spatial view of history will require us to begin at the beginning; that is at the most linguistically and culturally difficult part. A policy of selecting for interest and availability in class allows us to have a completely free hand to choose materials for their educational efficacy in a manner that might in other circumstances be considered merely arbitrary and random. We need works of literature that produce the best responses in class. Some teachers may feel that several pieces concerned with a single topic allow valuable cross-comparisons. Others may feel that selection might best be a sequence of plot incidents that deal with childhood, maturity, and age. Others may determine to find both poetry and prose that focus on the same attitude. It is perfectly possible to justify a variety of principles of selection.

No matter what the choice, the intention must be to accomplish a very close and accurate examination and interpretation of the work. That is why it is important to select a subject that is assumed to be of interest from the first. If further defense were needed of this random method of designing a curriculum like a string of beads—each beautiful but unrelated—one might point out that it can be happily sustained by the presently most accepted contemporary view of literary criticism. The so-called New Criticism insists that a work of literature be examined as a work of art in itself and not through the distorting observations relating to its historical significance nor through the personal biography of its writer. The principles of reading with close attention which are going to be advanced in the discussion of classroom methodology—the close and precise examination of language and its connotative and semantic force—is then, not only a technique that happens to be ideal for second language learners, but is at the same time in keeping with the principles of modern literary scholarship which are increasingly accepted in the regular classrooms of English literature. The technique is found to be most appropriate for opening up to students the skill and subtlety of the work of writing that they are immediately encountering on the page. In this mode foreign students are quantitatively different in their skills but not qualitatively different in the intellectual and social experience they bring to bear upon their studies.

There appear to be too many variables for one to advance a simple list of recommended books to a teacher. This is why the eternal plaint of "What shall I teach on Monday?" is unanswerable. A "good" piece is one that a teacher enjoys teaching and that will "work" in the classroom. One teacher told me of her success in using nursery rhymes with Puerto Rican children. I pointed out all the difficulties she must have encountered: the complicated syntax, the extraordinary situations, the bizarre vocabulary. She answered, "Yes, but I enjoy them so and the students keep asking for more." If teachers do enjoy a story or a poem it is probable that the students will too; such is the elation of interesting classes. Unless one gets into the unhappy though simple situation of receiving a formal booklist of texts required, which will call forth all one's pedagogic stamina and discipline, the free choice can be one's own subject only to some general recommendations.

First, it is probably best to use American literature and that of the twentieth century. If that seems obvious to the point of truism, even here many have discovered that the most unexpected and improbable texts are enthusiastically received because of some fancied association with students' experience. Some classics need not be dismissed out of hand, although others, perhaps *The Scarlet Letter* for example, deemed a masterpiece by critics, can be a disaster of bored miscomprehension. There is no reason not to experiment. After all, some societies in which a teacher might be working may be a lot closer to Elizabethan England, nineteenth century America or even Classical Greece than present-day California or New York! However twentieth century American writing can be most simply and readily defended. It is set in the culture with which the teacher is most familiar. It records elements in the target culture to which the students' language learning is directing them. It is also probable that, properly selected, the style represents excellent examples of efficient and emulable contemporary prose. The language will then make a good pattern for writing. Modern drama may be closer to the language of colloquial modern speech which may reinforce the oral learning with the written.

I am not yet convinced that there is any ready, mechanical way to measure the simplicity of a piece of literature. Until we know more about linguistic complexity in literature, I recommend that apparently casual but actually rather efficient measure that derives from a teacher's opinion of what would or ought to work. This is probably about the most accurate measure we have even though it is an emotive and private judgment. A list of successes and disasters from experience rapidly establishes a book list of titles that serve the needs. Probably in the final analysis every teacher must, and does, develop his or her own anthology.

POETRY

Ironically, often one of the most difficult things about teaching poetry to foreign students is handling the teacher's own deeply wrought unhappiness with verse, the result of experiences he or she has suffered. Many high school poetry courses can be credited with the achievement of spoiling for life any true enjoyment of poetry by requiring of the student false and unconvincing exhibitions of appreciation. It may be of some surprise, it is certainly of great comfort, to know that foreign students actively enjoy poetry. There does not have to be that introductory series of apologetic explanations as to why they should (all expectations and evidence to the contrary) find it interesting, with which one begins classes in poetry for American teen-agers.

No doubt many hints about poetry, its choice and presentation, could be given, but the various possibilities are all subsumed in two vital concepts of teaching poetry. The first is an interest in its subject matter—theme—thought. Second, and more significant, it is crucial to convey the counter concept that this theme is not detachable from, but is created precisely by the words employed; in technical terms: form and content are inseparable. Diction, an awareness and recognition of words and their multi-level semantic function, are all-important in the appreciation of poetry.

For foreign students there will invariably be the need for special attention to unexpected language and cultural complexities; the presentation will only need to be a more careful, detailed, and explicit version of those same devices used to elucidate poetry with native speakers. The approach does not entail that we invent either new targets or new techniques to guide, only that we employ the most effective ones with more charitable consideration and care and that we check the state and degree of understanding more carefully and repeatedly. We cannot expect those leaps of recognition that come out of the immense unacknowledged but extensive mine of cultural and linguistic passive recognition inbred in the native speaker.

In making a selection of poetry a teacher should not be unduly frightened by what might appear to be a difficult poem. No one wants to make the class a period of dismayed incomprehension to any student, but sometimes wrestling with somewhat complicated syntax necessitates that a student read with careful comprehension and attention to detail, which is exactly the technique one wishes to instill. Reading, close, detailed, precise reading is the vital core of interpreting poetry. It is certainly a most desirable linguistic discipline for the foreign student. Without wanting to make the task appear too much like completing a jigsaw puzzle, there is an agreeable sense of solution in gradually assembling the concepts out of the syntax of a poem. The discovery that superficial reading is only adequate for very superficial writing is important, especially when linked to the discovery that poetry requires every bit of one's capacity, both linguistic and emotional, for its appreciation. This is a thought to be balanced against the more obvious idea that the simpler the better is a good motto for the

selection of verse. Sometimes, in fact, a piece of poetry proves to be so simple that a teacher can have the helpless feeling that it does not provide much to teach. After two readings it becomes empty of interest.

There is the odd fact that one urgently advises contemporary prose as being most desirable for foreign students since it is natural and colloquial. By contrast, poetry, in general, has not become progressively more intelligible. Much contemporary poetry with its convoluted structure and highly esoteric metaphors can be more difficult than traditional verse, for all its apparent artificiality of fancy rhyme schemes and meter. I have had some good classroom experiences with such Victorian poems as Shelley's "Ozymandias" or Browning's "My Last Duchess," where the narrative element gives a connecting thread that aids understanding.

No matter the choice, the procedures are the same. There are two crucial aspects of language usage which must be understood before it is possible to begin to appreciate poetry—or teach it. A teacher may decide whether it is better to generate these poetic usages for the first time from a particular poem being treated in class or to attempt a separate lesson on poetic techniques. I prefer the latter in spite of all the usual warnings about giving information without context. I realize the danger of making dull theoretical lessons on very abstract issues not related to the need to interpret an actual poem. But to counter this view there is an obvious advantage in this preference. Anything that can be done "up front," as it were, clears a bit of ground prior to the introduction of a poem which it is hoped will be greeted with enjoyment and not made the subject of a series of disturbing tangential activities. Also, by selecting examples from a wide variety of several poetic works one can find examples that most specifically and effectively represent the form of poetic language that one wishes to demonstrate.

Two key elements regularly anticipated in introductions to teaching verse are *rhyme* and *rhythm*. These trappings are probably not of high consequence but they cannot be ignored. This is not at all due to their true importance but because foreign students, like many Americans, have already been so thoroughly indoctrinated with the belief that poetry in English is defined by its regularity of rhythm and rhyme that they will feel unhappy if this element is not discussed. Avoidance may provide the suspicion that the omission of this topic is explained by ignorance as much as by deliberate intellectual decision. It will be necessary to get all this stuff out of the way in order to eliminate the false expectations of poetry and poetic form which so preclude an open and intelligent assessment of the really important qualities of poetry.

Offer this technical information fairly quickly. Indicate that it is of passing interest only. Putting in rhyme schemes of the *abba* variety teaches nothing except observation and is precisely the kind of busy work that has spoiled poetry for many. However, one cannot avoid some explanation. Indicate what constitutes rhyme in English, i.e., a pair of words of similar sound differing only in their initial consonant. *Cat* and *bat* rhyme but not *cat* and *cab* nor *cap* and *cape*, and, in spite of the eye's counterevidence, *cuff* and *enough* constitute true rhymes. One can also mention other less specific assonanatal sounds of near but not perfect rhyme. Long lessons on, say, alliteration serve little purpose until they can be demonstrated as occurring in a specific poem and only then when their significant addition to meaning can be stressed rather than the mere peculiarity of the existence of the device. Similarly one might want to point out what an iamb is. It may even prove to be a good opportunity to reinforce the nature of English as a stress-timed language and indicate the inevitable predominance of the iambic light-heavy stress in English even in prose. But to get lost in maze-like detours of discovering anapests and spondees, etc., is probably unhelpful for anything but the most mechanical of delights. The consequences of the common use of iambics, however, does help to explain the manner in which poetry, although formally rhythmic, can sound so relatively natural and colloquial. Some lines of Shakespeare's most powerful verse have an easy, casual, air although the lines, in fact, could be scanned precisely. For this reason some appreciation of the underlying rhyme

scheme is one thing; marking in stress patterns, except for some immediate and justifiable purpose, is a waste of energy.

The first crucial topic in teaching poetry is the concept of the distinction between connotative and denotative elements of word meaning. The second is the use of the poetic image, essential to English poetry: the metaphor or simile. Connotation is not a difficult concept to understand but it is essential to articulate because it is a distinction thoughtlessly taken for granted. Words are not neutral. In the great aphorism of Aldous Huxley, "Any act can be made to appear saintly or disgusting if we clothe it in the appropriate words." One should give examples of how many words can mean approximately the same thing but carry overtones of attitude. Make a list of words that mean a place to live in: *house, home, shack, mansion, abode, cottage*, for example, and discuss the variations in meaning. In this task one is perhaps only teaching word discrimination and pointing out the limitations of synonyms rather than true connotation. Indicate how apparently functional, even scientific, words can have such overtones. *Blood*, for example, may be shown to encompass several symbolic reactions. In the case of ESL work, it is important to recognize that these attendant overtones may often be culturally tied to the British or American environment. A word like *mother* means denotatively a female who has bred. Obviously the word will precipitate a variety of reactions based on the personal and national experiences of the reader. Some terms have most curious associations. In America *apple pie* is not merely the alternative fruit composition to peach pie but includes home, motherhood and the flag! When a poet draws upon these associations there are particular difficulties for the foreign student. Consider "September Song" or some such association of mood with seasons. Recognize how inextricably its associations are tied to the Northern Hemisphere and its attendant seasons that could well be unfamiliar to all students from the tropics. At a deeper level, consider all the complex associations to be derived from Cleopatra's casual remark about her "salad days." As an exercise write on the board random words—

earth, tree, bread, fence, etc. See if you can elicit student reactions. Some of them may not be the least close to those expected from one's own cultural standpoint.

The second significant poetic device is the comparison, or poetic image. The analogy is at the heart of English poetry and perhaps most others (I detect it in translations of Zulu poems and in the subtle associations of Japanese Haiku). Again the teacher's job is likely to be alerting students rather than informing. The device is not so complex. Touch briefly on the underlying concept: similes move from the known to the unknown. A writer shares his or her private knowledge. (See how abstract definitions make the obvious complicated!) "He swims like a fish," assumes that one does not know how "he" swims but does know how a fish does. (Notice that the device operates if the writer can assume this joint knowledge; a fish comparison is meaningless in a fishless cultural environment.) By weighing one's knowledge, one is by comparison able to share the original observation. It is also obvious that at the same time one eliminates the many irrelevancies contained in such a comparison where only certain aspects of the items are compared and the differences are ignored. (The man presumably has no scales nor gills, etc.) Beginning with these simplicities one can go on to show how "My love is like a red, red rose" works; or, more subtly still, one can elucidate the meaning of John Donne's most famous simile of lovers as "twin compasses," one of the richest observations in English poetry.

When the presentation of these devices is behind one, then comes a poem. Since it is clear that I assume that one reads poetry for its emotional, intellectual, and sensual impact, it is essential that one devises a methodology of presentation that will allow the verse to be *enjoyed.* The word may shock in its enthusiasm, but what other justification can one decently have! My recommended methodology aims at one thing alone—pre-preparation to the degree that permits a first reading to have some measure of pleasure, which presupposes, naturally, some degree of initial comprehension. The teacher should review the poem and select the words likely to be new and difficult. These

should be divided into three categories for explication:

a.   New words that will have future use. These need some work, even drilling for use and comprehension.

b.   New words that are unlikely to be subsequently useful but which are essential to this particular poem. These can be explained without excessive general comment.

c.   Words that happen to appear in this verse but are going to be of minimal utility either in the poem or subsequently. As far as students will permit, these words may be ignored completely. Unfortunately there are always some fanatics who feel obligated to learn everything. For these method (b) avails.

With these divisions set up, a teacher can rehearse some of the likely problems and thus prepare the student to recognize and understand (or comfortably ignore) the vocabulary to be encountered.

At this point the poem should be presented. Now it will not be in a void of linguistic ignorance but with the students alert at least to vocabulary. Probably the best way to begin is with an oral reading by the teacher, as this supplies certain evidence of tone and meaning through the oral interpretation. This may subsequently be followed by another reading that is accompanied by the students reading along silently in their texts. In this manner they reinforce their ears with the vision of the written word and develop reading as well as aural skills. Perhaps some time should then be allowed for silent reading. Group reading is always tempting and some teachers handle this impressively. I admit with chagrin that my own experiences have been unhappy in this regard. A teacher should at least be aware that choral reading, even of the simplest poem, is a strangely complicated skill. It requires substantial rehearsal and can result in something of a muddle and a general embarrassment.

With the overall impression of the poem established, it is necessary to work through it at the very factual level. The first stage requires examination almost line by line to elucidate actual functional meaning. After this one begins to ask questions relating to the language usage and the basic imagery of the poem. With functional meaning now confirmed, it is time to press the discussion to a higher level of debate and draw out concepts of thought and the thematic content of the poem. It is at this stage that the true effect of the verse can be perceived.

To be specific, let us assume the students are of mixed cultural backgrounds, are adult in their age and intellectual development, and are competent at an advanced ESL level in their linguistic preparation.

A sample lesson

I suggest that an appropriate poem for an early class might be Robert Frost's "Mending Wall." Frost is one of the most famous American poets abroad, and it is probable that the students will have heard of him. There are some cultural difficulties deriving from his extreme localism, his total involvement with the New England landscape. On the linguistic level his words, like those of Hemingway, have at least a surface simplicity that assists initial student comprehension of his lines. (As in Hemingway, this simplicity is a highly sophisticated and subtle stylistic device. By no means is simplicity simple. At an introductory level one may not have to plunge in so deeply that one has to encounter the complicated issues that derive from this paradox.)

The theme of this poem is a good one for classroom discussion as it deals with the curious determination of men to build walls, and wall themselves off from others in an offensive-defensive gesture of misapplied independence. Frost suggests that there is "something" in the universe that opposes this very human characteristic. That idea of "wall" transposed to the more common concept of frontier is a provocative and important idea to argue with one's class.

At the purely technical level, I like the fact that this poem has a narrative chronological structure. This gives a peg of literalism to its organization that aids the students' initial understanding and makes a ready beginning for the first level of comprehension. The "story" of

this verse can be visualized before it is necessary that the student be made aware of the sophisticated and subtle levels of the symbolic interpretations.

One should begin, as I have suggested, with the immediate difficulties to be found in the vocabulary. The obvious words that would need pre-selection and definition are *boulders*, which is important, and *yelping, cone,* and *notion,* which all need some elucidation. *Spell* and *loaves* (there are few round ones these days) need glossing in the particular sense in which they are used here. *Elves* needs a comment, although it is important to realize that it isn't really a question of drawing some cute little big-eared Disney caricature so much as introducing the idea of the visible manifestation of those strange, non-human, inexplicable forces in the folklore of all countries. Some are beneficent and attractive, others hostile. This is important when it comes to Frost's investigation of what that "something" in the universe really is that deplores walls. The teacher at least has to bear in mind the tone. *Elves* are personified as rather quaint, charming, and harmless. They, therefore, make an unthreatening and safe manner of speaking of the unknown forces of the world. Yet, as Frost says, *But it's not elves exactly.* He has something much more serious than mischievous pixies in mind, though he will not name it.

There are a few oddities of syntax, though none, I think, formidable. Frost plays tricks with the phrase/clause position for emphasis. But rearrangement into conventional order, if necessary, is easy and immediately clarifies the statement. The position of *something* in the opening line is a case in point. Later there is: *The gaps I mean No one has seen them made,* where *them* has to substitute for the irregular placement of the opening noun phrase. There is also a minor irregularity of usage (important to the meaning) in the unexpected verbs of *He is all pine and I am apple.*

The title displays the eccentricity of avoiding the article. This will probably pass unnoticed by Asiatic students, but it has a semantic force that is developed throughout the poem. It suggests the generality rather than specificity of the activity that Frost is discussing and that is precisely what develops the incident from fact-event to symbol. I am never sure how much in the way of audiovisuals will help comprehension but perhaps a teacher will want to describe the stone boulder walls that divide the New England farms. The context of the lines supplies the essential information.

Begin by reading the poem through at least twice. Read aloud slowly, preferably after some private rehearsal so that the poem has some impact. Reading aloud is not an instinctive skill, so it requires practice for familiarity. The poem has a deliberately conversational force, and yet it is careful and contrived poetry, too. There is only minimal rhyme but there is a very regular ten-syllable measure that makes for an iambic pentameter blank verse form, yet those light/heavy stresses do not intrude emphatically into the rhythm of the spoken verse.

At the beginning avoid the debate on that "something." It is confusing to begin with a pronominal form that obviously has no immediate explanatory antecedent. But this unresolved query in the mind is precisely the idea that Frost is intending. The resolution of who or what that "something" is becomes the entire subject of this verse. Begin rather by testing comprehension at the purely factual level. What is it that can be seen to break down a wall? There are natural forces: *frozen ground swells*—a concept that may mean little to those from the tropics. There is the wanton destruction by hunters. (What are the hunters using to hunt? What are they hunting? etc.) Again do not try to press a conclusion of the conundrum at this stage. The teacher must be aware of how the poet dismisses these known damages and talks of *the gaps I mean* as being other than those explicably caused. What is their characteristic? How does one distinguish known from unknown causes? Only the bewildering, mysterious fact that *No one has seen them made or heard them made.* To return to the narrative of the poem; confronted by these gaps in his walls, what does he do? He calls on his neighbor and they walk the dividing lines together, roughing their hands putting back on the piles the stones that frost, hunting, and "something" have deranged. They walk along repairing. Notice that later you will want to stress the symbolic

fact that *we* keep the wall between *us.* At this stage the simple "where" questions are adequate. What grows on each side of this wall? Pine trees and apple trees? What does the neighbor say about the advantages of walls? *Good fences make good neighbors.* This is probably an old country saying. Like many pithy proverbs retained deep in folk wisdom, it may need questioning. Would it be a good idea to have walls if there were cows? This type of question, although somewhat speculative, continues to establish the informational level of description.

The second level of speculation concerning the information is particularly rich in this poem. Why does the poet feel that a wall is not necessary? Why does the neighbor say more than once his confident phrase *Good fences make good neighbors*? Is it true? Does saying it more than once lend it strength or doubt? Is the repetition deliberate or unthinking? Why does Frost suggest it is a *Spring* mischief that makes him want to ask why? Perhaps one will have to get to the questions of the nature of spring and the effects it is supposed to have on people. The links between seasons and mood may be very unfamiliar to those not aware of this symbolic seasonal response.

The ordering of the discussion of this poem is important. I would argue that it might be desirable to postpone questions of that "something" still further. After all, its solution by suggestion of its meaning is the final resolution of the poem. After the poet's discussion, we can go back to that opening word illuminated. Yet, if one prefers an approach that keeps closer to the line order, notice the nature of the poet's implicit question *I'd ask to know.* What is the actual question that would be asked? Make the students state it exactly. The *to whom* presumably begins to personify the "something." Its form suggests that certain busy human activities like this wall-mending are now an *offence against his concerns.* This issue becomes the most open-ended of questions and it is for this reason I urge its postponement after recognition of the personification. Before that one might prefer to move ahead to *elves* which is a deliberately light and comic version of the unseen powers of the universe that the poet is, in fact, in this poem taking terribly seriously, just because he is here treating it so lightly in this chosen vocabulary. Flippancy is a common Anglo-American device to conceal responses too difficult to articulate directly. (A sidetrack at this point might take one into some very revealing discussions of which are the friendly or childlike spirits, and which are the mighty ogre-demons, of the different cultures. We need to ask, perhaps later, why the poet feels he should not supply an idea, that he would *rather he said it for himself.* What is important about self-discovery rather than a mere telling? What a splendid educational statement is being made so casually here!)

The neighbor is now described. His appearance should have been ascertained by level one questions. What is he carrying? But why does Frost talk of this neighboring modern man as *savage armed* and by extension *stone aged?* It should not take long to see how the key vocabulary sets up a view of Neanderthal man, primitive, savage, cruel, and like him, armed with heavy rocks. Why is such an accusation made? He is not going to throw the rocks but build with them. Note the semantic input of *darkness* to add to the idea of uncivilized heathen, in that deliberate phrase which you may have to reverse into the more common syntactical order of *he moves in darkness as it seems to me, not of woods only.* (It is not only the shadowy woods that make his darkness.) What other darkness is there? What is the tone in which the poet says *He will not go behind his father's saying?* Is it critical? At this point the third level of questioning might begin.

Should you go "behind" your father's saying—questioning all the established truths? Can the foreign student detect without your assistance the slightly snide tone of *he likes having thought of it so well he says again Good fences make good neighbors!* Is repetition always bad? Is this unthinking repetition? Hopefully at this stage one can begin to pursue the questions that provide the theme of this poem and that elusive "something" that is breaking down these walls. Is it unreasonable for a person to try to build them up? Does that human decision contradict some elemental power in nature? What is the significance of his

concern that there are unnecessary walls that are being built that divide things and persons that can do each other no harm? Are men nearer to being cows—in this sense dangerously predatory—who will invade each other's estates unless restricted, or are they very different like pines and apples and so quite harmless to one another? The continuance of this line of discussion in the class may well provoke in the teacher some very healthy exasperation. Poetry is not a neutral art but demands highly provocative intellectual and emotional reactions. Teachers should not be immune in the confident carapace of their professional abilities. If student responses stimulate that teacher to angry involvement, it will invariably have a highly stimulating and beneficial effect on the interaction between teacher and student. Finally they will be on equal levels each defending urgently held principles rather than exhibiting that active/passive system of teller/listener that too often masquerades as education. A lively class may well teach the teacher to remember what poetry is all about. It is not a country garden art form but virulent and vehement in its presentation of consequent issues that affect everybody's lives.

For this reason, as one presses this important question of who builds walls and with what justification, do not expect to get the simple idealistic response of liberal American sophomores. Many foreign students will say that it is perfectly reasonable for Frost, living in "fortress America" to say walls are useless. How about those people living in Korea or Berlin? Can they reject walls? If they cannot, does this in any way invalidate the general principle that Frost appears to be arguing, for human neighborliness, or does it merely prove that not all men are "trees" and, like cows, they *do* stray destructively? If this is rational, why is Frost in his own gentle way so destructive of the beliefs of his hard-working neighbor who builds the wall? Why is that man called a savage and a fool without *a notion in his head*? Why is he drawn as unobservant and unfeeling? Is it because of a question not related to the actual building of the wall? Is the key to this poem the important thought advanced by Frost that before you start building you should know who you are *walling in or walling out*? That general philosophy can then be pressed into even more symbolic walls, perhaps those that surround the emotion of the human heart! At such an abstract level of human mutuality and affection a teacher of foreign students might be safe. But don't be surprised to encounter the argument from many foreign students more personally familiar than Americans with the disaster of local battle, that having decided who you should be walling out you ought to build a wall higher than any conceivably practical in New England.

What I have hoped to indicate by this perhaps over-elaborate exposition is the direction of the class lesson when one presents poetry. The factual observation is a matter of accurate reading. From this evolve the imaginative elements of the intellect which asks "why." Lastly, there is open and ongoing discussion that brings the significant theme and conclusion of the poet into the most fundamental conflict or support with opinions that have been engendered by personal training and experience. It is this approach that stresses the consequence of poetry. It is something far more profound than some pretty presentation of the charming and therefore inconsequent aspects of life. As in all presentation of literature, but particularly classes conceived for the foreign student, we begin with the recognition that is provided by the denotative aspects of language, but we do not stop at that level of clarification. We move on through the more subtle connotative elements, into a response that involves us in an interaction with the most urgent statement that poetry makes when it is written by a skillful and dedicated writer.

Before the end of the class, read this poem through at least once more, or better yet, play a recording of Frost reading it (records are available). Each fresh reading after the substantial discovery occasioned by the questioning will add a little more to the students' appreciative response and enjoyment. Probably at this point it may be desirable to rest the class and require subsequent readings. Suggest that when at home the poem be read, preferably aloud, for major effect. If there is a sincere willingness to attempt that, encourage it. Further cogita-tion may have provoked more theories and thoughts that will make the reopening of the discussion worthwhile. Further examples may have come to mind and accusations and defenses can be undertaken about certain heroes.

THE SHORT STORY

Obviously the short story can be regarded as the most suitable literary genre for the foreign student. It is brief, contemporary, interesting, and portrays a modern cultural environment that is either relatively familiar to the student or else is significantly attached to the target culture of the language s/he is studying. Brevity is a significant point because it allows the class to focus on the story within a single class period. This possibility is very important even if the story and its attendant preparation and discussion are carried forward effectively over a series of periods. A variety of activities around a fully known piece of literature is a very different thing if done from a serial! This preference for at least one aspect of the entire work to be tackled within a single class period is the reason my own experience with novels has not been entirely happy. Working through a novel chapter by chapter may build up suspense—if one is clever enough to keep boredom at bay for a month or two—but it does not allow one to talk across its total sequence until too late in the term. The payoff of general overall discussion is delayed to a point of educational disutility. For those desiring or being required to teach a novel I can only recommend that one regards its chapters or sections as short stories and teaches them by the methodology I recommend below, and then draws together the overall themes and issues in terminal class activities.

It is essential that a teacher have in his or her own mind the elements that allow the apprehension of a story. Again it is a matter of judgment and taste whether one makes an initial explanatory lesson specifically, for example, about how to understand a character in a story, or whether one allows one's own questions to form the desired approach inductively. There is something to be said for either method, but in both cases the essential aspects of the story have to be established for the full understanding of the tale. The common terminology cannot be readily dismissed because it is so specifically connected with meaning. "Setting," for example, may at one level be merely the obvious fact of geography and history, but it can equally be a significant dimension of the plot and form the major justification of the events. This is an area in which the foreign student will particularly need guidance, for events that are appropriate to one American environment will be quite differently perceived when transposed—from town to village, for example.

The most convenient initial handle for understanding a short story is through its characters. This requires that we have some idea as to how an author builds up his or her characters and how we learn of their nature. Our recognition and interpretation come from the character's words and deeds but more subtly the words and actions of those with whom he or she interacts. Characters are established in five ways: (a) the explanations of the author; (b) what the character says; (c) what is said about him or her; (d) what the character does; (e) what is done to him or her. It is important to indicate that (a) is always the truth; (b) and (c) can be true or false; (d) and (e) will be true in fact but interpretation may vary. Thus only the authorial asides require no qualification and discrimination on the part of the reader and it is this judgment that must be developed. This is not difficult to establish in class but it has to be handled slowly and precisely, pursuing the individual actions in specific detail. *Why did s/he do that? What does that show us about his or her character?*

It is not essential to go deeply into the definition and construction of the short story. I do try to get the students to recognize the relationship of the author to his or her tale because this is so often significant in the story. Is the author "omniscient" or working through a narrator? Is the narrator a clear mouthpiece or do his or her views counterpoise those of the writer? To appreciate a short story we are required to find evidence of the author's true belief and morality. Obviously this does not usually come from any one of the characters. They may be taking contradictory positions,

none of which match the belief of the author him- or herself. In a story such as Willa Cather's *The Sculptor's Funeral*, for example, the majority of the characters sit around bad-mouthing the dead sculptor. In so doing they only expose their own degenerate moral values and soon every further condemnation of the artist becomes evidence of the dead man's actual superiority. This is obvious and yet it is an aspect of writing that needs some initial explanation, especially as, in the final analysis, moral theme is the crucial element in any writing and justifies its consequence.

Again, as with poetry, the presentation should be designed as far as possible to eliminate the problems in advance, so that there is some impact possible in the first reading. Nothing is more pathetic than to see a student stopping at each line to look up a word in his or her dictionary. Of course this may mean nothing more than that the piece is too difficult—even six unknown words a page can be daunting. Perhaps more importantly s/he has to be encouraged (or commanded) to have the confidence to read doggedly through patches of miscomprehension waiting for the eventual support of overall revelation that comes as the sequence of the story provides its own momentum. It is essential to advise this course. In fact, it is quite another matter to get most foreign students agitated by linguistic incompetence to obey your request! This knowledge gives yet further support to the need to supply students in advance with the essential elements of the vocabulary they are going to encounter. Again, attempt to convince the students that some words are of minor significance and merely clutter the mind. Help them with others that may be of little utility by any reasonable word count but are essential to the story. It is not always easy to establish the individual difficulty level of vocabulary for many reasons; the varied background of the readers themselves, the degree of meaning illumination provided by context. If a teacher has some doubts about his or her ability to recognize probable gaps in knowledge, s/he might begin by asking the students to go through a page or two specifically marking up all the words that are unfamiliar. These can then be reported and discussed in class. This is not in contradiction to the assertion that the student should not get the story before the teacher presentation that includes explanation of difficult vocabulary, since this is not a suggestion for a regular and consistent methodology, but an occasional test of the perception that is occurring. If the page is selected pretty much at random it is seen as a checking exercise that does not constitute an alternative procedure in presenting the short story. What must be carefully avoided is the process of telling students to take home the story and work through it on the evening before—a task that requires from them a complete private initial reading that necessitates a dictionary and mires them in the discovery of the extent of their own incomprehension of the tale.

A further most significant element in comprehension will undoubtedly arise. (This in itself could make the subject for several theses but I will be brief.) It is regularly apparent that, when students have finally and painfully garnered all the requisite linguistic knowledge and can understand at the factual level the information provided by the sentences, they may still be far from any true comprehension of the overall meaning. They may be unable to discriminate the motivation and sequence of events through their own preconceptions and ignorance of American cultural attitudes. I would argue that just as vocabulary should be introduced in advance of a first reading it may be equally essential to go over some of the obvious assumptions that an author is making in the recognition that s/he commonly shares his or her response with his or her readers. The cultural identification assumed between reader and writer is fundamental to the nature of literary understanding. This casually assumed connection is interpreted by the ESL situation and considerable attention must be paid to cultural explication. However, the teacher's difficulty in cultural elucidation is far greater than in the explanation of vocabulary items. This is for two reasons. First, the teacher who can readily recognize unfamiliar words is far less likely to know what will prove to be a cultural difficulty since s/he is so immersed in his or her own culture that s/he is often unable to recognize its individuality—as someone color-blind needs an outsider to indicate his or her aberrant color sense. One's world view always seems a god-given norm. Second, and from the student side of the problem, it is far harder to detect what is not being grasped accurately. Lack of vocabulary is a very simple matter to discover. Cultural misapprehensions are more elusive. There may be almost as many culturally-determined responses to a story as there are students in the room. (Also, there are none of the comfortable means of diagnosing a direct "right" answer.) There will be a whole range of reactions that must be measured along an axis between the exactly known and the totally unfamiliar. In this context, complete ignorance is easy to establish but student miscomprehensions are often so confidently made that they are hard to discover since if students do not know that they are wrong it is unlikely that the teacher will even learn of the error and thus be in a position to attempt to correct it. "I do not understand" is an easy situation. "I know I understand" may be true or false but the teacher will not be able to decide upon that judgment without considerable investigation which s/he will be unlikely to undertake without some prior evidence that error is occurring.

In many cases some initial explanation of how Americans behave can be useful, provided that it does not develop into a separable lesson on the subject only lightly attached to the topic of the story being studied. Such information is only required to provide the minimal necessary introduction to the actual piece of literature being presented. An obvious example might be American treatment of the aged. Perhaps a story might describe how a grandmother enjoys being independent in her retirement home freed from all the demands made by her children and grandchildren. This is a view almost unimaginable to most of the rest of the world. In such a case students will seek for motivations appropriate to their own culture, not accepting the validity of the American social custom. Similarly a good girl can go out with her boyfriend even unchaperoned, and not immediately lose her reputation. The importance of recognizing such things as this rests not in the need to correct general error—that would be a life work—but because, without such awareness, distortions of authorial intentions will happen and the story itself will be rendered meaningless.

A short story should be prepared in the way I have indicated above with the pre-preparation of vocabulary and some explication of obvious points of cultural assumption. Then come the first two private readings. The first is a rapid reading for general gist, the second a slower one for deeper comprehension. This reading should be done at home as there is not much point in wasting classroom time on long periods of silent reading, in spite of the temptation of the few minutes of peace it provides a harrassed and overworked teacher on a long day. There is, I feel, in the case of the short story no obvious advantage in the teacher's lengthy oral presentation as there certainly is in providing an initial reading of a poem.

In the following period in class there should be an initial time when the teacher attempts to gauge the students' comprehension of plot events before passing on to other things more crucial to literature. The sequence should be as follows. Begin by asking direct questions of fact that can be answered by specific reference to the text of the story. Deliberately ask *how? what? when? where? who?* but not *why? Why?* questions are reserved for the second stage, after the factual background has been established and understood. With *why?* one begins to probe motivation. This requires that students develop their interpretation from the already firmly fixed knowledge of fact. It requires speculation about the most probable causes for decisions and events. It requires analysis and appreciation of the ideas, intentions, and obligations of the characters. After having established what a character actually did, one goes to the next stage by asking *Why did s/he think that was a good idea?* or *Why did s/he not do . . . ?* or *Why did his or her mother disapprove of this decision?*

Even at this stage, the answers can be related closely to the book itself, though interpretation is also required. The third stage is the point at which one takes the giant stride of involving the students—which is where literary study may be said to begin. *Would you have done this? Do you think s/he should have done it? What would you rather have tried?* Most specifically for the foreign student is the repeated question, *In your country what is s/he more likely to have chosen to have done?*

Sample lesson

I am selecting for discussion *The Sculptor's Funeral* by Willa Cather, although it is perhaps longer than ideal. The title is simple enough, although the circumstances may be a little strange: the tale concerns less the funeral than the antagonistic attitudes which the dead man's return provokes. The return of a dead body to its home is probably very common in many foreign societies, such as the Chinese. It may even be more readily acceptable to students than teacher. However, there is an ironic twist. You may begin by commenting on the cultural background. Willa Cather was from Nebraska and this story deals with certain commonly believed American attitudes. There is the opposition between small town and city which sets the narrowness and isolation of the small town against the intellectual stimulus of the metropolis (e.g., Sinclair Lewis' *Main Street*) or the opposition reverses itself and excoriates the sin and luxury of the city against small town virtues of sincerity, thrift, and honest toil. Both of these attitudes, paradoxically, exist simultaneously. Reinforcing this is the tension between East and West or Midwest that exists on very similar grounds. The East, many believe, is more cultured and elegant, but the West believes the East has lost true American virtues. There are many contemporary examples of this antagonism and polarization, political and economic. Attendant to this deployment is a similar controversy between business and liberal education, between practicality and art, that finds most intellectual ideals useless as the other side discerns business motives as discreditable. It is cruel and wrong to see this in geographic terms as Cather chooses to do in her exasperation with Kansas/Nebraska, but the often-remarked anti-intellectualism of American democracy is part of this tale. It is important that one provides the students with what one considers necessary of this background. Ask whether it exists in their own country. If one goes into it too deeply, with long explanation and discussion, one will in fact be anticipating material that ought to be derived from the presentation of the story itself.

The language of this story is fairly difficult by the level I have outlined, even if one does ignore the awkward patches of dialect. However, to indicate the technique with reference to the opening pages, I would suggest that the following selection would be typical: (a) words worth knowing: *conspicuous, bury, restless,* etc.; (b) words needed in the story: *siding, hearse, express,* etc.; (c) other words not likely to be known: (i) words appropriate only to the tale, *gait, dogged, grizzled,* etc., and (ii) words important, but difficult and fairly rare for the students' present level of reading, *impartiality, commiseratingly,* etc. Because of the significance of this geographical antagonism the setting is all-important and should be dealt with. The story takes place in Sand City, Kansas. It is soon seen to be isolated both physically and intellectually. Draw attention to the way in which that isolation is brilliantly suggested by the scenes of waiting for the train, the connecting link with the rest of the country. Consider atmosphere. From the hushed sounds and the small groups on the platform we know that some disaster has occurred but we are not told what it is until later, after our senses have been alerted to the tension. Mention too how Jim is not only *conspicuously apart* but the only one *who looked as if he knew exactly why he was there.* This indicates both the nature and reason for his isolation, and thus sets him apart from the others of Sand City from the very beginning of the tale. One other structural point of interest, though one may let the student discover this rather than provide it, is the presence of Steavens. He is the man who knew the sculptor in his other world of Boston in which he was so honored and lauded. Thus he constitutes the "outsider's" point of view and is the eyes of the world judging the localism in the attitudes of the Sand City people. As one works through the story, one should indicate how much we learn through Steavens' eyes. One may need to demonstrate the development of several individual characters or do one in class and have others treated at home. As an example of the technique, consider the mother. She is described in appearance as *tall and corpulent* and a little later as having *a kind of brutal handsomeness.* (Notice how we are getting the shocked view of the outsider. Mr. Phelps would not have seen her in this way.) Some students may well be taken in by the original scene: the dramatic advent of the woman in the snow shattered by the death of her son. After all, a common myth is that others are more emotional than Americans in these matters, and exceptional grief may be commonplace and admired behavior. Perhaps only Americans will see at once the contrast between the understandable grief of *"My boy, my boy!"* and the acid tone of *"And this is how you've come home to me."* (How does one read the tone of that remark? It is capable of several stresses and therefore innuendos.) Regardless of one's first response, Cather has Steavens guide us by his *shudder of unutterable repulsion.* This is an example of how we round out our view of character by discerning not only the person's act but the response that it occasions in others. More importantly, we begin to find that Steavens as the outsider is a person whose judgment we may accept, and thus we do not have to go through the dubious cycle of questioning the validity of the morality which sustains his judgment as we rapidly learn to do with the Sand City people. If we have any doubts, they are rapidly resolved. If we still imagine her grief might be truly intense, we are presented with a picture of her husband *with a full frightened, appealing expression, as a spaniel looks at the whip.* His sincere agony—the more real for being so inarticulate—is interrupted by her authoritarian call from the top of the stairs that solicits his immediate hangdog obedience. If this illuminates his defeated nature, at the same time it says much about hers. One judges a person by the influence and the reactions of others. She becomes more clearly the bully. Any lingering feeling we might have concerning the legitimacy of her grief is shattered by the violent sounds from the kitchen. *The mother was abusing the maid for having forgotten to make the dressing for the chicken salad.* Such preoccupations with inessentials are not the usual concommitant of grief, and in case we should not perceive this at once we are treated to confirming remarks from Steavens who makes *a shudder of disgust* and Jim who quite openly asserts that *the woman is a fury.* Perhaps the summary of her character only comes obliquely through Steavens' words *He was wonderful . . . but until tonight I never knew how wonderful.*

Although the mother makes a simple character for analysis, it is Jim the lawyer who is the most interesting. One can show the development of his personality in the same way. But the key to his character is the closeness of his association with the sculptor. This is seen in his very real understanding and concern at his death. It also explains that air of jealousy and guilt with which he admits he regards Harvey Merrick's success. They began with the same ambitions: *We meant to be great men.* But when Harvey went away and achieved success, *I came back here and became the damned shyster.* His dichotomy is openly expressed and very understandable in its ambivalence: *There have been times when the sight of Harvey's name on some Eastern paper has made me hang my head like a whipped dog; and again, times when I liked to think of him off there in the world, away from all this hog wallow.*

The rest of the characters are minor and act like a kind of chorus. They meet for the wake (and it may be necessary to explain the custom and perhaps elicit information concerning similar ritual in other parts of the world). Gradually we are filled in on the sculptor's early life. Take each remark in detail and show how it reinforces the fineness of Harvey's nature and diminishes the townspeople long before Jim has summed up the whole story for us. The story of swindling in the sale of the mule makes the seller seem merely a crook, not Harvey foolish. The accusation of drunkenness is made without the least factual basis. The sneers at his urge for education and the general scorn for education itself at least beyond the simple vocational training of the Kansas City Business College expose only the intellectual limitations of the speaker. All these brash confident assertions discredit the speakers although they would be surprised to know this. A point to check with the students as one reads this story is: how do we get from the tale the perspective which allows us to condemn these people? Is it from our own external view of justice, or in what way does the author convey her interpretation of the situation? With this discussion one gets into important questions of tone and the relationship between author and character in the structure known as "omniscient author." Because we do so clearly recognize the truth of the sculptor's virtue and distinction, perhaps we hardly need the last, long impassioned speech of Jim, except that it gives us some satisfaction to have our own burning indignation articulated so pungently. Perhaps, too, Jim deserves the last sense of righteousness for he has often, as he admits, fallen short of his ideals in this community. In this context his death is particularly ironic for it is caused by his continuing to serve the immorality of Sand City; defending a crooked son from a just accusation of theft.

Jim is certainly the most complicated character in this story and deserves close analysis by questioning, so that his very human mixed motives can be elicited. Why did he come back? What qualities did Harvey have that Jim lacked? How is it so easy for him to see the situation and not act upon the evidence? Being a subtle and complex story, the theme is not so easy to elicit. Why do the townspeople despise Merrick? He is famous. Should not they be proud of the glory he brings his town? Certainly they are ignorant. But if they knew more of his life would they change their minds? Probably not. Is this ignorance of a higher level that is not even corrigible? Is there anything to be said for their standards? Would the situation be any different if Harvey had not turned out to be a genius? Is the honor in his gesture or its success? What options does Jim have if he has not Harvey's spark of true brilliance? (I often wonder whether we would admire Gaugin half as much if his painting had been judged inferior.) Why are all the young men in Sand City apparently lacking in morality? (Even the minister's son, the previous corpse to arrive on the train, died after a gambling shoot-out.) Why, if all this is so, does the sculptor choose to come home? Can this wretched city be a home to such an artist?

These are the kind of questions that will undoubtedly occur to one as one reads. One's speculations must be translated into questions one can also ask the students. For some classes these queries may go too far, too fast. When one fails to elicit responses immediately, one should go back into the more comfortable area of factual questions with which one began.

The final concern of the teacher must be to elicit the student response to the entire presentation. One may find that they have a far higher and more ready approval of the artist's role in their own society and therefore a large measure of the motivation will be insignificant. Perhaps one can translate this simply into a tale of a young man leaving home. This will be understood and yet it misses much of the story, and may in fact build up an undue sympathy for the family neglected by Harvey's absence. Students will certainly assert that education is highly respected in their society. Check on the degree of vocational study necessary for such approval. In Africa there almost seems a higher measure of respect in ratio to the degree of disutility of the field of study! What does that suggest? After the teacher has gone over the regional cultural responses solicited from individual students, it is highly desirable to go back into the story again for the discussion will probably have ranged widely, and arguments between Asians and Latin Americans about the need for artists or farmers in developing countries will leave Willa Cather's concerns far behind. Returning to the American context, one can attempt to solicit opinions by encouraging students to consider their expectations and experiences in that situation. Perhaps, although it becomes dangerously speculative ground, one can discuss whether there is some identification between the author and the sculptor, and whether that might have biased the presentation of the events. This subject, like so many others, is open-ended, and the satisfactory resolution occurs only in the mind of the individuals who have interacted with the story with knowledge and enjoyment.

RESEARCH SUGGESTIONS

The somewhat tenuous link between the literature in an ESL program and that appropriate in formal English departments serves as the starting point for a discussion of possible research activities appropriate to the ESL scholar. One might rather simplistically begin by defining the task by means of a negative. Roughly speaking, any study that would be suitable for an English department thesis would not be a topic of interest to ESL. By that I mean that all formal studies of authors, genres, and themes are not central to ESL concerns even though it has to be urged that, to introduce literature to non-native speakers, a teacher should have an adequate background in the formal methodology of teaching literature and some awareness of the concepts and critical terminology that are required for the comprehension and elucidation of literature at an adult level. This training may be accomplished with varying degrees of efficiency in the teacher's own education, but formal training cannot be enough. We are presupposing that we need to add particular issues, questions, and approaches in the performance of this teaching function in ESL to the conventional skills, not make a substitute for them. The formal training in English literature is highly desirable, probably necessary, but most significantly not enough for the requirements of ESL. The foreign language situation imposes another extended series of problems to which a teacher must attempt the solution. It is to provide initial solutions to these problems that ESL researchers must address themselves.

Language

No formal research that I know of has been done on measuring or evaluating levels of difficulty in literature. This would be vital to establish the most suitable materials for choice. It would be ideal, though unlikely, if one could set up some kind of grid that allowed a teacher to estimate the degree of difficulty that a foreign student might encounter. In this way there would be some rational assessment in the selection of an appropriate story for a class. Every teacher inevitably develops some rough personal assumptions of difficulty; such opinions form a crude hierarchy that is only tested at best in an individual and casual way, without even the guidance of a rule of thumb. It would seem that some simple indications can be established, but these each raise questions and qualifications, and they have not been tested by experiment. For example, one would assume that one major evidence of difficulty would derive from the vocabulary used by the author. This is probably undeniable, and yet what is difficult in this context has not been defined. One could hypothesize that one could test the level of vocabulary difficulty by measuring the words in a representative page of the prose in a short story against one of the established word count lists. Examination against those standards would indicate the proportion of the most commonly used words actually employed by the author. One could then make the leap of faith that this count does in fact control the recognition factor. That this is likely to be untrue derives from more than one contradiction relating to the students' previous vocabulary acquisition and the means by which they recognize and incorporate new words into their existing vocabulary.

When one considers the reading of literature, two factors other than usage frequency will determine literary comprehension at word level. First, intelligibility may be supplied substantially by context, even more so than would be provided by a paragraph of merely expository prose assumed to be at the same level of difficulty. In this situation the meaning of even rare and exceptional words may be perfectly apparent. Second, not all words need to be known individually, nor definitions required, in order to achieve an adequate comprehension of the entire situation. There are many elements that enrich a reading but which are not required for basic understanding. Analogous might be the gradually increasing depth of perception that comes as native speakers read a work of literature at several stages in the maturation of their intellectual and literary sensibility. They do not require total understanding from the very beginning. Some pleasure is available immediately, even though much is ignored or misunderstood.

Similar studies might be attempted with issues of syntax. Can we decide what are the most readily or the least easily assimilable structures? A natural instinct is to assert that length is the most obvious complicating elements in clause construction. We know from

oral work that length of the sentence that can be retained in the memory and repeated back has proved a valuable indicator of language comprehension generally. It is for this reason, among others, that a teacher instinctively eschews the work of Faulkner in favor of Hemingway's short and spare sentences.

Here again it certainly cannot only be length that decides complexity of meaning. Surely a row of clauses in a compound sentence demarked only by commas would be no more difficult than a series of simple sentences divided by periods. More significantly, the complex embeddings and ellipses and arbitrary arrangements of clauses in brief lines of poetry present numerous difficulties even for the native speaker.

Culture
Beyond questions of linguistic comprehension the student can make an entirely different series of misapprehensions that derive from the cultural elements inherent in a work of literature. Some of the remarks offered concerning linguistic difficulties will most likely also be appropriate here. It is obvious that it would be advantageous if we could establish a hierarchy of difficulty appropriate to the cultural mode of a piece of literature. As before, one could unhesitatingly proffer an instinctive anticipated expectation of the qualities that one might imagine would make for difficulty and confusion. Just as certainly we cannot know that our expectations are correct or that they are founded on any more adequate or accurate a response than the ones initially offered concerning the vocabulary or syntactical hierarchy. For they are nothing more than opinions neither experimentally obtained nor rationally sustained.

Cultural associations within a piece of literature might be argued to range across a spectrum that extends from the most universal aspects of a work of literature to the most culture-tied. Obviously, neither absolute extreme on this measured spectrum is possible. No literature can be so entirely specific that it relates only to a single cultural locale. It must deal with human beings who, no matter what the peculiarities of their local and regional customs, share the mutuality of the human experience in those fundamental experiences of birth, procreation, death, and in the reactions to pain or delight. But how the appropriate reactions to such general experiences are exhibited are infinitely varied. They reflect the increasing particularity and localism of "that's the way we do it in my country, my religion, my town," and finally "my family."

One would naturally assume, yet again it is only an untested assumption, that the more universal the story, the less problem the foreign student would encounter. In contrast it would seem, at least on the surface, highly likely that the more American a story were in its setting and mores, the more difficult its interpretation would be to a foreigner. Obviously, in our own reading we find it far easier to share the experience and motivation of a protagonist who is acting within a context of a social and cultural environment similar to our own. Again we do not know if this is correct. There are a number of imponderables.

Firstly, American culture, in a superficial sense, has become the culture of much of the contemporary world, no matter the local modifications. Typically American things from freeways to ice cream, from jeans to rock music, are often familiar at first hand. This awareness is reinforced by the secondary experience derived from the media. Film and TV shows throughout the world tend to be dominated by American production. They give the foreign viewer a persistent if somewhat bizarre view of that American way of life which s/he will also encounter in contemporary literature with a feeling of recognition as much as of surprise. Probably some aspects of American culture are more familiar to a foreign student than the behavior encountered in a neighboring regional territory.

However, even if experimental research did prove to support the accuracy of our original expectation that a student might find a work difficult to the degree that it is embedded in the American cultural context, these data might not be decisive in our final choice of classroom material. We also have to consider the intention of our lesson. The American element that rendered the work difficult might become precisely the reason for the selection. A

teacher might find, in spite of the problems a work provides, a purely educational obligation to direct the reader to some understanding of the specialized and regional context. It could be argued that it is the teacher's duty to explore that American culture precisely because it is unfamiliar. Paradoxically, we might argue that it is the very difficulty encountered that exposes most obviously the students' need for assistance in their early acquaintance with the culture of the language they are attempting to acquire. The guidance in the appreciation of the uniqueness of the American culture supplied by literature might well be one of the arguable reasons for introducing such works into the ESL classroom in the first place.

Nothing that has been discussed above may be taken to indicate that such quibbles make the need for research less important. We need to know where the problems lie. But equally clearly, the pedagogical decisions that follow when we know the facts that experiment provides make quite a separate division of our work than the actual collection and testing of the data.

To investigate this problem, a number of cross-cultural studies suggest themselves. The first question would be to try to identify and then perhaps correlate difficulties of comprehension. The problems are likely to be similar to those arising from the same approach at the linguistic level. Undertaking this virtual contrastive analysis would be a very extensive and complicated task. Most importantly, it would prove applicable only to the single language cultural unit of the reader. We could reasonably expect in general terms that a European who is closer to the overall cultural heritage of America will have fewer problems than, say, an Asian whose range of history is more remote from the general Judaic, Hellenic, Christian tradition of Europe. If this is probably true, we cannot assume that such a view will prove precisely applicable: it may be that since the Japanese traditional culture is now significantly modified by the impact of a capitalistic technology that has close similarities with the American one Japanese students may find it perfectly simple to understand many aspects of American commercial and economic motivation. Similarly, an

African student reading an American novel that dealt with the exodus of the young, lured from small towns by the dangerous glitter of the metropolis, will find this action highly familiar, although s/he has encountered it in his or her own very different country. Obviously, not only are generalizations going to be difficult, but they will scarcely be likely to apply to more than one group. The isolation of individual problems cannot be applied to a heterogeneous class of foreign students for the same reason that in such a mixed class the element of phonological difficulty will not be similar. Stern (1977) does, however, begin to isolate some widely-shared cultural misconceptions and her work can serve as a useful starting point.

One early and ingenious study in the field of cross-cultural misinterpretation was Anita Pincas' analysis of difficulties that might be supposed to derive from ignorance of the background British culture that sustains a C. P. Snow novel (Pincas, 1963b). She asserts there are certain elements that will prove inexplicable without particular explanation. In fact, she gives no adequate rationale to justify the principles she has employed to determine what these difficulties would be. This is partially accounted for by the fact that presumably in order to make sure a nice lot of incomprehensions turn up she has decided to select, not a particular culture for contrasting, but a Culture X. This is some kind of imaginary compound that seems, in its concern for chaperones and admiration for football, to be a rough compendium of South American attitudes. If we agree to accept her assertions that these are reasonable examples of the problems likely to be encountered by X nationals, we must follow her argument one step further. She provides a "cultural" translation. That is, she *modifies the original events of the story* in order to make its concerns intelligible to the Culture X reader. There are at least two reasons why this is undesirable, a general and a specific one. The first question is simply that of putting the cart before the horse. If a teacher wants foreign students to enjoy English literature, s/he wants them to be able to understand it. The teacher prepares his or her lessons to illuminate the

situation and elucidate the difficulties by demonstration and explanation. This is only achieved in a most superficial way if the teacher has, in fact, deemed it his or her task to transpose the incidents out of the target culture the students need to encounter, and returned it to their own, with which they are perfectly familiar. This transaction might have some utility as a *student* exercise *after* the student has been made aware of the nature of the events s/he is reading about. Then the task could be an interesting test of the degree to which the student has comprehended the explanatory lesson—if, of course, the teacher was at least familiar enough with the student's native culture to judge the complex crossover that has occurred.

But even if the principle of this activity were deemed pedagogically acceptable, there is the more serious problem that the cultural translations provided simply do not work. One runs into the same problem encountered in the transposition of simple vocabulary, though at a much more complicated level. One is suspicious of one-word synonym transfer between languages and wonders whether even very obvious apparently one-to-one correspondent specificities like *wife* or *dinner* can transfer; how much more this is so when one is transferring cultural presuppositions. For example, Snow's protagonist is full of malaise and concern. He decides to visit a cricket match. Now a cricket match is a very relaxing activity—soporific, some might call it. It is, therefore, exactly right for a little introspection on a sunny afternoon. There is something soothing in its deliberate and traditional ritual. Pincas, finding no cricket in Culture X, substitutes the alternative local game, a football match. This makes nonsense of the author's intention, because a Latin-American football match is nearer a civil war than a sport for peaceful deliberation. In this way nothing has been achieved by the change except the introduction of another error. Clearly such comparisons must be undertaken at a level that exhibits far greater awareness of the overtones. But after this general warning has been offered, there remain a number of experiments along the lines of cultural translation that might be useful as initiating data. My own reports on experiments with Thurber's *Walter Mitty* and J. Updike's *A and P* suggest what might be uncovered when the veneer of apparent linguistic comprehension is pierced (Povey, 1972 and 1968).

Certain experiments with translation can be equally revealing and would make useful research projects. The attempt to find equivalents, both verbal and cultural, in a transposition by translation is valuable at least as evidence of the difficulties that are occurring. (As an example of this type of study, see Kurzdorfer, 1974.) With this concern in mind I felt it helpful to encourage two Asian students to demonstrate a kind of translation exercise to American students. The foreign students offered a criticism of a particular English translation and explained what was missing. American students were then forced into the role of the foreign student in relation to this literature. More important, they learned that on many occasions when they at first felt perfectly comfortable with the immediate responses they had made, it was healthy to have them discover how erroneous or exaggerated they were. It is necessary to admit that there is an element of artificiality in such experiments. They result finally in warnings of the problems. They may serve the valuable task of engendering great sensitivity and responsiveness in the English language teacher without necessarily supplying any particular technique that might provide amelioration of the misapprehensions that such close examination of texts has exposed.

Stylistics

There are two aspects of study that relate to the language of literature. There has been much discussion about the advantages and limitations of using simplified texts. It is obvious that many incorrigible literature teachers view such efforts as an intolerable liberty with the author's words. It is clear that if one accepts the most basic tenet of English departments, that "form and content are inseparable," then there can be little defense for simplification. Nevertheless, such books are used and it might be a revealing study to examine a series and check them against the original forms. What is being left out? What are the presuppositions that

dictate what is altered? Is it merely the restriction of vocabulary and is this sufficient to provide more reading comprehension? It might be useful to see if it is possible to prepare a simplified text that achieves an effective balance between closeness to the original with elimination of linguistic difficulties. Such a task would only be defensible if there were cognizance of the concerns I have raised earlier in this chapter. Otherwise, the justification of the simplification will be based on nothing more than the opinion that "it seems easier to me to make these changes. . . ." For one attempt in this direction see Strop (1971).

One exciting area of research is perhaps a far cry from the use of the literature in the classroom. But I feel we too often neglect what is actually being done with the language we are dedicated to teach. It is now well known that there is a very extensive second language literature in English. Where the English language has become the daily means of national communication in a country and the local tongues are reserved for regional needs, English may also be the language of creativity. Creativity in literature would appear to be a very intimate and personal activity, and it has been assumed to necessitate that special affinity that a writer inevitably has only for his or her native tongue. But the opportunities for a wider audience and connections to a range of genre forms more flexible and contemporary than those of an earlier local tradition that may well be primarily oral has led writers to make this unexpected but important language choice. Such literature is being written in Nigeria, India, Kenya, the Philippines, and many other countries. It is important to recognize the distinctiveness of these literatures that employ English as a second language. They are entirely separate from the new territories such as Australia or Canada which equally are generating new national literatures but where the English language is a first language and exhibits only relatively small variations from the British original. With truly second language literatures, a valuable literary study might be the analysis of the distinctions in the writing that derive from the intrusion of the first language not only at the level of diction but also of stylistics.

This would be useful as an example of what is happening to English abroad when it is being used at a sophisticated and complicated level. Obviously, it would be almost essential in such a task to have a knowledge of the first language—in this way it might be a research task particularly suitable for the foreign student. Yet it is not impossible to detect certain forms on a comparative basis provided one has access to a sufficiently large selection of items to eliminate the mere peculiarities of individual style. It seems possible to argue convincingly that there are differences of style between Nigerian writers depending on whether they are Ibo or Yoruba. The Ibo style in English appears relatively concise and formal, the Yoruba flamboyant and poetic. Perhaps such studies might include examination of structure at the paragraph level which might tend to reinforce Kaplan's hypothesis concerning the variety of culture-tied logical perceptions (Kaplan, 1966).

Selection

For many teachers the question of what to teach and what literature is appropriate for a certain level is crucial and can become a source of much agitation. Studies that assess the function and advantages of particular works might significantly assist them. However, as I indicated earlier, the mere listing of a series of "good" titles has no more validity than the opinion of the person who presents it, unless a specific and exact policy is being carried forward that is derived from previous experimental research on the subject of acceptability. There is nothing more useless than for a teacher to argue that Dickens is good or bad, "because I found it was well (or badly) received in class!" Extra votes of the "and my friend didn't like teaching it either" are hardly statistically convincing. Listing books to make up part of a syllabus will have to await some more serious studies of the elements that constitute difficulty as discussed in previous pages.

There have been several attempts to arrange materials around certain themes which are ingenious and valuable and might well be convincing after tests. One aspect of selection might focus around a single thematic issue. If it is argued that confusion will derive from the multiplicity of different social conundrums being provided by the motivations and decisions of the characters, then the situation might be easier if a single focus were selected which would gradually reveal itself as each separate version of the action was brought to the student's observation. In this way the illumination would be gradual and consistent. If the theme were deliberately selected to be representative of a major element of American cultural attitudes, such as the attitude toward the aged, there would be the advantage of an increasing familiarity with the American responses that may have previously been confusing. For example, one persistent theme in American literature, as in American folk consciousness, is the idea of the lone man. This individualism is seen as heroic rather than unhappy or deplorable and occurs in mythical stories of cowboys (Shane) and detectives (Philip Marlowe) and many Humphrey Bogart movies. The idea shocks students from areas having more socially cohesive social life patterns. Yet it is so central to American thought that it deserves a careful study. Because of the omnipresence of the subject, some of the finest American literature focuses on this theme, and, therefore, purely literary excellence can also be considered. Further attempts at this task would be valuable and would be relatively easy in that such arrangements are not as entirely dependent on analysis of difficulty levels as are more general courses. It is assumed that the various selections would, over the period of the program, clarify each other at least at the cultural level. For examples of studies dealing with problems of selection see Bengur (1973), which deals with selection for a heterogeneous university ESL class, and Band (1974), which deals with selection for one cohesive group, i.e., Hebrew-speaking university students.

Methodology

One practical area of literary research would be experiments to determine effective teaching methodologies. Initially, it would be valuable to make an adequate survey of the accepted methods of teaching literature in the various circumstances of native-speaking classrooms. I believe that it is important to examine this educational material, and it is something that is often neglected in TESL studies. It is true that ESL can be argued to be a new subject, but it is obviously related to the last few centuries of teaching the English language and literature to native speakers.

I have read several attempts by graduate students to offer a bibliography on the "Literature and TESL" field. They are always lamentably brief because the choice of sources has been so severely restricted. The defense of such brevity is usually "there hasn't been much done." This is simultaneously true in one sense and yet highly inadequate because such lists have not considered the possibilities inherent in the riches provided by previous research into methodology in the general field of literature teaching. Of course, the methods cannot necessarily be taken over wholesale. They may be quite useless or only suitable after adaptation and modification, but the work in this field should be evaluated.

If methodological experimental studies and tests are to have any validity, they will ideally require all the usual apparatus of control groups to balance the competing methodologies. It may here be argued that the relatively few people who can be examined for such a thesis may barely constitute a cross-section adequate to be statistically significant. The defense would be that, after all, we are undertaking fairly small first steps to test our hypothesis, the conclusions to which will themselves be subject to more extensive examination if they seem viable. In this way tests can be attempted, reformed, and reiterated, gradually becoming the exact and efficient testing instrument we seek.

There are obviously almost unlimited specifics of methodology. Approaches may be almost as varied as the individual teacher who undertakes them in his or her classroom. But it would seem that there are two particular questions that might be tested as a general issue underlying most of the approaches. The division in my mind would be the degree to which explications best preceded the presentation or would be confirmed inductively as the material is presented. The debate over this question must reconcile two opposing prospects: whether for there to be an initial exciting impact from the work of literature it is essential to provide extensive preparation prior to a first reading so that immediate understanding and pleasure is engendered, or whether the amount of explanation that necessarily has to precede the first reading is in itself so monumental and demanding of time and attention that interest is lost well before the student comes around to the enjoyment of the word.

There could be tests to decide the degree of comprehension that is achieved by the two methods and the variations that they seem to apply. Of course, even here we are getting back to those untested presuppositions of the earlier part of the paper. A teacher presents a series of words or sentence structures deemed to be difficult for the student in the particular class and prepares to explain unfamiliar attitudes and actions anticipated to be unintelligible or misleading. Yet again, that *deemed* and *anticipated* indicate the expectations of the teacher. These will only be as valuable and rational as his or her experience and special knowledge of the individual class can provide. These assertions are still locked in the dubious proof of opinion.

Methodology itself is, by definition, not an abstract. It can only be adequately defended in relation to an appropriate target. Bauman's proposals regarding a humanistic approach to teaching literature overseas (Bauman, 1972) constitute just one attempt. It is hard to see how such a project could be undertaken in a truly scientific or quantitative manner, but it is still obvious that we do not really have a clear knowledge of what we are doing with literature. If literature is at the service of language teaching in a basic and specific sense, then one might want to check whether there is anything in narrative prose that is more satisfactory for the teaching task than expository prose. Is the interest in the events of the tale superior to the interest sustained by a logical argument on some general subject such as space science or cooking? Unless this is true, one would question the utility of literature. If it proves true that literature commands more attention, one would assume that this is because a reader is enticed through the pages by the eager interest to discover the next development in the plot and ultimately the conclusion. Does this then mean that the best stories are those where the drive of the plot whips onward a linguistic attention that might otherwise lag, and does the plot supply that spur to the general level of competence that is usually barely adequate to the recognition of the ideas in newspaper articles? In my own case my reading in French was improved by a diet of Simenon. Likewise, is it possible that modern drama with its use of colloquial speech and human interaction is methodologically a good literary genre to use in the ESL classroom? Stern (1977) addresses this question and offers an affirmative response. Via (1976) in fact has written a book espousing the use of drama in the form of a play production in the ESL classroom.

The teaching of literature to the ESL student is in much the same place as the language teaching side of our subject was some thirty years ago, before it was liberated from native-speaking customs by the researches of linguistic scholars. Their studies indicated that experiment could determine how things could be more effectively done for the special circumstances of second language learners. In our satisfaction with the successes of the elementary language methodology in our field, we have neglected to investigate what alterations will be necessary in adapting the teaching of literature to ESL students. There are numerous research needs and perhaps some of the areas I have outlined will attract the attention of those who realize that the obligations of the ESL teacher do not end with success at the limited level of oral-aural discourse.

DISCUSSION QUESTIONS

1. What reasons are advanced to recommend literature in ESL classes? What particular complications arise from teaching literature in ESL classes?

2. What is the difference between a teacher of literature and a teacher of literature for foreign students?

3. What are the obvious differences between an ESL student and a native speaker of English of similar linguistic ability?

4. What are the practical difficulties that hinder the exact measurement of the level of difficulty of a piece of literature?

5. Is contemporary poetry usually as desirable in class as contemporary prose?

6. How does a simile work? In what way are similes sometimes "culture-tied"?

7. State the three levels of vocabulary distinguished by the writer to be found in a work of literature.

8. What problems remain for the foreign student after linguistic comprehension has been achieved?

9. Come up with a defensible educational theory to justify a particular principle of text choice for a class in literature and name examples of works that would exactly fulfill your criteria.

10. If background is a major element in miscomprehension, is there an argument for including in the works presented material from the students' own culture translated into English so that only the language would be unfamiliar?

11. Is the foreign student's unfamiliarity with American literature analogous with your own lack of knowledge of certain regional American literatures such as Black literature, or the Jewish novel, etc.? Why or why not?

12. Do you feel that in your selection of material you have any non-literary obligations? I.e., for offering a breadth of American experience or the good (or bad) face of the country only?

13. Discuss the advantages or disadvantages in using some of the major new world literatures employing English as a second language in ESL classes.

SUGGESTED ACTIVITIES

1. What methods could be used to measure with some mathematical exactness a student's degree of comprehension of a work of literature? Demonstrate with examples.

2. Undertake a contrastive analysis of the cultural presuppositions of a short story, against the cultural expectations of one foreign culture familiar to you (cf. Pincus, 1963b).

3. Effect a cultural translation of a short story into another national environment. Judge how much must be altered to make a similar impact.

4. Select two short stories that seem to you the clearest examples of "culture-tied" or "universal" situations. Show why you feel that the works justify their label.

5. Select a single story or poem and with minute attention to detail indicate the words and situations that require cultural explication. Perhaps do this task deliberately for one specific national or regional group.

6. Prepare a presentation of the cultural background required for teaching any poem by Whitman, Sandburg or Frost. What materials would be required—slides? films?

7. Select a major work of pre-twentieth century literature and justify it as being especially appropriate for inclusion in the syllabus for some specific cultural or national group you know well. Or do the same thing in reverse pointing out a most inappropriate work and indicating why it would not be well received.

8. Prepare a questionnaire that will establish the degree of comprehension that has been achieved after you have taught a short story to some students.

9. Prepare either a term's syllabus, or a book list, or a specific lesson plan that would be ideal for a certain group of foreign students. Justify the principles of your selection.

10. Study a piece of foreign literature in translation and see whether it provides you with similar difficulties that you imagine a foreign student might encounter in the reverse situation. Does this experiment permit generalizations?

11. Indicate how you might measure linguistic difficulty in a work of literature. Explain your theory by indicating a single work that might be judged particularly easy or difficult by your standards.

12. Set up some scale for the measure of cultural complexity in the work of literature. Apply your scale in an illuminating way to some work(s).

SUGGESTIONS FOR FURTHER READING

There is not a great deal of material on this subject as there has always been the belief that at an advanced level of English usage there is little need to make allowance for the second language situation.

Bright, J. A., and G. P. McGregor (1971)
Teaching English as a Second Language. Harlow: Longmans.
The literature chapters, pp. 201-36, have more useful discussion and examples than most TESL texts.

Dunning, Stephen (1968)
Teaching Literature to Adolescents. Scott Foresman. There is a volume each on plays, poetry, and short stories. They are excellent guides for teachers, though are not texts for students.

Imamura, Shigeo, and James Ney (1969)
Readings from Samuel Clemens. Waltham, Mass.: Ginn Co.
Has a teacher's guide. It can be regarded as a representative example of the simplification of reading material, and the use of literature for the development of general language skills.

Jenkinson, E. B. (ed.) (1967)
On Teaching Literature. Bloomington, Indiana.
Again, not directly focused upon TESL, but this is an important collection provided by the prestigious English Curriculum Study Center at Indiana University.

Press, John (ed.) (1963)
The Teaching of Literature Overseas. London: Methuen.
This brings together the papers delivered at a British conference. There are many distinguished contributors, but they generally take the assumption that the classics of English literature are a vital part of overseas teaching. The debate is on the means rather than the whethers.

Squire, James (ed.) (1966)
A Common Purpose. Champaign, Illinois: National Council of Teachers of English.
These are the papers delivered at an NCTE conference, and supply important background to the ESL situation, if only by implication.

Topping, Donald (1968)
"Linguistics or Literature: An Approach to Language," *TESOL*, Vol. 2, No. 2, 95-100.
A witty, scathing rejection of the place of *any* literature in ESL classes, which he argues belong to the linguist!

Via, Richard (1976)
English in Three Acts. Honolulu: University of Hawaii Press.
A manual showing the ESL teacher how to make a play production the focus of an ESL class. Good step-by-step instructions.

D. Writing

The ability to express one's ideas in written form in a second language and to do so with reasonable accuracy and coherence is no mean achievement, since many native speakers of English never truly master this skill. Gorman's chapter on teaching composition surveys the techniques that can be used to teach writing at different proficiency levels in the ESL classroom. Specific teaching suggestions are also discussed in terms of four progressively less manipulative categories: controlled writing, directed composition, guided composition, and free writing.

An adjunct to good writing is good spelling. Many ESL students (like native speakers) need special assistance and practice if they are to improve their spelling in English. Cronnell's article provides the necessary background and many useful suggestions.

THE TEACHING OF COMPOSITION

Thomas P. Gorman

A CRITIQUE OF SOME
METHODS OF TEACHING COMPOSITION

Composition involves the production and arrangement of written sentences in a manner appropriate to the purposes of the writer, the person or persons addressed, and the function of what is written. It is a complex activity requiring a variety of skills; and there is no general agreement among teachers regarding the methods to be used in teaching it.

To illustrate the point, I would like to outline and comment on some methods of teaching that have been or are being adopted, and subsequently to make detailed practical suggestions regarding techniques that might be used in a composition program.

The controlled expression method

A program that will serve to illustrate several of the features I associate with this method was outlined some years ago in an article by Pincas (1963a). She argued that "since free composition relies on inventiveness, on creativeness, it is in direct opposition to the expressed ideals of scientific habit-forming teaching methods which strive to prevent error from occurring."

Pincas outlined a course that served to reflect the methodological principles she accepted. She suggested that emphasis should shift progressively from the substitution of words in sentences of different patterns to the substitution of sentences in paragraphs of different types and finally to the substitution of what she termed "literary devices" in whole essays or stories. At first, students would be told what to substitute and where to substitute it. Later they would be encouraged to develop their own terms for substitution—but at no stage would free expression be permitted.

Naturally the program suggested is more complex than the above description might indicate. In the teaching scheme, multiple substitution exercises of this kind constitute only one stage in a scheme of training that includes: (a) practice in the recognition of different vocabulary and sentence constructions used in writing and speech; (b) practice in production involving contrasts of the "stages of speech and writing," and only when the student's recognition of the various features of English writing is fairly reliable should s/he begin to produce these; (c) practice in the recognition of different styles of writing for different purposes; and (d) composition writing involving multiple substitution.

The program reflects a theory of language learning that is in part superseded. One assumption underlying it is that "the use of language is the manipulation of fixed patterns which are learnt by imitation" and "not until these have been learnt can originality occur in their manipulation or variation." We now recognize that language is not a habit-structure and that pattern practice involving elements of surface structure cannot be so confidently assumed to be the obvious way in which to effect students' language competence. Additionally, while the writer speaks of practice in the recognition of the different vocabulary and sentence constructions used in writing and speech and in different styles, it is apparent that the categories she uses in discussing these—as, for instance, persuasive versus descriptive styles, or business jargon versus personal writing—reflect a rudimentary form of stylistic analysis.

The fact is that the theoretical basis for the description of personal and group registers and individual and "collective" styles of writing is only just being developed. Description of the ways writers organize the language system to compensate for the absence of a variety of paralinguistic elements such as voice dynamics and gesture or to compensate for the absence of feedback has only recently been undertaken; and an adequate pedagogical grammar of written English is not available. Teachers of writing, therefore, generally have to rely on their own casual impressions of the numerous differences between the grammatical features of the many varieties of speech and more numerous varieties of writing.

To follow Pincas' suggestions in detail is, consequently, far more difficult than may initially appear to be the case. Nevertheless, there are features of the program suggested that can be usefully applied in the classroom, and I will refer to certain of these in my concluding section.

The free expression method

Several of the features I associate with this method were outlined by Erazmus (1960) in his description some years ago of the "program of fluency," as he termed it, then used at the University of Michigan. One feature of the program he described was that students were "pushed and motivated to produce extensively with little regard to the number and type of errors and infelicities" and were directed to write rapidly with little revision or recomposition. In the system of values that was projected, greatest emphasis was placed on the length of the materials produced. In his commentary on the method, Erazmus argued that "it is more important to have the student produce large quantities of material than to produce perfect copy." He further justified the method on the grounds that "every new use by a student of a vocabulary item, a variation in syntactic sequence or a different structural combination is an enrichment of his language experience and an incorporation into his active language control of a new range of morphemes and their distribution. This is worth the errors that he makes. The next time he goes over similar territory he will do so with greater security and ease and with fewer mistakes." Erazmus supported this argument with the arguable state-

ment that "language is a self-correcting and self-expanding system, and the more it is used, the greater facility there is in the use of it."

Methods similar to the one described above have been discussed favorably by a number of commentators. Chastain (1976), for example, cites an experiment carried out some years ago at UCLA by Brière which, Chastain asserts, demonstrated the success of such a program of "fluency" emphasizing quantity rather than quality, and which indicated that such a program "resulted in students writing more materials with fewer errors than did a program in which essays had been carefully prepared and corrected."

The experiment as described by Brière had these features. In an experimental group, students wrote freely for at least six minutes during each class session on the subject of a cartoon. Regardless of the number of errors made, only two errors at the most were indicated by the instructor. Weekly compositions ranging progressively from 300 to 500 words in length were assigned and a term paper of a minimum of 1,000 words was required. Home and class composition and term papers were carefully corrected, and students receiving any grade below "A" were asked to rewrite their compositions.

The final tests showed that there was a decrease in error rate and an increase in quantity of output during the course. In his description of the experiment, Brière suggested that one interpretation of the results might be that "an emphasis on quantity will produce greater fluency and also have the concomitant effect of reducing error rate," and he posited that "an emphasis on quantity and fluency will produce far better results than any emphasis on quality." He concluded that although no definitive statements could be made concerning the efficacy of emphasizing quantity before quality on the basis of this pilot study, the results led him to "temporarily accept the hypothesis that in the beginning emphasis should be placed on the quantity of writing rather than the quality" (Brière, 1966).

In view of the experimental design of the study, these conclusions are, in my opinion, unjustified. The experimenter used two methods of teaching the one group of students—not two groups as Chastain infers (p. 236). One method involved an emphasis on fluency and quantity, the other emphasized the identification, correction, and revision of errors. There appears to be no way of deducing from the evidence provided in what measure either of the two methods contributed to the final result.

There is, in fact, no convincing evidence that requiring students to write freely and at length under circumstances in which their work is not corrected is likely to reduce the error rate. There is, indeed, some evidence to the contrary.[1] However, exercises in "speed-writing," in which students are asked to write as much as they are able to about a particular subject in a limited time may be helpful in encouraging them to organize the content of their work with greater facility and in preparing them to take examinations.[2]

The literary model method

This approach generally involves presenting students with extracts from the works of well-known writers and subjecting these to some form of stylistic analysis and imitation. The method as generally practiced is not, in my view, one that can be recommended for use with students of English as a second language as distinct from students of English as a second literature, so I will not discuss it further here. This is not to say, however, that there are no circumstances in which examples of contemporary literature might not be used to advantage to illustrate the use of particular stylistic features or to provide subjects for discussion and subsequent composition in advanced classes.

The rhetorical method

I refer here to that body of rhetorical theory and related practice concerning such matters as "invention," "arrangement," and "style" in written work. Characteristic of one popular rhetorical tradition is a recognition of forms of descriptive, narrative, expository, and argumentative prose—the division supposedly designating the different ways of ordering statements within paragraphs and paragraphs within complete passages. For the purposes of analysis, some practitioners also accept a distinction between three major sentence types—loose, periodic, and balanced sentences. More recent studies have isolated other types (Christensen, 1967). But since such distinctions do not derive from a coherent system of grammatical description, their pedagogical utility is limited.[3]

Many texts drawing on the rhetorical tradition also instruct students in the use of schemes according to which materials can be organized and arguments presented. Emphasis is given to different patterns of organization that paragraphs might assume through processes of analysis, contrast, analogy, etc. I think it is apparent that the application or imitation of such procedural patterns of paragraph development is unlikely to encourage students to write with any degree of spontaneity. Nor, in my opinion, is such exposure likely to teach students to think more clearly, as is occasionally suggested.

In particular, teachers should be aware of the tentative nature of the conclusions of studies that purport to have, in some sense, codified in rhetorical terms "the thought patterns which speakers and readers of English appear to expect as an integral part of their communication" and of the reduction of these to a limited number of types of paragraph structure. Kaplan, for example (from whom the above quotation is taken), suggested some years ago that "two types of (paragraph) development represent the common *inductive* and *deductive* reasoning which the English reader expects to be an integral part of any formal communication." He further suggested, on the basis of experimental evidence which appears to be tenuous, that speakers of other languages do not share the English preference or penchant for sequences that are "dominantly linear" in development (Kaplan, 1966). Bander interprets and paraphrases Kaplan's suggestions as follows: "In following a direct line of development, an English paragraph is very different from an Oriental paragraph, which tends to follow a circular line of development. It also differs from a Semitic paragraph, which tends to follow parallel lines of development. A paragraph in Spanish, or in some other Romance language, differs in still another way: its line of thought is sometimes interrupted by rather complex digressions. Similarly a paragraph in Russian often contains digressions . . ." (Bander, 1971). It will be apparent that such generalizations are greatly oversimplified.

These comments should not be taken to imply that in a course for university students it is not useful to discuss matters relating to the organization of research papers, for example, or to present students with essays that employ different types of organization or structure. I wish simply to question the value of much that passes for training in rhetoric and logical analysis and to reassert with Kitzhaber (1963) that "the majority of handbooks present a dessicated rhetorical doctrine that has probably done a great deal more over the years to hinder good writing than to foster it."

TEACHING COMPOSITION: SOME SPECIFIC TECHNIQUES

So far this commentary has been largely negative. I would now like to make some comments about procedures a teacher might usefully employ in teaching students to compose and in correcting what they write. The first step, of course, is for the teacher to define his or her long-term objectives in the light of the needs of his or her students and their proficiency-level in English, and of the length and intensity of the course. Since, as was mentioned earlier, writing involves the use of a variety of skills, the teacher will then need to decide on the skills to be taught and on the selection and sequencing of the exercises to be used.

It has been said that in the process of composition there are three principle areas of choice, namely what to say; how to sequence what is said; and how to express what is said. These can be termed the areas of content, organization, and expression, and the teacher needs to establish a set of criteria in each of these areas to determine how to evaluate a piece of writing.

Content
In undertaking some form of content analysis of written work, it is appropriate to consider whether the writer has dealt with the subject selected with a degree of adequacy, given his or her general abilities and the information avail-

able; and whether, as far as can be judged, s/he has said what s/he wanted to say with a measure of clarity.

Organization
The teacher will examine the structure which is imparted to the content both within paragraphs and in larger units of discourse, and might, for instance, ask such questions as: Is the proposition that is dealt with appropriately introduced and presented? If the propositions or observations have several facets, are these developed according to their relative significance? Is the paper appropriately concluded? etc.

Expression
The teacher might concern him- or herself with the accuracy with which students use devices of punctuation and other orthographic conventions. Second, s/he could concern him- or herself with whether what the student writes is grammatical. Third, s/he might consider the extent to which what is written is contextually appropriate, and ask, for instance, whether the selection of items of vocabulary and syntax is appropriate to the level of formality of the passage, or the register adopted.

There are other sets of skills not mentioned here that some teachers would consider relevant to the process of composition, particularly at more advanced levels, such as the conscious use of stylistic features for aesthetic purposes;[4] but my intention here is simply to identify certain areas of activity that are relevant to teachers of composition, as I have defined it, at all levels.

Having decided on the skill or skills to be taught at particular times, the teacher needs to decide on the types of exercises to use with his or her students. As an aid to the categorization of these I would like to suggest a distinction between *controlled*, *directed*, and *guided* exercises, and to apply the terms to activities which can be distinguished primarily by the degree to which the student is obliged to work independently. I will use the term *controlled composition* to apply to activities in which students are presented with a set of sentences or a written text and given directions regarding ways in which these should be modified. They should also be given information necessary to check the accuracy of what they have written. I will use the term *directed composition* to describe activities in which students originate the sentences, but in which they are given suggestions regarding the content and organization of what is written. These activities are generally appropriate for pair or group activity and require direct teacher supervision or involvement. In *guided composition* exercises, suggestions are given regarding the content of the written work, but students work independently. Each of these types of exercises is to be distinguished from *free* or *independent composition*.

Controlled composition

Most of the exercises mentioned in this subsection might best be regarded as pre-composition activities and for the most part they have the limited aim of ensuring that what the student writes is grammatically correct. I will illustrate them with reference to the following passage, and will refer to a text or texts in which examples of the techniques are discussed or illustrated.

The mayor walked to the microphone with a number of papers in his hand. He looked calm and relaxed. As he began to speak a man rose from his seat and moved toward the platform. He was holding something in his hand and facing in the mayor's direction. People in the audience began to shout at him. The mayor stopped speaking and raised his hand to ask for silence. One woman began to scream and another to shout a warning. Unfortunately it was too late. The tomato hit him on the ear with an audible thud.

Suggested exercises

1.   Alteration of model sentences changing a specific grammatical feature such as tense: e.g., *Rewrite the passage from the point of view of an observer describing the events as they happen. Begin as follows: "The mayor is walking to the microphone. . . ."* (Dykstra et al., 1966; Robinson, 1967; Dykstra and Paulston, 1967, etc.)

2.   Alteration of a set of related grammatical features: e.g., *Substitute "mayoress" for "mayor" and make the necessary changes to the text.*

3.   Simple substitution frames (all alternatives are acceptable); e.g., *Rewrite the sentence(s) using one of the words in each column.*

The mayor	*walked to*	*the microphone with a sheaf*		*of cards in his hand. . .*
speaker	went	dais	bundle	papers
guest of honor	moved	platform	number	folders

4.   Correlative substitution frames: e.g., *Rewrite the sentence(s) using one of the words in each column.* (In this exercise the selection of one alternative form such as *mayoress* requires the selection of the appropriate form of possessive pronoun):

The mayor	*moved*	*to the platform with a number of papers in his hand.*	
mayoress	stepped	stage	bundle	her

He looked calm and relaxed.
She   serene   at ease.

(Moody, 1965)

5.   Sentence-combining exercises: e.g., *Combine the following sentences into two sentences: The mayor walked to the microphone. The mayor had a number of papers in his hand. He began to speak. A man rose from his seat. The man moved toward the platform.* Generally it seems appropriate for the teachers to do the initial task of sentence analysis and for students to concern themselves with

sentence synthesis, but Rand, from whom these terms are derived, has found it feasible for students to do both activities at intervals of approximately one week. (Rand, 1967; Ross, 1968; Mellon, 1969;.O'Hare, 1971)

6. Sentence expansion with modifiers: e.g., *Rewrite the sentence and insert an appropriate modifier in place of each of the numbers.*

The (1) mayor walked (2) to the microphone, with a number of (3) papers in his (4) hand.

    (1) old; unpopular, ailing
    (2) quickly; slowly; confidently
    (3) folded; crumpled; colored
    (4) shaking; right; outstretched

(Spencer, 1965)

7. Selection of appropriate linking words and transitional devices: e.g., *Insert an appropriate word or phrase from the list below in place of each of the numbers. Make the first letter a capital letter and add any necessary punctuation marks to the sentence.*

The mayor walked to the microphone with a number of papers in his hand. (1) He looked calm and relaxed. (2) As he began to speak a man rose from his seat and moved toward the platform. He was holding something in his hand and facing in the mayor's direction. People in the audience began to shout at him. (3) The mayor stopped speaking and raised his hand to ask for silence. (4) One woman began to scream and another to shout a warning. (5) Unfortunately it was too late. The tomato hit him on the ear with an audible thud.

suddenly   but   at least   because of this   however

8. Sentence sense exercises: e.g., *Link the appropriate sentence in column B with one of the sentences in column A, and rewrite the linked sentences as one paragraph.*

A	B
The mayor walked to the microphone	a man rose from his seat and moved toward the platform
As he began to speak	and facing in the mayor's direction
He was holding something in his hand	with a number of papers in his hand
The mayor stopped speaking	with an audible thud
One woman began to scream	and raised his hand to ask for silence
The tomato hit him on the ear	and another to shout a warning

(Dacanay and Bowen, 1963)

9. Multiple substitution exercises: e.g., *Using the passage as a model write a paragraph beginning: "The policeman ran to the bank...."* (This is a difficult manipulative exercise which is primarily useful as a means of getting relatively advanced students to employ features of grammatical or rhetorical usage which they would be unlikely to use otherwise.)

Other types of exercises in which students are required to recall the content of materials previously read or heard (and subsequently consulted) can also be classified in the category of controlled writing. Two examples are (a) text dictation and (b) text reconstruction. Dictation can be used to check the accuracy with which features of spelling and punctuation are used; text reconstruction to check the accuracy of grammatical and stylistic choices made by the student. The latter technique was employed in an interesting fashion in Newmark et al. (1964). Students are presented with short passages of prose and asked to memorize these and subsequently to reconstruct the original in class from a partly obliterated version. In the incomplete version, alternative or synonymous items to those omitted are provided to serve as memory cues, to clarify the meaning of the original, and to expand the students' vocabulary range.

The dicto-comp, as it is sometimes called, combines features of both techniques. The teacher reads a short passage and asks questions on its content. S/he then rereads the passage and puts a number of key words on the board. Using these as cues, the students attempt to rewrite the story in as complete a form as possible (Hatch, 1971, and Wishon and Burks, 1968).

It would be a simple matter to devise exercises of this type that would require the student to choose between two or more synonyms, only one of which would be contextually appropriate. Several of the other exercises detailed here could also be adapted for this purpose. Arapoff, for example, has devised a form of correlative substitution table for testing the ability of advanced students to select an appropriate sequence of rhetorical devices (Arapoff, 1968).

Another type of controlled exercise can be used to practice and test the abilities needed to organize sentences sequentially within paragraphs and paragraphs within longer pieces of discourse. The teacher can simply rearrange the order in which the sentences or paragraphs appear in a passage and ask the student to attempt to reconstruct the original.

As I said above, in each of the activities the student should be in a position to check the accuracy of his or her own responses. One way to ensure that this is possible is to base the exercises on materials that have been previously read by the students or, at an earlier stage of language learning, on materials that they have learned in dialogues or oral exercises and seen written on the board.

Directed composition

I will list a number of activities under this heading. But in most cases, it will not be necessary, I think, to give a specific example of each type of exercise. As was mentioned earlier, many of these exercises lend themselves to group activity.

1. Written interviews with fellow students—a useful introductory exercise for a group of students meeting for the first time.

2. Exercises in which the content and sequence of events are provided by a series of pictures or cartoons; or by film strips or short movies.

3. Exercises in which a story or oral narrative told by the teacher is retold in written form.

4. Exercises involving note-taking from a lecture or a talk, followed by a subsequent written report. A language laboratory can be utilized for such activities if available.

5. Exercises in which the students complete a narrative relating to a particular event or a person's life (real or imaginary) in which they may be given the freedom to select from a number of possible alternative renderings of the narrative. *(The assassin was born in (St. James infirmary; Boston; Peoria). His father was (an acrobat; a successful writer; unknown). At the age of seven he (left home; caught the measles; composed a quartet). His mother who was a(n) (clergyman's daughter; New Yorker; English woman) never wholly recovered from the shock this caused her. . . .)* (Sandburg, 1967)

6. A similar exercise in which students are required to answer a series of questions about a person or event. e.g., *When was . . . born? Where was s/he born? Who was his or her father? Where did s/he go to school? What were his or her favorite subjects? When did his or her interest in vivisection become apparent? . . .* etc. (Hill, 1966)

7. Exercises in which the teacher and class, or students organized into writing groups, develop compositions following discussion and initial agreement on the composition structure.

It seems appropriate also to classify under this heading activities involving summary or paraphrase of a piece of writing, and exercises in which students are asked to report in writing on information given in a particular passage. Text-based activities of this kind can be associated with intensive reading exercises and can, of course, be of varying degrees of difficulty. Such exercises might involve the simple recording of information given in the passage, or the student might be presented with more difficult questions requiring the exercise of judgment and evaluation.

Guided composition
At this stage, I envisage the student working independently but being given suggestions regarding the content and, to a lesser degree, the form of what s/he should write. Exercises used at this stage might include:

1.   Situational compositions of various kinds. In these students are informed about a detailed set of circumstances which requires from them a written response. E.g., *You are the secretary of a basketball team. You have been asked by the captain to write a letter to a member of the team thanking him or her for his or her efforts but telling him or her politely that s/he has been replaced on the team by a younger member . . . , etc.* (Further details of the situation and of the character to be addressed could be provided.)

2.   Letter chains. This is a variation of the situational composition in which students might be asked, for example, to respond to letters sent by other students who are taking the roles of other characters in a particular situation.

3.   Text-based activities involving the discussion or refutation of an argument in a particular passage or the elaboration of such an argument. At an advanced stage, such elaboration might also involve utilization of stylistic features characteristic of the passage under discussion.

Independent writing
For the most part, the types of independent writing that teachers deal with concern writing that involves the student in some form of research activity or in some form of creative activity in the usual sense of the word. Under this heading, therefore, we might classify the following very different kinds of activities:

1.   The writing of term papers or research and other reports in which the basic intention is to convey information accurately and clearly. There are a considerable number of effective guides which discuss methods of approach and layout and give suggestions regarding the organization of footnotes and bibliographical data. The basic procedures in these respects are the same for students of English as a first or second language.

2.   Creative writing including (a) personal diaries and (b) original essays, short stories or poems.

Any inclination that individual students may show toward creative verbal activity should be strongly encouraged, and teachers should make an effort to develop such interests by exposing students to short stories or poems appropriate to their backgrounds and age group and encouraging them to write their own for the interest and entertainment of the class if this seems to be appropriate. In some circumstances it is possible to establish a class magazine or to set up a communications board through which original work can be shared with other students. Students should, when feasible, be encouraged to keep personal diaries. I have found repeatedly that foreign students away from their home and family frequently have much to say and no one to say it to. They sometimes welcome the opportunity of commenting on aspects of their daily lives and of the culture with which they are in contact.

With regard to occasional essays, teachers should generally avoid asking students to perform the extremely difficult task of writing on general topics (such as *Wealth* or *Capital punishment*) unless these have been thoroughly discussed in class beforehand. As a general rule they should not be asked to deal with topics which they otherwise would not conceivably be required to write about outside school.

I trust that what has been said so far will not be interpreted to mean that teachers should necessarily restrict themselves to the use of controlled exercises at beginning levels of instruction and only introduce exercises requiring greater independence at more advanced levels. A teacher could follow such a program of activities, of course, if his or her overriding intention was to ensure the grammatical accuracy of what is written. But even at an early stage of language learning some students will find certain kinds of directed composition feasible and interesting, particularly if they are working cooperatively in groups—and such enjoyment should not be wholly subordinated to the ideal of correctness.

A TEXT-BASED COMPOSITION METHOD

In the preceding sections I have outlined a number of methods and techniques at present in use in teaching composition. It is essential that teachers adopt an eclectic approach to this task and select such means as seem appropriate to their classes and their needs. In my own work, however, I have become increasingly convinced of the effectiveness of an approach that involves a closer integration of reading and writing skills than is evident in the methods discussed earlier. I have described such a text-based method elsewhere in the following terms (Gorman, 1973):

"Having specified his objectives the teacher should get hold of written materials from any sources that exemplify such written varieties as he considers might serve as a stylistic point of reference, and which will provide students with subjects for the class discussion that will precede most writing assignments. These will also provide a basis for substitution and extension exercises, and sentence-combining exercises if these are used.

"The initial stage in class activities will involve a reading of the article or passage selected and a discussion of this. Any vocabulary item that is not generally understood should be identified and exemplified in various contexts if an understanding of it is necessary for a full understanding of the text. At this stage the instructor might point out any item of grammatical structure that he wishes to draw attention to. His observations in this respect can be as detailed as he has the time and inclination to make them. He might, for instance, simply draw attention to items that might be misunderstood or that are characteristic of formal academic discourse or that are for one reason or other unusual in such prose; or he might systematically identify the various noun-replacement transformations in the passage.

"The teacher should give the members of the class such information about the writer and the readers to whom he addressed himself and, if relevant, the occasion on which he did so, as will provide a basis for brief discussion of the purposes he had in writing the article, the effects he wished to secure and, *in relation to these factors*, the style of writing adopted or employed. In this context I am using the term style to encompass the writer's choice from among the organizational, rhetorical, grammatical and lexical options available to him (given the restrictions imposed by the conventions governing the type of written work undertaken). One task the teacher should set himself is to get his students to repeatedly ask themselves the question: Why has the writer used this particular item? And subsequently in substitution-type exercises to get them to consider what other possible ways there are of saying the same thing—given the information they have already deduced or been given about the writer, his audience, and his purposes.

"Such discussion can serve as a prelude to the writing of passages on issues related to the theme of the passage in question. These might involve, for example, commentary on the topic discussed, or refutation or elaboration of particular points raised. At advanced level, the arguments might be presented by the students from a different point of view or with a different audience in mind. All assignments should be such as to require the student to make close and frequent reference to the text. Exercises that require students to paraphrase sections of text have much to recommend them as do summary exercises involving note-taking.[5] All such activities practice skills that the student needs to use in school and, at the same time, require him to restate in ways that are appropriate to his purposes materials that have been prepared by other writers. Time taken to identify the significant points in a passage and to summarize these in intelligible form is never wasted. Such exercises can, however, be tedious for the student and initially they can be best done by the instructor working with the class in building up the paraphrase or summary on a blackboard or overhead projector."

CORRECTING COMPOSITIONS

Before concluding this essay I would like to make a few comments on the correction of compositions. Students should be asked to set out assignments in such a way as to leave the instructor room for commentary and themselves room for revision. It is essential to encourage students to keep all assignments in the same file. This allows for a check to be made on recurrent errors and progress in revision, if necessary. Personally, I correct assignments in detail but do not assign grades to individual essays. If grades are required or requested they are best given on the basis of all the work done over a period of time. A single paper written by a student on a given topic at a particular time cannot, as is well-known, be considered a valid basis for evaluating his or her achievement, unless his or her level of writing attainment is relatively low.

In class, it is generally practicable to focus attention for revision purposes on a limited number of items of general importance. In each class students will be found, for example, who make errors in written work relating to the use of the modal auxiliaries or involving tense harmony. In a short-term course a number of such items can be isolated from student essays for class discussion, but to go some way toward meeting the need for individual instruction the teacher should, if possible, have on hand a number of texts to which additional assignments can be given to those who need these.

I use a set of symbols characterizing different types of errors (see appendix to this paper) and familiarize students with these at the beginning of the course. So as not to depress students unduly it is generally sensible to concentrate on a limited set of error types at one reading and focus attention on errors relevant to aspects of composition under study.

Whenever possible, students should be encouraged to collaborate both in the preparation of compositions and in their correction. They should also be encouraged to prepare initial drafts of their work and to get the advice of members of their writing group and subsequently of their teacher on such drafts on the understanding that if a grade is to be assigned it will be assigned on the basis of the final draft. After the final draft has been marked, it should be talked over with the student if this is feasible—in an after-class session if necessary. At this time, deficiencies or achievements that cannot be adequately indicated by corrective symbols can be discussed. The teacher should emphasize that good writing frequently requires a "fumbling for exactitude"[6] that can only be achieved by careful rereading and revision. It is sometimes a consolation for students who find it difficult to express themselves on paper to realize that their difficulties are to some degree shared by all those who are seriously engaged in what can be the immensely demanding process of saying clearly what they mean and communicating this meaning unambiguously to others. The teacher's basic responsibility is to get students to the stage when through practice in editing their own work and that of others they are capable of recognizing and removing features that lead to incorrectness, ambiguity, pretentiousness and redundancy in expression, triviality or banality in content, and incoherence or lack of sequence in organization or form.

NOTES

1.   For example, a study by Buxton at Stanford University on the work of 257 students indicated that college freshmen whose writing is graded and thoroughly marked and criticized, and who revise their papers in the light of these criticisms, can improve their writing more than freshmen whose writing receives a few general suggestions but no grades or intensive marking, and who do not revise their papers. The subjects were native speakers of English but the findings are nevertheless relevant. They are reported in greater detail in Braddock et al., 1963, p. 70.

2. See Celce-Murcia, 1974, pp. 63-70.

3. Rhetorical theory is, of course, undergoing constant development and elaboration. For a contemporary viewpoint of some interest see Young and Becker (1965).

4. Rivers, for example, states that the ultimate aim of the writer is to be able to express him- or herself in "polished literary form which requires the utilization of a special vocabulary and certain refinements of structure. This we shall call *composition*" (Rivers, 1968, p. 243). Clearly such a definition implies that the teacher of composition should be concerned to some degree with the teaching of features of literary usage such as are characteristic of belletristic prose.

5. In my usage, a paraphrase involves a precise restatement of the significant points in a passage, presented in the student's own words and generally in paragraph form. A summary involves an itemization of the points made in schematic and sometimes abbreviated form, using the writer's terms if necessary.

6. The phrase was used by William Faulkner in "A Note on Sherwood Anderson," *Essays, Speeches and Public Letters*, 1965, p. 5.

DISCUSSION QUESTIONS

1. What basic differences are there between controlled and directed composition—between directed and guided composition—between guided and free composition (or independent writing)? What types of activities are carried out at each level and under what circumstances should these different approaches be used?

2. Describe the free expression method. Why is it controversial?

3. Why would it be difficult to develop an adequate and detailed syllabus for a composition course around the rhetorical tradition?

4. What does the author include under the three headings of content, organization and expression? Can you suggest other areas?

5. According to the author, how might the skills of reading and writing be more closely integrated in a composition course? Do you have any additional suggestions to make on this subject?

6. Why should a classroom teacher develop a clear statement concerning his or her practices in grading and correcting compositions?

SUGGESTED ACTIVITIES

1. You and two or three colleagues should read the following passage in preparation for a cooperative writing exercise.

"All men ... desire to have, in the woman most nearly connected with them, not a forced slave but a willing one. ... They have therefore put everything in practice to enslave their minds. ... All women are brought up from the very earliest years in the belief that their ideal of character is the very opposite to that of men; not self-will and government by self-control, but submission, and yielding to the control of others. ... When we put together three things: first, the natural attraction between the opposite sexes; secondly, the wife's entire dependence on the husband; and lastly, that the principal object of human pursuit, consideration, and all objects of social ambition, can in general be sought or obtained by her only through him, it would be a miracle if the object of being attractive to men had not become the polar star of feminine education and formation of character. And, this means of influence over the minds of women having been acquired, an instinct of selfishness made men avail themselves of it to the utmost, as a means of holding women in subjection, by representing to them meekness, submissiveness, and resignation of all individual will into the hands of a man, as an essential part of sexual attractiveness." (John Stewart Mill)

Discuss the passage and decide whether you agree or disagree with the argument or proposition. If you agree you should jointly write a paragraph or paragraphs indicating why this is so. If you disagree, do likewise.

The purpose of this exercise is to alert you to some of the questions that need to be decided on in the process of cooperative writing. How was responsibility for the different aspects of the task allocated? (Such responsibilities can include background research or inquiry, notetaking on the discussion, preparation of a draft, revising, preparation and typing of a final draft, etc.) Did one student write the draft and the others comment on it, or did each student write a draft? Which is preferable in this case?

2. If possible, obtain a copy of an essay written by a foreign student. Correct his or her errors of expression, of content, and organization using appropriate symbols. Is the error classification scheme suggested in the appendix to this chapter adequate for this purpose? What additional symbols might be appropriately used? (If more than one copy of the student essay can be made, this exercise could be undertaken by a number of markers who could undertake to grade the essay. Prior discussion of the criteria to be adopted with regard to grading the paper and subsequent discussion of the differences, if any, in grades assigned would help to clarify some of the problems involved in such an undertaking.)

3. Using the following passage or an extract from it as a point of departure, prepare exercises involving the following activities: (a) sentence-combining, (b) sentence expansion with modifiers, (c) a sentence-sense exercise, (d) a multiple substitution exercise. Make whatever changes in the text you think are advisable.

> A woman in a white dress met us at the border-crossing as had been agreed. She looked frightened. We began to understand why as we walked toward the steel gate. There were three men at the crossing looking in our direction. One of them had his left hand behind his back in an unusual way. Suddenly, he turned and walked straight at us. Pulling his hand from behind his back he presented me with a bunch of carnations.

4. The following words are frequently misspelled. Can you suggest a rule of thumb that would help students to avoid each of these errors? Try also to think of exceptions to the rule that you suggest.

Correct form	Misspelled form
noticeable	noticable
hoping	hopeing
referred	refered
stopping	stoping

guidance	guideance
arrangement	arrangment
offered	offerred
believe	beleive
receive	recieve

5. Punctuate the following passage. Then discuss the "rules" or conventions relating to capitalization in these instances.

> john is a french student who is studying history and english at the university of california los angeles on friday he has to write a report on a book called all quiet on the western front

SUGGESTIONS FOR FURTHER READING

The following articles contain useful discussion and illustration of techniques of teaching composition.

Paulston, C. B. (1972)
"Teaching Writing in the ESOL Classroom: Techniques of Controlled Composition," *TESOL Quarterly*, March, pp. 33-59.
This article contains numerous examples of what I have termed controlled and directed exercises, and it provides detailed bibliographical information.

Slager, W. R. (1966)
"Controlling Composition: Some Practical Classroom Techniques," in R. Kaplan (ed.) *NAFSA Studies and Papers*, English Language Series, 12.

Hatch, E. (1971)
"Composition, Control, Communication," *Workpapers in TESL*, V, pp. 47-53.
This paper gives a helpful set of suggestions regarding the need for communicative activities in the teaching of writing, particularly at the elementary level.

The following books have specific chapters dealing with the teaching of composition. They are noteworthy for their practical emphasis. The first text is written with reference to teachers in the Philippines, and the other texts reflect the writers' experience in Africa, but all three books contain suggestions that are applicable in most ESL teaching situations.

Dacanay, F., and J. D. Bowen (eds.) (1963)
Techniques and Procedures in Second Language Teaching (Chapter V). Quezon City, the Philippines: Phoenix Publishing House.

Bright, J. A. and G. P. McGregor (1971)
Teaching English as a Second Language, pp. 130-76. Harlow: Longmans.

Gurrey, P. (1955)
Teaching English as a Second Language. London: Longmans.

These textbooks should also be consulted for examples of controlled, directed, and guided composition exercises.

Dykstra, G., R. Port, and A. Port (1966)
Ananse Tales: A Course in Controlled Composition. New York: Columbia Teachers College Press.

Robinson, Lois (1967)
Guided Writing and Free Writing. New York: Harper & Row.

Newmark, L. et al. (1964)
Using American English. New York: Harper & Row.

NCTE (1972)
English for Today. Book Six. New York; McGraw-Hill.

Hill, L. A. (1966)
Free Composition Book. London: Oxford University Press.

——— (1966)
Outline Composition Book. London: Oxford University Press.

Paulston, C. B., and G. Dykstra (1973)
Controlled Composition in English as a Second Language. New York: Regents Publishing Co.

Several books that have been prepared for the assistance of teachers of English as a first language contain information that is relevant to the teaching of composition in a second language at intermediate and advanced levels.

Braddock, R., R. Lloyd-Jones, and L. Schoer (1963)
Research in Written Composition. Champaign, III.: NCTE.
This is a report and evaluation of research into the subject up to the date of publication. It is an essential reference source for those interested in this field.

Tate, G., and E. Corbett (eds.) (1970)
Teaching High School Composition.
The article by D. Nichols in this collection on the organization of composition is excellent.

Mirrielees, L. B. (1952)
Teaching Composition and Literature in Junior and Senior High School.
Though somewhat dated, this is still a useful source of reference. One of the sections of the book deals with the preparation of term papers and research papers.

Ehrlich, E., and D. Murphy (1965)
Writing and Researching: Term papers and reporting.

The following book also relates to the teaching of composition in the United States.

Kitzhaber, A. (1963)
Themes, Theories and Therapy. New York: McGraw-Hill.
This text reports on an inquiry into the teaching of composition at universities. It is perceptive and well-written.

APPENDIX: ERROR CLASSIFICATION SCHEME

Spelling and Punctuation

⬭ Error in spelling, punctuation or capitalization (circle error).

_____ Grammatical error (underline)

Grammaticalness

a	Error in use (or omission) of article
t	Error in tense
aux	Error in use of Auxiliary
ag	Error in agreement
tr	Inappropriate sentence connector
w.o.	Incorrect word order

Lexico/semantic error

〰〰〰 Lexical/semantic error (underline)

∧ Insert a word or phrase

X Delete this word or phrase

Stylistic/rhetorical error

⟨ ⟩ Incomplete sentence

{ } Rewrite as a series of shorter sentences

Col. Colloquial: too informal for the context

Lit.	Literary: too formal for the context
Reg.	Not appropriate for the written register used
Aud.	Not appropriate for the audience addressed

Organizational error

?I	Inadequate introduction
?C	Inadequate conclusion
¶	Begin a new paragraph
TR	Inadequate transition or connection between paragraphs

Error in content

D	Inadequate development of a proposition or argument
?[ ]	Unclear proposition or argument
X[ ]	Proposition or argument inaccurate

Every teacher should develop his or her own scheme and an additional set of categories for indicating approbation and achievement.

SPELLING ENGLISH AS A SECOND LANGUAGE*

Bruce Cronnell

INTRODUCTION

Among the four skills that are the goals of ESL instruction—listening, speaking, reading, writing—writing is commonly last: last to be taught in the sequence of skills, and last to receive much emphasis. Writing includes several sub-skills, one of which is spelling.[1] Spelling is important for at least two reasons. First, a writer may not communicate well if s/he cannot spell; that is, a reader must be able to interpret marks on the page as meaningful words and s/he cannot do this easily when words are misspelled. Second, contemporary American society (and probably other educated English-speaking societies) considers misspelling a serious social error, marking a person as, at best, "illiterate," if not outright "ignorant." While a wide variation in speech is acceptable, variation in spelling is completely forbidden.[2]

ENGLISH SPELLING: ORDER OR CHAOS?

A common attitude, prevalent for several hundred years, is that English spelling is a chaotic mess and that it is a miracle anyone has learned to spell it correctly. The claim is that English is "not phonetic"; that is, English words cannot be spelled on the basis of their pronunciation as can, for example, words in Spanish or Turkish. It is true that not all English words can be spelled on the basis of sound. The spellings of a few words cannot be (synchronically) related to speech at all, e.g., *of, who*. In a number of other words, certain parts cannot be related to speech, e.g., the *a* in *was*, the *o* in *to* and *do*, the *oi* in *choir*. However, words with such idiosyncratic spellings account for probably fewer than ten percent of English words; thus many words can be spelled on the basis of sounds and of other principles of English orthography.

Much recent linguistic research supports the view that English spelling is a rule-governed system based on speech. Hanna, Hanna, Hodges, and Rudorf (1966) analyzed the sound-to-spelling relations in over 17,000 words; while flawed (cf. Reed, 1967; Roberts, 1967), their work and its extension by Bergquist (1966) have formed the basis of contemporary views concerning the regularity of English spelling. Some major studies of spelling-to-sound relations (Venezky, 1967, 1970; Berdiansky, Cronnell, and Koehler, 1969; Cronnell, 1971a) further support this conclusion; while these studies concerned letter-sound relations for reading and while such relations are not completely applicable to spelling (Cronnell, 1971c), they provide additional, albeit indirect, evidence for the regularity of English spelling. A linguistic study of English phonology (Chomsky and Halle, 1968) has been interpreted as further evidence for the regularity of English sound-spelling relations (Brengelman, 1970b; Chomsky, 1970; Schane, 1970).

However, English spelling is not a simple, straightforward system (cf. Vachek, 1945-9, 1959; Venezky, 1969); rather there are at least four subsystems to consider:

1. In one-syllable, one-morpheme words, sound-to-spelling correspondences can be used, e.g., /sæt/ is spelled *sat*: /s/-*s*, /æ/-*a*, /t/-*t*. Some of these correspondences are predictable in a one-to-one fashion; e.g., /æ/ is spelled *a* except in a very few words. Others are predictable, but application depends on recognition of word environment, e.g., the spellings of /k/ (see Appendix A). Other sounds may have two or more common spellings, but which to use in a particular word cannot be determined from sound alone, e.g., /ey/ spelled *a . . .e* or *ai* (*date*, *wait*). These unpredictable spellings often produce homophones, words pronounced the same but spelled differently, e.g., *made*, *maid*. However, knowledge of possible alternate spellings for the same sound can be used to limit the search for the correct spelling of words in a dictionary.

2. In one-morpheme words consisting of more than one syllable, the spelling of the stressed syllable can generally be determined as in one-syllable words. However, the spelling of the unstressed vowel is often unpredictable, but finding the correct spelling in a dictionary is generally not too difficult since there are only five options (*a, e, i, o, u*).

3. In polymorphemic words, the spellings are generally predictable (although sometimes complex) if each morpheme can be spelled independently and then appropriate morpheme-combining rules are used.

4. Finally, there are the words with unpredictable spellings—the irregular words which have to be memorized. As noted above, they represent probably less than ten percent of English words. While many of them are high-frequency words, their frequency—and thus familiarity—may make them less difficult to learn.

This outline suggests that English spelling is not a simple system; however, it is a system, and one that can be learned.

WHAT ARE THE RULES OF ENGLISH SPELLING?

One reason why English spelling is difficult to learn and to teach is that few people know explicitly what the rules are: what is regular and what is irregular, what is predictable and what is not. At present, no description of English spelling takes into account all the subsystems noted above; in Appendix A an outline is presented which attempts to provide an overview—albeit simplified and condensed—which may help teachers and students to utilize the system more fully. While not all the details of English spelling are given, and while irregularities are not noted, the summary in Appendix A can serve as a starting point for investigations into an understanding of English sound-to-spelling correspondences.

HOW CAN SPELLING BE DIFFICULT FOR ESL STUDENTS?

The description of English spelling in Appendix A is based on the phonological and morphological systems of Standard English (the educated form of speech described, for example, in Prator and Robinett, 1972). Thus the use of these spelling rules should hold for speakers of Standard English. Speakers of other dialects (even those standard dialects differing from the one used in this chapter) may have problems in spelling. Boiarsky (1969) found that the dialect of rural West Virginia tenth graders affected their spelling performance as opposed to that of comparable Philadelphians. Graham and Rudorf (1972) detected spelling differences related to dialect among sixth graders from Ohio, Massachusetts, and Georgia. Sullivan (1971) compared the speech and spelling of Black and White second graders in Texas and found differences which could be attributed to dialect. In California, Kligman and Cronnell (1974) also studied Black and White second graders; they tested the spelling of features known to occur commonly in Black English but infrequently in Standard English and concluded that dialect affected spelling performance.

Thus there is ample research evidence that differences in pronunciation can produce spelling errors related to these pronunciations. While the speech of ESL students is not generally considered a dialect of English, most ESL students do not speak Standard English. Therefore, we might expect their speech forms to affect their spelling. While /r/ and /l/ can be easily spelled in Standard English, their spelling could be a problem for speakers who do not differentiate between these sounds. Students who do not differentiate between /ɪ/ and /iy/ could have problems spelling these sounds—in addition to the problems which may already exist because of the complexities of the spellings for /iy/. The ESL student's pronunciation may result in more homophonous spellings, i.e., more cases of multiple spellings for one sound (Cronnell, 1972). Since English already has many homophonous spellings, this is not a different but a more prevalent spelling problem for ESL students than for native speakers. However, variant pronunciations may not always result in misspellings. For example, Kligman and Cronnell (ibid.) found that Black English speakers often used /f/ in speech where Standard English has final /θ/, but rarely misspelled *th*. Thus, predictions of spelling difficulty based on speech need verification in actual spelling performance.

On the other hand, the spelling and combining of affixes and bases may be a greater problem for the ESL student. While the native speaker generally can use the morphology of English, the learner may not have this ability. Chomsky and Halle (ibid.), in discussing morphologically-based phonology, contend that "Orthography is a system designed for readers, who know the language, who understand sentences and therefore know the surface structure of sentences." This assertion can reasonably be extended to the role of orthography for spellers. Kligman and Cronnell (ibid.) found that Black English speakers had their greatest difficulty in spelling inflectional suffixes, which are realized differently in Black English than in Standard English. For example, the past tense marker *-ed*, which has three phonological variations in Standard English (i.e., /d, t, ɪd/), is frequently realized with a zero morpheme in Black English (i.e., no phonological ending added) with the result that the child speaking Standard English will tend to write *I walked to school yesterday*, while the child speaking Black English will tend to write *I walk to school yesterday*. Similarly, ESL students who have incomplete command of English morphology and syntax might be expected to have particular difficulty in spelling words of more than one morpheme.

ESL students who can write their native language may have spelling problems because of this literacy.[3] If the native language uses a non-alphabetic writing system, then students must learn the notion that symbols (letters) represent sounds, rather than syllables (as in Japanese) or words (as in Chinese). If the native language uses an alphabetic writing system, but not the Roman alphabet (such languages as Hindi), a new alphabet must be learned, although the notion of sound-spelling relations would not be new. If the native language uses an alphabet related to the Roman alphabet (such as Greek and Cyrillic), a number of new letters must be learned; in addition, some native-language sound-to-spelling correspondences must be unlearned; for example, in Greek *P* represents /r/ and in Russian *H* represents /n/.

While literate ESL students from all these orthographic backgrounds may have difficulties, there is some suggestion that the greatest spelling problems may exist for students whose native languages use the Roman alphabet. Oller and Ziahosseiny (1970) found that at the college level such students made significantly more spelling errors in English than students whose native languages do not use the Roman alphabet. The sources of this problem are often clear; for example, in German /y/ is spelled *j* (English: *y*); in Spanish /ay/ is spelled *ay* (never in English). Literate language learners, when writing in a familiar alphabet, may continue using highly-learned native-language sound-to-spelling correspondences even when writing English, while students who must learn a new alphabet or writing system for English may be much more aware of how English spelling differs from their native orthography.

There is little empirical evidence concerning the effects of native language on spelling in English. Two studies of the spelling performance of Hebrew speakers have turned up conflicting results. Bassan (1973) found that the misspellings of third graders could be more easily accounted for by analysis of the English spelling system than by interference from Hebrew, thus suggesting that native language is not a problem. Michelson (1974) found that the vowel misspellings of college students reflected the pronunciation of Hebrew speakers. Broussard (1971) in her analysis of the spelling errors of a group of Mexican-American high school students found evidence of interference from Spanish as well as examples of the normal developmental errors that native speakers make. Additional controlled studies are needed with speakers from a variety of language backgrounds and at different age and language levels to determine more fully the effects of native language on spelling in English.

HOW SHOULD SPELLING BE TAUGHT?

As in all areas of language learning, there are no simple solutions to questions of how to teach; this section can only make some suggestions and provide some guidelines. We can begin with ten general features of English spelling which can be valuable for students to learn.

1. That English spelling is systematic.

2. Which spellings are predictable (e.g., /æ/-*a*).

3. Which spellings are not predictable, but are common (e.g., /iy/—*ea, ee, e, ei, ie*).

4. How frequent unpredictable spellings are (e.g., in one syllable words, /iy/—is most frequently spelled *ea* or *ee*).

5. How to use a dictionary to find the spelling of words with unpredictable spellings. Since, as noted above, ESL students may have more homophonous spellings than native speakers, this is probably a crucial skill.

6. How to spell useful, but irregularly spelled, words.

7. What bases and affixes are, and how to spell them individually.

8. How to combine bases and affixes.

9. How to use certain word-internal punctuation (e.g., apostrophes in contractions and possessives, capitalization of names, periods in abbreviations, hyphens in compounds).[4]

10. What is possible and what is impossible in English spelling (e.g., words do not end in vowel-*cke*, rather in vowel-*ck*, vowel-*ke*, or vowel-*k*).

Once students know all of the above, they should be well on their way to good spelling.

The approach to teaching depends on the learner's background. (See Appendix B for some sample spelling lessons.) For the illiterate learner, instruction might be similar to that used for English-speaking children (see Hanna, Hodges, and Hanna, 1971, for a detailed description of a graded organization for spelling instruction). For children learning English, a regular elementary school spelling series may be appropriate; however, a series should be selected which adequately reflects the nature of English spelling (Cronnell, 1971b).

For the literate beginning learner, many particular features of English will need to be mastered. However, the teacher may be able to take advantage of the student's native-language knowledge of the nature of spelling, particularly when the student can write a European language. For example, the German speaker who can spell *Hand* in German should have little difficulty spelling *hand* in English; the French speaker who can spell *air* and *nation* in French should be able to spell *air* and *nation* in English. Often the relations between spellings in two languages are less direct, but could be used in spelling instruction. For example, the Spanish speaker who can spell *accidente* and *rapido* in Spanish would need only learn not to include the final vowel when spelling *accident* and *rapid* in English. Being able to spell *proporcion* in Spanish would require learning only one letter to spell *proportion* in English.

Most literate ESL students do not need instruction in the complete range of the English spelling system. For them, diagnostic testing may be most useful. One approach used effectively with English-speaking students beyond the early grades is the test-study method (Gates, 1931): a preliminary spelling test is given and those words misspelled are specifically studied. However, rather than simply testing and studying random lists of words, a better approach is testing words that illustrate various spellings. Then students performing poorly on specific spellings could receive instruction and practice on their problems. For advanced students (with specific or general spelling difficulties) a programmed text may provide more individualized learning without creating a heavy burden on the teacher (e.g., Ryan, 1973; Smith, 1966).

All students who have a basic knowledge of English spelling should learn to use a dictionary (a) to find the spellings of words in which there are sounds with two or more possible spellings; and (b) to check words when they are unsure of the spellings. Literate students may be familiar with dictionary use from their native language, but they may need instruction in using an English dictionary to locate spellings of unknown words. Students without experience in dictionary use will need instruction; many dictionaries designed for ele-mentary school children have extensive sections on how to use a dictionary, which may be helpful for ESL students.

Teaching spelling is not the same as teaching composition. When the emphasis is on getting the students to write, too much concern with the spelling of individual words may inhibit their fluency and expression of ideas. Rather, spelling instruction may be best viewed as a separate subject, when individual words and rules are focused on. Correct spelling in composition should probably be a concern when editing written work; then students can carefully check their spelling. Since editing may not be an obvious process for students, practice might be of value, for instance, proofreading (and correcting) sentences with spelling errors.

CONCLUSION

ESL students' specific spelling needs depend on their language and educational background. However, all students should understand that English spelling is a system, and they should be able to apply the rules of this system. One of their most valuable spelling tools is the dictionary. Since teachers cannot always depend on reliable published resources for teaching spelling, they may need to become experts in English spelling to provide systematic and accurate instruction.

While this chapter has focused on spelling, spelling is only part of writing. Perfect spelling without ideas, knowledge, organization, and clarity is of little value; with these and other features of good writing, correct spelling is the finishing touch on all written communication.

NOTES

*The work upon which this chapter is based was performed pursuant to Contract NE-C-00-3-0064 with the National Institute of Education (NIE), Department of Health, Education and Welfare.

1. Additional sub-skills of writing might be letter formation, punctuation and other mechanics, fluency, organization, and style. These are not the domain of the present chapter, which is about spelling: the process of moving from spoken words to written words.

2. This was not always true; the development of printing seems to have given rise to standardization of

spelling. Vallins (1965) provides an interesting description of past spelling practice.

3. Illiterate ESL learners who must learn how to write may have needs closer to those of young, English-speaking children.

4. Other uses of punctuation operate at the phrase or sentence level and are thus not properly dealt with as part of spelling.

DISCUSSION QUESTIONS

1. What arguments can be made opposing the view presented in this chapter concerning the regularity of English spelling? What are the pedagogical results of the opposite view?

2. If the terms "long vowel" and "short vowel" (see Appendix A) are used in spelling, how can they be incorporated in the description of vowel and consonant spellings presented in this chapter?

3. Assess the relative importance of sound-to-spelling correspondences and of morphological spellings. How does their importance vary with the student's language level?

4. Many features of English spelling, which are problems for the speller, seem to help the reader. Identify some of them. Is the spelling system appropriately balanced between ease of spelling and ease of reading?

5. Suggest reasons why some differences in pronunciation may not result in spelling problems.

6. Assess the relative effects on spelling of pronunciation interference and orthographic interference for ESL students.

7. This chapter suggests ten general features of English spelling for students to learn. Are they all equally important? How should they be sequenced for instruction?

SUGGESTED ACTIVITIES

1. Make up lists of words to practice various spellings. Different lists might reflect various levels of language ability.

2. Prepare a list of major English prefixes. Separate them as (a) ones in which the vowel pronunciation changes, (b) ones in which the final consonant assimilates to the initial consonant of the base, (c) ones which do not change.

3. Prepare a list of major English suffixes. Identify those that are homophonous and indicate which of these may be differentiated on the basis of meaning or function. Identify suffixes which cause palatalization; some of these are the same as non-palatalizing suffixes, but with a preceding *i* or *u* (e.g., *al-ial*, *ate-uate*).

4. Revise English sound-to-spelling correspondences based on the commonly found speech patterns of ESL students from a specific language background (e.g., for Spanish speakers, the spellings for /ey/ might include *e* and *ea*, as well as *a . . . e*, *ai*, etc.).

5. For a specific native-language background, identify the sound-to-spelling correspondences which might interfere with English spelling.

6. If you have access to students, test their spelling with unfamiliar words to determine how their speech and/or first language orthography affects their spelling performance.

7. Identify possible vs. impossible spellings in one-syllable words.

8. Organize spellings for consonants or vowels in an instructional sequence.

9. Mnemonics are often useful for learning homophones and irregularly spelled words. Prepare some mnemonic sentences or phrases which could be used by ESL students.

E.g. a) The *principal* is my *pal*.
b) There is *a rat* in se*parat*e.

10. Survey spelling instruction in ESL or native-language textbooks. How accurately do they reflect the English spelling system? Would any of them be suitable for your ESL students?

SUGGESTIONS FOR FURTHER READING

Hanna, P. R., R. E. Hodges, and J. Hanna (1971) *Spelling: Structure and Strategies*. Boston: Houghton Mifflin.
This is the best book available on spelling. The first part discusses writing systems, the development of

English (language and spelling), spelling as a school subject, and the psychology of spelling. The second part describes a fully sequenced spelling program.

Hanna, P. R., J. Hanna, R. E. Hodges, and E. H. Rudorf (1966)
Phoneme-grapheme correspondences as cues to spelling improvement. Washington, C.C.: U.S. Government Printing Office.
This book should be consulted, although critically, for an understanding of spelling-sound relations. The Hanna, Hodges, and Hanna book above summarizes this larger study.

Venezky, R. L. (1970)
The structure of English orthography. The Hague: Mouton and Co.
This is another helpful book on the topic of spelling-sound relations.

Cronnell, B. (1971a)
"Annotated spelling-to-sound correspondence rules." Technical Report No. 32. Los Alamitos, CA: SWRL Educational Research and Development.
Another helpful piece on the same topic.

Venezky, R. L. (1967)
"English orthography: its graphical structure and its relation to sound," *Reading Research Quarterly,* 2:75-106.
This article contains a description of crucial features of English orthography.

Brengleman, F. (1970a)
The English Language. Englewood Cliffs, N.J.: Prentice-Hall.
A useful and accurate description of English spelling is found in chapters 7 and 8 of this book.

Chomsky, C. (1970)
"Reading, Writing and Phonology." *Harvard Educational Review,* 40:287-309.
The spelling applications of recent research into generative phonology are clearly developed here.

Vallins, G. H. (1965)
Spelling. Rev. ed. London: Andre Deutsch.
Provides a readable and interesting treatment of the history of English spelling, including many examples of previous spelling practices.

APPENDIX A: A BRIEF SUMMARY OF ENGLISH SPELLING*

1. Vowel categories

There are two main categories of English vowels:

Category A	Category B
/ey/	/æ/
/iy/	/ɛ/
/ay/	/ɪ/
/ow/	/a/
/uw/ or /yuw/	/ə/ (stressed)
/ɔy/	
/aw/	
	/ɔ/
	/u/

The first five sounds in each category are frequently paired in English spelling because they use the same letters, e.g., /ey/–/æ/, lady–lad. The sound /ɔ/ does not occur in many American English dialects where it merges with /a/.

There are many labels in use for these two categories as shown in Chart 1. All of these sets of labels have problems. The first four are rather technical and may not be very meaningful to students without some background in phonology. The last two actually cover only the first five sounds in each category. Choice of a category label depends on at least three factors; (a) students' backgrounds (those familiar with linguistics should be able to handle the first four); (b) students' future needs (children in American schools will likely find "long" and "short" used in many texts); (c) the textbooks being used.

In this chapter, "simple vowels" and "diphthongs" will be used, although not without recognition of the value of other terminology.

---

*This description is based to a large extent on the outstanding analysis being made by Paula Russell, to whom I am greatly indebted.

Chart 1

Category A diphthong	Category B simple	Source Prator and Robinett, 1972
glided (ends with a glide; i.e., is a diphthong)	unglided (does not end with a glide; i.e., is not a diphthong)	
tense (muscle tenseness in articulation)	lax (lack of muscle tenseness in articulation)	Chomsky and Halle, 1968
free (can end a word; includes /ɔ/)	checked (cannot end a word)	Kurath, 1967
name (the names of the vowel letters)	basic (most common pronunciation of the five vowel letters)	Allen, Allen and Shute, 1966
long (does not mean length)	short (does not mean shortness)	traditional; Prator and Robinett, 1972

2. Vowel spellings in single morphemes

a. Simple vowels (generally spelled with one letter)

/æ/	*a: pass*
/ɛ/	*e, less* frequently *ea: bed, head*
/ɪ/	*i: slip* (infrequent, *y*: myth*)
/a/	*o: pot*
/ə/	*u,* less frequently *o* or *o . . . e* (generally before /m, n, v, or ð/) and *ou: but, son, come, young*
/ɔ/	*o, a* before /l/, *au, aw* finally and before final *n* or *l: long, ball, sauce, saw* (infrequent: *augh, ough: caught, thought*)
/u/	*oo* (particularly before /d/ or /k/) or *u* (particularly after a labial): *look, pull*

b. Diphthongs (commonly spelled with two letters†, spellings are listed approximately in order of descending frequency)

/ey/	*a . . . e* or *ai, ay* finally, *a* in polysyllabic words: *date, rain, day, table* (infrequent: *ei,* and *eigh, ey, et** finally: *veil, weigh, they, ballet*)
/iy/	*ea* or *ee, y* finally in polysyllabic words: *heat, three, silly* (infrequent: *e . . . e, ie, ei, i . . . e,* e, i,** and *e, ey* finally: *scene, thief, deceive, machine, meter, museum, stadium, he, valley*)

---

*This is a foreign spelling; the words it occurs in are frequently marked semantically as technical, academic, or luxurious.

†The two letters are commonly the letter with the name corresponding to the vowel sound, plus *e* at the end of the morpheme. (Note that "final silent *e*" is usually part of a vowel spelling or a consonant spelling.) When the two vowels in the spelling are contiguous, the second is often *y, i, w,* or *u: y* or *w,* when morpheme final, before a vowel, or before final *l* or *n; i* or *u* elsewhere.

/ay/	*i . . . e, i* before consonant clusters and in polysyllabic words, *y* finally, less frequently *igh* finally or before *t: mine, mind, tiger, cry, light* (infrequent: *y . . . e,* * *y,* * and *ie, ye* finally: *type, cycle, pie, dye*)
/ow/	*o . . . e* or *oa, o* before consonant clusters and in polysyllabic words, *ow* finally: *hope, boat, most, open, yellow* (infrequent: *ou,* * and *o, oe* finally: *mould, go, hoe*)
/uw/ or /yuw/	*oo* (for /uw/ only), *u . . . e, u* in polysyllabic words: *boot, cute, super* (infrequent: *ui,* * *eu, ou,* * and *ew, ue* finally: *fruit, feud, group, new, blue*)
/oy/	*oi, oy* finally: *boil, boy*
/aw/	*ou, ow* finally and before final *n* or *l: found, allow*

c. Vowels plus /r/ ‡

Vowel-r combinations are sometimes spelled by applying the appropriate vowel correspondences before /r/—*r,* e.g., *hire* (cf. *hike*), *our* (cf. *out*). For some simple vowels, the spelling before /r/ corresponds to a diphthong spelling:

/ɛər/ cf. /ey/	*stare, air.* (In many dialects /ey/, /ɛ/, and /æ/ have merged before /r/, so the spelling for each of these vowels is found: *vary, berry, marry.*)
/ɪər/ cf. /iy/	*deer, fear*
/ɔr/ cf. /ow/	*more, board, torn.* (After /w/, /ɔr/ is spelled *ar: warm, quart.*)
/ur/ cf. /(y)uw/	*pure, poor*

Two vowel-r spellings are not related to other spellings:

/ar/	*ar: star*
/ər/	*er, ur, ir,* or after *w: her, hurt, bird, word* (infrequent: *ear: earn*)

d. The unstressed vowel /ə/ (or/ɪ/ or /ɨ/) may be spelled with any single vowel letter: *lapel, wallet, April, gallop, circus.* Initial /ə/ (when not part of a prefix) and final /ə/ are generally spelled *a: about, comma.* Syllabic consonants are best treated for spelling purposes as a vowel plus the consonant (e.g., *button, metal*); for syllabic /l/, the spelling *le* is most common, but *el* and *al* are also found: *battle, shovel, oval.* Unstressed /ər/ is most commonly spelled *er* (e.g., *butter, mother, clever*), but is sometimes spelled with other vowel letters: *collar, doctor, sulphur.*

3. **Consonant spellings in single morphemes**

a. Consonant sounds with one primary spelling (in addition to the doubling described in c below). The sounds /p, t, b, d, g, f, v, m, n, l, r, w, y, h/ are spelled with the corresponding letters: *p, t, b, d, g, f, v, m, n, l, r, w, y, h.* Several consonant sounds are spelled with digraphs (two-letter spellings):

/θ/ and /ð/	*th: thigh, thy, with*
/š/	*sh: shoot, bush*

---

‡Vowels before /l/ do not have special spellings (except for /ɔ/). Before /l/, the sounds /ie/, /ɪə/, /eə/, /ɛə/, and /æə/, are spelled the same as /iy/, /ɪ/, /ey/, /ɛ/ and /æ/, respectively.

/hw/	*wh: when* (for speakers who do not use /hw/, there are two spellings of /w/: *w* and *wh*)
/tš/	*ch: chin*
	The final cluster /ks/ is spelled *x: box, six*.

b. Consonant sounds with variant spellings (in addition to the doubling described in c below).

/k/	*c* before *a, o, u* or a consonant: *cat, cold, cute, act, cream; k* before *e, i, y: keep, kiss, sky; k* at the end of a word after a diphthong: *seek, make, strike; k* at the end of a word after a consonant: *milk, honk, bark*
/kw/	is always spelled *qu*
/s/	*s* at the beginning of a word: *see, sit, sat, said; c(e)* or *s(e)* at the end of a word: *ice, dance, else, base*
/z/	*z* at the beginning of a word: *zone, zero; s* before or after a consonant: *wisdom, pansy; s(e)* or *z(e)* at the end of a word: *wise, please, breeze, haze*
/dž/	*j* at the beginning of a word: *jewel, jam; g* (sometimes) if followed by *e, i, y: gem, giant, gym; g(e)* at the end of a word: *huge, large*
/ŋ/	*ng* at the end of a word: *ring; n* elsewhere: *thank*

c. Doubled consonants. *Note*: Consonants are not doubled after diphthongs, nor after two-letter vowel spellings.

i. Consonants (except *v* and *x*) are doubled when following a single letter spelling of a simple vowel and preceding another vowel or a syllabic consonant: *happy, follow, merry, paddle, bottom, butter*. The doubled forms of *c* (or *k*), *ch*, and *j* are *ck, tch*, and *dg*, respectively: *pickle, hatchet, midget*. *Note*: This rule has numerous exceptions, e.g., *copy, wagon*.

ii. /k, f, s, z, tš, dž, l/ occurring at the end of a morpheme following a single letter spelling of a simple vowel are spelled with a doubled consonant: *lick, puff, mess, buzz, match, edge* (*dge* is the doubled form finally), *tall*.

d. Some foreign consonant spellings (cf. Brengelman, 1971):
/k/ *ch: chlorine, chorus*
/f/ *ph: phone, graph*
/š/ *ch: chef, chauffeur*
Words with foreign spellings are often semantically marked as unusual—e.g., technical, academic, musical, connotating luxury.

e. Some infrequent consonant spellings:
/g/ *gu(e): guest, league*
/s/ *sc: scene*
/s/ *st: castle*
/ž/ *ge: rouge*
/m/ *mn: autumn*
/n/ *kn: knee, know*
/r/ *wr: writer*
/y/ *i: onion*

Word final /v/ is spelled *ve: give, twelve*.
Word final /ð/ is spelled *the: breathe*.

4. Spelling compounds

Graphic compounds are generally spelled by writing the individual words with no space or with a hyphen between them: *shortstop, short-term*. Some semantic compounds are written as two words: *White House*. Only by using a dictionary—and different dictionaries may give conflicting information—can one determine how a compound is written.

5. Spelling prefixes

While the pronunciation of a vowel in a prefix may vary, the spelling remains the same, e.g., *pronoun, prospect, promote*. Note that prefixes (and suffixes) are spelled according to the same principles, whether added to free bases or bound bases. However, recognition of the prefix (and/or the base) is often crucial to spelling it: in this, meaning is sometimes a clue, e.g., /prə/ meaning "before" spelled *pre* (e.g., *predict*) but /prə/ meaning "forward" spelled *pro* (e.g., *promote*). The final consonant in some prefixes assimilates to the initial consonant in the base; e.g., *in* is assimilated in *immature, impolite, illegal, irregular*; while this reflects pronunciation, it is relevant to determining consonant doubling, e.g., doubling in *assign* (*ad + sign*) vs. not doubling in *asleep* (*a + sleep*).

6. Spelling suffixes
a. Inflectional suffixes (often described well in dictionaries)

The plural, verbal, and possessive suffix /s/, /z/, /ɪz/ is generally spelled *s* (with appropriate apostrophe use for possessives). When following *s, z, sh, ch, x*, the plural and verbal suffix is spelled *es*; when following *o*, it is spelled *s* or *es*. When reflected in the pronunciation, base *f(e)* becomes suffixed *ves*. The past tense and past participle suffix /t/, /d/, /ɪd/ is spelled *ed*.

Other inflectional suffixes are spelled with one spelling: *ing, en, er, est*.

b. Derivational suffixes

There are many derivational suffixes. Some have homophonous spellings, which can frequently be distinguished on the basis of function or meaning; e.g., /ɪst/ is spelled *est* when a superlative adjective (e.g., *fastest*), *ist* when referring to a person (e.g., *artist*).

Some suffixes, beginning with *i* or *u*, palatalize the final consonant in the base. Thus the following spellings result:

/š/ *ci, ti, ss(i), si*: *official, election, pressure, permission, expansion*
/tš/ *t(i)*: *architecture, Christian*
/ž/ *s(i)*: *pleasure, explosion*
/dž/ *d*: *graduate*

7. Affix-aided spelling

In general, the spellings of bases do not change (except for regular suffixation rules listed below) when affixes are added, even if the pronunciation changes. A variety of examples of affix-aided spellings is listed below to suggest the possibilities.

secret-secretary	*athlete-athletic*	*Christ-Christian-Christmas*
differ-difference	*atom-atomic*	*magic-magician*
study-studious	*colony-colonial*	*please-pleasure*
grade-graduate	*invite-invitation*	*photograph-photography*
office-official	*relate-relative*	*human-humanity*
elect-election	*sign-signal*	*moral-morality*
press-pressure	*bomb-bombard*	*architect-architecture*

This feature of English can help in determining the spelling of unstressed vowels. For example, in *metal* (/mɛtəl/) the spelling of the first vowel is predictable (/ɛ/-*e*), but that of the second is not (/əl/-*le, el, al*); in *metallic* (/mətǽlɪk/) the opposite is true (/ə/-*a, e, i, o, u*; /æ/-*a*); using the predictable *e* in *metal* and the predictable *a* in *metallic*, the vowels in both words can be correctly spelled. Thus the spelling of unstressed vowels can be determined on the basis of the stressed pronunciation in related words.

8. Suffixation rules

Suffixes are commonly added directly to the ends of bases (e.g., *trying, played, soften*) but there are a few special rules. Many dictionaries provide good descriptions of these rules. The following is a summary of some major points.

a. When the base ends in a consonant and *e* and the suffix begins with a vowel, the *e* is dropped, e.g., *hoped, driving*.

b. When the last syllable is stressed and is spelled with a single vowel letter plus a single consonant letter, the final consonant is doubled, e.g., *hopped, occurring*.

c. When the base ends in a consonant plus *y* and the suffix does not begin with *i*, the *y* changes to *i*, e.g., *happiness, tried*.

APPENDIX B: SAMPLE LESSONS*

Lesson One

Purpose:

To teach the spelling a . . . e ("a and then e at the end of the word") for /ey/

Student level:

Young (about second grade), two-three years of ESL instruction

Spelling prerequisites:

Ability to spell simple vowels and consonants spelled with one letter

1. Write *mad* and *made* on the board. Say the words and note the differences in the vowel sounds. Explain that the vowel sound in *hate* is called a "long vowel sound";† it is the same as the name of the letter *a*. Explain that the vowel sound in *hat* is called a "short vowel sound"; it is spelled with a single vowel letter.

Have students tell whether words have a long or a short vowel sound: e.g., *fate, fat, name, made, mad, sat, wave, map.*

Have students tell whether words have the same or different vowel sounds; e.g., *made-came, hat-name, sat-red, sad-lap, wave-let.*

Written work: Provide a list of words with *e*, *a*, and *a . . . e,* and have students circle the words that have a long vowel sound.

Provide a list of words with *e*, *a*, and *a . . . e* and a picture of a word spelled with each of these; have students match vowel sounds in written and pictured words.

2. Explain that when the sound /ey/ is heard, it is frequently spelled with *a* and then *e* at the end of the word. Using one-syllable words spelled with *e*, *a*, and *a . . . e,* have students spell the vowel sound. (These words can also be used for reviewing the spelling of first and last sounds.)

---

*These sample lessons are based in part on instruction used in the *SWRL Communication Skills Program for the Elementary School: Spelling.* Lexington, Mass.: Ginn and Co. Copyright, 1975, by Southwest Regional Laboratory for Educational Research and Development.
†Students are assumed to be in United States schools, where this terminology is used.

Written work: Use pictures of words spelled with *e*, *a*, and *a . . . e.* Have students (a) circle the correct vowel spelling, given a choice; (b) write the correct vowel spelling.

Using only unambiguous strings, have students fill in either *a* or *a . . . e.* E.g., *n m , s d , sl p , g m .*

3. Have students spell whole words with *e*, *a*, and *a . . . e.* If students have difficulty, have them spell the individual sounds first:

Spell the first sound in *name.* (*n*—write on board)

Spell the vowel sound in *name.* (*a . . . e*—write on board with *n: na e*)

Spell the last sound in *name.* (*m*—write on board with previous: *name*)

Spell the word *name.*

Dictate words for students to write.

Written work: Have students spell pictured words.

Have students complete sentences; the missing words are spelled with *a* or *a . . . e:*

I am not happy; I am s _____ .
Her n_____ is Maria.

Lesson Two

Purpose:

To teach alternate spellings for /ey/ in monosyllables

Student level:

Older students; literate; large vocabularies, but poor spelling skills

Spelling prerequisites:

General familiarity with English spelling; knowledge of pronunciation symbols; ability to use a dictionary

1. Write the following words on the board; explain that the underlined letters are spellings of /ey/ and note the constraints on these spellings. Point out that the spellings with *a* are more frequent than those with *e*.

name: with single final consonants and with *st* and *ng* (*paste, strange*).

rain: especially frequent before *n* and *l;* medial

gay: final
vein: medial
weigh, weight: final or before final *t*
they: final

Be sure students can name the six spellings for /ey/ and can verbalize the constraints.

Written work: Fill in correct letters (see Lesson One, 2); use the following choices: *ai/ay; ei/ey; ei/eigh*. Encourage dictionary use for checking spellings with these choices: *a . . . e/ai; a . . . e/ei; ai/ei; ay/eigh/ey*.

Provide the pronunciation of nonsense syllables and have students circle all possible spellings. E.g., /bley/: *blai, blay, blae, bleigh, blei, bley*; /cleyn/: *clain, clayn, clane, cleighn, clein, cleyn*

2. Teach students several /ey/ words which they commonly misspell; e.g., *strange, weight*.

Written work: Complete sentences (See Lesson One, 3).

3. Teach homophones with /ey/, e.g., *main-mane, pray-prey, way-weigh, wait-weight, waste-waist*. Be sure students understand the meaning of each word. Use the words in sentences and have students choose the correct spelling.

Written work: Using sentence context, have students circle the correct word. E.g., *I know the weigh/way to school. He weighs/ways 70 kilos*. Complete sentences (see Lesson One, 3)

4. Say unfamiliar words and have students give possible spellings; e.g., /hwey/: *whay, whey, wheigh*. Have students check in a dictionary for the correct spelling.

Written work: Provide the pronunciation of words and have students spell them, checking their spellings in a dictionary; e.g., /geyn/, /fley/.

Lesson Three*

Purpose:

To use affixed words to determine the correct spelling of unstressed vowels

Student level:

Advanced; good spelling skills

Have students identify unstressed syllables in words (e.g., first, last).

Have students identify bases in suffixed words (e.g., *human* is the base of *humanity*).

Have students provide suffixed forms which change the stress in the base (e.g., *atomic* is a suffixed form of *atom* where the second syllable is stressed).

Write a pair of vowel-less words on the board, e.g., *h m n, h m nity, t m, t mic*.

Have students spell the stressed vowel in the base and write it in both the base and the suffixed word, e.g., *hum n, hum nity, at m, at mic*.

Then have students spell the stressed vowel in the suffixed word and write it in both the base and suffixed words, e.g., *human, humanity, atom, atomic*.

Written work: Have students identify bases and/or suffixes in suffixed words. Have students write the bases for suffixed words. Have students fill in the correct letter in pairs of vowel-less words (see above). In sentences, have students write the correct form of a provided word, e.g.,

Concern for *humans* is concern for all _____.
Another name for the atom bomb is the _____ bomb.

---

*This is an outline of some teaching possibilities; it is not developed as a full lesson.

E. Grammar and Vocabulary

Grammar and vocabulary have often been viewed as incompatible elements in language teaching. The Reading Approach elevated vocabulary and suppressed grammar with the result that language learners could not produce coherent sentences even after several years of language study. The Audiolingual Approach did the reverse: it elevated grammar and structure and suppressed vocabulary. The result was that ESL learners had generally poor comprehension of natural, unedited speech or written materials even after a year or more of intensive language instruction. Both grammar and vocabulary are important and both can and should be taught in the ESL classroom without sacrificing one for the other. Over the past decade, however, much more has been written about grammar than vocabulary. Larsen-Freeman's chapter covers the issues that have emerged in the teaching of grammar, and McIntosh's chapter suggests a pedagogical structural sequence for use with beginning ESL students; she also provides contexts for most of the teaching points, which should be of help to the teacher. The chapter on vocabulary by Celce-Murcia and Rosensweig reviews what is known about the teaching and learning of vocabulary and provides many teaching suggestions.

ISSUES IN THE TEACHING OF GRAMMAR

Diane Larsen-Freeman

INTRODUCTION

As is true in many areas of language teaching today, the teaching of grammar is fraught with controversy. Many of the issues are inexorably intertwined with a particular methodological approach to language teaching. Other issues on which there is greater accord relate more directly to the practical, or "how to" aspects of teaching grammar. Each of these major areas will be considered in turn.

METHODOLOGICAL ISSUES

Selection of a methodology
Perhaps the issue with the broadest ramifications for the teaching of grammar involves the selection of a methodological approach to language teaching. Throughout the history of language teaching, different methodologies have come into vogue, supplanting their predecessors and enjoying preeminence for a time.[1] This trend has by no means decelerated in modern times. Current literature in the language teaching field is replete with reference to innovative methodologies such as Gattegno's "Silent Way," Asher's "Total Physical Response," and Curran's "Counseling-Learning Approach."[2] Despite the evolutionary nature of the trend (i.e., one methodology becoming popularized because it purports to eliminate the weakness of preceding ones), many different methodologies are being practiced concurrently. Of all these methodologies, there are two approaches to language teaching—the audiolingual and the cognitive-code—which would appear to have exerted the most influence on the language teaching profession of today.

The audiolingual approach was a product of the theories of the behavioral psychologists and their contemporaries in linguistics, the structuralists. They saw language as a structured sequence of discrete units. It was the teacher's task to inculcate in the learner the grammatical patterns existing in the foreign or second language. For children learning their native tongue, this task was fairly straightforward since their minds were thought to be *tabulae rasae*. Eventually, with enough exposure to the language, imitation of the adult model, and positive reinforcement, the children were said to have acquired the "habits" of their native language.

By comparison, the second language learners' task was much more formidable. They operated under the handicap of having already acquired the habits of a first language; somehow these habits had to be overcome if learners were to have any hope of acquiring the second language.

In order to accomplish the acquisition of the second language, dialogue memorization, pattern practice, and structural drilling were the classroom techniques through which new habit response strength was built up. Overlearning of the pattern was the key to automaticity in communication. Maximum control of the linguistic material was exerted by the teacher to obviate, as much as possible, the learners' errors. This was done to avoid compounding the learners' task, i.e., having to overcome the bad habits that learner errors induced as well as the interfering habits of the first language. The selection of the items presented during a language course was dependent upon the outcome of a contrastive analysis—a systematic comparison between the native language and second language so that areas which could prove troublesome would be identified in advance and be given special attention. The presentation of vocabulary items was minimal because the most urgent task of the learner was to acquire the syntactic and phonological patterns of the second language. Since the structuralists saw speech as the primary manifestation of language, instruction in reading or writing in the second language was postponed until the learner was at a more advanced stage.

True to form, this behaviorist/structuralist perspective of language and language acquisition was ultimately challenged by adherents of a new approach to linguistics—transformational-generative grammar. They were joined in this challenge by their colleagues in the cognitive school of psychology. These theorists maintain that language is rule-governed behavior which allows speakers to create and understand utterances to which they may never have been exposed. Language is far too complicated, they argue, to ever be acquired through simple habit formation.

According to their model, children acquire their native language because they approach the language learning task equipped with an innate language acquisition device which predisposes them to find the linguistic system of any language they are exposed to. As children are exposed to natural speech, they adopt a process of gradual organization of what they hear. They do not simply imitate adult speech; they form rules from the speech to which they are exposed that they then use to produce their own speech. The rules get refined, as does their speech product, with increasing exposure to the target· language (Chomsky, 1959). Children pass through a series of stages, the first of which is characterized by their attempt to produce relatively simple syntactic structures. In later stages they add to their repertory other structures of increasing linguistic complexity (McNeill, 1966).

According to the cognitive-code approach which developed from this position, it is the second language learner's task to internalize the rules of the second language. The language must be presented naturally to allow the learner to extrapolate the rules. Thus instead of language input being strictly controlled, to prevent errors from occurring, learn-er errors are welcomed as evidence that the learner is testing hypotheses about the rules of the second language. Since the goal of studying a second language is defined as enabling the learner to achieve communicative competence, role-playing and communicative problem-solving are techniques practiced as part of this approach. The learner must learn the limits of a rule's application, the appropriate register to use in a given situation, and how to use the language naturally in context. In the cognitive approach, instead of postponing reading and writing in the second language, these skills play an integral part in the language learning experience from the start.

Although the Audiolingual and Cognitive-code Approaches seem diametrically opposed, it is probably the case that only the most zealous of adherents in the language teaching field have practiced one approach to the exclusion of the other. Anyone who views language teaching from a pragmatic perspective realizes that there is indeed a place for both approaches. Particularly at the initial stage of second language learning, there is a very real need for practice in the basic syntactic configurations of the language such as the order of the auxiliary elements or the formation of questions. However, once language learners have acquired certain of the formulae and have language data to work with it seems sensible to allow them to express themselves as much as possible in "real" communicative situations and problem-solving tasks designed to enrich their linguistic repertory.

The place of errors

Another issue very much bound up with methodological choice, and yet important enough to warrant independent consideration, is the place of errors in the language-learning process.

The point was made earlier that practitioners of the Audiolingual Approach would seek to control language input as much as possible to prevent learner errors from occurring. Errors were evidence that the correct automatic habits of the second language had not yet been acquired, and their eradication was thought to be realizable only by more intensive drilling in correct forms (Fries, 1945).

Theoretically, had the teaching process been perfect, no errors would have been committed; thus, errors were associated with some sort of failure.

Contrast this with the cognitive-code point of view, where the committing of errors is seen as a normal, healthy process in which the learner can be said to be testing hypotheses. Not only should the teacher accept their inevitability, s/he should also be sure to provide the proper feedback to the learner so that his or her hypotheses might be refined accordingly. The teacher should not simply reject the learners' contribution as being ungrammatical, but should supply him or her with the information necessary to form a more adequate representation of the rules in the second language (Corder, 1971).

Just as with the selection of a methodological approach, neither of these two extremes is profitably practical to the exclusion of the other. There are times when a teacher may simply reject a learner's ungrammatical utterance outright and supply him or her with the correct form without an explanation. Such behavior might be warranted for expediency's sake, because of the complexity of the error or because the grammar rule which the learner violated had not as yet been taught. There are other times when the teacher may want to provide the learner with a thorough explanation as to why what s/he has just uttered was unacceptable. Such an explanation might not always come from the teacher; the teacher may elicit an explanation from another member of the class or work to extract an explanation from the erring learner.

Inductive versus deductive learning

Another issue bound up in a less direct way with methodology is whether or not a teacher should adopt an inductive or deductive approach to the teaching of grammar. In inductive learning, the teacher presents examples from which the learner induces the relevant second language rule. In the Audiolingual Approach inductive learning is dominant, although typically the learner is never required to overtly state the rule. Conversely, in deductive learning the teacher states the rule and leads the learner in subsequently deducing examples.

Although different theorists and teachers may favor one way or the other, an interesting study by Hartnett (1974) would suggest that the best course to take would be to encourage both kinds of learning in any given second language class. Hartnett found a significant interaction between brain hemispheric dominance and the effectiveness of inductive and deductive teaching of Spanish. The brain is composed of a right and a left hemisphere. Different cognitive abilities are thought to be controlled by each. Furthermore, individuals are thought to be dominant in one hemisphere or the other. Hartnett discovered that inductive learning was as effective or more effective than deductive learning for right-hemisphere dominant students. Deductive learning, on the other hand, was more effective for left-hemisphere dominant students.

Since language teaching situations do not at present allow for the segregation of learners according to brain hemisphere dominance, one must conclude that a course designed to best meet the needs of all students would have to be one which included both inductive and deductive presentations of a language learning task.

The place of the first language in the second language classroom

Assuming that the students in a given second language class are homogeneous with regard to native language, should the teacher who has knowledge of the native language make use of it in the classroom? The cognitive-code proponents would probably be more tolerant than the audiolinguists with regard to the use of the mother-tongue in the classroom.

Despite methodological orientation, the common pragmatic viewpoint (Finnochiaro, 1974; Rivers, 1968) would be that judicious use of the native language for purposes of elucidation of a point that is apparently escaping the class would be acceptable. Both Finnochiaro and Rivers seem to see this as an efficiency measure, however, and one to be resorted to only when attempts at explication in the second language have failed (Finnochiaro) or for weaker students who are having difficulty in grasping a particular point (Rivers).

Frey (1970) warns that in early second language learning translation is not a good idea since it retards the ability of the student to think in the new language. Finnochiaro (ibid.), however, adds: "We delude ourselves if we think the new student is not translating each new English item into his native language when he first meets it."

Although most opinions would seem to suggest allowing some limited use of the native language in the *homogeneous* second language classroom, a point one ought to consider is that students should be encouraged right from the start to express themselves in the second language and to develop the ability to circumlocute whenever they cannot recall the exact word for which they are groping. Teachers might keep this in mind and, by way of example, minimize the use of the mother tongue in the second language classroom. It should be noted, however, that while this suggestion is applicable to a traditional class, it is contrary to the *modus operandi* of an "innovative methodology," Curran's Counseling Learning, which makes extensive use of translation in the initial stages of language instruction.

Sequence

The question of the order in which one should teach the grammatical structures of English meets with near unanimity of response: teach the structures in order from simple to difficult. At first glance "sequencing" does not seem to be a controversial issue in the teaching of grammar. Upon reflection, however, one realizes the accord of response belies the fact that not everyone agrees on how to define "simplicity" or "difficulty."

Lois McIntosh (in this volume) offers one possible sequence. She advocates the use of what I would call a "pedagogically-based" structural syllabus. Vocabulary which is concrete (i.e., the objects are present in the classroom) is used in conjunction with structures which can be easily demonstrated. Increasingly abstract vocabulary and structures are introduced so that the teacher moves from one structure to the next with each successive structure being built upon the ones before it.

Although this seems a reasonable approach, it is not always so easy to put into practice. Furthermore, it might very well be important to distinguish between what is difficult to explain and what is difficult to internalize—the two may not be the same. What follows are some other possible bases for sequencing grammatical structures. For the sake of brevity, I will only list and develop them briefly. The interested reader should consult Larsen (1975) for arguments, pro and con, on each.

a.   For the audiolingual proponents, the notion of difficulty would be easy to delineate. The most difficult structure for the learner of a second language would be the one which would be vulnerable to the most interference from his or her native language. As Fries and Fries (1961) put it:

In building any set of most efficient minimum materials to teach ESL, the structure of the native language of the learner is of prime importance. The ease or difficulty of learning any particular pattern of English rests not upon the intrinsic characteristics of the English language itself but rather upon the structural characteristics of the native language.

Thus, a contrastive analysis would have to be conducted to identify troublesome areas prior to constructing a pedagogical sequence.

b.   Approaching the same problem from an entirely opposing point of view would be the proposition that Fries rejects—that intralingual linguistic complexity be the basis for sequencing. Increasing complexity, perhaps based on the number of transformations needed to derive the surface form of a structure could be the means by which grammatical structures should be pedagogically ordered.

c.   Basing the pedagogical sequence on the order in which children learn the structures of their native language has also been suggested. Although certainly differences in cognitive maturity are apparent, some researchers believe that the processes of first and second language acquisition are sufficiently alike to allow second language learners to profit from an order of presentation identical with the first language order of acquisition.

d.   Although not yet fully expanded for all structures of English, we do have some evidence

(Dulay and Burt, 1973; Bailey, Madden, and Krashen, 1974; Larsen-Freeman, 1975, 1976) that learners of ESL, regardless of native language background, experience comparable difficulty with regard to certain grammatical morphemes in English. If a difficulty order could be established, impervious to language background, we might find the optimal pedagogical sequence to be the one that mirrors the natural order of structural difficulty for ESL.[3]

e.   Another possibility is to adopt a certain heuristic stance with regard to sequencing. For example, based on the assumption that a regular closed paradigm is somehow easier to learn than exceptional cases, we might want to teach the regular past tense construction before the irregular forms.

f.   If we had a fully detailed description of language universals and language typology, we might consider sequencing so as to emphasize within our syllabus those structures of English which are not widely found in other languages (Celce-Murcia, personal communication).

g.   Perhaps a pedagogical sequence of grammatical structures should be based upon the frequency with which native speakers of the language use the structures. Just as with vocabulary word-counts, the presupposition would be that those words/structures which appear most often are most useful for learners to acquire.

h.   Frequency, on the other hand, might be too global a measure—and based more on form than function. Perhaps, the *utility* of a particular structure to the students as viewed by its presence in relevant situations of the students' lives should be the criterion on which to base the sequencing of grammatical structures in a syllabus.

This is by no means an exhaustive list of contenders for the principal criterion of grammatical syllabus design. It would be foolish to belabor the point, however. No one knows what the optimum sequence should be. Furthermore, the consideration of some of the factors mentioned above might only tell us which structures we should emphasize in our course—not necessarily how we should sequence them.

Until (if ever) we resolve the issue of how to sequence grammatical structures, a language teacher can do several things:

i.   On the first day of class, survey your students' needs, interests and motivation for learning English. See if there is commonality across students and design your syllabus as much as possible to meet those common needs.

ii.   Avoid adhering to the way in which the textbook you are using sequences grammatical structures unless you feel it is a sensible order. Be careful not to skip around in the book, however, if it is of the type in which later lessons are dependent upon earlier ones.

iii.   Recycle. Do not assume that a syllabus has to be linear. After introducing a particular structure and practicing it, do not abandon it. Reintroduce it as necessary, particularly if it proves troublesome. (This suggestion will be further expanded below.)

Individual "bits" vs. "chunks"
A fairly new challenge to the traditional way of teaching grammar comes to us from theorists like Newmark (1966). It is Newmark's contention that we are doing our students a disservice if we even bother about the sequencing issue at all. Language acquisition, according to Newmark, is not simply an additive process. "Complex bits of language are learned a whole chunk at a time." While Newmark is not explicit in what he means by a "chunk" one could imagine it to be something like a speech act (Searle, 1970). In other words, a learner of a second language needs to learn the functions of language: how to make requests, apologize, ask for permission, etc., in the second language. Instead of teaching the learner how to use the present perfect tense, for instance, a teacher could make the object of a particular lesson a certain function of language and give students practice in all the forms necessary to realize that function. Indeed, that is what I believe Wilkins (1972) proposes when he says:
... the first step in the creation of a syllabus should be consideration of the *content* of probable utterances and from this it will be possible to determine which *forms* of language will be most valuable to the learner.
Wilkins' "notional syllabus" is one designed not

as a list of language structures, but rather as a list of "communicative units" (i.e., greeting, interrogating, leave-taking, etc.). The student learns how to do something with language rather than how to manipulate a certain syntactic structure.

While this approach is intuitively appealing, a thorough analysis of the functions of language and a pragmatic pedagogical sequence for these functions has not yet been accomplished. As Corder (1973) writes:

> The selection of what is to be taught is determined by what the learner wishes or needs to be able to do with his knowledge of the language, that is, it must be categorized in the first instance in terms of the communicative function he will need the language for. Until we have a theory which integrates an account of communicative functions into the account of linguistic structure, we shall have to look primarily to several sociolinguistic principles to guide our selection procedures.

Gaps

Before moving on to a discussion of practical issues, it might be helpful to acknowledge some *lacunae* in our understanding of language and language acquisition which affect the teaching of grammar. More information about the following areas would help considerably in teaching grammar:

a. *Language in context.* There is increasing awareness that language teachers must be equipped with a knowledge of how to convey language pragmatics to their students. Pragmatics is the knowledge that native speakers possess which enables them to know when to use one structure rather than another in a particular context. For example, when is the passive voice preferable to the active? In what environments does the native speaker use the quantifiers *lots of/lot of* rather than the quantifiers *many/much*, and why? (Celce-Murcia, 1975). Research in pragmatics and optional ways of conveying pragmatic knowledge to language students are very much needed.

b. *Second language acquisition strategies.* Within the last ten years, interest in the theoretical aspects of second language acquisition has flourished. Researchers have done much to increase our understanding of the process of second language acquisition. With a

better awareness of the strategies a learner adopts in tackling the second language, we might be able to capitalize on the natural abilities of learners by gearing our lessons to take advantage of these abilities.

c. *The treatment of errors by teachers.* If in fact, learners are hypothesis-testers, how should the teacher respond to their errors—supply the correct answers, lead them to discover it for themselves, call on a classmate for help, etc.? Allwright (1975) and Fanselow (1974) are but two of the researchers who feel this is an area worthy of investigation in the search for better language teaching practices.

d. *Linguistic model.* What is the best linguistic model for training language teachers to gain insights into the language they are to teach? For transmitting those insights to their students? Just as there is a divergence of opinion as to which is the best language teaching methodology, so is there a dispute over whether a more traditional grammatical model affords a better pedagogical basis for language teaching than say, a transformational-generative model. (See Celce-Murcia and Larsen-Freeman, 1977.) Some educators believe that no linguistic theory will serve pedagogical purposes, and instead a grammar constructed more for the purpose of elucidation in language teaching, such as Allen's sector analysis, will be the only way to satisfy language teaching demands. This too, then, is an area in which research would be enlightening.

PRACTICAL ISSUES

Manipulation to communication

Although the sequencing of tasks in the second language class from ones that are basically manipulative to ones that are basically communicative is not really a controversial issue, it is another aspect of the teaching of grammar worth considering.

Prator (1965) distinguishes between manipulative activities, where "the teacher controls the entire exercise, supplying students with both words and structures," from communicative activities where "the student is in control of the situation and supplies for himself the words and structures he needs."

Obviously, such activities would become the poles for a continuum along which activities which were predominantly manipulative and predominantly communicative would also have a rightful place.

Paulston (1971) in discussing drill types feels the need to make a finer distinction, and claims that there exists a middle ground, "meaningful" drill, in which "there is still control of response" by the teacher, but the student could correctly express an answer in more than one way. Furthermore, "the student cannot complete the (meaningful) drill without fully understanding structurally and semantically what he is saying."

However narrowly the distinction is made, the point worth noting is that the activities for every new lesson should be sequenced along this continuum. The teacher should give the students ample opportunity to manipulate the structure under the tightest of controls, and subsequently relax the controls, giving them the opportunity to use the structure communicatively.

This same continuum could probably equally well be considered characteristic of the progression in the overall language learning experience. When the learner is at a beginning level of language instruction, much of his or her time is preoccupied with learning to manipulate the structures in this new language. Little by little, automaticity develops and s/he feels freer to use the basic patterns of the language in creative, communicative ways.

Presenting a grammatical structure

a. *Dialogues.* The new grammatical structure is given a context in a conversation, usually between two speakers. The structure and vocabulary included in the dialogue (other than the new structure) should be ones that the students have already learned. The lines of each speaker should be kept fairly short, although natural. It is not necessary to establish a setting within the dialogue; the teacher can do this with a short introduction before the actual dialogue. This eliminates the need to begin each dialogue with

an exchange of greetings between each of the participants. Whether or not the dialogue is to be memorized should be left to the discretion of the teacher, but certainly ample practice should be given in its manipulation from choral repetition by a class to recitation by groups of students to practice by individual volunteers.

b. *Texts.* Grammatical structures can also be presented within the context of a story or some sort of text. The teacher can read or tell the story with or without the actual text in the students' hands. Again, natural language should be used. Resist the temptation to have the structure appear so frequently in the passage that it does so at the expense of authenticity.

c. *Rules.* For those grammatical structures which are not particularly conducive to presentation by one of the above means, it is certainly possible for the teacher to simply present the rule, as long as it is supplemented by plenty of examples and practice. Conversely, the teacher could follow the inductive approach with any of the above means, or simply give a series of examples to the students and lead them to induce the rule for themselves.

d. *Realia, pictures, pantomime.* Another possibility is for the teacher to follow the inductive approach, but rather than simply stating the examples, or writing them on the blackboard, to accompany or dramatize them with realia, pictures or pantomime. An obvious example which comes to mind is for the teacher to demonstrate the regular past tense by saying while acting: *I am walking across the room.* (Stop—turn to class and say: *I walked across the room.*); *I am smiling now.* (Stop—turn to class and say: *I smiled.*)

Drills and practice

Once the structure has been presented, keeping in mind our intention to give our students initial practice in manipulating the new item, our next procedure should probably involve some sort of drill. Although they are referred to by a variety of names, we will follow Paulston's terminology and hierarchy (manipulative, meaningful, communicative). The teacher can indicate the type of drill through words and gestures. Once the pattern has been established, a minimum amount of direction will be necessary by the teacher. The following, then are some of the possible drill types:

a. Manipulative drills

1. *Repetition.* The teacher simply provides the model containing the new structure and the students repeat it. The usual practice with this type as with many of the others is for the class to respond as a whole chorally, then for groups of students to respond (i.e., the males and then the females, students on one side of the class and then another, and finally response by individuals).

·2. *Substitution drill.*

i. Single-slot. In this drill the students are given a sentence (or question, etc.) and a cue word. They are to substitute the cue words into their appropriate place in the sentence. For example:

Teacher: *I go to the store every day. (every week)*
Students: *I go to the store every week.*
Teacher: *(every afternoon)*
Students: *I go to the store every afternoon.*

ii. Multiple-slot. This is a variation of the first type of substitution drill. The basic format remains the same but this time the cue could be a substitute for any item in the model. For example:

Teacher: *I go to the store every day. (every week)*
Students: *I go to the store every week.*
Teacher: *(the park)*
Students: *I go to the park every week.*
Teacher: *(he)*
Students: *He goes to the park every week.*

3. *Transformation.* For this drill the teacher supplies a certain English syntactic structure, for example, an affirmative sentence. The students are instructed to transform that structure into another—say, a question, or a negative sentence.

Teacher: *I go to the store every week.*
Students: *Do you go to the store every week?*

4. *Completion.*[4] This drill type would only be applicable for certain structural types. One

possible application would be with question tags. The teacher models the formal statement and the students repeat the model and complete the utterance with the appropriate question tag. For example:

Teacher: *He goes to the store every week.*
Students: *He goes to the store every week, doesn't he?*

5. *Expansion drill.* This drill can be used along with the other drills or can be employed whenever needed to help students with an especially troublesome sentence. It is primarily designed to aid in the development of fluency with a long sentence. For example:

Model sentence: *I went to the store and I bought a dozen eggs, a loaf of bread and a quart of milk.*
Teacher: *I went to the store.*
Students: *I went to the store.*
Teacher: *I went to the store and I bought. . . .*
Students: *I went to the store and I bought. . . .*
Students: *I went to the store and I bought a dozen eggs.*
Students: *I went to the store and I bought a dozen eggs.*

6. *Integrative drill.* Again, this drill is not appropriate for all structures of English. The students' task is to combine the two cues given them by the teacher into one utterance. For example:

Teacher: *I went to the store. He went to the store.*
Students: *I went to the store and he did, too.*

b. Meaningful drills

1. *Restatement.*

Teacher: *Abdul, ask Juan what he did yesterday.*
Abdul: *What did you do yesterday, Juan?*
Juan: *I went to the library.*

Drills such as this, which require individual responses can be conducted as "chain drills." A chain drill is one where the teacher begins the drill, but rather than giving all the cues, allows the students to carry on the drill by themselves. In the above example, Juan would turn to the student sitting beside him and ask the question he had just answered. The drill can be perpetuated until all have had an opportunity to answer or stopped at any time.

2. *Rejoinder.* This is a drill where the teacher makes a statement containing a certain syntactic structure and a student is asked to respond. The student's response may necessitate using another syntactic structure, but s/he will have to understand what is being said to him or her in order to respond accurately. Rutherford (1968) gives us an example:

Teacher: *What countries border on Spain besides Germany and Belgium?*
Student: *Germany doesn't border on Spain and neither does Belgium.*
Teacher: *I'm studying French and Italian now, so I'll be able to communicate a little when I go to Spain.*
Student: *French isn't spoken in Spain and Italian isn't either.*

c. Communicative drills

1. *Rejoinder.* The teacher makes a statement, but rather than the student simply replying with something factually correct, s/he communicates something about him- or herself. For example:

Teacher: *I like apples.*
Student: *You like apples, but I don't.*
Teacher: *I don't smoke.*
Student: *You don't smoke and I don't either.*

2. *Question and answer.* It is a moot point whether an exercise of this sort should be rightfully classified as a drill. What happens is that the teacher poses a question and the student responds by, again, having a free choice of answer.

Teacher: *What's your hobby?*
Student: *My hobby is collecting stamps.*
Teacher: *What's your favorite pastime?*
Student: *My favorite pastime is watching T.V.*

To guard against overuse or abuse in conducting drills, Rivers (1969) supplies us with the following evaluative checklist:

i. Drill is designed for teaching, not testing. The teacher should provide considerable practice in the use of each element before moving to another.

ii. Each drill should be concerned with one specific structural pattern.

iii. The structural feature to be drilled will have been encountered already by the students in recent material—for example, in a dialogue they have memorized.

iv. Changes made between one response item and the next will be minimal.

v. Each item in the series will be short.

vi. Each item will be a complete utterance of a type which could conceivably occur in a conversational interchange.

vii. The drill will be designed so that the cue will provoke only the desired response.[5]

viii. The variety of vocabulary should be kept to a minimum.

ix. Both cue and response items should be in English.

x. Drills will be conducted orally.

xi. They should not be purely imitative, but varied in type to alleviate boredom.[6]

xii. Some provision will be made for students to apply what they have learned in the drill series in a structured communicative situation.

Further practice

In between drills and communicative activities, the teacher might want to make use of the blackboard, the overhead projector, or handouts to give students an opportunity to complete exercises, oral and/or written, which relate to the new structure. One way of doing this as well as promoting peer correction and a good social climate is to make use of group work.

In this technique devised by Celce-Murcia (1977), homework exercises are distributed to the students on a particular day. The next day the teacher checks to see that all of the students have completed the exercises, and then divides the class into several groups. Within each group the students compare their responses and discuss any disagreement. Then they record the group's consensus. They give the teacher their consensus answers on a clean exercise sheet which the teacher has given to the recorder in each group. The teacher then corrects the groups' responses, gives the entire class feedback, and pinpoints general problems. Finally, the teacher develops follow-up exercises dealing with these residual problem areas.

Once the teacher is reasonably satisfied that most of the class has grasped the new structure in isolation, it is time to give students communicative practice using the new structure in context. There are many ways to accomplish this—the variety limited only by the teacher's degree of imagination. The following are two typical communicative activities:

a. *Role playing.* Role playing is one technique which affords much opportunity to practice a new structure in the context of "natural" communicative usage. For example, after the teacher has introduced *Wh*-questions for the first time and the students have had ample practice manipulating the form, the teacher can suggest that the students pair off and role-play the part of newspaper reporters. Their instructions are to find out as much as possible about their partner within a certain time limit. The "reporters" must later relate their findings to the class.

b. *Problem-solving.* Taking advantage of the second language learner's cognitive ability and desire to communicate, the teacher can present the learner with all sorts of problems that need to be solved through the manipulation of new language structures.

In one problem-solving task, for example, two students are asked to sit back to back or are separated by a cardboard screen. Both students receive colored pieces of plastic of various dimensions and shapes; however, one member of each pair is given them pre-arranged in some sort of simple geometric design while the other is given them scrambled. It is the responsibility of the first student to make use of the imperative form and the prepositions of English to enable the second student to construct a figure identical to the one already assembled for the first student. It is the second student's responsibility to request clarification whenever needed (Allwright, 1975).

This, then, concludes the suggested sequence of presentation: rule, drills, practice exercises, and communicative activities. The teacher trainee should not interpret this sequence nor the activities comprising each part of the sequence as being inflexible. Indeed, a key to any good teaching is holding the students' attention, and attention-holding is often enhanced by variety rather than conformity to a set pattern. Furthermore, the trainee should not conclude that this sequence was meant to be incorporated into a single lesson plan. The initial presentation of a new structure might very well take place over an entire week with each day containing some drill, some practice exercise, and communicative activities.

Linear versus cyclical

Another practical issue alluded to earlier has to do with the way in which the teacher designs the syllabus.

One approach, the linear one, would be to teach grammatical structures from start to finish through a syllabus, or book, covering each structure thoroughly at the prescribed time. Another possibility would be to "recycle" structures from time to time during the term. For example, in teaching a new verb tense, the previously learned tenses could be reviewed by contrasting their forms and functions with the form and function of the tense being introduced. By re-introducing material that has been presented previously in conjunction with a new, but similar pattern, the teacher would hopefully be minimizing the amount of intralanguage interference which could occur, as well as reinforcing the structures already presented throughout the term. The latter approach has obvious advantages and should be adhered to unless other factors suggest otherwise.

Is it necessary to follow the skills sequence (Listening-Speaking-Reading-Writing)?

Under the Audiolingual Approach it was considered imperative that the student learn to control a new structure aurally/orally before grappling with it in the printed form. Although this still is the common practice, there is nothing today that binds us to this sequence with such rigor. Indeed, some would advise the introduction of a new structure through a reading passage so that the correct context for its usage will have been established. Furthermore, because of the frequency with which they occur in the two media, some structures are far more natural in the written context, than the spoken.

Thus, although the emphasis in a second language classroom is still on an oral approach initially, we should not feel ourselves restricted to following the traditional skill sequence when it does not make sense. Van Syoc (1977) also expresses this point of view.

Heterogeneous class

When one is engaged in the teaching of ESL in an English-speaking country, as opposed to EFL in another country, one is likely to encounter classes which are heterogeneous with regard to language background.

It is not advisable for the teacher to use any native language in the classroom in this case, for it would only estrange the other students and make for a poor social climate in the classroom. What the teacher can do is conduct the entire course in English, using pictures, props, and pantomime to convey meaning.

Finocchiaro and Bonomo (1973) suggest teaching students (presumably through pantomime) the basic simple directional terms— *listen, repeat, say, ask,* and *answer*—with accompanying gestures, right from the first day of class. With these commands, beginning students should be able to participate in most any manipulative activities in the lesson. As they get more advanced, more complex instructions can be given in English with assurance of comprehension.

Another suggestion is to take advantage of some of the better students in the class to help out with the slower students of the same language background. The weaker students will gain from the individual attention they receive and the stronger students will gain from tutoring the language while avoiding any restlessness they may experience due to the slower pace.

Although usually it is wise to integrate members from different language backgrounds into different groups, the teacher could occasionally have the class break up into groups according to their native language to enable the teacher to work with each group and the

existing problems unique to that group (e.g., review of articles for the Oriental students and practice with phrasal verbs for the students of Romance language background).

CONCLUSION

Many issues of both a theoretical and a practical nature have been touched upon in this chapter. While teacher trainees might find the lack of resolution of some of these issues disturbing, the intention of this chapter was not to be prescriptive about the teaching of grammar, but rather to point out the issues which must be resolved by the individual teacher. Each teacher must take into consideration his or her own personality, the needs of his or her students and the situation in which teaching is to take place before deciding upon a suitable course of instruction. The best course design will be one that will help promote a positive social climate in the classroom, enhance student motivation, and make teaching enjoyable for the teacher—all indispensable if successful language learning is to be accomplished.

NOTES

1. See Prator with Celce-Murcia (in this volume) for a summary of the various approaches that have been used in the United States.

2. For a discussion of these and other innovative methodologies, see the Madsen article (in this volume).

3. Of course, one could argue that what we should do is teach in just the opposite order from the "natural order" so as to concentrate our efforts on those structures which take the longest to master. This debate would have to be resolved empirically.

4. Note that this type of controlled completion drill can be considered a special case of transformation drill.

5. Obviously Rivers is confining her comments to what Paulston would call "manipulative drills."

6. Other ways to alleviate boredom involve altering the tempo and volume in which drills are conducted—also the posture of the students, i.e., sitting or standing up. If drills are obviously boring, students are probably ready to go beyond the drill stage and to use the language more meaningfully in communicative situations.

DISCUSSION QUESTIONS

1. Explain the different views on errors held by proponents of the audiolingual and cognitive-code methodologies.

2. Would structure drills be appropriate for students at all levels of language proficiency? Why or why not?

3. Explain why the manipulation-to-communication continuum rule is appropriate for an entire program of instruction as well as an individual lesson.

4. Discuss the advantages and disadvantages of having students memorize a dialogue.

5. Why would it not ordinarily be advisable for a teacher to divide a heterogeneous class into groups for group work according to their native language backgrounds?

6. What would be some arguments against using the frequency of occurrence of structures as a basis for developing a pedagogical sequence?

SUGGESTED ACTIVITIES

1. Prepare a series of drills (manipulative, meaningful, communicative) relating to a particular grammar point. Practice conducting these drills on a group of peers.

2. Select an area of grammar which has several component parts, e.g., the verb tenses. Sequence the parts according to the order in which you would teach them. Be prepared to justify your order.

3. Examine several ESL grammar books. Read the preface in each to see if you can discover on what basis the lessons are sequenced. Does the sequence make sense? Is it flexible enough to be changed in order to meet the needs of your students as you perceive them?

4. Think of several role-playing situations you could assign your students to give them practice in producing negatives.

SUGGESTIONS FOR FURTHER READING

Celce-Murcia, M., and D. Larsen-Freeman (forthcoming)
An English Grammar for Teachers of ESL, Rowley, Mass.: Newbury House.
From a basically transformational grammar perspective, it seeks to guide teacher-trainees to an understanding of the grammar of those English structures they will have to teach, and offers useful teaching suggestions for these same structures.

Finocchiaro, Mary (1974)
English as a Second Language: From Theory to Practice. New York; Regents Publishing Co. 2d edition.
The section on "Basic Oral Practice Activities" (pp. 62-72) and the section on "Some Language-Teaching Myths" (pp. 168-72) are useful. The first section gives hints on how to conduct oral drills, lists different types of drills, and provides useful examples. The second section discusses some misconceptions about language learning and teaching that have been presented here as "issues."

Rivers, Wilga (1968)
Teaching Foreign-Language Skills. Chicago: Univ. of Chicago Press, Chapters 2, 3, and 4.
A good discussion of the audiolingual versus cognitive-code methodology. Helpful hints on constructing grammatical drills and exercises.

Slager, William R. (1973)
"Creating Contexts for Language Practice," *TESOL Quarterly*, Vol. 7, No. 1, pp. 35-50.
Argues the need for contextualization when teaching grammar and provides two examples: one for the passive voice, and one for the present perfect tense.

Wilkins, David A. (1972)
Linguistics in Language Teaching. Cambridge, Mass.: MIT Press, pp. 77-85.
Discusses syllabus design and textbook contents reminding teachers that language learning does not simply consist of the acquisition of a set of forms.

A GRAMMAR SEQUENCE FOR TEACHING ESL TO BEGINNERS

Lois McIntosh

INTRODUCTION

As long as languages have been taught, each prevailing philosophy underlying the teaching has yielded in time to a different theory. Every time this happens, the procedures and theories that went before have been largely ignored and each new approach has been hailed as the only way to go. The French have pointed out that the more things change, the more they are the same; and for language teaching there may be some application of that saying. However, the same things are never really exactly the same in language theory. Time and place change language usage, and circumstances—often political—force a language which was once foreign to become domestic in use.

We know that in the past grammar-translation was for a long time the only way to teach a language. Today it is still the only way in some countries where English is taught as a foreign language.

The structural grammarians like Bloomfield (1933), who flourished before 1960, tossed out grammar-translation and developed the Audiolingual Approach to language teaching. In this approach the structural linguist meticulously examined the spoken utterances of native speakers of a given language and made careful descriptions of its basic sentences. Such descriptions constituted the subject matter of language courses, and stimulus-response psychology underlay the teaching method used (Fries, 1945).

Some of these careful descriptions have survived as phrase structure rules in the transformational-generative grammatical theory of Chomsky (1957, 1965). This successor to the structuralist point of view came about in the late 1950s. It recognizes that language is limited to humans, and that it is a function of the human brain. It provides an abstract representation of language at the level of deep structure. By applying the natural processes of language—substitution, re-arrangement, addition, and deletion—in a series of transformations, surface structures are generated.

Meanwhile, as this grammatical theory begins to yield to a more pronounced emphasis on a science of semantics, the teachers in the classrooms are teaching the language as best they can. When we teach English to mixed groups of speakers of other languages in our schools and colleges in this country, we must, perforce, resort to direct methods. No other way is possible. If the teacher of the class knows one of the languages represented in that class, it would be most unfair to the other students if s/he translated and discussed lessons in that language.

By carefully sequencing the material of our lessons and presenting them in contexts that are directly meaningful to the learners, we manage without translations. At this moment, this pedagogical approach seems to be an effective way to proceed. The experienced teacher of English as a second or foreign language, in choosing a text, will discard one that presents a feature of the language only once, and never brings it up again. S/he will discard a text that has random drills, so that every sentence in an exercise, while being consistent as to the grammar in it, will vary widely in subject matter, thereby compounding the problem for the students as they adjust their minds to large amounts of semantically unrelated language material.

THE VERB *BE* AND
THE BEGINNING LESSONS

Most introductory lessons begin with the verb *be*. Although this verb has more forms than any other verb in English, it is basic to the language, and it must be presented early and recycled often.

It is used in sentences of identification: *This is a book.*

It is used in sentences of description: *The book is red.*

It is used in sentences of location: *The book is on the table.*

The full verb form in these examples is, of course, present tense + *be*.[1] Tense is always present in the finite verb in an English sentence, and its form (though not necessarily its meaning) is either present or past. To form a *yes-no* question with *be* sentences, we invert present tense + *be* with the subject, and to form a negative sentence, we insert *not* following *be*.

This *is* a book.
   pres. + *be*

Is this a book?
pres. + *be*

  Yes, it *is*.
   pres. + *be*

Is this a pencil?
pres. + *be*

  No, it *isn't*.
   pres. + *be* + neg.

Let me state firmly that the teaching of grammar must be based on truth. If you hold up a book and ask, *Is this a book?* and then require the class to answer *Yes, it is* and immediately after that, *No, it isn't* to that same question, you are doing the class and the language a disservice. A *yes-no* question calls for either a *yes* or a *no* in response, depending on the question and the context.

We have introduced the short answer with *it* as subject pronoun, to prevent the awkward spatial requirement of *this* and *that*. In normal speech, we do not answer the question, *Is this a book?* with *Yes, that is a*

book (unless perhaps the book is on a high shelf and looks like something else).

There are other situations where *that* can be brought in naturally: a map at the back of the class; the teacher's desk at a distance from the students; windows, doors, lights on the ceiling, and the blackboard.

With basic identification sentences based on the full verb *be* and the *yes-no* questions with appropriate short answers, in the affirmative and negative, we have introduced our students to a good amount of grammar for a beginning lesson. By confining our context to the visible and countable objects in the classroom, we eliminate the need to translate, which we can't do anyway in a multilingual classroom.

We must continue until every student has had an opportunity to ask a question about a countable object in the classroom, and the opportunity to answer a question with a short, truthful response. We can provide this practice by holding up (or getting the students to hold up) a book, a pen, a pencil, a map—but not *chalk* or *paper* as they are not countable in their base form. If the class has never had any previous encounter with English, the teacher can and should model the statement, the question, and the answer, and have a short choral repetition from the class as they adjust to the strange sounds of this language.

We begin by identifying the countable nouns in the classroom. We continue by asking about the color and size of these objects. Notice that in the second mention of the noun, *the* replaces *a/an* as the determiner. The second mention makes the noun specific.

Review: *Is this a book?*
       Yes, it is.
New: *Is the book red?*
       No, it's not. It's blue.

After the basic colors have been practiced, we move on to sizes:

Is the desk big?
  Yes, it is.
Is the pencil small?
  Yes, it is.
Is the pen long?
  No, it isn't.

Finally, we locate these same objects:

Is the book on the desk?
Yes, it is.
Is the book in my hand?
No, it isn't.

All this goes on in the first few lessons. It may take several class meetings to cover all the material. Don't rush it. It forms the basis of much of the language that follows.

One problem the teacher must solve here is which form of the negative to introduce first. The form with *not* (e.g., *No, it's not*) carries some special stress, and the form with contraction of the negative (e.g., *No, it isn't*) is necessary in later constructions. If we teach the *not* form first, we will have this paradigm: *am not, are not, is not,* [2] but some teachers point out that we will not be able to use it in tag questions, in sentences with the expletive (e.g., *there is/isn't*), and other constructions. However, other teachers feel that in the first lessons the material should be kept as simple and consistent as possible, and so they use *not* in the early lessons.

When we have thoroughly practiced the singular forms of present tense + *be* in the three basic sentences, in *yes-no* questions, and in short affirmative and negative responses, then we introduce three *wh*-questions: *what's this?* elicits a noun phrase answer; *what color is this?* brings out adjectives; and *where's the* (noun)*?* elicits the locative sentence.

Now we are ready to move into the plural, still using the verb *be*. In choosing the context for the plural, we can stay in the classroom, if we can find nouns that illustrate the voicing feature that permeates English (i.e., plural, third person singular of verbs, and possessives):

books—voiceless /k/ followed by the voiceless sibilant /s/

pencils—voiced /l/ followed by voiced sibilant /z/

and the syllabic demanded by nouns ending in /s/, /z/, /š/, /ž/, /tš/, /dž/: *classes* /əz/; *dishes* /əz/; *pages* /əz/, etc.

At this time we can also find this principle working in *be* sentences formed with *is*:

That*'s* a book.   /s/
The*re's* a book on the table.   /z/
This *is* a book.   /əz/

Later, when the noun shows possession, the voicing is present once more: *Kate's book* /s/, *Bess's book* /əz/, *Mary's book* /z/. (Appendix A summarizes the occurrence of this feature.)

By reminding your students each time this feature appears, and by practicing it with them, an important part of the sound system of English will be recycled. When you introduce plural + noun, you also reintroduce *this-these,* and *that-those.* In this way the nearness-distance feature is once more practiced with plural nouns.

As we introduce the other pronoun subjects, we can bring in people and their professions, work, or jobs, depending on their age and activity. Then we can tell where they work, and thus re-practice the *where* question again.

When we arrive at the possessive + noun, we can practice family relationships. We must remember that many languages form this construction differently from English. We say: *Mary is John's sister. She's his sister.* And: *John is Mary's brother. He is her brother.*

Before we leave *be,* we can have lessons on time and the weather. In the United States there is regional variation in telling time. Railroad and airplane schedules are fairly universal: 5:50, 2:20. The variations come in the wording of *before* and *after:* It's *ten to six* in some parts of the country; *ten till six* in other parts; *ten of six* in still other parts. It's *twenty after two*; and *twenty past two.* Find out what the accepted form is in the community you are teaching in, and use that. Don't try to teach all the forms, but if your class is full of world travelers, teach them the international time form where the hour is followed by the minutes: 10:30, 11:45, 20:45.

But now we must return to the noun phrases of English, since an important division of them should be introduced at a fairly early stage. This is the non-count category that contrasts with the count nouns that have singular and plural forms. The nouns that come in the non-count sets often classify a group of nouns, and, when they do, the members of the group are often countable. Consider the non-count nouns *meat* and *furniture*. Meat is a class of food; chops, steaks, roasts, etc, are countable parts of this class. Furniture is a class of objects; chairs, tables, beds, bookshelves, etc., are countable parts of this class.

However, in introducing this division to a beginning class, it is well to begin with food. A hearty breakfast (and pictures of it) could have both kinds of nouns:

Non-count: *coffee, milk, juice, toast, butter, jam*

Count: *an egg* (or *two eggs*), some *pancakes,* some *sausages*

For the non-count nouns we have counters (e.g., *cup, bottle, piece,* etc.), usually in the shape of a container. Thus we have *cups of coffee; glasses of milk* and *juice; pieces of toast; spoonfuls* or *helpings* or *servings of jam,* and *butter.*

When this feature has been thoroughly practiced with the help of pictures, and the food in other meals has been classified according to count and non-count, it may interest your students to explore another part of the house as they tell what they use to get ready for school:

Count: *a toothbrush, a comb, a hair-brush, a razor,* etc.

Non-count: *soap, powder, rouge, tooth-paste, shaving cream,* etc.

There are many other divisions of non-count and count nouns including natural events like *fire, rain, snow, thunder, lightning*; school subjects—*history, English, mathematics, geography.* While in geography, teach the English names of the countries of the world, and notice that those with plural names (e.g., *The United States, The Philippines*) and those with a description of their government (e.g., *The United Kingdom*) take the definite article, whereas more common proper names of countries (*England, France, Germany,* etc.) take neither a plural marker nor an article. (See Appendix B for a summary of determiner co-occurrence with count and non-count nouns.)

Next, we use *be* along with *-ing* as an auxiliary with intransitive verbs. We begin with intransitives as they are only optionally modified by adverbs and make no demands on the shape of what follows them. If we also choose those intransitives that later can function as transitives with an object, we get double mileage out of our vocabulary. Thus we can, while still in the progressive, talk about these people:

John is studying. Mary is reading. Professor Miller is teaching.

After practice with these, we can make the sentences transitive like this:

John is studying math.
  He's studying it.
Mary is reading a book.
  She's reading it.
Professor Miller is teaching the students.
  She's teaching them.

And other situations will occur to you and your students while you are still in the progressive. You can open and shut doors and windows; you can put pencils on desks, words on the chalkboard—all the while using *be* + verb-ing. Be sure to practice this with questions and negatives too.

When we combine present + *be* and *going to,* we have the planning future. This gives us one more lesson involving *be,* which is used here again as an auxiliary, carrying tense and making the same demands of agreement with noun phrase subject and verb. We can draw on our familiarity with its performance in questions and negatives, and we can supplement our vocabulary of verbs at the same time. The context here, depending on the age of your students, could be one of these. For adults and adolescents: *What are you going to be? What are you going to do next year? Where are you going to live?* etc. For younger students: *What games are you going to play? What things are you going to learn? What places are you going to visit?* and the like. And while in this planning future, be sure to practice questions, negatives, and short answers.

Finally, we turn away from *be* and take up the other present tense—the one that talks about habitual or recurring actions: *We get up every morning; the sun rises in the east; we go to school every morning,* etc.

The third person singular form of the verb needs to be practiced, and practiced hard.

Even students who have progressed a long way in English repeatedly fail to inflect that verb. So line up your plural sentences, and have the students change them to the singular:

Students study.
   A student studies.
Boys play.
   A boy plays.

If some of the verbs end in voiceless sounds, and some in voiced, and some demand an extra syllable, the voicing lesson can be recycled at this time.

A good context for questions and negatives is a schedule of classes that two different students follow—one student having classes in the afternoon, the other in the morning. Then extensive practice can be carried out with the answers to such questions as: *Does Y study English? When does X take math?* To elicit the negative, the teacher says, *Y has classes in the morning, doesn't she?* and the students will say, *No, she doesn't. She has classes in the afternoon.* And so forth. Again it is important that the question and negative transformations be practiced as well as the statement form. In a related writing assignment, provide a paragraph of daily activities carried out by two people every day. Then have the students rewrite the paragraph telling the story of what only one of them does every day.

When we have thoroughly practiced the two presents— the *be* + verb-ing and the present with the *-(e)s* ending on third person singular— we can take a fairly rapid trip through the simple past tense. Except for *be* and other irregular verbs, past tense in English is expressed with an affix (/t/d/əd/), and tense is carried by the past auxiliary *did* in questions and negatives.

However, the English verb system over its long history has acquired some irregular verbs that do not have the affix that the regular ones have. A summary of these is found in Appendix C. Some of them do not change in the three parts; some, and these are the most frequently used verbs, change all three forms. For example: *go-went-gone.*

But these verbs too can be learned, and when they are learned in sets of similar forma-tion, the task is made easier for the students. So look at Appendix C and start a brisk drill in which each student can form a *did* question, and a response. Where the first principle part differs notably from the simple past tense form, go back to the present tense and practice the questions and negatives with *do/does* and *don't/doesn't,* too.

Last year	This year
What did you do?	*What do you do?*
I taught French.	*I sell cars.*
Who sold cars?	*Who teaches French?*

PRE-VERBS OR MODAL AUXILIARIES

It is especially important to teach the meanings that modals bring to the sentence. The first set—*can, will,* and *may,* for example—varies greatly in meaning and use.

The modal *can* basically tells of ability. *X can swim; Y can sing,* etc. The question is often a request for permission: *Can I have a candy? Can I go out?* It is used by younger children and in informal speech. The negative form, *can't,* is difficult to hear when it precedes verbs that begin with /k/ or /g/. The main signal is stress: *I can go* /aý kən ɡów/; *I can't go* /aý kǽn ɡów/. If your students listen for the full, stressed vowel /æ/ in the negative, it will help them to make the distinction between affirmative and negative uses of *can.*

May is most frequent in first person use. It is slightly more formal than *can,* and it is used in questions like: *May I have this dance? May* also predicts: *We may be a few minutes late.*

Will belongs to the ways we talk about the future. It is sometimes referred to as the promising future. *I'll meet you at six o'clock.* Now *shall* occurs only as a somewhat quaint invitation: *Shall we dance? Shall we go? Shall I open that window for you?* or a request for advice or opinion: *Shall we ask John to the party?*

The past forms of modals do not neces-sarily signal past time. Consider *should.* It belongs in a list of obligatory actions. *Should* addresses our better natures and adjures us to do that which we might otherwise neglect. *I should write my parents. Had better, should, have to*, and *must* are the moralizers. In ascending order of severity, they present problems when their negative forms occur.[3]

> *Should he scold his child like that? He shouldn't frighten him.*
> *You'd better not have a second helping. You're quite fat enough.*
> *Do I have to take that medicine? Yes, but after next week, you won't have to take it any more.*
> *Yes, you really must. You mustn't neglect your health.*

Once modals have been introduced, they are never really abandoned. Their role in conditionals requires attention:

Future Possibility:
If I go by bus, it will/can take three days.

Present Improbability:
If I went by car, it would/could take even longer.

Past Impossibility:
If I had gone by plane, I would/could have been there by now.

What must be pointed out in this set is that the second and third sentences are negative in implication. The speaker probably won't go by car in sentence two. S/he definitely didn't go by plane in sentence three—s/he is merely speculating about the consequences of these two ways of traveling. This must be pointed out, and students should be encouraged to respond: *but s/he isn't going by car; s/he didn't go by plane.*
Would rather and *had better* require separate treatment. In offering a choice, *would rather* has a special intonation:

Would you rather eat or sleep?

Had better is part of the moral sequence, and the negative is contracted: *Hadn't you better take an umbrella? It looks like rain.*[4]

PASSIVE VOICE

The use of the passive voice is most frequent in those sentences where the agent is not important. Some texts give an example like this: *John ate an apple. An apple was eaten by John.* This is not a useful example, as nothing is gained by resorting to the passive voice. Academic writing, in which the author modestly keeps out of the limelight, is a place where the passive voice can serve usefully. Other good contexts for teaching this form are subjects like slum clearances, where old houses are being torn down, and new houses are being built; the restoration of a city; the provision of a new mass transit system, the construction of bridges. Be sure to teach modal passive and perfective passive forms too: *The bridge is repaired; was repaired; will be repaired; has been repaired. The building can be torn down; could be torn down; should have been torn down . . . etc.*

THE PERFECT TENSES

When we move into another part of the verb auxiliary—the perfective aspect—we have a construction that contrasts strongly with its use in other languages (i.e., the present perfect). The present perfect in English (*have* or *has* + past participle) has present time in its meaning. It is necessary to teach at least four lessons dealing with this construction:

(*since, for*) *The Smiths have lived in this city for twenty years. They have lived in the same house since 1970.*
(*ever, never*) *Mr. Smith has never traveled abroad. He likes to stay home. Has he ever left the country? No, he hasn't.*
(*already, yet*) *The oldest Smith son has already left the family. He is looking for a job, but he hasn't found one yet.*
(*have just*) *The youngest Smith child has just fallen down and sprained her ankle.*

And when these have been taught,[5] we need present perfect progressive for contexts that emphasize duration: *Mrs. Smith has been waiting for her husband for half an hour. She has been getting more and more impatient; but his plane is late, and she will have to keep on waiting until he arrives.*

The past perfect is more often encountered in writing than in speech. It is time in the past before some more recent past time: *The Jones family went camping last summer. They had just settled down in their tents, when a large animal came sniffing around. Mr. Jones had left his flashlight outside, and he had no way of identifying the visitor. It looked like a large bear, and it had been turning over pails and cans looking for food.*

The future perfect is hard to deal with in a natural conversational context: *By the time we get home from the airport, the plane on which our friends departed will have arrived in Florida. What do you think you will have accomplished by this time next year?*

CLAUSES

The foregoing discussion has centered on the demands made in one clause sentences and, in the case of the conditionals, two clause sentences. Beyond these demands, longer sentences simply consist of more clauses with the same requirements of concord and the same noun phrase divisions.

In a sequence that goes beyond single clause sentences we must include the following:

a. Sentences joined by *and, but, because.* These sentences cannot be random in each clause. There must be continuity, or they should not be joined together.

The boys played football all afternoon, and they went home tired and dirty.
Two women dropped in on a neighbor, but they did not stay long because he was busy.

b. Relative clauses—the embedding or addition principle of language. This part of the grammar needs careful preparation. The restrictive relative clause needs a division between human and non-human subjects as reflected in the relative connectors: *who, which.*

The man came to dinner. The man broke his leg and stayed all summer.
The man who came to dinner broke his leg and stayed all summer.

The man sat on a bench. The bench broke under his great weight.
The man sat on a bench which broke under his great weight.

c. Non-restrictive clauses are believed to be derived from compound sentences, the second clause of which is introduced by *and.*

For he's a jolly good fellow—and nobody can deny it.
For he's a jolly good fellow, which nobody can deny.

d. Beyond these clauses lies the possibility of expanding adverbial modifiers into clauses: *when, while, after, before* for time clauses; *where* for place; *why* for reason; *how* for manner.

e. Another difficult area of the grammar of complex English sentences deals with complementation and nominalization; namely, *that*-clauses, gerunds, and infinitives. The reader should consult the relevant chapters in Celce-Murcia and Larsen-Freeman (forthcoming) for an explanation of these sentence types, as well as for suggestions for teaching them to ESL students.

CONTEXTUALIZATION, DIALOGUES, AND REGISTER

Throughout the sequence of grammatical points proposed above, frequent suggestions were made concerning appropriate contexts for teaching these points of grammar. It must be emphasized that contextualization is not merely a nice decoration but a necessary and integral part of any effective language lesson. Very little is learned if the student is presented with a string of unrelated sentences all exhibiting the same structure. Developing a natural and appropriate context for each lesson can be quite difficult since the context must be compatible not only with the structural point being taught but also with the interests and needs of the students. A good textbook will suggest effective contexts, but in the final analysis, the classroom teacher is the best judge of what context will or will not be suitable for his or her students and should adapt the materials in the textbooks accordingly. (See Slager, 1973, for further discussion of this.)

The context can be provided in a number of ways. Celce-Murcia describes many helpful contextualizing tools in her article on Language Teaching Aids, in this volume.

One very common way to contextualize is in a short dialogue. The dialogue has its advantages. It is an exchange between two speakers of the language, and it can provide examples of statements, negated statements, questions, and short answers to questions.

Also a real conversation may take short-cuts, if the speakers know each other well.

Informal example

A: *Where are you going?*
B: *Downtown. Wanna lift?*
A: *Sure. Thanks a lot.*

Formal example

A: *Where are you going?*
B: *I'm going downtown. Would you like a ride?*
A: *Yes, I would. Thank you very much.*

The first exchange is that of two friends, and the language is very limited. Though it is undoubtedly realistic, the opportunities which it offers for language practice are also limited. The second exchange is somewhat more formal, and it provides considerably more opportunities for grammar drilling.

The question of register is a problem when one is creating language material. The teacher must be aware that his or her own speech in the classroom may be too formal to serve as a model for everyday exchanges. Conversely, if the dialogue is merely setting the context for a grammar lesson, it very likely has to be somewhat contrived.

Joos (1962) and others have pointed out that there are several registers of formality in languages. For English there are *frozen forms*, formulae acknowledging introductions and thanks and the like; *formal*, for a public lecture or a sermon; *consultative*, the language we use with people we deal with every day; *informal*, among friends who know each other very well; and *intimate*, within the family group. When you are delivering a lecture to a group, they must get all the information they need from you; they cannot ask questions or contradict. Therefore this more formal language is characterized by full sentences and specific details. The consultative register is more of an exchange, but the conversationalists need to be filled in rather specifically with little taken for granted. The use of the informal register suggests that there is rapport between the speakers, and that the background is familiar to both. This makes for half sentences, and attention noises. Intimate talk is in the family, and here the exchange is based on a long association. The choice of an appropriate register for classroom use will depend on many factors, among them the age and nationality of students and teacher, the purposes for which the language is being learned, etc.

Following the introduction of the material in the dialogue, drills should be used to reinforce the grammatical point being presented. An inventory of various kinds of drills is provided in McIntosh (1972)[6] and in Larsen-Freeman's article in this volume.

CONCLUSION

The foregoing suggestions are merely devices to help students control the English language better. They *can't* learn the language by talking about it. They *can* learn the language by using it in terms that they fully understand. We *do not* want them to imitate a teacher without having any notion of what they are saying. And we *do* want them to practice enough, and with full understanding, so that at the end of each lesson they have achieved control of a little more of the English language.

NOTES

1. The whole situation, of course, is further complicated by the fact that the number and person of the subject noun phrase are additional factors (other than tense) that determine the form *be* takes in any given sentence.

2. Note that the paradigm for the other pattern is incomplete: *s/he isn't, you, they, we aren't,* but not *I amn't.* (The non-standard gap filler here is *I ain't,* and a colloquial gap filler in tags is *aren't I?*)

3. Note that *have to* and *must* are similar in meaning in the affirmative; in the negative *mustn't* forbids, and *don't have to* excuses.

4. Hannah (1975) provides ESL teachers with a useful resource on the meaning and use of modals.

5. In reviewing these various uses of the present perfect, this would be a good context: *The Smith family has lived in this house for several generations. Mr. Smith left home last year, and he hasn't been seen since then. Mrs. Smith has recently decided to sell the house and move away. Her children have graduated from high school, and they have already left for college. Mrs. Smith hasn't told anyone about this yet. She has just decided to do it.* These examples stretch over time in such a way that they relate it to the moment of speaking. That is, with this aspect we express what the linguists call "current relevance"— nothing is over and done with. In contrast with the simple past tense, life is still going on.

6. The context in which these drill types are suggested is ESL materials for children.

DISCUSSION QUESTIONS

1. Why is it important to teach pronunciation along with grammar in a language lesson? What are the possible results of segregating these two language areas?

2. Should every language lesson be contextualized? Why or why not?

3. What could be used to provide context for a grammar lesson besides pictures or dialogues?

4. What are the advantages and disadvantages of using dialogues?

5. Why do irregular verbs pose a problem for ESL students at the beginning level? How would you deal with this problem when introducing the simple past tense? (Assume that you can devote several lessons to this topic.)

6. Why is it important to consider register when planning a grammar lesson for ESL students?

SUGGESTED ACTIVITIES

1. Extract and list the sequence of grammatical points in any ESL/EFL textbook. Is the sequencing logically acceptable? Is it linear or cyclic? What improvements could be made?

2. In what sequence and in how many different lessons would you present the structures shown in the following sentences to an intermediate or advanced ESL class? Justify your sequence. You may add other related structures to the sequence.

a. *I might have been working in the garden when you called.*

b. *The book has been reviewed by many critics.*

c. *John is reading a book right now.*

d. *You will have gone away and returned before he arrives.*

e. *This product has been being sold everywhere for three years now.*

f. *We have considered a new textbook.*

g. *The painting was being finished by George.*

h. *Bill may be visiting his grandparents.*

3. Evaluate any ESL/EFL textbook for quality of contextualization. Are all, some, or none of the lessons contextualized? Would you be able to use some of the contexts with your students?

4. Prepare a set of materials for a specific class based on the teaching sequence proposed in this chapter.

5. Devise a suitable context for intermediate level adult university students learning/ reviewing one of these constructions:

a. The quasi-modals: *would like, would rather,* and *had better.*

b. Restrictive relative clauses modifying the subject of the main sentence: *The flowers which were blooming in the garden were colorful. The students who were studying chemistry were very intelligent.*

c. The infinitive of purpose (*to/in order to*): *They all work to make a living.*

6. Prepare two lessons on the same point of grammar. One lesson should use the inductive, the other the deductive method. If possible, teach each version to a different class at the same level. Which method worked best? Why? What appear to be advantages and disadvantages of each method?

7. For the same point of grammar, devise three different introductions to a lesson using (a) pictures, (b) a prose passage, (c) a dialogue. Which introduction would be most effective with beginning students? With advanced students? Why?

8. Examine any grammar lesson in a currently used ESL text. Describe it in terms of (a) the type of introduction; (b) inductive or deductive approach; (c) number of rules vs. amount of exercises and drills; (d) amount of manipulative vs. communicative exercises provided. Evaluate the lesson in terms of (a) quality of contextualization; (b) variety and usefulness of exercises and drills provided; (c) overall effectiveness.

SUGGESTIONS FOR FURTHER READING

Chastain, Kenneth (1976)
Developing Second Language Skills: Theory to Practice, 2d ed. Chicago: Rand McNally College Publishing Company. Chapter 2: Audiolingual and Cognitive Teaching.
Discusses the Audiolingual vs. Cognitive-code Approach in relation to inductive and deductive language learning.

Joos, Martin (1962)
The Five Clocks, IJAL Publ. No. 22, Vol. 28, Part 2V, Research Center in Anthropology, Folklore, and Linguistics, Indiana University.
An extended discussion of the language registers that were mentioned briefly in the last two paragraphs of this chapter.

Liles, Bruce (1971)
An Introductory Transformational Grammar (pp. 1-113 only), Englewood Cliffs, N.J.: Prentice-Hall.
This text provides a good foundation in English grammar in the transformational framework—an orientation all language teachers should be very familiar with since transformational grammar reflects most closely the processes used in natural languages.

McIntosh, Lois (1972)
"How to Teach English Grammar," in Kenneth Croft (ed.), Readings on *English as a Second Language*. Cambridge, Mass.: Winthrop.
This article provides an inventory of drill types and is oriented toward teaching English grammar to elementary school children.

McIntosh, Lois (1967)
"Language Lessons Based on Transformational Analysis," in *UCLA Workpapers in English as a Second Language*, Vol. 1, pp. 15-26.
A series of lessons on relative clauses in English designed for native speakers of Tagalog. The lessons demonstrate how contrastive information may help determine a good sequence for a specific linguistic group.

Prator, Clifford H. (1965)
"Development of a Manipulation-Communication Scale," NAFSA Studies and Papers, English Language Series, No. 10, March, pp. 385-391. Reprinted in Allen and Campbell, *Teaching English as a Second Language* (1972). New York: McGraw-Hill, pp. 139-145.
One of the earliest criticisms of the overly manipulative and unproductive nature of teaching materials based on the Audiolingual Method. Calls for movement from manipulative to communicative drills in the language classroom.

Slager, William R. (1973)
"Creating Contexts for Language Practice," *TESOL*, Vol. 7, No. 1, pp. 35-50.
An excellent discussion of contextualization in language teaching and of ways in which it can be achieved.

Stevick, Earl W. (1959)
Helping People Learn English. Nashville, Tenn.: Abingdon Press.
One of the first and only sources to suggest a rather complete sequence of teaching points for use with students who are beginning their study of English.

APPENDIX A: VOICING FEATURES OF ENGLISH GRAMMAR

Sibilants

a. Contractions with *be*:
   This is a book /əz/
   That's a book /s/
   There's a book here /z/

b. Plural:
   classes, dishes, pages, vases /əz/
   books, hats, caps /s/
   pens, combs, cabs, bags, pencils /z/

c. Present tense + verb (3rd person singular):
   walks /s/
   runs /z/
   watches, washes, uses, passes /əz/

d. Possessive:
   Jack's /s/
   Mary's /z/
   Bess's /əz/

Alveolar stops

e. Past tense + verb:
walked /t/
moved /d/
waited, waded /əd/

APPENDIX B: DETERMINERS WITH COUNT AND NON-COUNT NOUNS

Count nouns

Singular: *a/an*. Plural: *some* identified and specific: singular: *the, this, that;* plural: *the, these, those*
Quantities: *lots of/a lot of, both, several, many, a few, few*

Non-count nouns

Singular form only: no marker, identified and specific: *the, this/that*
Quantities: *lots of/a lot of, much, little, a little, some*

Notes. 1. There are three determiners written as *some.* One, lightly stressed, is the plural equivalent of *a/an* in count nouns: *some pencils, some dogs.* In non-count nouns it replaces *a/an* to indicate a non-specific amount: *some coffee, some music, some peace and quiet.* Another *some* carries heavier stress, and it is used in connection with *other(s)* to divide the class in two: *Sóme men smoke; others don't. Sóme music is loud; other music is soft* (with non-count nouns, we must repeat the noun). The third *some* is very heavily stressed and used in exclamations: *Sóme party! That was sóme party!*
2. Note the change of unstressed *some* to *any*—obligatory in negated sentences, optional in questions:
A: *I'd like to buy some blueberries. Do you have any/some?*
B: *No, I don't have any right now.*

APPENDIX C: STRONG OR IRREGULAR VERBS ARRANGED IN PATTERNS

Three principal parts the same

hit	hit	hit
quit	quit	quit
split	split	split
bid	bid	bid
rid	rid	rid
bet	bet	bet
let	let	let
set	set	set
shed	shed	shed
spread	spread	spread
put	put	put
hurt	hurt	hurt
burst	burst	burst
cost	cost	cost
cast	cast	cast*

*But: forecast or forecasted; broadcast or broadcasted.

Last two principal parts alike

a. consonant change only

have	had	had
make	made	made
build	built	built
bend	bent	bent
lend	lent	lent
send	sent	sent
spend	spent	spent

b. vowel change

meet	met	met
bleed	bled	bled
feed	fed	fed
lead	led	led
mislead	misled	misled
read	read	read*
speed	sped	sped
light (also lighted)	lit	lit
slide	slid	slid
win	won	won
dig	dug	dug
stick	stuck	stuck
strike	struck	struck
find	found	found†
bind	bound	bound
wind	wound	wound /aw/

*Vowel sound changes although the spelling does not.
†But: *The city was founded in 1620.*

shine	shone	shone*
sit	sat	sat
hold	held	held
shoot	shot	shot
cling	clung	clung†

*Also: *shined*, transitive

†Similarly: *fling, sling, sting, string, swing, wring, slink*

c. vowel change and addition of /t/ or /d/

creep	crept	crept
keep	kept	kept
sleep	slept	slept
sweep	swept	swept
weep	wept	wept
buy	bought	bought
bring	brought	brought
fight	fought	fought
seek	sought	sought
think	thought	thought
catch	caught	caught
teach	taught	taught
mean	meant	meant
leave	left	left
flee	fled	fled

d. *Vowel change: addition; loss and addition*

tell	told	told
sell	sold	sold
lose	lost	lost
hear	heard	heard
stand	stood	stood
understand	understood	understood

Variation among the three principal parts

a. Three parts different:

be	was	been
go	went	gone
do	did	done

b. *Vowel change, addition of /ən/*

arise	arose	arisen
drive	drove	driven
ride	rode	ridden
rise	rose	risen
write	wrote	written

c. *Vowel change only*

begin	began	begun

sing	sang	sung
ring	rang	rung
drink	drank	drunk
swim	swam	swum

d. *Vowel change: first and third similar* (third may have addition of /n/ or /ən/)

blow	blew	blown
know	knew	known
grow	grew	grown
throw	threw	thrown
fly	flew	flown
run	ran	run
come	came	come
eat	ate	eaten
see	saw	seen
give	gave	given
forgive	forgave	forgiven
shake	shook	shaken

e. *Vowel change: second and third similar* (third has addition of /n/ or /ən/)

break	broke	broken
choose	chose	chosen
speak	spoke	spoken
steal	stole	stolen
tear	tore	torn
wear	wore	worn
swear	swore	sworn
bear	bore	born
get	got	gotten
forget	forgot	forgotten

Notes on the irregular verb list:

Some of these verbs are not used in everyday speech. The sun *rises,* but in conversational speech humans *get up.* This relegates *arise* to somewhat formal use in literature.

lie-lied-lied is a regular verb meaning to fail to tell the truth.

lie-lay-lay is an intranstive verb, frequently followed by *down,* as in *The child is lying down for her afternoon nap. The baby lay quietly in his crib.*

The other verb is *lay-laid-laid,* and it is transitive. *The hen laid an egg. We laid the table and had dinner.* (*Set the table* is more frequently used.)

TEACHING VOCABULARY IN THE ESL CLASSROOM*

Marianne Celce-Murcia *and*
Fred Rosensweig

INTRODUCTION AND BACKGROUND

The attitude that foreign language teachers have had toward teaching vocabulary and the classroom techniques they have employed have varied enormously during the past five or six decades. When the Grammar-translation Approach was in vogue at the turn of the century, the recognition of written words (i.e., vocabulary) as well as an awareness of each word's part of speech and attendant inflections (i.e., grammar) were among the primary objectives of language instruction. All languages were studied much the way Latin was studied. Then the later Reading Approach, while giving less attention to grammatical cases and declensions, nonetheless assigned a central role to the teaching of vocabulary. The primary objective of this method was the comprehension of written materials in the foreign language.

Learners using either of these approaches typically spent a great deal of time looking up words in the dictionary and translating texts from the foreign language under study into their native language. Neither of these approaches aimed at getting the students to understand and speak the foreign language they were studying. In fact following these approaches one frequently studied a foreign language for four, five, or six years without being able to produce or comprehend natural speech; i.e., students were unable to use the foreign language for communicative purposes.

Both the Direct Method and the Audiolingual (or Linguistic) Approach arose in reaction to this basic failure of the Grammar-translation and Reading Approaches. The Direct Method assumes that one learns a foreign language by active and meaningful use of it—especially by listening to it and speaking it, with some attention given to reading it and writing it. Using this approach one hears and uses only the target foreign language in the classroom. No translations into or explanations in the native language are tolerated. It is assumed that the students will acquire vocabulary in context as an integral part of each lesson. Often a preliminary part of the lesson consists of identifying or acting out vocabulary that is part of the context used in the lesson at hand, e.g., *These are keys; This is a keychain; This is a lock; I'm locking the door with a key; Now I'm unlocking the door,* etc.

The Audiolingual Approach, on the other hand, deliberately deemphasized the teaching of vocabulary in the initial stages, keeping it to a minimum until the basic structures and the sound system of the language have been mastered. The sequence of teaching points for beginning learners of English presented in Stevick (1957) is a good example of this audiolingual strategy, the theoretical underpinnings of which had been developed much earlier by Fries and others:

> In the early stages of language learning, there are many phrases and sentences to be practiced as complete wholes in the situations in which they are useful. These contain but few new content items at any one time. Thorough control and a feeling of confidence in the use of a limited number of items makes for more progress than an uncertain acquaintance with a large number of words, (Fries, 1945: p. 54)

There is thus no doubt that over the past thirty years the teaching of vocabulary has been of secondary importance. A few recent studies have also noted the paucity of research in the area of foreign language vocabulary acquisition. Twaddell (1973), while agreeing in principle with the use of a limited vocabulary in the initial stage of language learning, urges the immediate development of strategies for the massive expansion of vocabulary at the intermediate and advanced stages. He feels that this area has been a serious shortcoming of modern language instruction and suggests remedies such as teaching students of a foreign language to skim reading materials and to guess at words in context as part of this much-needed massive vocabulary expansion program. Henning (1973a) calls the recent lack of attention to vocabulary acquisition unfortunate since he believes that one's learning of the terms and expressions of a language (i.e., its vocabulary) is fundamental even in the earliest stages of the acquisition of that language.

We agree with Henning's contention that vocabulary should be recognized as a central element in language instruction from the beginning stages. From our own experience with non-native speakers of English we feel that a good amount of vocabulary—with a minimum of structure—often makes for better reading comprehension and more efficient survival communication than near-perfect structure with an impoverished vocabulary of 100 words or less. However, the point we would like to make here is that neither impoverished structure nor vocabulary is desirable. Even at the initial level, both should be properly taught since experience should show us that concentration on one of these areas—to the exclusion or near-exclusion of the other—has negative consequences.

Fortunately, human curiosity being what it is, our beginning students have, of necessity, always learned far more vocabulary than we—or the texts we have used—have explicitly taught them. However, they have probably not learned enough this way. Furthermore, as has been generally recognized, vocabulary is a language area that needs continued growth and development for both native and non-native speakers long after grammar and pronunciation are under reasonable control. Beyond the initial stage, the factors of motivation and intelligence become important because, like monolingual speakers of English, advanced foreign learners will exhibit proportionately larger or smaller vocabularies even though they may share the same type and amount of instruction in the language.

FACTORS TO CONSIDER

There is a useful distinction the language teacher must keep in mind concerning the teaching of vocabulary. First of all, s/he must be able to determine whether the vocabulary items at hand are needed by his or her students for active use (i.e., recall, production) or passive use (i.e., recognition, comprehension). Active use in speaking or writing is, of course, all-encompassing in that it necessitates co-existent receptive and productive facility, whereas the passive use of vocabulary for listening and reading purposes may exclude productive facility altogether. An understanding of this distinction will influence one's approach to the teaching of vocabulary. Likewise, vocabulary items necessary for the development of formal reading and writing skills may not be appropriate when one is learning the less formal vocabulary typical of listening or speaking. Another related consideration is that the teacher must decide whether passive vocabulary is to be learned permanently or temporarily (i.e., acquired merely to understand a given passage in a piece of writing or a movie with no consideration for later use). All these factors can influence the way vocabulary is presented and taught in the ESL classroom.

Word lists and selection criteria

The teacher concerned with vocabulary instruction must also be aware of the work that has been done in the area of word counts. There have been many word-lists based on frequency; e.g., Thorndike and Lorge (1944), Carroll et al. (1972), Kučera and Francis (1967). Word-lists based on both frequency and usefulness of the various meanings of a word have also been prepared, e.g., West (1959). The applications of these word-lists to ESL have been: (a) to guide teachers in the selection of controlled vocabulary used in beginning courses, and (b) to assist textbook writers in the simplification of texts for initial reading experience in English.

These applications—when carried to an extreme—have been criticized by Lott (1959-60), who feels that word-lists are biased due to the data on which they are based, e.g., they may be too literary. He also argues that the limitation or simplification of vocabulary does not materially facilitate production or comprehension since overuse of this procedure may make syntax very complex, often requiring many more words to express the same concept. This in turn makes it more difficult for students to learn to use the right word in the right place. Likewise, Fries and Traver (1940) caution the language teacher using word-lists to remember that few frequent words have one meaning—usually they have at least fifteen to twenty meanings. So the teacher must decide which meanings to present and which to ignore. They also point out that usefulness is not exclusively determined by frequency—i.e., frequency is only one factor determining usefulness—and beginning courses in English must include (regardless of frequency) important function words, substitute words, and words with affirmative and negative distribution (e.g., *some/any, already/yet,* etc.). Another seemingly unrelated factor may be the length or phonological form of a potential vocabulary item. Celce-Murcia (1977a), for example, suggests that initial teaching vocabulary should (whenever possible) avoid words that are difficult for the learner to pronounce since vocabulary that is hard to articulate will be avoided and/or will cause initial psychological problems that easy-to-produce words will not cause.

In summary, beginning with the *Interim Report on Vocabulary Selection* (1936), all those who have carefully considered the potential use and application of word counts in the teaching of English as a second/foreign language have reservations and suggest that teachers use them as a guide but that they temper their vocabulary selection with some feeling for what is natural use for native speakers, and what is useful in terms of the level, age, needs, and background of their own students. For example, an ESL course for Chicano housewives would at some point deal with supermarket vocabulary whether or not it is of high frequency.

Research

Although there is anecdotal evidence to suggest that contrastive analysis of the vocabularies of the source and target language of the foreign learners would be quite useful to the language teacher, little work has been done in this area, when compared with the amount of contrastive work that has been done in phonology and syntax; however, studies by Prator (1963), Vander Werf (1969), and Hagerty and Bowen (1974) provide examples of the useful work that can be done in this area.

Levinson (1975) in focusing specially on the lexical problems that Romance speakers have in learning English assumed that interference would be a major source of error. By doing a series of three error analyses (each analysis with a different corpus drawn from a different group of Romance speakers), Levinson found that his hypothesis was strongly confirmed but that the percentage of interference-induced errors diminished in number as the students' level of English proficiency became more advanced (p. 50).

Yoshida's (1977) study of the English vocabulary acquisition of a young Japanese boy, Miki (age at arrival in U.S. 3.5) found that Miki had acquired productive use of 264 words after seven months' of exposure to English in an English-speaking nursery school. His English syntax was almost non-existent, yet he was communicating effectively with peers. Almost 75% of Miki's words were nominals and his seven major semantic categories for these nominals were:

1. Food and drink	33 nouns
2. Animals	23 nouns
3. Toys and play things	19 nouns
4. Vehicles	17 nouns
5. Outdoor objects	13 nouns
6. People	10 nouns
7. Clothes	9 nouns

(Yoshida, 1977, p. 35)

Miki's three main strategies for the acquisition of words were (a) rote learning by imitation and repetition; (b) cognitive learning by association and recall; and (c) a translation mode that utilized mixing or confirmation of meaning by translation from Japanese. It would be useful to know how general Miki's strategies are, i.e., whether other children and adults also make use of these strategies; and if not, what strategies they use.

A related matter is the fact that Miki made use of large numbers of English words that exist as loan words in Japanese. According to Yoshida, this facilitated his overall learning of English but sometimes interfered with his pronunciation in that while many of the loan words changed phonologically to the English system, some were still being pronounced as if they were Japanese words. The whole issue of loan words or cognates,[1] which both Yoshida (1977) and Levinson (1975) discuss, deserves much closer attention. To what extent do second language learners use, misuse, or avoid cognates or loanwords in their overall vocabulary acquisition strategies? Further research is needed.

Henning (1973a) states that his experience with error analysis of foreign student compositions serves "to indicate that a high percentage, if not a majority, of errors committed are in the choice of appropriate words and idioms for the expression of the intended thoughts of the writers, rather than exclusively in areas of grammar and syntax and mechanics...." We have made similar evaluations based on correcting numerous students' compositions. Thus more and better strategies for teaching vocabulary to our students would no doubt also improve their written work in English.

There is a great need for research into the vocabulary learning strategies utilized by language learners of different proficiency levels, ages, etc., to guide us toward the more effective teaching of vocabulary. Henning (1973b), for example, gives experimental evidence which shows that adult beginners learning a foreign language tend to encode vocabulary in the memory on the basis of interrelated sounds (i.e., acoustic features) while more advanced language learners tend to encode vocabulary on the basis of associated meanings (i.e., semantic features).

Likewise, it remains to be demonstrated whether adults learning a second language under natural conditions employ the same strategies as children do. The earliest stage in a child's natural acquisition of a second language is often a relexification of the content words of the first language. For example, we have ob-served an English-speaking child learning French produce *I am faim* as a first approximation to the French utterance *J'ai faim* (*I am hungry*). This is not code-switching since the child was at the time incapable of producing the French utterance correctly. (See Hatch, 1978, for numerous other examples.)

Vocabulary-learning strategies operating on other parameters need to be explored too. For instance, we feel intuitively that it is easier to teach students words with concrete meanings than words with abstract meanings. Higa (1965) confirms this hunch as a general rule, but he also isolates five specific factors that make a word relatively easy or difficult to learn:

a. the intrinsic difficulty of the word to be learned;
b. the interaction between a group of words to be learned at the same time (optimal number is 5-7);
c. the interaction between groups of words to be learned in sequence;
d. the effect of repeated presentation of words to be learned.

Higa's suggested optimal number of vocabulary items to be taught in one session is similar to ours. However, not everyone agrees with this. Lozanov (1977), for example, claims that in the suggestopaedic method about 200 to 240 new words are introduced each 4-hour lesson and that this explains how in forty to fifty hours of instruction 2,000 new words can be covered. Lozanov further claims that students can use about sixty percent of this new vocabulary actively (in speaking) and about ninety percent passively (i.e., can translate it). If such claims are true, ESL teachers should utilize more innovative methods for teaching vocabulary such as suggestopaedia.

WHAT TO TEACH: TWO SAMPLE SYLLABUSES

Language syllabuses are typically concerned with a structured sequence, or a set of situations, or the development of a specific skill or skills. In such syllabuses there is usually no explicit mention of vocabulary objectives, even though vocabulary instruction is directly or indirectly part of any language course. An example of a general statement of vocabulary objectives for a beginning-level adult ESL class follows (developed by Marjorie Walsleben, personal communication). It is suggested that the ESL teacher dealing with beginning-level adult students follow such a plan if no provision has been made for teaching vocabulary in either the syllabus or textbook.

Vocabulary: A basic vocabulary of approximately 2,000 words including numbers will be utilized and taught in class. Flexible in content, the list includes such items as:

numbers: cardinal (1-1,000)
          ordinal (1st-100th)
          and the use of numbers to express dates, years, addresses, phone numbers, and certain other measurable concepts such as age, height, weight, time, distance, money, etc.

common foods
the telling of time, days of the week
months of the year, seasons
articles of clothing
eating utensils
parts of the body
furniture
family relationships
colors
shapes and sizes
cities, countries
common animals
common occupations
common actions/activities

A much more detailed and specific vocabulary syllabus was developed as part of a total language syllabus (structure points were also listed) at an in-service training program in Tegucigalpa, Honduras in the summer of 1944. Using the *Interim Report on Vocabulary Selection* (1936) as a guide, the program leaders and participants selected about 500 words to include in the first-year (i.e., 6th grade) syllabus for English instruction in Honduras. This was done to insure identical objectives would be used in materials development, teaching, and in testing instruments throughout the country. The 500-odd words were divided into 43 categories according to part of speech, meaning, and function; however, only the alphabetical list of these selected vocabulary items is reproduced here in the interests of time and space (this list comes to us courtesy of Clifford Prator's notes and materials from the conference).

ALPHABETICAL LIST

a	bird	corn
address	black	cost
after	blackboard	country
afternoon	blue	cow
again	boat	cup
air	body	cut
airplane	book	
all	box	dance
almost	boy	daughter
always	bread	day
also	breakfast	dear
am	bridge	December
an	bring	desk
and	brother	die
answer	but	different
any	buy	dining room
April	by	dinner
are		do
ask	call	doctor
at	can	does
attention	car	doesn't
away	care	dog
August	carry	dollar
	cat	don't
baby	cent	donkey
back	chair	door
bad /ly	chalk	down
ball	change	dress
bank	chicken	
beans	child /ren	ear
beautiful	Christmas	early
because	church	east
bed	city	eat
before	class	egg
begin	clock	England
behind	coat	English
believe	coffee	enough
between	cold	eraser
big	color	evening
bill	come	every
birthday	copper	eye

face	hard	line	night	question	son
fair /ly	has	list	no		song
fall	hat	listen	north	rain	sound
family	have	little	not	read	south
far	he	live	nothing	ready	Spanish
farm	head	living room	November	reason	speak
father	hear	long	now	receive	spell
February	help	look	number	red	spoon
feel	her	love		remember	spring
fifth	here	low	ocean	rest	stamp
find	high		o'clock	return	stand
fine /ly	him	mail	October	rice	star
finish	his	make	of	right /ly	station
fire	hope	man—men	old	river	stay
first	horse	many	on	road	still
five	hot	March	once	room	stop
floor	hour	market	one	ruler	store
flower	house	May	only	run	story
fly	how	may	or		street
for	hundred	me	order (in—to)	Saturday	strong /ly
forget	husband	mean	other	say	student
fork		meat	over	school	study
four /th	I	meet	our	sea	sun
foot—feet	ice	member	out	season	Sunday
freedom	in	milk		seat	supper
free /ly	ink	minute	page	second	sure /ly
Friday	is	Miss	pants	see	
friend	it	mistake	paper	sell	table
from		Monday	part	send	take
front (in—of)	January	money	pay	September	talk
fruit	July	month	peace	she	teacher
full	June	moon	pen	shirt	tell
		morning	pencil	shoes	thank
game	keep	mother	people	short	that
garden	kind	mountain	picture	show	the
get	knife	move	piece	sick	their
girl	know	Mr.	pig	side	them
give		Mrs.	place	sight	then
glad /ly	land	much	plants	silver	there
glass	large	my	plate	sing	these
go	last		play	sir	they
good	late	name	please	sister	thing
grade	learn	near	pleasure	sit	think
great /ly	leave	need	poor	sky	third
green	left	neighbor	post office	sleep	this
ground	lesson	never	pound	small	those
grow	let	new	president	snow	three
	letter	news	pretty	so	Thursday
hair	light	next	price	some	time
hand	like	nice /ly	put	sometimes	to
happy /ly					

today	wait	wind
together	walk	window
tomorrow	wall	winter
tonight	want	with
too	war	woman—women
town	warm	wood
train	was	world
tree	watch	word
trip	water	work
true /ly	we	write
try	weather	
Tuesday	Wednesday	year
turn	week	yellow
two	well	yes
	were	yesterday
under	west	you
understand	what	young
United States	when	your
up	where	
us	which	
use	white	
	who	
very	whose	
visit	why	
voice	wife	

These two sample syllabuses have been included to encourage ESL teachers/programs to make their vocabulary objectives explicit.

TEACHING THE ACTIVE USE OF VOCABULARY

Thus far this chapter has concerned itself mainly with factors to consider in choosing the vocabulary to be taught. Once the instructor has made a decision as to what items to teach, s/he has to decide on an appropriate technique. Whether engaged in teaching adults or children, it seems logical that different techniques are needed for teaching different item types; e.g., idioms, sets of related words, abstract words. This section, then, is organized according to the different problems that face the ESL teacher in the area of teaching vocabulary.

The underlying assumption is that different techniques are appropriate for different words and that the technique used depends to a large extent on the objectives the teacher has for teaching the vocabulary.

Teaching the active use of the meaning of a word: a general approach

Although there are many different ways to teach a vocabulary item (cf. Mackey, 1965, chapter 8), it is possible to recommend one general approach which can be used either with deliberate planning or for an impromptu explanation. The easiest and clearest way to present this approach is in a formula which, though not rigid, can be used as a guide. The approach allows the teacher to present five or six selected words in about twenty minutes. It is the most general of the techniques presented below and can be applied to teaching almost any word.

Step 1: lead-in. The teacher establishes a context in which to teach the word. This can be done by asking a question or by simply making a statement.

Step 2: convey meaning. The teacher can convey the meaning of a word through various devices such as definition, active demonstration, visual aids, synonyms or antonyms, or translation. These devices are self-explanatory and often two or more can be used to clarify the meaning. Once the meaning has been understood, the word should be used in a model sentence which will further convey the meaning.

Step 3: repetition of the word. The students should repeat the word in isolation until they have no difficulties pronouncing it. A difficult word should be repeated often enough so that most of the students can say it correctly if called upon.

Step 4: verification. The teacher needs to verify that the students have understood the word. This can be done by asking a question in which the students' response will show whether or not they have understood the meaning. The students are not yet required to use the word.

Step 5: use. The teacher asks the students some open-ended questions which will allow for varied student answers. Each question should explore the use of the word in context and allow the students to practice using it.

Step 6: model sentence. A model sentence using the word should either be put on the blackboard or dictated to the students. The model sentence should be constructed so that, when the students read the model sentence after class, they will understand the meaning of the word from the context of the sentence. Periodically the students' notebooks should be collected to check over their sentences.

An example will clarify the above approach. The item being taught is the figurative sense of the word *adamant*.

Step 1: lead-in. Professor Smith never changes his mind.

Step 2: convey meaning. Once Professor Smith makes up his mind about something, he is adamant. (The teacher might use the gesture of pounding a fist on a table to dramatize the meaning.)

Step 3: repetition. adamant, adamant . . .

Step 4: verification. When your father gave you orders, was he adamant?

Step 5: use. Do you think it's good for teachers and parents to be adamant? Who is more adamant, a man or a woman? (varied answers)

Step 6: model sentence. Because of the nature of politics, it is not wise for a politician to be too adamant.

In using this strategy the teacher should:

a. Use indefinite articles before count nouns. Thus, *car* is written *a car*, while *water* is written merely as *water*. This will help the students to learn which nouns are count nouns and which are mass nouns.

b. Use the infinitive marker *to* to indicate a verb.

c. If applicable, include the prepositions that go with the word being taught. Thus, when being taught a word like *bored*, students should be told that *with* goes with *bored* in sentences such as *I'm bored with school.*

d. Show the derivatives and related forms of the word. For example, in teaching the word *bored*, the verb *to bore* and the nouns *a bore* and *boredom* should also be taught. These should be introduced after the target word has been mastered.

These derivatives, if they form words belonging to the same part of speech, often differ from each other in meaning. Teaching students to use the appropriate derivative given one context or another is a teaching problem in and of itself. For example, one of our students used *discriminatory* to describe his friend's good taste instead of *discriminating*; another student described the weather in his country as *various* instead of *variable*. ESL teachers must anticipate such problems and teach such distinctions when presenting derivatives. When the derivative has a different meaning from the word being taught, it should be counted as a separate item. As a general rule, don't teach five to six words with three to four derivatives each, and don't teach too many derivatives of a single word stem in one session since this confuses students unnecessarily.

This approach can take a great deal of time if the teacher is not careful. Overexplanation of the word and meaningless questions should be avoided. Although it is difficult to predict exactly how much time should be spent on a vocabulary lesson of six or seven words, the limit for one lesson is twenty minutes. It is easy to spend thirty-five to forty minutes using this strategy, but carefully prepared explanations and questions can cut down on the time. The word should be presented in the simplest manner possible and wordy explanations should be avoided in favor of visual demonstrations and model sentences. Putting a word in context is often worth more than any verbal explanation of its meaning.

Teaching a text

Often a teacher is faced with the prospect of teaching a set text. This sometimes requires explicit pre-teaching of vocabulary and grammar before the text is read and discussed. Many courses or syllabuses for ESL/EFL are based on a series of literary texts, thus making the pre-teaching of vocabulary essential for the students' comprehension of each text. (See the chapter by Povey in this volume for more specific suggestions regarding the role of vocabulary in teaching literature.) In deciding what words should be taught from a text, guidelines such as usefulness and frequency, which have been discussed previously, should be followed. If a teacher chooses an article from a newspaper or magazine, s/he is likely to find fifteen to twenty words that the students will not know. In this case, s/he should choose for extended instruction only those which they should have active control of, and save the others for a brief explanation prior to or during the actual reading of the text.

Below is a sample text, an Ethiopian folk-tale, for use in an intermediate class of foreign students at the secondary level. Read it and try to pick out the words which should be taught for active use.

The Story of
Lightning and Thunder

In the olden days Thunder and Lightning lived on earth amongst mankind, but the king made them live at the far end of town, as far as possible from the people's houses.

Thunder was an old mother sheep, and Lightning was her son, a ram. Whenever the ram got angry, he used to charge about burning houses and knocking down trees; he even did damage to the farms, and sometimes he killed people.

Whenever Lightning did these things, his mother commanded him in a very loud voice to stop, but Lightning did not care in the least what his mother said, and continued his damaging behavior. His mother scolded louder and louder. At last the people could stand it no longer and complained to the king.

The king issued a special edict that the sheep (Thunder) and her son the ram (Lightning) leave town and live in the far bush. But this did not help matters, as the ram, when he got angry, still burned the forest, and the flames sometimes spread to the farms and consumed them.

So the people complained again and the king banished both Lightning and Thunder

from earth, and made them live in the sky, where they could not cause so much destruction. (Leslau, 1963)

Words that should be taught:

for active use	for passive use
damage	olden
to scold	to charge about
to complain	an edict
destruction	to consume
	to banish

If this same text were taught at the advanced level, some of the words selected for passive use could perhaps be taught for active use.

The actual technique for teaching each word is the same as the general approach outlined previously. The advantage, however, in choosing the words from a text is that the teacher can refer to them in a ready-made context. Since the words will be encountered by the students during the reading, they will be reinforced. The teacher should also ask questions during the discussion to elicit the new words. Teaching a text, then, offers a way of deciding what vocabulary to present and at the same time a way of reinforcing those words after they have been explained.

Teaching lexical sets and semantic functions

One of the major problems in teaching vocabulary is finding a situation or context in which the students can show if they can use the words properly. The general approach requires the teacher to ask open-ended questions to get the students to use the word, and the activity of teaching a text allows the students to encounter the word while reading the text and use it in the discussion which follows. However, both of these methods depend on the teacher's skill at asking appropriate questions which will elicit the word. The techniques proposed in this section deal with lexical sets or semantic functions; i.e., a set of words that are closely related to one another in meaning and use. An example might be the parts of a car or the vocabulary needed to rent an apartment. Since the words in any lexical set or semantic function deal with a particular topic, the problem is to find a situation in which the students can use all or most of the words taught. To do this, we propose the use of problem-solving or role-playing as teaching techniques.

Problem-solving is an activity that involves presenting the class with a problem that must be solved through small group discussions. The students are given a problem that requires them to rank order a list of alternatives in terms of criteria given in the problem. To talk about the problem, certain vocabulary items are needed. Before the students solve the problem, the teacher presents the necessary vocabulary. This activity, then, is not a way to introduce the vocabulary; it is rather a way to allow the students to use it in a natural context after it has been explained. The actual method of presentation of the words is the general approach previously outlined.

The following is an example of problem-solving used as a vocabulary exercise.

Describing Americans

Many adjectives have been used to describe Americans. Some are complimentary and others are not. Below is a list of fifteen adjectives often used by foreign students in describing Americans. Your task is to rank these adjectives placing the number 1 by the adjective which best describes Americans, the number 2 by the adjective which describes Americans second best, and so on through number 15, which is your estimate of the adjective that describes Americans least well. Remember that your ranking is from a *foreign student's viewpoint* and it should be based on your general overall impressions of Americans, not on a few specific examples or exceptions.

Do this ranking first individually at home. Then in class you will do it in small groups for 25 minutes. Do not forget that in the groups, you must reach a consensus on the rankings. Everyone must agree on the ranking that you give each adjective. (Rosensweig, 1974)

Discussion questions and suggested topics for writing follow this activity. In this exercise, the lexical focus is on adjectives. In the course of the problem-solving, the students will use the adjectives frequently, thus reinforcing their understanding.

	Rankings	
Individual at home	Groups in school	
		hurried
		efficient
		hospitable
		outgoing
		showy
		devious
		traditional
		polite
		punctual
		tolerant
		pushy
		friendly
		frank
		reserved
		cosmopolitan

Role-playing is the dramatization of a real-life situation in which the students assume roles. It presents the students with a situation that must be interpreted and acted out by them. In doing the role-playing, the students are likely to need certain vocabulary. These words can be introduced by the teacher prior to the dramatization, and will subsequently be used during the role-playing in the context of the situation.

An example of a role-playing situation follows (Rosensweig, 1974).

You haven't been feeling well the last week and, in spite of your efforts to take care of yourself, you still don't feel well. You decide to go to a doctor, but unfortunately, you don't know any. Your task is to go to a doctor's office, introduce yourself, and explain what is wrong with you. There are three characters: the nurse, the doctor, and the student who does not feel well. (A fourth character could be the student's friend who brings him or her to the doctor's office.) Decide on the roles and on the student's reasons for going to the doctor's office and then prepare a short skit.

Vocabulary:
  to be bothered by
  to feel terrible
  the flu
  as directed
  to make sure
  a sore throat
  achy
  to make an appointment
  to take your temperature
  to have a fever
  to fill out a form

Both of these activities provide natural contexts in which the students can practice the new vocabulary. Although both activities may also have other purposes, they allow for reinforcement of the vocabulary that has been taught. The words are put in a context; they are not taught in isolation. Most ESL teachers will agree that students remember vocabulary better when they experience the words and when the words relate to something relevant in their lives. Problem-solving and role-playing furnish strategies that contextualize vocabulary and implant it more firmly in the students' minds.

Idioms

Mastering the idioms of a language has long been considered essential for achieving fluency. Idioms are unlike most vocabulary items in that their meanings are typically different from the literal meaning of the same word(s) and that they are more difficult to figure out given the usual patterns of the language. Since a large number of idioms appear in informal conversation, it seems that the most effective way to teach idioms to ESL students is through dialogues. Idioms can certainly be taught by any of the strategies previously discussed, but dialogues seem particularly appropriate, since idioms often defy explanation or definition and can only be understood in context.

A dialogue the primary purpose of which is teaching vocabulary should contain no more than seven to eight new items. Not all of these items need to be idioms. In fact, eight idioms would be a lot for any student to handle at once. The dialogue should be relatively short, from six to twelve lines. To teach the dialogue, the teacher should:

a. refer to each sentence in the dialogue and have the students repeat it;
b. isolate the new item, convey its meaning, and have the students repeat it;
c. briefly verify the students' understanding of the new items;
d. refer back to the dialogue to use the items in context.

After the class has gone through the dialogue line by line and has practiced the new vocabulary, the whole dialogue should be either practiced, or memorized and acted out. This should help to reinforce the words in the context of the dialogue. If the dialogue is not acted out, then the advantage of a natural conversational context is lost. After the dialogue has been acted out, other uses of the idioms in new contexts can be explored.

An example of a dialogue used to teach idioms follows.

Vocabulary: *to be broke*
              to go my way
              to shape up
              to stick with it

George: *How have you been recently?*
Paul: *Not too good. I'm broke.*
George: *Why don't you shape up and get a job?*
Paul: *Well, I've been trying to, but things just haven't been going my way.*
George: *Stick with it. Things will improve.*

Numa Markee (personal communication) has suggested to us a technique whereby five to seven apparently unrelated vocabulary items—typically a mixture of idioms and straightforward items—can be presented for active use. Markee puts the items in the context of a story he himself devises. Finally, he prepares a series of pictures to illustrate the story. An example of the technique follows:

Vocabulary to be taught:
  set off   *barely*   *ashamed*
  end up   *cruel*   *scold*

First, the teacher shows the class the pictures and tells the story while the students watch and listen. Then the teacher distributes copies of the text or projects the text on an overhead transparency. Students read the story and explain the target vocabulary from the context:

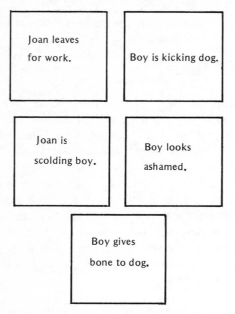

One day Joan set off for work. She had barely left her house, when she stopped because she saw a young boy kicking a dog. The young boy was cruel. Joan scolded him, and then he felt ashamed of himself. He ended up by giving the dog a bone.

Markee feels that much vocabulary can be taught this way without explicit instruction.

Words with multiple senses

Certain words in English, which are heavily used, have multiple meanings. Some of these words are *have*, *get*, *make*, *do*, and *fix*. The word *get*, for example, can be used in the following ways:

> *to get a job* (to obtain a job)
> *to get hired* (to be hired)
> *to get a good grade* (to achieve a good grade)
> *to get heavy* (to become heavy)
> *to get the ball* (to fetch the ball)
> *to get him to walk* (to make him walk)
> *to get it* (to purchase it)
> *to get there* (to be successful)

The list is incomplete, but it does serve to illustrate that mastering the word *get* in its

principal uses is a key to mastering the vocabulary of English. Indeed, without it a student would have quite a gap in his or her vocabulary.

Teaching the ESL student the multiple meanings of such words presents a formidable problem. How often have ESL teachers heard students misuse such words? One possible solution is to use the general approach for teaching vocabulary that this article proposes. This is possible, but the teacher must take care not to introduce too many uses in any one day. To do so would probably lead to confusion and misuse by the students.

It is proposed that the uses of a word like *get* be systematically taught throughout a quarter or semester; at the end of the term the teacher can check to see if the students can distinguish the different uses. Any of the strategies previously mentioned could be used to teach words with multiple uses. It is important to realize that such vocabulary problems do exist and that they should be taught systematically throughout a term, since they are one of the keys to learning idiomatic English.

Teaching the productive processes of word formation

Our last strategy for teaching the active use of vocabulary deals with the productive processes of word formation. Celce-Murcia (1973) calls one such process "incorporation." This refers to the syntactic nature of vocabulary. Examples cited by Celce-Murcia are given below.

a. *The cowboys led the horses into the corral.*
    The cowboys corralled the horses.
b. *They put the milk into bottles.*
    They bottled the milk.
c. *I put water on the plants.*
    I watered the plants.
d. *Mary took the dust off the furniture.*
    Mary dusted the furniture.
e. *The shortstop caught the ball with his glove.*
    The shortstop gloved the ball.

In the above examples, the several activity verbs in the first of each pair of sentences have incorporated the semantic function of one of the nouns to create a new verb in the second.

Other productive lexical processes include compounding, and the use of affixes. In using affixes, for example, when a native speaker says *unbutton,* s/he knows it means *to undo the button(s).* The prefix *un* is often used with verbs to denote a reversal of action (e.g., *tie/untie; fasten/unfasten; fold/unfold,* etc.) and can thus be termed a productive prefix. There are undoubtedly semantic restrictions on the use of such prefixes since they cannot occur with all verbs, but they are nevertheless common and should be taught. Although it is unrealistic to expect the students to be familiar with all the semantic restrictions, it is realistic to teach them to recognize the productive affixes when they occur and to be able to use the more common ones. For the teacher's reference, Willis (1975) empirically identifies those productive affixes that are used frequently in modern English word formation. She argues that they should (a) be distinguished from affixes that are only occasionally (or never) used in forming new words, and (b) be taught in the ESL classroom, i.e., be given priority in vocabulary instruction. Willis also suggests a sequence for teaching productive affixes as well as a procedure for presenting these affixes in the ESL classroom.

To teach the productive processes of word formation we recommend grammar-type drills. The drills that could be used to teach incorporation are illustrated above. Having first taught students to recognize and paraphrase incorporated nouns, the teacher could use a productive drill such as the following:

Teacher: *Paraphrase the following sentence: The decorator put the carpet on the floor.*
Student: *The decorator carpeted the floor.*

To teach productive affixes, practice could be constructed so that, after explanation and recognition of a pattern, productive drills such as the following could be pursued:

Teacher: *If a mother has tied her son's shoes, but the son did not want them tied, he would say:*

Student: *Please untie my shoes.*
Teacher: *If the door is locked and you want to get out, you would say:*
Student: *Unlock the door.*

Exercises for familiarizing students with compounding processes could be of a similar nature. Such exercises require the teacher to make up in advance sentences which will elicit the target affix or compound. By providing a model to show the students what they are to do, the teacher can make the drill proceed smoothly.

Many other ways of teaching vocabulary items are possible (and perhaps even preferable depending on the age and level of sophistication of your students). Songs and games (see the chapter in this volume by Waldman and Gasser) can be enjoyable and effective tools for introducing or reinforcing vocabulary. Field trips to zoos, museums, parks, and department stores also offer still other opportunities for teaching vocabulary in context. Finally, visual and audiovisual materials such as wall charts, film strips, slides, and movies are colorful and vivid means through which a large amount of contextualized vocabulary can be presented. (See the chapter on language teaching aids in this volume.)

TEACHING THE PASSIVE RECOGNITION OF VOCABULARY

Often students claim that their primary problem in acquiring English is a lack of vocabulary. Such students often have an adequate active vocabulary, but they lack an extensive passive vocabulary. Frequency counts indicate that about 2,000 words make up ninety per cent of the vocabulary that native speakers use in everyday conversation. However, a native speaker has a vast passive vocabulary which s/he uses in reading and listening. The foreign students' problem, then, is to extend their passive vocabulary to improve their reading and listening comprehension skills. Obviously, the techniques used to teach passive vocabulary will be different from those used to increase a student's active vocabulary. The next section of this article is concerned with such strategies.

Study skills

a. Using the dictionary.[2] To build an extensive vocabulary a student must know how to look up a word in the dictionary and how to use a thesaurus. Bilingual dictionaries are perhaps useful at very early levels, but, because they are often misleading, students should be encouraged to use a desk-size monolingual English dictionary as early in their language-learning experience as possible.

Ability to use a dictionary or a thesaurus should not be taken for granted. Often a student will not be aware of the information that a dictionary contains. Yorkey (1970a) itemizes such information when he says that a dictionary shows the accepted spelling of a word, the pronunciation, the syllable division, the derivatives, the definitions, the usage, synonyms, antonyms, and general information. To practice using the dictionary Yorkey proposes a variety of exercises. Particularly useful are the exercises that give students practice in alphabetizing, in using the dictionary for determining pronunciation, and in recognizing the different meanings and derivatives of a word. Such exercises are in written form and will primarily involve giving students tasks that make them use the dictionary.

An example might be the following:

Look up these words and recopy them in alphabetical order, indicating (1) the syllable division and (2) a synonym:
  difficult
  imagination
  unusual
  newspaper
  homework

To do this exercise, students would have to look up each word and take note of the syllable division and the list of synonyms, thus making them aware that a dictionary provides such information. It should be pointed out to students that most dictionaries also provide rules of spelling, syllable division, and rules of pronunciation in the introductory section.

b. Word stems and word formation. Another important aspect of building a passive vocabulary is the ability to guess the meaning of a word from context. This often entails a knowledge of word formation and word stems. To teach word formation, the teacher should select items for presentation at intervals from a list of the more common suffixes and prefixes in English. Students should then be asked to find example words in which these affixes occur. A follow-up to introducing the students to the common affixes of English is to give them practice in changing the parts of speech of root words. A student should be able to recognize without difficulty related nouns, verbs, adjectives, and adverbs. To do this, the students should be given a model and then be asked to provide derivatives based on that model. An example follows:

  to agree   *an agreement*
  to punish   _____
  to argue   _____

To teach word stems, the teacher should familiarize the students with the more common Latin and Greek roots. Yorkey (1970a) gives such a list along with their meanings. Students should be asked to find words that contain these roots and should then be given sentences that contain such words and asked to deduce the meaning.

After students have become familiar with the different parts of speech and with the more common word stems in English, they will become more adept at guessing the meaning of a word in context. Yorkey provides exercises in which the students guess the meanings of words in context, but they seem inadequate. Johnson (1977) carried out important exploratory research in this area. Using five volunteer subjects she addressed herself to the following questions:

a. What methods can teach students to guess word meaning from context?
b. Which second language learners improve their guessing of word meaning in context and which do not?
c. Which second language learners find this skill useful and which do not?

d. What conscious vocabulary acquisition strategies do students employ when attempting to learn a set of vocabulary items?

Among the most interesting of Johnson's findings was that tolerance of ambiguity (as measured by the Budner scale) did not correlate with an ability to guess word meanings from the context for Johnson's five subjects. Instead, Johnson suggests that aptitude and motivation were more important factors. Also, her subjects reported using several different conscious vocabulary-building strategies, the three most frequently mentioned being:

a. practice in generating the meaning of target vocabulary items using flashcards or lists;
b. teaching target items to peers;
c. attempting to use items in communicative contexts.

Johnson suggests that the relative effectiveness of these three strategies should be tested experimentally.

Extensive reading
More than any other strategy, extensive reading is the key to building an adequate vocabulary. Thus far, using a dictionary and familiarizing a student with word formation have been discussed. However, both of these should be considered merely as tools which will enable students to increase their vocabulary and thus make reading less of a chore and more of an enjoyment. An interesting procedure for encouraging students to do extensive reading is described in Carroll (1967)[3].

When native speakers read, they often come across words they do not know, but only occasionally do they have to refer to the dictionary. ESL students similarly should not take the time to look up each word that they do not know. Instead it is recommended that they look up a word only when they feel that it is central to their understanding of the passage. If the reading is a class assignment, then the teacher can supply some of the crucial vocabulary in advance, but if students are to read on

their own as much as possible, then it is not always feasible to have such advance notice.

A recommended procedure is for students to underline those words which they do not know, looking up a word only when it is absolutely necessary. After they have finished reading, they can go back and make a list of those new words. Often they will find that the word has reappeared and that the meaning has become clear. Students should develop a system for recording the meanings of words which they do look up. This could be done either using index cards or a notebook. Regardless of the method chosen, students should record the word, its derivatives, the pronunciation, the definition, and a model sentence. Students should review their records periodically and place check marks next to those words they forget. When they feel confident that they know a word, they can then remove the card or cross the word off the list.

Being systematic about new words encountered will help students enlarge their vocabulary. They should review their records regularly and try to use the words in speaking and in writing. Making such an effort will move some of the new words from ESL students' passive vocabulary to their active vocabulary.

The above technique applies not only to words encountered in reading, but also to words encountered in listening. Students, however, should be told not to panic when they do not understand a word. To look up or take note of every word they do not understand would be time-consuming, if not impossible. ESL students should be told that the second or third time they hear a new word in context, they are likely to be able to figure out its meaning. If a word reappears and they still do not understand, then they should use the dictionary. In fact, a series of listening comprehension exercises specially prepared to expand vocabulary would be a useful supplement to extensive reading exercises.[4]

Programmed texts and workbooks
Another technique for enlarging a student's passive vocabulary would be the use of a programmed text or workbook. Finding a suitable text is difficult, especially for inter-

mediate students, since one would have to decide whether general or specialized vocabulary would be most useful. However, if a sound programmed text or workbook is available (see, for example, Barnard (1971) as an example of a vocabulary workbook), it provides one additional way for ESL students to improve their passive vocabulary.

CONCLUSION

Just as it is important for an ESL teacher to be informed of the English sound system and grammatical system, it is also important for him or her to learn something about the English lexicon (i.e., words, meanings, derivations, productive lexical processes, etc.). S/he must be aware of the teaching techniques that are available, choosing carefully those techniques that contextualize word meanings best. Most important, perhaps, is the teacher's ability to arouse in his or her students a genuine interest in vocabulary, to develop the skills and the curiosity that will guarantee the growth of every student's vocabulary far beyond the spatial and temporal limits of the ESL classroom.

NOTES

*We are grateful to Clifford Prator for his comments on an earlier version of this chapter written in 1974.

1. There is, of course, the related issue of false cognates, i.e., words with the same or similar form but different meanings such as French *actuel* (current, present) and English *actual* (real) or German *fast* (almost) and English *fast* (quick). Apparently some language learners are bothered more by such items than others. It would be interesting to know why.

2. See Marckwardt (1973) for a full discussion of why ESL teachers should get their students more familiar with using dictionaries.

3. Twaddell (1973) also recommends extensive reading as a means of increasing vocabulary.

4. This suggestion was made by Peggy Robbins (personal communication) and we believe it has merit, although we know of no such listening materials currently in use.

DISCUSSION QUESTIONS

1. Why has the teaching of vocabulary been of secondary importance in ESL?

2. Why is it difficult to argue that either (a) grammar or (b) vocabulary is the most important element in mastering and using a foreign language?

3. Why does the teaching of vocabulary so often involve the teaching of grammar?

4. Why should the ESL teacher be familiar with word-lists? What are their uses and limitations?

5. Which ways for contextualizing vocabulary practice were suggested in this chapter? What other ways can you suggest to accomplish this?

6. Is the distinction made between active and passive vocabulary valid? Why or why not?

7. Suggest some research areas/projects that might help in the development of effective materials and techniques for teaching vocabulary.

8. Consider questions such as these: At what rate should a student learn vocabulary? How large should a learner's vocabulary be at various stages? Should new vocabulary and new structures be presented simultaneously? In what ways would vocabulary instruction for adults and for young children differ? How might answers to these questions be found?

9. Why is the use of a bilingual dictionary discouraged in this chapter? Under what circumstances might it be encouraged?

SUGGESTED ACTIVITIES

1. Analyze four compositions written (a) by one ESL student or (b) by four different ESL students with the same native language. What proportion of the errors made are lexical in nature? What types of lexical errors are made? How could these errors be corrected or avoided?

2. Prepare a problem-solving or role-playing exercise to teach vocabulary in one of the following areas to intermediate ESL students: English kinship terms, American English vocabulary relating to cars, vocabulary needed for shopping in a supermarket, vocabulary involved in preparing for and taking a final examination.

3. If you are familiar with a language other than English, select a general lexical area (e.g., colors, numbers, kinship terms, etc.) in which the lexicon of this language differs describably from that of English. Do a contrastive analysis and outline the most important teaching points that emerge from your analysis.

4. Select a reading text (300 to 500 words in length) that might be used in an advanced ESL class. Describe in detail how you would treat the teaching of vocabulary related to that text. Include all of the drills, etc., that you would use.

5. What would be your procedure during an academic term for teaching the multiple meanings of the word *fix*? Describe the drills and explanations you would use and outline your sequence of teaching points.

SUGGESTIONS FOR FURTHER READING

Brooks, Nelson (1964)
Language and Language Learning: Theory and Practice. Second Edition. New York: Harcourt, Brace, Jovanovich. Chapter 13: "Vocabulary."
An introduction with some practical suggestions for teaching vocabulary.

Croft, Kenneth (1972)
Readings on English as a Second Language. Cambridge, Mass.: Winthrop.
See Section 6: "Vocabulary." This section of the Croft anthology contains articles by Twaddell, Lado, and Higa with a general introduction and bibliography by Croft. One of the few texts that gives so much attention to vocabulary.

Francis, W. Nelson (1966)
"The Brown University Standard Corpus of English: Some Implications for TESOL," in *Series III on Teaching English to Speakers of Other Languages*, (ed.) B. W. Robinett, Washington, D.C.: Teachers of English to Speakers of Other Languages, pp. 131-137.
A description of a recent English word count with suggestions as to some potential ESL applications of such a count.

Fries, C. C. (1945)
"The Words: Mastering Vocabulary Content," Chapter IV in *Teaching and Learning a Second Language.* Ann Arbor: University of Michigan Press.
A clear statement of the structural approach to vocabulary analysis and teaching. Highly linguistic in nature; only a few explicit pedagogical suggestions.

McBride, Kenneth (1974)
An Analytical Evaluation of the Lexicon of an ESL Textbook. MA thesis in TESL, UCLA.
The lexical items of an ESL text undergoing revision are analyzed with regard to frequency, word class, entry rate, repetition, and several other factors. While giving the textbook generally favorable rating, McBride makes several recommendations for improvement of lexical content and pedagogy.

Petty, Walter T., Curtis B. Herold and Earline Stoll (1968)
The State of Knowledge about the Teaching of Vocabulary. Champaign, Ill.: The National Council of Teachers of English.
A valuable survey for anyone interested in the teaching of vocabulary.

Richards, Jack C. (1976)
"The Role of Vocabulary Teaching," *TESOL*, 10: 1, 77-90.
A good survey of the linguistic, psycholinguistic, and sociological aspects of lexical competence, and of teaching techniques that attempt to build up these aspects of lexical competence.

PART III
STUDENTS

Many of the preceding chapters have focused on what the ESL teacher should know or what the teacher can do to facilitate student practice (and hopefully improvement) in a language skill. However, unless the teacher is tutoring an individual, s/he must deal with a class—a group of individuals with different needs often growing out of their different linguistic and cultural backgrounds. The chapter by Peck recognizes class diversity and provides many constructive solutions. The two other chapters focus on special groups with fairly unique problems. Arthur's chapter on English for minority students covers the important issues and provides some teaching suggestions. Heaton's chapter focuses on the adult ESL classroom and the special activities and strategies that ESL teachers have had to develop to successfully cope with these non-academic, survival-oriented students.

DIFFERING NEEDS OF ESL STUDENTS

Sabrina Peck

INTRODUCTION

ESL students have widely different needs because of differences in cultural background, age, and previous education. Even if the students in one class are all from the same language group, they inevitably have different learning styles and needs. And if the teacher becomes sensitive to the needs of one group, for instance non-academic adults from many language backgrounds, s/he may still feel at a loss when his or her students are Eastern European senior citizens, or Navajo children, or Japanese businessmen, or highly motivated Taiwanese and Libyan electrical engineering students. The goal of this article, then, is to offer some suggestions on how to find out the needs of one's students, and how to adapt oneself, the management of the class, and the curriculum to meet those needs. All the examples represent classes in the United States; most of them are adult classes.

THE HOMOGENEOUS CLASS

Let's consider first classes that are homogeneous according to age and cultural background. Later, because it is more complicated, we can consider heterogeneous classes. The students in a homogeneous class—Arabic-speaking graduate students, or Cantonese-speaking non-academic adults, or Japanese high school students, or Puerto Rican first-graders, or Russian and Yiddish-speaking people in their 60's and 70's—are supposedly similar. But there are differences. Students have varied learning styles. And the teacher needs to be aware of the difficulties in teaching students with a common native language. The social needs, assumptions about the United States and about school, and the academic needs that are peculiar to each

group also need to be taken into account. One way to deal with these differences—perhaps the only way to do so creatively—is through the use of individualized instruction.

Individualizing instruction for different learning styles

Handscombe and others (1974) suggest that the teacher should individualize ESL instruction so that s/he teaches in the ways in which students learn. S/he should make for each student a profile with such items as age, previous education and attitude toward education, preferred learning style, previous language learning, personality, occupation, and home environment. The teacher can find out about these items through observation, class discussions, individual talks with students, and assigned essays or questionnaires. Then, ideally, s/he will have some idea about the students' needs, including these aspects of their learning style:

preference for learning alone, in small groups, and in large groups
ear/eye preference
preference for observation vs. participation
use of language analysis, rules and explanations
preference for immersion
use of translation
use of visuals
use of rote learning

Handscombe suggests a variety of activities for individualizing adult classes. Students could use the language lab alone during and outside of class. Even at the very beginning level, they could observe and note down the words they see on billboards and bring them to class for discussion. More advanced students could be assigned to find out prices and other information from restaurants or airlines, and later report back to the class. A variation of this would be to have students interview people in the community such as personnel managers for a factory or a social worker at a clinic, and report back to the class on what they find out.

A group of students with a teacher or aide could form an interest group to learn vocabulary and structures for describing one specific area. For instance, a group could discuss how to describe a child's illness to a doctor, or their previous experience to a prospective employer. Another suggestion is for a group to discuss with the teacher appropriate clothes for a party or the beach, and then collectively make up dialogues for the occasion. Also, the teacher could introduce material for memorization such as the language of weights and measurements, and then supervise groups as they weighed and measured items in the classroom.

One student with the teacher could work on individual needs. The student might need to learn the vocabulary for renting a house, or filling out an immigration form or job application.

Pairs of adult students could teach simple material to each other, such as numbers or colors, and could do projects which they later presented to the group. They could discuss values clarification problems (Simon, Howe and Kirschenbaum, 1972), or find out certain facts about each other, or make up a dialogue to present to the teacher before they present it to the class.

The Handscombe article gives a number of practical suggestions for individualizing ESL classes for adults, high school students, and elementary age children. Many of them could be adapted to use with any age group. Another good source of ideas to adapt are any of the books about open education in the United States, or the methods of the Leicestershire primary schools in England.

Guiding question: What degree of individualization will benefit your students?

Increasing the use of English among students who speak the same language: teaching ESL to children

With a homogeneous class of, for instance, all Puerto Rican children, or all Korean children,

the teacher can exploit the students' common cultural background as a natural source of subject matter, and plan interesting activities that are done in English. The children often enjoy studying aspects of life in their native country because they fondly remember their time there and because this material is something they can collectively explain to the teacher. Handscombe suggests role-plays such as acting out a day in a Korean school. Other ideas are to learn songs in the native language or in English, to make a mural or a model village, to cook native foods, and to talk about differences between life in the U.S. and life in the native country. Using culture as subject matter not only gives enjoyment and a clearer self concept to the children; it also allows the teacher to learn about the children's culture through their eyes. The teacher can gain a general idea of their assumptions about school and teachers, home and family, which would be impossible for him or her to arrive at through library research or asking children even the most expertly phrased questions.

If all the children speak the same language, how can the teacher encourage them to speak English to each other during the ESL class? One way is to use activities and materials that the children enjoy. If they are introduced to these materials in English, they will often continue to use English in connection with them, even to each other. For small children, the teacher could make flannelboard cutouts to represent the characters in a story such as "The Gingerbread Man." S/he could begin by telling the story him- or herself as s/he moved the cutouts around. S/he could encourage the children to learn the story, beginning with the parts that repeat (*Run, run, as fast as you can . . .*). Later steps could be for individual children or groups to tell the story, for the class to act it out, or for children to make their own paperdoll versions of the characters. The children could also learn some related songs, and of course, make some gingerbread men.

Some useful questions for planning lessons for ESL children of the same language background are:

(a) From what you know about the culture, and the individual children, what activities do they enjoy? (Example: Most Puerto

Rican children in New England come from rural areas, and like animals.)

(b) How could you plan activities that are keyed to the children's interests but presented in a slightly new way? (Example: The children have probably never raised fish, or hamsters, and have probably not had a chance to design and build their own cages or to use some of the new plastic, maze-like cages.)

(c) How will you present the language of the activity? (Example: Take snapshots of the children building the hamster cage and use them as the focus of a dialogue, or use them to make into a simple book.)

The teacher also needs to respect the frequent desire of such children to do some work with reading and writing, even though s/he may feel that they need oral work most of all. Second graders and children in higher grades will probably expect and want reading and writing in English. They may have had some schooling in their native language and assume that school is where one reads and writes; at any rate, they will know that their American peers are reading and writing. There are ways to take advantage of ESL children's interest in written work while still giving them the oral work that they need. The teacher can give beginning students dittos for handwriting practice with the vocabulary and structures from the current oral lesson. Other exercises can involve more than copying. The teacher can use the language of classroom routines and activities for writing and sight-reading practice, and can label parts of the room (wall, window, desk, plants, etc.). S/he can post the words for songs and poems the children are learning. Individual students or the entire group can dictate and then copy stories about the class hamster or the trip to the zoo. The Polaroid pictures of the class are good material to describe and write about.

When the children start to dictate stories to the teacher, s/he will have to decide whether correct English or the experience of copying or writing in English is more important. Some ESL teachers feel that they are fighting a battle twice by allowing children to dictate and copy such sentences as *Ms. Conlon, she coming down the stairs.* On the other hand, for an account of one teacher who used this technique very

successfully with non-English speakers, see Ashton-Warner (1963).

These few comments and suggestions on how to teach ESL classes for children of one language background, if stated in general terms, could be applied to classes for adolescents and adults as well. They are:

(a) Learn all you can about the students' culture, and use it as subject matter.

(b) Plan activities that will be interesting, fun, and slightly novel.

(c) Respect the students' attitudes about what "school" should be like, particularly the amount of reading and writing that should be involved.

The next three sections are examples of ESL classes in which teachers adapted their approach to meet the needs of one group. They give suggestions for meeting social needs (teaching ESL to older people), adjusting to students' assumptions about what school should be like (teaching ESL to Chinese non-academic adults), and meeting academic needs that are common to one native language group (teaching Arabic-speaking university students).

Meeting social needs:
teaching ESL to older people
Buzan (1972) describes a successful ESL program for senior citizens in British Columbia.

This group was heterogeneous in terms of language backgrounds, but homogeneous in the sense that all the students were older people. Many of them were lonely, and the ESL class was one of the few reasons for which they left their homes. Because of this, the teachers paid more attention than usual to the students' social needs. There was a coffee break at the halfway point of every evening. Students brought home-made cookies and breads, and the students from all levels gathered in one place. Friendships developed between people of different language backgrounds. Because the teachers allowed the students to socialize in a way in which they were comfortable, attendance was excellent, and students made new friends with whom they could practice their English. The teachers, the students, and their relatives thought that the coffee breaks and the friendships that developed out of them were vital in motivating the students, and giving them opportunities to practice English.

Guiding question: How can you help your students to make friends with other learners, and with native speakers?

Adjusting to students'
assumptions about school:
teaching ESL to Chinese non-academic adults

Asian assumptions about the United States, the student-teacher relationship, school, and finding a job are very different from our own (Asian Project Materials, 1972). Many teachers find that they need to adapt to attitudes which at first seem inexplicable.

Asians often think of the U.S. as a country that is rich in resources and opportunities for making money, but spiritually poor. Because they think of the U.S. as a young country without a mature culture, it is important to show them how our culture is derived from European cultures. Holidays would be good opportunities for the teacher to present lessons that make this point.

Asians have great respect for teachers and do not want to lose face with them. They are accustomed to rote recitation in the classroom, and may be reluctant to speak out or ask questions in class. Some suggestions for the teacher (Asian Project Materials, 1972) are:

(a) Explain the American customs concerning calling someone by a first or last name. Give the students a choice.

(b) Be friendly.

(c) Be non-threatening in oral activities. For instance, ask the students to repeat or to answer yes-no questions. Give them conversations to memorize.

Asians may feel that the teacher does not respect their maturity if the emphasis is on oral work with pictures. The teacher could explain the importance of oral skills. Oral drills should be contextualized, and each lesson could end with real communication utilizing the structures. With more advanced groups, the teacher should choose conversation topics with discretion. Many students may be uncomfortable discussing personal topics. The Chinese are particularly reluctant to talk about death, illness, or accidents (Asian Project Materials).

Handouts can relate oral and written work. To keep the student from being distracted, handouts could be distributed after the oral practice. Terrell (1971) suggests including Chinese translations of the English vocabulary, since students want translation and will otherwise waste time by noting the phonetic transcription in characters, or searching for the meaning in a bilingual dictionary.

Reading and writing should be included in the classwork and homework, even for beginners. Terrell notes that Chinese students can handle sight reading without phonics for a long time, since their system of writing with characters is basically a kind of sight reading. The teacher could have students practice writing the new words of each lesson on dittos with the model provided. The handwriting dittos make good homework assignments, as do review drills, narratives to read with new words translated, and comprehension questions to answer. Terrell feels that Chinese students want and expect homework. However, because they probably have jobs, it is a good idea not to plan class time around the successful completion of the homework.

In a job interview, Chinese adults often do not stress their talents and past experience. While respecting the students' humble attitude, the teacher could help them to see that such an attitude is harmful when seeking employment in this country. The teacher could explain that the job applicant in the U.S. mentions relevant work experience, and tries to prove that s/he is the best qualified applicant. The teacher could help Chinese students by doing role-plays of job interviews, and getting the students to write resumés.

Guiding questions: What assumptions do the students have about the U.S.? How do they think the teacher and students should behave? According to the students, what should be taught, and how? How can you, as the teacher, recognize these attitudes and adapt to them?

Meeting the academic needs of students from one language group: teaching ESL to Arabic-speaking university students

The Chinese example gives pedagogical suggestions arising from a sort of cultural contrastive analysis. In the next case, Yorkey (1974) predicts areas of rhetorical and grammatical difficulty for Arabic-speaking students. In Arabic there is use of coordination, not subordination, in written paragraphs. A tightly organized English paragraph, with its topic sentence, controlling idea, and supporting ideas, is a manner of expression which is foreign to them and which they often interpret as "cold and calculating." Modifying the Arabic student's rhetoric, however, could be as sensitive a task for the teacher as explaining the need for oral work to Chinese adults. Sometimes students feel that the way in which they express their ideas is a cherished part of their personality. They resent being told to write according to English rhetoric as much as if the teacher had told them to think and feel differently.

Yorkey suggests that the teacher give Arabic-speaking students practice in writing and identifying different paragraph components. They need practice with subordinate clauses (particularly adverb clauses of time, place, result, concession, cause, purpose and condition). They need practice in identifying the topic sentence and other components of a paragraph.

The correction of bad grammatical habits is usually not such an emotional process. Scott and Tucker (1974) state that most grammatical problems for these students are in the areas of verbs, prepositions, articles, and relative clauses. An almost universal problem is the presence of redundant object pronouns which are grammatical in Arabic and ungrammatical in English:

> *The teacher is the woman that you know her.*
> *The book which I am looking for it is sold out.*

Guiding questions: From your reading of contrastive analyses, conversations with other teachers, and study of students' work, what common problems in English do you think your students have? How will you give your students practice in these areas? How will you explain American ways of reading (skimming, for instance) and writing without offending the students?

THE HETEROGENEOUS CLASS

The preceding sections have given some examples of how to take individual needs and learning styles into account, and how to meet some needs of a seemingly homogeneous group. But the more usual kind of adult ESL class in the United States is composed of a wide variety of students, each with his or her own needs reflecting the amount of education s/he has had in his or her native language, the type of previous instruction in English, his or her age and emotional needs. When a teacher first meets with a heterogeneous class, it is easy to feel at a loss about what to do because the students seem to have nothing in common.

Amount of education in the native language

The same class may include students from ten different countries, ranging from some illiterate in their native languages to some with Ph.D.'s. The teacher will need some access to materials on basic literacy (see Lewis, this volume; and Eley and Lewis (1976)), and may want to use the backgrounds of the students as a resource in the class. A doctor from Iran, and a mechanic from Cuba each have access to a special vocabulary and a specialized body of knowledge. Each could explain some of this vocabulary, or present a dialogue that would get results if someone needed a physical exam or a tune-up for his or her car.

Guiding questions: What materials could you use to meet a range of academic needs? What kinds of group work and class projects would allow students to help each other, and you to help individual students?

Type of prior ESL instruction

Some differences in instructional needs are rooted in differences in the kind of ESL instruction students have had in their native countries. Many Japanese students, for example, have had rigorous instruction in grammar, but need listening and speaking practice. Arabic-speaking students often need extra help with spelling, handwriting and the mechanics of writing. And people who have been exposed to spoken English more than written English (some Chicano students from East Los Angeles fall into this category) may need reading and writing more than any other skills. All of these statements are simplistic and over-generalized, but together they give some idea of the range of differences the ESL teacher may encounter.

Guiding question: In what ways could interviews and written tests help you to find out the kind of previous ESL instruction your students have had?

Age

High-school-age or adolescent students may have vastly different needs from those of adults with more defined personal goals. Adolescents are usually exploring goals and identities, while adults are more settled in their goals. How can the teacher accommodate the needs of both groups in one class?

In night schools, some of the younger students register for an ESL class because they want to make friends, especially of the opposite sex. Assigning papers to be written as a group, or skits to be made up and presented in class by groups may satisfy some of their social needs as well as be a means for the teacher to guide their progress in English. Values clarification discussions and other activities in which students examine and express their own feelings are effective with adolescents (Maureen Schmid, personal communication).

These young students may also need some counseling about American culture. One teacher gives the example of an eighteen-year-old woman from an Arabic-speaking country. In her native country the woman had not been allowed to go out by herself or with friends. In the United States, however, she had her own car and was drinking and driving with her high school friends. She thought that she was acting like an American teenager. There are many ways to explore the myths and realities of American teenage culture, and still teach ESL. Students could discuss Ann Landers or Dear Abby columns, and make up their own responses to some of the questions, or view and discuss movies such as "Rebel Without a Cause."

The problem is, however, that there are not only adolescents in the class, but adults who are studying English in order to reach a specific goal: to get into a university, or become a dental technician, or join a construction workers' union. Generally, because their personal goals are definite, adults are less interested in group work and discussion activities, and intent on being taught and tested on specific points of English: grammar, vocabulary, spelling, reading, and writing. What many adult students want from the teacher are grammar explanations, assignments, and feedback. They have often had very little oral work, and may or may not feel that an ESL class is a place for them to practice speaking.

Obviously the teacher cannot please all the students all the time. The adolescents need some grammar work, and group work can be an effective way of giving adult students more chances to talk in class. It might help in motivating the adolescents to discuss with them the attitudes they think Americans have toward people with foreign accents or grammatical mistakes in their speech. The teacher could give these students some information about sociolinguistic experiments (Lambert and Tucker, 1969) and ask the students what they think the results were. Adults might show more interest in group discussions if the topics were relevant to their goals (how to act at a job interview, how to fill out an income tax form) or if they could use their own experiences as adults (what makes a good father, what makes people feel young or old). So in dealing with adolescents and adults in the same class, the teacher can try to make each group see why traditional activities and non-traditional activities are important, and s/he can sometimes gear the subject matter of the activity to the group that has less interest in the educational purpose of the activity. Other ways of dealing with this problem are to individualize as many activities as possible (the teacher will need to make or buy materials) or to group the students (if there is a teacher's aide or volunteer working in the class).

Guiding questions: What needs do the adult and adolescent students in your class have? Why are they studying English? How will you plan activities that meet the needs of both groups? How will you explain to each group the importance of doing some activities which they find boring or unnecessary?

Emotional needs

Teachers of young children have to be concerned with the different emotional needs of their pupils and the importance of meeting these needs. Unfortunately, texts for ESL teachers often do not discuss emotional needs, even though many writers compare the task of learning a language with becoming a child again. This discussion is limited to two common issues: students that are too loud or too quiet, and class reactions to a teaching style that seems too authoritarian or too free.

In one university-level class, students complained that one student talked too much, and was wasting the class time. They appealed to the teacher to control the student. Sometimes loud students need to feel more important. One suggestion would be to give such students extra responsibility in the class such as coordinating the transportation for a party or collecting money for extra materials. In group-work, it may be best to put all the loud students together. The teacher could chat with a loud student outside of class and, by listening to his or her comments and questions, make him or her feel that s/he does not need to bring them up in class. The teacher also might want to tell him or her what the other students had said, and ask him or her what s/he thought s/he

could do to avoid annoying them. In classes where students seem to be too quiet, some of the comments in the section on teaching Chinese adults may apply.

Even adult students may have a strong need for an authoritarian classroom atmosphere. Because of personality, cultural background, or age, some students want to be told exactly what to do and feel that a class is a place not for learning but for being taught. Other students want a democratic atmosphere; they want to contribute to discussions, give presentations, and make suggestions about what activities should go on in class. One way for the teacher to deal with this situation is to make his or her own objectives and standards clear to the students (e.g., by stating them in the course description, and by discussing them with the class at the beginning of the course or unit) and to accomplish some of these objectives through "democratic" teaching methods. For instance, if one goal of the course is that all students will write well-organized paragraphs, the teacher can lead a discussion in which the students are asked to come up with a set of defining qualities for a well-organized paragraph. The students will know, of course, that the teacher has his or her own ideas about what a well-organized paragraph is. Thus, the teacher has control over the content (and probably the outcome) of the discussion, but the students have a chance to consider, evaluate, and discuss the problem before the teacher gives his or her input.

Guiding questions: If students do not tell you that a certain student annoys them, how can you tell by their reactions? How will you balance the preferences of your students and yourself for a classroom that is "authoritarian" or "democratic"?

SUMMARY

Because of (and in spite of) his or her background, every student is unique. Some factors which combine to make him or her unique are his or her native language, cultural background, age, emotional and social needs, learning style, level of education, and previous instruction in English as a Second Language. One goal of this article has been to make new teachers aware of some of the differing needs that ESL students have. These needs form a continuum from the purely academic (e.g., poor reading ability) to the social or personal (e.g., fear of talking to native speakers). Another goal has been to give examples of some ways that the teacher can adapt the curriculum, and his or her style of managing the class, in order to meet the needs of more of the students more of the time.

Some ways to find out a student's needs are through individual and group discussions, forms or questionnaires, compositions, and an examination of his or her oral and written work. With children, asking them to make up skits or puppet shows can be an effective way for the teacher to find out about the child's culture and attitudes toward school. To have some idea about a student's social needs, emotional needs, and learning style, observation and intuition may be more productive tools than assigning questionnaires or essays to the students. Contrastive analyses may be very helpful for the teacher, not just in pointing out phonological, syntactic, and semantic problems, but sometimes in describing areas of cultural differences (Asian attitudes toward school) or discourse (Arabic rhetoric).

In adapting the curriculum to meet students' needs, the teacher can use different types of commercial materials, and make use of the interests and talents of his or her students. S/he can design units around a particular culture (e.g., a unit on the Taino Indians for a class of Puerto Rican children) or allow each student to teach the class something about his or her own culture in a heterogeneous adult class. The teacher can take social and emotional needs into consideration when s/he picks topics for discussion and assigns students to groups. S/he can plan lessons, choose commercial materials, and decide on groupings in order to meet students' varied academic needs.

In adapting his or her system of classroom management, the teacher will want to be aware of whether his or her students, as a group, can handle an authoritarian or democratic style of teaching. S/he will need to be aware of which students like to participate orally, and which do not. S/he may want to completely individualize the class instruction, or some part of it. Because older adult students and adolescent students have their own social needs, s/he may want to allow extra time for a coffee break during the class.

An ESL teacher is in one sense a juggler, juggling the needs of an astonishing variety of students—a computer scientist from India, a Taiwanese dental student, the wife of a Latin American diplomat, and an American Chinese high school dropout. Even the students in a "homogeneous" class may seem to have little in common. While the teacher cannot satisfy all of the students all of the time, s/he can make it his or her goal to identify and then (to whatever extent is possible) to meet their differing needs.

DISCUSSION QUESTIONS

1.   A university ESL class has Latin American, Korean, and Taiwanese adolescents (freshmen) and Iranian and Japanese adults (doctors and computer scientists). What might be some ways in which the adolescents have different needs from the adults? What sample activity for the whole class can you suggest?

2.   In what ways are written tests useful for determining students' needs?

3.   In thinking about good high school or college teachers, what do you think are some ways in which they find out and meet students' needs?

SUGGESTED ACTIVITIES

1.   Observe an ESL class for several consecutive days, in order to focus on one student. Watch that student and note his or her expression and body language as well as what s/he says. From your observations, make some hypotheses about what you think his or her needs are in the ESL class. If possible, discuss your ideas with the teacher or another observer.

2.   If you are not studying a foreign language, take a mini-course at the beginning level of a language, or ask a teacher for permission to sit in during the first few weeks of a class. As a learner, how do you feel in the class? Do you like the way the teacher treats you? What kind

of teaching is helpful to you? What do you want from the other students? What are your needs? Keep a journal of your reactions.

3. Interview an ESL student about what his or her needs are in the ESL class. Use questions that you have prepared. With the student's permission, tape record the interview. In listening to it later, ask yourself which of your questions received informative responses. Would other ways of phrasing them have been more effective? Would other questions have been more effective?

4. Interview ESL teachers to find out in what ways their students are different. Ask them how they deal with having a variety of students in the same class.

SUGGESTIONS FOR FURTHER READING

Ashton-Warner, Silvia (1963)
Teacher. New York: Simon and Schuster.
An account of how the writer taught Maori primary school children in New Zealand. Especially interesting is her individualized method of teaching reading and writing.

Holt, John (1964)
How Children Fail. New York: Pitman.

——— (1969)
How Children Learn. New York: Pitman.
Holt describes children's individual learning styles and needs. A good example of what a sensitive observer can find out about students by watching and listening.

Knapp, Donald (1972)
"A Focused, Efficient Method to Relate Composition Correction to Teaching Aims," in Harold B. Allen and Russell N. Campbell, *Teaching English as a Second Language: A Book of Readings.* New York: McGraw-Hill.
One method for individualizing composition teaching.

Logan, Gerald E. (1973)
Individualized Foreign Language Learning: Organic Process. Rowley, Mass.: Newbury House.
A detailed description of the author's system for individualizing the teaching of German at the high school level.

Sargent, Betsye (1970)
The Integrated Day in an American School. National Association of Independent Schools.
Describes activities and materials in an open classroom for five, six, and seven-year olds. Gives a specific idea of the kind of room arrangement, planning, and preparation that is necessary for an open classroom.

Simon, Sidney B., Leland W. Howe and Howard Kirschenbaum (1972)
Values Clarification: A Handbook of Practical Strategies for Teachers and Students. New York: Hart Publishing Company, Inc.
Includes topics for groupwork and discussion.

Wolfram, Walt (1969)
"Sociolinguistic Implications for Educational Sequencing," in Ralph W. Fasold, and Roger W. Shuy, *Teaching Standard English to Black Children.* Washington, D.C.: Center for Applied Linguistics.
Points out that grammatical features are a stronger sign of social class than are other features.

TEACHING ENGLISH TO MINORITY GROUPS

Bradford Arthur

BACKGROUND

Since teaching English as a second language is applied linguistics, it was assumed that the teaching of English to minority groups must be applied TESL. Techniques for teaching English as a second or foreign language were being applied to a domestic situation where English is sometimes a first rather than a second language and never entirely foreign. In such a situation we may question the appropriateness of using second language teaching techniques to teach English to minority groups.

This application of ESL techniques was first proposed by people trying to respond to a crisis in American education. During the 1950's when America was determined to produce a corps of scientists to rival the Russians' space exploration program, we believed that American education was the great catalyst in the melting pot, the most democratic of democratic institutions that could take the nationalities of Europe and the races of Africa and Asia and build scholars limited only by their own individual intellectual potential. This faith helped us to see education as a way out for the countless poor who were filling the urban vacuum created by the middle class exodus to the suburbs. The schools remained—surely the schools could educate these children as they had educated their middle class predecessors.

The teachers were probably the first to recognize that the schools couldn't do this, but many teachers rationalized: the children come from intellectually impoverished families; there are no books in the home; communication is primarily non-verbal, and consequently language development is stunted.[1] The effects were clear enough: low scores on tests—intelligence tests, achievement tests, tests of reading and composition skills; low college admissions—Americans of non-European ancestry were filling the cities but few were seen on the campuses of American universities; low employment figures—white Americans controlled more than their share of those high-paying jobs for which the union card is a college degree. The effects of this educational failure were clear enough. The difficulty was in linking causes with effects.

Why were the schools failing to educate children from ethnic minority groups? During the decade of the fifties, intellectuals, educators, politicians, and ultimately the Supreme Court had decided that segregation was the reason. But integration by National Guard or bus was not a panacea. The differences between minority groups and assimilated (majority group) Americans were and are real, and they create special educational needs for minority group children whether these children are in an integrated or a segregated classroom.[2]

It is these differences and the educational needs they create that may require the special skills and techniques of ESL teachers. To understand the complexity of an ESL teacher's role in an American school we must first examine these differences. What are the conditions that define American ethnic minority groups?[3]

Being a member of an ethnic minority group, a so-called "hyphenated American," is first and foremost a matter of how one conceives of oneself. How would you respond to the query *Who are you?* or *Tell me about yourself.* What facts would you choose to represent yourself, and, in what order of importance would you enumerate those facts? Your sex? Your age? Your occupation? Your nationality? A special interest or talent or infirmity? What about your race or the nationality of your parents? I suspect that the position of race or national origin would be low on the list for white Americans but near the top of the list for most non-European, non-white Americans.

Membership in a minority group is also a matter of how you are viewed. The hyphen has lasted longest for those Americans whose appearance or surname or native language or place of residence marks them as non-white or non-European. Hyphenated Americans frequently live in segregated residential communities—Chinatowns, ghettoes, barrios, inner-cities, or reservations.

Race, defined in purely anthropological terms, differs from race as a basis for ethnic groupings. Ethnically speaking, a man who is not totally white is black, unless he is willing and able to pass for white. For statistical purposes at least, being classified as Mexican-American in school depends on a child's name. To be classified officially as an American Indian, you must have at least one Indian grandparent.

Like an individual's race, his or her language may be related to his or her ethnic classification, but not in the neat consistent terms linguists prefer. Black English is a collection of linguistic features occurring within the Black community. But few if any such features are either universal within or exclusive to that community. The complexities of modern communication networks seem to preclude consistent use of language within clearly demarcated regions. Most ethnic minority groups (Blacks are the major exception) speak a language other than English but seldom if ever to the total exclusion of English. This situation could be confusing to a naive teacher. What sounds like English spoken with a Spanish accent may in fact be the first and indeed virtually the only language of an individual living in East Central Los Angeles.

America's economic class structure is related to its ethnic structure. A disproportionately large number of ethnic minority group members in the United States are poor, without jobs, or with little opportunity for advancement to a higher paying job. When politicians or educators talk about ethnic minorities as problems, they are really talking about the ethnic poor. It is the ethnic poor whose English is most likely to differ from the local standard and whose achievement level in school is most likely to sag well below the national norms.

A problem that is sociological, psychological, genealogical, geographical, economic, and educational, as well as linguistic, cannot be solved by a dose of ESL. But English teachers can contribute skills that reach some parts of the problem and, at the very least, they can avoid making the problem worse. To be a help, English teachers must keep their wits about them. The standard English curriculum has failed vast numbers of ethnic minority students, and standard techniques for teaching English as a second language abroad don't stand to fare much better. Applications of ESL techniques to the teaching of ethnic minorities in the United States entail adaptations and modifications. The teacher of English to minority students within the United States faces some unique problems balanced by some unique advantages and opportunities for innovation.

TAKING ADVANTAGE OF RECEPTIVE COMPETENCE

Ethnic minority students in the United States are likely to understand some English (or Standard English in the case of Black students) even when they do not speak it. Receptive competence outstrips productive competence to an extent not generally found among students whose sole contact with English is in an ESL classroom. Most ESL methods encourage students to say or write words and sentences almost as soon as they can recognize them. Only a few approaches to teaching a second language such as Asher's Total Physical Response encourage learners to listen to the target language for days, weeks or even months before trying their own hand at making sounds and sentences.

When learners hear language which intends to communicate (as opposed to language manipulation exercises) and when the speech act occurs in an environment containing sufficient non-verbal clues to meaning, extended listening generates a surprising amount of language learning. These learners finally do start speaking from an advantaged position: in a sense, they already know the language they are learning. In that same sense, children growing up in a so-called non-English-speaking community within the United States may already "know" English. They may not have perceived any great need to speak English, but through contacts with English speakers and especially through television and motion pictures they are generally assured a massive dose of English spoken at them—and this, especially among younger children, is bound to advance comprehension.

The challenge then is to take advantage of what the second language or second dialect learner already knows about the target language. ESL texts overemphasize skills that such learners already possess. Many ESL materials and techniques follow a sequence from manipulation to communication. Students begin by repeating the structure or sounds of English in drills that are either devoid of communicative value:

Teacher: *Clara is traveling to Chicago.*
Student: *Is Clara traveling to Chicago?*

or communicating at a primitive level:

Student A: *My name is Susan. What's your name?*
Student B: *My name is Lisette. What's your name?*

Such a beginning is *not* appropriate for students who can already comprehend a substantial portion of the English they hear. The task of the teacher then is to adapt existing materials and create new materials and techniques that will lead students from comprehension to production.

Teachers might experiment, for example, with play-acting situations. Younger children might act out a dinner with an English-speaking family. Older students might simulate a visit to a supermarket or a rock concert. In any case, students would begin by taking roles in which they respond non-verbally to the English spoken to them by a teacher or aide playing a linguistically more active role. Thus, the student would begin by exercising his or her ability to comprehend but would be expected to respond with actions rather than words—or at most with short responses repeating words in the question.

Teacher: *Please pass the catsup.*
Student: (Passes appropriate bottle.)
Teacher: *Do you want butter or sour cream on your baked potato?*
Student: *Sour cream.*

Gradually students could be encouraged to volunteer for more verbally active roles in the now-familiar dramatic situations.

Teacher: *Ask Lisette what she wants on her baked potato.*
Student: *What do you want on your baked potato, Lisette?* or *Do you want butter or sour cream on your baked potato?* or *Butter? Sour cream?*

The teacher in this dialogue combines an imperative with an indirect question. Students who can already comprehend English reasonably well will have no difficulty understanding this sort of command. The teacher should accept any semantically appropriate response from the student: the direct question form of the indirect question the teacher used; a repetition of a question form the teacher had used in previous dialogues; or single words with rising, question intonation perhaps accompanied by appropriate dramatic gestures. In a variant of this same technique, useful for providing speakers of non-standard English with a better productive knowledge of the standard language, the teacher creates situations in which some characters speak the student's non-standard dialect of English while others speak Standard English. The situation might be a group of students buying shoes or clothes, or it might be an enactment of the police questioning a group of teenagers. Initially, the teacher plays the Standard-English-speaking shoe salesman or policeman. Then the roles are reversed.

Students who have had extensive exposure to Standard or written English but who have difficulty writing the standard dialect themselves without lapses into their own dialect nonetheless have insights which, if developed, can lead them to the consistent use of Standard English in writing. For example, a student may suspect that what s/he has written is not Standard English even though s/he is not sure what the Standard English form is. Or a student may be able to identify errors in rereading that escaped him or her while s/he was writing the first draft. Or a student may catch an error in a fellow student's writing that s/he would miss in his or her own.

To develop this incipient command of Standard English some teachers have used a transcription of the students' spoken English as a first draft that the class working together (but without teacher assistance) converts into "correct" written English.[4] These students come to recognize and expand their knowledge of Standard English. They are later encouraged to use this knowledge in the independent editing of their own written work.

TAKING ADVANTAGE OF THE ENVIRONMENT

When English is taught overseas, the ESL classroom and language laboratory constitute an English-speaking island, an environment intended in part to simulate the conditions that exist in an English-speaking country. When English is taught here at home, the entire community can become a language laboratory. The teacher of English to minority students can devise techniques that structure the students' contact with the English-speaking community surrounding the classroom in such a way that the community becomes a natural laboratory. Virtually any student, let loose in an English-speaking community, will acquire some English. Clever teachers can guide students into especially effective language learning situations. Obviously the teacher, to be an effective guide, must recognize the differing needs of various individual students. If Juan has just arrived in this country and has had no previous contact with English, he should be given credit for the number of hours he spends watching English language television, or attending movies in English. If he enjoys a movie, he should be encouraged to see it one or more additional times. At a somewhat later stage in his development Juan gets extra credit in his ESL class by joining the school chorus. Still later, he receives ESL credit when he runs for an office in the student government.

Class work can be preparation for some activity outside of class. If students with limited English are going to a baseball game, class time can be used to prepare them to deal with the language-related situations they will encounter at the ball park: buying a reserved-seat ticket and finding their seat in the upper tier on the third base side of the infield; singing "The Star-Spangled Banner"; buying a hotdog with mustard and relish; keeping score; yelling at the umpire; finding their car in Lot 5, Section E-3 and getting back onto the Harbor Freeway South.

TEACHING LANGUAGE AND LITERACY SIMULTANEOUSLY

Non-English-speaking children entering an American elementary school must learn how to read and write English at the same time they are learning to understand and speak it. Similarly, many Black students must learn to read and write a dialect of English other than the one they bring to school with them. Most adult foreign learners of American English, on the other hand, have some degree of literacy in their native language. These existing literacy skills can be utilized in the decoding and production of written English.

The challenge in teaching language and literacy simultaneously is to sequence the learning of both skills so that children are learning to read the words and sentences that have become a part of their new language but are not forced to read words or sentences that are unintelligible. Other problems of sequencing are less obvious. Some educators believe, for example, that Black children should be taught to pronounce all of the final consonant clusters of Standard English before they begin learning to read, although another equally plausible alternative is for the children to be taught to consider some final consonants silent just as all English readers avoid pronouncing the *g* in a word like *sign*.

MAINTAINING THE FIRST LANGUAGE

Until recently the law of the State of California specified that all classes (with the exception of foreign language classes) should be taught in English. The result was that vast numbers of Americans whose native language was not English remained illiterate in their first language. Many came to be ashamed of their first language and the way they spoke it. In much the same way, students speaking Black English or some other form of non-Standard English were discouraged from speaking it and forbidden to write it. As a consequence, children came to be ashamed of their way of speaking English and to consider it somehow a result of their own laziness or carelessness.

Changes in the laws, and funding for bilingual education, in recent years have weakened the monopoly of Standard English in the schools. Most teachers now feel a responsibility to provide students with respect for and literacy in their native language. But a myriad of questions raised by bilingual education remain to be answered. What portion of the school day should be taught in each language? What languages should be used for what subject areas? Should students be taught to read two languages simultaneously, and if not, which language should they read first? Isn't a separate curriculum for bilingual students an enforcement of segregation? Why should bilingual education be limited to non-English-speaking students? What texts should be used? What dialect of the first language should be taught? (Southern California Spanish is different from standard Mexican Spanish—and is generally held in lower esteem.)

TEACHING STANDARD ENGLISH AND ATTITUDES TOWARD IT

In the United States being educated, being literate, and having social status are made to depend on dialect. Whether English teachers like it or not, a so-called "non-Standard" or "sub-Standard" dialect of English precludes admittance to higher education or higher society. No one knows this better than speakers of non-Standard English themselves.

For this reason ESL teachers have been encouraged to apply techniques developed for teaching English as a second language to the teaching of Standard English as a second dialect. (See Alatis, 1970; and Jacobson, 1971). A contrastive analysis will predict constructions that are likely to cause errors. Pattern practice drills, transformational drills, and so on, can also be adapted from the teaching of a second language to the teaching of a second dialect.

However, we can question whether the techniques should be applied in this way since a good deal of the student's class time is taken up in an effort to add another dialect. Increased facility in one dialect may decrease facility in the other. Because of the linguistic closeness of two dialects of the same language, this sort of interference is especially likely to occur in second dialect learning.

As most ESL teachers know, so-called sub-Standard English is not at all substandard from a linguistic (as opposed to a social) point of view. Linguistically speaking, all naturally-occurring dialects of English are equally systematic and equally capable of embodying and communicating human thought and emotion. One dialect is called Standard through accidents of history and politics, not by virtue of some inherent linguistic superiority. (See Shuy, 1964.) Teaching the standard language is, from this point of view, perpetuating irrational social standards.

KEEPING THE LOPEZES UP WITH THE JONESES

We began with the problem: test scores continue to indicate that ethnic minority students are not keeping up with the national average for school achievement. While some educators must work to provide students with the skills and understanding that will raise their test scores, other educators must examine the tests to be certain that they are fair measuring instruments for students of different linguistic and ethnic backgrounds. Tests can be unfair in subtle ways: a test designed to measure some non-verbal skill but which requires the testee to understand or produce language is also testing language ability. As long as the population being tested is relatively uniform in their facility with the variety of English used for the test, then the test may provide a valid measure of the non-verbal skill, but when the population differs in their knowledge of the English used for the test, the test is no longer valid. When verbal intelligence tests include a measurement of vocabulary size, the test is valid only when all students taking the test have had equal exposure to the vocabulary items used on the test. When college entrance depends on verbal aptitude tests that in fact measure the candidate's command of Standard English, then the candidates who are native speakers of Standard English are given a better chance of getting into college.

Finally, in our desire to keep the Lopezes up with the Joneses, let's not forget that we are expecting the Lopezes to learn everything that the Joneses learn *plus* a new language or dialect. Moreover, since textbooks are written in English and since teachers give their explanations in English, the new language is made a key to most of the rest of what is learned in school.... The ethnic minority student is acquiring the verbal tools for learning at the same time s/he is expected to employ those tools. Instead of condemning the low achievements of ethnic minority students, we should praise whatever success they might have achieved in meeting the unrealistic goals that the schools have forced upon them.

NOTES

1. See, for example, the various opinions expressed in Corbin and Crosby (1965).

2. For further discussion of these and many other general problems facing public education in the United States see Silberman (1970).

3. There is increasing irony in our use of the term *ethnic* or *racial minorities*. In most of America's largest cities (and even in a few states) white Americans of European ancestry are in the minority.

4. For a further description of this technique, see Taylor (1971).

DISCUSSION QUESTIONS

1. What are the arguments for and against the use of TESL methods and techniques in English classes for Americans belonging to minority groups?

2. What various subject matters should a teacher have knowledge of to ensure that s/he will be able to instruct the minority child wisely, compassionately, effectively? Give a reason for each field mentioned.

3. In what ways does the teaching of English or Standard English to minority group members differ from the teaching of English to foreign students here in the U.S. or to students in a foreign country?

4. What specific pedagogical suggestions does the author make? Can you suggest others?

SUGGESTED ACTIVITIES

To fully comprehend the task of teaching English to ethnic minority children, you must arrange to watch these children, to talk with them and to teach them.

1. Plan a series of visits to inner-city schools serving students of different ethnic backgrounds. In Los Angeles, for example, you should observe schools in Black, Mexican-American, Chinese, and Japanese neighborhoods. Make arrangements for such a visit by calling the principal and explaining your interest in the teaching of English to minority group children. Try to observe learners in different age groups. You might even include evening adult school classes. Write up a report on your experiences.

2. An even better way to confront the task of teaching English to ethnic minority groups is to volunteer as a tutor for public school students in the area. Tutorial services have been organized on many university campuses. Church groups and community centers also provide contact points between tutors and students who need help with their school work. Tutor one individual for one school term and keep a log of your lesson plans, comments, observations, etc.

3. Select one of the references cited in the "Suggestions for Further Reading" and prepare a critical book review for your class.

SUGGESTIONS FOR FURTHER READING

Aarons, Alfred C., Barbara Y. Gorden, and William A. Stewart, eds. (1969)
Linguistic-cultural Differences and American Education. The Florida FL Reporter, Vol. 7, No. 1.
A special anthology issue containing 43 articles expressing a range of different views on the problems of teaching ethnic minority students and the solutions.

Arthur, Bradford (1973)
Teaching English to Speakers of English. New York: Harcourt Brace Jovanovich.
Chapters 5, 6, and 7 elaborate many of the suggestions made above for teaching language and literacy skills to ethnic minority students.

Baratz, Joan C., and Roger W. Shuy, eds. (1969)
Teaching Black Children to Read. Washington, D.C.: Center for Applied Linguistics.
A collection of articles discussing such issues as the appropriateness of English orthography for speakers of Black English and the usefulness of reading texts written in Black English.

Evertts, Eldonna L., ed. (1967)
Dimensions of Dialect. Champaign, Ill.: National Council of Teachers of English.
An anthology of articles written from the points of view both of educational theorists and of classroom teachers.

Fasold, Ralph W., and Roger W. Shuy, eds. (1970)
Teaching Standard English in the Inner City. Washington, D.C.: Center for Applied Linguistics.
An anthology of articles concerned with the teaching of Standard English to speakers of Black English. "Some Linguistic Features of Negro Dialect," by Ralph W. Fasold and Walt Wolfram provides an excellent introductory description of Black English.

Labov, William (1970)
The Study of Nonstandard English. Champaign, Ill.: National Council of Teachers of English.
An introductory guide for teachers to the sociolinguistics of non-Standard English.

Pialorsi, Frank, ed. (1974)
Teaching the Bilingual. Tucson, Arizona: The University of Arizona Press.
Twenty-two articles discussing the theory and practice of teaching bilingual children, especially the Mexican-American and American Indian children living in the Southwest.

Williams, Frederick, ed. (1970)
Language and Poverty. Chicago, Ill.: Markham Publishing Company.
An important collection of articles presenting a range of theoretical perspectives on the development and nature of language in poverty situations.

THE ADULT ESL CLASSROOM

James Heaton

INTRODUCTION

To a large extent, one must be more pragmatic with methods and materials in the adult ESL situation than anywhere. Adult teaching situations and the types of students one encounters vary from place to place. What I'm going to describe mostly derives from my experience in Southern California, but the general needs of adult students and techniques for dealing with their needs apply to many parts of the country.

The major contrast appears when the typical adult ESL student is compared with the university foreign student. The latter comes to us with the needs and aspirations typical of university study—mostly clustering around linguistic survival in the classroom and library, and, to a lesser degree, general personal enrichment from his or her learning experience in a foreign country. His or her needs, *qua* foreign student, are specific, definable, and solvable in the conventional classroom mode—though not necessarily *only* in that mode. But the adult learner is becoming a more or less established member of a local community, and as such, the formula for defining his or her language needs may not be quite so simple.

Adult classes in ESL are generally organized as part of a community adult school program, funded by local school district taxes, and housed in local high school or junior college buildings. The only fee the students pay is an optional student body membership which is on the order of one dollar. Thus, the courses are available to anyone currently resident in the community, as long as they fulfill certain visa requirements. A record is kept of the students' attendance so that individuals can get credit, where appropriate, but registration is allowed continuously throughout a semester, allowing students to enter a class at any time. Another reason for concern with attendance records is that the schools receive money from the school district and from the state in direct proportion to student attendance hours (Average Daily Attendance). And ESL has traditionally been the "breadwinner" of an Adult Basic Education program (see California State Dept. of Education, 1970, and Preston, 1971). Often, the number of students in ESL classes is nearly as great as the enrollment in the rest of the ABE program. Since keeping up the attendance is one of the main rules of the game, adult school ESL is characterized by large classes of thirty to forty students at the beginning levels.

The "adult" students may range in age from a minimum of 18 up to 65, they may have been in this country for anywhere from a month to a decade, and their language backgrounds range from Korean to Native American. A typical class in the Southwest, at least, will be composed of about twenty Spanish-speakers (Mexicans, Cubans, Central Americans, and South Americans, in that order), four Orientals (Japanese, Chinese, Korean, and Vietnamese—with currently a larger proportion of the latter), and three or four Europeans. Some classes will be entirely composed of Spanish-speakers, so that the teacher may teach first and second semester beginners bilingually. Bilingual teaching may also occur where classes are predominately composed of Chinese.

The students in an adult class are usually working people. There are usually some mechanics, waiters, seamstresses, medical assist-

ants, painters, and truck drivers. Some are students in that they are just out of high school and need to learn English before they can proceed with technical training and a subsequent job. This situation may change somewhat when bilingual education becomes more of a reality. Commonly, Mexican young people come to the United States only temporarily, to work in more or less menial jobs while living with relatives, and they eventually return to Mexico. This phenomenon is something quite apart from the migrant labor scene, however.

There is currently a large influx of Vietnamese of all ages and all degrees of professional training. This is expected to have a significant effect on the size and constitution of ESL classes in Southern California especially. The special circumstances of the Vietnamese coming to this country have motivated some private tutorial programs and a few teacher workshops. Much more may have been done in the way of public programs for easing the transition of this special group of immigrants by the time this paper is published.

Some adult school students are in the United States on special visa programs which allow them to take a specific course of study at a specific school. They are, in fact, required to maintain a study program of 25 hours per week. While these "visa" students are typical of only part of the adult school scene they often make up a considerable proportion of daytime ESL classes, when most regular adult students are working. Visa students' ESL classes serve more or less the same purpose as university ESL—survival in an academic situation rather than, strictly speaking, survival in the community-cultural setting.

As one can see from this, it is not easy to make simple classifications of people attending adult school classes. The range of interests and learning goals of the students will be as widely varied as their occupations. While some students progress normally and successfully through a sequence of three to five "levels" of English, others seem to make little or no progress, sometimes repeating the same class two or three times. Some seem to enjoy attending the class simply as a social experience—perhaps as a temporary relief from a hectic household, no household, unemployment, or as a momentary break between a day job and a night job. Even classification by a common first language yields no particular basis for a teaching strategy, since variations in personal status are so great. Some of the students are fresh out of high school, while some haven't seen the inside of a classroom for twenty years. Some see the English class as a necessary evil, whereas to others it is one of the few places they can make themselves understood, and, consequently, the English class is highly valued as a social outlet—an end in itself.

Students are generally placed in a class-level by informal means: they attend a class of their choice, and the teacher decides on the basis of a brief conversation whether that person can work effectively in the class. Sometimes a paraprofessional teacher's aide (usually bilingual) will interview incoming students briefly as part of the registration process and in so doing will determine readiness for a given level. But too often a student will simply place him- or herself in a class where the teacher is thought to be good, regardless of level, and the busy teacher may not get around to checking the appropriateness of the student's placement. Normally, at least half the input at intermediate levels is from the preceding classes. These are from the group recommended for advancement by the previous teacher. The list of students who have "passed" given levels is circulated among all the teachers. But what appears on the surface to be an orderly process, with the student entering at Level 1 and exiting two years later at Level 4, is often anything but orderly.

Since one isn't dealing with a captive population who must pass Course 1 to Course 4 or some fraction thereof, in a neat, tested sequence, as at a university, the constitution of a class tends to be very fluid from one level to the next. Because of job moves, family obligations, military reassignment, or simply a return to the home country, many students drop out of the sequence at the end of a semester—or midway through the course. Some return after skipping six months or a year and are placed at the same or at a different level, depending on the relative sizes of the classes and the amount of time remaining in the semester, as well as the

processes described above. If they stay in this country, some students find another school in their new neighborhood. Or some simply go out and learn English by the school of hard knocks.

When these problems are compounded with insufficient motivation, the result is that, if you begin with a class of thirty students, by the middle of the semester you may still have thirty students, provided the students find you an interesting teacher (based, of course, on their own expectations). But these probably won't be the *same* thirty students. In fact only a third of them would probably have been in the original number. This situation is pretty well known, but the implications which a shifting student population has for the teacher's handling of the class material are still largely misunderstood. We'll get back to that aspect a bit later.

Another essential variant in the background which the students bring to an adult class is their degree of literacy. University ESL students have almost all had the best of secondary school education. If anything, their problem has been too much literacy in the foreign language, the reading method being a common methodological instrument and an eventual block to understanding the spoken language. Adult immigrant students, usually coming from a poorer segment of the population than university foreign students, have been self-supporting for a large proportion of their lives and, therefore, seldom have had the luxury of a "higher" education and the attendant facility with the written word. Most adult students have, however, had a high school education and are literate in their own language. Some have not finished grade school. These latter have considerable problems with the mechanics of writing and reading, both in their own language and in English. Sometimes a literacy problem is aggravated by the task of trying to learn a new orthography as well as getting along in the new culture. In many cases, the problem may not be directly related to degree of education at all.

To some extent the combined problems of teaching literacy and ESL are found in all but the most affluent adult school situations. Principals in the L.A. area often voice a desire to find teachers who can deal with both ESL and basic literacy. Yet schools in general cannot afford to recognize the ESL-literacy problem by setting up special classes to deal with it. Where there are available federal funds for hiring bilingual teaching aides (and this situation may be becoming more general with the enforcement of bilingual education), the aide usually gives special assistance to those who have writing problems. Unfortunately, teaching aides do not usually have the training necessary to really teach adults to read and write. If a large proportion of the beginning class seems to have this problem, the teacher will simply suppress the writing objectives of the class and concentrate on oral ESL, with some written vocabulary work requiring non-written responses—such as word-picture matching or sentence-building with word cards.

No class is a simple homogeneous group in any sense. The variety of students' needs demands the utmost of the teacher's understanding of our immigrant subcultures as well as the maximum resourcefulness in using appropriate methods for dealing with a variety of learning problems.

I have tried to sketch the heterogeneity involved in a typical adult classroom; compared to this a university class is quite homogeneous in terms of immediate needs. The variety of skill levels, learning rates, and general educational backgrounds in an adult class makes some sort of individualized approach a necessity. Not only a student's skills, but also his or her degree of experience with surviving in this country are important variables. Some students are old hands at the everyday aspects of working, driving, shopping, and raising children in a foreign situation. To others, all those areas are new and contain important blocks to communication which they may not have been able to deal with successfully. And if teaching is to be at all effective, the approach to the whole class has to be seen in a new light, as well.

Probably a word needs to be said about the nature of the teacher, as well, in an adult ESL situation. Adult school teachers are not generally hired on a full-time basis. They are usually paid by the hour and may actually lose their job if an insufficient number of students

turns up. So the teachers are encouraged not to depend on their adult school teaching as a major source of income. In fact, they sometimes end up having to do their own bush-beating for students! There is a small proportion of *contract* ESL teachers at community junior colleges (two-year degree institutions), but these are fairly rare. Up to quite recently, *most* adult school teachers were employed full-time at some other daytime job, as a high school teacher or as a professional in the area being taught. The adult education assignment of one or two courses was regarded as "moon-lighting," and the teaching went accordingly. Teaching being a profession which taxes both the body and mind, it was a rare teacher indeed who would be seen putting the same amount of creative effort into the adult school assignment as one would put in one's regular job. Adult ESL was straight from the textbook; a good deal of sympathy went to the students but little in the way of imaginative solutions to their problems. With the job market being what it is now, the $10 to $15 hourly pay looks fairly attractive and more young teachers fresh out of college TESL courses are entering the scene. Moreover, special concern is being voiced over the plight of particular groups, such as the Vietnamese refugees, where the old steamroller ESL techniques borrowed from remedial English classes simply will not suffice. With younger and better-trained staff, some new techniques of team-teaching and rotating classes are being successfully used. Still, one observes immense differences in the styles and qualities of teaching that a student is likely to be exposed to.

In the continuous enrollment situation outlined above, combined with a host of problems affecting class attendance for many students, the idea of being able to progress in an orderly manner from teaching point "A" to teaching point "G" becomes entirely unrealizable. Many teachers nevertheless follow such a linear sequence as Standard Operating Procedure, because the material in the book is that way. This is as much to maintain their own sanity as to actually claim that the majority of the students have *learned* the substance of the sequence of points. How else can you be sure you've *covered* everything? But if any material comes up which requires knowledge of intermediate points already taught (say, the forms of *be* in sentences identifying objects, taught before the present progressive tense) the teacher can't escape the awareness that something has gone wrong when half the class doesn't know the intermediate material and isn't able to respond accurately. Unless some sort of cyclical review program is built into the sequence, very little in the way of teaching effectiveness will be possible, except toward those few students who registered at the beginning of the course and have been present for every class meeting. If we consider a normal teaching sequence for some ideal academic class of language learners as being A - B - C - D - (Test) - E - F - G - H - (Test) . . . then a sequence for a continuous enrollment, inconsistent attendance situation should be A - B - C (+ review A) - D (+ review B and C) - E (+ review A and D). . . . until as much as half the time available for each lesson is taken by review of previous lessons, depending on how essential and difficult the previous material was. Implicit inclusion of grammar and phonological material will often comprise incidental review (e.g., the forms of *be* are reviewed in teaching the present progressive), but this sort of incidental work will not be sufficiently analytical for those who missed out on the original presentation and drill of the point in question. The students who have missed classes are then back in the school of hard knocks: they may be good enough learners to pick up the material they missed the first time around. But then again, they might not be. Time for the inclusion of explicit review for at least the essential points of previous lessons is an absolute necessity.

But this gets us into the problem of how one is to teach any new material when one's class time is already so cluttered up with review of old stuff? And how is a normal, noncomputerized teacher going to keep the ever-burgeoning number of review points in mind, and still ensure that all are given an appropriate amount of class concentration? And how does one keep the review material from crowding out the new points altogether in a slow class? In many classes this actually happens—as well it

should. The phenomenon is called "not making it through the book."

One wonders, when confronted with such obstacles to the classical model of teaching a linear sequence, if perhaps the concept of "linear sequence" teaching should itself be modified. Not only is the student population too fluid to allow such a neat scheme, but the learners as individuals have little time for home preparation and review, many are exposed only to their first language or to non-standard dialects of English at home, and the textbooks offer little support for people long out of school. Even if the students were "textbook oriented" the texts which have received the widest use are notoriously inappropriate in content, have poor review schemes, if any, and cover inadequately, if at all, the most needed "colloquial" grammar and vocabulary.

Several alternatives to the linear program have been tried in the continuous enrollment situation. One approach has been to teach *skills*, rather than a sequence of grammar points with subsidiary vocabulary and pronunciation objectives. Given the state of affairs that many of the students are borderline illiterates, such an approach is more direct than dividing up the program into levels. In many cases, a beginning class ("level one") is composed of some students who are very good in grammar, but encounter great difficulty when it comes to communicating in writing. Others can read and write, but need much more pronunciation work than is customarily given in their class level. Others may have vocabulary problems and need library materials as part of their program.

Sometimes a good teacher can handle a single class composed of students with such diverse skill-levels by organizing "break activities" which the students can pursue on their own after they have been introduced to the activities in class. Such activities range from games dealing with pronunciation, vocabulary, spelling, reading, and grammar structure, for beginner-intermediate levels, to programmed reading/vocabulary-building for specialized parts of the regular class routine, rather than specifically during break times only. Others can be set up in "stations," to which students are assigned or in which they work voluntarily. As with everything, the variety of ways of pleasantly motivating students to gain additional practice is limited only by the amount of imagination (and extra time) a teacher is willing to put into designing the activities.

GAMES

Following is a sample list of language practice games and activities that have been tried in a variety of adult school situations. Though many appear to be recreational activities—and, indeed, many are—they can all serve as intensive and peer-motivated teaching devices.

Board Games

These exist in many variants, of the "Monopoly" type, where a player throws the dice, moves a marker the indicated number of steps, and performs the activity written in the square he or she lands on. The player may also draw a card indicating an activity, such as saying what is happening in a picture, changing the verb tense of the sentence in the square, or simply responding to a command involving adjectives (*Go to the next blue square*), quantifiers (*Go back five spaces*), or adverbs (*Go directly to jail*). The others playing the game generally act as informal evaluators.

Bingo

This is played in groups like the familiar game, except that the spaces are filled with pictures of vocabulary items, words (usually built around a theme such as professions), or colors. Thus it can be used to involve either readers or non-readers.

"Grid" Games

Similar to the "Silent Way" type of exercise, these are played by two people. The first person chooses a picture from a pile of picture cards and places it on a grid (a piece of cardboard marked in squares), names the picture and describes its position. The second player, who is separated by a partition from the first, has to then identify the correct vocabulary item from another pile of picture cards and place it in the correct position on his or her grid as described. The first person then identifies and describes the position of another picture, which the second student has to find and place correctly according to the description, as before. The game proceeds this way until the second player's grid is filled up. It should look the same as the first player's. The grid can be made more complicated, with four or more squares on a side, presenting a more difficult task in identifying positions.

First player's grid   Partition   Second player's grid

"The car is in the upper-left corner."

"Silent Way" Games

This genre derives from a method described by Gattegno in his book *The Silent Way*. The name is deceptive, since at least one of the players has to use quite a lot of language in order to describe a construction which he or she has built of wooden rods and which the second

player can't see.[1] As in the grid game, a partition separates the two players, though, if this is played as a class game, the partition is arranged so that the class can see the work of both players and participate in giving instructions to the "engineer." The game is finished when the engineer has successfully completed a replica of the "instructor's" work. No pointing or gesturing is allowed.

From the structural viewpoint, such an activity would perforce give an especially large amount of practice in the correct use of adjectives and prepositional phrases of location. The instructor player would have to use—and the engineer would have to understand—such sentences as:

Stand two green rods next to each other. Lay a yellow rod on top of them.

Stand an orange rod to the right of the two green rods.

Lay another yellow rod on top of that. The green rods are under it.

In actual practice, the students will find ways of simplifying the grammar and still communicating the information necessary, and this is indeed a valid objective of this stage of language learning. The stress is laid on *getting the information across,* not on *saying it correctly.* There is an important distinction between the two—one which is central to this kind of teaching, but which is usually swept under the rug in TESL methodology. That is, although it is recognized that all language learning goes through stages of successive approximations to the "mature" language, much TESL methodology has it that students should not be allowed to use *any* incorrect structure, i.e., structure which does not coincide with the grammar of an adult native speaker. The beginning second language learner, then, is confined to learning a language in which he or she is effectively forbidden to *say* anything! In communicative games of the type described here, the student is no longer obliged to fulfill an obligation to the teacher to juggle phonemes and morphemes, but is practicing the art of saying what he or she *means.* Certainly the task itself is artificial in being "made up," and is of no pragmatic consequence as other than a class activity. However, one could say this about all class activities, the difference here being that the materials provide visual reinforcement for the spoken language, the physical action correlates with the language at all points, and the learners can practice saying what they *mean* to say.

Concentration

As with bingo, there are manifold variations on the ways one can adapt this traditional board game as an ESL activity. The basic game consists of a checkerboard where the squares are filled with a set of numbers, words, or pictures. Each square is covered with a blank card. The two players share a deck of cards. They take turns drawing a card from this deck and then lifting a blank card from one of the squares on the board to see if it matches the one they have drawn. If so, that player keeps the card and gets to take another turn, until he or she fails to come up with a match. If the player doesn't match the drawn card, the other player takes a turn. The game is more difficult if, after each try, the blank side of the card is put back on its square. The object is to *concentrate* on remembering what was in each square, so as to acquire as many matched cards as possible.

The ESL application requires the players to remember something about the words in the squares rather than simply matching them. For example, one version has English male and female names on the board. The draw cards have male and female possessive and pronominal forms, *his, her, hers, he,* and *she,* etc., and the players have to match these with the names on the board. Lots of other tasks are possible, such as matching vocabulary items with their pictures, cardinal or ordinal number-words with their numerals, artifacts with appropriate professions (*carpenter—saw,* etc.), synonyms or antonyms. The level can then be varied according to the task.

Gossip

This is a less formal variation of a chain drill exercise and needs a large group or the whole class. The teacher or leader gives a note to the first person in a row of players. This note might contain a statement about someone in the class, such as *Mary is wearing a red sweater,* which the first person has to read and whisper to the second person, who has to whisper it to the next person, and so on, to the end of the row. The leader must confirm that the last person got the information correctly. The gossip statement might contain a pronunciation point the students need to work on, such as /l/ and /r/ in *Larry left the ladder on the lawn.*[2]

"Envelope" Sorting Games[3]

An assortment of word or picture cards about a given class of objects is contained in an envelope. For example, a "furniture" envelope would contain pictures of various common furniture objects, perhaps with the name written on the reverse side. The aim is to identify each of the objects with its English name and to say what room you would find each of them in. Food items might be sorted by the units you buy them in; tools by what you do with them, etc.

Dominoes

This is another type of matching game, using cards divided into halves. Each half of a card has a word or phrase on it which has to be matched, domino style, to another card to complete a phrase or sentence, to match a synonym or antonym, or to match count nouns and mass nouns with other words of the same category.

These are only a brief selection of the many types of language games that can be invented or adapted. While some may be set up in semi-permanent "stations," if space permits, the usual case is that adult classrooms are shared with high school or college classes which occupy them in the daytime. In this case materials have to be carried in or kept in storage cupboards, with the games being set up before each class.

The main advantage of games is that they provide the students with an informal opportunity to gain further practice in specific areas of need, such as vocabulary, reading, grammar, or pronunciation. If the games are well chosen or adapted for the level of the class and the kinds of skills the students bring to it, the activities are self-motivating, and many of them are a constructive way of simulating real-life language use.

But there is still a great deal that we don't know about how effective games are in teaching language. Research carried on with simulation games indicates that these are about as effective in teaching *factual* knowledge as conventional teaching methods. But, more to the point, research also indicates that games increase motivation and are interesting to the students. And these are two major attractions of this kind of language learning (see Heinkel, 1969).

READING LAB MATERIALS

Other activities are also available which can help individualize learning along skill lines. The literacy problem mentioned previously is one area which requires particular resourcefulness. Reading lab materials of the SRA type are used where the school can afford them. These are the well-known programmed sets of short reading passages sequenced into progressively more difficult levels, with built-in comprehension questions, vocabulary building exercises, and progress testing devices. Usually the students work with the lab with a minimal amount of supervision from the teacher, whose main job it is to chart their progress and check out the booklets. The reading lab has been used with success in a wide variety of situations, though it is aimed mainly at American grade school and junior high students who are behind in their reading skills. Still, the fact that the reading lab is somewhat bound to the American "school culture" (as apart from matters of immediate community significance which are of more concern and usefulness to adults) and the fact that each lab costs around $200 makes this approach a less than fully satisfactory solution to adult literacy.

LANGUAGE EXPERIENCE APPROACH

One of the main problems with teaching reading/composition skills is getting the students interested in the reading material and making them able to express what they *want* to express. Kennedy (1973) advocates an approach to the literacy problem that uses student-created materials:

In a reading class based upon the Language Experience Approach, the curriculum consists of the articulated experiences, thoughts and feelings of the students. The first words that are learned are those of the students themselves. Words become something useful, personal and exciting; they tell about our lives and how we feel when we fall asleep at night. They belong to all of us, not just to teachers and authors. They are symbols of sounds and images rather than conglomerates of phonetic parts.[4]

The approach is humanistic in that it stresses communication and helps relieve the feeling of failure that students have built up from previous experiences. Briefly, the language experience approach involves several alternative techniques:[5]

Dictation
The student dictates to the teacher a short passage, such as a recent movie he or she has seen, a daily activity, or a special family event. The teacher prints the passage, word for word, with a magic marker on a large sheet of paper and reads it back to the student. Difficult words are picked out and printed on 3" x 5" cards for recognition drill. These can be filed for home study, as well. Sentence completion exercises can also be derived from the story, and the student is asked to recognize words which are randomly pointed to. I would add that this kind of activity can be done with the whole class as well and the resultant passage can be later dittoed up for further work, or as part of a class journal.

Directed Writing
This gets the students to do their own writing, if only minimally so, by filling in sentences such as: *When I think of my children, I feel (happy and worried).* The activity can also extend to a more communicative exercise, like the "Gossip" game above, where a student writes a question and passes the piece of paper to the person on the right, who then answers the question on the paper and writes another question for the next person:

A: *What is your favorite TV program?*
B: *"All in the Family."*
B: *What do you like to eat?*
C: *Potato chips and ice cream.* etc.

Though some problems may arise with the students not being able to read each other's handwriting, the communicative context provides natural motivation for doing so, given that they already have some word recognition skills.

Free Writing: The Class Journal
This resembles the traditional class composition exercise except that, again, it is done primarily for the purpose of communicating something to somebody. The students write about topics of immediate interest—their homes, their daily lives or an important event therein—and share the work with others in the class as a reading journal dittoed by the teacher, but for the most part preserving the students' own style and wording.

In all cases, the exercises can be more or less structured as to vocabulary, spelling patterns, and grammar by controlling the topic and prior oral work, and by providing students with individual vocabulary lists to work from. In most cases the language experience approach will mean more work for the teacher, but it has also been known to solve literacy problems that had been seen as almost incurable. Students who had dragged through class after class without making any apparent progress with their blocks toward writing have been able to improve significantly because of the capacity of this method to motivate communication.[6]

THE CLASSROOM ENVIRONMENT

The classroom environment itself is an important teaching device in the adult situation, as with any age group. And individualized break activities often include work with displays of various kinds. Charts and displays of temperatures, weights, and measures are valuable for semi-permanent display to refer to during the regular class as well as for special "research" assignments. (One teacher I know posted in graphic style the height, weight, and shoe size of some favorite basketball stars.) Maps are an invaluable stand-by and should include blow-ups of the local streets as well as road maps of the state and region. The usual world map is also a useful tool, but less so than in a university class. Pictures of traffic signs are an important aid and make a useful display for discussion and vocabulary activities.

Other types of displays can include colors, textures (samples of silk, wool, sandpaper, rubber cement, etc.) and even tastes and smells.

One should note that none of the above constitutes a methodology which is guaranteed to work with all students, or, for that matter, with all teachers. Unfortunately, there are no infallible recipes in the ESL business: you just have to choose carefully among the available resources. Some teachers have classes where they can make effective use of practically all these game activities; other teachers seem to be able to *create* classes in which they can use their favorite methods, even though, to an external observer the methods don't always seem to fit the situation. One sometimes has to suspend judgment, but it appears that the needs of the students must be kept in focus in this challenging situation.

SOME ADDITIONAL ACTIVITIES

Descriptions of other activities which are more adapted to whole-class participation can be found in my chapter on "An Audiovisual Method for ESL," also in this book (p. 38). But here are a few class techniques and media which seem to me to be especially well-adapted to adult ESL, and which do not draw too heavily on technical expertise.

Pictures

Magazines and the Sunday supplements are the best sources for these. They should be as large and as simple as possible, depicting a simple action (*smiling, eating, getting married*), nouns (*man, boat, house, hand*), or adjectives (*fat, tanned, happy, obnoxious*) or phonological items (*cot/cat, fly/fry, cat/cut, ch*-words, *sh*-words, etc.). The pictures must be mounted on medium weight cardboard with rubber cement or dry mounting tissue, and they should also be protected with clear contact paper. The last and most important requirement is that the pictures must be grouped and filed in some orderly and retrievable fashion, e.g., alphabetized under Nouns, Colors, *sh*-words, etc.

A variation of magazine pictures is do-it-yourself photographic prints in which one can depict exactly what one needs, and with local significance. If at all possible, a lot of composition work will be stimulated by having the class photograph and assemble its own picture story of some place or event. Educational publishing houses also sell sets of large prints depicting situations suitable for oral and written composition.

The "Scroll" and Comics

A nice variation on stick figure vocabulary cards has been devised by Celce-Murcia, in which the whole "life history" of an imaginary individual—or at least the most important parts of it—are depicted with representative pictures, dates and years on a long roll of white shelf paper, which is hung up over the blackboard for contextualized grammar practice. A good deal of tense practice is possible when, for example, the date and the picture representing the present (*She's attending UCLA now, in 1979*) is used as the reference point to past and future pictures. Given a specified reference point, all the other tenses can be practiced, as well:

> *How long has she attended UCLA?*
> *Had she bought a car before 1979?*
> *When will she get married?*

Comic strips cut out of newspapers, with the words "whited out" and the panels cut apart and mounted on thin cardboard, also make a good device for working with verb tenses and putting events together in logical sequence for oral and written composition in small groups. *Peanuts, The Little King, B.C., Basil,* and *Heathcliff* are good ones to try.

SURVIVAL ENGLISH

Some materials are especially well adapted toward helping the newly-arrived student obtain and exchange information as readily as possible within the same natural contexts and from the same sources available to native speakers. The type of lesson material dealing with such information is loosely called "survival English," since the contexts which are taught are those in which one must become immediately involved to get food, transportation, emergency services, clothing, and general community information. The technique used is to teach the language of a specific situation or "unit" of situations, with attendant vocabulary and grammar being thought of as clustering about the situation rather than being handed down by a frequency list and a structural sequence. For example, if one were teaching a unit on bus transportation, one would use real bus schedules and deal with such vocabulary as *driver, passenger, transfer* (v. and n.), *transfer point, route, get on, get off, just miss, angry, stupid*, etc. And the grammar would similarly deal with some items, such as the present perfect (*Have you seen the Number Three bus yet?*) out of "normal" sequence. Some more materials which are associated with survival English are:

Realia

Newspaper advertisements are a good source of many kinds of survival material, such as mass/count and comparison shopping exercises. The Dear Abby columns are useful for discussion, role-play, and writing replies. The *T.V. Guide* furnishes practice in time adverbials and vocabulary. Magazine articles and picture stories are often useful, as are the old standby, real objects (cooking utensils, tools, common hardware, fruit, clothing). One possible class activity is assigning a group to pick out a prop, sight unseen, from a bag of old artifacts you've brought from home. The students' task then is to organize a skit around this prop.[7]

Slides and A-V Material

Projected photographs are another quick, easy, and cheap way of bringing in local experience as well as impressively displaying graphic material such as advertisements, weights and measures, and short reading passages. One thing that many people don't realize is that slides don't have to be photographic. Using 35mm clear leader, available from editing supply houses, and the permanent type of felt tip pen, one can make pictorial and graphic slide lessons in the slide or filmstrip format. Such projected materials are also probably the most compact and easy to store of any medium. Some lesson formats are suggested in the chapter on "An Audiovisual Method for ESL" in this volume.

It also is not common knowledge that most adult schools and junior colleges are exceptionally well provided with audiovisual equipment: projectors of all types, tape recorders, duplicating machines, and the like can either be obtained from a central storage room at the school, or can readily be ordered on loan from the school district. The teacher usually requests equipment from an administrative assistant, and frequently a custodian will even set the equipment up for him or her in the designated room.

School districts have a central audiovisual materials center with lots of filmstrip and motion picture film materials gathering dust because teachers don't know about them or regard them as inappropriate. A little exploration through such places can turn up some very adaptable lesson materials—if not exactly the kind one was looking for. For example, grade school filmstrips for teaching numbers and letters can be turned into vocabulary and pronunciation lessons.

Although most adult schools aren't equipped with much in the way of video playback equipment, it is a fact that the programs *Sesame Street, Villa Alegre*, and *Pochtlan* contain a lot of English teaching material, the latter being principally aimed at adult learners in a bilingual/bicultural program. Students even report watching the Saturday morning cartoons! If they are that hard up for English experience, they should certainly be watching *Villa Alegre* and *Pochtlan*. Program guides for these are easily obtainable through the broadcasting station so that specific out-of-class assignments can be made in advance to facilitate classroom discussion activities.

Recorded Listening Comprehension: Conversations, Sound Effects, News Broadcasts, and Songs

The first task a newly arrived student has is to understand the new language, with all its "colloquialism," speed, dialectal variation, and interference factors such as poor quality sound transmission (as on a telephone or radio) and noise. And, from the classroom standpoint, such real-sounding language can be brought into the lesson materials for practice under controlled conditions through the use of audiotape.

Survival conversation material (e.g., dialogues with the grocery clerk, the hamburger seller, the woman at the bank) can be either faked to sound real or, better yet, genuine recorded and edited material can be used.

(These days *anybody* can be a CIA man with a hidden tape recorder!) In either case, when the material is used in the classroom, it may need a lot of repeated playing, or a "breakdown" stage, for full comprehension of the normal-speed material. But the students will thank you that you didn't try to feed them warmed-over ESL soup when what they needed was the live animal. Neither should such material avoid contemporary slang and local colloquial levels of phonology and grammar, since that's exactly what the students will have to cope with. If the material is properly presented, in short, manageable chunks, the material itself won't have to be idealized.

The first stage of a presentation is simply listening comprehension and discussion. The students are given a list of questions or points of information to look for in the conversation passage. The tape can be played two or three times, as needed. Second, the students can work in pairs with copies of the script itself, with the objective of ironing out as many pronunciation problems as possible—at least at the level of correctly understanding the segmentation of the words. Note that some types of classes might play down the productive stage, if the main and most immediate aim is listening comprehension. Otherwise, after practicing the given material, the next stage will be either an in-class role-play which is an improvised version of the lesson tape, practiced and "performed" by the students in groups. Or that stage can be replaced by a field trip (if time and transportation allow), in which the students are taken (or sent) out to deal with the required language *in situ*. We'll get back to the ESL field trip below. But one way of having the students perform a real information-gathering task without having to leave the school building is to work with survival telephone conversations (how to ask for information of various kinds or how to contact directory assistance in various cities), which also provides beginners good practice in dealing with numbers. Their "field trip" can be a short walk to the nearest telephone. Another such local task, modeled by a vérité conversation on audiotape, would be finding out school enrollment or current event information from a secretary or administrator. If the class is held during the working hours of the "resource" people, then the follow-up might even be completed during the class period, instead of as an overnight assignment. Such exercises are interesting to the students, self-motivating, self-checking (either they come back with the information or they don't) and, needless to say, straight to the point.

Some news broadcasts also provide a source of information and listening comprehension practice which the students need. Going from the premise that foreigners need access to the public information channels just as much as we do, work on this type of material also becomes of survival significance. It is possible for a teacher to collect a whole set of short news features of more or less undated material (on employment, technology, strange facts, food environment, medical matters) which are edited for use at x level. One then has to extract the vocabulary which will need advance "priming," and the crucial points of information that the students need to look for.

Songs, current pop and folk music, are widely used as a way of teaching all the usual elements of language, plus perhaps some of the more poetic features that ESL usually sifts out. Most students enjoy at least listening to our music, and many enjoy participating in singing such old dinosaurs as "I've Been Working on the Railroad." The basic material is a matter of selection rather than editing. The commercially recorded song should generally be chosen to be as simple as possible musically, with a minimum of production embellishment. The lyrics should also be straightforward if the song is to be used for teaching a grammar or pronunciation point, although poetic usage will not particularly surprise anybody, since songs in other languages have poetry as well. Usually one would select the song for a number of occurrences of the teaching point and present it both as music which the class can participate in and as a sample of the language which can be discussed against some cultural background. Many songs lend themselves to reinforcement with visual images, and this has been successfully tried at UCLA, using slides, with "Old Friends" (Simon and Garfunkle) and "Rocky Racoon" (The Beatles). There are also some collections of songs especially written or edited for ESL. Such collections attempt to control language but often do so at the expense of cultural authenticity, which is important.

Sound effects, obtained from real life or from commercial discs, provide an interesting source of composition material for intermediate classes.[8] Sounds such as a thunderstorm may be used to elicit a list of adjectives (*wet, cold, windy, frightening*) or a story (*It was a dark night. Suddenly there appeared a big, horrible . . .*). Household sounds, street sounds, and factory sounds can also be used for vocabulary identification, adjective work, and descriptive composition. It is also a nice way to get people to talk about their feelings and what they associate with certain sound impressions.

The Field Trip

More and more, teachers are beginning to regard the classroom as only a starting point for the teaching of language. In our situation, where the English is all around us, there are many opportunities for the students to go out and gather information straight from the community. A few such opportunities have been noted above in passing. If English is to be regarded as a medium of communication, it is possible that a major proportion of the assignments of beginning and intermediate work should include some sort of information-gathering outside the classroom. As a teacher-led group or as individuals the students can find out from the horse's mouth such things as: *What is the bus fare to East LA? Does the Number 8 stop at 4th and Pico? How much is a large cheese pizza at (restaurant)? What number do you call to get Information in San Francisco? How do you get to the airport? What does 'to split' mean? How much does it cost to mail a two-pound package to Mexico City?*

Another assignment is an interview of a school official or of other teachers. In such cases the students bring the information to class, compare notes, and discuss the results of their enquiries. Though the questions don't seem to be of world-shaking importance to a jaded native, most of them will involve vital basic information about the ins and outs of the community. And, at the same time, the stu-dents have been practicing communicating in English in the ultimate authentic context.

A program in San Francisco called the Asian Newcomer Parent Program, for Chinese immigrants, made heavy use of both the community field trip approach and a novel way of organizing the curriculum which may be the solution to the problem of how to march ever onward through the structures of English when you've got new beginners (who, in this case, were also new immigrants) entering the class every few days. The scheme stresses a situational approach, including cultural information, akin to "survival English." The program simplifies things considerably by abandoning the fiction of sequenced learning from A to Z and by *holding constant* a set of structural patterns which are retaught throughout a whole series of contexts, at a given proficiency level. The course is organized as a series of cycles, with the grammar being constantly repeated—but as new *information.* The grammar advances in the next course-cycle, where the same situation modules are repeated. A student may enter at any part of a cycle and still eventually go through the whole course, and similarly students who must be absent still have the opportunity to pick up the material they missed the next time around. A sample of the scheme[9] is shown on page 289.

The basic classroom techniques are audiolingual. New material is introduced by a short conversation or a listening passage. Grammar structures are focused on via pattern drills, commands, questions and "guided conversation" (which allows fill-in modification). The lesson module ends with a short story which contains the structures practiced. Since the students must also learn the English writing system, attention is given to sentence copying and other minimal written work after the oral material has been studied. All of this is carried on within the situation and using its vocabulary. The students are given additional "Community Information" handouts and exercises as part of the regular course. A good bit of this is bilingual since the information is fairly vital and too complex to be dealt with in beginning English. Cultural events are introduced and more detailed information is given regarding the

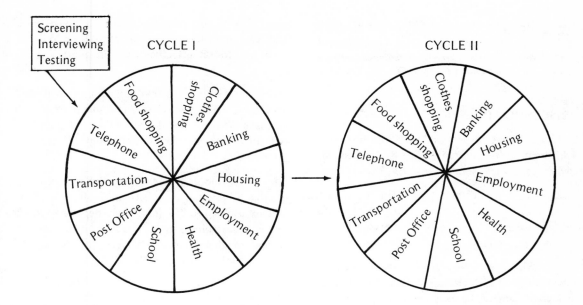

Screening
Interviewing
Testing

CYCLE I

Food shopping
Clothes shopping
Telephone
Banking
Transportation
Housing
Post Office
Employment
School
Health

CYCLE II

Clothes shopping
Food shopping
Banking
Telephone
Housing
Transportation
Employment
Post Office
Health
School

situation modules in the local areas (transportation: bus routes, fares, transfer points, etc.; banking: cost of checks, statements, minimum balance, etc.).

Beginning with the second cycle (after 100 hours of instruction) the context modules are accompanied by field trips in the local community, after the students are prepared with the language they will need for the particular situation. On a field trip they do with the Cycle II Transportation module, the students ride the cable car from the school in Chinatown down to a transfer point. From there they proceed to the central bus station where they ask the ticket clerk about fares to specific destinations. This field trip is done with a teacher's help, but they have a number of specific opportunities to apply the language they have just learned.

Like the Asian Newcomer Parent Program, any situational approach has to be designed for the area where the students are living, which is *not* Anywhere, USA. Moreover, the materials and approach must reflect at least the age group and general interests of the students, even if it is not possible to consider them a homogeneous language group.

The area of Adult ESL is a broad, frustrating, vital, and fascinating part of the profession and one that still needs serious study and innovation. I hope I have been able to show, however sketchily, how much language needs to be treated as a communicative tool when one is dealing directly with people who are settling into a more or less permanent local community. Indeed, sometimes the teacher has to become part social worker, but if we think about it a while, I imagine we will be forced to the conclusion that we have never really been anything else. Many people still learn this new language by the school of hard knocks—and many people fail. The task of the teacher in adult ESL is to soften the blows however one can.

NOTES

1. Blocks will also serve. But when the rods come in color-coded lengths, they are called Cuisiniere Rods.

2. I am indebted to Dayle Hartnett for this and other ideas regarding organizing games.

3. The "Envelope" and "Dominoes" games are by Evelyn Hatch.

4. Kennedy and Roeder (1973), p. 1.

5. *Ibid.*

6. See also the Teachers and Writers Collaborative Newsletter (New York) for many further ideas and experiences in composition work with problem learners.

7. I am indebted to Judy Olsen (1977) for this idea.

8. This idea also was presented by Judy Olsen (1977).

9. Adapted from *Everyday English*, vol. 1 (San Francisco Asian Newcomer Parent Program, Education Center for Chinese, 1973), p. 3.

DISCUSSION QUESTIONS

1. In what respects is the adult ESL class different from the university ESL class? In what respect is it similar?

2. What would your general approach be if you had an adult school ESL class at the beginning level where some students are literate in their native language while others are not?

3. What are the results of continuous enrollment in adult ESL classes? What can be done to alleviate some of the negative results?

4. Why is the use of games and other similar activities especially important in adult ESL classes?

5. Why should the oral communication aspect of language necessarily be stressed more in adult ESL than in university ESL?

SUGGESTED ACTIVITIES

1. Develop a game or an adaptation of a game described in this chapter designed to teach one of the following points:

a. The difference between the phonemes /i/ and /iy/ as in *bit* and *beat* respectively.

b. The inherent countability of nouns like *book, chair, fork* as opposed to the inherent non-countability of semantically similar nouns like *paper, furniture, silverware*.

c. The fact that action verbs such as *run, walk, talk* take the present participle whereas stative verbs such as *seem, hear, see,* etc., usually do not.

d. Contextualized practice with the principle parts of common irregular verbs such as *be, have, take, put,* etc.

2. Visit an ESL class in your area several times. Describe what is going on in the class and make several suggestions for curriculum improvement.

3. Take a grammar lesson from a university ESL text and indicate how it would have to be modified to be effective with an adult ESL class.

4. Get a copy of a textbook in current use in a local adult ESL class. How much of the language used in the dialogue material could one conventionally classify as "slang" or colloquialisms?

5. Take the above textbook and rate each of the situational contexts in it from "1" (totally useless) to "5" (extremely necessary) in terms of usefulness to a person who has just arrived in this country. What is the average survival context rating for the book?

SUGGESTIONS FOR FURTHER READING

Altschuler, Thelma (1970)
Choices. Englewood Cliffs, N.J.: Prentice-Hall, Inc.
Presents a variety of controversial situations to stimulate discussion and composition among students with motivational problems.

Battung, Diane (1972)
A pilot study for the development of a learning resource center format. M.A. thesis, UCLA.
A sound argument for an individualized media approach to ESL.

Carlson, Eliot (1969)
Learning through games. Washington, D.C.: Public Affairs Press.
Surveys the types and applications of simulation games.

Dalkin, Julian (1968)
Songs and Rhymes for the Teaching of English. London: Longmans.
Collection of traditional children's songs and a teacher's guide giving suggestions for teaching pronunciation.

Finocchiaro, Mary (1971)
"Myth and reality in TESOL: a plea for a broader view," *TESOL Quarterly,* 5, 1, pp. 3-17.
Opposes rigid adherence to the myths of "applied linguistics" and advocates a flexible learner-centered approach.

Johnston, Letitia M. (1972)
A study of student turnover in adult ESL classes. Unpublished M.A. thesis, UCLA.
Surveys some of the teacher-student communication problems that lead to a high dropout rate.

Kennedy, Katherine (1975)
Games and Butterflies. Cambridge, Mass.: Community Learning Center for Adults.
A compendium of detailed game descriptions, organized by skills and levels.

Norris, William E. (1971)
TESOL at the beginning of the 70s. University of Pittsburgh.
Summarizes the various justifications for flexible methodology.

Pomeroy, Carol (1974)
Songs for ESL. Unpublished M.A. thesis, UCLA.
A selection of songs and a rationale for their use in the adult ESL situation.

Salisbury, Lee (1970)
"Role playing—rehearsal for language change," *TESOL Quarterly, 4,* 4, pp. 331-336.
Role-playing may enable non-standard speaking students to obtain facility with a standard dialect.

Smith, Larry E. (1971)
"Don't teach—let them learn," *TESOL Quarterly, 5,* 2, pp. 149-151.
Describes an individualized ESL class at the East-West Center, University of Hawaii.

Valdes, Joyce (1970)
"Starting English late," *TESOL Quarterly, 4,* 3, pp. 277-282.

PART IV
TEACHERS

This book ends with a section devoted to the ESL teacher. What does the teacher need to know in order to perform his or her job professionally and efficiently? What are the skills all too frequently left undiscussed in an ESL methods course or a methods textbook? In the first chapter Celce-Murcia and Gorman spell out a procedure for preparing ESL lesson plans, and in the next chapter Daoud and Celce-Murcia provide the ESL teacher with a system for selecting and evaluating language textbooks. An overview of the audiovisual aids that the ESL teacher has at his or her potential disposal (along with teaching suggestions) is provided in Celce-Murcia's chapter on language teaching aids. Bailey and Celce-Murcia in their chapter then provide the ESL teacher with many classroom activities designed to improve four aspects of the teaching-learning situation: social climate, variety in learning activities, opportunity for student participation, and ways of accomplishing feedback and correction. Cohen covers many issues in second language testing (kinds of language tests, types of test items, test administration, reliability, validity, etc.) and provides hundreds of sample items in his chapter. Finally, Thompson reminds the ESL teacher of all the possibilities s/he should exploit to keep up to date. The field is growing rapidly, and a big part of any ESL teacher's responsibility is to keep abreast of new developments.

PREPARING LESSON PLANS

Marianne Celce-Murcia *and*
Thomas P. Gorman

INTRODUCTION

For the inexperienced teacher in an ESL/EFL teacher training program often the most difficult task is not the assimilation of different methods and techniques of teaching but the ability to use his or her knowledge of the English language and the four skills to write creative and effective lesson plans.

This is especially true if the teacher trainees have had no previous experience with general pedagogy yet must engage in an extended supervised teaching experience prior to certification. In such cases, presenting the points that must be attended to before and during the preparation of lesson plans—along with appropriate example lessons—can be very helpful, especially if this knowledge is applied regularly throughout the training period in the preparation of sample or hypothetical lesson plans. This is not to say that normal apprehensions can be completely eliminated prior to a trainee's first teaching session; but the inevitable initial feelings of disquiet can be allayed considerably if an appropriate procedure and format—as well as many good example lesson plans—have been presented right from the start as part of the training program. In addition, the preparation of lesson plans that receive careful study and comment from the instructor should be a regularly scheduled activity. In this way the trainee will have a good notion of what a lesson plan is and how to go about preparing one.

PRELIMINARIES

The first step in planning a lesson for an ESL class involves the determination of essential background information: Who are the students? How old are they? What is their level of proficiency in English? What is the linguistic (and, if relevant, ethnic) composition of the class? How motivated are the students? Who is the regular classroom instructor? What is his or her syllabus? What textbook, if any, is being used? etc. Such background information should influence a teacher's strategy and selection of materials in the presentation of any teaching point. This is why trainees should prepare some sort of cover sheet such as the following one to accompany any lesson plan(s) submitted for evaluation.[1] (See cover sheet on page 296.)

THE LESSON PLAN

Certain information should be provided at the top of any lesson plan: the student teacher's name, the intended date of presentation, the estimated time of the lesson (or the time allotted for the lesson), and the teaching point. The teaching point should be stated briefly and should specify the general topic of the lesson (e.g., the use of the indefinite article, the present perfect, /i/ vs. /iy/, common uses of the comma, etc.).

The next section of the lesson plan deals with justification and elaboration of the teaching point. Where appropriate, it also relates the teaching point to any relevant preceding lessons and to the unit of instruction in which it occurs. More precisely the following kinds of information should be provided:

(a) *Pre-assessment activity.* What activity or activities did the student teacher carry out to determine that the class, in fact, needs a lesson on this particular teaching point? (The "activity" might involve the use of error analysis, diagnostic tests, informal observation or following the directives of the regular teacher, etc.)

(b) *Relationship to current unit.* How do this particular teaching point and the lesson

COVER SHEET

The following set of lesson plans should all be evaluated in terms of the following information:

Student Teacher _____

Regular Teacher _____

Supervising/Coordinating Teacher _____

School _____

Class _____

Learning Stage of Class _____

Age Level of Class _____

Size of Class _____

Linguistic/Ethnic Composition of Class _____

Other Relevant Factors _____

(e.g., syllabus, class texts, examination system, degree of student motivation, reason(s) for studying English, literacy level, etc.)

Note: A cover sheet of this kind is suggested to help the student teacher avoid needless repetition of information on the actual lesson plans. Ordinarily, such information would be provided with each lesson plan.

plan fit into the current unit of instruction being presented to the students? Why is it being taught at this time?

(c) *Pre-entry performance.* What, if anything, was covered in previous lesson(s) that will be reviewed or applied in the course of this lesson?

(d) *Performance objectives.*[2] State very precisely the behaviors you expect the students to be able to perform as a result of the lesson. For example, if your teaching point is /i/ vs. /iy/ your performance objective might be: Students will be able to discriminate aurally and orally between /i/ and /iy/ in the following minimal word pairs: *meat/mitt; heel/hill; Sid/seed;* and in the following minimal sentences: *Do you think he will live/leave? Johnny beat/bit his sister.*

(e) *Criterion level.* The teacher can decide in advance that the lesson will be considered successfully completed if X percent of the students can perform the objectives X percent of the time. (This level normally should be fairly high, e.g., 80-100%.) The criterion level may be set for the whole class, groups of students, or individuals.

(f) *Materials.* This includes the textbook, if any, hand-outs, the use of the blackboard, audiovisual aids, etc.

The next section (Procedures), which is the core of the lesson plan, specifies the procedures or activities that the students will engage in to accomplish the objectives of the lesson. The actual number of steps used by the teacher depends on factors such as the teaching point, objective(s), time set aside for the particular lesson, etc. In the development of student activities, the student teacher should try to sequence carefully and be sure that all exercises are contextualized and meaningful to the fullest extent possible.

The first step should be an appropriate introductory activity, and the final step should be a concluding activity that permits at least informal testing of the criterion level established earlier. Within this general framework the student teacher should plan activities that will be interesting to and profitable for his or her students, given the teaching point at hand.

The final items on the lesson plan should specify the assignment (if there is one relating to the lesson) and contingency plans (i.e., What alternate activity or activities has s/he prepared so that a change of plan can be made if this is necessary?), and comments or self-evaluation. The comments or self-evaluation should note whether or not the lesson was successful, what the teacher would improve if s/he could re-teach the lesson, how well the teacher feels s/he performed as an ESL teacher, etc.

After receiving such suggestions on how to plan a well-prepared lesson, the reaction from trainees often is, "That's so time-consuming and complicated. Do I have to do all that?" One way of alleviating such complaints is to provide copies—as many as required—of the lesson plan form so that the student teachers will be able to save time by filling in the material specific to each lesson plan. Experience indicates that facility and speed increase daily as such a form is used.

The following is an example of what such a form might look like. A sample lesson plan following this format is provided in the Appendix.

LESSON PLAN

Student teacher's name _____

Date of presentation _____

Estimated Time of Lesson _____

Teaching Point_____

- -

Pre-assessment Activity _____

Relationship to Current Unit _____

Pre-entry Performance _____

Performance Objectives _____

Criterion Level: _____

Materials: _____

- -

PROCEDURES (Student Activities)[3]

    Step 1 — Introduction
    (time:)

    Step n. (Concluding activity that permits informal testing of criterion level established above.)
    (time:)

- -

Assignment (optional):

Contingency plans:

Comments/Self-evaluation: (Fill out after lesson is taught.)

Having a set format to follow is desirable not only for the trainee but also for the teacher trainer. The trainer must often evaluate and correct dozens of lesson plans per week, and his or her task is considerably simplified if all plans submitted adhere to the same format. Another advantage of using a set format is that it facilitates collaboration on lesson plans and group discussions of them. One drawback that arises from using such a rigorous format, however, is that the novice who has gone to great lengths to prepare thoroughly will often be reluctant to alter his or her lesson plan during the class period even though change or modification is obviously necessary. The only way around this problem is for the supervisor to emphasize from the very beginning that even the most elaborate lesson plan is a flexible guide, not a fixed itinerary, and that it must always be viewed as being subject to change if the circumstances call for such a decision.

CONCLUSION

A logical and necessary extension of the individual lesson plan is the unit or the entire syllabus. For a discussion of the issues and problems involved in syllabus design see the chapter by Allwright in Celce-Murcia (forthcoming).

NOTES

1. Prior to having an actual practice teaching assignment this background information may be fictional. Trainees should be encouraged, however, to write up cover sheets that reflect the teaching situation(s) they expect to encounter.

2. For certain kinds of language learning it may not be possible to state objectives in performance terms exclusively, in which case you may want to add one or two cognitive objectives to the lesson plan at this point (e.g., "The students will demonstrate their understanding of the poem by writing a paragraph explaining its meaning.").

3. Use the back of the sheet or separate, attached sheets to spell out the steps.

DISCUSSION QUESTIONS

1. What are the advantages and disadvantages of following a set format for lesson planning?

2. Should lesson planning be optional? Why or why not?

3. Do you feel that all of the pre-procedural information required by the lesson plan format is necessary? Why or why not? Might some of it not be applicable at times?

SUGGESTED ACTIVITIES

1. Visit an ESL class and fill out a cover sheet similar to the one provided in this chapter. Interview the teacher and students if possible. Say how the information obtained could be used in lesson planning.

2. Using the lesson plan format presented in this chapter, write a lesson plan for a point of grammar or a set of vocabulary items.

3. Using the format presented in this chapter, write an alternate version of the sample lesson plan that you feel would be equal to or better than the sample.

SUGGESTIONS FOR FURTHER READING

Popham, James W. (1970)
The Teacher-Empiricist. Santa Monica, Ca.: Tinnon-Brown.
An excellent resource on behavioral objectives—why they are important and how to write them.

Stevick, Earl W. (1957)
Helping People Learn English, Nashville: Abingdon Press.
Helpful suggestions on how to prepare for one's first class, classroom activities, etc.

Finnochiaro, Mary, and Michael Bonomo (1973)
The Foreign Language Learner: A Guide for Teachers, Chapter VI, Regents Publishing Company, Inc.

APPENDIX: SAMPLE COVER SHEET AND LESSON PLAN

Cover Sheet

Student Teacher _____ Caroline Morris _____

Regular Teacher _____ Ms. Bolter _____

Supervising/Coordinating Teacher _____ Mr. Evans _____

School _____ Lincoln Jr. High _____

Class _____ 9th grade _____

Learning Stage of Class _____ Intermediate _____

Age Level of Class _____ 14-17 years _____

Size of Class _____ 29 students _____

Linguistic/Ethnic Composition of Class _____ Chicano and Mexican _____

Other Relevant Factors _ Negative attitude toward English, low motivation _____

Lesson Plan

Student teacher's name _____ Caroline Morris _____

Date of presentation _____ Oct. 27 _____

Estimated Time of Lesson _____ 30 minutes _____

Teaching Point _ Vowel length differences before voiced and voiceless final stops _

- -

Pre-assessment Activity _ Analysis of student pronunciation errors from _____

taped conversations. _____

Relationship to Current Unit _ (None. One general listening-speaking problem is _

being treated per week.) _____

Pre-entry Performance _ Students have had a lesson on voiced and voiceless stops _

in initial position with focus on aspiration of voiceless _____

ones. _____

Performance Objectives

a. To distinguish aurally and orally between the two members in the following word-level minimal pairs using vowel length as the main factor (i.e., stops not fully released):

rope	beet	wick
robe	bead	wig

b. To distinguish aurally and orally between the two members in the following sentence-level minimal pairs using vowel length as the main factor (i.e., stops not fully released):

Where is the cab/cap?   Look at my back/bag.   I hid/hit the dog.

Criterion Level: <u>80% of the students will perform as specified at least 80%</u>

<u>of the time.</u>

Materials: <u>Blackboard, objects, pictures.</u>

— —

PROCEDURES (Student Activities):

Step 1 — Introduction
(1 minute)

	1	2
on board:	*rope*	*robe*
	beet	*bead*
	wick	*wig*

a. Students listen to teacher read words.
b. Students describe differences between words in (1) and (2): voiced, long vowel—voiceless, short vowel
c. Teacher notes that such words have been a problem and erases words on the board.

Step 2 — Students are shown a rope and a robe.
(3 minutes)

a. Teacher pronounces the words and puts the rope on one side of the blackboard, the robe on the other. Teacher says words at random and the students (class, then individuals) point to the appropriate object.
b. Students listen and repeat each word several times after teacher—emphasis on vowel length.
c. Teacher points to the objects at random and the students (class, then individuals) say the word.
d. A student comes up and points to the object and calls on classmates to respond.

Step 3 — Present a picture of a man with a cap on his head and another one of a taxi on a highway. Attach them to opposite ends of the blackboard.
(6 minutes)

a. Teacher: *Where is the cap?*   *On his head.*
               Where is the cab?   *On the highway.*
    (Several times while pointing to appropriate picture.)
b. Students (class, then individuals) respond with either *On his head* or *On the highway*, depending on teacher's question.
c. Students (class, then individuals) respond with either *The cap* or *The cab*, depending on whether teacher says: *What's on his head?* or *What's on the highway?*
d. One student comes to the front and teacher goes to the back (others look only at student in front). If teacher taps her head, student says: *Where is the cap?* If teacher pretends to drive, student says: *Where is the cab?* Several other students do this.

Step 4 — Show a beet (a picture or a real vegetable) and a large bead (from a necklace) to the class. Repeat procedure used for *rope* and *robe* in Step 2.
(3 minutes)

Step 5 — Show class a stuffed toy dog. Hide him behind the desk and then hit him on the nose. Follow procedure of Step 3 using the following phrases and rejoinders:
(6 minutes)

> *I hit the dog.*   *(on the nose)*
> *I hid the dog.*   *(behind the desk)*

Step 6 — Show a candle with a large wick and a wig to the class. Repeat procedure used with *rope* and *robe* in Step 2.
(3 minutes)

Step 7 — Arrange in advance for a student to come up to the front (he has a broad back and a bag full of books, papers, pencils, etc.). Follow procedure of Step 3 using the following phrases and rejoinders:
(6 minutes)

> *Look at Juan's bag.*   *(It's full.)*
> *Look at Juan's back.*   *(It's broad.)*

Step 8 — Students take a short listening quiz utilizing all words practiced to see if they all hear the distinctions. (Skill in production can be judged informally from individual class performances.)
(2 minutes)

Assignment: None

Contingency plans: Let students make up their own question and answer sequences to present to the class using the words or sentences I have prepared.

Comment/Self-evaluation: The lesson took longer than expected. One more pair of words and sentences needed for each contrast. Some students dominated—others got unruly. A fairly good though not brilliant lesson. Contingency plan should have been the final part of the lesson.

SELECTING AND EVALUATING A TEXTBOOK

Abdel-Messih Daoud *and*
Marianne Celce-Murcia

INTRODUCTION

In any language teaching-learning situation success depends on giving proper consideration to both human elements, such as the role of the teacher, the nature of the learner(s), etc., and also to non-human elements such as the textbook, the syllabus, the number of hours allocated to language study, etc. In this chapter the problems involved in selecting an English language textbook will be discussed and a procedure for textbook evaluation will be presented.[1]

We feel that this information is useful since it is sometimes part of the ESL/EFL teacher's responsibility to select the textbook s/he will use in a given class. Such a decision should be made carefully and systematically, not arbitrarily. Furthermore, even in countries and school systems where the choice of the textbook does not directly involve the teacher (i.e., adoptions are the responsibility of the school board or the state), teachers are often asked to submit reports on the value and usefulness of the prescribed language texts they are using. Most of the information given here would also be helpful in the preparation of such an evaluation.

PRELIMINARY INFORMATION

Before one even begins to look for potentially appropriate texts, certain information should be gathered and explicitly stated. This preliminary information includes:

**1. Background Information on
    the Students:**
a.   age range;

b.   proficiency level in English;
c.   sex distribution (segregated, or if mixed, what percentage of M/F?);
d.   level of general education;
e.   background language(s) (homogeneous, heterogeneous);
f.   reasons for studying English (is it required or optional, is it professionally or socially advantageous?).

**2. Course Syllabus
    (whether predetermined or left to the
    teacher):**
a.   relative emphasis given to each skill (listening, speaking, reading, writing);
b.   those tasks each skill is needed for most (e.g., reading technical literature in physics);
c.   relative emphasis given to each language area (grammar, vocabulary, pronunciation);
d.   the use to which the language material will be put (e.g., how much of the vocabulary will be used for recognition or for both recognition and production purposes?);
e.   relative attention given to mechanics (penmanship, spelling, punctuation).

3. Institutional Data
a.   typical class size;
b.   time: years and/or hours per week allocated to the study of English;
c.   type of physical environment/support (i.e., classroom size, flexibility of the

seating arrangement, blackboard space, audiovisual equipment);

d. preferred dialect of English (British, American, other);

e. institutional or national objectives for English instruction;

f. nature and form of any required internal/external English language examination.

SURVEY, ANALYSIS, AND JUDGMENT

Once this background information has been clearly spelled out, the ESL/EFL teacher who is free to select his or her own textbook should try to find five to ten texts that appear to be superficially appropriate for a given class. This initial selection process can be done as a survey.

The First Step: Survey

Skim through the Introduction, the Table of Contents, the Text, and the Glossary or Index in order to get an idea about the purpose, organization, and method of presentation, as well as the range and kind of materials that the book includes.

Texts that seem to agree with the previously specified preliminary requirements should be set aside for further consideration.

The next step in the evaluation process requires more careful analysis of the textbook and also of the teacher's manual, if there is one.

The Second Step: Analysis

Carefully examine and state the content of the Textbook and the Teacher's Manual. These data should be recorded and organized in the following way:

The Textbook:
a. Subject matter (topics, contexts)
b. Vocabulary and structures covered
c. Exercises
d. Illustrations
e. Physical make-up (cover, size, binding, paper, printing, type, lay-out of the page)

The Teacher's Manual:
a. General features (Is a rationale provided? Is there a useful index with references made to the textbook? Are answers supplied for all textbook exercises?)

b. Type and amount of supplementary exercises for each language skill (i.e., listening, speaking, reading, writing)

c. Methodological/pedagogical guidance in the presentation of lessons/exercises and the use of aids, etc.

d. Linguistic background information— perhaps from contrastive analysis or error analysis (grammar, vocabulary, pronunciation)

The Third Step: Judging

The above analysis may narrow down the choice to two or three textbooks. To arrive at a final decision, the teacher must make judgments about certain quantitative and qualitative elements of the textbook and the teacher's manual (if there is one). If a distinction can be maintained between steps 2 and 3, namely the recording of the data and the evaluation of the same, subjective error, which is often the reason for difference of opinion among raters, can be minimized to a great extent. To this end the suggested checklist that follows may prove useful as a tool to use in the judging process. Each question raises a point that should be taken into account in each category. The teacher/rater evaluates the textbook for each question by making a check in the appropriate column according to the following rating scale:

Excellent	4
Good	3
Adequate	2
Weak	1
Totally lacking	0

The three processes—surveying, analyzing, and judging (rating the questions)—form one integrated whole, which aids in objective selection of textbook(s).

THE CHECKLIST

The Textbook

	Excellent	Good	Adequate	Weak	Totally lacking
	4	3	2	1	0

a. Subject matter
    1. Does the subject matter cover a variety of topics appropriate to the interests of the learners for whom the textbook is intended (urban or rural environment; child or adult learners; male and/or female students)?
    2. Is the ordering of materials done by topics or themes that are arranged in a logical fashion?
    3. Is the content graded according to the needs of the students or the requirements of the existing syllabus (if there is one)?
    4. Is the material accurate and up-to-date?

b. Vocabulary and structures
    1. Does the vocabulary load (i.e., the number of new words introduced every lesson) seem to be reasonable for the students of that level?
    2. Are the vocabulary items controlled to ensure systematic gradation from simple to complex items?
    3. Is the new vocabulary repeated in subsequent lessons for reinforcement?
    4. Does the sentence length seem reasonable for the students of that level?
    5. Is the number of grammatical points as well as their sequence appropriate?
    6. Do the structures gradually increase in complexity to suit the growing reading ability of the students?
    7. Does the writer use current everyday language, and sentence structures that follow normal word order?
    8. Do the sentences and paragraphs follow one another in a logical sequence?
    9. Are linguistic items introduced in meaningful situations to facilitate understanding and ensure assimilation and consolidation?

c. Exercises
    1. Do the exercises develop comprehension and test knowledge of main ideas, details, and sequence of ideas?
    2. Do the exercises involve vocabulary and structures which build up the learner's repertoire?
    3. Do the exercises provide practice in different types of written work (sentence completion, spelling and dictation, guided composition)?
    4. Does the book provide a pattern of review within lessons and cumulatively test new material?
    5. Do the exercises promote meaningful communication by referring to realistic activities and situations?

d. Illustrations
    1. Do illustrations create a favorable atmosphere for practice in reading and spelling by depicting realism and action?
    2. Are the illustrations clear, simple, and free of unnecessary details that may confuse the learner?
    3. Are the illustrations printed close enough to the text and directly related to the content to help the learner understand the printed text?

e. Physical make-up
    1. Is the cover of the book durable enough to withstand wear?
    2. Is the text attractive (i.e., cover, page appearance, binding)?

3. Does the size of the book seem convenient for the students to handle?

4. Is the type size appropriate for the intended learners?

The Teacher's Manual

a. General features

1. Does the Manual help the teacher understand the rationale of the Text-book (objectives, methodology)?

2. Does the Manual guide the teacher to any set syllabus for that level?

3. Does the index of the Manual guide the teacher to the vocabulary, structures, and topics found in the Textbook?

4. Are correct or suggested answers provided for all of the exercises in the textbook?

5. Is the rationale for the given sequence of grammar points clearly stated?

b. Type and amount of supplementary exercises for each language skill

1. Does the Manual provide material for training the students in listening and understanding the spoken language?

2. Does the Manual provide material for training the students in oral expression?

3. Does the Manual suggest adequate and varied oral exercises for reinforcing points of grammar presented in the textbook?

4. Does the Manual provide drills and exercises that enable the teacher to help the students build up their vocabulary?

5. Does the Manual provide questions to help the teacher test the students' reading comprehension?

6. Does the Manual provide adequate graded material for additional writing practice?

c. Methodological/pedagogical guidance

1. Does the Manual help the teacher with each new type of lesson introduced?

2. Does the Manual provide suggestions to help the teacher review old lessons and introduce new lessons?

3. Does the Manual provide practical suggestions for teaching pronunciation and intonation?

4. Does the Manual provide suggestions to help the teacher introduce new reading passages?

5. Does the Manual provide guidance to the teacher for introducing various types of written work?

6. Does the Manual provide guidance to the teacher for evaluating written work and identifying the students' most serious mistakes?

7. Does the Manual advise the teacher on the use of audiovisual aids?

d. Linguistic background information

1. Does the Manual provide contrastive information for the teacher on likely pronunciation problems?

2. Are English vocabulary items and English structures well explained?

3. Are lists of cognate words (true and false cognates) provided for the teacher?

4. Does the Manual provide information on grammar to help the teacher explain grammatical patterns presented in the lessons and anticipate likely problems (i.e., data from contrastive analysis and error analysis)?

Such an evaluation process, especially if it is carried out by three or more experienced teachers, should clearly reveal the most suitable text. Any rating disagreement(s) would become obvious by comparing the Checklists of the raters and could then be reconciled by discussion and further examination of the text(s) in question. Also, there may be other important questions to consider that we have not included, such as the cost of the text (Rivers, 1968), i.e., it should not be so expensive that the students or the school district cannot afford it. Weighting is another important factor we have not mentioned, i.e., teachers may well feel that certain of the items on the above checklist are more important than others; when this is the case, these more important items should be given correspondingly more weight in the judging process. Likewise, it may also be important to consider the teacher's personal preferences along the lines suggested by Chastain (1976: 529):

By selecting a text with a content which can be personalized to the student's interests, the teacher can more readily provide opportunities for real language practice. . . . By selecting a text which includes the people as well as the language, the teacher can more readily help his students to relate to the language. And by selecting a text in which provision is made for daily homework, the teacher can more easily expand the number of student contact hours with the language.

A strictly objective checklist may not adequately emphasize such factors, but where they are important, they must also be considered.

Of course, "no text or set of materials has all the answers, and no reviewer can foresee all the situations in which the textbook might be used" (Cowles, 1976). The ultimate evaluation of a text comes with actual classroom use. It would, therefore, be useful for the ESL/EFL teacher using a newly adopted text to evaluate it at the end of the term (as well as prior to selection), perhaps using the identical checklist both times, so that the selected text could be re-evaluated on the basis of classroom experience. This will help the teacher to decide whether to continue with the adopted text or to look for a new one. And even if the ESL/EFL teacher is satisfied, s/he should always be on the lookout for new and better texts since no existing textbook is perfect. To

do this s/he should visit book exhibits at professional conventions, make regular checks at the nearest libraries containing ESL/EFL materials, and look at the textbook advertisements in publications intended for teachers of English to speakers of other languages.

NOTE

1.   Relatively little has been published on this topic. One of the authors has done research in this area: A. M. Daoud (1970). In addition to the references and the suggestions for further reading, some information from Clifford Prator's unpublished guidelines for textbook evaluation, regularly distributed in his ESL methodology courses, has been incorporated into this chapter. Some other information comes from suggestions made by Lois McIntosh (personal communication).

DISCUSSION QUESTIONS

1.   If you have taught/are teaching ESL or EFL, how were/are textbooks selected? How much responsibility (if any) did/do teachers have in this area? Is the selection systematic or arbitrary? Explain.

2.   If several ESL/EFL instructors are all teaching the same course and they are jointly responsible for selecting the textbook, what do you feel the optimal selection procedure would be?

3.   What are the various things you could do if you were teaching an ESL/EFL class for which there was a prescribed but totally inadequate textbook?

SUGGESTED ACTIVITIES

1.   If you have taught, are currently teaching, or will soon be teaching an ESL/EFL class, evaluate the textbook you have used/are using/ or will be using according to the checklist provided in this chapter. What are the text's strengths and weaknesses? How much work does it demand of the teacher?

2.   Describe in detail the type of ESL/EFL class you expect to be teaching next. (Use the outline for background information provided at the beginning of this chapter.) Go to the library and find two or more suitable texts. Then use

the checklist in this chapter to evaluate the texts. Which is the most appropriate text? Why?

3. Suppose that you are an EFL teacher in Europe and that you have been hired to teach a basic English conversation class for adults who speak no English but who want to learn some English before they spend a month's vacation in the U.S. The class will run three months and will meet two nights a week. What will your teaching priorities be? State them. Then go to the library and survey texts. Find at least two suitable texts. Analyze them according to step two (i.e., Analysis) of the evaluation procedure described in this chapter. State which one of the texts would be more appropriate, and why.

SUGGESTIONS FOR FURTHER READING

Chastain, K. (1976)
Developing Second-Language Skills, second edition. Chicago: Rand McNally.
In Appendix 2, "Selecting a Basic Text: A Subjective Evaluation," pp. 523-530, Chastain gives some broad and general assumptions and guidelines for selecting a language textbook.

Cowles, Hovy M. (1976)
"Textbook Materials Evaluation. A Comprehensive Checklist," in *Foreign Language Annals*, Vol. 9, No. 4.

This checksheet was created and progressively refined at Vermont Academy in Saxtons River, Vermont. According to the author, it has been of assistance for several years in evaluating supplementary materials as well as materials being considered for revised foreign language curricula. It has also been used to evaluate sample materials which arrive in the mail and for which no immediate use is planned.

Dubin, F., and E. Olshtain (1977)
Facilitating Language Learning: A Guidebook for the ESL/EFL Teacher, New York: McGraw-Hill.
A section entitled "Shopping for Textbooks," pp. 231-234, provides 27 questions that the teacher should consider in textbook selection.

Papalia, Anthony (1976)
Learner-Centered Language Teaching: Methods and Materials. Rowley, Mass.: Newbury House.
The checklist (pp. 176-179) presented by Papalia is based on the criteria established by the Modern Language Association in the appendices of its selective list of Materials, for judging basic texts. Papalia's checklist has been developed to provide guidance for the selection of foreign language textbooks.

Rivers, Wilga M. (1968)
Teaching Foreign Language Skills, University of Chicago Press, pp. 368-371.
The reader can find a set of guidelines which s/he could easily convert into a format usable for an actual textbook evaluation.

For further discussion of several of the issues involved in textbook use and selection, see the articles by Buckingham, Durrance, Kottmeyer, and Lodge in *The Phi Delta Kappan*, vol. 33, no. 5, Jan., 1952.

LANGUAGE TEACHING AIDS

Marianne Celce-Murcia

INTRODUCTION

In an earlier chapter of this textbook (p. 38), Heaton justifies and develops an audiovisual method for ESL; he also outlines the five basic media that are used in most language lessons:

1. the teacher
2. the students
3. the chalkboard
4. the textbook
5. the classroom.

Heaton convincingly argues that, even in language classes where these five basic media are appropriately exploited, they provide neither enough realism nor an adequate variety of contexts to ensure optimal language learning on the part of the students. Heaton's solution is to use professional quality slide shows with realistic, synchronized tape-recorded dialogues or narratives accompanying them as the core of a language course. He also suggests that many other audiovisual resources be tapped for additional verité materials (i.e, radio, television, movies, etc.).

Heaton's proposals, however, are not always feasible. For example, if appropriate slide shows and tapes are not already available, much time and labor are required to prepare them. Furthermore, not all ESL teachers have the time and/or skill and/or financial resources to prepare high quality technical materials. Alternatively, the ESL syllabus may be so tightly structured around a given textbook or a given skill (e.g., reading) that such elaborate audiovisual materials would not be the most efficient materials to use. In addition, in some areas of the world where ESL is taught, there may be no technical equipment—in some places, even no reliable source of electricity. Other similar situations could be cited; however, this chapter argues that even in those situations where a highly intensive and technically-oriented audiovisual method would not apply for one reason or another, the ESL teacher can still improve any given language lesson for any given group of students by using one or more well-selected teaching aids to supplement the five basic media listed above.

Stevick (1957:74) has defined an "audiovisual aid" as ". . . anything audible or visible which helps your student learn the language more quickly or more accurately. . . ." Sight and hearing are the two senses used most in human teaching and learning activities of any kind, and thus receive primary consideration in the development and/or selection of language teaching aids. However, the ESL teacher should not forget to exploit the other three senses—touch, taste, and smell—where appropriate. For example, the meaning of adjective oppositions such as *rough* and *smooth* or *wet* and *dry* are taught most efficiently through the sense of touch. And what better way is there for an ESL teacher to give a class an idea of what a chocolate-chip cookie or peanut brittle is than to give each student a taste of the item under discussion. Likewise, herbs and flowers can be identified by their odor as well as their appearance—something that should be exploited where relevant. However, the typical language teaching aid is something that is visual, auditory, or both, as the following discussion of such aids indicates.

For our purposes language teaching aids can be divided into two main categories: *Technical* and *Non-technical*. The technical aids involve machinery and/or require electricity while the non-technical aids require neither machinery nor electricity but are simple, inexpensive aids that the resourceful teacher can acquire or make on his or her own.

TECHNICAL PROJECTED AIDS

As Allen and Valette (1974) have suggested, the technical aids can be further subdivided into projected and non-projected aids. The projected aids include the following, each of which will be briefly discussed in turn:

a. The overhead projector, and overhead transparencies
b. The opaque projector
c. Slides
d. Filmstrips
e. Movies
f. Videotape
g. Television

The Overhead Projector

The overhead projector allows the ESL teacher to project on a wall or screen printed or pictorial materials that are reproduced either professionally or by the individual teacher on 8" x 11" acetate transparencies (clear or colored). Felt-tipped pens of different colors but with small tips are used for preparing teacher-made transparencies.

This aid is extremely flexible: the teacher may use it without turning his or her back to the class. Answers or blanks can be left in a text to be filled in by hand by the teacher (or a student) while the lesson is in progress. Likewise, it is easy for the teacher to cover up an answer while showing just the question to a class. After a student has volunteered an answer, the teacher can uncover the correct answer and use it either as a confirmation or a correction. Materials with blanks to be filled in can be prepared using permanent ink pens and then filled in with washable ink pens in class so that they can be used several times (with different classes or different teachers). Also the acetate sheets can be cut into small strips to provide vivid graphic practice in carrying out word-order changes or the addition, deletion, or substitution of words or grammatical elements—e.g.

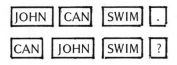

The possibilities for using this aid effectively in the ESL classroom are virtually limitless: it has been used for class/group correction of composition errors, for spontaneous class/group composition of a paragraph, for explanation of grammatical or phonological rules, for presentation of exercises to practice grammar, for teaching composition, reading, or vocabulary, and many other things. In addition there is a thermofax process that allows typed materials to be transferred to transparencies, giving this aid added possibilities.

The Opaque Projector

The opaque projector is useful in that it permits the ESL teacher to project in enlarged form for the whole class to see: a picture, a map, paragraph, etc., from a book or magazine. Naturally, language exercises from textbooks that the students do not have can also be directly projected, as can paragraphs or compositions that the teacher wishes to use as models, or student-written work that the teacher wants to use as a basis for a class correction exercise. This aid is useful in that many existing printed materials (texts, pictures, charts, etc.) that are too small for all the students to see if the teacher holds them up in front of the class, can

be projected in an enlarged form and used to good advantage with the whole class seeing them clearly at the same time.

Slides

Slides, whether purchased commercially or shot and developed by the individual teacher, can make a unique contribution to the ESL classroom. They can be used for cultural orientation as well as for teaching grammar, vocabulary, pronunciation, and for providing the stimulus for practice in speaking, reading, or writing skills. Slides are usually in color and provide large, life-like images and stimuli for practicing language in real-world contexts. As Heaton has indicated in his chapter, when coordinated with a well-written, well-recorded sound track on audiotape, they are even more effective. However, this sound-track is not necessary. The ESL teacher can read an accompanying script (i.e., dialogue, narrative, exercise cues, etc.) while showing the slides and still be extremely effective. Also many media centers will prepare slides of printed materials quickly and inexpensively for the ESL teacher who particularly enjoys using this medium. Thus colorful maps, charts, exercises, etc., can all be projected using slides.

Filmstrips

Commercial filmstrips exist in large numbers (some have an accompanying audiotape sound track), and they are fairly inexpensive to purchase and easy to use (i.e., the machinery is not complicated); however, many of the available commercial filmstrips have been developed not specifically for language instruction but for teaching science, history, or some other subject. Even in such cases, a good filmstrip can—in the hands of a resourceful teacher—be used for practicing language skills. Some ESL teachers even make their own filmstrips on blank strips of the filmstrip acetate with the pre-punched holes on each side. They draw small stick figures, objects, words, etc., using the colored ink pens that have the finest points. The process is inexpensive and the product is colorful, amusing, and especially effective if the teacher can actively involve the class in discussing the content of the filmstrip.

Movies

Most schools or universities have a library of English-language movies that teachers can use or the schools have access to a service through which movies can be inexpensively rented for use in the classroom. Even where such facilities are not available, the local cinema can be used for a class field trip. This medium is especially effective with intermediate and advanced students although use with beginners should not be ruled out. I know of individuals who have literally learned English by watching hundreds of movies. If well selected, commercial films are a good source of information on American life and language. Educational films may also be available. The teacher should always preview films and prepare the class with background information on what they are about to see (and hear) and should ideally give them tasks to perform or questions to answer while viewing the film. Home-made movies or movies made by the teacher and the class offer possibilities if the teacher has the interest and skill to lead the class in such an activity.

Television

Television has been used in the ESL classroom in two ways. The main use has been to air professionally developed English language lessons to large numbers of students in remote classrooms on a regular basis. These students, if they have an English teacher at all, typically have an ill-qualified teacher and/or poor classroom materials, so they can profit from viewing and perhaps even participating in a TV class led by a native or near-native speaking teacher skilled in using ESL techniques. Such language lessons have also been used in situations where teachers are well-trained but in short supply so that additional language study time could be provided for the students.

A secondary application of television in the ESL classroom has been the use by some teachers of regular programs that are produced by commercial or educational television and that are on the air during classtime. Regular viewing of a short program followed by discussion of events, vocabulary, etc., can greatly enrich the language learning experience of the students and can establish a context that exists outside the classroom for use in speaking and writing exercises.

Videotape

The videotape recorder when used with a monitor and playback capability is much more useful and flexible in the ESL classroom than a television set. If the teacher has pre-recorded videotape and the playback equipment, a given language lesson can be shown to the class at the most suitable time—not just when it is on the air. In addition, the VTR is extremely effective when used to record during the class itself. The students can be videotaped giving speeches or doing exercises, and this can then be played back for self-evaluation or self and peer correction, etc. A given segment can be viewed as many times as necessary. If the whole class is videotaped (teacher and students), the teacher can observe his or her own teaching and look for areas to improve, as well as noting with greater accuracy the most serious language performance errors of his or her students. Previously, such elaborate equipment was too expensive for all but the richest, largest schools; however, now small, inexpensive portable VTR systems are available, and can be used profitably in many ESL instructional situations. It should be added, however, that the cost of repair and maintenance is fairly high and must also be considered at the time of purchase; i.e., it is no use investing in such equipment if it can't be properly maintained.

TECHNICAL NON-PROJECTED AIDS

Technical but non-projected aids usually can operate on batteries as well as on electricity, and are thus more reliable in some situations than projected technical aids. These are the phonograph, the tape recorder (which on a large, multiple scale is the language laboratory), the radio, and multi-copied materials, i.e., dittos, mimeographs, photocopies. We shall briefly discuss below each of these aids in the language teaching context:

The Phonograph

Many commercial phonograph records are available to supplement instruction in the language classroom. Record libraries where teachers can check out records exist at most schools and universities. Here we do not simply mean dialogues and songs recorded in the language being studied, but also readings of short stories, poems, essays, speeches, etc. (often available in the voice of the author). The resourceful ESL teacher who has access to a phonograph can make good and regular use of this aid in the classroom to enrich the language learning experience of his or her students.

The Tape Recorder

The tape recorder was the first technical aid to be used extensively in the language classroom. It was used to bring in the voices of native speakers and to bring in the songs and stories representing the culture of the language being learned in the classroom. And with the advent of the audiolingual method, where pronunciation and repetition drills become so important, came the language laboratory—a complex of tape recorders set up for individual use by all members of a class at the same time.

As Stevick points out (1957:76) a tape recorder is like a phonograph in that it makes it possible for the students to listen to English spoken by a native speaker, even when the teacher is doing something else. Stevick continues:

... unlike the phonograph, the tape recorder lets you record exactly, the stories, the sentences, or the words you want your students to hear. It also lets you erase what you no longer need or what you don't like, and record something else in its place. The tape recorder can be invaluable in multiplying your students' listening hours. The tape recorder offers one other advantage: your students can listen to themselves as well as to a recorded native speaker. Hearing oneself on a machine is a wonderful way to become vividly aware of one's own shortcomings. That is particularly true if the native speaker's voice is recorded together with one's own.

There are two ways to get the two voices on the tape together. One, of course, is for the native and the student to record together. The other is through use of a "binaural" recorder. The binaural recorder uses two sound tracks instead of one. The native can put his voice on one track while the student uses the other. When the tape is in use, only the student's track is erased and re-recorded, whereas the master track remains.

At the present time a tape recorder uses audiotape that is either on reels or in cassettes,

the latter being especially handy for the mechanically inept teacher. Even where electricity is not available, battery-operated tape recorders can be used. The binaural system described above by Stevick is, of course, a feature commonly built into each individual console in a language laboratory. For a specific and detailed discussion of the way a language laboratory is set up and used, see Lado, 1964, pp. 173-193.

The Radio

The radio was and is being used in the language classroom in much the same way and for much the same purposes as television, which has already been discussed above—i.e., to air language lessons or regular programs. Many ESL teachers make special use of tape-recorded radio broadcasts, especially short news features (i.e., two to three minutes) dealing with current problems, important personalities, or current events, etc., to give their students guided practice in listening comprehension. In such a radio broadcast the rate of speech is usually faster than normal speech. Thus with less than advanced students it helps if the ESL teacher prepares the students for what they are about to hear and then allows them to listen to the broadcast several times over, telling them what to listen for each time, e.g.

i. listen for the general theme;
ii. listen for general facts—a, b, c;
iii. listen for specific details—a, b, c.

More detailed instructions for use of this procedure can be found in Brinton and Gaskill (1978).

Reproduced Materials

The possibility of quickly and easily producing multiple copies of materials—reproduced with a ditto machine, a mimeograph machine, or a photocopier—can greatly increase an ESL teacher's creativity and flexibility and can also save a lot of time. Texts or pictures that the teacher wants to use with a copy for each student must be typed, handwritten or drawn on ditto masters or mimeograph stencils. Ditto masters usually produce about a hundred legible copies and then wear out. They also age rapidly.

Mimeograph stencils, on the other hand, can be used to produce many more copies and they produce good copies for a long period of time. Photocopies are quick and easy to produce. The master can be a typed, handwritten or hand-drawn page or a combination of these; it can be a page out of a magazine or a collage/composite specially prepared by the teacher. It is the most flexible reproduction process the ESL teacher can use. Its disadvantage is that it is much more expensive than dittoed or mimeographed copying. However, a ditto master can be made from a clear dark photocopy through a thermofax process, and this possibility can save the ESL teacher time and money when producing copies.

NON-TECHNICAL AIDS

Next, I would like to discuss non-technical teaching aids very briefly to remind the ESL teacher of the wealth of materials s/he can develop in this area—especially if s/he is in a school or area where none of the previously mentioned technical aids are available. Detailed suggestions and instructions concerning the production and use of non-technical aids can be found in Finocchiaro (1974:100-116) and in Dubin and Olshtain (1977:106-110).

Board-based Aids
The universal board-based aid is the chalkboard, to which the teacher can introduce greater flexibility and variety by using colored as well as white chalk, and by writing things on the board and covering them up for later use during the class hour. If there is plenty of chalkboard space, students can profitably do some of their practice at the board instead of at their desks.

Three other commonly used board-based aids are the *flannel board*, the *magnetic board*, and the *pegboard*. When flannel is stretched tightly over a piece of plywood, pictures, letters, and words that also have a piece of flannel glued to the back adhere to the flannel board easily and also can be moved around with ease by either the students or the teacher. This aid lends itself especially well to practicing the ordering of linguistic or visual elements, e.g., (spelling) letters in a word, (alphabetizing)

words in a list, (grammar) words in a sentence, (composition) sentences in a paragraph, furniture in a house or room, a table setting for a meal, etc.

The magnetic board is a large sheet of aluminum or a large cookie sheet. Letters, numbers, and pictures with small magnets on the back can then be placed on the board and manipulated much in the manner described above for the flannel board. Colorful plastic letters with magnets, numbers, and objects are available from several commercial toy firms. Small magnets can also be purchased inexpensively for glueing or attaching to the back of pictures.

A pegboard can be purchased at most lumber yards. It is a large flat piece of treated and pressed wood or paper with a small hole every two inches. The pegboard can be mounted on the wall and small wooden pegs or nails can be used to hang numbers, pictures, letters, etc., on the board. These visuals can also be moved around easily from hole to hole on the board.

Pictures
Pictures are a very flexible language teaching aid. They should be large and clear enough to use from the front of the room with the whole class (i.e., about 7" x 10" or larger with a clear, uncomplicated image). The teacher should always check for clarity in the pictures s/he wants to use from the back of the classroom in advance of presentation to the class.

It is good to mount the pictures on pieces of posterboard larger than the pictures themselves so that they can be held up without the hand covering part of the picture. In this way the pictures can also be lined up along the shelf of the chalkboard for reference and/or discussion. Pictures can be black and white or colored. They can be cut out of magazines or drawn by the teacher, by friends of the teacher, or perhaps by the students themselves. Pictures can be used, whether the students are children or adults, for teaching vocabulary, practicing grammar, stimulating writing practice, and for many other activities. Every ESL teacher should be actively developing his or her own picture file.

Flashcards and Sentence-strips

Flashcards are words or simple pictures (or both) mounted on posterboard-weight cards. For use in a class, they should be at least 7" x 10" in size: smaller flashcards may be used for tutorial/small group work. Flashcards can be used to teach or review vocabulary, pronunciation of difficult sounds, sound-letter correspondences, etc. It is always a good idea for the ESL teacher to develop sets of flashcards to review points covered in previous lessons. The cards can then be used whenever there is a bit of extra classtime available. Flashcards extended to the sentence level are sentence strips, i.e., sentences written on long narrow strips of posterboard.

John went to school yesterday

These strips are useful aids in reading lessons. They can also be used to present model sentences or sentences that the students should copy, i.e., sight dictation.

Charts and Scrolls

Charts are a natural extension of pictures and flashcards. They are an organized composite that allows the ESL teacher to present several pictures or objects simultaneously so that grammatical objectives such as count vs. mass nouns can be practiced (if, for instance, all the usual breakfast food items are represented) or a particular verb tense can be practiced (if a series of related activities is presented). A series of contextually related and physically connected charts is often called a flip chart—this is where the first chart might give the rule or the model sentence and following charts might supply contexts for practice. Some ESL teachers apply the same concept using a large artists' sketch pad. They prepare drills and examples on successive pages of the pad and just flip the pages over as the lesson progresses. Another similar idea is use of the scroll technique. A story or an extended exercise can unfold in front of the class while the exercise is in progress. Aids such as flip charts and scrolls create suspense and thus help arouse interest in the students.

Word and Picture Pockets

In classrooms where there is no chalkboard ledge or other long shelf for the language teacher to use, a word and picture pocket should be made. The teacher can use sturdy cloth (i.e., felt, denim) or posterboard for this purpose. The pocket should be 5 or 6 feet long and deep enough to easily support 7" x 10" pictures and flashcards. The pocket can be used to reorder words in sentences, to practice vocabulary and pronunciation, and for many other purposes. Also, several pockets can be attached to a very large chart so that words and cards can be manipulated up and down as well as back and forth.

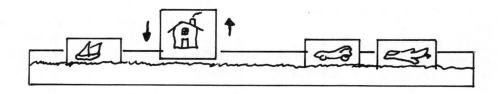

Realia

The final category of aids that I will discuss, realia, is truly limitless. The more of the following items that the ESL teacher can incorporate into language lessons, the better. I will merely list some suggested realia and give a few teaching implications for each item suggested as a reminder of all the commonplace resources that could be very effectively used in the language classroom:

- A large calendar: to teach dates, days of the week, months of the year, past tense, present tense, future tense, etc.
- Large maps and/or a large globe: to teach English names of countries, regions, continents, oceans, etc.
- Puzzles: crossword puzzles to reinforce vocabulary; interesting picture puzzles for group work and oral discussion centered on guessing what the finished picture will look like.
- A large clock with movable hands to teach the language of telling time in English (and to teach numbers, if necessary).
- Menus: to talk about food and how one orders food and pays for it in a restaurant.
- A suitcase full of clothing: to teach clothing vocabulary for common items, and to practice certain count and noncount nouns.
- Postcards, letters, stamps: the whole vocabulary of correspondence and the post office could be introduced in this manner.
- Magazines, newspapers: to stimulate reading and discussion of current events.
- Travel posters and brochures: to discuss means of transportation, travel vocabulary, or perhaps just points of interest to visit in the area.
- Food (or food containers): to practice food vocabulary and what to expect at the local supermarket.
- A large paper thermometer where the mercury reading can be changed by hand: to practice temperature readings

and to discuss the weather (e.g., a roll of red crêpe paper that one can roll up and down).

- Hand puppets: a way for the teacher to model a dialogue more realistically. Also, with hand puppets some shy students will practice language more willingly when hiding behind a puppet than they will without a guise.
- Money (play or real): to learn the vocabulary of American currency, asking for change, giving change, counting money, etc.
- Mirrors: to practice pronunciation of sounds like /æ/ and /ð/, and grammar objectives such as reflexive pronouns.
- Pictures of traffic signals and signs: to practice the vocabulary of road safety.
- A table setting: to discuss the vocabulary involved in the tableware and the eating habits of Americans.

The responsible and well-trained ESL teacher must be aware of all the teaching aids that s/he might have at hand. S/he must then select and use those aids that best serve the objectives of the lesson, the needs of the students, and his or her own teaching style.

To conclude this brief overview I quote Dubin and Olshtain (1977:110) on the value of language teaching aids:

... if used effectively, they add a very important dimension to classroom activities. The modern language classroom must contain a variety of such aids, if it is to provide the learner with an active teaching-learning situation.

DISCUSSION QUESTIONS

1. Should the ESL teacher make a conscious effort to use teaching aids in the classroom? Why or why not?

2. What are the arguments for and against the use of technical teaching aids in the ESL classroom?

3. Some ESL teachers have no artistic ability. Are they justified in claiming that they should not use drawings as aids in the ESL classroom?

SUGGESTED ACTIVITIES

1. Observe an ESL class. What was the objective of the lesson? What aids did the teacher use? Think of additional aids that would have improved the lesson.

2. Explore the potential use of either the overhead projector or videotape in the ESL classroom. Go into greater detail than was done in this chapter. Examine the advantages and the drawbacks. Develop a number of original teaching applications for the teaching aid you are exploring.

3. Buy a stack of magazines at a used book store and begin a picture file. Be sure to clip out only those pictures that can be seen well at a distance (i.e., from the back of the room). Develop a lesson using some of the pictures you have selected.

SUGGESTIONS FOR FURTHER READING

Dubin, F., and E. Olshtain (1977)
Facilitating Language Learning. New York: McGraw-Hill, pp. 106-110.
The authors present several clear, simple suggestions concerning the construction and use of teacher-made aids.

Finocchiaro, Mary (1974)
ESL from Theory to Practice. New York: Regents, pp. 100-116.
Her section "Some Materials of Instruction" is one of the best and most complete statements on this topic concerning what's possible and available.

Lado, R. (1964)
Language Teaching. New York: McGraw-Hill, pp. 194-203.
Lado provides a useful list of visual aids and makes some especially interesting comments on the use of television. See also chapter 17 on the language laboratory.

Stevick, Earl (1957)
Helping People Learn English. Nashville: Abingdon Press, pp. 74-78.
In addition to general remarks on the use of audiovisual aids, useful specific suggestions are offered on the use of the flannelgraph (board), opaque projector, filmstrips, tape recorder, and movies.

CLASSROOM SKILLS FOR ESL TEACHERS

Kathleen M. Bailey *and*
Marianne Celce-Murcia

INTRODUCTION

Teaching English as a second language has now come to be recognized as a legitimate profession. Many people realize that being an effective ESL teacher demands training and practice. Being a native speaker of English, or a fairly fluent non-native speaker, is not enough. Yet because of credentialing policies and financial pressures on school districts, many ESL teachers in the public schools have gained experience without much formal training. On the other hand, young teachers just entering the profession may leave their university training with limited practical experience, in spite of strong theoretical preparation.

It is the purpose of this chapter to address both groups of teachers by considering some current research findings and exploring their possible classroom applications. We will first suggest four significant areas of classroom interaction that ESL teachers should be aware of in planning a language lesson and in analyzing their own teaching: the social climate, the variety in learning activities, the opportunity for student participation, and the need for feedback and correction. We will also offer suggestions as to how to implement various teaching strategies related to these important topics. Finally, we will suggest a framework for self-evaluation following a language lesson. It is hoped that the information presented here will provide teachers with ideas for putting currently available theory into useful practice.

SOCIAL CLIMATE

Recent research in language acquisition both in natural environments (Schumann, 1975) and in instructional situations (Stevick, 1976) as well as in teacher effectiveness (Moskowitz, 1976; Moskowitz, Benevento and Furst, 1973; Moskowitz and Hayman, 1974) indicates that the social environment in which a person learns a language is one of the most important facets of the language learning experience. The belief that a good social climate promotes communication is widely accepted in modern language teaching. In research conducted at UCLA the ESL faculty chose social climate as the most important among eleven factors related to language teaching (Bailey, 1976). Hunter (1974) has suggested that the teacher is the single most important variable in the classroom. In reviewing the literature on teacher effectiveness, Brophy and Good (1974) found that teacher warmth and enthusiasm consistently show a positive correlation with student achievement. What the teacher says and does is so significant in establishing classroom atmosphere that it can outweigh the effects of materials, methods, and educational facilities. Given the pressures of curriculum demands, the differing needs of the students, overcrowded classes, and too little time, what can the ESL teacher do to promote a good social climate in the classroom?

The first thing the teacher must do is to learn the students' names, no matter how large the class enrollment is. The teacher should also make it clear that the students will need to know one another's names during the course.

Furthermore, the teacher should respect each students' wishes about what s/he will be called in class. For example, a student who is not comfortable with the generally relaxed relationships between teachers and students in the US, or one who is older than the teacher, may prefer to be called Mr. Kim or Mrs. Castillo instead of functioning on a first-name basis. By the same token, a teacher should not undertake to change a child's name from *Ng* to *Henry* unless the child himself expresses a desire for a new name. Our names are such integral parts of ourselves that to forget, mispronounce, or alter a name can be taken as a personal affront.

Learning the students' names can be facilitated by knowing something about the individuals in the class. Many teachers find it useful to solicit information from the students about their background, interests and reasons for taking the course. Using this information, the teacher can compile a class information sheet which gives each student's full name, the name s/he wishes to be called in class, his or her interests, his or her country or origin, the language s/he speaks, etc. If students are intermediate or advanced and can read, distributing copies of the sheet will help the students learn their classmates' names. It will also help to break the ice socially. Furthermore, the class information sheet provides meaningful contexts for many grammar lessons. For example, it can be used in forming *wh*-questions (*Who is from Venezuela? What is Marta's hobby? Where was Hilda born?*), comparatives and superlatives (*Jaime is older than Werner; Jose is taller than Yvonne; Kyung Sook is the youngest person in the class*) or relative clauses (*The student who likes tennis is Fumiko; The student who speaks Persian is Hamid*). Even in exercises that don't utilize the information on the sheet, the students' names can be used to make them more interesting. Of course, if the students are beginners and/or cannot read, the information on the class sheet will be taught as part of class content, bit by bit.

It is likely that the students will gradually get to know one another during the course, especially if the teacher uses information about members of the class for language practice. However, the teacher can take a more active role in insuring that students get acquainted. An interesting introductory activity during the first class meeting can establish a friendly tone for the course. In one variation of this activity the teacher gives each student a card on which s/he neatly prints his or her name. The teacher collects the cards and redistributes them to different people. Each student must then locate the person whose card s/he holds and prepare to introduce him or her to the class. The teacher can tell the class ahead of time what information is needed (name, country of origin, academic major or profession, favorite food or pastime, etc.) or leave it up to the individuals. Normally this distribution of cards means that each student will talk to at least two new people during the class: the person whose name s/he has, and the person who has his or her name. The students also speak briefly to several other people in the process of finding their person because it is sometimes difficult to tell whether the gender of a foreign name is masculine or feminine. When the students have had time to identify and interview one another, one student comes to the front of the class and introduces another, who in turn introduces another, and so on. This activity helps the students and the teacher to match names with faces, but it also gives the teacher a chance to hear each student speak during the first class period. Normally students find it easier to speak about someone else for a few minutes than to talk about themselves. In the class periods to come this interviewing activity can be expanded to include other sorts of information. For example, after a lesson on *wh*-questions, the students can interview one another to get the answers to several questions and have practice in posing them: (*What is your name? Where do you live? How old are you? Where were you born?*). The information learned in the interview is then reported to the class as a follow-up activity.

In intermediate or advanced classes any language activity which involves the entire class cooperating on a specific task can enhance the social climate. For example, a story-sorting activity can provide the impetus for a cooperative problem-solving lesson in which the students must use pronoun reference, adverbial time clues, and verb tenses. In planning this activity, the teacher must first choose an interesting story and divide it into as many sentences as there are students in the class. In order to accommodate late-comers or absent students, the teacher should include a few sentences that can be added or deleted without disrupting the story. The sentences are then printed on index cards, which are shuffled and distributed randomly to the students. Each student has only two or three minutes to memorize his or her sentence. The cards are then collected and the students try to sort themselves into a logical story line. In order to do this, they must listen carefully to one another's recitations and discuss the syntax as well as the content of each sentence. This task usually involves a great deal of positive communication. It also gives the class a feeling of community accomplishment when the finished story is finally presented. In a large group the teacher can split the class into two groups working on the same task by providing a double set of cards. The value of such an activity is that it involves the students using English with one another rather than with the teacher.

The physical environment of a classroom can greatly influence the social climate in an ESL class. Rooms with fixed desks and/or laboratory-like partitions on the tables have an isolating effect on the students. It is difficult, at best, to promote small group interaction in a room full of barriers. Frequently a teacher has little or no control over the facilities, but within certain limits much can be done to improve the environment. First of all is the classroom clean and comfortable? Do the decorations (e.g., bulletin boards, displays, posters, etc.) and the arrangement of the furniture make the students feel at ease? The teacher may not always have time to create bulletin board displays, but students can be given interesting and productive assignments to develop a display around a grammar point, a vocabulary set, minimal pairs, etc. If there are no bulletin boards, the teacher and students can contribute travel posters or drawings to brighten up the room.

Regardless of the classroom layout, the teacher must be aware of the influence the environment can exert on classroom interaction. For example, research has shown that teachers tend to call on people sitting in particular areas of the room (Brophy and Good, ibid.). It is up to the teacher to avoid this pattern by calling on people in the back row or in the corners as often as those in the front or center of the room. The atmosphere of the class can be severely affected if the teacher seems to have "pets" or favor some students over others. The way the teacher manages grouping or the arrangement of desks can prevent the formation of cliques and involve the students in new communicative situations.

Whatever the physical set-up of the classroom may be, the teacher can do much with it to promote learning. Even in a bare classroom one can be imaginative. For example, in a windowless room, the teacher can ask students to imagine a window in a blank wall and then ask individuals to tell the class what they "see" through the window. When no materials are available through the school system, it is up to the teacher to either bring in items of interest or creatively use what little is available to stimulate student interest.

All of these factors—careful attention to names, the student information sheet, introductions and interviews, cooperative learning tasks, and the physical arrangement of the room—can contribute greatly to the social climate of an ESL class. Throughout the course, as well as at the beginning, the teacher should plan activities in which students can pursue and share their own interests. Field trips, oral reports, research projects, and media presentations will be more meaningful if they are in some way related to the students' lives. With adult classes, or in any situation where the curriculum is relatively flexible, the teacher can solicit input from the students about the course content. An informal mid-term evaluation can provide the teacher with valuable feedback about the students' perception of class activities. Using a brief written questionnaire which the students answer anonymously can determine which activities have been most helpful, which have been least helpful, and what there should be more of during the remainder of the course. The social climate can be improved if the

students have some voice in what they are learning and feel that the teacher is reponsive to their needs.

Ultimately, the responsibility for the classroom atmosphere lies with the teacher. It is important to begin each class period with some expression of interest in the students as individuals: *Maria, is your baby better now? Ahmad, did you get your car fixed? Yoko, the revision of your composition was a big improvement.* Opportunities for humor should be exploited as well. If there is a cartoon, joke, or anecdote that pertains to the lesson, the teacher should share it with the group. In a study that compared outstanding teachers with beginning and "typical" teachers in inner-city schools, Moskowitz and Hayman (ibid.) found that the best teachers used humor in their initial contacts with students. Social climate is affected by the teacher's behavior both inside and outside of class. Whenever time permits, the teacher should be available to discuss problems with students before and after class.

Finally the teacher should project an enthusiastic and positive image. It is unlikely that the students will become actively involved in the material if the teacher doesn't seem to enjoy teaching the course. In another study that compared outstanding and typical language teachers, Moskowitz (ibid.) found that outstanding teachers smiled more than typical teachers, and there was more laughter in their classrooms. In looking at the whole issue of social climate, one must ask whether the teacher's behavior, the physical arrangements, and the class atmosphere work together to create a pleasant learning environment.

VARIETY IN LEARNING ACTIVITIES

Research and common sense suggest that variety makes a language lesson more interesting. A variety of activities can reinforce the teaching point without boring the students. Research by Moskowitz (ibid.) and Politzer (1970) has shown that good language teachers (whether "good teaching" is defined by student achievement records or student evaluations of teaching) use a variety of activities in language lessons. Furthermore, a well-selected variety of activities prevents boredom, minimizes classroom control problems, and even encourages student achievement (Medley and Mitzel, 1963; Moskowitz, ibid.; Politzer, 1970; Politzer and Weiss, 1970).

Traditionally ESL teachers have followed the suggested sequence of activities of listening, speaking, reading and writing, because it is thought to parallel the natural language learning process; however, even the validity of this sequence has recently been questioned (Van Syoc, 1977). In using substitution drills, for example, we have often begun with the entire class repeating, then moved to one row at a time, and then individual students. These are certainly good ideas, but the whole question of using a variety of activities in a language lesson is much broader and more complex than this. Stevick (1959) was one of the first to recognize this fact in a very useful article on the rhythm of classroom activity and the need for variation in pacing.

At this point it is important to note that here *variety* does not mean a hodgepodge of unrelated activities. In this chapter, variety in learning activities refers to the number and effectiveness (i.e., quality *and* quantity) of the different language tasks the teacher provides for the students to do in mastering the teaching point. In lower level classes, in particular, it is important that these activities be sequenced from easy to difficult, and manipulative to communicative (Prator, 1965). In planning a lesson, the teacher should consider what types of activities would enable the students to understand, practice, and internalize the teaching point.

Nowadays a great deal of variety can be introduced through the use of audiovisual aids. Videotape and audio recordings, filmstrip and movie projectors, overhead projectors and sound-on-slide programs all make the teacher's job easier, but at the same time more challenging and complicated. The thought of coordinating and operating these machines and keeping a language lesson going at the same time can be intimidating. However, with a little practice and some careful planning, the use of such equipment can add variety and interest to a language lesson that would be impossible to achieve in a

"one-man show." In fact, Moskowitz and Hayman (ibid.) found that those teachers identified as outstanding by their students used a variety of AV aids, while new and typical teachers did not use many.

Beginning with the traditional sequence of listening, speaking, reading, and writing, we can ask ourselves what variety can be included in these different activities. For example, much of the language lesson involves students in listening, even if it is just listening to the teacher explain a grammar point. But students quickly become adjusted to their own teacher's voice. They may be able to understand the teacher perfectly well and yet have trouble understanding a neighbor, a bus driver, or a clerk in a store. For this reason, the teacher should provide opportunities for the students to listen to other people speaking English. Tape recordings of live conversations or radio broadcasts are useful, as are videotape recordings of lectures and television programs. Recordings of songs in English can be used with cloze passages of the lyrics to give students guided practice in listening for particular words in context. Films, sound-on-slide programs, or filmstrips with cassette recordings, can provide listening practice reinforced by visual images. Having a guest speaker in class gives the students the chance to hear an entirely new voice. In this situation they can also ask questions of the speaker, which isn't possible with a film, videotape or audio recording. The variety of activities possible in a listening exercise is limited only by the teacher's imagination and the equipment available.

There is also the potential for great variety in speaking activities. In addition to participating in regular live classroom discourse, students can record themselves reading a passage, telling stories, or performing dialogues. Videotaping oral reports or skits provides the students with instant feedback on their pronunciation, fluency, and body language. Such recordings can later be used as student-generated listening materials.

Teletrainers can also be used for a variety of speaking (and listening) activities in the ESL classroom. The teletrainers are a set of two telephones with long cords and a control box which produces a ring and a busy signal. The conversation can be limited to just the two parties on the line, or it can be projected to the entire classroom. Placing the two parties where they can't see each other simulates telephone speech in which the students must get or convey information without the assistance of gestures or facial expressions. The teletrainers also provide a realistic situation for the students to ask questions, rather than just responding to the teacher's questions. Several telephone companies loan the teletrainers to schools free of charge as a public service.

Even when such sophisticated AV equipment is not available, the average teacher has access to thousands of inexpensive items that students can talk about. Pictures cut from magazines can be used in grammar lessons, pronunciation practice, in telling stories or writing dialogues. Common household items can be hidden in a bag while one student describes an item so that his or her classmates can guess its identity.[1]

In introducing more variety into the speaking component of a lesson, the teacher should consider the objectives of the lesson and the language proficiency of the class. Activities should be carefully planned to encourage the students to use the language for communicative purposes. If the proposed activity is too easy, students may become bored, but if it is too difficult they can get discouraged. In planning a lesson, the teacher should ask him- or herself what communicative activities could be used to get the students talking and give them realistic practice with the teaching point.

Like listening, reading is involved in many language lessons because textbooks are the sources of much of the information students get in class. Research by Politzer (ibid.) has shown that good language teachers are not "book-bound." There are hundreds of things for students to read other than textbooks. Newspapers, magazines, signs, maps, schedules, travel brochures, catalogs, letters, and comic books—in short, anything the students would want to read anyway—can be adapted for use in language lessons. Regardless of the actual material to be read, students may read silently or aloud (to the class, to themselves, to a partner, or on tape). In silent reading, the student can skim for specific information, read to find the main idea, read for entertainment, or do in-depth reading for details.[2] Reading in English is vital, whether it is the main objective of the lesson, or a means to another end.

Sometimes the reading component of a lesson may be as simple as reading the directions to an exercise aloud. In a grammar lesson, students may read what their classmates have written on the blackboard as a lead-in to peer correction. In more advanced classes students can read one another's compositions, which have been duplicated or put on overhead transparencies. Whatever the purpose of the exercise, there are numerous ways in which reading can be used to add variety to a language lesson.

Like the other language skills, writing may be the primary objective of a lesson, or it may be secondary or incidental to the teaching point. For example, grammar and vocabulary lessons often involve some amount of writing in English. But writing can also be a powerful means of adding variety to a language lesson. For instance, even at the early stages of English instruction, stories written by the students themselves can provide reading materials and excellent topics for discussion. Before or after a grammar lesson, a brief writing assignment can provide the teacher with data for error analysis. Students can write as a follow-up to almost any other language activity.

Much has been written about the value of controlled, guided, and free composition. Dicto-comps (Wishon and Burks, 1968) and speed-writing (Celce-Murcia, 1974) can also be used to get students started on writing compositions. However, classroom writing should not necessarily be limited to formal expository writing. Students can also use their English in writing short stories, poems, plays, radio dramas, advertisements, dialogues or role-plays, business and personal letters, editorials or jokes. Many teachers find it useful to allow ten minutes of class time for students to write in their own cultural journals, describing their experiences in living in a new place and learning a new language. Keeping a journal not only provides the student with an outlet for personal expression, but also prompts him or her to write about those things which are most important to him or her at the time.

Although independent writing is extremely important, students can also benefit from collaborating on written work. Pairs or groups of students writing a paper together can share ideas, suggest vocabulary, and correct one another's grammar problems. Or the entire class can contribute to one large group composition which is written on the blackboard or an overhead transparency. An anthology of student writings can be produced by the teacher, or it can be edited and developed by the students themselves.

Whatever the particular teaching point may be, in planning the lesson the teacher should consider several ways of making the lesson interesting and stimulating. Careful sequencing of the activities (easy to difficult, manipulative to communicative) will insure that the basic presentation is logical and coherent. Audiovisual equipment, pictures and realia, communication games, student-generated materials, flexible reading and writing assignments, cultural journals and anthologies of the students' work are all means of adding variety to the language classroom. The teacher should utilize whatever activities and equipment will help the students learn the material. However, careful planning and some practice are needed to insure that the activities and AV aids work *with* the lesson and not against it. The objective is to get the students' English out of the textbooks and into the real world. With a little research into the professional journals and a trip to the local educational resource center, the ESL teacher can discover hundreds of useful ideas for adding variety and interest to his or her lessons.

OPPORTUNITY FOR STUDENT PARTICIPATION

It is an axiom of modern language teaching that active use of the language is crucial to good language learning. Yet as ESL teachers we are often faced with anywhere from twenty to sixty students in a class. Given these numbers, how can the teacher involve all the students in the use of the language? Choral repetition has traditionally been used to get many students speaking at once, but can we say students are really *using* the language if they simply repeat en masse?

A possible solution to this dilemma is to increase the opportunity for student participation by cutting back on the amount of "teacher talk" in the lesson. Careful preparation can change the classroom interaction from teacher-dominated activities to teacher/student communication and finally to student/student communication. It stands to reason that planning opportunities for student/student communication will involve a greater number of students in an active, *cognitive* use of the language than does choral repetition or even a mathematically even distribution of turns by the teacher.

How can one plan opportunities for student participation? A simple way to start is to get the students involved in classroom management tasks. Students can call the roll, return corrected papers, develop a bulletin board display, read announcements, etc. Although these are minor details, involving the students in these chores can promote interaction, a sense of teamwork, and the learning of names. The important thing is for the teacher to begin to loosen his or her hold on the total domination/management of the classroom.

Those activities which are teacher-led should be carefully planned to involve all the students. Sometimes teachers are able to call on students randomly, or strike a balance between calling on volunteers and drawing out the quieter students. In a large class it may be helpful for the teacher to use a set of index cards with a student's name on each card. The teacher can flip through the cards, calling on each student as his or her name appears. This simple system can help to ensure a fairer distribution of turns since research (Allwright, 1977) has shown that ESL teachers typically do not distribute turns evenly among students (e.g., we sometimes rely too heavily on bright students or call on those who "look ready").

Another way to involve more students more often is by using a chain-drill approach to grammar. Even at the early stages of language instruction, chain drills can be used to cut down on "teacher talk" and maximize student participation. For example, asking and answering questions has traditionally been a teacher-dominated activity:

Teacher: *Juan, what time do you get up in the morning?*
Juan: *I get up at seven o'clock every morning.*
Teacher: *Very good. Beatriz, what time do you get up in the morning?*
Beatriz: *I get up at six-thirty every day.*
Teacher: *Good. . . .*

When a chain drill is used in the following situation, "teacher talk" is minimized and the students are able to say more:

Teacher: *Juan, what time do you get up in the morning?*
Juan: *I get up at seven o'clock every morning.*
Teacher: *Very good. Find out when Beatriz gets up.*
Juan: *Beatriz, what time do you get up in the morning?*
Beatriz: *I get up at six-thirty every day.*
Juan: *She gets up at six-thirty every day.*

This exchange would be followed by Beatriz finding out when a third student eats breakfast, and so on. With this small change in the teacher's strategy Juan's involvement in the language lesson grew from a simple response to phrasing the question himself (using the *do* auxiliary, rising intonation, and the correct pronoun) and rephrasing the other student's response (employing the correct pronoun, using the third person singular *-s* marker, and reporting the information). Thus the student was not only given more time to talk, but the opportunity to engage in a much more complicated language task as well. Although it takes careful preparation by the teacher, a chain drill format can be applied to many grammar lessons to increase the opportunity for student participation in the English lesson.

The next logical step in increasing the opportunities for student participation is to ask oneself what *language* activities can be done by the students just as well as by the teacher. Phrased in another way, how can the teacher say less and utilize the students' knowledge more? The opportunities for using such an approach are numerous, even in a lesson that isn't specifically planned to include student/student interaction. For example, teachers are quick to answer questions, when the students themselves could answer many of their peers' questions. Inquiries about vocabulary, spelling, or grammar can easily be thrown back to the class: *That's a good question. Who can answer it?* As opposed to a straightforward teacher response, this strategy involves more people in the use of the language, it keeps the entire class alert and listening, and it provides more chances for hypothesis-testing by the students. Furthermore, it allows the teacher to monitor the production of more students more often.

Taking this idea one step further, the teacher should sometimes plan opportunities for various students to play the part of the teacher. Following presentation and practice of a grammar point, for instance, one student can come to the front of the class and ask questions or distribute the turns in an exercise. Or one student can come to the blackboard and write the answers given by his or her classmates. Those at their desks must speak clearly and the student at the board must listen and write carefully. The entire class must negotiate the spelling of words that are problematic for the "teacher." This sort of activity also works well in using an overhead projector. One student can arrange words or sentences on the screen with directions and feedback from the class. Such a task involves more people more *actively* than if the teacher were simply standing there soliciting the input from one student at a time. This technique can be utilized for almost any word order problem (passive, question formation), practice in paragraph unity (arranging sentences in a logical order, deleting extraneous material), or organization (outlining, grouping by part of speech, etc.).

There are many cases in which students can benefit from working in pairs instead of having the attention of the entire class focused on the teacher. For example, after a lesson on the future tense, students can find out what their partners plan to do that evening or over the weekend. This interview activity is followed by each student reporting the information s/he has learned to the class. During the reporting step, students receive feedback on their use of the future tense. Of course, there is the possibility that some of the questions and answers in this type of activity will involve errors that go uncorrected, even if the teacher circulates and listens during the interviews. But the technique is useful in that the students are utilizing the structures learned in gaining information, a situation which approaches genuine communication.

Pairs of students can also jointly produce information. After studying irregular past tense verbs, for example, students can collaborate on writing a story using those verbs, after which they can read the story to their classmates, who then give them feedback on the correct use of the past tense forms. After working on a pronunciation lesson, pairs of students can write dialogues, then present them before the entire group. These are just a few of the many ways pairs of students can accomplish the same things the teacher would do with individuals or with the entire class.

In using students in pairs, the teacher should first provide the basic information (i.e., the data or rules to work with) and then carefully structure and define the task the students are to perform, so as to give clear and concise directions to the class. In some cases it may be useful for the teacher to determine the pairings in advance (for example, to avoid getting two students from the same language background together, to evenly match English fluency levels, or to put a more advanced student with one who is having problems). Once the pair work begins, the teacher is free to monitor the language production, or respond to questions. Since the idea here is to let the students do most of the talking, the teacher must remember not to interfere, unless the pairs have problems accomplishing the task.

Some language learning or language practicing activities are more appropriate for small group work than for pairs of students. Students can also prepare stories or dialogues in groups of three or four. Many role-playing and problem-solving tasks lend themselves well to groups of three or four students (for example

exercises, see Rosensweig, 1974). The well-known "values clarification" exercises (see Simon et al., 1972) and other tasks that involve debatable issues are better suited to groups of three or more than to pairs. Age is also a factor. In elementary classes, students can either complete worksheets individually and then compare answers in small groups, or work in small groups from the start. Some teachers prefer to give only one paper to each group to insure that the students do, in fact, discuss the topic (Allwright, personal communication).

A teacher who decides to try using small groups should consider the effects of various grouping strategies on student participation. It is often helpful to use heterogeneous grouping by language background to guarantee the use of English as the medium of discussion. If students always choose their own groups they may easily come to rely on their friends too much in producing the language. In some language tasks it may be useful to try to have the groups evenly divided between men and women. It may also be desirable to have one talkative person in each group to stimulate discussion. In other cases the teacher may decide to put all the talkative students in one group, so the quieter students will have more opportunity to participate. The method of dividing the class into groups depends largely on the students' background and proficiency and the objective of the lesson. In planning the lesson the teacher should consider which approach would be most appropriate for the activity. As with pair work, during group work the teacher's role is to assist when help is needed, to keep the students working on the task (by offering encouragement, settling disputes, etc.) and to observe the students' use of the language. Normally it is not the teacher's role to interfere or to direct the groups. For this reason it is extremely important that the original explanation of the task, and the students' responsibility for completing the job, be made explicit from the beginning of the exercise. If there is a follow-up activity, for example, the group may choose a spokesperson, or the teacher can choose someone who was relatively passive during the exercise.

Like group cooperation, competition can be used to provide opportunities for student participation. There are many variations on the old spelling bee, which can be used to get the students involved in the language. If the language task is appropriate for the students' ability, adults will enjoy these games as well as children. For example, each student can win points for his or her team by correctly spelling and defining a word with a given prefix. In such a competition, each person is encouraged and coached by his or her teammates. The teacher merely serves as the authority or checks the dictionary. Team competition can be used with hundreds of lesson plans: anything from basic grammatical structures (using the correct preposition, changing a present tense sentence to past tense, etc.) or using a vocabulary item correctly at the lower levels, to asking and answering questions about a classmate's oral report at the upper levels. Whatever type of competitive team activity is used, it is important that the teacher think through the game process and define the rules ahead of time, to insure maximum participation and to prevent confusion.

All of the teaching strategies discussed above—utilizing classroom management chores, name cards and chain drills, turning students' questions back to the class, having a student "play teacher" at the blackboard or overhead projector, pair work, small group work, and team competition—are ways of increasing the opportunity for student participation. The thing to remember is that ESL students need practice in using the language, as well as formal instruction. For the child who speaks no English at home or for the adult learner who works all day among non-English-speaking colleagues, the English class may provide the only opportunity to actively use the language. Keeping this in mind, teachers should learn to minimize the amount of time they spend talking in order to increase the opportunities for the students to utilize their English.

FEEDBACK AND CORRECTION

Although much has been written about feedback and correction in language classrooms, these issues continue to be hotly debated in discussions of methodology. Recent studies have investigated the effectiveness of various feedback and correction strategies (Zahorik, 1968; Lucas, 1975; Fanselow, 1974). Other writers have advocated a policy of non-interference (Castaños and Long, 1976). Others have investigated teacher and learner preferences regarding correction (Cathcart and Olsen, 1976).

The fact remains that many students enroll in ESL classes expecting to be corrected. The teacher is faced with the problem of deciding what to criticize, what to praise, and what to ignore. It is generally accepted that correct responses in a language lesson should be positively reinforced, either by simple confirmation or extended praise, but there is little agreement on what to do with problem utterances. Traditionally, it has been the teacher's role to correct errors in syntax, pronunciation, and vocabulary. But teacher correction may be the least effective form of feedback in terms of student retention and improvement. Students can repeat corrected words or phrases without internalizing them. In fact, when a student is concentrating on conveying a particular message, s/he may not focus on the correctness of the form. It can be frustrating to have an agreement error corrected after struggling to produce the proper vocabulary items in the correct word order.

Should the teacher be concerned with the medium (the form of the utterance) or the message (the content) or both? Certainly severe problems that interfere with communication must be resolved before the listener can interpret the utterance of the speaker. These problems include cases of severe mispronunciation, confusion of minimal pairs in context, or grammatical errors that interfere with the transmission of the message. If the objectives of the class include improving the students' accuracy as well as their communicative competence, then steps should be taken to help the students monitor their own output. In general, it is our feeling that students should only be held responsible for the correct production of material that has already been covered in class (i.e., performance errors rather than competence problems). One other important area for feedback and correction has to do with the question of competence, however. Competence errors can provide a springboard for highly context-ualized learning. For example, in a case where the language learner is groping for exactly the right word but is apparently unfamiliar with the appropriate vocabulary item, the teacher can profitably provide the word or lead another student to supply it. Being receptive and alert to this type of error can enable the teacher to meet students' individual needs in the class-room situation. Thus we suggest that teachers concentrate on three different types of errors: those which interfere with communication, those which involve a self-monitoring process in producing structures and vocabulary which have already been studied, and finally, those errors which involve queries—i.e., the student takes a stab at the question but uses rising intonation in his or her response. Whenever possible the teacher should lead the students to self-correct. Allwright (1975) feels that forcing learners back on their own resources all the time may actually give them more precise help than does simple teacher correction. Asking a student to repeat a phrase may be enough of a signal to the speaker to re-process the utterance while checking for errors. The teacher can also give more specific guidance as to the location of the errors:

Student: *After school he go to work.*
Teacher: *After school he —*
Student: *Goes to work.*

Sometimes gestures can be used to help the student identify problems (Susan Greenwood, personal communication). The students quickly learn to recognize a system of hand signals for indicating errors. For example, pointing with your thumb backward over your shoulder can represent past tense. Teachers who use such gestures report that the visual cue that some-thing is wrong seems to be less disruptive than verbally indicating an error.

Recent research in discourse analysis (Schegloff, Jefferson, and Sacks, 1977) shows that repairs in native-speakers' conversations are often initiated extralinguistically—with body movements, gestures, or changes of facial ex-pression. They also found a preference for self-initiated self-correction. In examining con-versational repair strategies among non-native speakers, Schwartz (1977) found that in natural discourse listeners signal confusion or need for correction by leaning forward when seated and/or raising their eyebrows. Although research has not yet determined the effective-ness of teaching such extralinguistic cues, we as teachers should attempt to expose ESL stu-dents to the types of feedback they will get in natural conversation.

Another correcting strategy which can be particularly effective with an adult learner who is unable to determine the source of the error is to diagnose the error and then have the student correct the utterance himself. This procedure gives the student guidance as to the location and nature of the error, but also gives him or her the responsibility for correcting it:

Teacher: *Where did you go last night?*
Student: *I go to the movies.*
Teacher: *What tense do you need?*
Student: *I went to the movies.*

Clearly not every language problem in the classroom is so easily dealt with as this example would indicate. As Allwright points out (ibid.), the language teacher's task is difficult because s/he cannot always wait to see whether or not an error is significantly frequent, develop-mental, caused by interference, or simply care-less. An ESL teacher must be constantly diag-nosing and reacting to errors because everything that is said in the language classroom can be considered input. We will learn more about effective feedback strategies as more research is done on language acquisition, classroom inter-action, and teacher effectiveness.

Regardless of the way in which it is instigated, we prefer self-correction to other correction strategies because it should eventu-ally contribute to weaning the student away from the need for overt correction. It forces the student to be more responsible for the original output if no one constantly supplies the correct form for him or her.

If a student is not able to self-correct, for whatever reason (forgetting, competence, ner-vousness, etc.), the teacher can turn the job of correction over to another student. We feel this strategy is preferable to straight teacher correction because it affords another language learner practice at locating, diagnosing, and repairing a problem. Input from peers can be less intimidating than teacher correction, but it must be handled carefully. The teacher should manipulate the distribution of turns so as to avoid embarrassing a student with constant correction from the same classmate. When a student supplies or corrects an answer that another student missed, the teacher should return again to the student who made the error and give him or her another chance, either with the same question or with another question involving the same potential error. Thus peer correction can be utilized in oral work when the self-correction process breaks down or isn't negotiable. Although peer-correction is external and therefore less desirable than self-correction, it has the advantage of giving all the students more opportunities for language production and hypothesis testing. It also promotes communication among students and decreases the teacher's domination of classroom discourse.

Peer correction can also be used effectively with written assignments. In an advanced class a composition can be dittoed and distributed or viewed by the entire group with an overhead projector. The composition could be a composite developed by the teacher to include representative writing problems, or an actual composition written by a student. In correcting the problems it is important that the teacher maintain a constructive atmosphere so that no one feels embarrassed or unduly criticized. For other ideas regarding different ways of organizing peer correction of written work, see Witbeck (1976).

Some teachers find it useful to have the students read one another's compositions before the teacher sees them. Students can actually write their compositions on ditto masters or bring photocopies to class for small group discussions. Some teachers have found that such a filtering process eliminates many of the mechanical errors common in the writing of intermediate students (Dermody, personal communication).

Peer correction can also be useful in analyzing spelling, reading, or grammar exercises, even at the more elementary levels. For example, following a homework assignment, groups of three or four students can compare answers without a key to determine points of disagreement. Such small group correction activities promote peer teaching, hypothesis testing, and student talk. The teacher's role becomes one of resolving conflicting ideas and referring students to sources of information rather than being the authority figure (e.g., *Look at the example on page thirty-eight. What does that tell you about your answer to number four?*). And yet, when the authority is needed, the teacher can quickly prevent the spread of misinformation.

The issues of feedback and correction in classroom interaction are extremely complex. Further study of interlanguage, student achievement, and teachers' reacting moves are needed before we can definitively state what ESL teachers should and should not do. However, our experience suggests that leading a student to self-correct, and ultimately to monitor his or her own language production, is an effective means of promoting learning. Peer-correction can also be used to advantage, but must be carefully managed either in a small group or with the entire class. Finally, teacher correction of errors should be selective. Haphazard errors of performance or errors that block communication demand attention but the teacher should also be alert to gaps in the learner's competence. Because everything that is said in the target language can be considered to be input, the way a teacher responds to what the students produce appears to be extremely important, although not enough is known about this area yet.

A CHECKLIST FOR LESSON PLANNING AND SELF-EVALUATION

Let us pause a moment here to summarize and to consider how the ESL teacher might use much of the preceding information. Obviously, the four areas discussed above (i.e., social climate, variety in learning activities, oppor-

	Yes, Good to Excellent	Yes, Average/ adequate	No, needs improvement	Not Applicable
Social Climate				
a. Does the teacher demonstrate interest in and concern for each student (e.g., does s/he know and use their names?)				
b. Does the teacher project a friendly, positive attitude in the classroom?				
c. Are the students comfortable and relaxed with the teacher and each other? (e.g., is there humor?)				
d. Do the students know each other by name and enjoy exchanging information?				
e. Do the students volunteer and cooperate in carrying out group responsibility delegated by the teacher?				
f. Does the teacher use the physical environment to enhance language learning and social interaction?				
Variety in Learning Activities				
a. Is appropriate use of several language skills required in this lesson (listening, speaking, reading, writing)?				
b. Are audiovisual aids or other supplementary materials used to enhance the lesson?				
c. Is there appropriate variation in student grouping (together or individuals, whole class, pairs, groups, etc.)?				
d. Is there appropriate variation in input (e.g., teacher input vs. student input, voices of different native speakers, different written models, prose passage, dialogue, etc.)?				
e. Is there appropriate variation in pacing (i.e., easy activities/fast pace; harder activities/ slower pace)?				
f. Is there appropriate variation in the nature of the task (manipulation to communication)?				
Opportunity for Student Participation				
a. Does the teacher delegate tasks to students whenever possible (e.g., call roll, answer questions of other students, pass out papers, etc.)?				
b. Does the teacher distribute turns evenly among all students in the class?				
c. Does the teacher appropriately utilize techniques and drills that maximize student talk time and minimize teacher talk time?				

(continued on next page)

Self-Rating of Lesson Plan or of a Live Language Lesson (continued)	Yes, Good to Excellent	Yes, Average/ adequate	No, needs improvement	Not Applicable
d. Does the teacher develop appropriate tasks for pairs and groups of students to maximize student participation and lessen teacher domination?				
e. Does the teacher make use of games/ competitions/songs to enhance student participation?				
Feedback and Correction a. Does the teacher help the students to monitor their own output whenever the focus is on form or accuracy?				
b. Does the teacher effectively elicit self-correction of errors whenever possible (e.g., gestures, asking for repetition, etc.)?				
c. Does the teacher elicit constructive peer correction when self correction has not been effective?				
d. Does the teacher pinpoint the source of error without actually correcting the error?				
e. Does the teacher strike a happy balance between (i) correcting so much that students become inhibited and (ii) not correcting any of the errors that occur?				

tunities for student participation, and feedback and correction) should be actively considered and exploited as the teacher is going about planning a particular language lesson. This can be accomplished most efficiently if the essential questions are listed for easy reference and if the questions are presented as a checklist or matrix that permits relatively easy self-evaluation. The checklist given here is our suggestion and derives from the preceding discussion. It is presented as a sample for individual ESL teachers to adapt or modify as necessary.

It is obvious that not all of the above questions are applicable to lesson planning. Many of the questions under social climate, and feedback and correction, for example, can only be answered during an evaluation of a class (teacher and students) in action. However, many of the points raised under "Variety in Learning Activities" and "Opportunity for Student Participation" must be carefully and deliberately planned. To this extent, the above

checklist can serve as a useful reminder to an ESL teacher when s/he is in the process of planning a lesson.

Perhaps an even more useful function of such a matrix is that it provides the ESL teacher with a framework for self-evaluation. If shortly after teaching a lesson the teacher can refer to the matrix and judge his or her own performance, then areas of strength and weakness should emerge and the teacher will know which areas are in need of improvement. If the teacher can be videotaped in order to critique his or her performance in the classroom, this is even better. Alternatively, the teacher can ask another ESL teacher, a friend or trusted colleague, to observe his or her class and make ratings with reference to the matrix.

Several such ratings of different lessons taught over a period of time usually indicate patterns: areas of progress and areas where improvement does not seem to be taking place. This type of rating is much more useful to a teacher genuinely interested in self-improvement than a one-shot experience with self-evaluation or peer evaluation. The important thing for all teachers to realize is that further improvement is always possible, and that some form of critical self-evaluation should be an ongoing, never-ending process.

EIGHT ADDITIONAL SKILLS

In addition to the teacher skills we have discussed above, there are eight others that we should mention. Four of them are fairly self-evident, and four of them are not.

The four self-evident teacher skills that many beginning and experienced teachers find problematic to some degree are:

a. *Volume level*: does the teacher maintain an appropriate volume level when speaking?
b. *Clarity*: does the teacher give clear instructions?
c. *Eye contact*: does the teacher maintain eye contact with the students whenever talking to them or listening to them?
d. *Legibility*: Are the teacher's materials neat and legible (e.g., clear dittoes and overhead transparencies, legible handwriting on the blackboard, etc.)?

A "no" answer to any of the above questions indicates that the teacher's overall effectiveness is probably being compromised due to inattention to the particular skill involved.

Four other important skills which are somehow less self-evident are the following:

e. *Question posing*: does the teacher pose the question first and then call on a student to respond (a volunteer or someone s/he selects)?
f. *Pause*: does the teacher allow an appropriate pause between posing the question and calling on the student?
g. *Wait time*: does the teacher give the student enough time to answer the question before calling on someone else? Are all students given equal time to respond?

h. *Physical movement*: does the teacher provide an opportunity for appropriate physical movement during the lesson?

In small-group or one-to-one verbal interaction, people instinctively say the addressee's name before posing a question. This gets the person's attention and helps lead up to the question. However, using the same strategy in front of a classroom with twenty to fifty students can be disastrous since many of the students will not even listen to the question if they know that someone else will be responsible for answering it. Posing the question and then pausing appropriately, before calling on someone, encourages each student to listen and to formulate an answer. Also this procedure often encourages students to volunteer whereas the reverse procedure (i.e., name first and then the question) tends to discourage volunteers.

The third question concerning "wait time" is extremely important since previous research involving science and math teachers (Rowe, 1969) and English teachers (McNeil, 1971) indicates that after posing a question, the teachers in these studies instinctively waited *less* for poor students to answer the question than they did for good ones. When the teachers were made aware of this tendency and were properly trained to slow down for all students, the quality of all their students' responses improved.

In many language classes the students sit at their desks the whole hour and the teacher moves along the board or around the room. In some classes even the teacher remains seated at his or her desk or stands in one spot during the course of a lesson. Such a static format is especially unwise in a language class. One of today's highly effective language teaching methodologies is based on the premise that the learner must listen to imperatives (*stand up, sit down*, etc.) and immediately produce the appropriate physical response (i.e., s/he stands up or sits down) (see Asher, 1965 and 1974). Without adopting Asher's methodology completely, the ESL teacher should be appropriately mobile throughout most of the lesson, whether pantomiming or just moving around to monitor different students. The teacher should—as frequently as appropriate—provide individual students, groups of students, and sometimes even the whole class, with an activity that involves the need for some purposeful physical movement (e.g., going to the board, passing out papers, moving into pairs/groups, role-playing in front of the class or in small groups, etc.). Such activities keep students attentive and alert and insure better learning and retention.

The ESL teacher who is interested in knowing how s/he performs regarding the above eight questions should probably write them out on a sheet and ask a fellow ESL teacher to come and observe a class and to rate him or her with respect to these eight skills. Moreover, the areas of legibility and physical movement (if deficient) can usually be improved merely with proper advance planning.

CONCLUSION

Obviously, not even the best ESL teacher can perform all of the skills and behaviors discussed above perfectly and consistently. Also, additional research will reveal other important skills we have not even mentioned here. The essentials for any teacher are: (a) that s/he be aware of effective teaching skills and behaviors; and (b) that s/he know how his or her own performance compares with the ideal—this means knowledge of one's performance on any one particular lesson or of one's performance in general. Doing this also implies (c) the need to keep up with current classroom research applicable to ESL. All three types of information, when coupled with a sincere desire to improve, should facilitate a change for the better.

NOTES

1.   For more ideas on ways to add variety to the speaking component of a language lesson see Olsen (1977).

2.   See the textbook by Gorman and Walsleben, for further ideas along these lines.

DISCUSSION QUESTIONS

1.   Why do you think that Stevick argues in *Memory, Meaning and Method* (1976) that social climate is the single most important factor in the language classroom—more important, for example, than the textbook, syllabus, or method being used?

2.   In this chapter which suggestion(s) for encouraging variety in learning activities did you like the best? Why? Can you think of any parameters—other than those mentioned—that offer possibilities for introducing variation in teaching/learning procedures?

3.   Why should the ESL teacher be concerned about keeping up with the results of classroom research?

4.   Discuss the ways in which one might research the issue of feedback and correction in more detail. What should serve as data? What would constitute evidence?

5.   If you were a teacher trainer, what advice would you give to a student teacher having the following problems?
a.   S/he speaks too softly to the class.
b.   S/he avoids eye contact with the students.
c.   S/he writes illegibly on the blackboard.

SUGGESTED ACTIVITIES

1.   Compare the suggestions concerning opportunity for student participation in this chapter and in Sue Mockridge-Fong's chapter oh "Teaching the Speaking Skill." Write a two-page summary bringing out the similarities and differences in the two chapters.

2.   As a prelude to self-evaluation or peer evaluation, arrange to go and observe several other ESL teachers using the checklist provided in this chapter. What did you learn from the experience? What changes would you suggest in the checklist?

3.   Ask another ESL teacher to observe one of your classes or *vice versa*. As soon thereafter as possible, both of you should independently fill out a form rating the teacher's performance of the following skills:
a.   volume level
b.   clarity
c.   eye contact
d.   legibility

e. pause

f. wait time

g. physical movement

After you have both filled out the form, compare ratings. What are the areas of agreement? Or disagreement? How do you feel about this evaluation procedure?

4. Meet informally with several other ESL teachers. What possibilities for teacher self-improvement—other than those discussed in this chapter—can your group suggest?

SUGGESTIONS FOR FURTHER READING

For practical suggestions we suggest the following sources:

Moskowitz, G. (1978)
Caring and Sharing in the Foreign Language Class. Rowley, Mass.: Newbury House.
This book has lots of suggestions that would contribute to the improvement of social climate in the ESL classroom.

Olsen, Judy Winn-Bell (1977)
Communication-Starters and other Activities for the ESL Classroom. San Francisco, CA.: Alemany Press. There are numerous activities provided here for introducing variety into the language classroom.

Witbeck, Michael C. (1976)
"Peer correction procedures for intermediate and advanced ESL composition lessons," *TESOL Quarterly,* 10:3, 321-326.
This article gives useful ideas concerning the development of feedback and correction strategies for dealing with the written work of ESL students.

In the way of more research-oriented references we suggest the following sources:

Brophy, J. E., and J. L. Good (1974)
Teacher-student relations: causes and consequences. NY: Holt, Rinehart, and Winston.
This reference is an excellent survey of research on teaching in general (e.g., all subjects) but many of the findings apply to ESL.

Fanselow, J. (1977)
"Beyond RASHOMON—Conceptualizing and Describing the Teaching Act," *TESOL Quarterly,* 11:1.
Fanselow presents an instrument (FOCUS) for getting all the people involved in ESL teaching to give similar accounts of the same event as a starting point for fruitful communication.

Allwright, R. (1975)
"Problems in the study of the language teacher's treatment of learner error," in Burt and Dulay (eds.), *New Directions in Second Language Learning, Teaching and Bilingual Education,* Washington, D.C.: TESOL.
This article discusses the study of the "feedback-error correction" at work in the ESL classroom; it raises questions and provides suggestions.

SECOND LANGUAGE TESTING

Andrew D. Cohen

INTRODUCTION

Testing is perhaps one of the more misunderstood areas of language teaching and learning. Students and teachers alike cringe when they hear the word "testing." Students see tests as a threat to their competence, because they are afraid they won't perform well on them. Teachers, on the other hand, often don't like to construct tests, and are not altogether satisfied with their results when they do. They are also suspicious of the standardized, professionally designed tests because they don't understand what these tests are really trying to measure.

This chapter is intended as a reference guide to language test construction. It is also intended to better equip the ESL teacher to understand and scrutinize tests prepared by others. Beginning with a theoretical framework for types of tests and types of items, this chapter should help the teacher determine just what kind of test s/he is constructing or reviewing, as well as give him or her insights into the types of items that are involved. What follows next is a thorough discussion of approaches to testing the listening skill. A similar discussion of approaches to testing speaking, reading, and writing is given in the appendix to this chapter. The chapter concludes with a discussion of test construction and administration techniques.

THEORETICAL FOUNDATIONS

Types of Tests

In order to properly construct or assess a test, it is helpful to have some explicit notion of what the test is testing and of how it might be labeled. The diagram below provides a schema for labeling a test. Experts in testing use a variety of frameworks for describing tests. The schema in this diagram is based largely on Clark (1972a). A basic distinction is made between tests that deal with prediction of a student's performance, "prognosis," and tests that assess the current level of accomplishments, "evaluation of attainment." Prognostic tests include aptitude tests, which assume no prior study, and placement tests, which assume some prior study, however little. Tests of attainment include achievement tests, which assess the student's performance in a given course, and general proficiency tests, which assess a student's skill for real-life purposes.

Another distinction is made between norm-referenced and criterion-referenced assessment. A test can be used, for example, to compare a respondent with other respondents, whether locally (e.g., in a class), regionally, or nationally. Classroom, regional, or national norms[1] may be established to interpret just how one student compares with another. A test can also be used to see whether a respondent has met certain instructional objectives or criteria, hence the term "criterion-referenced" assessment. Aptitude, placement, achievement, and proficiency tests can all be normed (see the diagram). However, only placement and achievement tests can be considered criterion-referenced, because the other types are not generally linked to prior study of specified objectives.

As with any schema, this one is somewhat simplistic. It can be argued, for instance, that there is overlap between general proficiency and achievement tests. Also, the same test could serve both as an achievement test and as a placement test. Thus the *intended* purpose is of prime importance in labeling a test.

Not only is there potential overlap *across* categories, but *within* categories as well. There is need for further clarification, as in the case of general proficiency and aptitude, for example. In testing general proficiency, the current concern is over distinguishing *linguistic* proficiency from *communicative* proficiency, often referred to as "competence" and "performance" respectively (see Savignon, 1972). Clark (1972b) points out that, in assessing speaking proficiency, the relation between linguistic and communicative proficiency is tenuous. Informational redundancy in language, a student's ability to paraphrase and thus avoid his or her linguistic weaknesses, and varying degrees of

	Prognosis		Evaluation of Attainment	
	Aptitude	Placement	Achievement	General Proficiency
Norm-Referenced				
Criterion-Referenced	XXXX			XXXX

listener tolerance to faulty speech (depending on social and situational control) distort the relationship between competence and performance.

According to Pimsleur (1966), language aptitude includes verbal intelligence (knowledge of words and the ability to reason analytically in using verbal materials), motivation (an expression of interest in studying a second language), and auditory ability. After surveying what existing language aptitude tests actually measure, Smolinski (1970) added the following: short-term auditory and visual memory span, grammatical analogy or flexibility (ability to deal with new grammatical structures), and sound-symbol associative skill (ability to associate familiar sounds with new symbol assignments). Clark (1972a) notes that aptitude tests are now being used more for individualizing instruction than for selection of students into programs of language study.

Classifying an Item

Tests usually consist of a series of items. An item is a specific task to perform, and can test one or more points or objectives. For example, an item may test *one* point such as the meaning of a given vocabulary word, or *several* points, e.g., an item which tests the ability to obtain facts from a passage and then make inferences based on these facts. Likewise, a given objective may be tested by a series of items. For example, there could be five items all testing one grammatical point, say, tag questions. Items of a similar kind may also be grouped together to form "subtests" within a given test.

Skill Tested

The skills being tested are, in order, listening and reading, then speaking and writing. The ordering stresses that listening and reading are the more receptive skills on a continuum while speaking and writing are the more productive skills. Non-verbal skills can be both receptive (interpreting someone else's gestures) and productive (making one's own gestures). "Receptive" and "productive" are used instead of "active" and "passive" because it is misleading to think of listening, for example, as a passive activity since it calls for attentiveness, quick reflexes, etc.

Nature of Item

Items can be more discrete or more integrative in nature, just as they can be more objective or subjective. A completely discrete-point item would test simply one point or objective, while an integrative item would test more than one point or objective at a time. Sometimes an integrative item is really more a procedure than an item, as in the case of a free composition which could test a number of objectives.

The objectivity of an item refers to the way it is scored. A multiple-choice item, for example, is objective in that there is only one right answer. A free composition may be more subjective in nature if the scorer is not looking for any one right answer, but rather for a series of factors including, say, creativity, style, grammar, and mechanics.

Intellectual Operation

Items may call for different levels of intellectual operation (Valette, 1969, after Bloom *et al.*, 1956). They can test for the following intellectual levels: (a) knowledge (bringing to mind the appropriate material); (b) comprehension (understanding the basic meaning of the material); (c) application (applying the knowledge of the elements of language and comprehension to how they interrelate in the production of a correct oral or written message); (d) analysis (breaking down a message into its constituent parts in order to make explicit the relationships between ideas, including tasks like recognizing the connotative meanings of words and correctly processing a dictation, and making inferences); (e) synthesis (arranging parts so as to produce a pattern not clearly there before, such as in effectively organizing ideas in a written composition); and (f) evaluation (making quantitative and qualitative judgments about material). It is thought that these levels demand increasingly greater cognitive control as one moves from knowledge to evaluation. It may be that effective operation at more advanced levels, such as synthesis and evaluation, would call for more advanced control of the second language.

Tested Response Behavior

Items can test different response behavior. A respondent may be tested for fluency, for example, without concern for grammatical correctness. Or s/he could be told that the concern is for accuracy—phonological or grammatical correctness. Some items may call for a speedy response to determine how effectively the respondent replies under time pressure.

Characteristics of Respondents

Items can be designed specifically to cater to populations with certain characteristics. For example, items may be written differently for different age groups (e.g., pre-schoolers, children, adolescents, adults; see Kennedy, 1972), for different socioeconomic levels, and for different ethnic or language groups (e.g., English-language items for Amerindians or specifically for native speakers of Navajo). Intentional cultural bias has been identified in certain test items (see, for example, Brière, 1973; Messick and Anderson, 1974).

Item Stimulus Format

The format for the item stimulus has to be determined. An item can have a spoken, written, or pictorial stimulus, as well as any combination of the three. A tester should be aware that a listening test in which respondents answer oral questions by means of written multiple-choice responses is testing reading as well as listening. (One can avoid this if the multiple-choice responses are also presented orally.)

Item Response Format

The item response format can be fixed, structured, or free. Those with a fixed format include true/false, multiple-choice, and matching items. Those which call for a structured format include ordering (where, say, respondents are requested to arrange words to make a sentence, and several orders are possible), duplication—both written (e.g., dictation) and oral (e.g., recitation, repetition, mimicry), identification (e.g., explaining the part of speech of a form), and completion. Those calling for free format include composition—both written (e.g., creative fiction, expository essays) and oral (e.g., a speech) as well as other activities such as free oral response in role-playing situations.

Elements of Language to be Tested

Finally, items can test a variety of elements of language, including (a) phonology; (b) grammar

(morphology and syntax); (c) lexicon (vocabulary and idioms); (d) pragmatics (contextualization of language—e.g., appropriate language for a given sociocultural situation could involve dialect and register; see Oller, 1979); (e) mechanics (handwriting, spelling, punctuation, capitalization); and (f) stylistics.

The preceding overview of test types and item types was intended to lend perspective to the following discussion of approaches to testing the skills of listening, reading, speaking, and writing. The discussion includes a wide variety of item types, including different item response formats as well as a number of technical variations of a given format (e.g., different spatial presentation of the same item). No attempt is made to evaluate the effectiveness of one approach as opposed to that of another. Effectiveness depends largely on the use to which the testing technique is to be put. The reader is encouraged to make his or her own judgments as to the value of various types of test items and procedures. The examples are presented in list form to facilitate easy reference.

TESTING LANGUAGE SKILLS

The following is an enumeration of ways of testing language skills. The approaches described are a compilation and synthesis of techniques described by Harris (1969), Clark (1972a), Valette (1967), Lado (1961), Brooks (1966), and Oller (1973b), as well as those developed by the author.

TESTING LISTENING SKILLS

Auditory Identification and Discrimination

1. Identification of sounds:
    a. The student hears a sound in isolation and must identify it. (Taped stimulus): [æ] (Written response choices): *[2] (a) [æ], (b) [ɑ], (c) [ɔ] [3]
    b. The sound is in the context of a word, possibly in a sentence. (Taped stimulus): *The boy has a cat. What is the vowel in the final word?* (Written response choices): *(a) [æ], (b) [ɑ], (c) [ɔ]
2. Discrimination of foreign sounds from similar native-language sounds: e.g., the

respondent is to indicate which words are not in English. (Taped stimulus): (a) *mes* (Fr.), (b) *may*, (c) *may* (Response choices): *(a), (b), (c)

3. Discrimination of English sounds among themselves:

a. The respondent is to indicate whether two vowel sounds are the same or different. (Taped stimulus): *sun/put* (Response choices): (a) same, *(b) different

b. The respondent indicates which sound of three is different from the other two. (Taped stimulus): (1) *sun*, (2) *put*, (3) *dug* (Response choices): (a) 1, *(b) 2, (c) 3

c. These sounds could be in sentence context. (Taped stimulus): (1) *It's a sheep.* (2) *It's a sheep.* (3) *It's a ship.* (Response choices): (a) 1, (b) 2, *(c) 3

d. The respondent could choose the distractor(s) that is (are) the same as a stimulus. (Taped stimulus): *The cat was soft.* (Response choices): (a) *The cot was soft.* *(b) *The cat was soft.* (c) *The cot was soft.*

4. Implicit discrimination: The respondent hears a phrase and then must indicate the appropriate continuation. (Taped stimulus): *He was given the sheep as a present.* (Response choices): *(a) *He likes farm animals.* (b) *He likes sea vessels.*

5. Rhyming:

a. The respondent is to indicate whether two words rhyme. (Taped stimulus): *fit-seat* (Response choices): (a) rhyme, *(b) don't rhyme

b. The respondent is to mark the one of the three words that doesn't rhyme with the others. (Taped stimulus): *fit/hit/meat* (Response choices): (a), (b), *(c)

6. Intonation:

a. The respondent is to indicate whether two phrases have the same intonation. (Taped stimulus): *You're coming?/You're coming.* (Response choices) (a) same, *(b) different

b. The respondent is to mark the linear pattern that most closely depicts the intonation curve of the speaker. (Taped stimulus): *Who's there?* (Response choices): *(a) ⌣ (b) ⌢ (c) ╱

c. The respondent must determine the meaning of the phrase from the intonation. (Taped stimulus): *Good morning!* (Response choices): (a) happy to see employee, *(b) annoyed that the employee is late to work

7. Stress and accent:

a. The respondent must choose the word that is accented on a different syllable from the other two. (Taped stimulus): *cónvert/convért/convért* (Response choices): *(a), (b), (c)

b. Respondents of the same native language group could be asked to translate an English phrase into their own language. (Taped stimulus): *It's the dessert.* (Response choices for Spanish speakers): (a) *Es el desierto.* (*It's the desert.*) *(b) *Es el postre.* (*It's the dessert.*)

c. The respondent is to mark the sentence that indicates correct primary stress (word in bold letters) for a stimulus sentence. (Taped stimulus): *It's* **this** *boy's hat.* (Response choices): *(a) *It's* **this** *boy's hat.* (b) *It's this* **boy's** *hat.* (c) *It's this boy's* **hat.**

Listening as it Relates to Grammar

1. Pictorial relationships: The respondent must determine grammatical relationships. (Taped stimulus): *The pen is on the box.* (Response choices—pictures): (a) A pen in a box. *(b) A pen on a box. (c) A pen under a box.

2. Morphological endings: The respondent has to listen carefully for the inflectional markers. E.g., the respondent must determine whether the subject and verb are in the singular or the plural. (Taped stimulus): *The boys sing well.* (Response choices): (a) singular, *(b) plural, (c) same form for singular and plural

3. Agreement:

a. Respondents must determine whether two sentences are in agreement with respect to verb tense, noun-pronoun reference, subject-verb, etc. (Taped stimulus): *My sister went to the store. He bought a dozen eggs.* (Response choices): (a) agreement, *(b) lack of agreement *b.* A variation of this would be as follows: (Taped stimulus): *Joe find California very attractive.* (Response choices): (a) agreement, *(b) lack of agreement

4. Grammatical labels: The respondent indicates knowledge of grammatical labels. (Taped stimulus): *You are to identify the tense of the verb in the following sentence: That politician has received a good deal of criticism recently.* (Response choices): (a) pluperfect, (b) simple past *(c) present perfect

Listening as it Relates to Vocabulary

1. Action: The respondent performs a command (e.g., getting up, walking to the window) or draws a picture according to instructions (e.g., coloring a picture a certain way, putting hands on a clock to indicate a specific time, etc.).

2. Translation: The respondent hears a word in his or her native language and must write an English equivalent, or s/he hears a sentence and must translate the last word. Instead of writing the word, the respondent could be asked to select from multiple-choice alternatives. (Taped stimulus in Spanish): *El novio está celoso.* (Response choices): (a) *joyous,* (b) *upset,* *(c) *jealous,* (d) *conceited*

3. Pictorial representation:
a. The respondent hears a stimulus, sees a picture, and must indicate whether the picture represents what was heard. (Taped stimulus): *This is a tree.* (The number 3 is depicted.) (Response choices): (a) true, *(b) false

b. Another approach involves the careful scrutiny of a picture and indication of whether a set of sentences do or do not describe that picture. E.g., the listener sees a picture of a house with a chimney, three windows, two doors, and a two-car garage. (Taped stimulus): (a) *The house has three doors.* (b) *There is room for two cars in the garage.* (c) *The house doesn't have a fireplace.* (Response choices): *Indicate which sentences are true about the picture.* (a) *(b), (c)

4. Sentence completion or definition: The respondent is to complete the sentence with the appropriate vocabulary. (Taped stimulus): *I guess John's really upset about something because he's ....* (Response choices): (a) *sleepy,* *(b) *crying,* (c) *singing,* (d) *laughing.* A definitional format would be as follows: (Taped stimulus): *I think John's really* **anxious** *about something.* (Response choices): *(a) *worried,* (b) *happy,* (c) *unconcerned,* (d) *listless*

Auditory Comprehension

This is a catch-all category to encompass a host of activities involving the decoding of speech samples.

1. Questions and answers:
a. The respondent hears a question and must choose a correct response. (Taped stimulus): *What time did Mary get in last night?* (Response choices): (a) *Tomorrow at noon.* *(b) *At midnight.* (c) *A new Ford station wagon.*

b. The respondent indicates whether a response to a question is appropriate. (Taped stimulus): *How're you gonna get home? At about 3:30 p.m.* (Response choices): (a) appropriate, *(b) inappropriate

2. Paraphrasing or continuation:
a. The respondent hears a statement and must indicate the appropriate paraphrase for the statement. (Taped stimulus): *What'd you get yourself into this time?* (Response choices): (a) *What are you wearing this time?* (b) *What did you buy this time?* *(c) *What's your problem this time?*

b. The respondent is to find the appropriate continuation for a statement. (Taped stimulus): *The opera star didn't perform up to snuff.* (Response choices): (a) *That is the mark of a true performer.* (b) *Her performance was not bad.* *(c) *She probably was quite tired.*

3. Dialogue/telephone conversation:
a. The respondent hears a dialogue and is asked questions about it. The dialogue and the questions are taped. The response choices are written on the answer sheet. To avoid requiring extensive read-

ing skill in answering questions, the response choices themselves can also be taped.

b. The respondent listens in on a telephone conversation between two people and at appropriate times must indicate what s/he would say if s/he were one of the speakers in the conversation. (Taped stimulus): Mother: *Well, Mary, you know you were supposed to call me last week.* Mary: *I know, Mom, but I got tied up.* Mother: *That's really no excuse.* Mary: (Response choices): (a) *Yes, I'll call him.* *(b) *Well, I'm sorry.* (c) *I've really had nothing to do.*

4. Lecture: The respondent hears a lecture, with all the false starts, filled pauses, and other features that make it different from oral recitation. After the lecture, there are taped questions for which the respondent must select the appropriate multiple-choice alternative on his or her answer sheet.

5. Dictation: Dictation can serve as a test of auditory comprehension if it is given at a fast enough pace so that it is not simply a spelling test (Oller, 1972). The pace is determined by the size of the phrase groups between pauses, the length of the pauses, and the speed at which the phrase groups are read. The non-native respondent must segment the sounds into words, phrases, and sentences. It has been found that s/he makes errors of word inversion, incorrect word choice (through misunderstanding of grammar or lack of vocabulary), insertion of extra words, and omission (Oller, 1972).

For a similar listing of test items dealing with reading, speaking, and writing, see the Appendix, p. 345.

TEST CONSTRUCTION AND ADMINISTRATION

Inventory of Objectives

The test constructor first makes an inventory of the discrete points and integrative areas s/he wants to test. This involves distinguishing broad objectives from more specific ones. Important objectives are distinguished from trivial ones. Test items are then developed for each objective. If the objectives are broad, the test designer needs more items for each in order to assess the full range of performance. Varying the difficulty of the items testing a particular objective helps distinguish one student's grasp of the area covered by the objective from that of another student.

The number of test items used to measure any given objective depends on several things. First, is the test intended to assess *mastery* of the objectives or simply some attainment? If mastery is being assessed, there should be a large enough sample of items to allow measurement of this. For example, including only one item on tag questions doesn't assure the examiner that the respondent has a firm grasp of tag questions. But if the tester does not have the testing time to allow for, say, three items on tag questions, then s/he should at least be aware that s/he is not really testing for mastery. A respondent's correct answer on one item could be a result of guessing. A tester may not have time to cover all the objectives s/he would like to. Thus, s/he may simply sample from among the objectives s/he wishes to cover.

If the test is being designed for use in a course, then the objectives covered might be those most emphasized in the course, those of greatest utility value for the students, and those causing major difficulty for the students. The teacher must decide how to apply these criteria. In order to differentiate among the better and poorer achievers, it may be necessary to use some of the difficult items—items which may have only marginal value because of their low frequency in the language, their possible difficulty for natives as well, etc.

Constructing an Item File

Potential test items should be written onto file cards, perhaps color-coded into different categories (e.g., listening grammar, general reading comprehension, etc.) so as to make the items easily accessible. It is also easy to revise the items and reorder them for different tests if they are on cards. In the case of a reading comprehension procedure, the passage could be stapled to one card and the multiple-choice items accompanying the passage would follow on successive cards. Each card in the item file should contain the following information:

a. The skill or combination of skills tested.
b. The language element(s) involved.
c. The item stimulus and item response formats.
d. Instructions as to how to give the item.
e. The section of the book or the part of the course that the item relates to (if applicable).
f. The time it took to write the item (which gives an estimate of the time needed to prepare a series of such items for a test).
g. The answer, on the reverse side of the card to encourage the test constructor to try out the item in reviewing the item file. This procedure may prompt item revision. An item may seem easy or well-written when it is generated but may exhibit glaring inadequacies upon later inspection. For this reason, also, piloting of items on sample groups is a good idea before including items in actual tests.

The item file should be ample enough to provide, say, thirty percent more items than actually desired in the final test to allow for discarded items.

Test Format

One basic issue of format is whether the test progresses to increasingly more difficult items or whether easy and difficult items are interspersed. There are arguments on both sides. If items get increasingly more difficult, the respondents may give up after a while and not attempt items after the first one they get stumped on (Educational Testing Service, 1967). Yet if respondents experience failure too frequently at the outset of a test because of difficult items, they may be discouraged from attempting the remainder of the items in a section. Thus, there may be a psychological advantage to pacing the items so that they become progressively more difficult (Rivers, 1968). A compromise is to start the test with relatively easy items and then to start interspersing easy and difficult items.

Another issue of format relates to multiple-choice items. Such items lend themselves to guessing. Increasing the number of alternatives (from say, three to four) decreases the likelihood of getting the item right by chance alone. There is a thirty-three percent chance of getting a three-choice item right by guessing, and a twenty-five percent change of guessing correctly on a four-choice item. This of course assumes that all choices are equally attractive to the respondent who does not know the answer to the item. This condition is not always met.

Instructions

The instructions should be brief and yet explicit and unambiguous. The respondents should be informed as to whether guessing counts against them. They should also know the value of each item and section of the test. Finally, the time allowed for each subtest and/or for the total test should be announced. If speed is a factor for a subtest, the respondents should be aware of this. Harris (ibid.) discourages timed tests that leave more than ten to fifteen percent of the group behind.

Scoring

If an objective is tested by more than one item—say, five items—then it is possible to speak of mastery of the objective. If Juan gets four of the five items right, he has displayed eighty percent mastery of that objective, according to the test. The test may be a series of such items. If Juan's test performance is stated only in terms of his mastery of objectives, then the test is being used for criterion-referenced evaluation. What constitutes mastery of an objective is a difficult question to answer. Is it four out of five items correct on that objective? What about three out of five? Further, what constitutes notable achievement? It could be that mastery of one objective reflects far more learning than mastery of another. For this reason, items covering one objective may be weighted more than items covering other objectives. For example, three questions asked after presentation of a lecture on a tape may count more than ten short-answer multiple-choice reading or grammar items. Weighting also involves consideration of the ease of the task and the time spent on it.

The test constructor has to consider how long it will take to score particular types of items, as well as the easiest procedure for scoring (e.g., machine scoring vs. hand scoring). The more objective the item, the higher the scorer reliability is likely to be (i.e., the likelihood that two different scorers would come up with the same score for a particular respondent's test). Machine scoring involves separate answer sheets. Separate answer sheets may be desired in any event if the same test is to be given again.

Reliability

The reliability of a test concerns its precision as a measuring instrument. Reliability asks whether a test given to the same respondents a second time would yield the same results. Brière and Brown (1971) point to three crucial factors relating to test reliability:

a. Test factors: types of items, content of each item, length of the total test (the longer, the more reliable). Harris (ibid.) provides an easy-to-calculate measure of reliability. More sophisticated measures are found in statistics books and are included in computerized programs.[4] Some reliability measures call for correlating the odd-numbered items on the test with the even-numbered ones as a measure of inter-item consistency. Other measures involve more complex calculations. Some reliability coefficients are more suited for certain types of tests, e.g., timed tests (Medley's Kudar-Richardson 21). For most purposes, a reliability coefficient of .75 and up is good. A perfect coefficient is 1.0. Lado (ibid., p. 332) offers suggested reliability coefficients for tests of different skills. For example, he suggests that acceptable reliability for a speaking test may be lower (.70 to .79) than for a listening test (.80 to .89) than for a reading test (.90 to .99).

b. Situational factors: The manner in which the examiner presents the instructions, the characteristics of the room (comfort, lighting, acoustics), outside noises, and other factors can have a bearing on how well the respondents perform on the test.

c. Individual factors:
i. *Transient*: factors such as the physical and psychological state of mind of the respondent (motivation, rapport with examiner, etc.).
ii. *Stable*: factors such as mechanical skill, I.Q., ability to use English, experience with such tests.

Validity

Validity refers to whether the test actually measures what it purports to measure. Thus, the test must be reliable before it can be valid. Assuming that the test is producing a reliable measure of something, the question is then, "What is that something?" and "Is it what the test is supposed to be measuring?"

a. Face validity: This aspect of validity refers to whether the test *looks* like it is measuring what it is supposed to measure. For example, a test which measures a respondent's own English pronunciation by assessing the respondent's rating of others' pronunciation of English may not be readily accepted as a valid measure in the everyday sense of the word. The measure may appear to be too indirect. The fact that it is indirect may confuse and distract the respondent. Also, a test's title may be misleading. For example, a test entitled "Pragmatic Syntax Measure" may deal more with morphology than with syntax and may use stilted grammar-book English rather than the language of everyday situational interactions.

b. Content validity: This type of validity refers to the adequacy of sampling of content or objectives in a test. Sometimes even commercial tests constructed by experts fail to state what objectives are being covered in the test and which items specifically are testing each of these objectives. Valette (1967) notes that, "For the language teacher, the degree of test validity is not derived from a statistical analysis of test performance, but from a meticulous analysis of the content of each item and of the test as a whole."

c. Criterion-related validity: A test can be validated by seeing how closely a respondent's performance on specific sets of objectives on a total test parallels his or her performance on another test which is thought to measure the same or similar activities.

i. *Concurrent validity.* Validation is concurrent if test results are compared with results from another test given at about the same time. For example, a teacher may wish to see how student performance on a test that s/he constructs compares to student performance on some criterion measure of reading obtained from a commercial test of reading.

ii. *Predictive validity.* Validity is predictive if test results are compared with results from another test or another type of measure obtained at a later date. For example, a language aptitude test may be validated by a test of a student's achievement in the language class in which s/he was placed on the basis of the aptitude test.

d. Convergent validity: Validity in testing a given construct, such as listening comprehension, may be attained by testing the same phenomenon in a variety of different ways. The classroom teacher can practice this kind of validation. The discussion of item types presented earlier in this chapter provides a number of techniques for testing the same objectives differently. Varying the item stimulus and response formats, as well as the discreteness and integrativeness of the items can produce items testing the same objectives in different ways.

Item Analysis

a. *Piloting the test.* If time and resources permit, a test should be piloted on a population similar to that for which it is designed. The pilot administration provides the test constructor feedback on the items. On timed subtests, pilot respondents can be instructed to mark how far they got when the time ran out and then to complete the test so that there is feedback on all the items in the test.

b. *Item Difficulty.* Item difficulty refers to the proportion of correct responses to a test item. A test which aims to differentiate among respondents should have items which forty to sixty percent of the respondents answer correctly. (If ten out of twenty respondents answer an item correctly, the item difficulty is fifty percent.) If the purpose of the test is to determine whether nearly all students have achieved the objectives of, say, a course, then the item difficulty should be ninety percent or better.

c. *Item Discrimination.* The item discrimination index tells how well an item performs in separating the better students from the poorer ones (Valette, 1967). The index is intended to distinguish respondents who know the most or have the skills or abilities being tested from those who do not (Harris, ibid.). Knowledge of the material is determined by the respondent's performance on the *total* test (i.e., all subtests combined).

An item discrimination level of .30 or above is generally agreed to be desirable. One way to calculate item discrimination is to distinguish the top twenty-five percent of the test papers and the bottom twenty-five percent (Harris, ibid.). For example, if there are twenty papers, the top five and bottom five are identified. These are labeled the "high" and the "low" groups respectively. The others are called "middle." There are three steps in the calculation. First, for any given item, the responses of the high and low groups are tabulated as "correct" or "incorrect."

	No. of Respondents	Correct	Incorrect
High	5	4	1
Middle	(10)	(4)	(6)
Low	5	2	3

Second, the number of "lows" who answered correctly is subtracted from the number of "highs" who answered correctly. Third, the difference (here 2) is divided by the number of papers in the high or low groups (here 5). The result is the item discrimination coefficient (here, $2/5 = .40$). If there are an uneven number of papers in the high and low groups (e.g., 6 and 5), then the average (5.5) is used for calculations.

Another way to calculate item discrimination is by means of a point-biserial correlation, a measure of an item's reliability (Clark, 1972a). A correlation is made between all respondents' performance on a given item (a dichotomous variable—right or wrong) and their performance on some more general criterion, usually scores on the test as a whole (a continuous variable). The higher the point-biserial correlation for a given item (the maximum is 1.0), the more the respondents getting a particular item right are also those who perform best on the total test (or other criterion measure). A correlation coefficient of .30 or better would make the item acceptable with respect to discrimination.

d. *In-Class Item Analysis.* The teacher can calculate item difficulty and discrimination for a test in class with the students' help (Valette, 1967). For item difficulty, the students can switch papers and then raise their hands if the item the teacher announces is incorrectly answered on the test they are correcting. The teacher keeps a tally. Obtaining item discrimination is more complex. The teacher must divide the papers into a high and a low stack (with or without middle group) and then must ask for a show of hands from each group as to the number who got a particular item correct. The item discrimination coefficient is then calculated by means of the computational steps enumerated above.

Test Revision
If an item has a difficulty coefficient of lower than forty percent and higher than sixty percent or so,[5] and if the discrimination coefficient is below .30, then the item should probably be eliminated. But it is difficult to select or reject borderline items. Especially if the item analysis is performed on a small sample, only one or two responses will change the index considerably. There may be good justification for leaving an item in the test if, for example, it is a lead-off item used to give students encouragement to continue on. Also, *where* an item appears in a test may effect performance on it. For example, students may do best on the items in the *middle* of an exam, after they have warmed up to the test and before fatigue sets in.

Multiple-choice items can be improved by examining the percent of respondents who selected each choice. If some distractors draw no responses or too many, then they should be omitted or altered. This task requires both rigor and intuition. For instance, it may be necessary to change the syntax or vocabulary of a distractor, or perhaps its semantic thrust. In piloting the test, it is possible to ask the respondents what their rationale was for choosing a particular distractor instead of the correct answer.

The results of item analysis can be added to the item cards in the card file if one has been established. If a particular test item comes under challenge by respondents or other examiners, it is useful to be able to check the item analysis information on the item. Perhaps it will turn out to be a borderline item that should probably not have been included in the test.

Test Administration
The following checklist of administration tips applies primarily to large-scale examinations, e.g., fifty or more students. Yet many of the suggestions apply to classroom tests as well. The word "should" is used liberally but the "shoulds" of test administration will vary from setting to setting. These are only suggestions, not prescriptions:

- The room should be carefully checked out to see that there is adequate ventilation or heat, light, seating, acoustics, etc. The name of the exam should appear on the blackboard.
- If a public address system or any mechanical device (e.g., tape recorder) is to be used, it should be set up and tested in advance to make sure it works. It is embarrassing to announce a dictation that doesn't materialize because the equipment isn't working. Presenting a dictation "live" may favor the students in the front rows and subsequently draw protests from some of those who were in the back once the results are announced.
- Proctors should guide students to their seats. It may be best to have one door through which the students are to enter. There are various seating possibilities, but every other seat is usually good enough. For example, one way is to use every other seat and every other row, with people sitting directly behind the person two rows in front of them.

- Pencils should be available for the students who didn't bring one.
- Staplers may be handy for reassembling exams that come apart. There may be other useful odds and ends to have on hand, such as a watch or even a stop watch, red pencils for scoring, etc.
- Latecomers should *not* be allowed to take the exam. They should be informed as to the date of the make-up (if there is one). Inevitably, the latecomer who is permitted to take the exam will use his or her tardiness as an excuse if s/he performs poorly on the test.
- The test administrator should present him- or herself as affable but stern. A few smiles help to put the respondents somewhat at ease. S/he should introduce him- or herself and perhaps give a little background on the test if applicable. The sternness is necessary to make it very clear that the proctors will not stand for any cheating. Much as the tester might wish that such activities didn't go on, they do. Proctors should issue warnings, report the incident to the person in charge, and even confiscate the exam if necessary.
- It is important to preserve test security, and very hard to do so. Inevitably one or two exams are missing at the end of the session, whether by a student leaving "for the bathroom" with his or her exam or ducking out the door at the end of the exam period, clutching his or her exam and planning to study up before the make-up. Passing multiple copies down a row is one way that a respondent can obtain an extra copy of the test, so care should be taken in test distribution.
- The concept of first and last names may be difficult to explain to students, particularly those with weak English skills. Some students, particularly the Asians, have first and last names that appear identical to the American. It may help to tell the students to put a box around their last name, using a model such as James Bond, or Bond, James.

- The time that the exam begins and the total time remaining for the test and/or subtests should be written on the blackboard.
- If the instructions are to be read aloud, they should be read slowly with no departure from the established wording. If questions arise, the tester can use paraphrasing but should not add anything substantive to the instructions (Harris, ibid.).
- Announce the number of pages the exam has. If students are missing pages out of their exam, they should raise their hand in order to obtain a new exam or the missing page. Often the student will simply disregard, overlook, or be too panicked to do anything about the missing page, and the result is an incomplete exam.
- Proctors should make sure that no one starts the exam until told to do so. This sounds obvious but there are always several students who do just that.
- Students may have a variety of problems during the exam, illness, hearing disorders, and the like, that may make the listening comprehension or dictation activities impossible for them. The best procedure may be to have the respondent take the test at a later date in a special sitting, or to allow him or her to skip the aural sections of the test, with his or her score becoming a prorating of the other sections of the test.
- Students should be informed as to how they can obtain the results of the exam. If it is a classroom test, students may be told to exchange papers and do the correcting right in class. One innovative approach is to assign a student a grade not only for his or her own work but for how well s/he corrects someone else's paper, as, for example, on a dictation.
- When students are ready to leave—and usually the bulk of them finish at the same time—proctors should check for several things such as: *a.* Signature on exam matching signature on some other

identification (some people may take exams for others). *b.* Return of pencil. *c.* Name printed on every page of the exam. *d.* All biographical data on cover sheet filled out (if applicable). *e.* No one taking copies of the exam with him or her. *f.* All sections of the exam completed (students may forget to do several reading passages, for example).

NOTES

1. Sometimes teachers speak of using a "curve," which simply means they evaluate a student's performance with that of other students in the same class or in other classes.

2. Throughout this paper unless otherwise indicated the correct answer will be preceded by an asterisk to distinguish it from the distractors.

3. [æ] = *a* as in *cat;* [ɑ] = *a* as in *father;* [ɔ] = *au* as in *caught.*

4. For example, one test analysis package program available is called Testat (Veldman, 1967). It provides all the basic statistics for tests, questionnaires, and rating scales.

5. Unless a high difficulty coefficient, e.g., ninety percent or better, is desired.

DISCUSSION QUESTIONS

1. Is there such a thing as a general proficiency test that isn't somewhat testing achievement in language learning as well? What would you consider the main differences between achievement tests and general proficiency tests? Think of such tests that you have taken. Were they actually testing what they purported to test?

2. Can there be a test that is culturally fair for all ethnic and social-class groups? How might tests be biased against certain groups?

3. Are the productive skills (speaking and writing) harder to assess than the receptive skills (listening and reading)? Why or why not?

4. What are the trade-offs between choosing more objectively scored vs. more subjectively scored items or procedures?

5. Can a test be valid if it is not reliable? Why or why not?

SUGGESTED ACTIVITIES

1. Take an ESL/EFL test—either your own or someone else's—and review it, using the review checklist of questions provided below:

a. Instructions:

i. Are the instructions for each section clear? Do all the items in a section fit the instructions for that section?

ii. Is the vocabulary in the instructions and in the items at the desired level of difficulty (or too hard—particularly in the instruction section)?

iii. Are there good examples of how to complete each section (where applicable)?

iv. In structured or free-response sections, do the instructions indicate the approximate length of the response that is to be made?

v. If the test is timed or timed in certain sections, is the timing realistic?

vi. Are the respondents informed in the instructions as to whether the section is timed and how long they will have?

vii. Do the instructions indicate the value of the particular section with respect to the overall test score? Is the overall value of the test clear to the intended respondents? What is the purpose of the test?

viii. Is the method of administering the test/quiz carefully established (i.e., so that someone else would administer the test exactly as you would, if you were not able to give it or intended others to administer it)?

b. Content:

i. (With reference to achievement tests): Is the test adequately covering the instructional objectives for the course? Is it testing material *not* taught/learned in the course? (Remember that a good test should reveal gaps in the instructor's teaching as well as in the student's learning.)

ii. Is the test testing the desired receptive/productive language skills? Has the test adequately isolated the desired skill (if this is what it purports to do)?

iii. Does the content of the test cover the intended elements of language (phonology, grammar, vocabulary, mechanics, etc.)? Is the test intending to get at *mastery* of a set (or sampled subset) of objectives or simply some attainment of these objectives? Is the actual test consistent with the expressed design?

iv. Is only one style (formal, casual, intimate) or dialect (standard or non-standard) considered correct in one or all sections of the test? Are the respondents aware of this (with reference to the "Instructions" section above)? If the intent is to keep the language "conversational" in, say, short-answer listening comprehension items, do the items reflect this intent?

v. Might some or many items be testing more points than you thought originally (if you constructed the test)? Would it then help to simplify these points so as to give greater prominence to exactly the points intended to be measured?

vi. Are any of your sentences "linguistic curiosities" in an effort to test certain lexical and/or structural points? (E.g., "My brother has something beautiful and I have nothing ugly."—from Rivers, 1968, p. 300.)

vii. After all is said and done, does the test have the right title or might it mislead both the respondents and potential test administrators and interpreters of the results?

c. Item format and layout of the test:

i. Is the test as a whole too long or too short? (If too short, it may not be reliable.)

ii. Is one objective or another being tested too much or too little? (Over-testing may start giving away the answers and under-testing may not give enough diagnostic information.)

iii. Are the items testing the same objective spaced such that one doesn't provide a give-away for the others?

iv. Are any items or sections clearly too difficult or too easy to answer? (Of course, item analysis helps answer this question. The difficulty of an item is often hard to determine on an *a priori* basis.)

v. Have the correct true/false and multiple-choice responses been adequately randomized so as not to set up a response pattern? (E.g., all t/f items shouldn't be "true" and all multiple-choice items shouldn't have either "b" or "c" as the correct answer.)

vi. Are the items paced so that even the poorest student will experience at least a modicum of success at the outset?

vii. Are the item response formats the most appropriate for what you want to be testing? (E.g., would matching be a more efficient means of testing vocabulary, say, than completion or multiple-choice, or would you wish to use several formats?)

viii. Is the item stimulus format appropriate? (E.g., should the stimulus be taped, rather than written, or should both be used?)

ix. How good is the layout?
(1) Is the technical arrangement of the items on the printed page easy to follow? (E.g., are the multiple-choice alternatives horizontal or vertical, in the sentence itself, or to one side, etc.?)
(2) Is the spacing between and within items adequate?
(3) If dittoed, is the print legible?

x. Have the items been adequately reviewed by other native speakers (and non-natives, if possible) to eliminate poor distractors and deceptive or confusing items?

d. Scoring:

i. Have the methods for scoring the test or grading a procedure or section been adequately determined?

ii. Are the items and/or sections weighted appropriately in scoring—i.e., do they coincide with your notions about the most important objectives, the ones given the most emphasis in the class, the most useful elements, etc.?

SUGGESTIONS FOR FURTHER READING

Clark, John L. D. (1972)
Foreign language testing: theory and practice. Philadelphia: The Center for Curriculum Development, Inc.
This text provides a thorough coverage of foreign language testing, using a theoretical framework developed for the book. Sample items are drawn mostly from the testing of French. Chapters discuss prognostic testing, achievement resting, proficiency testing, knowledge testing, and the role of published tests. The author evaluates the testing techniques he discusses and is critical of a number of approaches to testing, enumerating their shortcomings.

Harris, David P. (1969)
Testing English as a second language. New York: McGraw-Hill Book Company.
This text provides perhaps the only book devoted solely to construction of English-as-a-second-language tests. The organization is not as easy to follow as that of the Clark text. For example, Harris has a chapter on testing grammar without distinguishing listening from speaking items, as Clark does. Harris is somewhat prescriptive, not too critical, and a little simplistic in an attempt to present test construction issues simply.

Valette, Rebecca M. (1967)
Modern language testing: a handbook. New York: Harcourt, Brace and World, Inc.
This book is more directed at the classroom teacher than the Clark or the Harris books. The author provides many helpful suggestions for teachers, as well as numerous examples of item types (from English, German, and the Romance languages). The more theoretical issues treated in depth by Clark are treated more superficially, if at all, in this text.
See also the second edition of Valette's text (1978).

Lado, Robert (1964)
Language testing: the construction and use of foreign language tests. New York: McGraw-Hill Book Company.

Although slightly outdated (this book was first published in 1961), this text still provides many useful sample items in English and Spanish. The coverage is thorough, with much space devoted to testing pronunciation and auditory comprehension.

Valette, Rebecca (1969)
Directions in foreign language testing. New York: Modern Language Association.
This pamphlet primarily applies the Bloom taxonomy of educational objectives to language testing. The author also discusses language aptitude tests and the role of testing in teacher evaluation.

Clark, John L. D. (1972)
Measurement implications of recent trends in foreign language teaching," in Dale L. Lange, and Charles J. James, eds. *Foreign language education: a reappraisal.* Skokie, Illinois: National Textbook Company, pp. 219-257.
A recent review of the state of the art in foreign language testing. The author discusses some of the current issues in language testing, such as the relationship between linguistic and communicative performance, redundancy in language, and the cloze procedure.

Tyler, Ralph W., and Richard M. Wolf, eds. (1974)
Crucial issues in testing. Berkeley, California: McCutchan Publishing Corporation.
A collection of articles concerning testing in general, including sections on testing minority groups, using tests to select students for programs and for grouping, and criterion-referenced testing.

Tuckman, Bruce W. (1972)
Conducting educational research. New York: Harcourt Brace Jovanovich, Inc.
Although the author only devotes 20 pages specifically to testing (136-156), the book provides an excellent guide to research methodology, with a chapter on the writing of a research report (chapter 11).

APPENDIX: EXAMPLE TEST ITEMS FOR MEASURING READING, SPEAKING, AND WRITING SKILLS

Testing Reading Skills

(a)   *Grammar: Morphology and Syntax*
    1. Multiple choice: This format can be effectively used to test a number of discrete grammatical points, such as adjectival order, a particular verb form or preposition, as well as to test grammatical function or the correctness of forms. A variety of technical variations can be used, as indicated by the following examples:
       a. Part of a sentence is left blank and choices with alternative word order are provided:
       Mary likes her . . . . . . hats very much.
        (a) *little four French* (b) *French little four* *(c) *four little French*

b. Either using the form in *a.* above or expanding the item to include a rejoinder or an answer to a question, a set of alternative grammatical forms is presented:

Did you go to the movie last night? No, I . . . .

                       *(a)   *didn't go.*
                       (b)   *haven't gone.*
                       (c)   *hadn't gone.*

With respect to format, testers vary in their preferences. Not only is there variation in the *number* of multiple-choice distractors (note that two are used above), but also in how they are displayed. The following are alternate approaches:

No, I (A. didn't go) (B. haven't gone) (C. hadn't gone).

                   (a)   *didn't go.*
No, I . . . . . .   (b)   *haven't gone.*
                   (c)   *hadn't gone.*

c. This item is similar to *a.* and *b.* above, except that the alternatives are complete sentences, rather than forms intended to complete sentences. The respondent is to choose the correct one:

*(a) *I can't stop looking at her.*
 (b) *I can't stop looking her.*
 (c) *I can't stop looking on her.*

d. The respondent must indicate the alternative which correctly indicates how an underlined form functions in a sentence:

When Mary and Jack went out, Jack didn't mind having his mother come along with <u>them</u>.

 (a) *the mother and Jack*
 (b) *Mary and the mother*
*(c) *Mary and Jack*

A variation involving both multiple-choice and identification entails a series of, say, four underlined words in a sentence and the respondent is asked to indicate which one is grammatically incorrect:

<u>The class</u> <u>has</u> <u>went</u> to the art mus<u>eum</u> <u>today</u>.   <u> c </u>
    a   b   c   d

2. Ordering: Four sections of a sentence are presented in a random order and must be ordered correctly to reconstruct the sentence:

(a) *that*   (b) *it was clear*   (c) *the book*   (d) *he liked*
(b) (a) (d) (c)

This type of item tests a knowledge of word order in the surface structure of sentences.

3. Identification and Written Composition:

a. An item which calls for a respondent to determine whether an item is grammatical would involve the process of identification: Grammatical?

He would have went to the movies, had he known Jane would be there.

Yes _____   No   X_____

A variation on this item would involve the underlining of that portion of the item that is incorrect grammatically.

b. An item combining identification with written composition could consist of the respondent reading a sentence and determining whether there is a grammatical error. If not, s/he marks a check in the margin. If so, s/he must underline the ungrammatical form and write the correct form in the space at the margin:

George and Mary couldn't look after theyself.   themselves

The production of the correct form constitutes the written composition phase of the response.

c. A sentence completion item may provide a rootword in parentheses to be used in the correct form, rather than multiple choice responses:

He . . . . . . (go) to the movies, had he known that Jane would be there.
(Answer: *would have gone*)

Or items may ask for sentence transformations:

(Task): Write the sentence, *John hit the ball,* as a question.
(Response): *Did John hit the ball?*

Both of the above are examples of written composition, from the production of the correct verb form to the entire transformation of a given sentence.

(b) *Lexicon: Vocabulary and Idioms*

1. Multiple choice: There are a series of vocabulary items utilizing the format of sentence followed by multiple-choice alternatives.

a. The stem or stimulus may be a question or a statement with an underlined word or phrase (e.g., an idiom). Then the respondent must choose the best synonym, antonym, definition, or association for the underlined form:

The new mayor effected many programs.
   (a) *influenced*
   (b) *gave impetus to*
  *(c) *put into operation*
   (d) *improved*

b. A word is left blank and the respondent must select the appropriate word for the context:

Mary thought Tom was dead serious, but really he was only being . . . .
(a) *somber*   *(b) *facetious*   (c) *critical*

c. A word is given in the second or foreign language and multiple-choice alternatives are given in the respondent's native language:

gift   (a) *dolor*
           *(b) *regalo*
            (c) *deber*
            (d) *carro*

d. The same as *c.* except that a whole sentence is used, instead of a single word.

Se lo diré cuando lo sepa yo.
   (a) *I'll tell you when I know.*
   (b) *He'll tell me when he finds out.*
  *(c) *I'll tell you when I find out.*
   (d) *I'll tell him after he knows me.*

This item differs from the others in that it tests a knowlege of more than one vocabulary item (*sepa*). It also tests for a knowledge of grammatical structure. This could be considered a more integrative item.

The following are some guidelines for writing multiple-choice vocabulary items. First, there is an advantage in making sure that the multiple-choice synonyms for a stimulus word are *less* difficult than that stimulus word: an incorrect answer is less likely to be the fault of difficult vocabulary in the distractors. Second, keeping the article out of the stem sometimes helps to avoid providing unnecessary clues. For example:

An agreement is. . . . . .

*(a) *an understanding*
 (b) *a promise*
 (c) *a compromise*

When writing responses for multiple-choice items, ascertaining that the *best* alternative is indeed among these choices is an important, though sometimes overlooked step.

Distractors can be designed to serve different purposes. Lado (1964) suggests that distractors can be either "context-induced," "meaning-induced," or "form-induced." Consider the following item:

He wears glasses. . . . . .

 (a) *for gardening*
*(b) *to see with*
 (c) *to drink with*

Alternative (a) may be considered context-induced because *for gardening* provides a context for *wears*. Response (c) is meaning-induced because *to drink with* represents a different meaning for *glasses*, namely drinking glasses. With regard to form-induced distractors, consider the following item:

He is <u>*actually*</u> *generous.*

(a) *right now*   *(b) *really*   (c) *apparently*

Distractor (a), *right now*, may attract speakers of Romance languages in which a form of the same structure means *currently* or *right now*. Such lexical items with the same structural use but different meanings are *faux amis* ("false friends") and are form-induced.

2. Matching: A list of words could be matched with a list of definitions. The number of words may exceed the number of definitions or vice versa:

   (a) *booming*   (b) *unbelievable*
   (b) *incredible*   (c) *calm*
   (c) *placid*   (a) *expanding rapidly*

3. Identification:
   a. The respondent circles or underlines the irrelevant or misplaced word in a sentence:
      Bill went home <u>*these*</u> *in spite of the bad weather.*
   b. From lists of word pairs, the respondent must indicate whether the words are the same/opposite:

      meticulous—casual   <u>opposite</u>
      facetious—funny   <u>same</u>
      mundane—unusual   <u>opposite</u>

4. Completion: The respondent reads a definition, followed by the first letter of a series of words, one of which begins the word defined. The respondent is to complete the word:

A special place or building for eating meals.

m . . . . . .

h . . . . . .

restaurant

b . . . . . .

a . . . . . .

5. Written composition:

   a. The respondent must add prefixes to words to give them the opposite meaning:

   legal ___illegal_____

   important ___unimportant___

   b. Translating a sentence from a foreign language:

   (Task): Translate into English: *Se lo diré cuando lo sepa yo.*

   (Response): *I'll tell you when I find out.*

(c) *Pragmatics*

   1. Multiple choice

      a. Select the appropriate answer to a question or the appropriate rejoinder to a statement, in multiple-choice form:

      A: *It's really hot today.*

      B: (a) *We better put on real warm clothes.*

         (b) Yeah, it's a good day to go swimming.

         (c) *Yes, I've got a nice baby.*

         (d) *Maybe he'll be home soon.*

      b. Select the statement that is the logical continuation of or explanation for a given statement:

      She had a bad sore throat on the night of her vocal recital.

        (a) *She sang beautifully because of it.*

        (b) *All the same, she sang poorly.*

       (c) Nonetheless, she sang fairly well.

        (d) *As a result, her singing was most pleasant.*

   2. Oral Composition: The respondent reads a passage describing a situation and must respond orally in an appropriate way. Ideally, the response would be based on a careful reading and understanding of the passage. The following might be an example (see Levenston, 1975, for others):

      You take your girlfriend to a fancy restaurant and have every intention of impressing her with the elegance of the place. After you and your girlfriend have been sipping wine for a long time, your main dish finally arrives. You notice that your girlfriend's plate has a dirt smudge on it. Needless to say, you are quite upset. What do you say to the waiter?

(d) *Mechanics: Character Recognition, Spelling, Punctuation (Item Response Format: Identification)*

   1. The respondent is to discriminate among characters in print or in script: For example:

      cad   **(a) lousy person*   (b) *taxi*

      Such a test of reading would be most appropriate for students who are becoming literate in a language, particularly when the alphabet is new to them. The above item tests for discrimination between *b* and *d* (assuming they know the meaning of both *cad* and *cab*).

2. The respondent reads a passage and underlines the misspelled words and circles the misplaced or omitted punctuation marks and capitalization problems: For example:

The man⊙with the big cane⊙was known to <u>excell</u> in a variety of <u>endevors</u>. His friends would exclaim⊙⊙⊙hat a talented man!⊙

(e) *Stylistics (Item Response Format: Identification)*

The respondent reads a passage and must indicate stylistic deficiencies by means of a series of marginal notations. The list of notations might include: incorrect paragraphing (¶), lack of clear transition from one sentence or paragraph to the next (*tr*), deficiency in word choice (*WC*), and inappropriate level of prose (*pr*)—e.g., too flowery given the nature of the passage.

(f) *Integrative Items and Procedures (Based on Reading Passages)*

1. Style and content of passages: The purpose of the test will dictate the appropriate style and registers to use in the passages. For example, if a test is intended to assess the ability of students to read university-level texts in English, then the test should have reading passages comparable to such texts. Material taken from university course work, such as passages from biographies, prose and/or fiction, encyclopedia excerpts, and non-technical articles would be possible sources. Other sources would be newspaper and magazine feature articles and technical manuals.

   Avoiding or simplifying overly difficult lexicon and structures (depending, once again, on the purpose of the test) may eliminate distractions which could keep the respondents from the primary task of completing the test. A sensational topic will also distract respondents. Passages depicting situations related to a particular cultural group among the respondents will give that group an advantage. If the content of the passage is familiar to any particular group (e.g., chemists, musicians) or is based on common knowledge (perhaps more "common" for some respondents than for others), the results may be skewed accordingly.

2. How the passage is read: In certain cases, the passage may be read aloud by the respondent. The purpose would be to rate the subject on his or her ability to match correct sounds with printed symbols, his or her sense of phrase groups, and his or her control of stress, intonation, and juncture patterns. Such a reading could provide an integrative measure of oral recitation, plus some indication of the respondent's grasp of grammar, semantics, pragmatics, etc. However, in group testing particularly, the respondent usually reads the passage silently. The test or subtest may be timed or may not be. If questions accompany the passage, they may be placed before or after the passage. Placing the questions before the passage may encourage skimming for answers to the questions. Placing the questions after the passage may encourage the student to read the entire passage before considering the questions. Thus, placement of the questions may put the emphasis on different skills—skimming vs. thorough reading of a passage.

   The respondent may be instructed to refer back to the passage in answering the questions, or s/he may be told not to refer back. It is also possible for him or her to answer the question both ways, without looking back and then looking back, as for example:

What does _delinquent_ mean in line 7?	Without referring to passage	Reference to passage permitted
(a) _naughty_	_____	_____
(b) _haughty_	_____	_____
(c) _sinful_	_____	_____
(d) _subtle_	_____	_____

In this last example, the respondent would receive separate scores for his or her responses in the two columns. The obvious problem here would be to ensure that the respondents avoid the temptation to cross reference their answers.

3. What the reader must do: After reading or while reading the passage, the respondent is required to respond using one or more of the following item response formats—true/false, multiple-choice, recitation, identification (of unnecessary words), completion (filling in the blanks), or written/oral composition.

4. True/false and multiple-choice items: One consideration for the test constructor is the length of the passages that are accompanied by true/false and multiple-choice response items. Longer passages encourage faster reading, and shorter ones encourage respondents to read more slowly. Thus, the test constructor can use passage length as a means for testing reading speed. Harris (ibid.) suggests that 100-250-word passages with four to seven items per passage are about right. He points out that whereas it is inefficient to have a long passage and few items, there is a possibility of overlap between items if the passage is too short and has many items. Actually, it is difficult to write several good items for a short passage, so that passage size provides a natural check on the number of items. Both Harris and Perren (1967) seem to prefer several short passages to one or two long ones.

Another consideration is the type of information that the passage is intended to provide test material for. The following is a list of some of these possible testing areas:

(a) facts, details—who? when? where? what?
(b) relationships, causes—why? how?
(c) order, sequence of facts
(d) drawing conclusions
(e) summary, main idea
(f) inference, implication
(g) evaluation, judgment of reader (based on additional information, outside experience)
(h) tone (e.g., humor, irony)
(i) style
(j) author's/characters' personalities
(k) author's/characters' feelings
(l) synonym or definition of words or phrases

A third consideration is that the items accompanying the passage be well written. The following are some problem areas that test constructors need to keep in mind:

_a._ The test constructor needs to avoid having material in both the stem and the keyed response that is is identical to that in the text, because the respondent can easily answer the item without necessarily understanding the material in the text. It is acceptable to have the same wording in the keyed response as in the passage if the behavior being tested is the ability to answer questions in the same words that are given in the text. Thorndike and Hagen (1961) point out that if the intent is to measure understanding or insights, then the items should be presented in novel terms.

b. The answer to one item will be given away if it appears in another item: *Who went to the beach?* (a) *Mary and her sister* (b) *George and Tom* *(c) *Mary and George*

(Next item—poorly chosen) *What did Mary and George find at the beach?*

c. If an item has more than one correct answer, the results may prove of little value. In any event, instructing respondents to select the *best* answer is often better than asking them to select the one that is absolutely correct, since good distractors often are somewhat or even largely correct.

d. To allow more than one correct answer per item invites scoring problems. Such troublesome items often start out as follows: (Directions): *Indicate all the statements that are true about the above passage. . . . Which items do not apply to the above passage?*

e. Short responses save time for both respondent and scorer.

f. If distractors are obviously wrong to a respondent without ever having to consult the reading passage, they are not contributing anything to the item. Ideally, all distractors should attract the same number of wrong answers (Perren, ibid.). True statements that do not provide good answers are good distractors. Choices stated in such a way that the correct one can be selected only if the respondent comprehends the problem in the stem are ideal. Ideally, all alternatives are plausible to anyone who failed to comprehend the reading passage. Thorndike and Hagen (ibid.) note that it is better to have only three good alternatives for an item than five with two obviously wrong.

g. Bormuth (1970) advocates the use of *parallel* structures for the multiple-choice for an item because *alternate* phrasing can influence the respondent's answer.

h. An item can be made more difficult by making the stem more scientific and the responses more similar. The converse is also true. In using multiple-choice items, Harris (ibid.) suggests establishing the problem in the stem:

(bad): *John was*   (a)   *worried about his car.*
              (b)   *afraid about his grades.*
              (c)   *concerned about his brother.*

(better):   *John was particularly worried about his*   (a)   *car.*
                                        (b)   *grades.*
                                        (c)   *brother.*

Thorndike and Hagen (ibid.) state that the stem should formulate the problem, and add that it shouldn't include any irrelevant material. Stems with *not* for what is *not* correct or what is *not* in the reading section are confusing, and should be used sparingly if at all.

5. Completion: The basic "cloze" procedure (Taylor, 1953; Oller, 1973a) consists of a passage in which every nth word (5th, 7th, 10th, etc.) is

eliminated. Sometimes the order is varied slightly so that the same article or preposition isn't tested repeatedly. The respondent is required to produce a word to fill a blank and therefore complete a sequence. In doing so, s/he is using both productive and receptive language skills. One of the active or productive skills is formulating the hypotheses or expectations about information that is to follow (Oller, ibid.). Choice of which word goes in a particular blank depends upon what precedes and follows:

John went to the (1) ＿＿＿＿＿＿ *to buy a loaf* (2) ＿＿＿＿＿＿
bread. He needed bread (3) ＿＿＿＿＿＿ *the sandwiches which he* (4)
＿＿＿＿＿＿*to take to school* (5) ＿＿＿＿＿＿*day.*

Variations on this model include the following:

a. Fill in words performing certain syntactic functions (e.g., prepositions, articles) or lexical functions (e.g., nouns, adjectives):
   John walked (1) ＿＿＿＿＿＿*the street and bumped* (2) ＿＿＿＿＿＿
   a lamppost. He put his hand (3) ＿＿＿＿＿＿*his head and felt a lump*
   (4) ＿＿＿＿＿＿*the middle* (5) ＿＿＿＿＿＿*his scalp.*

b. Fill in phrases, clauses, sentences, even whole paragraphs that have been deleted (Oller, ibid.):
   *The workers went on strike because. . . . . . They insisted . . . . . . until
   their demands were met. As a result of the strike. . . . . . .*

c. Select the correct word/phrase for each blank from a list (possibly alphabetized for easy reference). Respondents could be instructed to use a word from the list only once or as often as necessary.

herself	*attention*	*were*
intention	*himself*	*want*
had been	*many*	*was*
much		

   Mary (1) ＿＿＿＿＿＿ *amazed at how* (2) ＿＿＿＿＿＿*leaves were in
   the yard. She had every* (3) ＿＿＿＿＿＿ *of raking them up* (4)
   ＿＿＿＿＿＿.*

d. The first letter for each deleted word in the passage is provided. The respondent completes the words.
   *When Joe a. . . . . . home, he found Jane k. . . . . . a sweater. He
   a. . . . . . her who it was for. She i. . . . . . him that it w. . . . . . be for
   their new b. . . . . . He was s. . . . . .*

6. Written/oral Composition: Respondents may be asked to paraphrase or summarize a reading passage, either in their native language or in the foreign language. They may also be asked to describe a particular phenomenon in a passage, give the chronology for a series of activities, or answer a series of questions concerning the passage. Another kind of task is to have them formulate specific kinds of questions about the passage, perhaps similar to those suggested by the categories for question types in *d.* above. However, since respondents may understand a passage without being able to compose an answer in that language, items which ask respondents to compose their own responses may end up testing *written composition* more than *reading comprehension.*

   Respondents may also be asked to explain or provide synonyms for words or phrases in the passage, either in their own language or in the foreign language. Such exercises would be checks on knowledge of vocabulary. The respondents could even be asked whether they feel that a translation from foreign to native language or vice versa is accurate by some agreed criteria, and if not, to elaborate on the problems with the translation.

Testing Speaking Skills

(a) *Pronunciation*

    A. Oral tests of phonemic and phonetic production, intonation, and stress:

        1. *Phonemic-level pronunciation*: This type of item tests for pronunciation that is comprehensible to native speakers, although not necessarily perfect. (Pictorial and oral stimuli): *Name the object.* (Internal response): *A ship.* (Used to test for the /I/ phoneme.)

        2. *Phonetic-level pronunciation*: Such items test how closely the response approximates native pronunciation.

            a. (Pictorial and oral stimuli): *Name the object.* (Internal response): *A chair.*

            b. (Stimulus): *Translate the following into English. Veo una silla.* (Response): *I see a chair.* This item tests for the phoneme /č/.) Such items can take into account native speakers' modifications of vowels and consonants in various positions within words and across word boundaries.

        3. *Sentence or word repetition, mimicry*

            a. (Oral stimulus): *Jack always likes good food.* (Response: repetition with examiner listening for the distinction between the /U/ in *good* and the /u/ in *food.*)

            b. (Stimulus): *Did you forget your lunch money again?* (Response: repetition with examiner listening for appropriate stress and intonational patterns.)

        4. *Oral recitation.* The respondent is given familiar or new material to read and is tested for speed and accuracy in handling the material. Scoring can be for general ability or for specific points such as vowel quality, final consonant realization, and intonation.

        5. *Structured Oral responses.*

            a. Pattern practice format. (Stimulus): *I come to visit every Friday. Jim . . . .* (Response): *Jim comes to visit every Friday* (testing for the realization of the third person present tense marker, *-s*)

            b. Question and answer format. (Stimulus): *Did she leave a chair for Tom?* (Response): *Yes, she did* (testing for the /ɛ/ in *yes* and for the /I/ in *did*)

            c. Completion format. (Stimulus): *Ham and . . . . . . are a typical American breakfast* (testing for appropriate use of the final consonant cluster /gz/ in *eggs*)

        6. *Memory.* The respondent recites a poem or passage from memory. The examiner listens for phonemic and phonetic production, intonation, and stress.

    B. Written (indirect) tests of phonemic and phonetic production, intonation, and stress:

        1. *Comparing sounds.* Such tests involve assessing whether two or three sounds or words are the same or different, or whether they rhyme, as in the listening comprehension items above.

2. *Comparing sounds with letters omitted.*
   a. (Written stimulus): *In which words is the omitted sound the same?* (a) *r.consideration* (b) *r.construction* (c) *r.tribution* (Response): (a) (b)
   b. The respondent determines which words have the same sounds as the sound of the letters omitted from the stimulus word in context. (Stimulus): *The men weren't gone very l . . .g.* (a) *song* (b) *wonder* (d) *wrong* (Response): (a) (d)
3. *Locating stress.*
   a. The respondents indicate the primary stress in a sentence, either directly (Stimulus: *The boy kissed the doll.* Response: *boy*) or through multiple-choice responses, as in the listening comprehension section above.
   b. The respondent could be asked to mark the two words that have the same stress patterns. (Stimulus): (a) *independent* (b) *intelligent* (c) *unusual* (Response): (b) (c)

(b) *Grammar*
1. Multiple substitution: The respondent is given a model sentence and a sample answer. The stimuli can be oral or written and may be in the native language or target language. A change of one element in the stimulus obliges the respondent to change one or more elements in the response.
   a. The following is an example of one change in the response. (Stimulus): *I go swimming on Wednesdays. Jack. . . . . . .* (Response): *Jack goes swimming on Wednesdays.* (Testing for the third person present tense marker, -s.)
   b. The following is an example of two changes in the response. (Stimulus): *There is a book on the table. Five books.* (Response): *There are five books on the table.* (Tests for change of copula to the plural and for the addition of the plural morpheme in *books.*)
2. Modified substitution: The respondent is given the base form of the new element but must inflect it before substitution is possible. (Stimulus): *He acquired two new friends. Make.* (Response): *He made two new friends.*
3. Replacement: The respondent is to replace nouns and noun phrases with pronouns. (Stimulus): *The children are going to school.* (Response): *They are going to school.*
4. Transformations: The respondent is to change the sentence with respect to number (e.g., singular to plural), negation, interrogation, verb (person, tense, mode). (Stimulus): *The boy hit the ball. Question.* (Response): *Did the boy hit the ball?*
5. Imperative: The respondent is to tell or ask someone to do something. (Stimulus): *Sitting* (Response): *Sit down./Will you please sit down.*
6. Joining sentences: The respondent is to join two sentences to make one complex sentence. (Stimulus): *Johnny went to the store. His brother loafed around the house.* (Response): *Johnny went to the store while his brother loafed around the house.*
7. Directed responses: (Stimulus): *Do you think he knows how to sing? Yes.* (Response): *Yes, I think he knows how to sing.*
8. Statement and rejoinder: If the stimulus is provided by the test administrator, then a gesture or facial expression can be used to prompt an

appropriate response. Both a live and taped stimulus can be used to signal intonation. (Stimulus): *I can't go to the party. (sad)* (Response): *Oh, what a pity!* (Responses would be scored, say, for appropriateness and promptness of response and accuracy of intonation.)

(c) *Vocabulary*
1. Picture stimulus: A respondent must identify a noun or an action, or choose an appropriate response from several alternatives.
2. Word stimulus: The respondent is to translate a word into his or her native language or define it in the target or native language.
3. The respondent is to fill in the missing word in an oral or written sentence. (Stimulus): *A tool used for cutting paper is called a. . . . . . .* (Response): *scissors*
4. Word naming by domain: The respondent is given a period of time (e.g., 45 seconds) to name all the words s/he can that pertain to a given setting (say, kitchen) from a specified domain (say, home). (Stimulus): *Name all the objects you can which are found in the kitchen, such as "salt," "plate," and "sink."*

(d) *Pragmatics*
1. Directed conversation: The respondents are given a situation and instructions. (Stimulus): *You have been stopped by a policeman for speeding. You know that you were, in fact, speeding. What do you say?* (The response is scored for situational appropriateness, and could also be scored for pronunciation, grammar, and vocabulary.)
2. Oral translation or paraphrase of something heard or read: the scoring is for speed, accuracy, and/or fluency.
3. Free response:
   a. *Monologue.* The stimulus is one or a series of pictures, a film, or a set of instructions. The respondent is asked to retell a story, or to make up a story (e.g., *What happened? What is happening now? What will happen?*). The respondent may be given specific instructions to tell the story in, say, the past tense or in the future. The response could be scored for approximation of native fluency, for grammar, for fluency, etc.
   b. *Conversation.* The respondents are given a dialogue or a role-playing situation which they are to enact. Certain vocabulary items and structures may or may not be provided. Performance could be scored on a series of scales, including situational appropriateness, overall fluency, pronunciation, grammar, and vocabulary. Such performance is often taped for careful examination. Rating scales usually consist of five scale points. Establishing the difference between, say, a "3" and a "4" on a grammatical scale is simplified somewhat through more precise designation of levels (e.g., two to four errors is a "3," five to seven errors is a "4"). The use of more than one rater to rate the responses helps make the scoring more reliable.

Testing Writing Skills
(a) *Dictation*
Dictation is a testing tool that can tap problems of mechanics, grammar, or pragmatics, and thus deserves special mention.

1. Partial or spot dictation: The respondent has an answer sheet with only certain function words, prefixes, suffixes, or inflected endings omitted. Testing is for selected problem areas only; respondents are not requested to write what it is assumed they have already mastered.
2. Prepared dictation: The respondents know the exact page to be dictated or know that it is among a series of possible passages (to avoid memorization of a passage).
3. Paraphrase of familiar material: The dictation represents a modified form of a dialogue or selection that the respondents are familiar with through, say, the language classroom.
4. Original or new dictation: An original dictation is created, using material that is known to cause difficulties for the respondents, either in mechanics or grammar, or both.
5. Administration of a dictation: Usually, dictations are read first at a normal pace, then again with pauses at the end of phrase groups for the student to write, then once again at a normal pace. The longer the phrase groups and the shorter the pauses between them, the more taxing the dictation is on listening comprehension skills, as noted above under testing of listening comprehension.

(b) *Focus on Mechanics*
   1. Character formation:
      a. The respondent is to copy or produce from memory printed or cursive letters.
      b. Respondents are asked to transform printed words into script.
   2. Spelling: The respondent is given a list of words or a dictation and the responses are corrected for spelling.
   3. Punctuation:
      a. The respondent must use the proper punctuation in a dictation exercise.
      b. It must be determined which of a series of alternative punctuation marks belongs in each indicated place in a sentence. (Stimulus): *After the train had pulled out of the station . . . we went home.* (Response):
      (a) ;   (b) :   *(c) ,

(c) *Grammar*
   Items to test grammar in writing differ only slightly in format from those testing grammatical awareness in reading. For instance, the respondent could be asked not only to underline an incorrect form in a statement, but also to write the correct form in the margin. (Written stimulus and correct response):
   The boy didn't found his father.   find
   If the multiple-choice format is used, then items testing grammar in writing are indistinguishable from those testing grammatical knowledge in reading.
   1. Structural parallelism: (Stimulus and correct response):
      She liked singing, walking, and to read her favorite books during the summer.   reading
   2. Grammar and style: (Stimulus and correct response):
      While watching from the shore, the large sailboat slowly came into view, its sails flapping in the breeze.   As we watched

3. Sentence modification:
   a. *Sample or multiple substitution, transformation.* The respondent is to select the best way of completing a sentence in terms of grammar, choice of vocabulary, tone, and sense. (Stimulus): *He is going to the store. Bob and Mary . . . . . . ?* (Response): *Are Bob and Mary going to the store?*
   b. The respondent chooses the sentence completion which is most consistent stylistically with the stimulus. (Stimulus): *I would be inclined to suggest that your handling of this court case* (a) *ain't no good.* (b) *is far out.* (c) *leaves something to be desired.* (Response): (c)

(d) *Vocabulary*

The format for testing written vocabulary differs little from that for testing speaking vocabulary. The only real difference is that in testing writing ability, the respondent must write out the word or expression, providing an opportunity for assessing his or her proficiency in making the proper sound-symbol correspondences. Sometimes, non-native speakers can use common words in an oral statement but have little idea of how they are written. In fact, respondents may not recognize even common words when reading them for the same reason. Hence, a test of written vocabulary can provide a useful check. Items could be exactly like those under the speaking vocabulary section above: (Stimulus): *The tool for cutting paper is called a . . . . . .* (Written Response): *scissors*

(e) *Written Composition*
   1. Structured:
      a. *Completion.* Words or phrases are left out of a passage. The respondent is to write them down. Responses could be scored for structural accuracy alone (e.g., correct inflections) or for mechanical accuracy as well (e.g., spelling, capitalization).
      b. *Transposition.*
         (1) The respondent is to transpose a passage into another tense.
         (2) The respondent is to change a dialogue into indirect discourse.
      c. *Organization.* The order of sentences in a paragraph or essay is scrambled and the respondents have to give the proper order (either by writing out the correct version or by numbering each sentence). The task of reorganization is made easier the more sequence indicators there are in the text, such as *first, also,* and *consequently.*
      d. *Composition from base words.* The respondent must complete a sentence or make a complete sentence from a series of words which appear in their uninflected form.
         (1) (Written stimulus): *He make/three/paper/plane/yesterday.* (Response): *He made three paper planes yesterday.*
         (2) (Stimulus): *Make a sentence following the model. Model: The suggestions offered in the introduction to the text are designed to help the reader. warning/print/label/intend/prevent/misuse/medicine.* (Response): *The warning printed on the label is intended to prevent misuse of the medicine.*
         (3) (Stimulus): *Since you are a stranger in town, I/take/you/where/wish/go.* (Response): *I'll take you where you wish to go.*

2. Semi-structured:
   a. *Sentence termination.* The respondent is given the first part of a sentence and is to terminate it however s/he chooses.
   b. *Dialogue paraphrase.* A dialogue is read and the respondent is requested to write out a retelling of it. (Other activities are similar to those used in testing speaking.)
3. Free written composition: The more specific the instructions, the less likelihood that the respondent will incorrectly execute the composition through misunderstanding. The following are some of the specifics the examiner may wish to include:
   a. An appealing choice of topics. (The respondents may have been given the topics in advance of the exam.)
   b. An outline to be utilized in writing the composition.
   c. A set time for organizing and writing.
   d. A specified purpose for the exercise (e.g., creative writing, straight description, personalized narrative, etc.).
   e. A suggested length.
   f. Tense (e.g., future) and person (e.g., first person).
4. Correcting compositions: The examiner can give three kinds of feedback concerning compositions—grammatical, mechanical, and stylistic. A series of conventions are often used to indicate performance mistakes and basic errors of competence, as well as strengths. Conventions help streamline the correction process, since the examiner uses them to point out problem areas, not to copy edit or rewrite the composition. In fact, sometimes only certain types of problems may be corrected in a given composition.

   If conventions are used, the respondents should have a list of the conventions in order to interpret the corrections (assuming the compositions are returned to the respondents).
5. Grading compositions: It is advisable (but not always practical) to have at least two raters for each composition. The scorers should scan all the papers to get a feel for the range of responses before starting to grade. It is helpful to keep a model of a composition at each level of performance and refer to these regularly while grading since it is possible to forget the criteria for assigning grades or to inadvertently alter the criteria while grading.

   Knapp (1972) asserts that grading a composition is unnecessary and undesirable. There are times, however, when a grade is necessary, as in a formal examination. For classroom purposes, a compromise to grading could be the +, √, − system. This system encourages improvement. "−" would mean that the composition needs rewriting—that it is unacceptable as is (by some criteria, say, what is expected at a certain course level). "√" means average, O.K. "+" means that the composition is excellent, above average. The teacher could offer to change a "−" to a "√" or a "+" upon rewriting (if rewriting is extremely well done).

   The criteria used to determine +, √, −, just as those for assigning letter grades, depend on how the teacher wishes to weight the various kinds of errors and good points—e.g., how much the grammatical and mechanical aspects are weighted vs. the stylistic aspects. If the composition is a criterion-referenced achievement test, then the teacher may simply wish to measure how well certain points were learned, such as paragraphing and/or parallelism.

The relative importance in a total course grade, say, of one composition vs. another could be determined on the basis of various criteria:

a. time spent on it (number of pages or amount of work demonstrated);
b. performance under pressure in, say, a timed in-class composition;
c. occurrence during course (giving more weight to compositions written later in the course).

KEEPING UP TO DATE AS AN ESL TEACHER *

Laura Thompson

INTRODUCTION

An important part of being an effective ESL teacher is keeping abreast of developments in the field. You need to keep up with current research and new techniques after you have completed your studies and your training. It is not too difficult to do this if you know where to turn for information. A few resources may be apparent, such as keeping in touch with the school you attended; however, more resources are needed for optimum progress. In addition to having the latest information pertaining to your area(s) of interest, you also need to have channels that will open up new interests.

This chapter is designed to open up such channels of information. To accomplish this, four major resource areas will be considered: professional organizations, periodicals, publishers, and colleges or universities. For each of the four areas specific references and general information are provided.

PROFESSIONAL ORGANIZATIONS

This first channel of information is an important one. Such organizations may be your best

link with other professionals and their work. The ESL/EFL teacher needs contact with other teachers and with researchers. This can often be accomplished through professional organizations as this is their primary aim. There is almost always a membership fee, but it is usually nominal. These organizations hold conventions and seminars, publish journals and newsletters, and generally do all they can to disseminate information. They are listed here according to the geographical area that they cover. Most teachers will belong to organizations at several levels: national, state or regional, and local.

International
International Association of Applied Linguistics
Address:
    c/o Prof. Dr. Gerhard Nickel
    Institute of Linguistics
    Schlosstrasse 26
    D-7000 Stuttgart 1
    West Germany
The aim of this association is to coordinate and encourage research in the field of applied linguistics. It publishes two bulletins a year and holds triennial conventions. (Also known as the

Association Internationale de Linguistique Appliquée or A.I.L.A.).

International Association of Teachers of English as a Foreign Language (IATEFL)
Address:
    16 Alexandra Gardens
    Hounslow
    Middlesex TW3 4HU
    England

The aim of this association is to encourage better teaching of English as a Foreign Language. It holds annual conferences and meetings. It is affiliated with the Féderation International de Professeurs de Langues Vivantes. It publishes a newsletter five times a year that is free to members only.

National and International
Teachers of English to Speakers of Other Languages
Address:
    202 D.C. Transit Building
    Georgetown University
    Washington, D.C. 20057

Membership includes subscription to the *TESOL Quarterly* and the TESOL Newsletter. It holds annual conventions and sponsors many meetings, conferences, and workshops.

National Association for Foreign Student Affairs, Association of Teachers of English as a Second Language
Address:
    Membership Office
    1860 19th St. N.W.
    Washington, D.C. 20009

This organization publishes a newsletter and Occasional Papers in TESL. It is oriented toward teachers of university or college level ESL. It sponsors state and national conferences and workshops.

State
There are many organizations at the state level. An example is the California Association of Teachers of English to Speakers of Other Languages. Many other states and at least one neighboring country (i.e., Mexico) have TESOL affiliates. Write to the national organization (see above) for the most recent information on state and regional TESOL affiliates. These organizations send out newsletters and sponsor conferences and workshops.

Local
There are also organizations operating at the local level. Sometimes these are within a school district, sometimes within a city, and sometimes these are within a small regional area. An example is the Los Angeles chapter of CATESOL. The state affiliate should be contacted for information regarding such local chapters. These organizations may also put out newsletters. They typically sponsor workshops and seminars especially suited to local needs.

PERIODICALS

The second channel of information that we shall consider is periodicals. This area overlaps somewhat with the first one as many organizations publish their own journals. Periodicals help you keep up with information in the general field of TESL/TEFL and also with many specialized areas of interest.

The periodicals listed below are grouped under ten headings according to content.

ESL/EFL or Language Teaching in General
English Language Teaching Journal
For English as a Second Language. Published by Oxford University Press in association with the British Council.
Address for new subscriptions:
    Subscription Department
    Oxford University Press
    Press Road
    Neasden, London NW 10
    England

Earlier reprints are available and the contribution of articles from classroom teachers is encouraged. See the journal for details.

English-Teaching Abstracts
Published by the British Council
Address:
    English-Teaching Information Centre
    State House
    High Holborn
    London

English Teaching Forum

Available free of charge through the United States Information Agency to Teachers who reside and work outside the United States; Those living in the U.S. may subscribe to *The Forum* through the U.S. Government Printing Office. Contributions from classroom teachers are encouraged.

    English Teaching Forum
    English Teaching Division
    Information Center Service
    ICA
    Washington, D.C. 20547

Educational Resources Information Center (ERIC)

Documents on the teaching of foreign languages (including ESL/EFL)
    Address:
    Clearinghouse on Languages and Linguistics
    American Council on the Teaching of Foreign Languages
    62 Fifth Avenue
    New York, NY 10011

The bulletin announcing their publications is published semi-annually and is distributed free of charge.

Foreign Language Annals

Published 4 times per year by the American Council on the Teaching of Foreign Languages (ACTFL)
    Address:
    62 Fifth Avenue
    New York, NY 10011

Language Learning

Published semi-annually by the English Language Institute, University of Michigan
    Address:
    2006 North University Building
    University of Michigan
    Ann Arbor, Michigan 48104

Modern Language Journal (MLJ)

Published monthly September through April by the National Federation of Modern Language Teachers Association
Address (Business Office):
    Richard S. Shill, Bus. Mgr.
    Dept. of Foreign Languages
    University of Nebraska
    Omaha, NEB 68182

TESOL Quarterly

Published by TESOL four times a year.
Address:
    202 D.C. Transit Building
    Georgetown University
    Washington, D.C. 20057

Rates are included in TESOL membership. Back issues are available and contributions from classroom teachers are encouraged.

UCLA Workpapers in TESL

One volume of faculty contributed articles was published annually by the ESL Section of the English Department at UCLA, Los Angeles, CA 90024. Some back issues are available.

Audiovisual Aids

Audiovisual Language Journal

"Journal of Applied Linguistics and Teaching Technology"
Address:
    Miss D. P. Wood
    Berenice
    1174 Highlane
    Burslen, Stoke-on-Trent
    Staffs, England
Published three times a year.

Media and Methods

Exploration in Education
Address:
    North American Publishing Co.
    401 North Broad Street
    Philadelphia, PA 19108
Published monthly during the school year.

System

A Journal for Education, Technology, and Language Learning systems. Printed and published January, May, and October.
Address:
    Department of Language and Literature
    University of Linkoping
    Sweden
Available free of charge from the editors.

Bilingual Education

Proceedings of Southwest Area Languages and Linguistics Workshop (SWALLOW)
Address:
    M. Reyes Mazon
    Institute for Cultural Pluralism
    School of Education

San Diego State University
San Diego, CA 92115

Working Papers in Bilingualism
Address:
  The Ontario Institute for Studies in Education
  252 Bloor St. West
  Toronto, Ontario M5S 1V6
Distributed free upon request. Some back issues are available.

Child Language
Journal of Child Language
Cambridge University Press
Address:
  32 E. 57th Street
  New York, NY 10022
Published three times a year.

Language Policy/Sociolinguistics
English Around the World, published by the English-Speaking Union of the United States
Address:
  16 East 69th Street
  New York, NY 10021

International Journal of the Sociology of Language, published by Mouton
Address for subscriptions:
  Co-Libri
  P. O. B. 482
  The Hague
  Netherlands

Language in Society, published three times a year by Cambridge University Press
Address:
  32 East 57th Street
  New York, NY 10022

Language Planning Newsletter, published by the East-West Center
Address:
  University of Hawaii
  Honolulu, Hawaii 96822

Sociolinguistics Newsletter, published by the Research Committee on Sociolinguistics of the International Sociological Association
Address:
  Institute of Behavioral Science
  University of Colorado
  Boulder, Colorado 80302

Linguistics: Theoretical and Applied
International Review of Applied Linguistics in Language Teaching (IRAL)
Address:
  Julius Groos Verlag
  Postfach 10 24 23
  D-69 Heidelberg
  Germany
Published quarterly.

Journal of Linguistics, published twice annually by the Linguistics Association of Great Britain.
US address for subscriptions:
  Cambridge University Press
  32 East 57th Street
  New York, NY 10022

Language, Linguistic Society of America
Address for subscription/membership application:
  Subscription Service, LSA
  428 Preston Street
  Baltimore, MD 21202
Published quarterly as part of society membership.

Lingua, an international review of general linguistics published by the North Holland Publishing Co.
Address:
  P. O. Box 211
  Amsterdam, Netherlands

Linguistic Reporter, newsletter of the Center for Applied Linguistics, mailed nine times annually to subscribers
Address:
  Center for Applied Linguistics
  3520 Prospect St, NW
  Washington, DC 20007

Literature in a Second or Foreign Language
English Language Teaching Journal (See previous entry)

English Teaching Forum (See previous entry)

Second Language Acquisition
Language Learning (See previous entry)

IRAL (See previous entry)

Working Papers in Bilingualism (See previous entry)

Second Language Acquisition Notes and Topics (SLANT) Newsletter, a newsletter for Researchers, published by the Linguistics Program at least twice yearly.

Address:

San Jose State University
San Jose, CA 95192

TESOL Quarterly (See previous entry)

Testing

American Education Research Association (AERA)

Address:

1126 16th Street N.W.
Washington, D.C. 20036

Publications with membership

Focus, Publication of Educational Testing Service

Address:

ETS
Princeton, New Jersey 08540

Include name, title, organization, and address.

General Interest

(Similar regional Educational Research Laboratories are located all over the U.S.)

Northwest Regional Educational Laboratory
Products, services and publications, especially for adult education and bilingual education.

Address:

Office of Marketing and Dissemination
710 S. W. Second Avenue
Portland, OR 97204

SWRL (Southwest Regional Laboratory)

Address:

4665 Lampson
Los Alamitos, CA 90720

PUBLISHERS

The third channel of information consists of those publishers that produce most of the commercial ESL/EFL materials in use. This can be a very helpful area as the publishers of these materials need to be in contact with ESL/EFL teachers. They must have accurate lists of people in the field so that they can contact potential customers. It is suggested that you write to the following publishers, specify what levels and skills and students you are teaching and your areas of interest. You should ask to be put on a mailing list. Also, publishers often display their books and materials at conferences, conventions and workshops. Such exhibits offer a good opportunity for you to examine materials, talk to publishers' representatives, sign up on mailing lists, and sometimes to get examination copies.

Addison-Wesley Publishing Company
Jacob Way
Reading, MA 10017

The Collier-Macmillan Co.
School Division
866 Third Avenue
New York, NY 10022

Harcourt Brace Jovanovich, Inc.
757 Third Avenue
New York, NY 10017

Holt, Rinehart, and Winston
383 Madison Avenue
New York, NY 10017

Institute of Modern Languages
1666 Connecticut Avenue, N.W.
Washington, D.C. 20008

Longman, Inc.
19 West 44th Street
New York, NY 10036

McGraw-Hill Book Company
330 West 42nd Street
New York, NY 10036

National Council of Teachers of English
1111 Kenyon Road
Urbana, IL 61801

National Textbook Company
8259 Niles Center Road
Skokie, IL 60070

Newbury House Publishers, Inc.
54 Warehouse Lane
Rowley, MA 01969

Oxford Book Company
11 Park Place
New York, NY 10007

Oxford University Press
200 Madison Avenue
New York, NY 10017

Prentice-Hall, Inc.
Englewood Cliffs,
New Jersey 07632

Random House Inc.
457 Madison Avenue
New York, NY 10022

Regents Publishing Co.
Two Park Avenue
New York, NY 10016

Scott, Foresman and Company
1900 East Lake Avenue
Glenview, IL 60025

Teachers College Press
Columbia University
1234 Amsterdam Avenue
New York, NY 10027

Thomas Y. Crowell Company
201 Park Avenue, South
New York, NY 10003

The University of Michigan Press
615 East University
Ann Arbor, MI 48106

University Press of Hawaii
2840 Kolowalu Street
Honolulu, Hawaii 96822

Winthrop Publishers
17 Dunster Street
Cambridge, MA 02138

COLLEGES AND UNIVERSITIES

The last channel of information to be discussed involves those schools that train ESL/EFL teachers and/or offer such courses for foreign students. A good listing of teacher-training institutions can be found in a book put out by the TESOL organization entitled: *TESOL Training Program Directory*. This book has been compiled and edited by Charles H. Blatchford. There is a new edition every two years. Copies may be obtained through TESOL, 202 D.C. Transit Building, Georgetown University, Washington, D.C. 20057. This book has a very complete listing of ESL teacher training facilities in the United States and Canada. A more general resource book is published by the Center for Applied Linguistics. It is called *University Resources in the U.S. for Linguistics and Teacher Training in ESL*. CAL's address is 3520 Prospect St, NW Washington, DC 20007.

There may also be schools near you that are not listed in these two references, which offer ESL courses for foreign students. Any college or university near the teacher should be considered a potential source of information. These schools may offer courses for teachers. They may also sponsor colloquia, conferences, or workshops of interest. They may have mailing lists for sending out announcements of such events. They will probably have visiting faculty of special interest to you. Also, the resident faculty may be a very helpful resource. There may be lectures or demonstration classes that you can attend free. Finally, their library may contain books and journals of interest.

CONCLUSION

Working with these four channels of information you can keep well-informed about what is happening in your field and in any of several particular areas of interest. You can keep up to date on your current interests and develop new ones. Given a little curiosity and effort, and if you use all of these channels, you can become and/or remain an effective and well-informed ESL teacher.

NOTE

*I gratefully acknowledge the input of several colleagues in the preparation of this chapter; Kathi Bailey, Russell Campbell, Marianne Celce-Murcia, José Galvan, Evelyn Hatch, Jim Heaton, Diane Larsen-Freeman, and Clifford Prator.

DISCUSSION QUESTIONS

1. Which of the four channels of information discussed in this chapter are/will be most helpful to you in keeping up with the field? Why?

2. Get together with a group of fellow ESL teachers (in training) to see if you can think of some ways to keep abreast of developments in the field other than the four channels described in this chapter.

3. What are some of the reasons why ESL/EFL teachers fail to keep up-to-date? Do you think any of these factors might prevent you from keeping abreast of developments in ESL/EFL?

SUGGESTED ACTIVITIES

1. Whether or not you are a member, attend a national, state or local convention of a professional organization for ESL/EFL teachers. Try to attend lectures, demonstrations, and to visit the book exhibits. To what degree was it a valuable professional experience for you?

2. Draw up a form letter to send publishers describing your background and interests (teaching level, student age range, skill areas you teach, etc.) as an ESL/EFL teacher. Type it neatly on letterhead leaving space for the address. Then Xerox several copies so that you only have to type in each publisher's name and address and sign your name. This will get you on several mailing lists quickly and easily.

3. Visit the library of the institution nearest you that trains ESL teachers. Examine several periodicals listed in this chapter that are unfamiliar to you but that seem interesting. Did you find a journal you would like to subscribe to? Why or why not?

SUGGESTIONS FOR FURTHER READING

Dubin, Fraida and Elite Olshtain (1977)
Facilitating Language Learning: A Guidebook for the ESL/EFL Teacher, New York: McGraw-Hill.
This text provides useful information on publications and professional organizations, pp. 234-236.

Finocchiaro, Mary (1974)
English as a Second Language: from Theory to Practice. New York: Regents. Appendix VII, "Some Additional Resources," pp. 213-216.
Finocchiaro provides lists of agencies and associations periodicals and journals, texts, where to write to arrange for penpals, etc.

Saville-Troike, Muriel (1976)
Foundations for Teaching English as a Second Language: Theory and Method for Multicultural Education. Englewood Cliffs, N.J.: Prentice-Hall.
Saville-Troike's chapter 9, "Preparation for Teaching," offers useful suggestions and good references for additional reading on this topic, pp. 142-143.

REFERENCES

Agard, Frederick B., and Harold B. Dunkel (1948) *An Investigation of Second Language Teaching.* Boston: Ginn & Co.

Alatis, James E. (1970) (ed.) "Linguistics and the Teaching of Standard English to Speakers of Other Languages or Dialects." *Report of the 20th Annual Round Table Meeting on Linguistics and Language Studies.* Washington, D.C.: Georgetown University Press.

Allen, E. D., and R. M. Valette (1977) *Classroom Techniques: Foreign Languages and ESL.* New York: Harcourt, Brace, Jovanovich.

Allen, Harold B. (1966) *TENES: A Survey of the Teaching of English to Non-English Speakers in the United States.* Champaign, Ill.: National Council of Teachers of English.

Allen, Harold B., and Russell N. Campbell (1972) *Teaching English as a Second Language.* Second edition. New York: McGraw-Hill.

Allen, Robert (1968) "A Reassessment of the Role of the Language Laboratory," *Journal of English as a Second Language* 14:1, 49-59.

Allen, R. L., V. F. Allen, and M. Shute (1966) *English Sounds and their Spellings.* New York: Thomas Y. Crowell.

Allen, V. F. (1973) "Trends in the Teaching of Reading." *English Teaching Forum* 11:31, 8-12.

——— (1975) "The Teaching of Reading." Workshop presented at the 10th Annual TESOL Convention, Los Angeles.

Allwright, R. (1975a) "Problems in the study of the language teacher's treatment of learner error," in Burt and Dulay (1975).

——— (1975b) "Language learning through communication practice." Paper presented at the 4th International Congress of Applied Linguistics, Stuttgart, Germany.

——— (1977) "Turns, Topics and Tasks: A pilot

investigation for a case-study approach to classroom language learning." Paper presented at the 11th Annual TESOL Convention, Miami Beach, Florida.

Altman, Howard B., and Robert L. Politzer (1971) (eds.) *Individualizing Foreign Language Instruction.* Rowley, Mass.: Newbury House.

Amble, B., and S. Muehl (1959) "Perceptual span training and reading achievement," *Journal of Educational Psychology* 57:192-206.

Anthony, E. M. (1965) "Approach, Method and Technique," *ELT* XVII, 63-67.

Arapoff, N. (1968) "Controlled Rhetoric Frames," *English Language Teaching* 23:1.

Arthur, Bradford (1973) *Teaching English to Speakers of English.* New York: Harcourt, Brace, Jovanovich.

Asher, James J. (1964) "Toward a Neo-Field Theory of Behavior," *Journal of Humanistic Psychology,* 4:85-94.

——— (1965) "The Strategy of the Total Physical Response: An Application to Learning Russian," *International Review of Applied Linguistics in Language Teaching,* 3:291-300.

——— (1972) "Children's First Language as a Model for Second Language Learning," *The Modern Language Journal,* 56:133-139.

——— (1977) *Learning Another Language through Actions: The Complete Teacher's Guidebook.* Los Gatos, CA: Sky Oak Productions.

Asher, James J., Jo Anne Kusudo, and Rita De La Torre (1974) "Learning a Second Language Through Commands: The Second Field Test," *The Modern Language Journal* 58:24-32.

Ashton-Warner, Sylvia (1963) *Teacher.* New York: Simon and Schuster.

Asian Project (1972) *Bridging the Asian Language and Cultural Gap.* Volume 7. Los Angeles City Schools, Division of Career and Continuing Education (ERIC ED 095 709).

Bailey, K. (1976) "The use of two observation instruments in supervised ESL teaching." Unpublished MA thesis. University of California, Los Angeles.

Bailey, N., C. Madden, and S. Krashen (1974) "Is There a 'Natural Sequence' in Adult Second Language Learning?" *Language Learning* 24:2, 235-244.

Ball, W. (1966) "An analysis of the sentence patterns of conversational English," *English Language Teaching* 20:55-67.

——— (1968) "Let's start talking," *English Language Teaching* 22:106-119.

Band, Ora (1974) "Selected Readings in English for Hebrew-speaking students." Unpublished MA thesis in TESL, UCLA.

Bander, R. G. (1971) *American English Rhetoric.* New York: Holt, Rinehart, and Winston.

Barbe, W. B., V. H. Lucas, C. Hackney, and C. McAllister (1975) *Creative Growth with Handwriting.* Columbus, Ohio: Zaner-Bloser.

Barik, H. C., and M. Swain (1972) "Bilingual Education Project: interim report on the 1972 testing programme." Toronto, Canada: Modern Language Centre.

Barnard, Helen (1971) *Advanced English Vocabulary, Workbook 1.* Rowley, Mass.: Newbury House.

Barrera-Vasques, A. (1953) "The Tarascan project in Mexico," *UNESCO Monographs on Fundamental Education* 18:61-76.

Bassan, H. F. (1973) "Spelling Difficulties of Hebrew Speakers of English: An error analysis of third graders in three bilingual schools." Unpublished MA thesis, UCLA.

Bauman, Lynn Charles (1972) "A humanistic approach to the teaching of English literature overseas." Unpublished MA thesis in TESL, UCLA.

Beardsmore, H., and A. Renkin (1971) "A test of spoken English," *IRAL* 9:1-11.

Been, S. (1975) "Reading in the foreign language teaching program." *TESOL Quarterly* 9:3, 233-242.

Belasco, Simon (1965) "Nucleation and the audio-lingual approach," *The Modern Language Journal* 49:482-489.

——— (1967) "The plateau; or the case for comprehension: the concept approach," *The Modern Language Journal* 51:82-86.

——— (1969) "Toward the acquisition of linguistic competence: from contrived to controlled materials," *The Modern Language Journal* 53:185-205.

——— (1971) "C'est la guerre? or can cognition and verbal behavior co-exist in second-language learning," in Lugton and Heinle (1971).

——— (1972) "Language teaching—help or hindrance," *The Canadian Modern Language Journal Review* 28:10-20.

Belyayev, B. V. (1964) *The Psychology of Teaching Foreign Language* (translated from the Russian by R. F. Hingley). New York: Macmillan.

Bengur, Belkis (1973) "Selection of literature for the ESL classroom: a project involving student evaluation." Unpublished MA thesis in TESL, UCLA.

Berdiansky, B., B. Cronnell, and J. Koehler, Jr. (1969) "Spelling-sound relations and primary form-class description for speech-comprehension vocabularies of 6-9 year-olds." Technical Report No. 15. Los Alamitos, Calif.: SWRL Educational Research and Development.

Bergquist, S. R. (1966) "A comparative index for the linguistic based patterns of American English spelling." Doctoral dissertation, Stanford University. Ann Arbor, Michigan: University Microfilms, no. 67-4319.

Berko, Jean (1958) "The Child's Learning of English Morphology," *Word* 14:150-177. Reprinted in Saporta (1961).

Berman, R. (1975) "Analytic syntax: a technique for advanced level reading," *TESOL Quarterly* 3: 243-251.

Best, B. Z. (1971) "The use of cloze techniques in remedial reading." Paper presented at the American Educational Research Association conference, New York.

Bever, T. G. (1970) "The influence of speech performance on linguistic structure," in D'Arcais and Levalt (1970), 4-30.

Bever T. G., and T. G. Bower (1970) "How to Read without Listening," Project Literacy Report 6. Reprinted in Lester (1970), 305-314.

Bloom, Benjamin S. et al. (1956) *Taxonomy of Educational Objectives: The Classification of Educational Goals, Handbook I: Cognitive Domain.* New York: David McKay Co.

Bloomer, R. (1962) "The cloze procedure as a remedial reading exercise," *Journal of Developmental Reading* 5:173-181.

Bloomfield, Leonard (1933) *Language.* New York: Holt, Rinehart, and Winston.

Boiarsky, C. (1969) "Consistency of spelling and pronunciation deviations of Appalachian students," *The Modern Language Journal* 53:347-350.

Bolinger, D. (1968) "The theorist and the language teacher," *Foreign Language Annals* 2:30-41. Reprinted in Allen and Campbell (1972).

Boni, M. B. (1947) (ed.) *Fireside book of Folk songs.* New York: Simon and Schuster.

Bormuth, John R. (1970) *On the Theory of Achievement Test Items.* Chicago: University of Chicago Press.

Bowen, J. Donald (1972) "Materials Designs for Intermediate and Advanced Second-Language Classes," *UCLA Workpapers in TESL.* Reprinted with modifications in *English Teaching Forum* (1974) 12:1 under the title " 'Lecturettes' for Mature Learners."

——— (1975) *Patterns of English Pronunciation.* Rowley, Mass.: Newbury House.

Bower, T. G. (1970) "Reading by Eye," in Levin and Williams (1970), 134-146.

Bowman, M. (1966) "Some Relationships Between Flexibility and Reading Gains at the College Level," *Journal of the Reading Specialist* 1:6, 20-25.

Braam, L. (1963) "Developing and Measuring Flexibility in Reading," *The Reading Teacher* 16:4, 247-351.

Braddock, R., R. Lloyd-Jones, and L. Schoer (1963) *Research in Written Composition.* Champaign, Ill.: NCTE.

Brengelman, F. (1970a) *The English Language.* Englewood Cliffs, N.J.: Prentice-Hall.

——— (1970b) "Generative phonology and the teaching of spelling," *English Journal* 59:1113-1118.

——— (1971) "English spelling as a marker of register and style," *English Studies* 52:201-209.

Brière, E. J. (1966) "Quantity before Quality in Second Language Composition," *Language Learning* 16:3 and 4, 141-151.

——— (1973) "Cross-cultural biases in language testing," in Oller and Richards (1973), 214-227.

Brière, E. J., and Richard H. Brown (1971) "Norming Tests of ESL among Amerindian children," *TESOL Quarterly* 5:4, 327-333.

Brinton, D., and W. Gaskill (1978) Using News Broadcasts in the ESL/EFL Classroom. *TESOL,* 12:4, 403-414.

Broadbent, D. E. (1958) *Perception and Communication.* New York-London: Pergamon Press.

Brooks, Nelson (1960) *Language and Language Learning: Theory and Practice.* New York: Harcourt, Brace and Co.

——— (1967) "Making your own language tests," in Donoghue (1967), 285-302.

Brophy, J., and T. Good (1974) *Teacher-student Relationships: Causes and Consequences.* New York: Holt, Rinehart, and Winston.

Broussard, N. C. (1971) "The Spelling Errors of Mexican-American Students Tested at UCLA." Unpublished M.A. thesis in TESL, UCLA.

Burns, Richard (1971) "Methods for Individualizing Instruction," *Educational Technology* 2:55-56.

Burt, M., and H. Dulay (1975) (eds.) *New Directions in Second Language Learning, Teaching and Bilingual Education.* Washington, D.C.: TESOL.

Bushman, Robert W. (1976) "Effects of a full- and modified suggestopedic treatment in foreign language learning." Unpublished MA thesis. Provo, Utah: Brigham Young University.

Buswell, G. T. (1957) "The Relationship between Perception and Intellectual Process in Reading," *California Journal of Educational Research* 8:99-103.

Buzan, Jean Mary (1972) "Teaching English as an Additional Language to Older People: A Case Study." Vancouver, Canada: Adult Education Centre, British Columbia University. (ERIC ED 106 535)

California State Department of Education (1970) *Adult Basic Education in California: A Progress Report.* Sacramento.

Campbell, Russell (1967) "The Language Laboratory and Teaching Pronunciation," *UCLA Workpapers in TESOL* 1:69-77.

Capretz, Pierre J. (1971) "Criteria for Audio Training Aids," *Audio in the 1970's* 19-21:45-66.

Carroll, George (1967) "The Battle for Better Reading," *ELT* 22, 34-40. Reprinted in Allen and Campbell (1972).

Carroll, John B. (1955) *The Study of Language.* Cambridge, Mass.: Harvard University Press.

Carroll, J. B. (1966) "Some Neglected Relationships in Reading and Language Learning," *Elementary English* 577-582.

Carroll, J. B. et al. (1972) *The American Heritage Word Frequency Book.* New York: American Heritage Publishing Co.

Castaños, F., and M. Long (1976) "Towards non-interference: making second language learning more like the first," *MEXTESOL Journal* 1:1, 36-48.

Cathcart, R. L. (1972) "Report on a group of Anglo children after one year of immersion in instruction in Spanish." Unpublished MA thesis, UCLA.

Cathcart, R., and J. Olsen (1976) "Teachers' and Students' Preferences for Correction of Classroom Conversation Errors," in Fanselow and Crymes (1976).

Celce-Murcia, Marianne (1973) "Incorporation: A Tool for Teaching Productive Vocabulary Patterns," *UCLA Workpapers in TESL.*

——— (1974) "Report on an Informal Classroom Experiment on Speedwriting," *UCLA Workpapers in TESL.*

——— (1975) "English Structure in Context: An Area of Research for ESL Specialists," *UCLA Workpapers in TESL* 83-94.

——— (1977) "Integrating group work with the teaching of grammar." Paper presented at the 1977 CATESOL Convention in San Diego, March 26. Published in the *UCLA Workpapers in TESL*, Vol. 12, 1978.

——— (1977) "Phonological Factors in Vocabulary Acquisition," *Working Papers in Bilingualism*, 13. 27-41.

——— (forthcoming) (ed.) *Selected Research Areas in ESL.* Rowley, Mass.: Newbury House.

Celce-Murcia, M., and D. Larsen-Freeman (1978) *An English Grammar for Teachers of English as a Second or Foreign Language.* Prepublication version. UCLA, ESL Section. Rowley, Mass.: Newbury House (forthcoming).

Chall, J. (1967) *The Great Debate.* New York: McGraw-Hill.

Chastain, K. (1970) "A Methodological Study Comparing the Audio-Lingual Habit Theory and the Cognitive Code-Learning Theory: A Continuation," *The Modern Language Journal* 54:257-266.

——— (1971) *The development of modern language skills: theory to practice.* Philadelphia, Pa.: CCD.

——— (1976) *Developing Second Language Skills: Theory to Practice.* 2nd ed. Chicago: Rand McNally College Publishing Co.

Chiu, R. (1972) "Measuring register characteristics: a prerequisite for preparing advanced level TESOL programs," *TESOL Quarterly* 6:129-141.

Chomsky, C. (1970) "Reading, writing and phonology," *Harvard Educational Review* 40:287-309.

Chomsky, N. (1957) *Syntactic Structures.* The Hague: Mouton.

——— (1959) Review of Skinner's Verbal Behavior in *Language* 35:26-58.

——— (1965) *Aspects of the Theory of Syntax.* Cambridge, Mass.: MIT Press.

Chomsky, N., and M. Halle (1968) *The Sound Pattern of English.* New York: Harper & Row.

Christensen, F. (1967) *Notes Towards a New Rhetoric.* New York: Harper & Row.

CITE (Consultants in Total Education), (1974) "Composition," Mimeo, Los Angeles, CA 90024

Clark, A. D., and C. J. Richards (1966) "Auditory discrimination among economically disadvantaged and nondisadvantaged school children," *Exceptional Children* 33:259-262.

Clark, John L. D. (1972a) *Foreign Language Testing: Theory and Practice.* Philadelphia: The Center for Curriculum Development.

——— (1972b) "Measurement implications of recent trends in foreign language teaching," in Lange and James (1972), 219-257.

Cohen, A. D. (1973) "The Culver City Spanish immersion program—the first two years," *UCLA Workpapers in TESL* 7:65-74.

Coleman, Algernon (1929) *Teaching of Modern Foreign Languages in the United States.* New York: Macmillan.

Coleman, Algernon, and Robert H. Fife (1933-49) *An Analytical Bibliography of Modern Language Teaching*, III (1937-42), 3 vols. Chicago: Univ. of Chicago Press and New York: King's Crown Press, Columbia University.

Corbin, R. K., and M. Crosby (1965) "Language programs for the disadvantaged," *The Report of the NCTE Task Force on the Teaching of English to the Disadvantaged.* Champaign, Ill.: National Council of Teachers of English.

Corcoran, D. W. (1966) "An acoustic factor in letter cancellation," *Nature* 210:39-43.

Corder, S. P. (1971) "Idiosyncratic Dialects and Error Analysis," *International Review of Applied Linguistics* 9:2.

Corder, S. P., and E. Roulet (1973) (eds.) *Theoretical Linguistic Models in Applied Linguistics.* Brussels/Paris: AIMAV/Didier.

Cornelius, Edwin T. (1953) *Language Teaching.* New York: Thomas Y. Crowell Co.

Cosgrave, Desmond (1971) "From Pattern Practice to Communication," *The Modern English Journal* (Seido Language Institute, Ashiya, Japan) 1:2-3 and 2:1 (June 1970, Oct. 1970 and Feb. 1971). Reprinted in the *English Teaching Forum* 9:6.

Cosper, R., and N. C. Kephart (1955) "Retention of Reading Skills," *Journal of Educational Research* 49:211-216.

Cowan, J. R. (1974) "Lexical and Syntactic Research for the Design of EFL Reading Materials," *TESOL Quarterly* 8:389-400.

Cowles, H. M. (1976) "Textual Materials Evaluation: A Comprehensive Checksheet," *Foreign Language Annals* 9:4.

Croft, Kenneth (1972) (ed.) *Readings on English as a Second Language.* Cambridge, Mass.: Winthrop.

Cronnell, B. (1971a) "Annotated spelling-to-sound correspondence rules." Technical Report No. 32. Los Alamitos, Calif.: SWRL Educational Research and Development.

——— (1971b) "Beginning spelling: A linguistic review of six spelling series." Technical Report No. 35.

Los Alamitos, Calif.: SWRL Educational Research and Development.

—— (1971c) "Spelling-to-sound correspondences for reading vs. sound-to-spelling correspondences for writing." Professional Paper No. 12. Los Alamitos, Calif.: SWRL Educational Research and Development.

—— (1972) "Spelling-sound relations in ESL instruction," *Language Learning* 22:11-27.

Crymes, R., and W. Norris (1975) (eds.) *On TESOL '74.* Washington, D.C.: TESOL.

Cummings, Thomas (1916) *How to Learn a Foreign Language.* Privately published.

Curran, Charles A. (1972) *Counseling-Learning: A Whole-Person Model for Education.* New York: Grune and Stratton.

—— (1976) *Counseling Learning in Second Languages.* Apple River, Ill.: Apple River Press.

Cuyer, Andre (1972) "The Saint-Cloud Method: What it can and cannot achieve," *English Language Teaching* 27:19-24.

Dacanay, F., and D. Bowen (1963) (eds.) *Techniques and Procedures in Second Language Teaching.* Quezon City, the Philippines: Phoenix Publishing House.

Daoud, Abdel Messih (1970) "Evaluating an English textbook for the preparatory stage." Unpublished doctoral thesis. Cairo: Faculty of Education, Ain Shams University.

—— (1977) "Evaluating an English Language Textbook." *UCLA Workpapers in TESL* 11:113-118.

D'Arcais, Flores, B. Giovanni, and W. J. M. Levalt (1970) (eds.) *Advances in Psycholinguistics.* London-Amsterdam: North Holland.

Davis, F. B. (1968) "Research in Comprehension in Reading," *Reading Research Quarterly* 3:499-545.

Deyes, A. F. (1973) "Language Games for Advanced Students," *English Language Teaching* 27:2, 160-165.

Dickinson, Leslie (1970) "The Language Laboratory and Advanced Teaching," *English Language Teaching* 21:1, 32-47.

Diller, Karl C. (1975) "Some new trends for applied linguistics and foreign language teaching in the United States," *TESOL Quarterly* 9:65-73.

Disick, Renée S. (1973) "Individualized Instruction: Promises versus Reality," *The Modern Language Journal* 57:248-250.

Dodge, J. W. (1973) (ed.) *Reports of the Working Committees.* Northeast Conference on the Teaching of Foreign Languages.

Dolch, E. W. (1941) *Teaching Primary Reading.* Champaign, Ill.: The Garrard Press.

Donoghue, M. R. (1967) *Foreign Languages and the Schools: A Book of Readings.* Dubuque, Iowa: Wm. C. Brown and Co.

Dorry, G. N. (1966) *Games for Second Language Learning.* New York: McGraw-Hill.

Dubin, F., and E. Olshtain (1977) *Facilitating Language Learning: A Guidebook for the ESL/EFL Teacher.* New York: McGraw-Hill.

Dulay, H., and M. Burt (1973) "Should we teach children syntax?" *Language Learning* 23:2, 245-258.

—— (1974) "A New Perspective on the Creative Construction Process in Child Second Language Acquisition," *Language Learning* 24:1, 37-53.

Dumler, M. J. (1958) "A Study of Factors Related to Gains in the Reading Rate of College Students Trained with the Tachistoscope Accelerator," *Journal of Educational Research* 52:1, 27-30.

Dykstra, Gerald (1967) *An Investigation of New Concepts in Language Learning:* Research Report. New York: Teachers College, Columbia University; Boston: Council for Public Schools.

Dykstra, G., and C. B. Paulston (1966) "Guided Composition," *English Language Teaching* 21:2, 136-141.

Dykstra, G. et al. (1966) *Ananse Tales: A Course in Controlled Composition.* New York: Teacher's College Press.

Educational Testing Service (1967) *Handbook: Cooperative Primary Tests.* Princeton, N.J.

Eley, V., and D. Lewis (1976) *Learning Center Activities for Beginning ESL Language and Reading Development.* Long Beach, CA: Harris Publishing Co.

English Language Institute, Univ. of Michigan (1943) *An Intensive Course in English for Latin-American Students* 4 vols. Ann Arbor: Wahr Publishing Co. (There have been several revised editions.)

Enkvist, N. (1969) "On defining style," in Love and Payne (1969), 120-132.

Erazmus, E. T. (1960) "Second Language Composition Teaching at the Intermediate Level," *Language Learning* 10:1 and 2, 25-31.

Eskey, D. (1970) "A New Technique for the Teaching of Reading to Advanced Students," *TESOL Quarterly* 4:315-321.

—— (1971) "Advanced Reading: The Structural Problem," *English Teaching Forum* 9:15-19.

—— (1973) "A Model Program for Teaching Advanced Reading to Students of English as a Foreign Language," *Language Learning* 23:2, 169-184.

Evans, Lyn (1970) "The Use of the Language Laboratory for Phonetics at Advanced Levels of English," *Language Learning* 20:1, 109-121.

Everyday English vols. 1 and 2 (1973) San Francisco: Asian Newcomer Parent Program, Education Center for Chinese.

Falk, Julia S. (1973) *Linguistics and Language: A Survey of Basic Concepts and Applications.* Lexington, Mass.: Xerox.

Fanselow, J. (1974) "The Treatment of Error in Oral Work." Paper presented at the Eighth Annual TESOL Convention, Denver.

Fanselow, J., and R. Crymes (1976) (eds.) *On TESOL '76*. Washington, D.C.: TESOL.

Faulkner, W. (1965) "A Note on Sherwood Anderson," in Meriwether (1965).

Finocchiaro, M. (1974) *English as a Second Language: From Theory to Practice*. New York: Regents.

Finocchiaro, M., and M. Bonomo (1973) *The Foreign Language Learner: A Guide for Teachers*. New York: Regents.

Finocchiaro, M., and V. H. Lavenda (1966) *Selections for Developing English Language Skills*. New York: Regents.

Fisher, Mary-Margaret (1973) "The Nuts and Bolts of Individualization: Classroom Management," *The Modern Language Journal* 58:179-185.

Forster, K. I., and I. Olbrei (1974) "Semantic Heuristics and Syntactic Analysis," *Cognition* 2 and 3:319-347.

Freeman, S., and J. McDonough (1975) "English for Science at the University of Essex: The Venezuelan Scheme," *ELT Documents* 2:11-23. London: ETIC.

Frey, B. (1970) *Basic Helps for Teaching English as a Second Language*. Tucson, Arizona: Palo Verde Publishing Co.

Fries, C. (1945) *Teaching and Learning English as a Foreign Language*. Ann Arbor, Michigan: University of Michigan Press.

Fries, C., and A. Fries (1961) *English Teaching*. Tokyo: Kenkyusha, Ltd.

Fries, C. C., and Aileen Traver (1940) *English Word Lists: A Study of Their Adaptability for Instruction*. Washington, D.C.: American Council on Education.

Gage, N. L. (1963) (ed.) *Handbook of Research on Teaching*. Chicago: Rand/McNally.

Gates, A. J. (1931) "An experimental comparison of the study-test and the test-study methods in spelling," *Journal of Educational Psychology* 22:1-19.

Gattegno, Caleb (1963, 2nd edition 1972) *Teaching Foreign Languages in Schools: the Silent Way*. New York: Educational Solutions.

——— (1976a) "The Silent Way." Conference Address and Demonstration at the 1976 National TESOL Convention, New York.

——— (1976b) *The Common Sense of Teaching Foreign Languages*. New York: Educational Solutions, Inc.

Ghiselin, Brewster (1964) *The Creative Process: A Symposium*. New York: New American Library.

Gladwin, T., and W. Sturtevant (1962) (eds.) *Anthropology and Human Behavior*. Washington, D.C.: Anthropological Society of Washington.

Gleitman, L. R., and P. Rozin (1973) "Teaching reading by use of a syllabary," *Reading Research Quarterly* 8:4, 447-483.

Goodman, K. S. (1970) "Reading: a psycholinguistic guessing game," in Gunderson (1970), 107-122, and in *Journal of the Reading Specialist* (1967 4: 126-135).

Goodman, Y., and C. Burke (1972) *Reading Miscue Inventory*. New York: Macmillan.

Gorman, T. P. (1964) *A Reading Improvement Course for Students of English as a Second Language* (12 films). Syracuse, N.Y.: Syracuse University Instructional Materials Center.

——— (1969) *Preliminary Report: Research Project on Reading Skills of University Students*. Nairobi. Mimeographed.

——— (1973) "Methods of Teaching Writing to Students at Advanced Level," *UCLA Workpapers in TESL* 7:41-52.

Gorman, T., and M. Walsleben (In press) *Advanced Reading and Composition Skills*. Englewood Cliffs, N.J.: Prentice-Hall. (Prepublication version available from UCLA Bookstore.)

Gough, P. B. (1972) "One Second of Reading," in Kavanagh and Mattingly (1972), 331-358.

Gougher, Ronald L. (1972) (ed.) *Individualization of Instruction in Foreign Languages: A Practical Guide*. Philadelphia, Pa.: The Center for Curriculum Development.

Graham, R. T., and E. H. Rudorf (1970) "Dialect and spelling," *Elementary English* 47:363-376.

Green, J. D. (1973) "What the Recording Manuals Don't Tell You," *UCLA Workpapers in TESL* 7: 117-122.

Gunderson, D. V. (1970) (ed.) *Language and Reading: An Interdisciplinary Approach*. Washington, D.C.: Center for Applied Linguistics.

Gurrey, P. (1955) *Teaching English as a Foreign Language*. London: Longmans.

Hagerty, Timothy, and J. Donald Bowen (1973) "A Contrastive Analysis of a Lexical Split: Spanish *hacer* to English *do/make/*etc.," in Nash (1973).

Hall, Eugene J. (n.d.) *Situational Reinforcement*. ERIC ED 024935.

——— (1978) Situational Reinforcement, *TESOL Newsletter* 12:2, April.

Hall, Eugene J., and Sandra Constinett (1970-71) *Orientation in American English*. Washington, D.C.: Institute of Modern Languages.

Halliday, M. A. K., and R. Hasan (1976) *Cohesion in English*. London: Longmans.

Handscombe, Jean et al. (1974) "Individualizing the ESL Program (or Teaching in the Ways in Which Students Learn)," *TESL Talk* 5:1, 23-35. (ERIC ED 105 762)

Hanna, P. R., J. Hanna, R. E. Hodges, and E. H. Rudorf (1966) *Phoneme-grapheme Correspondences as Cues to Spelling Improvement*. Washington, D.C.: U.S. Government Printing Office.

Hanna, P. R., R. E. Hodges, and J. Hanna (1971) *Spelling: Structure and Strategies*. Boston: Houghton Mifflin.

Hannah, Kay (1975) "Towards a systematization of English modals." Unpublished MA thesis in TESL, UCLA.

Harris, A. J. (1961) *How to Increase Reading Ability.* 4th ed. New York: David McKay, Co.

Harris, David P. (1966) *Reading Improvement Exercises for Students of English as a Second Language.* Englewood Cliffs, N.J.: Prentice-Hall.

——— (1969) *Testing English as a Second Language.* New York: McGraw-Hill.

Harrison, Grant Von (1976) *Beginning English* I. Salt Lake City: Interact.

——— (1977) *Beginning English I.* Orem: Metra.

Hartnett, D. (1974) "The relation of cognitive style and hemispheric preference to deductive and inductive second language learning." Paper presented at UCLA Conference on Human Brain Function, Los Angeles.

Hatch, E. (1971) "Composition $<$ Control Communication," *UCLA Workpaper in TESL* 5:47-53.

——— (1978) *Second Language Acquisition.* Rowley, Mass.: Newbury House.

Hatch, E., P. Polin, and S. Part (1974) "Acoustic scanning or syntactic processing," *Journal of Reading Behavior* 6:3, 275-285.

Heinkel, Otto A. (1969) "Evaluation of simulation as a teaching device," *Journal of Experimental Education* 38:3, 32-36.

Heise, Edward (1961) "Let's Talk Sense about Language Teaching," *The French Review* 35:176-184.

Henning, Grant (1973a) "A Research study in vocabulary learning: literature, experimentation, and ESL lessons." Unpublished MA thesis in TESL. University of California, Los Angeles.

——— (1973b) "Remembering Foreign Language Vocabulary: Acoustic and Semantic Parameters," *Language Learning* 23:2.

Herschenhorn, Suzanne (1975) "A rationale and suggested schema for teaching listening comprehension in the classroom using 'live' language." Unpublished MA thesis in TESL. University of California, Los Angeles.

Higa, Masanori (1965) "The psycholinguistic concept of 'difficulty' and the teaching of foreign language vocabulary," *Language Learning* 15:167-179. Reprinted in Croft (1972).

Hilgard, Ernest R. (1956) *Theories of Learning.* 2nd ed. New York: Appleton-Century Crofts.

Hill, L. A. (1966a) *Free Composition Book.* London: Oxford University Press.

——— (1966b) *Outline Composition Book.* London: Oxford University Press.

Hirasawa, L., and L. Markstein (1974) *Developing Reading Skills: Advanced.* Rowley, Mass.: Newbury House.

Hochberg, J. (1970) "Attention organization and consciousness," in Mostofsky (1970).

Holmes, Richard B. (1966) "What's Wrong with Our Tape Recordings?" *The Modern Language Journal* 50:7.

Hornby, A. (1950) "The situational approach to language teaching," *English Language Teaching* 4:

150-156. Reprinted in Allen and Campbell (1972), 83-88.

Hunter, M. (1974) "Piagetian theory applied to assessment of the teaching process." Unpublished manuscript. University Elementary School, University of California, Los Angeles.

Hymes, D. (1962) "The ethnography of speaking," in Gladwin and Sturtevant (1962).

Igarashi, J. (1971) "Application of question and answer drills to group work." *UCLA Workpapers in TESL* 5:55-67.

"Individualizing Foreign Language Instruction: Report of the Second Annual Texas Conference on Coordinating Foreign Languages" (n.d.) (ERIC ED 063 823).

Jacobson, Rodolfo (1971) "English to Speakers of Other Languages and Standard English to Speakers of a Non-Standard Dialect," *The English Record, Special Anthology Issue and Monograph* 14. Binghamton, N.Y.: New York State English Council.

Jakobovits, L. (1968) "Implications of recent psycholinguistic developments for the teaching of a second language," *Language Learning* 18. Reprinted in Lugton and Heinle (1971), 53-79.

——— (1970) *Foreign Language Learning: A Psycholinguistic Analysis of the Issues.* Rowley, Mass.: Newbury House.

Jespersen, Otto (1972) *The Philosophy of Grammar.* London: Allen and Unwin.

Johnson, F. C. (1973) *English as a Second Language: An Individualized Approach.* Singapore: Jacaranda Press.

Johnson, Gayle C. (1977) "Vocabulary Acquisition in ESL." Unpublished MA thesis in TESL, UCLA.

Johnston, V. A. (1972) "Some effects of acoustic input on reading comprehension." Unpublished MA thesis in TESL, University of California, Los Angeles.

Joos, Martin (1957) (ed.) *Readings in Linguistics I.* Chicago: University of Chicago Press.

——— (1962) *The Five Clocks, IJAL* Publ. No. 22, Vol. 28, Part 2V.

Kaplan, R. (1966) "Cultural Patterns in Inter-Cultural Education," *Language Learning* 16:1-20.

Kellaghan, T., and J. Macnamara (1967) "Reading in a Second Language," in M. D. Jenkinson (ed.) *Reading Instruction: An International Forum,* IRA, 231-340.

Kennedy, Katherine, and Stephanie Roeder (1973) "A guide to using language experience with adults." Unpublished manuscript. Cambridge, Mass.: Community Learning Center.

Kennedy, Graeme (1972) "The language tests for young children," in Spolsky (1973), 164-181.

King, F. M. (1976) *Easy to Teach Series.* Schaumburg, Illinois: A. N. Palmer Co.

Kitzhaber, A. (1963) *Themes, Theory and Therapy: Teaching of Writing in College.* New York: McGraw-Hill.

Kligman, D. S., and B. Cronnell (1974) "Black English and spelling." Technical Report No. 50. Los Alamitos, CA: SWRL Educational Research and Development.

Knapp, Donald (1972) "A focused, efficient method to relate composition correction to teaching aims," in Allen and Campbell (1972), 213-221.

Kolers, P. A. (1966) "Reading and Talking Bilingually," *The American Journal of Psychology* 79:3, 357-376.

Kučera, H., and W. N. Francis (1967) *Computational Analysis of Present Day American English*. Providence, R.I.: Brown University Press.

Kunihira, Shirou, and James J. Asher (1965) "The Strategy of the Total Physical Response: An Application to Learning Japanese," *International Review of Applied Linguistics* 3:277-289.

Kurath, H. (1967) *A Phonology and Prosody of Modern English*. Ann Arbor: University of Michigan.

Kurzdorfer, Christian (1974) "Problems in translating a German short story into English: a comparative/contrastive study." Unpublished MA thesis in TESL, UCLA.

Lackstrom, J., L. Selinker, and L. Trimble (1970) "Grammar and Technical English," in Lugton (1970), 10-134.

Lado, Robert (1964a) *Language Testing: The Construction and Use of Foreign Language Tests*. New York: McGraw-Hill. (First published in 1961 by Longmans, Green and Co., Ltd.)

——— (1964b) *Language Teaching: A Scientific Approach*. New York: McGraw-Hill.

La Forge, Paul (1971) "Community Language Learning: A Pilot Study," *Language Learning* 21:45-61.

——— (1977) Uses of Social Silence in the Interpersonal Dynamics of Community Language Learning, *TESOL* 11:4, 373-382.

Lambert, Wallace (1961) *A Study of the Roles of Attitudes and Motivation in Second Language Learning*. Project Report. SAE-8817. Montreal.

Lambert, W. E., M. Just, and N. Segalowitz (1970) "Some cognitive effects of following the curricula of grades one and two in a foreign language." Language Research Group, McGill University.

Lambert, W., and G. Tucker (1969) "White and Negro Listeners' Reactions to Various American-English Dialects," *Social Forces* 8:463-468.

Lane, Harlan (1964) "Programmed Learning of a Second Language," *International Review of Applied Linguistics in Language Teaching* 4:249-301.

Lange, Dale L., and Charles J. James (1972) (eds.) *Foreign Language Education: A Reappraisal*. Skokie, Ill.: National Textbook Co.

Langmuir, C. R. (1967) "English Language Reading Ability of Haile Sellassie 1 University Freshmen and Law Students." Technical Memorandum 1967-68. Addis Ababa: University Testing Center. Mimeo.

Larsen, D. (1975) "A Re-evaluation of Grammatical Structure Sequencing," in Crymes and Norris (1975), 151-162.

Larsen-Freeman, D. (1975) "The Acquisition of Grammatical Morphemes by Adult ESL Students," *TESOL Quarterly* 9:4, 409-420.

——— (1976) "An Explanation for the Morpheme Acquisition Order of Second Language Learners," *Language Learning* 26:1, 125-134.

Lawrence, M. (1972) *Writing as a Thinking Process*. Ann Arbor: University of Michigan Press.

Laycock, F. (1958) "Flexibility in Reading Rate and Einstellung," *Perceptual and Motor Skills* 123-129.

Lee, R., L. McCune, and L. Patton (1970) "Physiological responses to different modes of feedback in pronunciation training," *TESOL Quarterly* 4:117-122.

Lee, W. R. (1968) *Language-teaching Games and Contests*. London: Oxford University Press.

Leslau, C., and W. Leslau (1963) *African Folk Tales*. Mount Vernon, N.H.: The Peter Pauper Press.

Lester, Mark (1970) *Readings in Applied Transformational Grammar*. New York: Holt, Rinehart, and Winston.

Levenston, E. A. (1975) "Aspects of testing the oral proficiency of adult immigrants to Canada," in Palmer and Spolsky (1975), 67-74.

Levin, H., and J. P. Williams (1970) *Basic Studies in Reading*. New York: Basic Books.

Levinson, Stan M. (1975) "Problems of Romance Language Speakers Learning English: Theory and Practice in Lexical Analysis." Unpublished MA thesis in TESL, UCLA.

Lipson, Alexander (1971) "Some New Strategies for Teaching Oral Skills," in Lugton and Heinle (1971).

Lopate, Philip (1973) "How to use videotapes when you don't know the first thing about it," *Teachers and Writers Collaborative Newsletter* 4:4, 81-104.

Lott, Bernard (1959-60) "Graded and Restricted Vocabularies and Their Use in the Oral Teaching of English as a Second Language," *ESL* 14:1 and 2.

Love, G., and M. Payne (1969) (eds.) *Contemporary Essays on Style*. Glenview, Ill.: Scott, Foresman.

Lozanov, Georgi (1973) *Suggestology*. Sofia, Bulgaria: Nauka I Izkistvo. (Bulgarian) (Translated publication pending: *Suggestology and Suggestopedia*. New York: Gordon and Breach Science Publishers, ISBN 6-677-07170-0; One Park Avenue, New York, N.Y. 10016)

——— (1977) "The Suggestopaedic Method of Teaching Foreign Languages," in O'Brien (1977).

Lucas, E. (1975) "Teachers' reacting moves following errors made by pupils in post-primary English as a second language classes in Israel." Unpublished MA thesis. Tel Aviv University.

Lugton, R. C., and J. Heinle (1971) (eds.) *Toward a Cognitive Approach to Second Language Acquisition*. Philadelphia: The Center for Curriculum Development.

Mackey, W. F. (1965) *Language Teaching Analysis.* Bloomington, Ind.: Indiana University Press.

Macmillan, M. (1965) *Efficiency in Reading.* ETIC Occasional Paper 6. London.

Macnamara, J. (1966) "Comparative studies of reading and problem solving in two languages." Language Research Group, McGill University.

Macnamara, J., and T. Kellaghan (1967) "The teaching of reading in a second language," in *Reading Instruction: An International Forum,* proceedings of the 1st World Congress on Reading, Paris.

Madsen, Harold S., and Robert W. Bushman (1976) "Lozanov's Suggestopedic Method: What it is and how it works," In Fanselow and Crymes (1976).

Makita, Kiyoshi (1968) "The rarity of reading disability in Japanese children," *American Journal of Orthopsychiatry,* Vol. 38, 599-614.

Marckwardt, Albert H. (1973) "The dictionary as an English teaching resource," *TESOL* 7:4, 369-380.

Marks, L. (1972) "Interaction analysis in the English as a second language classroom." Unpublished MA thesis in TESL. University of California, Los Angeles.

McIntosh, L. (1967) "How to teach English grammar," *UCLA Workpapers in TESL* 1:39-55. Reprinted in Croft (1972).

McKillop, A., and E. Yoloye (1962) "The reading of university students," *Teacher Education* 3:93-107.

McKinley, C. (1974) "A study of ESL reading difficulties and their possible effects on academic achievement." Unpublished MA thesis in TESL. University of California, Los Angeles.

McLuhan, Marshall, and Quentin Fiore (1967) *The Medium is the Message.* New York: Random House.

McNeill, D. (1966) "Developmental Psycholinguistics," in Smith and Miller (1966).

McNeil, J. (1971) *Toward Acoustic Teachers: Their Appraisal and Improvement.* New York: Holt, Rinehart and Winston.

Medley, D., and H. Mitzel (1963) "Measuring classroom behavior by systematic observation," in Gage (1963), 247-328.

Mellon, J. C. (1969) *Transformational Sentence Combining.* Champaign, Ill.: NCTE.

Melnik, A., and J. Merritt (1972) *Reading Today and Tomorrow.* London: The Open University.

Mercier, Louis J. (1930) "Is the Coleman Report justified in its restatement of objectives for modern languages?" *The French Review* 3:397-415.

Meriwether, J. B. (1965) (ed.) *Essays, Speeches, and Public Letters.* New York: Random House.

Messick, Samuel, and Scarvia Anderson (1974) "Educational testing, individual development, and social responsibility," in Tyler and Wolf (1974), 21-34.

Meyer, George A. (1965) *Speaking Fluent American English.* Palo Alto, CA: The National Press.

Miami Linguistic Reader Series (1964) Board of Public Instruction, Miami, Florida.

Michelson, S. E. (1974) "An analysis of phoneme-grapheme correspondence in the spelling of English monosyllables by adult Israelis." Unpublished MA thesis in TESL. University of California, Los Angeles.

Miller, George, and J. A. Selfridge (1950) "Verbal context and recall of meaningful material," *American Journal of Psychology* 63:176-185.

Mills, Helen (n.d.) "A do-it-yourself kit for individualized instruction." (ERIC ED 064 740)

Modiano, N. (1968) "National or mother language in beginning reading: a comparative study," *Research in the Teaching of English* 1:32-43.

Mohrmann, C., A. Sommerfelt, and J. Whatmough (1961) (eds.) *Trends in European and American Linguistics 1930-1960.* Utrecht: Spectrum Publishers.

Moody, K. W. (1965) "Controlled composition frames," *English Language Teaching* 4:146-155.

Morley, Joan (1972) *Improving Aural Comprehension.* Ann Arbor: University of Michigan Press.

Morton, J. (1959) *Occupational Psychologist* 33.

——— (1964) "The effects of context on the visual duration threshold for words," *Quarterly Journal of Experimental Psychology* 55:2.

Mostofsky, D. I. (1970) (ed.) *Attention: Contemporary Theory and Analysis.* New York: Appleton-Century-Crofts.

Moskowitz, G. (1976) "The Search for Excellence." Paper presented at the tenth annual TESOL convention, New York.

Moskowitz, G., J. Benevento, and N. Furst (1973) "Sensitivity in the foreign language classroom," in Dodge (1973), 13-57.

Moskowitz, G., and J. Hayman (1974) "Interaction patterns of first year, typical and 'best' teachers in inner-city schools," *Journal of Educational Research* 67:5.

Mott Basic Language Skills Program (1967 to present). Allied Education Council, P.O. Box 78, Galien, MI 49113. (*Editor's note: Various materials have been and are being produced.*)

Moulton, William (1961) "Linguistics and Language Teaching in the United States, 1940-1960," in Mohrmann, Sommerfelt, and Whatmough (1961).

Nash, Rose (1973) (ed.) *Readings in Spanish-English Contrastive Linguistics.* Puerto Rico: Inter-American University Press.

National Defense Language Development Program, U.S. Office of Education (1964) *Completed Research, Studies, and Instructional Materials,* List No. 4 OE 12016-64. Washington, D.C. U.S. Government Printing Office.

Neisser, V. (1967) *Cognitive Psychology.* New York: Appleton-Century-Crofts.

Newmark, L. (1966) "How not to interfere with language learning," *International Journal of American Linguistics* 32:77-83. Reprinted in Allen and Campbell (1972), 37-43.

Newmark, L. et al. (1964) *Using American English.* New York: Harper & Row.

Ney, James (1973) "Towards a Synthetization of Teaching Methodologies for TESOL," *TESOL Quarterly* 7:3-11.

——— (1976) Harris Winitz and James Reeds: Comprehension and Problem Solving as Strategies of Second Language Training, *TESOL* 10:4.

Nida, Eugene (1952-53) "Selective Listening," *Language Learning* 3 and 4:92-101. Reprinted in Allen and Campbell (1972).

Noble, J. H., and the Handwriting Research Institute (1971) *Better Handwriting for you.* New York: Noble and Noble Publishers.

Norris, W. E. (1970) "Teaching Second Language Reading at the Advanced Level: Goals, Techniques, and Procedures," *TESOL Quarterly* 4:17-35.

O'Brien, Maureen Concannon (1977) (ed.) *Second Language Acquisition and Maintenance: World Views.* ATESOL: Dublin, Ireland.

Ohannessian, Sirarpi (1960) *Interim Bibliography on the Teaching of English to Speakers of Other Languages.* Washington, D.C.: Center for Applied Linguistics.

——— (1965) "ATESL Report," *NAFSA Newsletter* 16:7-13.

O'Hare, F. (1971) *Sentence-Combining.* Champaign, Ill.: NCTE.

Oller, John W., Jr. (1972) "Dictation as a test of ESL proficiency," in Allen and Campbell (1972), 346-354.

——— (1973a) "Cloze tests of second language proficiency and what they measure," *Language Learning* 23:1-105.

——— (1973b) "Discrete-point tests versus tests of integrative skills," in J. W. Oller, Jr., and J. C. Richards (eds.) *Focus on the Learner: Pragmatic Perspectives for the Language Teacher,* 184-199. Rowley, Mass.: Newbury House.

——— (1978) "Pragmatics and language testing," in Spolsky (1978).

Oller, J. W., Jr., and S. M. Ziahosseiny (1970) "The contrastive analysis hypothesis and spelling errors," *Language Learning* 20:183-189.

Olsen, Judy E. Winn-Bell (1977) *Communication-starters and Other Activities for the ESL Classroom.* San Francisco, Calif.: The Alemany Press.

Osterberg, T. (1961) *Bilingualism and the First School Language: An Educational Problem Illustrated by Results from a Swedish Dialect Area.* Umea, Sweden: Vasterbottens Tryckeri AB.

Ostrander, Sheila, and Lynn Schroeder (1970) *Psychic Discoveries Behind the Iron Curtain.* New York: Prentice-Hall.

Palmer, Adrian (1971) "Teaching Communication," *Language Learning* 1:1. Reprinted as "Communication Practice versus Pattern Practice," *English Teaching Forum* 9:4.

Palmer, L., and B. Spolsky (1975) (eds.) *Papers on Language Testing.* Washington, D.C.: TESOL.

Paulston, C. B. (1971) "The Sequencing of Structural Pattern Drills," *TESOL Quarterly* 5:3, 197-208.

——— (1974) "A Biased Bibliography," *Language Learning* 23:129-143. Reprinted in the *English Teaching Forum* 12:1.

Paulston, C. B. et al. (1975) *Developing Communicative Competence: Role-plays in English as a Second Language.* Pittsburgh: University of Pittsburgh.

Paulston, C. B., and Mary Newton Bruder (1976) *Teaching English as a Second Language: Techniques and Procedures.* Cambridge, Mass.: Winthrop.

Perren, George (1967a) "Testing ability in English as a second language: two techniques," *English Language Teaching* 21:3, 197-202.

——— (1967b) "Testing ability in English as a second language 3. Spoken-language," *English Language Teaching* 22:22-29.

Perry, W. G., and C. P. Whitlock (1957) *Instructor's Manual.* Harvard University Reading Course. 5th ed.

Philipov, Elizabeth Risova (1975) "Suggestology: the Use of Suggestion in Learning and Hyperamnesia." Unpublished Ph.D. dissertation. San Diego: United States International University. (Available through Xerox University Microfilms, Ann Arbor, MI 48106.)

Pierce, M. E. (1973) "Sentence-Level Expectancy as an Aid to Advanced Reading," *TESOL Quarterly* 7:269-277.

Pimsleur, Paul (1959) *Report of the Conference on Psychological Experiments Related to Second-Language Learning.* Unpublished. (Available in mimeographed form from Language Development Program, U.S. Office of Education.)

Pincas, Anita (1963a) "Structural Linguistics and Systematic Composition Teaching to Students of English as a Foreign Language," *Language Learning* 12:185-194.

——— (1963b) "Cultural translation for foreign students," *Language Learning* 13:1, 15-26.

Plaister, T. (1968) "Reading instruction for college level foreign students," *TESOL Quarterly* 2:164-168.

Politzer, R. (1970) "Some reflections on 'good' and 'bad' language teaching behaviors," *Language Learning* 20:31-43.

Politzer, R., and L. Weiss (1970) *The Successful Foreign Language Teacher.* Philadelphia: The Center for Curriculum Development.

Pomeroy, Carol A. (1974) "Songs for Intermediate ESL." Unpublished MA thesis in TESL. University of California, Los Angeles.

Postman, N., and C. Weingartner (1969) *Teaching as a Subversive Activity.* New York: Delacorte Press.

Povey, John (1968) "A guide to the study of the short story for non-native speakers," *UCLA Workpapers in TESL,* Vol. 2, 53-62.

——— (1972) "Walter Mitty: the all-American hero," *UCLA Workpapers in TESL,* Vol. 6, 51-58.

Prator, C. H. (1952) *Manual of American English Pronunciation*. New York: Holt, Rinehart, and Winston. New ed. 1972.

——— (1963) "Adjectives of Temperature," *ELT* 17: 158-164. Reprinted in Allen and Campbell (1972).

——— (1965) "Development of a Manipulation-communication Scale," *NAFSA Studies and Papers, English Language Series* No. 10. 385-391. Reprinted in Allen and Campbell (1972).

——— (1967) "Guidelines for planning classes and teaching materials," *UCLA Workpapers in TESL* 1-27-31;

Prator, C. H., and B. W. Robinett (1972) *Manual of American English Pronunciation*. New York: Holt, Rinehart, and Winston.

Preston, Dennis R. (1971) "ESL in adult basic education programs," *TESOL Quarterly* 5:5, 181-196.

Public Service Commission of Canada, Staff Development Branch, Studies Division, Suggestopaedia Programme (1975) *A Teaching Experience with the Suggestopaedia Method*. Ottawa: Information Canada. (Catalogue No. SC82-6/1975)

Racle, Gabriel L. (1977) *Suggestopaedia and the Teaching of Languages: Key Points* (Stockholm, Sweden), ERIC Microfiche ED 149 632.

Radice, Francis (1973) "Using Board Games," *English Language Teaching* 10:385-396.

Rand, E. (1967) "Analysis and Synthesis: Two Steps Toward Proficiency in Composition," *UCLA Workpapers in TESL* 1:87-91.

Rankin, E. F. (1963) "Sequential Emphasis and Speed and Comprehension in College Reading," *Journal of Developmental Reading* 46-65.

Ray, D. D. (1964) "Permanency of Gains in Reading Speech," *Proceedings of the Annual Convention*, American Psychological Society. 9:192-193.

Reading Attainment System. Grolier Educational Corp., 845 3rd Ave., New York, NY 10022.

Reed, D. W. (1967) "Roundtable review," *Research in the Teaching of English* 1:207-215.

Reed, J. (1970) "Improving the Effectiveness of Language Laboratory Work," *Journal of Applied Linguistics and Language Teaching Technology* 3: 1, 25-37.

Renard, Colette, and Charles H. Heinle (1969) *Implementing Voix et Images de France*. Philadelphia: Chilton Books.

Richards, J. (1969) "Songs in Language Learning," *TESOL Quarterly* 3:2.

Rivers, Wilga M. (1964) *The Psychologist and the Foreign Language Teacher*. Chicago: University of Chicago Press.

——— (1966) "Listening Comprehension," *Modern Language Journal* 50 (ERIC Microfiche ED 028-665)

——— (1968) *Teaching Foreign-Language Skills*. Chicago: University of Chicago Press.

——— (1972a) "Talking off the tops of their heads," *TESOL Quarterly* 1:71-81.

——— (1972b) *Speaking in Many Tongues*. Rowley, Mass.: Newbury House.

——— (1973) "From Linguistic Competence to Communicative Competence," *TESOL Quarterly* 7:25-34.

Roberts, A. H. (1967) "Roundtable review," *Research in the Teaching of English* 1:201-207.

Robinson, Francis P. (1946) *Effective Study*. New York: Harper & Row.

Robinson, Lois (1967) *Guided Writing and Free Writing*. New York: Harper & Row.

Rosensweig, Fred (1974) "Improving the communicative competence of advanced ESL students." Unpublished MA thesis in TESL. University of California, Los Angeles.

Rosenthal, Blanca (1973) "Developing a Foreign Language Learning Activity Package," *The Modern Language Journal* 57:195-199.

Ross, Janet (1967) "The Language Laboratory in a Small TESOL Program," *TESOL Quarterly* 1:1, 15-29.

——— (1968) "Controlled Writing: A Transformational Approach," *TESOL Quarterly* 2.

Rothkopf, E. Z. (1972) "Structural Text Features and the Control of Processes of Learning from Written Materials," in Carroll and Freedle, 315-335.

Rowe, M. (1969) "Science, silence and sanctions," *Science and Children* 6:6, 12-13.

Rudell, R. (1965) "The effect of oral and written patterns of language structure on reading comprehension," *The Reading Teacher* 18:1.

Rutherford, William (1973) Paper presented to the 1973 TESOL Convention, San Juan, Puerto Rico.

——— (1975) *Modern English* 2nd ed. Vol. 1. New York: Harcourt, Brace, Jovanovich.

Ryan, C. W. (1973) *Spelling for Adults*. New York: Charles Wiley and Sons.

Samuels, S. J. (1968) "Effect of experimentally learned word associations on the acquisition of reading responses," *Journal of Educational Psychology* 57:159-163.

Sandburg, K. L. (1967) "Drills for Writing Laboratories," in Wigglesworth (1967).

Saporta, Sol (1961) *Psycholinguistics: a Book of Readings*. New York: Holt, Rinehart, and Winston.

Savin, H. B. (1972) "What the child knows about speech when he starts to learn to read," in Kavanagh and Mattingly (1972), 319-326.

Savignon, Sandra J. (1972) *Communicative Competence: An Experiment in Foreign Language Teaching*. Philadelphia: The Center for Curriculum Development.

Schane, S. (1970) "Linguistics, spelling, and pronunciation," *TESOL Quarterly* 4:137-141.

Schankweiler, D., and I. Y. Liberman (1972) "Misreading: a search for causes," in Kavanagh and Mattingly (1972), 293-317.

Schegloff, E., G. Jefferson, and H. Sacks (1977) "The preference for self-correction in the organization of repair in conversation," *Language* 53:2, 361-382.

Schlesinger, I. (1968) *Sentence Structure and the Reading Process*. The Hague: Mouton.

Schramm, Wilbur (1973) *Big Media, Little Media: A Report to the Agency for International Development.* Palo Alto: Stanford University Press. Also available through ERIC.

Schumann, J. (1972) "Communication techniques," *TESOL Quarterly* 6:143-161.

——— (1975) "Affective Factors and the Problem of Age in Second Language Acquisition," *Language Learning* 26:135-143.

Schwartz, J. (1977) "Repair in conversations between adult second language learners of English." Unpublished MA thesis in TESL. University of California, Los Angeles.

Scott, Margaret Sue, and G. Richard Tucker (1974) "Error Analysis and English Language Strategies of Arab Students," *Language Learning* 24:69-97.

Searle, J. (1970) *Speech Acts.* Cambridge, Mass.: University Press.

Serpell, R. (1968) "Selective attention and interference between first and second languages," *H.D.R.U. Reports.* University of Zambia.

Shuy, Roger W. (1964) (ed.) *Social Dialects and Language Learning.* Champaign, Ill.: National Council of Teachers of English.

Silberman, Charles E. (1970) *Crisis in the Classroom: the Remaking of American Education.* New York: Random House.

Simon, Sidney B., Leland W. Howe, and Howard Kirschenbaum (1972) *Values Clarification: A Handbook of Practical Strategies for Teachers and Students.* New York: Hart Publishing Co.

Skinner, B. F. (1957) *Verbal Behavior.* New York: Appleton-Century-Crofts.

Slager, William R. (1973) "Creating Contexts for Language Practice," *TESOL Quarterly* 7:1, 35-50.

Smith, F. (1971) *Understanding Reading, A Psycholinguistic Analysis of Reading and Learning to Read.* New York: Holt.

Smith, F., and G. A. Miller (1966) (eds.) *The Genesis of Language.* Cambridge, Mass.: MIT Press.

Smith, G. L. (1966) *Spelling by Principles.* New York: Appleton-Century-Crofts.

Smith, H. P., and E. V. Dechant (1961) *Psychology in Teaching Reading.* Englewood Cliffs, N.J.: Prentice-Hall.

Smith, Phillip (1971) "Audio: State of Art," *Audio in the 1970's.* 19-21: 21-26.

Smolinski, Lois K. (1970) "Foreign language aptitude in children: an investigation of current theory and research in interrelated disciplines." Unpublished MA thesis in TESL. University of California, Los Angeles.

"Songs to sing in class" (1966) *English Teaching Forum* 4:4.

Spearritt, D. (1972) "Subskills of Reading Comprehension," *Reading Research Quarterly* 8:1, 92-111.

Spencer, D. H. (1965) "Two Types of Guided Composition Exercises," *English Language Teaching* 19:4, 156-158.

Spolsky, B. (1973) (ed.) *The Language Education of Minority Children.* Rowley, Mass.: Newbury House.

——— (1978) (ed.) *Advances in Language Testing: Series 2 Approaches to Language Testing.* Arlington, Va.: Center for Applied Linguistics.

Sprenger, Arnold (1973) "Group Work in Foreign Language Learning: A Report," *English Teaching Forum* 11:5.

SRA Materials. Science Research Associates, 57 West Grand Ave., Chicago, IL 60610.

Stack, Edward M. (1971) *The Language Laboratory and Modern Language Teaching.* New York: Oxford Univ. Press.

Stafford, C. (1976) "A psycholinguistic analysis of ESL reading difficulties with teaching application." Unpublished MA thesis in TESL. University of California, Los Angeles.

Staton, T. F. (1950) "Preliminary Evidence on Permanency of Reading Rate Increases Following Intensive Training in a Reading Laboratory," *American Psychologist* 5:341-342.

Stern, Susan (1977) "The teaching of contemporary American drama in advanced ESL." Unpublished MA thesis in TESL, UCLA.

Stevenson, R. (1973) "Using slides to improve reading comprehension," *English Teaching Forum* 11: 2, 10-15.

Stevick, Earl (1957) *Helping People Learn English.* Nashville, Tenn.: Abingdon Press.

——— (1959) " 'Technemes' and the Rhythm of class activity," *Language Learning* 2:3, 45-51.

——— (1967a) "UHF and microwaves in transmitting language skills," *IJAL* 32:84-93.

——— (1967b) "The modular mousetrap," *TESOL Quarterly* 1:3, 3-10.

——— (1971) *Adapting and Writing Language Lessons.* Washington, D.C.: Foreign Service Institute, Department of State.

——— (1972) "Evaluating and adapting language materials," in Allen and Campbell, 101-120.

——— (1973) "Review Article: Curran," *Language Learning* 23:259-271.

——— (1974) "Review Article: Gattegno," *TESOL Quarterly* 8:305-314.

——— (1976) *Memory, Meaning and Method.* Rowley, Mass.: Newbury House.

Stockwell, R., J. D. Bowen, and J. Martin (1965) *The Grammatical Structures of English and Spanish.* Chicago: University of Chicago Press.

Strop, Joanne C. (1971) "A rationale for the simplification of literature for use in English as a second language classes and simplification of 'The great mountains.' " Unpublished MA thesis in TESL, UCLA.

Suggestology and Suggestopaedia (1975) Bulletin of the Suggestology Research Institute under the Ministry of People's Education 1:1-55.

Suggestopaedia-Canada, Information Letter (1975) 1: 1-6. (Gabriel Racle, Director: Suggestopaedia-Canada, Aselford. Martin Building—Room 420, 1725 Woodward Drive, Ottawa, Ontario. K1A OM7 Canada.)

Sullivan, R. E. (1971) *A comparison of certain relationships among selected phonological differences and spelling deviations for a group of Negro and a group of White second grade children.* USCE Project No. 1F038. University of Texas at Austin.

Swales, J. (1968) "Language Laboratory Materials and Service Courses: Problems of Tape Course Design for Science Students," *Journal of Applied Linguistics and Language Teaching Technology* 6: 1, 17-22.

Taylor, Joseph A. (1971) "Teaching English to Chicano students." Unpublished MA thesis in TESL. University of California, Los Angeles.

Taylor, Wilson L. (1953) "Cloze procedure: a new tool for measuring readability," *Journalism Quarterly* 30:4, 415-433.

Terrell, Anne (1971) "Writing English Lessons for the Non Academic Adult." Paper presented at the 5th annual TESOL convention, New Orleans, Louisiana (ERIC ED 052 655).

Thonis, E. W. (1970) *Teaching Reading to Non-English Speakers.* New York: Macmillan.

Thorndike, E. L. (1917) "Reading as Reasoning: A Study of Mistakes in Paragraph Reading," *Journal of Educational Psychology* 8:323-332.

Thorndike, E. L., and I. Lorge (1944) *The Teacher's Word Book of 30,000 Words.* New York: Teachers' College, Columbia University.

Thorndike, Robert L., and Elizabeth Hagen (1961) *Measurement and Evaluation in Psychology and Education.* 2nd ed. New York: John Wiley and Sons.

Tinker, M. A. (1965) *Bases for Efficient Reading.* Minneapolis: University of Minnesota Press.

Tullius, J. (1971) "Analysis of reading skills of non-native speakers of English." Unpublished MA thesis in TESL. University of California, Los Angeles.

Tulving, E., and C. Gold (1963) "Stimulus information and contextual information as determinants of tachistoscopic recognition of words," *Journal of Experimental Psychology* 66:319-327.

Turkevich, Ludmilla B. (1972) "Suggestology," *Russian Language Journal* 26:8-84.

Twaddell, W. Freeman (1935) "On Defining the Phoneme," *Language Monograph* No. 16. Reprinted in Joos (1957).

——— (1973) "Vocabulary Expansion in the ESOL Classroom," *TESOL Quarterly* 7:1, 61-78.

Tyler, R. W., and R. M. Wolf (1974) (eds.) *Crucial Issues in Testing.* Berkeley, CA: McCutchan Publishing Corp.

Unoh, S. O. (1968) *The Study of Reading: An Introductory Survey.* Ibadan, Nigeria: Ibadan University Press.

Upshur, J. (1971) "Objective evaluation of oral proficiency in the ESOL classroom," *TESOL Quarterly* 5:47-59.

Vachek, J. (1945-9) "Some remarks on writing and phonetic transcription," *Acta Linguistica* 5:86-93.

——— (1959) "Two chapters on written English," *Brno Studies in English* 1:7-34.

Valette, Rebecca M. (1967) *Modern Language Testing: A Handbook.* New York: Harcourt, Brace and World. See also the second edition, 1978.

——— (1969) *Directions in Foreign Language Testing.* New York: Modern Language Association.

——— (1973) "Developing and evaluating communication skills in the classroom," *TESOL Quarterly* 7:407-424.

Vallins, G. H. (1965) *Spelling.* Rev. ed. London: Andre Deutsch.

Vander Werf, William C. (1969) "Lexical analysis and comparison: English and Persian: an exploratory study for ESL purposes." Unpublished MA thesis in TESL. University of California, Los Angeles.

Van Syok, B. (1977) "A new arrangement of textbook materials might help." Paper presented at the eleventh annual TESOL Convention, Miami Beach.

Veldman, D. J. (1967) *Fortran Programming for the Behavioral Sciences.* New York: Holt, Rinehart, and Winston.

Venezky, R. L. (1967) "English orthography: its graphical structure and its relation to sound," *Reading Research Quarterly* 2:75-106.

——— (1969) "Linguistics and spelling," Working Paper No. 15. Madison: Wisconsin Research and Development Center for Cognitive Learning. (Also in *Yearbook of the National Society for the Study of Education,* 1970, 264-274.)

——— (1970) *The Structure of English Orthography.* The Hague: Mouton.

Via, Richard (1972) "English through Drama," *ELEC Bulletin* No. 33. Tokyo: English Language Education Council. Reprinted in the *English Teaching Forum* 10:4.

——— (1976) *English in Three Acts.* Honolulu: University of Hawaii Press.

Wakeman, Alan (n.d.) *Jabberwocky: the Mastery/Mystery of English Game.* Essex: Longmans.

Walsleben, M. C. (1975) "Improving advanced ESL students' reading comprehension: an analysis and evaluation of materials and procedures." Unpublished MA thesis in TESL. University of California, Los Angeles.

Wardhaugh, R. (1969) "TESOL: current problems and classroom practice," *TESOL Quarterly* 3:105-116. Reprinted in Allen and Campbell (1972).

Watson, Goodwin (1961) *What Psychology Can We Trust?* New York: Bureau of Publications, Teachers' College, Columbia University.

West, Michael (1959) *A General Service List of English Words.* London: William Clowes and Sons, Ltd.

——— (1968) "The minimum adequate (a quest)," *English Language Teaching* 22:205-210.

White, R. (1971) "Activating advanced ESL students: a problem and a solution," *TESOL Quarterly* 5: 231-238.

Widdowson, H. G. (1972) "The Teaching of English as Communication," *English Language Teaching* 27:15-19.

Wilkins, D. A. (1972) "Grammatical, Situational and Notional Syllabuses." Paper presented at the Third International Congress of Applied Linguistics, Copenhagen.

Willis, Mary A. (1975) "Affixation in English Word Formation and Applications for TESL." Unpublished MA thesis in TESL, UCLA.

Wilson, L. I. (1973) "Reading in the ESOL Classroom: A Technique for Teaching Syntactic Meaning," *TESOL Quarterly* 7:259-267.

Wingfield, R. J. (1972) "Conversational Responses to Statements," *English Language Teaching* 27:24-27.

Winitz, Harris, and James Reeds (1973a) *Comprehension and Problem Solving as a Strategy for Language Training—The OHR Method.* Prepublication monograph. Kansas City, Missouri: University of Missouri.

——— (1973b) "Rapid Acquisition of a Foreign Language (German) by the Avoidance of Speaking," *International Review of Applied Linguistics* 10: 295-317.

——— (1975) *Comprehension and Problem Solving as Strategies for Language Training.* The Hague: Mouton.

Wishon, G., and J. Burks (1968) *Let's Write English Book 1.* New York: American Book Co.

Witbeck, M. (1976) "Peer Correction Procedures for Intermediate and Advanced ESL Composition Lessons," *TESOL Quarterly* 10:3, 321-326.

Wolkowski, Zbigniew William (n.d.) *Suggestology: A Major Contribution by Bulgarian Scientists.*

(Christopher Bird, tr.) Monograph 10. Washington, D.C.: Mankind Research Foundation.

Woodcock, R. W. (1968) "Rebus as a medium in beginning reading instruction," *IMRID Papers and Reports* 5:4, 1-34.

Woodworth, Robert S. (1948) *Contemporary Schools of Psychology.* Rev. ed. New York: Ronald Press Co.

Wright, P. (1968) "Reading to Learn," *Chemistry in Britain* 4:10, 445-450. (Reprinted in Melnik and Merritt, 1972.)

Yorio, C. A. (1971) "Some Sources of Reading Problems in Foreign Language Learners," *Language Learning* 21:107-115.

Yorkey, Richard C. (1970a) *Study Skills for Students of English as a Second Language.* New York: McGraw-Hill.

——— (1970b) "A Study Skills Course for Foreign College Students," *TESOL Quarterly* 4:2, 143-154.

——— (1974) "Practical EFL Techniques for Teaching Arabic-Speaking Students." Paper delivered at the Defense Language Institute, English Language Branch, Lackland Air Force Base. (ERIC ED 117 990)

Yoshida, Midori (1977) "A Japanese Child's Acquisition of English Vocabulary." Unpublished MA thesis in TESL, UCLA.

Young, R., and A. Becker (1965) "Towards a Modern Theory of Rhetoric: A Tagmemic Contribution," *Harvard Educational Review* 35:450-468.

Zahorik, J. A. (1968) "Classroom feedback behavior of teachers," *Journal of Educational Research* 42: 147-150.